THE
GREAT
MAYOR

ALYN BRODSKY

THE
GREAT
MAYOR

Fiorello La Guardia
and the Making of
the City of New York

TRUMAN TALLEY BOOKS
ST. MARTIN'S PRESS
NEW YORK

For the little Burtons:

Blake, Elena, Grant, and Jack

www.stmartins.com

All photos courtesy of AP/Wide World Photos.

Library of Congress Cataloging-in-Publication Data

Brodsky, Alyn.
    The great mayor : Fiorello La Guardia and the making of the city of New York / Alyn Brodsky.—1st ed.
        p.   cm.
    Includes bibliographical references (p. 491) and index (p. 521).
    ISBN 0-312-28737-2
    1. La Guardia, Fiorello H. (Fiorello Henry), 1882–1947.   2. Legislators— United States—Biography.   3. Mayors—New York (State)—New York— Biography.   4. New York (N.Y.)—Politics and government—1898–1951. 5. United States. Congress. House—Biography.   I. Title.

E748.L23B76   2003
974.7'1042'092—dc21
  [B]

                                                    2003041007

10   9   8   7   6   5   4   3   2

CONTENTS

PART III: 1922-1933
Return to Congress,
Champion of the People

PART IV: 1934-1943
The Great Mayor

CONTENTS

PART V: 1943–1947
The Last Years

PREFACE

Fiorello H. La Guardia was arguably the last great paradigm of honesty and incorruptibility in American political history to date. Elected to Congress for seven terms as a Progressive Republican, he opposed Prohibition, supported women's suffrage and child labor laws, lashed out at blatantly racist immigration laws, and cosponsored the Norris–La Guardia Act (1932), which reined in the power of the courts to ban or restrain strikes, boycotts, or picketing by organized labor. As spokesman for the nation's poor, he demanded the regulation of business interests, arguing that laissez-faire was no more than an excuse for ignoring the economically disadvantaged. Condemned by many as an abhorrent political iconoclast, he was in fact an agitator for political reform whose motivation lay not in radical ideology but in moral indignation.

In 1929, La Guardia made his first run for mayor of New York City against the darling of the people, the press, and the pols, James "Jimmy" Walker, a lovable rogue who had raised knavery to a fine art. To Jazz Age New Yorkers, "Beau James" was more attractive than the peppery firebrand in the outsized Stetson hat La Guardia always wore to memorialize his childhood on the western frontier. He suffered the most humiliating defeat by a major mayoral candidate in the city's history.

In 1933, La Guardia ran again, determined more than ever to clean up the corruption that was the legacy of Tammany Hall, for which read the New York Democratic Party, which had ruled, and bled, the city for close to a century. The dazzling summer of the twenties had evolved into the stygian winter of the Depression-ridden thirties. The people were ready for a reformer of La Guardia's caliber. He broke the grip of "boss" politics, depoliticized the Civil Service, replaced an antiquated city charter, expanded relief and social services, and undertook a program of slum clearance, park construction, public housing, and road and bridge building that literally recast the city physically. More: He unified and updated mass transit, expanded education, developed public health programs, and initiated a new labor policy, while cleaning out the police and other departments and commencing a vigorous assault on the racketeers and the crooked politicians who gladly served their nefarious purposes in return for appropriate under-the-table compensation. Not to be overlooked is how he orchestrated the great 1939 World's Fair dedicated to the World of Tomorrow (which became the World of Today), opened the City Center for Music and Drama (with tickets priced to accommodate the culturally starved cash-strapped masses), developed special secondary schools for the city's talented youth, and brought New York its first commercial airport.

His influence as a proven visionary in the area of social reform extended beyond the city's confines. He defined the concept of— and need for—a federal-urban relationship. Where others bore to the White House and Capitol Hill vague proposals and inflated budgets, La Guardia showed up with carefully detailed blueprints and hard figures. He was not only New York's greatest mayor; he was the nation's. In the words of Rexford Guy Tugwell, "He aspired greatly, and we ought to find out all we can about such people. They make a vast difference in our lives."

INTRODUCTION

"That's when I got sore"

On a balmy spring Wednesday in the year 1904, three functionaries bounded up the steps of a nondescript building on the Corso, the main street of Fiume, the port city of the Italian province of Trieste, at the time a component of the Austro-Hungarian Empire and its only outlet on the Atlantic, by way of the Adriatic. They were the chief local agent of the Cunard steamship line, the director of the port, and Count Szapari, the governor-general of Trieste. Their destination: the United States Consulate, a two-room suite, of which one was the consul's office, the other his bedroom. Their target: a twenty-two-year-old American-born Italian, Signor La Guardia, who in his four years as resident U.S. consular officer had earned a reputation his superiors at the embassy in Budapest found downright embarrassing at times.

The three visitors were in a rage. Consul La Guardia had grievously offended the Imperial Archduchess Maria-Josepha, a niece of Emperor Franz Joseph. How? By threatening to prevent her partaking in the entertainment of choice among the Fiume aristocrats: standing on the first-class deck of an outward-bound steamship and staring down in amusement upon pitiable emigrants boarding the steerage section with all their earthly possessions in carpetbags and sailing off to a new life in America.

It started the evening before when La Guardia, without whose certificate of medical clearance no foreign ship could enter an American port, learned that the Cunard liner *Panonia*, scheduled to sail the following Saturday, would be embarking steerage passengers the following afternoon. United States quarantine regulations required medically cleared passengers to board ship as close to sailing time as possible. Had the sailing date been advanced, he inquired of Cunard? No. The archduchess, having heard about the "amusing pastime" of watching an embarkation, was visiting the city and desired a special viewing. La Guardia suggested the archduchess wait till Saturday to be "amused," or seek her "amusement" elsewhere.

But, he was told, Her Imperial Highness was in Fiume only for the day. La Guardia replied that confining some five hundred poor souls in close, fetid quarters below decks for three days simply to "amuse" some titled lady was not only a contravention of American law, it was inhumane. The director of the port sputtered that these were only peasants. Surely American immigration regulations could be overlooked this one time. Not possible, replied the consul. The Cunard agent offered a compromise: Instead of embarking all the "peasants," a token embarkation of, say, one or two hundred might suffice. No, replied the consul; rules must be adhered to scrupulously.

The governor-general told the consul Her Imperial Highness had invited him to take tea with her aboard ship, after which they would watch the embarkation. The consul declined the invitation. The governor-general insisted that to deny an imperial archduchess an "amusement" was a grave enough offense, but to refuse her invitation to tea was an insult to the Hapsburg crown. There would be an official protest to Washington.

"That's when I got sore," La Guardia would recall in his memoirs. "I told them to tell their precious Archduchess that maybe she could boss her people around but she couldn't boss the American consul."[1] Count Szapari replied that the embarkation would take place, insisted that the subject was closed to further discussion, and stormed out, with the director of the port in his wake. La Guardia told the Cunard agent to warn the *Panonia*'s captain that if he took on passengers three days before sailing time, the requisite Bill of Health would not be issued. The captain canceled the embarkation. La Guardia realized that the best thing he could do was make himself scarce.

Runners from Governor-General Szapari fanned out around the town with the order "No excuses—find him!" They sped in and out of every café, restaurant, club, and hotel the young bachelor consul was known to frequent when on the prowl for entertainment or relaxation. He was nowhere to be found. When the *Panonia*'s captain flatly refused to permit the embarkation, the archduchess flounced off the ship in an imperial rage. The imperial court did, of course, lodge an official protest with Washington, but it was diplomatically ignored. Consul La Guardia had simply been following official guidelines.

And where did young Fiorello spend the afternoon while the port director was personally leading a cadre of police all over town looking for him? Sipping tea and chatting with a friend. The friend was the port director's wife.

The story epitomizes Fiorello's public life. Here was a man who assiduously defended the "little people" against "the Interests." A resolute stickler for rules and regulations when he truly believed he was in the right. A man who outfoxed his antagonists with impish satisfaction. Above all, a man who took great delight at being in the vanguard of any battle in which he could equate himself with the Forces of Light trouncing the Forces of Darkness. By the time of what we may term the Saga of the Imperial Archduchess and the Aborted Embarkation, Fiorello La Guardia's character—all his traits, all his virtues, and all his warts—had been fixed in its totality. Like a great actor who has mastered his lines and stage business and is only awaiting the raising of the curtain, he was ready to leave Fiume and step onto the world stage.

PART I

1882-1914

The Early Years

CHAPTER ONE

"I loathe the professional politician"

1.

Fiorello H. La Guardia was not only a man of many traits and attitudes; he was a man of many religions. His father was a lapsed Roman Catholic, his mother a nonpracticing Jewess, his first wife a devout Catholic, his second a Lutheran, and he himself an observant though unconfirmed Episcopalian. What a person believed theologically was to him of monumental unimportance. La Guardia's concern was not with one's religious orientation but with one's ethical orientation.

His father, Achille Luigi Carlo La Guardia, was born on March 26, 1849, to a government functionary and his wife in Foggia, at the time part of the Kingdom of the Two Sicilies, where the trade and migration routes linking Europe, Africa, and the Middle East intersected. This might account for the difficulty in fixing the La Guardia ethnicity. The name is both Spanish and Italian; the family dates back to the Spanish conquest of the Sicilies in the fifteenth century. Having shown from early childhood an aptitude and great love for music, Achille decided to pursue a career in that discipline. He also showed an aptitude for mischief. One day he put a pointed object on his teacher-priest's chair, not to cause harm but simply to elicit a reaction. The reaction it elicited was the demand that he do penance by making the sign of the cross on the floor—with his tongue. Rage over being publicly humiliated became exacerbated when he complained about the priest to his parents and they replied they would do the same thing if he ever again misbehaved.[1] He ran away, vowing never to return home and never again to partake of the Roman ritual. With an obstinacy he would pass on to his famous son, Achille kept both vows.

For the next twenty years he traveled the world studying music and acquitting himself admirably as a composer, arranger, accompanist, and cornetist. At the age of twenty-eight, he toured the United States as accompanist for the legendary opera diva Adelina Patti. After the tour, Achille decided to settle down in America. But first, like so many European immigrants, he returned to his homeland to find a bride. At a dance in Trieste he met Irene Coen, ten years his junior. The two fell in love at first sight, were married on June 3, 1880, in a civil ceremony, and sailed almost immediately for the United States. On the marriage certificate under the heading "Religion," Achille identified himself as *nessuna*—"nothing." His bride declared herself as—the word needs no translating—*israelita*.[2]

Irene's mother, Fiorina (born 1833), was a Luzzatto, from a family of Sephardic Jews who may have settled in Trieste following the expulsion from Spain of the Jews when she was nine years old. After Italy's unification, Fiorina's family produced many university professors, civil servants, and military leaders.

Irene's father, Abramo Isacco Coen, was born, in the same year as Fiorina, in Spalato (now Split), a small trading center on the Dalmatian coast, which at the time belonged to Austria and is today part of Serbia. When the Coens became a part of the small Jewish community there cannot be determined; in 1942, the Mussolini government destroyed the community's archives. Possibly they arrived during the eighteenth century, following the expulsion of the Jews from both Venice and the Papal States. Thus, like the La Guardias', their emergence in Italy may be a consequence of the Spanish Inquisition. When Abramo Isacco was twenty-one his family relocated to Trieste, then emerging as a thriving commercial center. The Coens were merchants who never enjoyed great success but never suffered failure. Three years after settling in Trieste, Abramo Isacco married Fiorina; Irene was the first of their six children.

Born in Trieste on July 18, 1859, Irene claimed through her mother a pedigree that suggests that in becoming Achille's bride she was "marrying down." To her credit, Irene never believed it. She passed on to her famous son the unalterable conviction that all people were to be judged solely on *what* they were, as opposed to *who* they were.

Austrian by citizenship, Italian by culture, Irene was raised in the Orthodox Judaism of her father but did not remain active in the faith. She was at ease in Gentile as well as Jewish circles.

Irene and Achille's marriage was a happy one. On arriving in New York City, the two settled in Greenwich Village, long an area favored by Italian immigrants, where they took an apartment at 7 Varick Place, just two blocks south of fashionable Washington Square. It was there that their first child, a girl, Gemma, was born on April 24, 1881. Fiorello Enrico Raffaele was born nineteen months later, on December 11, 1882. He was named, respectively, for Irene's mother, Achille's brother, a civil engineer back in Italy, and Achille's father. In time, he would anglicize the Enrico to Henry and drop the Raffaele altogether.[3]

Having already visited America, Achille La Guardia knew what arriving immigrants were to learn, to their profound disappointment and sorrow: The streets of America were not paved with gold. But this was no impediment to the incoming tidal wave of humanity that was part of the first great U.S.-bound migration. Between 1880 and the outbreak of the First World War, more than fifteen million from Eastern and Southern Europe—mainly Russia, Italy, and the dozen nations comprising the Austro-Hungarian Empire—increased the American population by more than 25 percent and, in the process, trebled the size of New York City. New York was not only assuming leadership in growth among all other cities of the Western world; it was assuming leadership in terms of criminal arrests, catastrophic illnesses, and deaths per capita, due to the overwhelming influx of destitute immigrants. But still they came. Horrendous as life proved to be here, it simply had to be better than the misery they'd left behind. Here they stood a better chance to improve themselves and thereby share, however humbly, in the glory and wealth that was the New World.

2.

When Fiorello was almost three his father enlisted in the U.S. Army and was posted to the Eleventh Infantry Regiment as bandmaster at Fort Sully, a military oasis amid an expanse of barren scrublands peppered with Indian encampments in what four years later became the state of North Dakota. The post commander, Colonel Richard Dodge, took a liking to his bandmaster, assigning the family a house well apart from the company area—an honor indeed for an enlisted man. In gratitude, the third and last La Guardia child, who was born there, was named in the colonel's honor. Irene had a flair for making friends, transcending not only the barriers of culture but those of language as well. A tribe of Sioux Indians who lived just outside the fort brought her handmade blankets, moccasins, and beads. She, in turn, gave them sugar and staples.[4]

In the fall of 1889, the Eleventh was transferred to Madison Barracks at Sackets Harbor, near Watertown, New York, on Lake Ontario's eastern shore. As with Fort Sully, Fiorello had no memories of life at Sackets Harbor—or perhaps he chose not to record them—but others did. The wife of the commissary sergeant recalled how little Fiorello "used to torment my girls by pulling their hair ribbons off and such pranks." She did go on to note, though, that "he was honest and truthful" and "such a quick, keen little fellow." Prefiguring lifelong character traits, he "had the instinct to take the part of the underdog," and "even in his play he was a leader, and many an argument was the outcome of his desire for leadership." Though the smallest, he "was the most persistent, and the other children eventually capitulated and followed."

His first teacher, Mrs. Estelle Littlefield, recalled that the young Fiorello "was impetuous and full of fight, and his vocabulary was well-stocked with words of profanity." An above-average student, he had "a rather volcanic personality," demonstrated when a group of visitors came to observe a lesson and Mrs. Littlefield began calling the student roll. Each replied with a pleasant "present"—except Fiorello. When he refused to respond, he was told sternly, "You're supposed to answer 'present.' " He responded, "You haven't called my name yet—which [is] *not* 'Fie-o-rello.' " Miss Littlefield realized he didn't mean to be difficult. He simply thought it was time she learned to pronounce his name properly.[5]

———

In 1890, the Eleventh was transferred back to the frontier, this time to Fort Huachuca in the Arizona Territory. Located just north of the Mexican border, it was a stockade in the middle of an uncultivable, dust-blown desert. Recalled Fiorello, "Its barren hills and bleak surroundings made it exceedingly unpleasant and undesirable for grown-ups, but a paradise for a little boy." He would later say nostalgically, "All my boyhood memories are of those Arizona days." He "had a happy, wholesome boyhood"; he and his contemporaries "could do just about everything a little boy dreams of," such as learning to shoot "even when we were so small the gun had to be held for us by an elder."

When Fiorello was ten, the regiment was transferred 250 miles north to Whipple Barracks, still in the Arizona Territory. Situated on a high plateau just outside Prescott (population two thousand), the fort had originally been built to protect the town against marauding Apaches and other dangerous tribes by then either subdued or dispersed. Today a prosperous city, in La Guardia's time this former territorial capital could be placed in terms of economy and growth potential somewhere between moderately thriving and barely surviving—less a town with a glorious future than a romantic vestige of the once but quickly vanishing Wild West. To young Fiorello it was "the greatest, the most comfortable and the most wonderful city in the whole world." Prescott would always be his "hometown," where he spent his most formative, and happiest, childhood years. In the early 1920s, when president of the New York City Board of Aldermen, he reminisced, "Some of the lessons I learned about self-reliance in taking care of myself as a boy in Arizona are coming in handy now."[6]

He learned more than self-reliance during his six years in Prescott. He learned that there was more than a semantic difference between the haves and the have-nots. He learned to despise purveyors of racial hatred and ignorance and to identify with the underdog and the downtrodden. He learned to hate social injustice and, perhaps the most acute of his hatreds, political corruption: "Many are the things on which I have such strong feelings—feelings which some of my [political] opponents have regarded as unreasonable obsessions—were first impressed on my mind during those [Arizona] days, and the knowledge I acquired then never left me."

The adult Fiorello La Guardia did not play by the rules if the rules were to him a contravention of fairness and common decency.

This was especially true in his political life if those who might be taken advantage of comprised the class with which he would always identify: the people. But before we examine what catalyzed La Guardia's attitudes, let us see how a Jewish-Catholic Italian family fared on the vanishing American frontier, where anyone belonging to any one of these categories was held to be, for the most part, an oddity, an emissary of Satanic forces, or a wayward pilgrim from an evil alien world—if not a combination thereof.

According to Gemma, the family suffered from an ambiguous social status. Though Achille ranked third among the regiment's NCOs, his pay was but nine dollars a month, augmented by giving private music lessons. He was welcomed in the homes of some of the regimental officers in his capacity as music teacher to their children, but he and Irene were not welcomed as visitors. They were socially unacceptable within the Army caste system. Not so to the townspeople, many of whom exchanged visits with the bandmaster and his wife.

Achille performed at every important municipal function—almost always, music of his own composition—accompanied by Gemma and Fiorello. Gemma he taught the violin, mandolin, and piano; Fiorello, the banjo, cornet, and trumpet, which became the boy's instrument of choice. A demanding taskmaster, Achille would scream at the children whenever they made a mistake, no matter how trivial. Gemma invariably burst into tears. Her brother absorbed the reprimand and told Achille, "Keep on screaming, Papa, in this way I'll learn."[7] It was also from Papa that Fiorello "learned" to be temperamental and excessively demanding in adulthood.

Besides teaching his children musical instruments, Achille taught them Hebrew prayers, out of love for his wife and respect for her religious traditions (and perhaps out of disrespect for his own). Though neither parent ever attended church or synagogue, they wanted their children to be like other native-born children, most of whom were Protestant, so they sent them to the Episcopal Sunday school. Fiorello would become an observant Episcopalian, but there is no evidence that he was baptized or otherwise received in that faith.

Fiorello was from earliest childhood a precocious speaker who insisted on being heard—another trait he carried into adulthood. Often he would break in on Gemma and her friends at play, announce peremptorily, "I am going to speak," and jump up onto a table. Recalled Gemma, "He would speak on how teachers should teach children, on how parents should treat children, on this and that. If we appeared to be interested and paid attention, it was all right. But if we didn't, oh my, it was terrible!"[8]

Presumably the reason he wouldn't speak without a table was not the fear of going unheard but the fear of going unseen. Even among his shortest contemporaries Fiorello came across as midget-like. It didn't stop him from fighting bigger boys and opting to be walloped instead of backing down. Once, while fighting a schoolmate who was so much taller that Fiorello's fists couldn't even connect with his opponent's face, he ran into the schoolhouse sobbing uncontrollably—and reappeared with a chair. He plopped it down in front of his jeering tormentor, jumped up on it, and flailed away.[9]

Achille insisted that his children, unlike the others on the post, attend the town public school because he believed they would receive a better education there. Fiorello, not a brilliant student but a bright one and quick to learn, "was a headache to every one of" the five or six teachers. On his first day at the Prescott school he exhibited yet another of his character traits, the conviction that authority was always to be challenged. The incident involved Lena Coover. Prescott was her first job, and she "was jittery about it." Her pupils were quick to pick up on her nervousness and to make the most of it. Correcting Fiorello's arithmetic paper, she failed to notice that some of his examples were wrong. Next day, he purposely gave some wrong answers, which she marked as correct. "Like the fresh kid that I was," Fiorello approached her the following day and, pointing out the mistakes, said, "Look here, teacher, you better learn arithmetic if you are going to teach us." The upshot was that "she did learn arithmetic, and [when] we were through with her she could put us through our mechanical ropes." Fiorello and "Miss Lena" remained in contact over the years. In tribute to her former—and ever favorite—pupil, Miss Coover flew to New York to attend his funeral.

Of all the people who made impressions on Fiorello during his Arizona childhood, none aroused in him more loathing than those who practiced political chicanery and ethnic intolerance. The genesis of that loathing lay in his first observance, at Huachuca, of Bureau of Indian Affairs employees who were selling to miners, and even to general stores for resale, food provided free by Washington for the Native Americans. It was his first contact with politicians, for whom he harbored a lifelong detestation. Often he would yell aloud, "I loathe the professional politician!" A favorite La Guardia epithet for crooked officeholders in particular and politicians in general was "tinhorn." The term was originally applied to professional gamblers of the Old West. "If a 'tinhorn' in the West was caught cheating," Fiorello recalled, "he would never play another game—and there was no coroner's inquest." As mayor of New York, he made life unpleasant for all tinhorns who fed illicitly at the municipal trough. "They did not have to worry about being shot when caught red-handed. But they were made to fear the law."

Another early experience that left a mark was watching immigrant laborers build the railroad connecting Prescott with the territorial capital, Phoenix. If a laborer was injured, he lost his job. If killed, he went unidentified, as there was no record of his address or next of kin—or even of a name; he had just a number. As construction progressed, it left behind injured, jobless, stranded victims. There was always an immigrant labor pool available to draw from down the line. As a congressman, La Guardia fought to abrogate antiquated laws in favor of concepts we now take for granted: employers' liability, workers' compensation, guarantees of safe and sanitary conditions in the workplace, and unemployment insurance. It was Fiorello's early glimpse of these railroad builders—legally exploited, totally unprotected—that motivated his concern for the rights of laborers.

By the age of fourteen, Fiorello had determined to carry out his boyhood dreams of "going to work against corrupt government." If it can be said that his boyhood in Arizona was, in a sense, his prep school, his textbook was Joseph Pulitzer's *New York World*. Prescott had two papers, the *Journal Miner* and the *Courier*. But these were "typical Bret Harte Western newspapers" whose content was mostly local news. Pulitzer's *World* covered national events with a compulsion to expose corruption in high places. When the Sunday edition arrived at Prescott on the following Friday or Saturday, Fiorello would rush down to Ross's drugstore for a copy, rush home, and "carefully read every word" of the paper's fight against the nation's most crooked political machine, New York's Tammany Hall. For boys raised in the city, such revelations were not even of passing interest (unless their fathers' names and photos made the papers), but "the amazing discoveries hit" the frontier-bred Fiorello "like a shock. I could not understand how the people of the greatest city in this country could put up with the vice and corruption that existed there."

Though his Sunday reading created in Fiorello a resentment against Tammany that became in time an obsession, he did not become cynical or lose faith in government. Still in his pubescent stage, Fiorello "was certain that good people could eliminate bad people from public office." As he accrued years and wisdom and, above all, practical experience, his hatred of corrupt politicians and feelings against dishonest and inefficient government increased exponentially.

CHAPTER TWO

"I want to be somebody and do something really worthwhile"

1.

Fiorello's plans to enter high school ended when the Spanish-American War broke out and all dependent women and children of the Eleventh were sent to Jefferson Barracks in St. Louis, Missouri, while the regiment went off to Mobile, Alabama, for combat training. The fifteen-year-old was "restless" and "wanted to join the Army," but three factors precluded the possibility: He was too short, too underweight, and too young. Determined to join his father at Mobile, he persuaded a *St. Louis Post-Dispatch* editor to finance his journey there in return for some articles on the troops being trained for Cuba.

The new war correspondent made the front pages even before leaving St. Louis—not as the author of an article but as the subject. One of the Jefferson barracks caught fire, and loss of life was averted only because "a bright boy and an exceptionally fine cornetist ran into [the] blazing building [for] his cornet to blow the fire call." Accompanying the story was a picture of the ninety-pound, under-five-feet young man, hair parted down the middle, holding a cornet in his left hand, clothed in short pants, knee socks, and—typical of

Irene's fastidiousness in outfitting her children—a middy blouse with white bow-tie.[1]

His first dispatch from Mobile, ten days later, appeared under the headline "F. La Guardia, the *Post-Dispatch*'s Youthful Correspondent Heard From." Its theme was announced boldly: "EVERYBODY'S IN FINE SPIRITS." The troops were "a nice lot of spirited boys and the right sort of men to defend their country." All were "ready and anxious for the orders to go to Cuba." Equally anxious to get to Cuba, Fiorello got no closer to the war-torn island than Tampa, where, as the Eleventh was preparing to embark, Achille became violently ill.

After suffering for years from a digestive ailment, he had contracted malaria. This was followed almost immediately by a violent stomach disorder caused by eating some of the "embalmed beef" sold to the Army by corrupt contractors, so called because some of it was preserved ("embalmed") with boric acid and nitrate of potash. So rotten was the meat (five tons of it had been rejected for sale in England the previous year), much of it actually began exploding from its tins and spreading its poison all over the cases. Achille was honorably discharged for service-incurred "disease of stomach and bowels, catarrh of head and throat and malarial poisoning." Three weeks later he was awarded a pension: eight dollars a month.[2]

Though Achille would live another six years, his son would ever after maintain that his father died a victim of condemned Army meat. To young Fiorello—indeed, to just about everyone except Armour, the dishonest purveyor of the diseased meat, and the company's moral kindred among Army purchasing agents—this was "one of the worst scandals of our entire military history." It "made a lasting impression on me," he recalled. Moreover, it imbued him with a hatred for big corporations that would infuse his congressional career and make him the scourge of what he contemptuously referred to as "the Interests."

When he was strong enough to travel, Achille took the family back to Italy. Having exhausted his savings, and with only his meager Army pension to rely on, he believed he had a better chance at a new life in Europe, where the pension would go further. The La Guardias moved in temporarily with Irene's widowed mother while Achille set about attempting to make a living. Unable to establish himself in music, he tried a number of jobs, but the work demanded a physical strength he lacked. A friend, Raymond Willey, the American consular agent at Fiume, offered him a job with the consulate, but he had to decline because it didn't pay enough to support a family of five. According to Gemma, Fiorello "kept plugging away at the college books he had brought from America, preparing himself to enter the university someday. He was always so ambitious and smart."[3] When Fiorello turned eighteen the American consul in Budapest, through the good offices of Willey, hired him as his clerk-secretary. Meanwhile, with financial assistance from friends and relatives, Achille had leased a hotel on the island of Capo d'Istria near Trieste, which he quickly made flourish—so much so that he was soon in a position to purchase it. One week after completing negotiations to do so, on October 21, 1904, he died of heart disease.

There now began for the grief-stricken Irene and her children two years of frustration bound in red tape as she sought a pension to which she was entitled as the widow of an honorably discharged Army NCO. As required, she proved she had been lawfully married to Achille, had not remarried, and was "without other means of support than her daily labor and an actual net income not exceeding $250 per annum." A physician's affidavit attested that Achille's fatal heart disease had been caused by pulmonary emphysema, which had in turn derived from "hard labors in the military service (marches and wind instruments)." Washington denied Irene's application on the grounds that her husband did not die due to a service-incurred disability. Irene appealed, and on October 11, 1906, the United States government settled the case by awarding her the arrears of her late husband's pension. Total settlement: $12.80!

Irene's case created in Fiorello an irremediable disgust with and contempt for red tape and the bureaucrats who thrive in it. However, despite his negative feelings about the whole sordid business, and his disappointment for his mother's sake with the outcome, he did not condemn the government. It was, he insisted, the bureaucrats who treated his mother so shabbily, and the Interests—the vendors of that poisoned meat—who were the ultimate cause of his father's death.

Of the four or five underpaid, untrained secretaries and clerks at the Budapest embassy, Fiorello ranked lowest, at a paltry yearly salary of one hundred dollars, because of his age and lack of formal education. Thanks to a quick mind and an innate curiosity that amounted to a thirst for learning "useful things," he was able not only to advance himself but also to gain valuable experience. His duties included making out consular invoices, processing visa applications and American passports, and gathering and compiling statistics for the quarterly and annual reports to the State Department.

Also contributing to his rapid rise to the top of the heap was the mentorship of his superior, Consul General Frank Dyer Chester, a supercilious, misogynistic Harvard-educated Boston Brahmin, who assured Fiorello that because he lacked a Harvard degree he would never rise any higher than a position of clerk in the American foreign service. Still, Chester liked his young clerk despite his lack of polish, his impishness, and, as his career progressed, his penchant for rubbing others, including high-ranking Austrian and Hungarian aristocrats, the wrong way.

Chester appreciated Fiorello's thirst for knowledge, in particular his study of history and languages and the fact that he kept informed about current events at home by reading every newspaper and magazine he could find. Chester soon guided Fiorello in his study of languages. Having picked up Italian at home, he began to study both it and German systematically under Chester's tutelage. Because Chester wanted at least one of his clerks to learn the language that was one of the most spoken throughout the Austro-Hungarian Empire, and Fiorello seemed the logical choice, Chester sent him to Zagreb for four months to immerse himself in Croatian, a highly complicated language.

Temperamentally, each was the other's antithesis. Chester, reserved, exquisitely dressed and mannered; La Guardia, rambunctious, a haberdasher's worst nightmare, often out late with the ladies. About the only thing they had in common was their flair for languages. La Guardia picked up enough of the Hungarian language, like the Croatian, to be able to address his many Hungarian and Croat immigrant constituents when he entered New York politics.

2.

When Raymond Willey returned to the United States, he arranged for Fiorello to succeed him as consular agent at Fiume. It was a one-man operation, under Chester's supervision from Budapest. Though the salary was a meager eight hundred a year, Fiorello managed to "hold my own socially with the local government officials and junior Army officers with whom I associated." By year's end he "just about broke even. I had no debts, and I had no cash." His responsibilities were limited to such routine matters as consular services and bills of health for America-bound ships clearing Fiume. Any matters concerning the rights and problems of American citizens covered by treaties and protocols between the United States and Hungary were considered diplomatic in nature and came under the purview of the embassy at Budapest. At times he overstepped his authority, invariably stepping on the toes of local government officials.

Chester complained constantly to the State Department that Fiorello's behavior was "detrimental to the good relations that ought to exist" between Washington and Budapest.[4] The State Department decided he was Chester's problem, not theirs. Besides, Fiorello was not acting out of willfulness or caprice but out of genuine concern for the less fortunate with whom he came into contact on an official basis. Nowhere was that concern greater than when it came to the emigrants who passed through Fiume in an endless stream, to be shipped off to America.

When Fiorello first went to Fiume, in the autumn of 1903, the Cunard Line had just inaugurated a semimonthly passenger service of four slow-speed ships between Trieste and New York, geared predominantly for the burgeoning emigration traffic. Since no one in the Budapest embassy had had any experience with America-bound emigrants, Fiorello had to start from scratch. All he knew was that he must attest to the health of all passengers and crew and give the ship a certificate that it had cleared Fiume free from contagious diseases or illnesses consonant with U.S. quarantine regulations. But, although there were many causes for excluding of immigrants and many health and other restrictions on their being admitted into the United States, there existed no provisions for inquiry, investigation, and physical checkup in the country of origin or at the port of embarkation. Every ship that left Fiume returned with from a dozen to fifty passengers who had been turned back by U.S. Immigration doctors at Ellis Island, mainly for trachoma, a then widespread, highly contagious, untreatable ocular infection that caused blindness. Thousands were rejected yearly, from this or another of the many unacceptable conditions, and were forced to return to their native lands impoverished, having sold whatever they owned to finance their passage in the first place.

How much more humane, La Guardia felt, if passengers were examined at their source of embarkation. He discussed the matter with Chester, who agreed that Fiorello could retain a physician to inspect all emigrants and prevent from sailing anyone afflicted with a contagious or loathsome disease that would preclude admission at the other end. La Guardia retained the services of a physician, Dr. S. de Emili. When the two boarded the Cunard liner SS *Aurania* for La Guardia's first embarkation, the captain believed it would be business as usual: a get-acquainted cup of tea with the new American consular agent, to be followed by the pro forma issuance of the requisite Bill of Health.

La Guardia passed up the cup of tea, introduced Dr. de Emili, and inquired about the health of the passengers and crew, in particular the approximately eighty emigrants, whom he now intended Dr. de Emili to examine personally. The captain and the company agents insisted vigorously that they would not permit such an examination. The Hungarian officials present said that detecting anyone who would be found inadmissible in New York and weeding him out before the ship sailed made perfect sense. The captain and the Cunard officials remained adamant. Advising them that he had come to do his job, not engage in a pointless debate, La Guardia motioned to the doctor to join him as he walked off the ship.

Barely had he returned to his office when a Cunard agent came for the Bill of Health. When he returned to the ship with word of La Guardia's refusal to issue it, the Cunard officials realized that he was serious. The *Aurania*'s captain went to the consulate to protest personally—but to no avail. Giving up after an hour, he escorted La Guardia and Dr. de Emili back to the ship, where each of the emigrants was examined and properly certified. The line paid the requisite five-dollar fee for the Bill of Health but refused La Guardia's demand that they pay Dr. de Emili's fee. When another Cunard vessel came in a few days later, La Guardia insisted that the line pay the doctor's bill for both ships before he would clear the second one. Cunard paid—and added this little stunt to the formal protest it insisted the British consul file with Chester against La Guardia's actions. Chester wrote to Washington for instructions. The State Department replied that consular agents had the power to execute and enforce immigration laws.

La Guardia knew from the outset that he had only vague authority for his actions, and he had no idea whether he would be backed up by Chester, let alone the State Department. He had acted out of the conviction that what he was doing was not only humanitarian, it was right. Here was the singular conviction by which he would operate throughout his political career: doing what he believed to be the right thing—even on those rare occasions when he was wrong. Since Washington never did give a definite decision regarding his insistence on presailing physical examinations, he kept on with the practice. Even the steamship companies complied, after Fiorello pointed out to them the obvious: that they had to bring back the rejected penniless emigrants at company expense.

For some time thereafter, Fiume was the only port that inspected emigrants prior to embarkation. During his three-year posting, La Guardia personally oversaw the inspection of some ninety thousand emigrants. It was no small satisfaction that while the rejection rate for trachoma from other ports averaged two dozen for each ship reaching the United States, a total of just four from Fiume were rejected at Ellis Island. An even greater source of satisfaction for Fiorello came twenty-five years later when Congressman La Guardia got legislation enacted making such examinations mandatory worldwide, under the management of the Public Health Service.

In April 1906, La Guardia petitioned Washington to upgrade Fiume to a consulate, independent of Budapest, and to upgrade him in rank, due to the rising flow of emigrants being handled by his office, plus the rising export-import trade between Hungary and the United States. Chester supported the petition when forwarding it to the State Department. Despite his complaints, he considered Fiorello not only the best of his subordinates but the one most likely to make the consular service a career if accorded higher rank and pay. He added that although La Guardia was at times "contentious," he was prompt and diligent in the discharge of his official duties, totally honest and fair, eager to learn, and—no small consideration here—proficient in the local languages. The request was denied. Fiorello then requested transfer to Belgrade as consul general of Serbia.

When this too was denied, he wrote, on March 7, 1906, that if his "knowledge and six years service are not sufficient to counterbalance his total lack of political influence, the undersigned begs for a special examination or appointment to a post within the United States (Department of State or Immigration Service, N.Y.). If none of the above can be practically granted there remains no doubt that the diplomatic service is not the place for a young man to work up."[5]

Again refused, Fiorello realized he had hit a dead end. "Don't be angry, Mother," he told Irene, "but I'm going to return to New York. I am ambitious. I want to study and to get somewhere in my own country. I want to be somebody and do something really worthwhile."[6] On June 5, 1906, Chester wrote to the Secretary of State that La Guardia had left for the States in hopes of obtaining from the department by personal interview "a higher position in the service than his indiscretions seem to fit him for."[7] Chester was right about Fiorello leaving but wrong about his intentions. He worked his passage home as a steward on a British ship, also acting as interpreter and assisting the ship's doctor in vaccinating 1,800 emigrants on board. His brother, Richard, was made acting consul at Fiume. Irene went to live with Gemma and her new husband in Budapest.

CHAPTER THREE

Interlude: Portrait of a corrupt metropolis

1.

By the time La Guardia returned to the city of his birth it was second only to London in population, second to none in corruption. When New York was the nation's first capital, what lay north of present-day Canal Street was a scattering of small settlements and villages (one of which was named Greenwich). Throughout the rest of the eighteenth century and well into the nineteenth, the city—which was in fact only Manhattan Island—expanded northward, incorporating those villages and settlements, taming the land and annexing much of the boroughs of the Bronx, Queens, and Staten Island. Outward growth was complemented by upward growth, with the development of steel-frame construction and invention of the elevator dramatically altering the city's skyline. On January 1, 1898, with the annexation of Brooklyn, the boundaries were fixed.

Thus came into being the New York we know today. Anomalously, the counties (New York, Kings, Queens, Bronx, and Richmond) remained subdivisions of the state, while the corresponding boroughs (Manhattan, Brooklyn, Queens, the Bronx, and Staten Island) were now subdivisions of the city. Here let it be noted that, contrary to common assumption and usage, there is no such entity as "New York

City." The proper term is "the City of New York," but popular custom demands the use of "New York City" or "New York" when referring to what has also acquired the appellations "Gotham" and "the Big Apple."

Under the reorganization, the city was to be governed by a more powerful mayor than in the past. This was the Republican-controlled state legislature's way of reining in the numerically superior Democrats. An assembly of two chambers, the Board of Aldermen and the Board of Estimate and Apportionment, was created to support the mayor. Consisting originally of the mayor and two commissioners, the Board of Estimate and Apportionment was organized in 1864 to supervise the regional police force and was given some say in the annual budget. Three years later, in response to a public outcry that the mayor's power be curbed, the chief executive of each borough (today the borough president) was added to the board. Corruption in the Board of Aldermen led at the turn of the century to its loss of power; the restructured Board of Estimate would wield the true power in the city until the 1980s, when the Supreme Court ruled it unconstitutional on the grounds that it violated the principle of one man, one vote.

The 1898 amalgamation created a metropolis of 320 square miles with 578 miles of waterfront that within two years contained a population of over 3,437,000—twice the population of Chicago and more than all but six of the then forty-six states. Over a third of the resident population was foreign born. Of these, the largest group was the Germans, whose immigration dated back to colonial times, followed by the Irish, whose early numbers were increased dramatically as a result of the Great Potato Famine of the 1840s. The Italians and European Jews, who by the outbreak of World War I constituted the city's two largest ethnic blocs, would soon outnumber them.

Enlarging the city led to the building of connecting subways. The first was completed in 1904 at a cost of thirty million dollars and the labor of twelve thousand men, many of them recently arrived Italian immigrants. A few years later Manhattan was connected to the other boroughs by bridges, and subsequently to New Jersey by the Holland and Lincoln tunnels so that travelers from beyond the Hudson need no longer detrain at Hoboken on the Jersey side and be ferried across.[1] As the city moved northward, the moneyed class followed, dragging along like the train on a dowager's gown the emporia and cultural venues that catered to their every taste and diversion. Novelist Edith Wharton recalled the elegance of Fifth Avenue uptown, "along which genteel landaus, broughams and victorias, and more countrified vehicles of the 'carry-all' and 'surrey' type moved up and down at decent intervals and a decorous pace." To respectable New Yorkers, politics was looked down upon with the same haughty contempt in which those engaged in "trade" were held. "No retail dealer, no matter how palatial his shop-front or how tempting his millions, was received in New York society until long after I was grown up," Wharton remembered.[2]

Situated between the aristocracy and, to the south, the nation's financial center, named for a street that had once been walled, lived what Danish-born ex-police reporter turned sociologist Jacob Riis termed collectively "the other half." And what a pathetic half it was! When the upper class moved out, leaving only pockets of middle- and lower-class residents, the poor, in many cases destitute, immigrants moved in. Avaricious landlords replaced single houses with a surfeit of sordid multiple-residence edifices. These tenements, as they were called, were so crowded, so filthy, so utterly unfit for human habitation that to read Riis's descriptions of them is almost like an exercise in masochism.[3]

The first European to view the island that would become Manhattan was Giovanni da Verrazzano. In April 1524, while seeking the Northwest Passage in the service of Francis I of France, he dropped anchor in the Lower Bay, below the point where the Narrows Bridge that bears his name would one day be erected. Presumably due to a threatening storm, he never set foot on the island. Before sailing off, he named what we now know as the Hudson River the Vendôme to honor the king's ducal brother; the island he named Angoulème to honor Francis's heir. The next European to approach the island was a Negro named Esteban Gómez in the service of King Charles of Spain. Arriving on January 17, 1526, he didn't go ashore either, due also to inclement weather. Like Verrazzano, however, Gómez gave a name of his own to the river up which he sailed: The Angoulème now became the San Antonio, to commemorate the date of his arrival, the feast day of St. Anthony.

The river's present eponym, as every schoolchild knows, was the next European to visit. This was, of course, Henry Hudson, who sailed his *Half Moon* up what he called simply "the Great Stream" on September 2, 1609. Unlike his two predecessors, Hudson did go ashore, where he found a number of natives with whom he bartered knives and beads for beaver and otter furs. From this paltry beginning came a trickle that would burgeon almost three centuries later into a massive invasion, predominantly by Europeans: not explorers or adventurers but emigrants, in quest not of beaver and otter pelts but of freedom from the political and economic oppression and privation of their native lands and a chance at a new and infinitely better life.

Between 1880 and 1919 there occurred the greatest population transfer in history as more than twenty-five million immigrants came to America. More than seventeen million of them landed at New York. Many went no farther. So great was the influx that Castle Garden, the main reception station at the Battery dating from 1855, was taken over by the federal government in 1890. Two years later the operation was transferred to Ellis Island, near the Statue of Liberty, where a number of buildings were constructed specifically for the processing of immigrants.

The earlier immigrants had been mainly from Northern and Western Europe: Scots, English, Irish, French, Dutch, German, and Scandinavian. The next great wave was from Southern and Eastern Europe, at first mainly Italians, then more and more Russians, Poles, Austrians, Hungarians, and refugees from the eternally contentious Balkans. More so than those who had preceded them here, these later immigrants were, for the most part, in flight from poverty or oppression. Of these immigrants, the two ethnic groups to which New York is most indebted for its dramatic population growth are the two from which Fiorello La Guardia was descended and his political core constituency derived: the Italians and the Jews.

Until the 1860s, the city's Italian population was very small, made up largely of peasants and landless laborers from Italy's economically depressed southern half. The year 1870 saw the phenomenon of entire villages emigrating, a movement that went on for two decades. By 1900, there were 145,000 in the city. Twenty years later the number had more than doubled to 391,000. Most came from the land but had no desire to return to it. Not all, however, had been tillers of the soil. Some were masons, who had no difficulty getting jobs, with all the construction taking place. Their work can be seen on the façades of the many buildings dating from that period that survive to this day. Most, though, were not only uneducated but illiterate. Possessing hardly any skills, they became day laborers, taking the places of those earlier Irish immigrants who had moved on to other occupations or, in some cases, achieved upward mobility.

Many of the southern Italians who settled in the Fourteenth Congressional District moved into the barely habitable Five Points area below Canal Street that had been abandoned by the Irish; they also settled into neighborhoods north as well as south of Canal. Taking a dislike to the new arrivals, whom they looked down upon, those from northern Italy decamped to an area in the northwest section of Greenwich Village, centering on Bleecker Street, known today as Little Italy.

Of all the immigrant groups, the Italians were the most cohesive. This was owing to their inborn distrust of strangers and outsiders, perhaps a psychological consequence of having lived in isolated rural communities back in the old country. As their numbers increased, they formed other "Little Italies" in East Harlem, in the Red Hook section of Brooklyn, and eventually in the Bronx south of Fordham Road. Unlike the Jewish immigrants, these early Italians dismissed higher education as not only a waste of time but an unjustified delay in assuming the responsibilities of adulthood. Many who were naturalized did not even vote until La Guardia—a *paisano*, one of their own—came on the scene.

The first settler in what was to become the largest Jewish population in the world was Jacob Bar Simon, a Dutch Jew, who arrived in July 1654, followed weeks later by twenty-seven of his brethren from Brazil. These were Jews who had fled to South America after their expulsion from Spain and Portugal. Peter Stuyvesant, the city's first director general, objected to the decision of his masters, the Dutch West India Company, that the Jews be permitted to reside in "Nieuw [New] Amsterdam," as the island was now known, if able "to take care of their own poor." He barred them from most trades, forcing them to subsist by slaughtering and butchering cattle. By the time Stuyvesant departed, they were permitted to buy property, engage in trade, and enjoy most privileges of a citizen except the right to hold public office.[4]

In 1801, there occurred what, more than any other factor, precipitated the mass Jewish exodus from Russia and, to a lesser extent, Poland, at the time under Russian domination: the assassination of Czar Alexander II, who had eased many statutes discriminatory toward the Jews. The consequent pogroms against the Jews (who had absolutely nothing to do with the assassination) and the imposition of severe restrictions sanctioned by the murdered emperor's morally bankrupt heir, Alexander III, prompted some 150,000 of them to flee in that decade alone, mostly to the United States. As the pogroms intensified after 1890, the exodus gained momentum.

In 1906, the year La Guardia resettled in New York, 259,000 Jewish immigrants were processed at Ellis Island. Within three years there were 1,100,000 Jews in New York City alone, and they now made up roughly a quarter of the city's population. Most of these Eastern European Jews came not from the farmlands but from towns and cities. More than two-thirds—men and single women—qualified for employment in the various trades, an unusually high percentage among immigrants regardless of ethnicity or site of origin. Some 145,000 gave their occupation as tailor, 23,000 as shoemaker, 17,000 as clerk or bookkeeper. Eager to advance themselves in their new homeland, they settled on the Lower East Side, in buildings owned by many of the "uptown" German Jews who had arrived earlier, assimilated and moved uptown, and tended to look with disdain upon their Eastern European brethren, whose outlandish dress and use of Yiddish instead of German they found not only an embarrassment but a threat to their own status. Their squalid tenements were overcrowded to the extent that the habitation density was 524 per acre, the city's highest. One block alone contained thirty-nine tenements housing 2,781 people who were forced to share but 264 toilets and one bathtub.[5]

These immigrants were the dominant labor force in the garment industry, known colloquially as "the rag trade." Most—the so-called sweaters—were forced to work in either the sweatshops of subcontractors or, for the most part, in their own dingy rooms on a piecework basis. They were underpaid and overexploited. Those unable to find jobs resorted to peddling, which became a big business on the Lower East Side. Streets like Hester, Ludlow, Orchard, and Essex were awash with women and men hawking from pushcarts everything from dry goods, used clothing ("I cash old clothes!"), and perishable foodstuffs to candles and matches—in short, whatever they bought from a wholesaler and retailed for whatever the traffic would bear. Because so many of the men dressed in "funny" long black coats and large furred hats (*stremels*) and spoke with a thick strange accent, and they had come in such numbers, many Americans—even those not long here themselves—began to feel somewhat threatened. Ere long, the first signs of anti-Semitism appeared.

The nation, and in particular New York, had been free of this evil. The more economically secure uptown German Jews, in their desire to conform and assimilate, had escaped such condemnation. Now many of them joined in the chorus of contempt. The Eastern European newcomers, unlike the Western Europeans who had preceded them, were perceived by other ethnics, both already assimilated or newly arrived, as a disturbing, alien force. Soon there arose the stereotypical "Jew as an Oriental figure hoarding secrets of recondite wisdom and trained in the arts of commercial deception" and "as a figure of surreptitious accumulation, gothic or medieval in style, performing mysterious rites in the dives of the modern city."[6]

Persecution at the hands of Russian authorities had turned many into political radicals—Socialists—thus magnifying the threat exponentially. As a consequence, all Jews, including those who had long since been accepted, were soon faced with discrimination, such as finding certain neighborhoods along with clubs and societies closed to them. This, in turn, reinforced the argument for proposals to limit Jewish immigration, primarily by establishing quotas. With quotas also established at the major universities and colleges, the children of these immigrants wound up at the publicly supported College of the City of New York, familiarly known as City College. Enrollment was open to all who could pass its entrance exams regardless of ethnic background, even if they could not afford the tuition.

The children of the Eastern European Jews by 1900 made up 85 percent of the student body—a figure that would remain constant for decades until major universities began opening their doors to Jews. In time, those who could manage it decamped the Lower East Side ghettos for Brownsville and Williamsburg in Brooklyn, where a number of clothing concerns had their factories. The more prosperous, many of whom were achieving upward mobility in the professions, moved to Harlem or the Bronx—and eventually to Central Park West on Manhattan's Upper West Side, which became, as it remains to this day, a cluster of Jewish intellectuals and creative artists who helped make the area an epicenter of the city's cultural life.

2.

Now that we have looked at the two major constituencies to whose protection and betterment Fiorello La Guardia would dedicate himself, let us look at Tammany Hall, whose stranglehold on his beloved city he would dedicate himself to eliminating. It was founded innocuously enough, immediately following the American Revolution, as a fraternal and charitable organization. The name derived from the mythic Tammany, or Tammanend, of Native American folklore, who lived beyond the Appalachians and was said to have been a warrior and hunter of great renown as well as a paragon of benevolence and doer of noble deeds who discovered bread and tobacco, taught his people how to make canoes from birch bark, improved the design of the bow and arrow, and, as a grand finale of sorts, created the five Great Lakes. Or so the legend goes. Another, more logical source of the name was Tamanend, a colonial Delaware Indian chief known for his wisdom, munificence, and love of freedom.

Initially called the Society of St. Tammany ("Saint" was intended as an anti-Catholic slur), it first met in 1786, though it was not officially organized until three years later. Its generally nonpartisan membership was made up primarily of tradesmen, artisans, and workmen and included a number of more affluent citizens who subscribed to its antiaristocratic tenets. According to its manifesto, which was about as far as one could get from what the club evolved into eventually, it was "instituted primarily as a social, fraternal and benevolent organization, based on democratic principles [whose] membership was not determined by caste, but that all might mingle on the basis of manhood rather than on that of wealth and culture."[7]

Its first Grand Sachem, as their leader was called, was an upholsterer and paperhanger named William Mooney, rumored to be an ex-soldier who had deserted the Continental forces in 1776 and gone over to the British. The charge was never proved (or disproved, for that matter). However, Mooney was probably just a figurehead. From all evidence it was a prosperous, liberal-minded merchant and philanthropist named John Pintard who gave Tammany Hall (its later, more popular locution) its initial form and substance. In framing the Society's constitution, Pintard defined its most significant principle, an aversion to aristocratic privilege and a belief in the common man: "a political institution founded on a strong republican basis whose democratic principles will serve in some measure to correct the aristocracy of our city." It was apparently also Pintard who devised the medley of Indian-style officers, titles, and ceremonial. Members—"braves"—elected yearly thirteen sachems to rule the Society, plus a scribe (secretary), treasurer, sagamore (master of ceremonies), and wiskinsky (doorkeeper). The thirteen, who chose one of their number to be Grand Sachem, each ruled a "tribe" within the Society with its own okemaw (warrior), mackawalaw (hunter), and alank (clerk). These were little more than planners of social events and ceremonies.[8]

For meetings, all members dressed in beads, feathers, and blankets, exchanged the secret handshake, and passed the peace pipe. In parades, they marched, like Indians, in single file and carried tomahawks or bows and arrows. Such trappings were abandoned during the War of 1812, when it became known that American Indians had sided with the British and committed atrocities against American soldiers. Also, within a generation, Pintard's desire that Tammany "correct the aristocracy" had slowly evolved into Tammany's determination to "correct the masses." Its cunning leaders became expert in exacting graft from those who wanted political help or favors and in otherwise circumventing any and all municipal codes. One city official, with Tammany's blessing if not outright collusion, embezzled $1,250,000 in city funds, truly a cosmic sum for the times, and departed for sites unknown.

Originally restricted in membership to "native-born patriots," Tammany did not wish to fraternize with the lower economic groups, in particular the immigrant Irish who poured into the city during this period. All that changed on April 24, 1817, when hundreds of them tried literally to pull down the Wigwam, as the Society's headquarters, or hall, was called. It was deemed prudent to abandon the anti-immigrant policy. Within a couple of years the Irish were sharing parity with the propertied element. Within a few years, they were in the majority—and in control. Letting in the immigrants proved over time to be a propitious move. They helped their economically and politically deprived fellow braves, along with those who came after, to obtain naturalization. By thus increasing its numbers, Tammany increased its strength and political influence. Every naturalized citizen represented a vote—more often than not, two or three. Ironically, these braves became the chiefs who went on to become a—perhaps *the*—paramount factor in transmuting the gold of Tammany's initial good name and intent into the dross of political venality. Touching all bases, as the century progressed the Wigwam moved into prostitution and other socially unacceptable commercial ventures, while concurrently tightening its grip on the city and on the Democratic Party.

Two factors above all others contributed to the rapid and expansive growth of Tammany's power and influence: massive immigration and an exploding economy. With its economic strength, begun by the South Street merchants and subsumed by the Wall Street bankers, New York became indeed the mother of all metropolises—or, to put it in Tammany context, the mother of all cookie jars. Concurrently, the immigrants fairly inundating the city formed a new constituency whose needs—food, clothing, jobs, assistance in adjusting, protection against discrimination and persecution—were not being met. The city's government was unequal to the task, and its old-time governing elite turned away from involvement. Thus another vacuum had been created. And since nature's abhorrence of vacuums must be resolved, Tammany was happy to oblige.

As the old ruling class abdicated from practical politics, visiting the lower wards only to deliver moral manifestoes, the professional pols moved in.[9] In exchange for votes, Tammany saw to the basic needs of the newcomers. (The term "votes" as used here requires qualification. In return for Tammany's concern and largesse, many of the immigrants were happy to serve on election day as "repeaters"—running all over town casting ballots again and again, under the names of registered voters who either had not yet made it to the polling places or were unable to because they were dead.)

From that power base the most capable and least principled of its leaders arose to take command of the city. There was money galore ("oodles of boodle") to be manipulated. Two factors militated in Tammany's favor: the paucity of effective election and conflict-of-interest laws to inhibit the sachems; and the fact that the time had passed when "the best, the most intelligent, the most active men of the city, of all classes and vocations, did not hesitate to devote hours, and days, and nights of their time, without hope or desire or remuneration, to the affairs of the city."[10]

As there was yet no Civil Service, New York's aldermen controlled all city jobs. Since they owed their election to Tammany, the Hall was soon staffing the municipal government with its people. This was especially true of the Police Department, which by 1855 was more than a third Irish. Their willingness to look the other way whenever Tammany goons trashed the opposition was a continuing scandal. City politics was in a state of chaos, thanks in large measure to the splinter parties that had not yet departed the national political scene. The Whigs were in decline. The Republicans, into which they would evolve as a result of the Kansas-Nebraska Act and the *Dred Scott* decision, had yet to be born. Other groups like the anti-Catholic (and just about anti–everybody else but their own bigoted selves) Know-Nothing Party came and went. Moreover, Tammany did not yet dominate the Democratic Party in New York and was itself split asunder by internal dissention.

Then along came John Kelly, known as "Honest John" for putting graft on a smooth-running, businesslike basis. Each Democratic candidate for a municipal office guaranteed his election with an obligatory "assessment," as bribes were termed euphemistically, to the Hall. Kelly himself, whose influence extended north to Albany through his control of the downstate delegation to the state legislature, effected the absolutely mesmerizing fiscal miracle of stashing away eight hundred thousand dollars (some fifty million dollars in today's purchasing power) during his six-year leadership of Tammany as the unsalaried sheriff of New York County. His popularity among the faithful climaxed when he secured the election of William R. Grace as the city's first Irish and first Catholic mayor.

For the first half of the nineteenth century, when Tammany was consolidating its power as a political force, no one man had come along to bring order out of chaos. Were it to avoid eventual self-destruction, what was needed was one sachem powerful and corrupt enough to unify the Democrats under the Tammany banner preparatory to solidifying control of the city. Fortunately, into the Wigwam slithered such a man: William Marcy Tweed. That Tweed aspired to so lofty a position, let alone succeeded, was due to his avoiding the mistakes made by the most venal, most corrupt mayor the city was ever to know. His name was Fernando Wood (1812–81), and he stands historically as Fiorello La Guardia's polar opposite.

Son of a bankrupt Philadelphia merchant who had relocated to New York, the suave and handsome Fernando was an actor, wine dealer, cigar maker, and proprietor of a waterfront grocery and grog shop. Joining Tammany in the 1830s and working his way through the system, Wood was elected to Congress in 1840. Looking on this less as a career than as a career move, he retired back to New York after one term, devoted the next few years to making a fortune as a merchant shipper by means less fair than foul, and in 1850 ran for mayor with Tammany's blessing and backing. But the knowledge that he had cheated a local bank and swindled a partner in his shipping firm of profits from the California trade, plus the allegation that he was a secret member of the Know-Nothing Party, which hardly endeared him to the Irish voters, cost him the race.

Four years later, the sachems helped the unpopular Wood narrowly defeat three other candidates, thanks primarily to their absolute control of the Sixth Ward, which gave him four hundred more votes than the district's total number of registered voters. In a bid to buy respectability, he championed a number of civic reforms. These included closure of saloons on Sundays (a standing law that had gone unenforced, mainly because most of them were owned by Tammanyites), clearing Broadway of the doxies who considered that major artery their exclusive trawling grounds by right of eminent domain, and insisting that hack drivers abandon their custom of overcharging fares shamelessly. He supported the construction of Central Park—on a site where stood the city's largest agglomeration of shantytowns and human-inhabited pigsties that, it is said, even the pigs who roamed the area would not be caught inhabiting—proposed establishing a city university (a notion that his Tammany puppeteers considered downright ridiculous), and instituted a "complaint book" in City Hall where citizens could register their gripes about municipal services. (Wood did not promise those gripes would be addressed, and suffice it to say they weren't. He just promised people were free to come in and write 'em down.) Perhaps Wood's most audacious move was to make the police directly responsible to him.

When the sachems complained about the Sunday closings, he deemed it prudent to let the saloons stay open. Also, word went out that the whores were free to again cruise Broadway. Seeking reelection in 1856, Wood not only ordered the police to contribute to his campaign fund, he used them to bar voters opposed to him and allow supporters to walk off with the ballot boxes. Winning, albeit narrowly, Wood discarded like a vermin-infested nightshirt his earlier veneer of righteousness. City offices were sold to the highest bidder, with the understanding that the buyer was entitled to get his money back by any means he deemed appropriate—or possible. Bills to the city were padded, the excess going to Wood. It was business as usual.

Responding to outcries that the city was as lawless as ever, the state legislature voted to abolish Wood's municipal police force and institute in its place a Metropolitan Police, to be run by five commissioners, appointed by the governor. Wood refused to recognize the new force or disband his own. This left the city with two rival police forces that expended more time and effort fighting each other than fighting crime. When the mayor's force prevented a newly named commissioner from entering City Hall to take office, a donnybrook broke out between the two rival forces. "The scene was a terrible one," according to the *New York Times*. "Blows upon naked heads fell thick and fast, and men rolled helpless down the steps, to be leaped upon and beaten until life seemed extinct." Joining in the melee, a horde of passersby improvised clubs by tearing branches off trees and whacked away.[11]

Fortuitously, troops of the Seventh National Guard Regiment marching down Broadway en route to embarkation for a ceremonial visit to Boston happened by, and their commander, realizing the state's authority was in jeopardy, ordered them to disperse the mob and storm City Hall on behalf of the Metropolitans. When order had been restored, the commander entered the building and personally arrested Mayor Wood. A month later the courts upheld Albany's authority to impose the Metropolitan force. Though Wood never stood trial—Tammany "owned" the judges—his authority had been severely compromised by the whole affair, and he had become a source of public ridicule and condemnation. Within the year he made a complete fool of himself by urging that New York protect its commercial interests by befriending the southern states then seceding from the Union. He somehow managed to get back into Congress, where he served nine more terms. His wings now clipped, he was unable to do any more damage; but then; it can be asked, what further damage *could* he have done?

Fernando Wood established the norm for all subsequent crooked mayors. It was William Marcy Tweed who established the norm for all subsequent city bosses. Indeed, he was the first to have imposed upon him the cognomen "Boss." He wore it with pride, this "last vulgar Protestant to win a prominent place in the city's life." (All the other Tammany bosses were Roman Catholic.)[12] Tweed was elected to the Board of Aldermen in 1851 after a previous failed attempt. The aldermen were responsible for all municipal patronage, public franchises, and civic improvements, of which a greatly expanding New York City was in dire need at midcentury. They also exercised a powerful judicial function, appointing grand juries and trying election violators.

One of Tweed's more memorable lines was "There never was a time when you couldn't buy the Board of Aldermen." Tweed and his fellow aldermen were so easily "bought" that they became known as the Forty Thieves. City contracts were padded (one five-hundred-dollar batch of Fourth of July fireworks was billed at four thousand dollars); appointments to city jobs were sold on the open market (the franchise for a new horsecar line on Third Avenue cost the bidder eighteen thousand dollars in bribes). Then there was the "strike legislation," a Tweed innovation that reaped the Forty Thieves a windfall through sheer volume. A fictitious resolution would be introduced threatening some merchant, whereupon the alderman sponsoring the bill would call upon the distressed merchant and promise that for $250 he'd make sure the bill was killed in committee. The merchant gladly paid, never realizing he had been taken.

As eponymous head of a band of four known to history as the Tweed Ring, the Boss set an all-time record for municipal plunder, investing himself with a patina of legality by becoming one of the city's leading property owners. But the real money was earned the old-fashioned way: Lumber worth $45,000, for example, was sold to the city for $460,000; eleven thermometers, which cost pennies each, went for $7,500; a pile of mops and brooms cost $41,191. The Ring took 65 percent off the top of each transaction, with the balance of the profit going to the cooperating merchants and middlemen.

While his activities were widely known—though not the number of millions he stole from the city—only two journals, *Harper's Weekly* and the *New York Times*, went after Tweed.

They didn't get far. With a shrewdness that you just had to admire in the man, he named a blue-ribbon panel comprised of the city's biggest landowners, headed by the biggest of the lot, John Jacob Astor III, to examine the allegedly tainted municipal books. The panel found the books to be in good order. Historical gossip has it that the panel either was not shown the real books or was threatened with property assessment increases were the members to find anything amiss. End of investigation.

Tweed's downfall came as a result of a classic tradition: a falling-out among thieves. When one Tammany ward heeler, jealous of the Boss's power, demanded a payoff and was refused, he gained access to the books and to incriminating documents, which he turned over to the *Times*. The many judges Tweed had bought either resigned or were impeached. Two of his three co-Ringmasters escaped to Europe; the third escaped conviction when the jury was unable to reach a verdict. Of the millions that went south, the city managed to recoup a comparatively paltry $876,241. Tweed died in jail on April 12, 1878, taking to his grave a most tantalizing secret: what became of the millions he personally had pocketed, said to equal some five billion dollars in today's purchasing power. Much of it is believed to have wound up in the pockets of a number of Tweed confederates, including his successor, the aforementioned Boss "Honest John" Kelly.

As George Washington Plunkitt, the Hall's philosopher-in-residence, put it, "See how beautiful a Tammany city government runs, with a so-called boss directin' the whole shootin' match! The machinery moves so noiseless you wouldn't think there was any. If there's any differences of opinion, the Tammany leader settles them quietly, and his orders go every time."[13] Plunkitt—who had he not been born to woman would have probably been created by Damon Runyon—was the Democratic ward boss on Manhattan's Lower East Side at the time of Achille and Irene La Guardia's arrival. Gracious, garrulous, above all unpretentious, he maintained his "office" at the bootblack stand in front of City Hall even though he harvested four salaries—simultaneously—as a magistrate, alderman, county supervisor, and state senator. It was said one could count on the fingers of either hand the number of times the man who coined the phrase "honest graft" attended to any of his salaried tasks.

It was left to Kelly's subordinate and successor, Richard Croker, to sum up, if not the Hall's justification, then certainly its philosophy. Commenting to an English editor that New York's wealthy, educated citizens were incapable of municipal governance because they disdained "political work," he posited that it was obligatory upon the city's leaders to interest the masses in politics, and the only way to accomplish that was through the spoils system (to give the term "graft" its more respectable euphemism).[14]

Around the time Croker was expounding this mind-set, the pudgy little ex–American consular agent at Fiume with the high-pitched voice and large Stetson hat was preparing to prove that such reasoning was not only fallacious, it was downright abhorrent.

CHAPTER FOUR

"The more I got to know about lawyers and their ethics, the less respect I had for them"

1.

La Guardia arrived back in America determined to complete his education, get admitted to the bar, then enter public life. But first he needed a job. Raymond Willey, who had gotten him the consular post at Fiume, offered him one with his brick-manufacturing company in Portsmouth, Ohio. Realizing after a few weeks that making bricks in Ohio was hardly the ideal launching point for a projected ascent into public life, Fiorello returned to New York. He found lodgings in the home of an old friend of Irene's who still lived in the Village, got a job with the Society for the Prevention of Cruelty to Children that paid ten dollars a week, and quickly moved on to clerking for a steamship company at fifteen dollars a week. Anxious to make more money, and knowing this was impossible without marketable employment skills, Fiorello invested forty-five dollars in a six-week stenography course at the Pratt Institute, which got him a job as stenographer with the clothiers Abercrombie & Fitch at twenty dollars a week.

He then took the U.S. Civil Service examination in an area for which his job experience at Fiume qualified him: interpreter at the

Ellis Island Immigration Center. Placing highest among three candidates, he was immediately put on the eligibility list due to his command of—in addition to Italian and German—Hungarian and Croatian, languages spoken by many immigrants but understood by few, if any, immigration officers. That, plus quickly endearing himself to the commissioner of immigration in New York, Robert Watchorn, won him an appointment to the service on November 12, 1907, at $1,200 a year.[1] Through his contacts with so many Jewish immigrants, Fiorello quickly mastered Yiddish. Meanwhile he applied for entrance to New York University Law School. Told that his credits earned in Arizona schools were unacceptable and that he would have to pass Regents' Examinations for the equivalent of prelaw school courses, he signed up with the New York Preparatory School. He easily passed the exams in time to be admitted to the NYU Law School evening-session fall semester, around the time he began his day job at Ellis Island.

For the first two years, 1908 and 1909, La Guardia worked seven days a week, taking the subway to the Battery and then the 8:40 government ferry to Ellis Island. Immigrants were pouring in at the average rate of five thousand a day. From the moment they were herded ashore they were caught up in a processing routine that must have made many feel they were about to enter not Uncle Sam's Land of Opportunity but Dante's Hell. Clutching for dear life all their worldly possessions and, if they had any, their children, they were carried along in a line of jostling bodies up an iron staircase into the massive main hall. There they learned either the good news (admission) or the bad news (rejection). As they shuffled past the bank of doctors, struggling to suppress a cough of nervousness that might be interpreted as incipient galloping pneumonia, an average of one in six had his or her outer garment chalk-marked: *H* for heart irregularity, *L* for lameness, *X* for suspicion of mental illness or defect. These were shunted aside for further examination and ultimate determination, which could result in being deported. End of dream.

Compounding the horror of it all, some were questioned by officials whose knowledge of their language was at best rudimentary, at worst nonexistent. Are you a polygamist? they were asked. Have you a job? Have you any money? Who is meeting you? Fearful of being rejected, unable to understand, praying they might by some miracle come up with an acceptable answer, they invariably came up with an unacceptable one. La Guardia recalled in his memoirs one pregnant woman with four small children in tow, in all probability a widow in quest of a new life, who sought to impress her interrogator with the claim that her husband had been in America fifteen years and worked very hard to bring her and the children here. Not realizing the obvious interpretation of moral turpitude, she and her brood were returned to Europe on the next eastbound ship.

In his three years at Ellis Island, Fiorello "never managed to become callous to the mental anguish, the disappointment and the despair I witnessed there almost daily." Most despairing were those suffering trachoma, which made their exclusion mandatory. If, for instance, a year-old child was found to be suffering from the disease, one of the parents had to return with the child to their native land, thus breaking up the family. When they learned their fate, they were stunned. Not only had the victims never felt ill, they were ignorant of the disease. Worse, not only could they see perfectly well, in practically all cases the family had sold everything to emigrate and therefore had no home to return to. The steamship company underwrote their return voyage—in steerage. At its termination, they were put ashore and left to fend for themselves.

Trachoma may have been the primary disease, but cases of favus (a chronic fungal infection of the scalp and nails) and other highly contagious scalp diseases were fairly common. To allow immigrants thus afflicted to meld into the general population, especially given the indescribably overcrowded tenement conditions, would have been, from the point of view of hygiene, simply catastrophic. Had the Immigration Service, La Guardia insisted, ordered that all consular agents at the European ports follow his example of obligatory preembarkation physicals, much misery would have been avoided. He bombarded senators and congressmen with letters describing his innovation and urging legislation to remedy the situation. Not until 1919 was appropriate legislation enacted—through the efforts of by then Congressman Fiorello H. La Guardia.

La Guardia recalled that he "always suffered greatly" when assigned to interpret for mental cases—and what were perceived to be mental cases. He was convinced that more than half the deportations for "alleged mental disease" were unjustified. Many were so classified because of ignorance, on the part of the immigrants or the doctors, and the inability of the doctors to understand the particular immigrant's native tongue. Aside from the horrors of the system there were the seeming inanities, of which pride of place went to two provisions of the immigration law. One excluded any immigrant who had no immediate prospects of a job. The other excluded any immigrant who came in as a contracted laborer, that is to say, one who had been induced, assisted, encouraged, or solicited by agents in the country of origin to migrate to the United States by offers or promises of "guaranteed immediate" employment.

Common sense would dictate that anyone coming to settle in the United States had come to work. Except for Jews fleeing the vicious anti-Semitic pogroms of czarist Russia, practically all came to escape economic deprivation. The immigrant had to tread a fine line when responding to official inquiry about job prospects. Were he too enthusiastic in verbalizing expectations, he might be presumed to have entered the country in violation of the contract labor provision. Were he too vague, knew not a soul here, and hadn't a clue where, let alone how, to get a job, he was excluded as likely to become a public charge.

While the application and interpretation of these laws would seem on the surface to be illogical, they were justified in the light of America's history of immigrant labor. Prior to their enactment in the 1880s, the nation's incredible industrial expansion was compromised by shameful criminal exploitation of labor. Industrial plants, and in particular railroads, were built by immigrants imported by the shipload by agents who had already contracted for their services at disgracefully low wages averaging under $1.50 a day, twelve hours a day, seven days a week. The wage scale, set by the agent, was well below what he had contracted for with the corporations, thus earning him more in "kickback" than in legitimate commission. Moreover, the corporation provided room and board, likely at exorbitant rates, which were deducted from the laborer's meager pay. Often it owned a company store, usually the only such establishment available in the general area, in which supplies were sold at excessive prices.

La Guardia described in his memoirs how his first brush with the "tinhorns" who would be the bane of his political life came as a result of one of his duties at Ellis Island. This involved young immigrant men who had already established themselves and sent for their fiancées. Legally, the prospective bride could be admitted only as the wife of a resident. She would be met as she stepped ashore by the groom-to-be and his witnesses. An immigration official would then rush the bridal party off to City Hall to certify the young lady's matrimonial eligibility for entry. Alderman Big Tim Sullivan, boss of the East Side, controlled the "wedding chapel," situated in the basement. He and his Tammany cronies liked to punctuate the granting of the marriage license and actual ceremony with dirty jokes, repulsive references to the anatomical features, apparent or assumed, of the bridal pair—understood, if not by them, then certainly by their interpreter—and filthy comments about immigrants in general, unless, of course, they were Irish. ("Dago," "guinea," "wop," "kike," "bohunk," and "Polack" were the epithets of choice.)

Their comments were interspersed with drunken guffaws as bottles of whiskey were passed around and cigar smoke all but obscured the proceedings. The state legislature had given these sleazy aldermen the right to perform marriages, a gift they turned into a tidy racket that yielded annually some thirty thousand dollars. Invariably on hand to partake of the disgusting fun and games were other aldermen and City Hall functionaries who seemed to have nothing better to do than go down to the "chapel" for a few laughs—and a few drinks. Usually the officiating alderman—sometimes even Big Tim himself—would not only make a mockery of the proceedings at the expense of the bridal couple, he would demand a fee in excess of the legally established two dollars: "No fee, no wedding, your little bitch goes back on the next ship." Should a groom protest this extortion, the alderman would shout something along the lines of "Get out o' here! Don't ever let me see your face again—you cheapskate—where the hell do you get off to get married?"[2] The alderman's cronies would roar in drunken laughter, adding a few choice remarks of their own, while Fiorello could do little more than stand by, powerless against these "red-faced, cheap, 'tinhorn' politicians" and those "who hung around to watch the so-called fun," and try to find words that might allay the poor immigrants' understandably negative feelings about their new country.

In 1910, Fiorello was transferred to Magistrate's Night Court as an interpreter. This enabled him to do his final year at law school as a regular day student, since it spared him the time it took commuting to and from Ellis Island. It also introduced him to the legal system and its inherent corruption as practiced in Tammany-controlled New York City. Night Court dealt exclusively with "commercialized vice" (prostitution practiced both in the streets and in the brothels), with a fair leavening of pimps and madams and, here and there, the occasional assault-and-battery case. The Immigration Service's interest was not in attempting to cleanse the city of its whores—a labor compared to which Hercules' celebrated cleansing of the Augean Stables was a simple hosing down of a holding pen for newborn colts. Rather, concern was with the aliens engaged in the business. La Guardia's task was to interview those hauled in by the wagonload for arraignment in order to ascertain their place of birth and, if foreign born, their date of arrival in the country. He interviewed thirty or forty people on an average night. Those resident less than the five years required to become eligible for naturalization were deported.

In this work, Fiorello got a liberal education in the ways of the Police Department. He now found himself in a substratum of society where huge profits were exacted through shakedowns by law enforcement authorities of indigent, ignorant, destitute women—many of them immigrants, of whom many were young girls. Arrests were made nightly to inflate the police blotter, but few of the girls ever went to prison. And while fines were levied—it was important to show the public that their guardians of the law were doing their duty—such fines were insignificant when measured against the wholesale bribery, in itself a growth industry.

Nightly—especially Saturdays—paddy wagons would pull up to Night Court in a seemingly endless caravan and discharge the latest haul. The going rate to mitigate judicial punishment was five dollars for the arresting cop plus whatever the traffic would bear for the shyster lawyers who infested the scene like maggots on a decomposing corpse and, in some cases, as much as five *hundred* dollars for a judge who had been slipped his share of the spoils to send the offender back to the streets or the parlors "with a stern warning." The dregs of the judicial system, they were known as "fining judges." (Though some of the so-called courthouse lawyers were eventually disbarred, quite a number of them went on to enjoy thriving practices and even, in a few cases, achieve important posts, by election or selection, in the city and state judiciary.)

Most of the action was in the White Slave Division of the Immigration Service, where Fiorello was assigned. Passage of the Mann

Act that year, which made it illegal to transport a woman across state lines for "immoral purposes," led to a precipitate decline in white slavery—up to that time a thriving industry in New York on a par with tourism. While the Mann Act also led to a diminution of activity in the city's red-light district along Sixth Avenue—today the Avenue of the Americas—the streetwalkers continued to flourish, thanks in equal measure to the corrupt cops and judges who provided protection and to the johns who provided patronage.

The chief inspector of the Immigration Service's White Slave Division, one Andrew Tedesco, stood up to the crooked politicians involved in this traffic and sought to clean up the red-light district. When La Guardia was first assigned to Night Court, Tedesco took him aside: "You can get experience in this job, or you can make a great deal of money. I don't think you'll take the money. But, remember, the test is if you hesitate. Unless you say 'No!' right off, the first time an offer comes your way, you're gone." La Guardia repeated Tedesco's advice to many men entering public service where they were subject to temptation. Anna Kross, a law school classmate whom Mayor La Guardia would make a city magistrate, said "he was always positive that the city could be run honestly and well, and that he would have a hand in making it happen."[3]

2.

Fiorello was admitted to the bar in October 1910, four months after receiving his law degree by racking up grades that would obviate the remotest consideration for a law review editorship. "I had no particular passion for the practice of law," he recalled. He did, though, find it "most useful," as it gave him the opportunity to learn a great deal about conditions in New York courts and New York politics in relation to the courts. On the day of his admission, he resigned from the Immigration Service.[4] With a total capital of sixty-five dollars, he rented space for fifteen dollars a month and access to the firm's law library in the offices of McIlheny and Bennett at 15 William Street. He had some stationery printed, picked up some secondhand furniture, and set upon his desk a six-inch idealized plaster bust of Napoleon Bonaparte. Was there any psychological or philosophical connotation here, be it intended or sublimated? We'll let the psychobabblers wrestle with that one, and move on to a more interest-

THE GREAT MAYOR

ing, less complex aspect of La Guardia's initial reaction to the profession he had just entered: "The more I got to know about lawyers and their ethics, the less respect I had for them."

He never accepted a retainer unless convinced of the client's probity. The idea of knowingly filing a suit that amounted to fraudulent or malicious prosecution was insupportable. He also refused to accept cases when he was confident that, while the cause of action was legitimate, the prospective client could settle the problem himself and thus save a legal fee. La Guardia's fees were minimal—ten dollars each—since most of his clients were from the lower socioeconomic strata. Some cases, which he believed to be legitimate but for which he knew the client could not afford the retainer, he took on a contingency basis; if he lost the case, he would forgo any fee. Without impugning La Guardia's altruism, it must be conceded that a healthy dollop of calculation can be imputed to him. He never intended the practice of law to be an end in itself but viewed it, like his linguistic talents, as a stepping-stone to the career in public service he planned before his return to America. He was building a constituency from among the lower-echelon laborers and indigent immigrants who comprised the overwhelming preponderance of his clientele.

La Guardia's first awareness of the corruptibility of trial judges came with his first case in the Municipal Court. He had prepared it carefully and presented it properly, yet the court decided against him. As he stood trying to figure out why, he was called to the bench by the judge. Knowing Fiorello to be recently admitted to the bar, he congratulated him on his presentation. "Well," asked the young lawyer, "if I did so well, why didn't you decide in my favor?" Replied the judge, "Oh, young man, I'll give you a break some other day." It didn't take La Guardia many cases to learn that "knowing the judge did not injure any lawyer." Another lesson quickly learned was the range of judicial incompetence, running the gamut from ignorance of the law to malfeasance, which the offending judge frequently took little or no pain to conceal.

The judges with whom La Guardia clashed outright were mostly those he appeared before in the role of criminal lawyer. Actually, criminal law did not appeal to him, and of the dozen or so cases he tried, he did "not remember ever taking a fee." Nor did he solicit any. Some were assigned by the court on a pro bono basis. Others were brought to him by friends or social workers who knew that the families involved could not afford to retain legal counsel. It didn't take Fiorello long to learn that the New York judges, whether elected or appointed, were invariably partisans vetted by Tammany. The state or county bar association, depending upon which purview the nomination fell under, would then go through the motions of either endorsing or turning down the candidate. There were some excellent judges: scholarly, upright, hardworking, fair. These were, though, the exceptions. He encountered a number, including many in the high federal courts, who belonged not on the bench but in a jail cell.

3.

In the late spring of 1912, having expanded his practice to include immigrants safely settled in their land of adoption but facing a host of other problems, Fiorello sought to form his own partnership with an attorney who shared his principles, his morality, and his integrity. The "people's attorney," as he was now becoming known, found what he wanted in Raimondo Canudo. The two opened an office at the corner of East Thirteenth Street and Third Avenue, limiting their practice to immigrants, primarily in and around the Greenwich Village area. An idealist attorney and a fiery orator and journalist, Canudo championed Sicilian immigrants, who were the most impoverished, least educated, and thus most vulnerable to discrimination and abuse by everyone from immigration officials to landlords to employers, along with bigoted merchants and Irish policemen who considered them the lowliest of the low. Through Canudo, La Guardia enjoyed something he had not known since childhood: a semblance of family life. Canudo took him home for dinner often, cementing a friendship that embraced his son Eugene, at the time two years old, who would as a young adult join Fiorello's congressional and mayoral staffs and be appointed by him to the bench. Also through Canudo, Fiorello was introduced into, and quickly won the admiration and support of, the large, tightly knit Italian community on the Lower East Side.

Wanting to touch all bases in the immigrant community, and with the blessing of Canudo, who preferred handling only Italian cases,

La Guardia also joined two Jewish lawyers with a general practice—estates, mortgages, and the like—whose clients were predominantly Jewish immigrants. Obviously he was building a bridge to the other of the two major immigrant blocs. He quickly endeared himself to the Yiddish-speaking clients with his ability to advise them in their own tongue. As in his continuing practice with Canudo, La Guardia accepted whatever fee the client could afford—even if it was nothing. What income this sacrificed he more than compensated for in the reputation he was building rapidly in the ever-expanding immigrant communities as that most anomalous of creatures: a lawyer who wasn't in it for the quick buck.

But Fiorello's two partnerships were, in a sense, of minimal significance for a man in whose head danced visions of holding high office. Granted, he was building a solid power base. What was lacking, however, was a more expansive, thus more efficacious, constituency. Naturalized immigrants voted, but while their votes counted heavily in any election, they did not—could not—count enough to win one. Fiorello had a "name" in the immigrant arena. Now he had to win a "name" in the political arena. While still maintaining the two partnerships, in 1914 he formed with two fairly upscale attorneys the firm of Weil, La Guardia & Aspen, at 50 Broad Street.

This association not only enhanced his reputation in court circles, it extended his social connections beyond Greenwich Village and its environs. Of the firm's three secretaries, the one assigned to Fiorello was Marie Fisher, a svelte New York–born eighteen-year-old blonde who managed from day one to cope with the two most pronounced of her boss's catalogue of personality traits: an energy that was positively manic and a predilection for volcanic outbursts that could cause rodents to flee the premises. Marie served Fiorello for the rest of his life, first as secretary, then as invaluable and superbly instinctive political aide, and, in time, as his second wife.

Disliking the routine of law almost as much as he disliked those who practiced it, whom he looked upon as "leeches and crooks," Fiorello joined with Weil and Aspen only to earn a living and further bind himself to the Italo-American community. For a guaranteed ten thousand dollars a year plus fees for cases he brought in, his main contribution to the firm was attracting clients not only from New York's Italian colony but from many back in Italy wishing, and financially able, to conduct legitimate business dealings in the States. Though he demanded and received equal voice as a partner, he rarely followed a case through to its conclusion, leaving that to an associate. He continued the same routine when in 1924, during his fourth term as a congressman, he formed yet another partnership, Foster, La Guardia & Cutler, located at 233 Broadway. Marie, who was his congressional office manager, doubled there as his personal secretary and kept him up to speed on the firm's business. Fiorello would make brief stops in the office when Congress was not in session and—a favorite form of communication, whether as an attorney or a legislator—fired off letters and telegrams with abandon.[5]

La Guardia had by now moved into his own four-room apartment at 39 Charles Street. There he liked to preside over dinners that he personally prepared from Irene's recipes, delivering what amounted to open-ended one-man talkathons while stirring the sauce and boiling the pasta. Having expanded his legal horizons, he now set about expanding his social horizons. Through one of his Broad Street clients, Miss Cyd Bettelheim, who ran a girls' finishing school, he gained entry into the cultured uptown German-Jewish circle of writers, artists, and professionals who met Sunday evenings for a buffet and to debate the issues of the day. Fiorello soon came to dominate these weekly exchanges of ideas. His new friends loved him for the passion he brought to his contempt for corruption and charlatanism and for the mesmerizing (or was it not perhaps overwhelming, even exhausting?) spell he cast.

Among the creative people in this circle with whom he formed lifelong friendships was Fannie Hurst, a young writer from St. Louis who had recently relocated to New York and was attending graduate school at Columbia. Today a forgotten author but in her day a popular novelist, she saw in Fiorello "a magnificent unrest, coupled with a desire to be a leader on his own terms." For his part, Fiorello saw in Hurst a fellow laborer in the field of social injustice. He showed her how politics worked at the pavement, which is to say basic, level, introduced her to the lives and vicissitudes of the lower classes, and took her to Ellis Island and Night Court, where she found raw material for the stories and novels that would make her reputation. Hurst wrote that he was "always about to explode in indignation against social injustice." She described him as " 'a blazing rebel' who moved through New York 'like a doctor with a stethoscope' which he pressed against the hearts of passersby to better understand their human, social, industrial and political pain. A man who cared."[6]

PART II

1912-1921

Congressman and Warrior

CHAPTER FIVE

"I joined the Republican Party because I could not stomach Tammany Hall"

1.

Even before he began the practice of law Fiorello La Guardia joined the Madison Republican Club of the Twenty-fifth Assembly District, headquartered at 251 West Fourteenth Street. Why the Republicans? In New York City they were so outnumbered by the Democrats that, come election time, the party would nominate a token candidate, thus all but conceding the office in question to Tammany, in exchange for a few crumbs of patronage. Moreover, Fiorello, the son of an Italian father and a Jewish mother, was a self-proclaimed, highly visible champion of the underdog. And the GOP was now the party of Protestant America. "I joined the Republican Party because I could not stomach Tammany Hall," said La Guardia, wanting it "understood" that by Tammany Hall he meant the Democratic political machine in all of New York's five boroughs.

The mile-square Twenty-fifth Assembly District encompassed the northeast corner of Greenwich Village, from Twenty-eighth Street to south of Washington Square, and from Third to Eighth avenues, and embraced four component groups. In Washington Square and just north of it were, respectively, the old-line Republican aristocracy and the combined left-wing radicals and intellectuals. South of the Square was the Italian colony, which, with its admixture of immigrants, intellectuals, and firebrands, seemed incapable of arriving at an overall cohesive identity beyond ethnic origin. On the West Side—the notorious Gas House District—were the Irish, led by saloonkeeper and reigning Tammany Grand Sachem Charlie Murphy.

The better-bred, better-educated Republicans of the Twenty-fifth looked upon the Democrats as a dowager might look upon a gang of street people who had established unlawful residency in both her front and back yards. Their leader was attorney Frederick Chauncey Tanner, who could trace his ancestry back past the American Revolution to one of the *Mayflower*'s passengers. Most of the Tammany leaders could not trace their ancestry back past their own grandparents. Fiorello brought with him no recommendation and no reputation. All he brought was a sincerity, a sense of social commitment, and an aura of someone willing to labor in the vineyard of Republicanism. Plus, of course, a contempt for Tammany, which impressed Tanner and his party.

Fiorello was not a complete unknown. While working at Ellis Island he had met, and greatly impressed, the man who within the year would become New York County's omnipotent Republican chairman, Samuel S. Koenig. Koenig, a Hungarian-born Jew, had risen to leadership of the Sixth Assembly District, which, along with the Tenth, embraced the Lower East Side contiguous to the Twenty-fifth and were inhabited predominantly by Jewish immigrants. Hardly a liberal philosophically, Koenig believed that "sometimes there's a fault in being too idealistic." Nor was he interested in issues, dismissing, for instance, the Wilsonian demand for a League of Nations as "over my head." What he liked—what he lived for—was playing the game of politics, with the give-and-take of campaigning, brokering deals, dispensing patronage, and, above all, the thrill of winning.[1]

Fiorello was assigned to the Twenty-fifth's Italian quarter. Directly to the south of what was for all intents and purposes a self-imposed ghetto lay the Democratic bailiwick run by their fellow nationalist Al Marinelli, whose cadre of professional bullies, goons, and criminals of every stripe enjoyed a twofold reputation: They voted more times in any given election than many people vote in a lifetime, and they made sure the Republicans realized that to so much as walk through the district, even accidentally, might well result in serious bodily harm.

Studying diligently under the tutelage of Tanner and Koenig, Fiorello quickly learned the basic empirical truism of politics: Party platforms are no more than a litany of campaign promises to be dismantled, plank by plank, and consigned to the woodpile (or victory bonfire) once their transitory purpose has been served. What counted was an engaging personality and a sympathetic ear. Fiorello made it his business to get to know every family in his assigned district by attending weddings, baptisms, confirmations, bar mitzvahs, funerals—in short, every occasion of a familial nature. Such efforts counted for infinitely more than spouting the party line on street corners and making grandiloquent promises that were as substantial as the contents of a clown's balloon. In less than a year, he was fully conversant with the joys and troubles and aspirations of what was emerging as his core constituency. These people sensed that he had their best interests at heart.

Of the men with whom La Guardia worked closely and who saw in him a definite "comer," three deserve mention. Most influential was the ward's elder statesman, Mike Kehoe, an Irishman in his seventies and Fiorello's chief mentor. The other two, both Kehoe protégés, were Louis Espresso and Harry G. Andrews. Coming from poor families, and inhibited from rising in the business and professional worlds by lack of education and access to financial backing and connections, they sought to achieve their desired place in the political sun through clubhouse participation. Neither was interested in political science, not even the rudiments of government. Their only interest was raw politics, complemented by a determination to offend no one who could serve their purpose and to back winners.

Espresso was a bail bondsman who sidetracked his plans to buy a saloon in order to instruct and serve La Guardia purely out of racial pride: "I figured that with a man like La Guardia I was making a steppingstone for the other Italians in this great city. . . . I wanted to do something for my forefathers that came to this country, understand that their sons and daughters etc. would get a better chance in politics because in those days the Italians was [sic] a nonentity."[2] Andrews, a cut or two above the streetwise Espresso, was a polio victim who did most of the district's clerical work. La Guardia would convince him to study law and would have the pleasure of seeing him grow and develop, so much so that he appointed Espresso a magistrate when he became mayor. La Guardia enjoyed the company of these two above all other members of the Twenty-fifth. Through them, he met the district captains, learned the importance of re- membering names, attended any and all gatherings that might prove politically useful, and otherwise studied the ways of ward heeling— "pavement politics."

In the beginning, Fiorello was the consummate party loyalist. In 1912, when district captain William Chadbourne bolted the party, which was backing Taft for the presidency, in order to support Teddy Roosevelt in his run as candidate for the ad hoc Bull Moosers, La Guardia joined in the chorus of "Shame on you" and was rewarded with the apostate's post as district captain.[3] The next year, John Pur- roy Mitchell, an attractive thirty-four-year-old independent Democrat who hated Tammany, ran for mayor on a fusion ticket, which the Republican machine agreed to support. La Guardia protested in a letter to Tanner, "It seems hard that with everything coming our way we should be compelled to play into the hands of a few disgruntled Republicans, now calling themselves 'Progressives,' and at the same time build up an organization for independent Democrats who are creating an organization of their own to capture the State election next year."[4]

This from the man who would become one of the most militant Progressives of his time! However, he assured Tanner, other than supporting the fusion ticket, he would be "pleased to . . . help the [Republican] organization all I can." Mitchell, who had uncovered buried scandals in the municipal government directly traceable to Tammany, was elected by a large plurality, along with a fusionist Board of Estimate. As for Fiorello, he sat out the campaign—a cam- paign that bore a pronounced resemblance to the one he would wage, successfully, in 1933.

Are we dealing here with a hypocrite who, not unlike so many office-seekers who litter the political killing fields to this day, reinvent themselves whenever it suits their purpose? Perhaps. But a more plausible assumption is that as Fiorello matured politically, he ma- tured philosophically and realized that, whereas the road to hell is paved with good intentions, the road to success is paved with prag- matic reality. La Guardia's letter to Tanner—in itself an act of cour- age—appears not to have bothered the Big Boss in the least. He may even have appreciated the young man's honesty. In addition to being an election district captain, Fiorello was made the district's assistant treasurer. Earning enough money in his law practice to maintain a comfortable bachelor's flat, and developing into another rough-and-tumble pol, the Little Flower was now "one of the boys," high on a list of those worthy of reward should the party, by some miracle, topple the Democrats from control of the city.

So far as the hierarchs were concerned, Fiorello was an open book.

In fact, he wasn't.

There was to this presumed paragon of a political foot soldier one aspect of which they were blissfully ignorant, an aspect that would in time cause the party considerable perturbation. This was La Guardia's unwavering commitment to social reform. Inwardly he abhorred the very ward-heeling style of politics he was mastering so rapidly.

2.

Pre–World War I Greenwich Village can be likened to an exotic greenhouse in which two bohemias flourished symbiotically. One was that of the philosophically militant—in some cases defiantly anarchistic—writers, artists, and intellectuals, idealists all, who fled their small-town, predominantly Protestant environments to coalesce in the Village, there to make common cause. The other, to which La Guardia belonged, was home to young, ambitious, likewise culturally and intellectually gifted, and equally militant Italo-Americans. It can be said that the former were societal insiders who wanted out, the latter societal outsiders who wanted in.

This dual bohemia was symptomatic of a movement dating back to the 1880s to which historians have assigned the label "Progressive." It was begun by a small but influential group of reformers, primarily Republicans, whose priority was to battle the corruption rampant in the rapidly expanding urban industrial United States following the Civil War. As the nation moved into the twentieth century, the banner of reform was taken up on every level by the likes of Theodore Roosevelt and Robert La Follette in politics, Charles Beard and John Dewey in education, Theodore Dreiser and Upton Sinclair in social-protest literature, and those two remarkable ladies Lillian

Wald in New York and Jane Addams in Chicago, who dedicated themselves to raising the living standards of the poor. These reformers, "in exposing and proposing changes for the worse aspects of thought and society in the United States," believed that "by tinkering with the environment, one could bring out the best in man. More specifically, they wanted to curb the plutocracy, to make government representative of the needs of all the people, and to provide opportunities for a life based on values other than those of the market place."[5]

The first group of Village bohemians—notably Eugene O'Neill, John Reed, Floyd Dell, and Max Eastman—all have received their due, and then some, in the countless biographies and histories of the period. Not so the second group, the Italo-Americans, known as the Green Geniuses. Their empathy with society's underdogs was complemented by a determination to guarantee their own inclusion in the American dream. Fiorello was introduced into this circle through his law partner and friend Raimondo Canudo. Prominent among them were sculptor Attilio Piccirilli, best remembered for his epic monument in Columbus Circle memorializing the men killed on the *Maine* in Havana harbor; Antonio Calitri, poet and ex–Catholic priest married to a Jewish woman, who translated into the language of his fellow Italian immigrants Walt Whitman's celebration of their adoptive nation's democracy; Arturo Giovannitti, syndicalist, journalist, and poet; Giovanni Fabrizio, flautist with the New York Philharmonic; and Onorio Ruotolo, perhaps the most fascinating of the lot. Painter, sculptor, poet, and editor of *Il Fuoco*, an Italian-language magazine devoted to "art and discussion," Ruotolo was a self-proclaimed *uomo universale* (Renaissance man) whose credo was "Society will tolerate anything but genius." Of this tightly knit circle, only La Guardia chose politics as the medium for expressing their common ideal of making this a better world. His friends made sure La Guardia became known in the Italian colony, thereby constructing a formidable political following.

Fiorello La Guardia was, first and foremost, a professional pol—though God help any man who so defined him to his face! In allying himself with the movers and shakers of the Italian immigrant community, he was emulating his political nemeses—the Irish in Tammany Hall—by staking out his own ethnic group through whom to ascend to power. His friends saw to it that his speeches were dutifully printed in the community's Italian-language papers. And they made sure that the immigrants were brought to realize that though he had been born and spent his formative years in the United States, Fiorello's "Italian origins, mind, and heart" made him the perfect point man round whom must rally all who yearned to raze the walls of bigotry and poverty that enclosed them.

The Green Geniuses met often at Fiorello's apartment to eat Italian food, drink Italian wine, and speak through the evening and well into the following morning of life, love, art, music, poetry—and political philosophy. While cooking, chattering, and gesticulating characteristically to emphasize a point nonstop like a bipolar chef on the verge of total dementia, Fiorello would argue that in America reform could succeed only within the two-party system and capitalism; this despite contentions to the contrary by the more radical of his *paisanos*, most of them Socialists, syndicalists, and anarchists. To believe otherwise, he insisted, was at best impractical, at worst a menace not only to the nation but to themselves.

Through Cyd Bettelheim he was now also moving in the uptown world of the German-Jewish intelligentsia, where the efforts of those laboring in the vineyards of the Progressive movement was as pervasive a subject of conversation as art, culture, and high ideals. Yet Fiorello was either unaware of or indifferent to the great liberal upheaval going on outside his own constricted world. That would come in time. For now, his concern was the world of the immigrants in his own backyard. While the twenty-sixth and twenty-eighth presidents, Roosevelt and Wilson, were leading the crusade against the menace to the nation posed by the big trusts, La Guardia was crusading in behalf of the tribulations being endured by the immigrant masses packed sardine-like in New York City's slums. Through his friend August Bellanca, he now commenced his lifelong association with and support of organized labor.

August Bellanca and his brother, Giuseppe, were among the closest of Fiorello's friends. August, a crusading labor organizer, dedicated himself to agitating for improving the lot of the working man and woman; Giuseppe devoted his efforts to designing and building bigger and better aircraft. Intuiting that the United States must eventually be drawn into the European war that had broken out in the previous year, Fiorello wanted to "be prepared." Every chance he got that summer of 1915, Fiorello took lessons from Giuseppe—free in return for doing his company's legal work—in what was at the time the company's only "flying machine," out at Mineola on Long Island. Even before Giuseppe turned him into a pilot, August turned him into an active labor advocate by involving him in the Garment Center Strike of 1912–13.

By 1912, the nearly 250,000 employees of New York's garment industry, the world's largest, situated in Manhattan's slum-ridden Lower East Side, belonged to newly organized so-called needle-trade unions. Ninety-five percent were recently arrived immigrants; they worked in crowded, dark, unsanitary workshops for extremely low wages ten to twelve hours a day, seven days a week. Compounding their misery, the work was seasonal. For between fifteen and twenty weeks a year they were unemployed. Still, rent had to be paid on their overcrowded, disease-infested tenements. And there were the basic necessities of food and clothing and the hope for some warmth during the city's harsh winter months.

The most successful of the alliances was the International Ladies' Garment Workers Union (ILGWU). But success was a relative term. The manufacturers were all-powerful, the politicians refused to become involved, and the threat of being fired was enough to send the workers back to their machines. Ironically, it was the increasing greed of the employers that made it possible for these unions to become effective. If individual employees, even small groups, were fired, there were other impoverished immigrants waiting to take their place. But if enough of them, without even waiting to be fired, simply halted their work, and the employers were unable to replace them, the workers would gain the upper hand. Without labor, the employers would have nothing to market.

The first strike in the garment trade was by women, in the fall of 1909—the largest walkout and picket by their gender in the United States up to that time. It started with about a hundred, the total membership of Local 25, Ladies' Waist Makers Union, whose employers were the Leiserson Company and the Triangle Shirt Waist Company. (Triangle was on the eighth, ninth, and tenth floors of its building. Firemen's ladders could reach only to the seventh—a level above which a half-million New Yorkers worked, in one edifice or another. Two years after the walkout, on March 25, 1911, a fire in Triangle's building took 164 lives, mostly women and girls, who died of burns or suffocation or were killed when they threw themselves out of windows to escape the flames. It was later learned that the building had no fire exits or outside fire escapes and that, contrary to law, workroom doors were locked, so that an employee had to ask permission to go to the bathroom, and could not be opened when the conflagration began.)

In the 1909 strike the employers hired thugs to beat up the strikers. The thugs were supplied by the Tammany sachems, who not only supported the employers but in many cases *were* the employers. Lest they be accused of being not only bullies but sexist bullies, they hired burly prostitutes to help the burly goons attack the all-female pickets. Lending a hand were the Tammany-controlled police, who cooperated with the manufacturers not only by joining in the head bashing but by carting the bruised strikers off to jail. The charge? Picketing. Peacefully. This brought members of the Women's Trade Union League to the picket lines, adding numbers and drawing the public's attention to their plight. Mass meetings were held throughout the city at which prominent men and women from every walk of life supported the strike and protested the actions of the police.

Though these protest meetings raised public awareness, they failed to deter the abuse to which the strikers were subjected by those charged with upholding the law. Typical was the case of one striker sentenced to the workhouse by a Tammanyite magistrate with the strangest theological argument: "You are on strike against God and Nature, whose law is that man shall earn his bread in the sweat of his brow."[6] Between September, when the strike started, and Christmas Day, 723 women were arrested (and manhandled) by the police. Of these, nineteen were sent to the workhouse—again, for daring to "strike against God and nature."

An end to the strike was brokered by the president of the United Mine Workers, whereby the employers agreed to improved conditions, a fifty-two-hour week, the promise not to discriminate against union members, and reinstatement of the strikers. While the workers failed to win recognition of their union, their strike did awaken the public to the realization that workingwomen were capable of successfully engaging in furtherance of their industrial welfare. Moreover, the strike resulted in many more workers of both genders joining the ILGWU. This in turn strengthened that union so that in time it became the single most powerful in the garment trade and a major force in national politics. It also laid the foundation for wider union organization and more successful union activity. Other garment-trade laborer groups were inspired by the strike to form unions. The original total membership of Local 25, Ladies' Waist Makers Union, grew from one hundred to ten thousand.

Busy working at Ellis Island and attending law school, La Guardia did not take any part in the strike. He did, though, follow its progress. What he found most disturbing was that Tammany lawyers were retained by the unions—and sided against the very people they had been hired to defend. These so-called political lawyers also selected the bail bondsmen. The unions soon learned two prudent tactics: Retain the right political lawyers and bondsmen and hire their own goons to go up against those of the employers. This, recalled La Guardia, often resulted in real battles which were costly to both sides. It wasn't long before he became caught up in the conflict.

When the dress and shirtwaist makers struck, they knew they could not expect any support from the mighty American Federation of Labor. The AFL, which comprised 80 percent of all unionized Americans, was almost all white, and its membership was closed to women and "all foreign born," gender notwithstanding. Three years later, in December 1912, sixty-five thousand Jewish and Italian men's clothing makers who labored sixty hours a week for between $5 and $14.50 (a few skilled workmen got $15 to $18 a week) struck for a forty-hour week, a living wage, and recognition of their own union. These workers belonged to the United Garment Workers, an affiliate of the AFL. But being "foreign born," they felt compelled to organize their own union, the Amalgamated Clothing Workers of America. That the AFL, or the UGW, for that matter, did not allow the other nearly two hundred thousand garment workers to join or even support the strike more than suggests that while the unions gladly accepted dues from the foreign born, they gladly ignored their plight.

What was urgently needed was a lawyer to fight picket cases who could explain conditions to the strikers in their mother tongue. Approached by his friend August Bellanca, head of the new union's Italian section, La Guardia readily agreed to assist in both phases of this work. The employers, having enjoyed some success in pitting the Jewish and Italian laborers against each other even before the strike, now resorted to spreading baseless rumors that each group was selling the other out. They certainly had not counted on a fiery professional sympathizer who could counteract this ploy by explaining to the strikers—in their own language—what was being done to them and what their rights were and, what's more, was willing to take on the manufacturers in court, unintimidated by their high-powered legal teams.

Fiorello's maiden speech was made from the balcony of Cooper Union. Speaking alternately in Yiddish and Italian but concluding in English, he exhorted the capacity crowd to abandon their mutual prejudices and unite against the bosses and their Tammany-financed strikebreaker thugs and goons. The strikers embraced this little firebrand in the string tie and ten-gallon Stetson. Here was a son of immigrants like themselves, born and raised in America, and thus one of their own but not quite, telling them what they wanted to hear, what they needed to hear, in their own tongues.[7]

Now fully committed, La Guardia took to navigating the Lower East Side, moving from rally to rally, street corner to street corner, persuading the strikers that their best hope—their *only* hope—for achieving improved working and living conditions lay in working *with* instead of *against* one another. But that wasn't even the half of it. There were the meetings he attended night after night with the union leaders, helping coordinate their efforts for maximum effect. During the day, he appeared in court in defense of the pickets and to litigate related charges. He even went on the picket line outside one of the struck factories and defied the police to arrest him as they were doing with others, "but they refused to touch me and just went on daily interfering with the right of the workers to engage in peaceful picketing."

Barely two months into the strike, on February 28, 1913, La Guardia and the others were horrified to read in their morning papers that the UGW leadership had settled with the manufacturers—without first consulting the strikers. Not only had no terms of the alleged settlement been submitted to the workers, the terms were not even known at strike headquarters. As the leaders and rank-and-file screamed "Betrayal!" Fiorello organized protest meetings to be held that very day throughout the city. Every available hall was booked. The union had no treasury, let alone a strike fund. Money for the rentals was "picked up in nickels and dimes" from the indigent strikers themselves. Each meeting selected a delegate, all of whom then met to select a committee of about fifteen men; these in turn gathered around noon in Stuyvesant Hall on Second Avenue, where, after meeting in session until four o'clock the next morning, they selected three arbitrators to negotiate directly with the employers. One was Socialist laborite Jacob Panken, later named a judge of the Domestic Relations Court when La Guardia became mayor. Another was Socialist leader Meyer London, later a congressman, whom La Guardia would come to loathe. The third was La Guardia himself.

The three had a difficult time making contact with the employers, who had nothing but contempt for the "foreign-born" workers and their representatives. As the negotiating team sought to get the employers to at least meet with them, the strike continued despite the bitter cold, personal privations, and a phalanx of opposition. Mayor William J. Gaynor, believing, like the courts, that the strike had been settled, ordered the police to terminate further picketing. Lending a hand, with a wink and a nod from the police, were the employers' hired goons. But to no avail. Realizing that their struck shops were going to remain so, the employers expressed a reluctant willingness to arbitrate. After extended negotiations a settlement was finally reached: a fifty-three-hour week, to be cut by an hour the following January first, a dollar-a-week salary increase, and de facto though not official recognition of the new union. Convinced by their leaders that it was the best settlement they could hope to get, the strikers went back to work.

3.

La Guardia came out of the 1912–13 strike with a determination to translate his newly won reputation as a champion of labor into political gain. "I had been storing up knowledge, and I was eager to bring about better conditions, particularly a more equitable economic situation and less favoritism to special interests in the administration of the law. That was why I determined to become a Congressman." From the time he returned to New York after living in Europe, he had read the *Congressional Record* habitually and kept abreast of activities on Capitol Hill. "Somehow—I did not know how—I had a feeling I would get into Congress. I kept my eyes open."

The choice of congressional districts to run in was his own, the Fourteenth, which extended south from Fourteenth Street to Third

Street and from the East River to the Hudson. With Broadway as the north-south dividing line, the district's eastern sector was one enormous slum comprised of row upon row of six- and seven-story walk-up tenements set amidst mounds of trash. Here lived more than a dozen national groups that had been part of the America-bound exodus from Southern and Eastern Europe over the preceding quarter of a century, predominantly Jews, Italians, Poles, Ukrainians, Russians, Czechs, and Romanians. This eastern area was a major stronghold of Socialist thought, led by a few immigrant intellectuals who had been part of that sizeable influx, reinforced by the recently arrived second generation.

The district's western sector was a study in contrasts. Around Washington Square were the mansions and ornate apartment-hotels that lined clean, spacious thoroughfares like University Place, Lower Fifth Avenue, and Waverly Place. Below the Square, between Sixth Avenue and the Hudson River was a perplexing patchwork of narrow streets, running in all directions and at all angles, peppered with broken-down houses and stores. Here lived newly arrived Italians and native Irishmen of the laboring class vying, often with open hostility, for jobs on the waterfront or in the factories farther downtown.[8]

Fiorello doubted any chances of getting the party's support. Never in the fifty-eight-year history of the Republican Party had a Republican won this seat. The party Brahmins knew that whoever they put forward would be but a token candidate. And the last kind of token they would consider putting forward was a non–Ivy Leaguer from an ethnic minority who ran around in a ridiculous string tie and black hat making enough noise to resurrect the dead. He was, went the political wisdom, the stuff of which ward heelers were made, not congressional candidates.

Besides the Republicans and Democrats, yet another group figured in what was essentially an ongoing three-party struggle for political power in lower Manhattan: the Socialists. La Guardia had labored heroically, and at great financial self-sacrifice, in support of the very people whose concerns the Socialists held dearest to their hearts. But philosophically, he was cut from an alien bolt of cloth. His fellow Green Geniuses, a heady brew of Socialists and Marxists, insisted that their problems could be resolved only through a radical third party. Fiorello reiterated doggedly that the solution lay only within the two-party system, that is, a two-party capitalist system.

He dismissed their suggestions that he run under the Socialist banner, if only as a short-term expediency.

Fiorello was not interested in a token run. Fighting the good fight for a lost cause was not his style. And not to be overlooked was his detestation, amounting almost to a pathological hatred, of the Socialist Party's powers-that-be. Leading the list was Morris Hillquit, a national leader of the party and his principal East Side rival. (A few years after the garment strike, while representing a client in a case against Burns Brothers Ice Company, which Hillquit not only represented but also held shares in, Fiorello accused him of "talking big" while treating his workers like "slaves in the days before the Civil War" and forcing indigent East Side "mothers . . . to pay prohibitive prices for ice, while the little independents were being frozen out." The Hearst papers played up the story with such headlines as "Young Ice Trust Laid to Morris Hillquit."[9] Hillquit never forgave La Guardia, which was perfectly fine with him. Fiorello was one of those who take delight in knowing that anyone they thoroughly abhor reciprocates.)

Fiorello had Harry Andrews, now secretary to state party chairman Frederick Chauncey Tanner, pass along a note in which he pointed out that some of the assembly districts in the Fourteenth were overwhelmingly inhabited by new voters, especially the Twenty-fifth (Italians) and the Sixth and Tenth (Jewish). "Hardly a family down there has not a member, a relative or a friend in the tailoring business," he advised Tanner, adding, "I am well known in those circles." Tanner liked Fiorello and was familiar with the solid reputation he had earned, as well as his following among the immigrants. But he felt that all the immigrants in all six assembly districts comprising the Fourteenth could not elect a Republican.

Indeed, Tanner had given up on the idea that even divine intervention could ever bring about a miracle of that magnitude. Consequently, the designated candidate was invariably an aging party leader or major contributor who was willing to be humiliated at the polls by the Democrats as recompense for a few weeks of local celebrity. This time around, Tanner gave the nod to a prominent physician, Dr. Frederick Marshall, who had made a large contribution to the party exchequer. But Marshall declined to offer himself up as that year's sacrificial lamb. To complicate matters, it was now late summer, and the requisite petitions for various state and county offices had already been printed and the names of nominees for most

offices filled in. The need was urgent to decide on nominees for the
State Senate and Assembly and the U.S. House of Representatives.

Legend has it that Fiorello won the nomination because he just happened to be at the right place at the right time. But Fiorello H. La
Guardia rarely, if ever, "just happened" to be anywhere or do anything in his political career. In fact, he had written to Tanner, after
his petition transmitted through Andrews had been rejected, "I am
out for the nomination for Congress in the Fourteenth District." He
admitted he would not "dare dream of the nomination, were it not
for the fact that the District is absolutely against us and my only hope
is in bringing up the Republican vote." He pointed out that the
Democratic Irish population was declining as many, having made
their way into the middle class, were moving north; new immigrant
groups of various ethnicities liked him; and in the Italian districts he
was confident of "unusually good support and will cut the Tammany
vote considerably." He was "well known" in the areas "mostly populated with the Hebrews," owing to his connection with the garment
workers' union. "I can go down there and campaign in 'Yiddish' and
put one over on" the incumbent, Jefferson Levy, "who, although a
Jew, refrains from doing so." In a tone suggesting determination
more than supplication, he told Tanner, "I want your O.K. I have
spoken with some of the boys and as far as I know they are in sympathy with me." Even asking for Tanner's okay was pro forma. Fiorello ended the letter with "This is my official declaration."[10] With a
smile, Tanner dismissed the declaration as just another instance of
unrealizable resolve on the part of this energetic party loyalist who
may have been small in stature but was beyond measure in confidence.

On the night "the boys" in the club room of the Twenty-fifth were
filling in petitions for the nomination for Congress, no one came
forward to offer himself as a replacement for Dr. Marshall. And "the
boys" were in a bit of a quandary. Suddenly Clarence Fay, the district
leader, came out from the back office and shouted, "Who wants to
run for Congress?" Fiorello jumped up and shouted back, "I do." Fay
told the scribe filling out the nominating petitions, "OK, put La
Guardia down." Asked the scribe, "Hey, La Guardia, what's your first
name?" "Fiorello." The scribe told Fay, "Oh, hell, let's get someone
whose name we can spell!" La Guardia stormed up to the desk and

shouted, "I am going to spell my name for you. Listen: F-I-O-R-E-L-L-O space L-A space G-U-A-R-D-I-A!"

"I took my nomination seriously," recalled the candidate. "I soon learned that I was not supposed to." At the district's first election rally all the party's candidates for the various offices were introduced and asked to say a few words. All, that is, but the candidate for Congress. After the rally he protested to the chairman. How come, he demanded, he had been treated like the Invisible Man? "Everybody," he later recalled, "had a good laugh." Then the chairman said, "Why, Fiorello, you haven't a chance of winning. We've never elected a Republican to Congress from this district. Now, what you should do is go out and campaign for the State Senator and Assemblyman, help elect the ticket. That is all you can do."

"Could I try?"

"Oh, no, don't be foolish. You just go out and help the others, and some day you may get a nomination for an office you can win."

Though just about everyone agreed, Mike Kehoe told him, "Kid, don't be discouraged, but go out and try."

Try he did, backed to the hilt by Espresso and Andrews and a cadre of dedicated volunteers. As for any help from the party, no such luck.

Attilio Piccirilli provided campaign headquarters on the ground floor of a family-owned Sixth Avenue building. La Guardia bought a secondhand Ford for a hundred dollars, plastered it with campaign posters, and rode up and down every street in the district, jumping out to dash up tenement stairs and knock on doors to introduce himself with a hearty handshake for the adults and a pat on the head for the children. Plus, of course attending all baptisms, first communions, bar mitzvahs, weddings, and wakes. Should he chance to notice two or three people engaged in a sidewalk chat, be it about the weather or the price of eggs, he would jam on the Ford's brakes, jump out, insinuate himself into their conversation, and steer it into political channels. Ere long, with his sheer magnetism and penetrating voice, he'd draw a sizeable crowd and start speechifying. A favorite gambit was to climb atop the hood of his broken-down car and, flailing his arms like a windmill caught in a gust, attract a crowd from among people leaving regularly scheduled meetings of the opposition.

More than once, Fiorello and his accompanying loyalists were showered by Tammany goons with epithets and rotting vegetables. More than once, these improvised rallies ended in a brawl. Still, he managed to get across, in six languages, that he was defending the rights of labor and immigrant groups, recalling his contribution to their cause during the great strikes of the recent past. With a prodigious knowledge of facts and figures, he could cite, say, the cost of a chicken or cut of meat by way of emphasizing how the workers living in squalid tenements were being exploited by absentee bosses and landlords who lived uptown in luxurious mansions and apartments.

Of the six assembly districts that made up the Fourteenth Congressional District, two were safely Republican: Fiorello's own predominantly Italian Twenty-fifth, and Samuel S. Koenig's predominantly Jewish Sixth. As he "worked" the other four, he showed what the electorate could expect in all future La Guardia canvasses. Driving here, there, everywhere, shouting and hectoring in that high-pitched voice to draw an audience, jabbing with a finger—sometimes with an entire hand—to drive home a point, he avowed both a sensitivity to the tribulations of the underprivileged and a willingness to deal with his Tammany antagonists on their own knuckle-busting, down-and-dirty, in-your-face level. This first time out, Fiorello was more the verbal bruiser than the polished orator. Moreover, he had yet to articulate the philosophy that would brand him for all time, and for which he is wistfully recalled and sorely missed to this day: a confirmed militant reformer who not only promised but delivered.

His Democratic opponent was not, as La Guardia had anticipated, Jefferson Levy. Tammany decided to run, instead, one Michael Farley, a saloonkeeper and president of the National Liquor Dealers Association, who was woefully deficient in social or political views and moral compass. In fact, he lacked all three. He was, to use a favorite La Guardia Yiddishism, *dreck*. Tammany had no illusions about the man, who did as commanded by the sachems (especially not making any political speeches or otherwise actively campaigning). So far as they were concerned, "Farley may be *dreck*, but he's our *dreck*."

Fiorello went after him with both proverbial barrels, calling him an illiterate *goniff* and accusing him of refusing to run bar tabs for even his best customers. His attacks on Farley—whom he called "the bartender"—became so ferocious that some of the Republican hierarchs, fearing retribution from Tammany and a possible backlash, pointed out to Fiorello that the retail liquor business was a lawful occupation and urged that he not disparage Farley for being in that business. La Guardia recalled in retrospect, "I did not disparage him. I merely pointed out that he [would not make] a good Congressman—and wasn't even a good bartender."

The election played out as anticipated. Farley won with votes to spare. The sachems made sure all the braves, along with Bowery drunks whose services had been purchased with a few drinks and a few bucks, cast two or three votes in their own names, plus names taken off tombstones of a number of residents in the district's graveyards. La Guardia was not only swamped at the polls in the Irish wards, which hardly came as any great surprise, he ran behind "the bartender" in the heavily populated Italian Third, which did. Not that some voters of the Third arbitrarily turned their backs on one of their own. Tammany had wooed them with Thanksgiving and Christmas turkey dinners. Also as anticipated, Fiorello carried his own Twenty-fifth and Koenig's Sixth and—somewhat surprisingly—did better in the predominantly Jewish Tenth than the Socialist and Progressive candidates, to whom this district was home turf.[11]

Totally unanticipated was that Fiorello cut down the normally large Democratic margin, reducing Farley's plurality from 6,000 to 1,700. And he amazed the pros of all parties by winning more votes than any Republican had ever won in the Fourteenth. His showing, not to mention his campaign style, was now a matter of some concern to the Democrats, and more so to the Republicans. How, they wondered, were they going to keep tight rein on this feisty La Guardia? It was one thing to be a good party man but something else to be as manageable as a bull in a china shop; to take the metaphor to its logical conclusion, a mad bull.

The answer? They weren't.

The thirty-two-year-old mad bull was already planning for the next congressional election.

CHAPTER SIX

"You just can't control him"

1.

While Andrew, Espresso, and Piccirilli—who again donated a head-quarters, manned by Marie Fisher—dealt with the details of organizing for the 1916 campaign, La Guardia sought a job that would augment his rather meager income and also give him much needed exposure beyond the bounds of the Fourteenth Congressional District. State GOP chairman Frederick Tanner, who was in charge of patronage for governor Charles S. Whitman, got Fiorello an appointment as deputy attorney general of the State of New York in New York City. While he genuinely liked La Guardia, Tanner assumed that this would effectively finesse La Guardia's chances—perhaps even his ambition—in the 1916 race. The Republicans and Democrats had a tacit agreement whereby, in exchange for the Republicans mounting a token congressional campaign in the Fourteenth, the Democrats would reciprocate on the gubernatorial level. This had contributed to Whitman's being sent to Albany. The Republicans of La Guardia's district, anxious to maintain that rather cynical gentlemen's agreement, had more reason to fear him now than they did in 1914. They certainly had no intention of supporting a 1916 run.

La Guardia gladly accepted the appointment, probably less for the added income it provided than for the opportunity it gave him to garner experience in public office in his home state. It also gave him the opportunity to learn a great deal about practical politics. What he learned imbued him with a chronic rage that would inform his political career. One of his first cases involved what was known as the "New Jersey fume nuisance." Several factories on the Jersey shore of the Hudson River had for years been emitting noxious fumes, to the great discomfort of the inhabitants of the heavily residential areas of Washington Heights and Riverside Drive on the city's Upper West Side and parts of Staten Island. Much money and time had been expended, and many briefs filed over the years, by a Riverside Drive Association seeking relief. Though there were three or four lawyers in the attorney general's office who were senior to him, and this was, after all, a major case, La Guardia didn't stop to consider why it was given to him, a political neophyte. He would soon learn why.

After familiarizing himself for months with all the facts of the case, wading through over a thousand relevant records and poring over pertinent case law, La Guardia made his move. He rushed down to Washington and filed with the U.S. Supreme Court simultaneous complaints in the name of the State of New York against each of the seven offending companies. The filing attracted attention both in legal circles and in the press. Fiorello, "quite proud of having finally started the action that had been kicked around the office for at least five or six years," was soon told by his superiors that, while the complaint had been verified by the attorney general, he had no right taking action before the Supreme Court.

In fact, the seven corporations had used their considerable influence with the acquiescent Governor Whitman to block the litigation. It seems there had been "some sort of stipulation" that the case would not be pursued while the companies were given "a liberal amount of time to make necessary changes." The "noxious fumes" case made La Guardia more determined than ever to beard the politically corrupt lions in their luxuriously appointed dens. There were other cases in which he was to learn "law is all right so long as big interests are not disturbed," thanks to inept or corrupt judges and officials in high places, be they Republicans or Democrats. But he "just could not be a regular." He could not "comply and accept the established custom [that] to raise a howl and kick" branded one as an insurgent. Summing up his career in the attorney general's office, he wrote, "[I] left it much wiser and not so innocent as when I entered it."

With his congressional campaign gearing up, he continued to cultivate political connections. "There was not a meeting of five or six people in that congressional district that Fiorello and I didn't attend for two solid years," recalled Andrews, who personally covered the tough Irish West Side, securing, through connections with a judge, the release from jail of petty offenders, on the theory that in politics a favor granted is a vote expected. And every vote counted. Meanwhile, Sam Koenig exploited his grip on the Lower East Side, where the old-time loyal Tammany Irish had been supplanted by the Jews and Italians, who were more amenable to Republican influences.[1]

Before Fiorello could get his campaign properly launched, a bombshell was tossed by Clarence Fay, who beat the drum by which the Fourteenth Congressional District marched. Fay designated Hamilton Fish Jr., of Putnam County, as the district's candidate, in return for a hefty contribution by his conservative family and friends to the party coffers. Bypassing Fay, Fiorello went to see state party chairman Tanner. Tanner disliked the idea of a carpetbagger coming in from another county. But he did like the dollars the carpetbag contained. He told Fiorello to be a good fellow, go along with the party, help wherever he could, and someday he'd "be a judge, or something big like that."

Fiorello argued that he deserved the nomination on the basis of his 1914 showing and that he was sure he could deliver an even bigger vote, certainly one much bigger than a wealthy carpetbagger from another county, which to the majority of those living in the Fourteenth was the same as another planet. Tanner was sympathetic. He even offered to reimburse Fiorello for expenses thus far incurred. Fiorello "hit the ceiling. . . . I blew up, and that just about ended our talk." As he started to storm out of the office, Tanner shouted to him, "Fiorello, hold your horses. Damn it, if you want to run again, go ahead and do it. Don't blame me if you're licked again."

Fiorello went ahead and did it.

Fay had to accept Tanner's order that the nomination was Fiorello's. But he did not have to accept it with grace. Though Fiorello never got a nod or a word from party leaders, no opposition developed. To circumvent opposition from one of the major splinter par-

ties, which would have siphoned off votes that might otherwise have
been his, La Guardia came up with a shrewd gambit that subsequently became standard practice among New York mayoral candidates: running simultaneously as candidate of one of those splinter
parties. He filed for and won a second spot on the ballot representing the Progressive Party.

A pleasant interlude for Fiorello halfway through the campaign
was the visit of his mother, who had been living in Budapest with
Gemma and her husband. As Irene was suffering from advanced
diabetes, it's likely she wanted to see her favorite son one last time.
It was around this time that Fiorello met Thea Almerigotti, a dress
designer, in a garment union picket line. Trieste born, twelve years
younger, and a few inches taller, the twenty-one-year-old Thea, a practicing Catholic, was described by Fannie Hurst as a "Rosetti-like girl,
porcelain-like, frail, blonde, and willowy." For Fiorello, it was love at
first sight. For Thea, it would take a little more time. She was not
only far removed from the world of politics Fiorello thrived on, she
"provided an enchanting contrast with his brash, conniving environment." They began dating steadily toward the end of the campaign.
Fiorello knew they would marry, but matrimony must cede precedence to the demands of his political career.[2]

2.

In his memoirs, La Guardia describes the 1916 campaign as "hot."
"Dirty" would be closer to the mark. There was quite a bit of mudslinging—much of it by La Guardia himself at his opponent, who
was again Mike Farley. Dealing with him more savagely than he had
in 1914, Fiorello accused the congressman of selling "rotgut" in his
saloon and, after the victims passed out, of tossing them into the
snow to freeze to death. On one occasion he climbed atop the back
of a truck in front of Farley's saloon and challenged him to come
out from behind the bar and debate the issues. When Farley refused,
Fiorello shouted to the crowd that had gathered that the president
of the National Liquor Dealers Association, and a member of Congress yet, was so ignorant he couldn't read a speech if it were written
for him. His tactic here was to get Farley to speak out and thereby
reveal his unfitness for garbage collector, let alone congressman.

But Tammany, knowing their man, didn't want him opening his

mouth. They even brought in stump speakers from other districts. La Guardia kept after Farley until, in hopes of shutting him up, Farley issued a ten-plank platform of legislation he proposed to introduce if reelected. La Guardia gleefully rushed around the Fourteenth in his beat-up Ford chortling that four of the proposals had already been enacted by City Hall, another four by the state legislature, and the remaining two had already been introduced in Congress—but when they came up for consideration Farley was back in his district tending bar!

For every abuse Fiorello flung at Farley, the latter's loyalists flung back the taunts "wop" and "guinea" and "dago." When things got really nasty, as they did fairly regularly, Fiorello could rely on a flying cadre of young campaign volunteers with flying fists. At times it appeared the Little Flower was running not for Congress but for the penitentiary. But still he kept at it. And in his campaign he had at least one kind of support he lacked in 1914. "The fighting Irish were helpful to me in that campaign. I knew more about the history of Ireland than Mike Farley did, and some of the Irish thought Mike Farley had not been anti-English enough," La Guardia recalled.

This brings us to the main thrust of La Guardia's campaign: the war in Europe, which was now in its second year.

The Fourteenth Congressional District was Europe in microcosm, with its ethnic neighborhoods and nationalistic feelings, especially among the recent immigrants, intensified by what was happening back in the Old World. The Irish prayed for England's defeat; the Italians wanted the return of Trieste, which could be effected only if the Allies defeated and broke up the Austro-Hungarian Empire; the Jews, the Poles, the Germans, the Hungarians, the Romanians— all had vested interests in the great conflict and were themselves in conflict with those of their immediate neighbors who favored the German-led Central Powers. Here were tumultuous, hazard-strewn waters that any candidate in so diverse a district must navigate at great peril. La Guardia navigated them brilliantly.

To the immigrants and children of immigrants from the many nationalities comprising the Austro-Hungarian Empire, he promised that the lands of their fathers would achieve independence. To the Italians he insisted that no peace would be an equitable peace unless Trieste were returned to Italy; to the Jews that the virulent anti-Semitism of the czars would end, and the collapse of the autocratic

Russian Empire would bring freedom to the Russian people. To the pro-Tammany English-hating Irish he showed where his sympathies lay by coming down squarely in support of that year's Dublin Easter Uprising.

The only area of the Fourteenth that La Guardia felt he could take for granted was the upper-class section of lower Fifth Avenue and Washington Square. There, interest in the campaign focused on the close, tense struggle between Woodrow Wilson, seeking re-election, and Charles Evans Hughes, the popular former governor of New York and U.S. Supreme Court justice. Fiorello was confident that these "silk-stocking" Republicans would vote the straight party ticket, so he need do very little campaigning there. Also to be counted on were many Democratic leaders in the ethnic communities. Outraged by Wilson's denunciation of the so-called hyphenates (Italo-Americans, Jewish-Americans, German-Americans, et al.) for their "divided loyalties," and disgusted by Farley's failure to speak out against the president, these Democrats decided to support La Guardia. Also climbing aboard the rapidly accelerating La Guardia bandwagon were the rabidly anti-Republican trade unionists led by those two social visionaries August Bellanca and Onorio Ruotolo, along with fellow Socialists. Emphasizing his role in the 1912–13 garment strike, Fiorello publicly pledged that although a "lifelong Republican" he would, if elected, vote and act independently, putting logic and fairness ahead of party loyalty. Those who joined in his crusade sensed what time would prove to be an incontrovertible truth: Unlike most politicians, who will say anything to get elected, Fiorello La Guardia never made empty promises but, rather, pledges he fully intended to honor.

Tammany was not concerned about the outcome. The Fourteenth was Democratic boss Charlie Murphy's home district. Under his aegis the machine-made party seemed invincible. Besides, the threat of those Democratic defections was more than offset by Republican leaders on the West Side who were feeding from the same trough of corruption as the Tammany swine and had no burning desire to see their party's candidate score. Besides, if, by some unforeseen jest of the gods, "the dago" should pull in more votes, the final tally could always be "adjusted" after the polls closed. Final tallies from all the polling places were recorded at Tammany-controlled police headquarters. They might as well have been recorded in the basement of Boss Murphy's home.

But the overconfident sachems underestimated "the dago." Reports were coming in daily to the Wigwam that the people, including many of *their* people, were taking to heart the reforms he preached and the concerns he expressed regarding their welfare and ambitions. Three days before the election, Tammany began to fear that "adjusting" the final tally was not just *an* option, it was the *only* option. The German hyphenates, Tammany's largest bloc aside from the Irish, had boarded the La Guardia Congressional Express.

A week before the election, La Guardia had been asked to meet with Victor and Bernard Ridder, publishers of the city's largest and most influential German-language newspaper, the New York *Staats-Zeitung,* pro-Democratic since its founding in 1834. The Ridders knew that the incumbent Farley, a loyal Democrat, shared President Wilson's negative feelings on the hyphenates. Now they wanted to hear from his opponent on the matter. Asked by Victor Ridder, "What's your opinion about hyphenated Americans? America isn't at war," Fiorello shot back instantly, "German-Americans have as much a right to be for Germany as the Plymouth Rockers have to be for England."

Satisfied with the response, Ridder said, "We'll support you. I'd like to have a picture of you to run in the newspaper."

Replied Fiorello, "I don't have one."

"You don't have any picture at all?"

Fiorello broke into German. "*Ich habe es nicht.*"

Exclaimed Ridder in astonishment, "Why, you speak German!"

"Of course I do," continued La Guardia in that language. "Nowadays every educated American should speak German." Years later, when Ridder asked how it was that he knew German so well, Fiorello said jokingly that he'd picked it up during his consular days in a Fiume whorehouse.[3]

Three days later, to the shock and horror of Tammany, the traditionally Democratic paper urged editorially that La Guardia replace Farley in Congress. Written in English and addressed to workingmen of Irish, German, and Italian descent, the editorial described the Republican candidate's interest in and concern for labor and immigration, emphasized his endorsement by the Progressive Party, and promised that he would be everything that Farley should have been but wasn't.[4] In addition, Victor Ridder personally stumped for his choice in heavily German-speaking neighborhoods.

"We had to get up very early on Election Day," recalled La Guardia, "for we had a job to do." The "job": to ensure that Tammany did not steal the election.

By five o'clock in the morning, after but three hours of sleep following last-minute campaigning, he and a band of supporters bearing platters of rolls and doughnuts and pots of coffee appeared at the district flophouses where Tammany traditionally procured votes with platters of sandwiches and alcoholic refreshments. After the denizens had been served breakfast, Fiorello personally walked them to the polling place. By the time the Tammany caterers showed up at eight o'clock, the flophouse crowd had already voted. It was not a personal thing, they assured the infuriated Tammanyites, who felt betrayed. They had voted for the little guy who'd been the first to show up at their domiciles with breakfast! It was the first time in years they voted sober. Many of them found it a novel experience.

Fiorello still had his work cut out for him when the polls closed and the count began. In those days, before machine-processed ballots, paper ballots were used and tallied by hand. The count was long and tedious—and allowed ample opportunity for marking ballots so that they could be disqualified, substituting phony ballots, and every other kind of dirty political trick. La Guardia ran around the district ordering his poll watchers to ensure an honest count and stay put until the returns were officially signed and the ballot boxes sealed. The volunteers ran the gamut from schoolteachers, doctors, and businessmen to longshoremen "and some tough guys," should things get dicey. Fiorello took it upon himself to cover personally the toughest district on the waterfront. Informed that he had shown up at police headquarters to watch the ballot count, Democratic district leader Charles Culkin, one of the Tammany sachems, rushed over and asked, "Why, La Guardia, what are you doing here? You shouldn't be here. Everything is all right."

"Everything is not all right. And what is more, Charlie, you sit here and help me watch this count. This is going to be an honest count, and, if not, someone is going to go to jail, and I mean you, Charlie!" Charlie sat. Ballot counting was commenced. The district, which usually went five to one against the Republicans, went to La Guardia.

This was one election Tammany failed to steal. Sam Koenig, who carried the Sixth Assembly District for Fiorello, gave him a rousing victory party even before the official results were announced. In Fiorello's own Twenty-fifth, the crowd was hysterical with joy over his election. By the time he got there, though, everyone had left except a few ward heelers engaged in a dispirited postmortem. As Fiorello walked into headquarters he overheard someone on the phone in the rear office telling a Democratic boss, "No, Joe, we didn't double-cross you; we didn't do anything for this fellow. You just can't control him." Fiorello went home in a bifurcated state of exultation and bitterness. "An apology for my victory is what I heard instead of congratulations!" he later recalled, adding philosophically, "Those are just some of the little things that have made me an incurable insurgent."

Of 18,670 ballots cast, La Guardia and Farley accounted for a total of 14,187, with Fiorello winning by a plurality of 357.[5] More than a third of his total came from his home district, where, as anticipated, silk-stocking Republicans, who normally ignored off-year elections, voted for Hughes and the entire party ticket. His greatest strength lay in the predominantly Jewish Sixth, where the socially concerned immigrants, unlike so many of their somewhat apathetic Italian co-evals, were quick to become citizens and thus eligible voters. Though predominantly Socialist-oriented, they believed that the staunchly pro-hyphenate Little Flower, whose image was that of a Liberal, could accomplish more in their behalf than the Socialist Party. Moreover, they realized that voting Socialist would split the vote and return the intellectually challenged Farley to Congress. La Guardia's margin of victory may have been what today would be termed chump change, but it made him the first Republican (as well as the first Italian-American) to be sent to Congress from the Fourteenth Congressional District—and not because of his party's bosses but in spite of them. He was not beholden to the party machine, which in the future would have one devil of a time keeping a tight rein on him. Or even a loose one, for that matter.

According to Louis Espresso, early the next morning he and the usually inexhaustible yet now bone-tired congressman-elect went to a Turkish bath "for a much-needed soaking and steaming out." Suddenly Fiorello broke down. Falling to his knees, his eyes brimming with tears—the first such display of emotion Espresso could recall—he said, "Louis, this is the happiest moment of my life, but if my mother were only alive to see this now." Irene had died the previous year shortly after returning to Budapest.[6]

CHAPTER SEVEN

"Don't blame me if you don't like the way I vote"

1.

Whether supporting or condemning pending legislation, offering amendments to the bills of others or presenting those of his own creation, lauding or hectoring colleagues, flooding the chamber with eloquent oratory or drowning it with coruscating sarcasm, resorting to show-and-tells and dog-and-pony shows to drive home a point, the member from the Fourteenth elicited from other members, be they of his own party or the opposition, praise, condemnation, cheering, jeering, laughs, catcalls, and an inability by many to decide in the final analysis whether the Little Flower was a noble statesman or an ignoble irritant. He was not concerned with winning prizes for congeniality. His concern was what best served the nation he loved and the constituency whose interests he had sworn to protect. He was congenitally incapable of accepting any man's doubts that his attitudes were the only acceptable ones. He was convinced that history would vindicate him.

When the Sixty-fifth Congress convened on March 5, 1917, the Republicans and Democrats were evenly divided, having each elected 215 members, which meant that whichever party won the support of any three of the five independents would gain control of the House.

The five, who would thus command special influence, were Meyer London, the New York Socialist; one Progressive each from Louisiana and Minnesota; Jeannette Rankin, from Montana, the first woman elected to Congress; and La Guardia. Though nominally a Republican, his having also run as a Progressive subjected him to intense pressure by the Democrats to caucus with them. Ever the party loyalist, he voted with the Republicans. It didn't help. Two independents voted for themselves, the other two merely answered "present," which counted as abstentions, and a few Republicans defected, wanting to see Congress organized so that President Wilson's policies could be more easily acted on. The Democrats won control by a plurality of twelve, and consequently every office from Speaker of the House down to and including Doorkeeper. Thus Fiorello's legislative career began in the minority. He would remain there—if not always in party designation, certainly in spirit—until the conclusion of his congressional career in 1932.

Attaching himself to the Progressives, throughout his congressional career he would collaborate more often than not with Senators (formerly Congressmen) George Norris, William E. Borah, and Hiram Johnson, in addition to Senator Robert La Follette, a particular role model. And herein lay an incongruity. American progressivism prior to World War I was to a great extent dominated by bellicose nationalists, of whom Teddy Roosevelt was the paradigm; La Follette and Norris led a strong antiwar wing.[1] La Guardia during this period shared both the radical domestic views of the La Follette wing and the Rooseveltian idea of an aggressive foreign policy. But while the Roosevelt wing's justification for America becoming involved in the European war was jingoistic, La Guardia insisted that our involvement must be dictated by a higher morality: democracy and freedom, and liberation for the millions of Central Europeans of diverse nationalities and ethnicities still under the domination of the Austro-Hungarian, German, and Russian autocracies.

Wilson had just been inaugurated a second time, his success at the polls due largely to the fact that, despite the sinking of the *Lusitania* by a German submarine in 1915 and the loss of many American lives, "He Kept Us Out of War." But now Germany had resumed unrestricted warfare, sinking four American ships. Then came to light the so-called Zimmerman Telegram in which Mexico was promised that in return for supporting Germany against the United States she would be rewarded with the return of all territory forcibly ceded in the Mexican-American War of 1846–48. The promise was an abysmal admixture of wishful thinking and prototypical Teutonic arrogance, with a suggestion of abject lunacy. Still, it left Wilson with no option but to call for Congress to meet in special session on April 2, 1917, and break his 1916 campaign promise. While waiting for the special session to open, La Guardia rushed back to his district to take part in a series of patriotic gatherings on the Lower East Side. "These are days," he insisted at one rally, "when we must renew our love for the land and the flag that flies over us." Calling for American participation in the European conflict, he told a thousand Italo-Americans at another mass meeting, "We've got to fight hard; we've got to take a man's part in this war."[2]

Wilson arrived for the joint session of Congress escorted by a troop of cavalry to ward off pacifist demonstrators positioned en masse on Capitol Hill. He noted that, as he had informed the Congress on February 3, Germany's resumption of unrestricted submarine warfare was "a warfare against humanity." In a subsequent message (February 26), he said, he had advocated a policy of "armed neutrality." But that policy was "now impracticable." Wilson asked that Congress declare war against Germany and act most expeditiously to prepare the nation to prosecute it.* Pronouncing an end to America's traditional isolationism, he made it patently clear that he had no quarrel with the Germans, only with their aggressive rulers. "We fight for the ultimate peace of the world and for the liberation of its peoples, the German peoples included," he emphasized, insisting in peroration, "The world must be made safe for democracy."[3]

Next morning the House Committee on Foreign Affairs reported out a resolution declaring war on Germany. Then commenced three days of impassioned debate. On the second day La Guardia introduced his first bill—a radical contravention of the unwritten rule that freshman members remain silent in deference to their seniors. Echoing his bitterness over the death of his father during the Spanish-American War, he called for "making the fraudulent sale of

---

*Serbia, which had started the whole hideous mess, was moribund. The United States would later declare war on the other Central Powers partner, Austria-Hungary, but this was pro forma, as the Hapsburg Empire was by then falling apart.

war materials a felony punishable by imprisonment in time of peace and by death in time of war." Newspaper comment was favorable, as in the *New York Evening Mail* in its following day's edition (April 4, 1917): "There is undoubtedly a strong public sentiment behind the measure. . . . The country has not forgotten the paper-soled shoes that were sold to the army in the [Civil War]. It remembers vividly the rotten beef that was disposed of to our soldiers in the Spanish [-American] war." The bill was referred to the Judiciary Committee, where it was allowed to expire. Republican lack of support was not so much out of opposition to the bill itself as a strong disinclination to support a member who was, for all intents and purposes, a party "irregular."

La Guardia's failure to partake directly in the raging debate over the war resolution was rooted in a personal quandary. While he wished to support American intervention, he knew there was a strong antiwar sentiment in his home district among the Irish and Germans, and especially among the Italian immigrants who wanted no further part in Europe's endless conflicts. Two days later he realized that to resist the mounting tide against Germany was politically obtuse. Congress was going to declare war anyway. Not supporting it would leave him open to the charge that he and his hyphenate constituents were disloyal to the country that had taken them in. At 3:14 in the morning of Good Friday, April 6, 1917, the House adjourned. The United States had officially entered World War I.[4]

France was rapidly approaching exhaustion, Great Britain was rapidly approaching depletion of its replacements pool, Italy was hard pressed to hold on to her sector, and Russia was coming apart at the seams through defeat on the field and internal chaos. American involvement was desperately and immediately needed if the Central Powers were to be defeated. But our standing army numbered 125,000 men—fewer than the French lost at Verdun. Our navy had expanded little since the Spanish-American War. And, with the airplane emerging as a vital weapon of warfare, the nation not only lacked an air force, it lacked a single combat plane. An emergency war appropriations bill was rushed through Congress, and Wilson called for an immediate draft of all able-bodied men.

Even before the conscription bill was introduced, La Guardia conducted a postcard referendum in his district soliciting his constituents' opinions. Explaining that the proposed legislation treated everyone equally, save for the aged and physically infirm, he also circulated a letter to the effect that, with bills pending "which would exempt the farmer from service, or the cotton grower, or the tobacco grower," if New York did not "watch out" she would have to "supply as large a proportion of the Army as she now does of the taxes, which is one-third. The only way to avoid this is to institute compulsory service. It is up to you to respond." The letter concluded with a caveat: "Don't blame me if you don't like the way I vote."[5]

La Guardia had his say in the draft bill debate, and what he had to say was quite a lot. He did not believe that anyone should be exempted from the draft, even on grounds of conscientious or religious objection. He introduced an amendment that provided for such conscripts to be excused only from combat and "be assigned to clerical, hospital, agricultural or manual work of a noncombative nature." The amendment was defeated. Another amendment, which avoided being shot down in flames only because he allowed colleagues to talk him out of even introducing it, opposed exemptions for physical deficiencies "if those people could perform clerical or other less strenuous work than field or combat service." Still another amendment he failed to get through was to oppose any young man holding officer's rank during the first six months of his service, "so that all would be trained on a basis of absolute equality, and we would have a really democratic army."

As Congress set about the prodigious task of mobilizing the nation's resources, La Guardia assumed the role of congressional gadfly. The House was by tradition the arena for legislation through compromise. To him it was an arena in which to fight for moral principles. Also by time-honored tradition, his colleagues believed in doing things in committee, through accommodation and compromise. La Guardia believed in making speeches on the floor defending or assailing, depending upon the cause. That he was frequently voted down was a matter of monumental unconcern; so, too, was criticism of his tone, which was one of superiority commingled with truculence and condescension. Being reprimanded for taking himself too seriously reinforced the ideologue in La Guardia. What was the business of a congressman, he demanded, if not serious business? And in his speeches, which were more often than not harangues, he considered as particularly serious business the mission America must play in what was being hailed as the War to End All Wars. Paramount in his thinking was self-determination for minority peoples, civil liberties at home as well as abroad, the problems involved in fighting and financing the war—and his ancestry.[6]

Readily identifiable by name and appearance as the Congress's sole Italo-American, Fiorello was determined that everyone realize he was (his own words here) "just as good as any Nordic." When Congress passed, over Wilson's veto, the Literacy Test Bill to curtail "new immigration" from Southern and Eastern Europe, La Guardia perceived it as official Washington not only rejecting the "melting pot" concept after 150 years of unrestricted immigration but positing instead that the United States was a fixed Anglo-Saxon culture into which only Protestants from Northern Europe need apply for inclusion. Not many of his colleagues were prepared to openly disagree. Straddling two cultures as both an immigrant by ancestry and a native American by birth, La Guardia was both defensively proud of his Italian heritage and belligerently assertive that he was as American as anyone lineally descended from a *Mayflower* passenger.

In the winter of 1916–17, he forged full steam ahead into the so-called Americanization movement. At loyalty demonstrations on the Lower East Side, he called for "100 Per Cent Americanism." He advised Italo-Americans to take a leaf from their Irish neighbors and organize themselves politically as a means of combating prejudice, urging that they follow his lead and look upon themselves as being as American as "the first inhabitants of New Amsterdam."[7] Many among his fellow legislators, convinced that nonnaturalized Italo-Americans were draft dodgers, considered this absurd. This encouraged Fiorello to rail passionately—and in vain—against enactment of a bill that would empower Allied governments to recruit troops in the United States among resident aliens born in their respective countries.

As he saw it, the bill made a distinction between citizens and noncitizens in order to get rid of the latter. Since, as he pointed out, Italy was prepared to confiscate the property of such aliens resisting military service, America's cooperation was ipso facto "the handmaid of shanghaiing these men back." That he was not being paranoid is borne out by an accusation by one Indiana representative that La Guardia "wants to protect a few Italians from going back to their own country. What did they come here for? Why do they not go back and stay there?" When the representative from North Carolina, who was piloting the bill through the House, explained that there was nothing coercive about it, La Guardia retorted angrily that volunteers were free to go back without such a law. To this the gentleman from North Carolina had no reply.[8]

In his home district, the locus of considerable antiwar sentiment, La Guardia sang a different tune: "I want to drive it home and impress it upon you, if I can, that we are in the midst of the most cruel war in the history of the world ... and those who prefer Italy to America should return to Italy. I know there are some of you in my district who won't sacrifice themselves for any country, and if I thought I owed my election to that sort I would resign." To which the audience responded lustily, in Italian, "We'll all fight." The Selective Service Act passed the House on April 28 by a vote of 397 to 24 with abstentions. Fiorello was one of the 397. Quite a few of his constituents, mainly the Socialists and others opposing the war, did not like his vote. "But I started the policy I used ever afterwards of voting as I thought right, explaining my views frankly to my constituents, and taking the consequences," he remembered. Three days later, he joined with Jimmy Walker and others in a parade through Greenwich Village, which, reported the *New York American* (May 21, 1917), "ceased being Bohemian long enough to demonstrate it was thoroughly American." Much as he hated war in principle, Fiorello saw this war as imperative if democracy was to survive.[9]

Though a certifiable social liberal, La Guardia parted ways with the many liberals of his generation who insisted that social problems were best approached with systematic theory compounded in equal doses of politics and economics. La Guardia's approach was compounded in equal doses of incontrovertible suspicion of powerful men ("the Interests") and immutable empathy for "their victims," the masses. He stood as a sentinel for democracy: a sentinel driven not by social design but by innate temperament. A case in point was the Lever Food and Fuel Control Act, which gave the president authority to regulate the production, conservation, and distribution of food and fuel supplies during wartime. Offering an amendment to place food inspectors under Civil Service, and warning against "7,000 men roaming all over the country with the ostensible purpose of preaching about hog cholera and incidentally extolling the virtues of the Democratic Party," La Guardia next introduced a constitutional amendment granting the federal government identical powers in time of peace.

Here was an instance when the Little Flower, for all his reading, betrayed a rather meager knowledge of American history. When doubts were raised on the House floor about the constitutionality of a national food control bill, he argued that "the far-sighted, liberty-loving men who worked on the Constitution and the Bill of Rights just couldn't imagine that the day would ever come in this country when food would be cornered, or they would have made provision to assure to every American willing to work, the right to food and shelter and clothing among his inalienable rights."[10] There was, to be sure, much that those "liberty-loving men" could not possibly have been "far-sighted" about. Their concern was for the creation of a master plan for governance; an organic master plan, not one fixed in marble. Unstated, but not unrecognized, was the fact that so much would have to be done in so many areas and on so many levels, much of which they could not possibly have imagined, to be achieved through government planning and applicable legislation, including amendments.

Clearly La Guardia either was unaware of the existence of this great American tradition or actually believed that the Founding Fathers should have imagined the day would come when, as he phrased it, "the right to food, shelter, and clothing at reasonable prices is as much an inalienable right as the right to life, liberty and the pursuit of happiness." Still, he is to be excused, given the fear uppermost in his mind: that the swindlers and speculators, whom he was confident would be conducting business as usual once the war was over, would make "the robust, full-blooded, red-cheeked American fade into a weak, anemic, underfed, disgruntled individual." The amendment was put to death by the Judiciary Committee.[11]

La Guardia's florid, empty rhetoric continued as he ventilated an innately illimitable resentment against the privileged few that derived from an immutable conviction that rich people cheat as a matter of course with impunity, thanks to the stupidity or duplicity—or complicity—of public officials. This conviction compelled him to jump all over one component of the Liberty Loan Bill whereby the secretary of the Treasury was authorized to dispose of unsubscribed bonds at his discretion instead of at par value. La Guardia warned the House that this was a loophole for "speculators and financial slackers" to buy bonds under par, something forbidden the general public. His mistrust was a key factor in the section being deleted from the bill.

Also symptomatic of this mistrust was the way he regarded the War Revenue Bill, which taxed personal income, commodities, services, and corporations. (This was a wartime measure supplementary to the Sixteenth ["Income Tax"] Amendment of 1913.) While there is no denying that the law worked hardships on low-income groups, it was burdensome to people in all economic strata, and despite its many shortcomings it was the most progressive tax bill in the nation's history. Still, La Guardia, with the tunnel vision to which he so often fell victim, saw it as a piece of soak-the-poor legislation and offered a litany of amendments, of which all but one met with failure: inclusion in the 10 percent admission tax for boxes, subscriptions, and season tickets at opera houses and other entertainment venues. "Otherwise," he argued, "only people in the orchestra, gallery and cheaper seats would have paid taxes."

Neither a utopian nor a cynic, Fiorello La Guardia was a pragmatist who tended to expect less from human nature rather than more. Nowhere is this more evident than in the three-billion-dollar Foreign Loan Bill. He was in the vanguard of support for it: "Our Allies [are] in need of the money. It [is] our duty to lend it." Assurances and promises were received from the president, the secretary of the Treasury, the chairman of the House Ways and Means Committee, and member after member who argued for the loan that it would cost the United States nothing, nor ever be a burden to the American taxpayer, inasmuch as the money would be "returned with interest in full." On April 14, La Guardia told the House he did not share this belief. He conceded that a good portion would in due time be returned, but he was certain that some of it would have to be written off as a loss. "Let us understand that clearly now and not be deceived later. Even so, if this brings about a speedy termination of the European war and permanent peace to our own country it is a good investment at that."

As he explained in his memoirs, La Guardia was all for foreign loans, but he "did not want Congress and the country to kid themselves about getting the money back with interest in full and then being disappointed and bitter about it." When there was opposition to refunding on any basis but the full principal and interest, he told the House, "Take it. Be lucky if you get it at all. I doubt that you will get even this much." Time proved him to have been remarkably prescient. Only tiny Finland repaid the loan in full, with interest; Great Britain made considerable restitution. Loans to all the other Allied nations, as he predicted, had to be written off as a loss. Still, as he stressed regarding all forms of aid to our allies in both world wars, by all means give them everything they need—but consider it a gift, not a loan.

Just as time bore out La Guardia's misgivings about the Foreign Loan Bill, so would his strong opposition to the Espionage Act vindicate his stand in defense of civil liberties. He was adamant in his conviction that the "right of individuals who could be falsely accused of impeding the war effort by over-eager legislative warriors had to be protected." Someone had to make an attempt "to curb hysteria so that we did not destroy, in the war we were engaged in, the rights we were anxious to preserve." To his mind, the Espionage Bill as originally introduced was too severe: "It could be used to cause abuses of individual liberty and contained possibilities of persecution and miscarriage of justice." He felt that some provisions would prevent legitimate criticism of misadministration in the military and the government in general. Such criticism was not necessarily advantageous to the enemy, while lack of such criticism could, as he saw it, be "of disadvantage to our own efficiency." Any ban on the right to indulge in it "would deprive American citizens of their traditional privilege to criticize their government even in military affairs."

On May 2, 1917, in his most eloquent speech of the Sixty-fifth Congress, La Guardia "sought to put some sense into the measure." Defining it as the most important to come before the House during this and previous sessions, he warned, "Gentlemen, if you pass this bill and it is enacted into law you change all that our flag ever stood and stands for, even though we do not change her colors. . . . This country will continue to exist after this war, and I want to do my part that it may exist a free and independent nation, a Republic of republics, a model and inspiration to the oppressed people of the world. We all have our heart and soul in this war, but because we have our heart in it is no reason why we should lose our head. . . . We have the responsibility of carrying this country through this war without impairing or limiting any of her institutions of true liberty or losing her identity as an ideal Republic."

La Guardia had no objection to any provisions of the bill that guarded against the activities of spies and traitors. What he most objected to was Section 4, which permitted the president to prohibit publication or communication of any information relating to the "national defense." His fear here was that even Wilson might resort to despotism if so empowered. The term "national defense" embraced reference to "any person, place, or thing in any wise having to do with the preparation for or the consideration or execution of any military or naval plans, expeditions, orders, supplies, or warfare for the advantage, defense or security of the United States of America." Even mere discussion of any such matters could subject a citizen to imprisonment for ten years.

La Guardia insisted that under Section 4, which violated the First Amendment to the Constitution, any critic of, say, inadequacy of food, contract frauds, and inefficiencies in the War Department could be put in jail. Reminding his colleagues that the infamous Sedition Act of 1798 was the last previous attempt "to shackle the minds of the American people" in the way some members of Congress were now trying to do, he expressed particular concern that a muzzled press would be tantamount to "a green light [to] the domestic enemy who is willing to turn American blood into gold, and will sell rotten corn beef, wormy beans, paper shoes, defective arms for our American boys."

> The people of this country [he said in peroration] are united in their demand that the scandals, abuses, graft and incompetence of 1898 are not to be repeated, and the press is their medium of detecting and exposing these abuses and crimes. It is our duty as their representatives to do nothing which will impair, restrict, or limit the press in the fulfillment of that duty. This alone, without considering the determination of our basic fundamental principles of liberty, is sufficient justification to arouse the indignation of this House and send this bill back to the committee, where it should die in shame and neglect.[12]

Though the House voted to strike out the whole of Section 4 by a vote of 221 to 167, La Guardia still voted against the Espionage Act as a whole because he "thought it still contained too many dangerous provisions." The act became law on June 15, 1917, and remained on the books, "a potential danger to our liberties thereafter." La Guardia's deep misgivings about the act were borne out in the number of people who were deprived of their civil rights during the war simply "because of their utterance of criticism." Throughout the 1920s, he worked with the American Civil Liberties Union to have those rights restored but came up against a stone wall during the Hoover administration. More than ten years after the war ended, 1,500 men and women convicted under the Espionage Act "for their utterances" still were unable to vote, serve on juries, or hold public office. The majority of those convicted were, for the most part, pacifists, Socialists, and IWW migratory workers ("the Wobblies"). In some states they were denied licenses to practice professions or engage in certain trades, to hunt and fish, even to operate an automobile. Ultimately, more than two thousand persons were prosecuted under the act, and more than eight hundred jailed—not a one of them for actual espionage.[13]

Other measures considered by the House during those first months following America's entry into the war also contained provisions La Guardia considered "dangerous to our civil liberties." One he was quite vocal in opposing was a provision of the Trading with the Enemy Act that allowed the president to include "anyone he saw fit" in the term "enemy." La Guardia insisted it was both unnecessary and pernicious to give the president such powers. Individuals could be deprived of their right of habeas corpus, denied due process, even held in custody until the termination of the war on the say-so of the president, or any other officer of the government to whom he might delegate this broad authority; evidence sufficient to warrant indictments was not required, merely suspicions. He offered many additional amendments "altering" the broad—indeed, almost limitless—powers inherent in the Trading with the Enemy Act. All were rejected. It was "a period when zeal and fervor were not always properly channeled," he recalled with characteristically understated irony.

La Guardia "also objected without success" to a provision in the act giving the federal government extensive powers over the railroads in wartime, which included empowering the president to order armed forces into any locality, for whatever reasons he saw fit, without first consulting with local authorities. "There was absolutely no necessity for this provision," La Guardia argued. "Under it an inexperienced, excitable or ignorant United States marshal could ask the

President for use of the armed forces and get it." He termed it "a vicious precedent to establish." Moreover, it was typical of what he called the "ghoulish legislation" being passed in that first wartime session of Congress—measures that "carried in [them] pet fads and hobbies of some members."[14]

A great number of civilian jobs were being created, and La Guardia made every effort to have as many of these jobs as possible subject to Civil Service regulations. He feared that the whole system, based on appointment by examination and strict adherence to regulation, would break down if "the excuse of war emergency" could be used by "greedy politicians. There were plenty of cases where the excuse that we could not wait for [the candidate to take] a Civil Service examination was being used to get political henchmen jobs whether or not they were qualified for the work." He failed, though not for want of trying, to prevent exemption from Civil Service regulations for the large increase in personnel at the Bureau of Mines to handle the greatly expanded production of explosives. The majority party in Congress, he charged, "wanted as many 'deserving' Democrats as possible to get those jobs, no matter what their abilities or qualifications."

One project that particularly raised La Guardia's ire derived from the creation of an air force. There was no opposition to the program, though the bill called for $640,000,000, the largest amount ever appropriated up to that time for any one branch of the armed services. The problem was the Liberty motor. Though proved to be obsolete and antiquated, it was put into manufacture on a large scale. It was the hope of her allies that the United States, with so much raw material and manufacturing skill at its disposal, could produce enough planes to relieve them of any further plane production. The Liberty motor, though, was "a miserable failure." The Allies had to go on making their own planes, at the expense of other armaments. Aggravating the problem, the United States had to devote a large portion of very scarce shipping tonnage to deliver the raw materials.

Though only American pilots agreed to fly them, and only for observation or light bombing, production continued in large numbers. "The boys did not like them. They soon got the name 'Flying Coffin,' and the Liberty motor was considered a jinx." When La Guardia returned to the House from war service, he was horrified to learn that the War Department had requested appropriation for the purchase of another ten thousand of these "Flying Coffins." He introduced a resolution of inquiry in the face of intense lobbying by General Motors and other manufacturers that the nation "would never be caught again with an airplane shortage" if the ten thousand were purchased, packed in oil, and held in reserve. He succeeded in getting the resolution through, the deal was killed, and the country saved millions of dollars as well as potentially hundreds, perhaps thousands, of lives. As for the manufacturers, their activities were subsequently investigated, but nothing ever came of it. La Guardia's explanation: "There were just too many people with good connections involved."

CHAPTER EIGHT

"I can't take the buzzard off, but I CAN FLY the son of a gun!"

1.

La Guardia had told the young men of his district that if he voted for drafting them into the Army, he would also go. By the beginning of July, with conscription, foreign-loan and trading-with-the-enemy acts, the espionage laws, and the food and aviation bills "out of the way," Congress adjourned for the summer. Confident that whatever further war measures might be needed could easily pass the House "without my vote," the thirty-four-year-old congressman "was ready to go to the front and determined to do so."

Precedent militated against a man holding a congressional seat and an Army commission simultaneously. Supported by Speaker of the House Champ Clark, a bill was introduced granting La Guardia a leave of absence and letting him retain his seat so long as he was in uniform. He was, though, not entitled to his pay as a congressman of $7,500 per annum, which was $5,500 above that of a first lieutenant. "If the Germans don't get me," he vowed, "I'll get that pay!"

When La Guardia presented himself at the recruiting office of the Aviation Section of the U.S. Army Signal Corps in mid-July, it was as a lawyer "with some little flying training." He felt that nothing should be said about his being a member of Congress until he had actually received his commission. The recruiting officer didn't think much of lawyers as material for the Air Service, especially a pudgy little overage one. But the chief of the Air Service, learning that the candidate could not only pilot a plane and speak Italian but was the very congressman who had helped create the Air Service, had other ideas. Plans were under way to send American aviation cadets to Italy for training; the first contingent was to leave for Europe shortly. On August 17, 1917, Congressman La Guardia became First Lieutenant La Guardia. Leaving Marie Fisher to handle the routine business of his congressional office with an assist from Harry Andrews, and his colleague from East Harlem, Isaac Siegel, with whom he would remain in constant telegraph contact while overseas, to cast his votes on any issues before the House, the nation's first aviator-legislator went off to war.

Sam Koenig and Fred Tanner honored him with a dinner attended by a hundred or so assorted politicians and prominent Republican bigwigs—most of whom had opposed his election to Congress. They hoped he would forget the past. He didn't, of course. But he pretended to. New York's Italian colony launched a series of "hot demonstrations of patriotism" in his honor. At one such event, in Washington Irving High School, he urged his hyphenate followers to fight; in so doing, they would be serving both their native land and their adopted land, now allied in common cause against Germany.[1]

Because of the reflected glory the Army was enjoying by having in its corner a congressman of his reputation for waging battles on Capitol Hill, La Guardia was quickly promoted to captain. At Mineola, on Long Island, where he first learned to fly, he reported to Major Leslie McDill, commanding officer of the war-bound cadets. McDill, wisely deferring to a subordinate officer who was, after all, a member of Congress, allowed La Guardia to "run the show," from organizing the contingent to getting it to Europe. It was probably just as well. He would have "run the show" anyway.

The handpicked cadets, students on leave from or graduates of major universities, were to be commissioned upon completion of training. One exception was the noted American violinist Albert Spalding. Assigned to the unit because of his command of Italian (he was also proficient in French and German), Spalding was asked why he was not an officer. He explained that he'd sought a commission, but the results of his examinations had somehow gone astray. "I've heard you play, and I know what a good fiddler you are," said La Guardia. "Will you be as good a soldier?" "Yes, sir." "I believe you." With a hearty handshake, La Guardia promised the twenty-nine-year-old Spalding that he'd have his commission—but would not be a flyer: "There is an emphasis on youth for flying. I agree with that emphasis [La Guardia was himself six years older], and why jeopardize talent if you don't have to?"[2]

One other noncom worthy of mention who appeared at Mineola, and all but joined himself to La Guardia at the hip, was Frank ("Ciccio") Giordano, owner of a small barbershop in Greenwich Village that Fiorello had patronized since 1906. Giordano, who would be slavishly loyal to La Guardia till his death, was eager to enlist though hardly Army material: he was married, over the age at which married men were being taken, with three children and, in the bargain, two flat feet. But Ciccio would not be put off, and he hounded La Guardia. As it happened, the contingent had to establish its own mess, and La Guardia was ordered to find a cook. He thought immediately of Giordano and arranged to get him the necessary waivers. Giordano's lack of culinary talents—"He was a mighty fine barber, but not much of a cook"—posed no problem. Except for breakfast, the men ate in local restaurants. He did, however, make himself "very useful," barbering the cadets and running errands.

La Guardia's first opportunity to demonstrate he could take on the War Department and emerge the victor came when he was ordered to arrange steamship passage for the contingent. He went down to the Cunard Line, produced his orders, and requested 156 first-class tickets on the SS *Carmania*. Though the ship would be carrying a large detachment of American troops, the head of the passenger division was dubious about noncommissioned officers traveling first class. Identifying himself as the congressman who had shaped the law that created the U.S. air branch, La Guardia "told him I knew it was the intent of Congress that these cadets were entitled to first-class passage. (At least I thought so!)" When Major McDill was shown the tickets, his "eyes almost popped out [and he said] that if we got away with that, we were good, but he warned me that the responsibility was mine." They "got away with it," establishing a precedent, which was later approved by the comptroller general of the United States. La Guardia was relieved: "Otherwise I would have been stuck for the difference between soldier rate—third-class or steerage—and first-class," a difference of about $150 a ticket, and he would have been "hard put to it to find $23,400."

But that wasn't the end of it. Even before they sailed, the Army embarkation port commander ordered the cadets down to steerage at once. La Guardia "pulled rank" as a congressman and carried the day. He did, though, reluctantly agree to send Giordano, Spalding, and the unit's clerks down to steerage. A week later, he had Spalding moved up to first class after telling the commanding officer of all U.S. Army personnel aboard that Spalding's services were required "to pound the rudiments of Italian into the cadet-students," who were headed for flying training at Italian camps where the pilot instructors would speak only Italian. "No time must be lost in giving them an elementary knowledge of the language." The officer, a West Pointer, became "revolted at this threat to a rigid caste system" and refused. La Guardia insisted—forcefully. The commander "faltered under the barrage of political persuasion, hesitated, gave way." Buck Private Spalding was moved up to first class.[3]

2.

La Guardia wore five hats while overseas from October 1917 to October 1918, some of them simultaneously. He was second in command (though he behaved as if he were first) of the Eighth Aviation Instruction Center at the Italian base where he also supervised the training of American airmen. He was a combat flyer. He served as the U.S. Army's representative on the Joint Army and Navy Aircraft Committee in Italy. He was a propagandist for the American Expeditionary Force. And he was a smuggler for the Italians, with the blessing of the U.S. State Department. Throughout it all, to the officials with whom he dealt he was an American congressman with clout. To his men he was mentor, protector, and best friend.

A change of plans awaited the Mineola contingent upon arrival at Liverpool. Major McDill received orders to send the cadets to British flying schools instead (so much for Spalding's Italian lessons) and to report with La Guardia and their medical staff to Allied headquarters in Paris. There they learned that another cadet corps, numbering some seven hundred, was being formed to go to Italy for flight training. A group of 125 had already been detached from their original outfits. McDill was assigned to Allied headquarters at Paris. La Guardia would take the contingent to their training camp at Foggia—the city of fifty thousand on the eastern plain near the Adriatic that was, ironically, the birthplace of his father, Achille.

On October 16, 1917, Captain La Guardia, attended by Ciccio Giordano, now upgraded to his personal orderly, settled into fairly comfortable quarters at what came to be known as Camp Foggia. The base, which lay in a funnel-shaped valley opening toward the Adriatic from which came the high easterly winds essential for air operations, was divided into two components: the West Camp, commanded by La Guardia, and the South Camp, commanded by a West Point–trained cavalry officer, Major (later Major General) William Ord Ryan. Being "regular army," Ryan found it a bit trying that La Guardia did not hold sacred the military tradition of doing things "by the numbers" and, worse, often went outside the chain of command to get what he wanted.

Since the United States lacked enough flying instructors and planes to send to their allies, Italy agreed to provide instructors, housing, and all flying equipment, along with camp discipline and overall command. The Americans were subject to discipline only by their own officers. Though the Italians were "a splendid group of instructors," their training methods seemed to La Guardia "childish and risky and dangerous." If a cadet, with his instructor in the rear seat, spent ten minutes in the air at one time, it was "considered quite a bit of training." After three hours of air time, the cadet made his first solo flight. If he and the plane landed in one piece, he was given his wings and commission and declared fit and ready for combat. Classification of flyers as fighter pilots, bombardiers, and navigators was, by today's standards, as primitive and crude as the training itself. The flyer's own preference was the deciding factor.

La Guardia endeared himself to his cadets ("my boys") by giving them the protection a tigress would give her newborn cubs. Learning that the surrounding population was anti-American, he rushed to Paris and returned with revolvers his men were ordered to carry at all times. When a colonel at Paris headquarters was about to court-martial one of his favorite lieutenants, La Guardia threatened to use his power as a congressman to bust him in rank: "He's one of my boys, lay off him!" The colonel laid off him.[4] And then there was the jock-like camaraderie. Off duty, there were baseball games between the South and West camps; these not only added to morale, they were consonant with La Guardia's insistence that his cadets be in top physical condition. Of course, they wished he would confine his participation to that of onlooker. But La Guardia never "onlooked" any activity in which he felt it was in everybody's best interest that he partake—even if "everybody" failed to share this view. Appointing himself first-base coach, he invariably kept up a strident, constant chatter to distract the other side. It distracted his own side as well. Still, they loved him.

"The Italians living up to their end of the agreement," La Guardia was able to report to American authorities. "Facilities for training are excellent."[5] As much could not be said for the food. His cadets were getting the same rations as Italian enlisted men. Breakfast was a kilo of "dark black bread" and "a canteen of a black fluid substitute for coffee." The big meal of the day, served at noon, consisted of "a boiled macaroni pasta or some such starch dish, a ladle of melted lard, and a handful of salt." Once a week the men were given "a diminutive piece of boiled meat and some soup." For the evening meal they received a bowl of gruel or vegetable soup and some more of the black bread. La Guardia was not only concerned that such a diet could not keep his men healthy, he doubted it could keep them alive.

Handling the problem in his own no-nonsense fashion, he came up with the novel idea of having meals catered. He worked out with a local vendor "a regular American breakfast, or as near to it as we could get under existing conditions"; a midday "big, well-balanced meal, with a meat or fish course every day"; and "a typical American supper." Out of consideration for Ryan's fear of a possible court-martial as overall base commander, La Guardia signed the contract on his own authority—and told the caterer to bill the Italian government! Several months later, with the catering system "functioning satisfactorily," La Guardia was suddenly ordered to appear at the chief quartermaster's office at Tours, France, with all data, records, and the contract for feeding the cadets.

Fiorello recalled in his memoirs that he had barely been ushered into the general's office by an aide when the general, who did not recognize him:

opened up on me right away. He stated that he was reporting the matter to the Judge Advocate General and charged me with violating the law, disregarding Army regulations, squandering public funds and acting generally like a convict, or something like that, rather than an officer and a gentleman. Then he pulled out papers and said the Italian government had paid the bills I had contracted and was now trying to collect their money from the American government under the master agreement between Italy and the United States for the training of cadets.

"Is that all that is troubling you, General?" I asked. "If so, I can have all that changed very easily."

I thought the man would burst with rage. He pounded the desk violently, called me insolent, impertinent, and demanded to know what I meant by saying that I could change Army regulations, which would take an act of Congress to accomplish.

At that point, the general's aide identified La Guardia. "You never saw a man change as fast as that general did when he heard that I was a Congressman. For the first time since I had come into the room, he asked me to be seated."

When La Guardia explained "in pretty straight language" the food situation at Foggia, the general cited Army regulations, pointing out that "some hardships are necessary." La Guardia stopped him practically in midsentence and said that it was not a question of some hardships but of feeding "my boys," who were "starving." The general insisted that the quartermaster's office could not pay for the catering because such an arrangement was not in accordance with regulations. Assuring him not to worry about having the bill paid, La Guardia rushed off to Paris and presented the problem to General Charles H. Dawes, chairman of the Interallied Finance Commission. Dawes, later vice president under Calvin Coolidge, "enjoyed a big laugh" when he heard of La Guardia's interview at Tours and arranged to have the Italian government bill the Interallied Finance Commission for catering services to Camp Foggia.

Having taken on the U.S. Army Quartermaster Corps, La Guardia now took on the Italian government.

Washington had agreed to purchase a thousand reconnaissance planes of Italian manufacture. They had been used on the Italian front for some time and proved effective. Those on order for the American airmen were newer models, with increased air speed and efficiency. But they were structurally weak, as shown by the number of test pilots who crashed to their death, and the Italian government did not want to make delivery until it was sure of the plane. When at last delivery began, the craft proved to be as dangerous—and disastrous—as the test models. La Guardia took it upon himself to inform the manufacturer that he "did not care to receive any more of them at Foggia" and recommended to the major American airbase at Tours that their order also be canceled. An agreement was reached whereby the United States would accept those already on hand and cancel the balance of the order; the delivered planes were not to be used in combat but only for training purposes. The Italians were quite put out about the cancellation of the order and appealed to La Guardia to lay off the manufacturer, which of course he would not do.

Having resolved the food and equipment quality problems at Camp Foggia, La Guardia next directed his attention to safeguarding the health of the American personnel. Foggia was located in a malarial district; the flat country provided no natural drainage, and the sewage system was primitive. La Guardia had his medical officer, Dr. Oliver Kiel, establish the camp's own public health service. Orders were issued to boil all drinking water; instructions were drawn up for the proper preparation of raw vegetables; the countryside was scoured for screens; each man's bunk was provided with mosquito netting. "The Italians thought we were crazy," La Guardia remembered, but the result was that there was only one case of malaria in all the time the Americans were at Foggia—"much to the surprise of the Italians."

That first Christmas at Foggia, with training at a standstill due to lack of equipment, and Major Ryan off on special duty in France, La Guardia, in command of the entire camp, discovered that his men had accumulated leave and back pay. As there was nothing to enjoy in Foggia, he arranged that some go to Rome, where he and Dr. Kiel set up a clinic to handle sexually transmitted infections. Those who could not be accommodated in Rome were sent to Naples, but lack of necessary personnel and supplies precluded setting up a similar clinic. La Guardia extracted from each man going to Naples his word that he would not expose himself to infection. When the unit's senior medical officer, Captain Sprague, insisted that Army regulations precluded the use of supplies or personnel for the clinics, La Guardia wrote out an official order countermanding Sprague's written authority. When Sprague refused to accept the order, La Guardia placed him under arrest and appointed Kiel acting senior medical officer. Once the men had gone off on their leaves, with the precautions in place, La Guardia released Sprague and restored him to his official duties. When the men returned from leave, not one man was infected.

Not long afterward La Guardia was ordered to report to Surgeon General Merritt Ireland at AEF General Headquarters in Chaumont, France. Ireland had heard about La Guardia's venereal disease control program and wanted more details and a report on results. Quite satisfied with what he now learned, Ireland instituted the program throughout the European theater. Asked what duties Captain Sprague could best perform, La Guardia could not resist telling the general that Sprague was "a stickler for paper work." Replied the general, "I think I can find a place for him." Sprague was soon transferred—into the Supply Corps. His replacement, a Swedish-American doctor from Minnesota, worked cooperatively with La Guardia "except when he got drunk, when he wasn't good for anything." The story has a piquant postscript. When La Guardia returned to France in 1919 with a delegation of the House Committee on Military Affairs for an inspection tour of American military installations, he ran into the Minnesota doctor. "Why don't you go home?" asked La Guardia. "I can't go home," came the reply. "This is a venereal disease center; I'm a prisoner here and can't go home until I am cured."

His men may have adored La Guardia, but as much could not be said for his immediate superiors, in particular Major Ryan and Colonel De Siebert, the senior Italian officer in charge of flight instruction. Ryan wrote a report to the War Department condemning La Guardia for conduct unbecoming an officer and a gentleman for making him and his other superiors "feel inferior," and denouncing him as "a roughneck." De Siebert complained in writing to American liaison headquarters in Paris that La Guardia was signing all his letters " 'Commander of the American Detachment' detached to Foggia," that he dealt directly with the uppermost echelons of command at Rome and Paris "in regard to questions neither disciplinary nor administrative," and that he claimed that "to him are attributed functions of a representative of the United States Government in Italy, and therefore it is up to him and no one else to treat with the Italian authorities for the better reciprocal relations in the preparation of the American pilots."[6]

The reports were duly read, filed, and forgotten. The men who counted—U.S. Army top brass and Italian government leaders—not only appreciated La Guardia's ideas and his ability to effect them, his personality, and his sense of consummate fairness, they also appreciated an even more important aspect of the man that both Ryan and De Siebert either could not or would not accept: Fiorello La Guardia was more than a mere captain. He was a United States congressman on leave of absence in Italy and, as the American generals never forgot, had important connections back in Washington. La Guardia never flaunted this. He did, though, issue subtle reminders when he felt it necessary.

Moreover, and this also worked to the American authorities' advantage, he had cultivated important connections at the highest level of the Italian government. Even Eugenio Chiesa, the minister of aviation, had "forgiven" La Guardia's cancellation of the Italian airplane contract—because of his unique position and because La Guardia was particularly admired by Minister of the Treasury (and later Prime Minister) Francesco Nitti. With Chiesa, Nitti made sure La Guardia got to know the highest-ranking Italian civil and military officials.

On January 23, 1918, while still retaining his command at Foggia, La Guardia was designated by General John J. "Black Jack" Pershing, commander of the AEF, as official Army representative on the Joint Army and Navy Aircraft Committee in Italy. His primary responsibilities included the delivery of aircraft and related matters. Within four months he was virtually chief of U.S. Army aviation in the boot of Italy. On May 30, Major Ryan almost threw a fit on being advised that Captain La Guardia would handle all problems relating to production of planes, procurement of raw materials, and "diplomatic relations," while Ryan was to supervise the training of pilots—who when qualified for combat would be assigned to La Guardia in his capacity as their commander.[7]

It was around this time that La Guardia had Spalding, at last a lieutenant, transferred from Paris to be his adjutant. Spalding again sought permission to be trained as a pilot. "I didn't ask you to come [here] for that purpose," he was told. "I wanted a good adjutant—not a mediocre pilot." Spalding was hurt at what he assumed to be an unfair prejudgment but then realized that La Guardia's "real preoccupation was with a fiddler's fingers, which must be kept safe against the return of peace."[8] Spalding, whose memoirs are a valuable source on La Guardia's activities during this period, found him an "unpredictable man. A dynamo of energy [who] appeared to be immune to fatigue. Apart from his military duties, the retention of his seat in Congress meant a constant flow of correspondence on political matters at home." His memory was "prodigious and irritatingly accurate, and he expected the same faculty in his subordinates." Though the two men were poles apart socially, intellectually, and temperamentally, Spalding found it "incredible that he should like me, but he did. We lived together almost like brothers."

3.

When the Battle of Caporetto, with a total loss of three hundred thousand men and a third of Italy's war materiel, culminated in the near-collapse of the Italian army, the panic that ensued throughout Italy was such that there was a strong feeling within the government that a separate peace might be necessary. What remained of the army retreated to Piave for what was feared would be its last stand. Miraculously, on Christmas Day, with the aid of British and French troops who had been rushed to the front, the last enemy attack was repulsed, thus turning the tide that had threatened the entire Allied cause. There was a lack of decent food for civilians and sufficient supplies for the war effort; coal and steel for making munitions were in perilously short supply; and such was the shortage of shipping in the Allied world that adequate supplies could not be sent to Italy from the United States. Furthermore, General Pershing refused to commit any American troops until they had their own front and were trained enough to maintain it. America was viewed with suspicion by the Italians, which the Germans exploited propagandistically.

La Guardia was summoned to Rome by the American ambassador, Thomas Nelson Page, who was determined to fight propaganda with propaganda by reassuring the Italians that they had America's support, and would have American troops as soon as humanly possible. Page believed Congressman-Airman Fiorello H. La Guardia was the only man capable of delivering the proper propaganda "couched in short, simple words and short, simple sentences, much on the order of the editorials of the Hearst newspapers in America, which can be understood by everybody."[9] No sooner had Page explained his predicament than La Guardia, accompanied by his aide, Spalding, was off and running:

> I hot-footed it to Genoa, and I spoke to a huge crowd there on the part the United States was playing in the war. Luckily for me they were very enthusiastic. Thereafter, I addressed huge mass meetings in Rome, Milan, Naples, Bologna, Turin, Florence, and Bari. I discussed American motives and intentions, which the Germans branded as selfish greed and a predatory effort to protect our money loaned to the Allies. The Germans were also telling the Italians that we had entered the war to prolong it, while I stressed that we had entered the war to finish it. I carefully explained in simple terms President Wilson's peace aims, discussed the purposes for which we were fighting, outlined our food and fuel policies and appealed passionately for full support by Italians of their war loans. Warm demonstrations occurred in favor of the United States at all these meetings.

Up and down the Italian boot he moved, exhorting the Italians to fight and assuring them that Americans would soon be on their way. According to Spalding, "La Guardia was very much in demand as a public speaker." Speaking fluent Italian, "terse, direct—even astringent," he "had, moreover, a gift for holding and moving his audience. . . . The crowds stamped and roared their approval of this fiery little man." Covering every major city between Naples and the Piave trenches, he interpreted the United States to the Italians "as, perhaps, no one ever has done before" and drove "home those truths which are ventured very rarely by orators."[10]

Along with reassuring the Italians, La Guardia gave them holy hell for eating too much, drinking too much, playing too much, and not working hard enough. As reported in the *New York Times*, in Milan he tore into " 'financial slackers' in terms not often heard in Italy." It was also the opinion of the *Times* that "President Wilson and the United States could not have chosen a better representative in Italy than this brave soldier." After the United States declaration of war against Austria and the announcement of Wilson's Fourteen Points (January 1918), La Guardia promised that America would help Italy in its irredentist aspirations. In Rome, "his words brought about an enthusiastic demonstration in favor of America amidst frantic cries of 'Viva Wilson!' 'Viva America!' " Also in Rome he told a group of Yugoslavs that if they broke the Hapsburg yoke America would "play fairy godmother who runs to your rescue." When a committee representing Trentino refugees petitioned him that they be annexed to Italy, he forwarded it to both houses of Congress.[11]

Even before donning the hat of propagandist, and while simultaneously wearing his hats as delegate to the Joint Army and Navy and Aircraft Committee and administrator at Camp Foggia, Fiorello had donned the hat—actually, an airman's cap with goggles—of combat flyer. After a fashion. In November 1917, while the Battle of Caporetto was still raging, he led a token detachment of U.S. airmen suggested by Pershing to the Italian front to report for duty with the Italian Army. Since he had not yet qualified, he could only function as the unit's ground commander. Their targets were principally airfields, munitions dumps, and freight centers. Obsessively desirous of qualifying as a combat pilot, La Guardia earned his wings by the middle of the following March, having attended the obligatory lectures and logged the requisite three hours of air time. The day of his final flight test was a particularly windy one, and on the last leg of the flight he ran into serious trouble. The wind speed was greater than the forward speed of his plane, and soon it was completely out of control. La Guardia was not only off course, he was beyond the limits of his map—and running low on fuel. When he tried to land in order to get his bearings, the plane was overturned by a wind squall and crashed. Only the fact that he was wearing a safety belt prevented his being crushed to death under the motor. Luckily, a more experienced pilot had been tracking him, and La Guardia was soon in the hospital, where he remained (against his will) for three weeks with concussions of the hip and a spinal bruise that would bother him the rest of his life. During his confinement, according to Gino Speranza of the American Embassy, sent to convey Ambassador Page's concern and hopes for a speedy recovery, he "kept about a dozen orderlies on the jump."[12]

On his release from the hospital, Fiorello donned another hat—that of a smuggler.

4.

Italian factories were producing planes, plane motors, trucks, and automobiles for senior commanders contingent on the United States supplying the necessary raw materials, primarily copper, steel, and ash wood for propellers. While these raw materials were already arriving in Europe in a steady stream despite the German U-boats, they were being allocated to British and French factories. The Italian government had, in addition, a contract with neutral Spain for delivery of several thousand tons of urgently needed steel. The lira, however, had depreciated. The Italians suggested that the United States take over the contract and get the steel to Italy, thus saving tonnage from the United States. But there was a hitch in getting that steel out of Spain, where there was also an abundance of desperately needed copper and ash wood. Fearing Germany's displeasure more than any Allied pressure, Spain had embargoed exports to all belligerent nations. To La Guardia the situation was impossible. There must, he insisted, be a solution for it. There was.

After outlining his plan in a telegram to the chief of the Air Service, General Benjamin Foulois, La Guardia and Spalding were summoned immediately to Paris and authorized by the enthusiastic Foulois to proceed to Spain, in civilian clothing, armed with letters of credit, to get what they could from that forbidden source of supply. Final authorization, however, had to come from General Pershing. Foulois was confident the authorization would be granted. But there might be some delay—perhaps ten days—before the two could be on their way. Though he didn't tell Foulois, La Guardia had no intention of waiting.

Once outside Foulois's office, he ordered Spalding to secure, by hook or by crook, tickets, civilian clothes—and official orders for departure the following evening. Spalding recalled that La Guardia didn't specify what kind of orders but merely told him, "You have an imagination—use it! Any kind of orders that will do the trick. I shan't ask any questions; nor do I expect any questions from you." Next day, while La Guardia went off to the American Embassy for their passports and to General Dawes's office for a letter of credit, Spalding went off to the office of General Foulois to secure the bogus secret orders. He charmed the secretary into "looking out of the windows for the next five minutes" while he typed a set of orders that he and La Guardia were to proceed to Spain "to such points as may be necessary, to carry out the instructions of the Commander-in-Chief" (i.e., General Pershing). He stamped them SECRET, thanked the secretary profusely, and rushed off to purchase two civilian suits—"cheap, serviceable, nondescript. I had to guess at La Guardia's measurements. . . . As a matter of fact, his uniform always looked as if it had been made for someone else."

Next came getting the bogus orders countersigned by the Military Police. Spalding succeeded through sheer bluff, telling the sergeant, "If you want further confirmation, you may, of course, ring up Air Service headquarters. . . . If that does not satisfy you, perhaps you would like to call up Chaumont and talk to General Pershing himself. Do it if you want to—but, seeing the nature of this document, I do not envy you the experience! But go ahead and try."

The sergeant countersigned, and Spalding, at this point a nervous wreck, rushed off to make train reservations and secure the requisite French signatures, which "were child's play" after what he'd just gone through. La Guardia, in the meantime, had secured passports and two letters of credit totaling five million dollars. Over breakfast next morning at their Barcelona hotel, cautioning that they were to behave like tourists, La Guardia ordered Spalding to make a thorough examination of newspaper files for the past two years and list all merchant shipping lost by Spain to German U-boats and the respective losses of each large shipping company. La Guardia was looking for one that was pro-Ally. When Spalding returned to the hotel, he was able to inform his chief that one company, the Taja Line, had lost more than all the others combined.

Next morning the two called on Señor Taja. His only son had been lost at sea when his ship was sunk by a U-boat, and his "hatred of the Hun was an unquenchable flame." He outlined whom La

Guardia was to see, whom to avoid, whom to trust, whom to suspect. Over the next few days the two Americans visited metallurgical factories, called on agents for ash wood, negotiated for the all-important steel, established quantities, and settled on prices. Taja himself undertook "the ticklish business of port clearance or evasion." La Guardia had decided it was prudent not to see Taja any more than was necessary, as he and Spalding were being followed and spied upon. On more than one occasion they returned to their hotel to find that their room had been broken into and searched during their absence.

Satisfied that all their purchases had been safely loaded aboard Señor Taja's ships in the harbor (roughly a million and a half dollars' worth eventually reached an Italian port safely), the two took the night sleeper to Madrid—shadowed by a man and wife in the adjoining compartment. More than once during the night, the door to the lavatory between the two compartments was stealthily tried, but La Guardia had securely bolted it on their side. Also, several times the corridor door to their compartment was unlocked and partly opened, presumably with the connivance—bribery, perhaps—of the sleeping-car attendant. But an instantaneous high-pitched "Who's there?" from La Guardia, who had a knack for sleeping with one eye open, generated a muttered apology and the closing of the door. At Madrid, the two smugglers reported to the American Embassy, where the entire story of their mission was written up and sent on to Paris in the embassy pouch. Also at Madrid they were handed their legitimate orders, forwarded from General Pershing's office, for the mission they had successfully completed. Nothing was ever said, nor were questions asked, about the two undertaking their mission before receiving proper authority. What mattered was that the mission was accomplished.

Shedding anonymity, La Guardia gave an interview to *La Publicidad* in which he told the Spanish people that they were injuring themselves by their friendliness toward Germany, whose propaganda in Spain was harping on the Spanish-American War. He pointed out that German submarines had sunk seventy-eight Spanish merchant ships with a total tonnage of over 160,000 and that Spain's factories could not continue to operate unless they got raw materials from the United States. He stressed that "our victory meant their prosperity, but that a German victory meant domination and exploitation of Spain in the interests of Germany." The next day's headline in New York City read "Shun Kaiser, Spain is Told by La Guardia."[13]

Following his return from Spain, La Guardia was urged by the Italian cabinet to continue as a propagandist, while Allied headquarters at Paris offered him a staff position. But now he wanted only to be a combat flyer. Since December 1917, he had been urging American headquarters to send Foggia-trained pilots to the Austro-Italian front instead of only to France, as had been the case. In June 1918, Pershing finally acceded, and on July 20, La Guardia was named commanding officer of the American Combat Division in Italy and, concurrently, a pilot-bombardier with the Fourth Group, Fifth Squadron, based at San Pellagio. A rather unorthodox flyer who "roared through the sky like a bull through a china shop," La Guardia was the first to admit, "I can't take the buzzard off, but I CAN FLY the son of a gun!" It was customary for an American to be paired as left-hand pilot and bombardier with an experienced Italian flyer for five sorties, after which he would assume command of the craft with the help of a left-hand Italian sergeant pilot. La Guardia never became a right-hand pilot; his superior officers deemed it best that "the buzzard" remain left-hand and bombardier.[14] Shortly after being promoted to the rank of major in August 1918, La Guardia attended a General Staff luncheon at Padua, at which King Victor Emmanuel III awarded him and six other American flyers Italy's Flying Cross. After the ceremony, he and the king enjoyed a private chat about the war. La Guardia addressed His Majesty as "Manny."[15]

His brilliant war record was complemented by marvelous press stateside. Said the *New York Times* (June 30, 1918), "Up to a year ago he was an unknown." Now he rated a profile in that paper's magazine section and a double profile with Spalding in *Literary Digest* (July 23, 1918). His bombing of enemy troops, his crashing, his friendships with the likes of General Pershing, Ambassador Page, and King Victor Emmanuel, his success in training pilots, serving as liaison between the Italians and the other Allies, even his exploit in Spain: It added up to a near-hagiographic portrait of this Arizona-bred New Yorker who had acquitted himself so admirably as a congressman, diplomat, propagandist, and flying ace. La Guardia not only cherished every word of it, he realized how vital it could be to his political career.

On September 25, 1918, General Pershing received a cabled order from the War Department to send Major La Guardia home "for duty in connection with Caproni bombing instructions."[16] The midterm congressional elections were coming up. Whether the order was legitimate or a machination on the part of a high-ranking, influential government official who wanted to be assured of La Guardia's reelection has never been determined. If the order was indeed a ruse, the culprit could well have been Champ Clark, a great admirer of La Guardia's, so much so that he was prepared to do anything to save his seat for him. As Speaker of the House, Clark wielded enough clout to pull off such a stunt.

CHAPTER NINE

"When I make a mistake, it's a beaut"

1.

La Guardia's reelection campaign began on January 8, 1918, nine months before his return, when a coalition of three thousand Socialists, pacifists, social workers, and suffragettes petitioned Clark to declare Major La Guardia's seat vacant and call for a special election to fill it. Clark lacked the authority to do so. Asked in Rome to comment about the attempt, La Guardia replied with characteristic flippancy, "You might say that if any signers of the petition wish to take my seat in a [not too reliable] Caproni biplane, I shall be glad to resume my upholstered seat in the House."

Meanwhile, Sam Koenig, Harry Andrews, and Louis Espresso launched a ferocious verbal assault against the treacherous extremism to which Greenwich Village had fallen victim. Bohemianism, went their argument, had given way to Bolshevism. "Socialists Imperil La Guardia's Seat" was typical of the headlines they generated with their warnings that radicals were out to punish La Guardia, who had served the district so well, for no other reason than for serving his country—which was more than *they* were doing. On March 21, La Guardia wrote from Rome to Isaac Siegel that he had every intention of seeking reelection in November on "an anti-yellow, anti-socialist, anti-German and true-blood American platform." So far as he was concerned, "the Socialist Party doesn't pretend to be 100 per cent loyal."[1]

Several months later, the Socialist Party nominated its choice to contest La Guardia in November: Scott Nearing. It was an extraordinary choice. A former professor of economics who had been dismissed from two universities because of his Socialist views, Nearing had been indicted under the Sedition Act for his screed "The Great Madness," in which he denounced war as "imperialistic" and demanded an immediate negotiated peace in which Socialists worldwide would participate. Other planks in his platform included forced conscription of wealth to retire the national debt and a socialism-based economy in order to achieve an "industrial co-operative commonwealth." He also demanded recognition of the new regime in Russia.[2] Since Fiorello was not on the scene to reply, the New York press took up the fight for him. Typical was the October 30 *New York World*, which editorialized that "while Major La Guardia was making a record fighting for democracy, Professor Nearing was establishing a record at home fighting democracy," and that should be reason enough to return Fiorello to Congress.

Koenig and Tammany chief Charlie Murphy agreed to run Republican and Democratic fusion candidates in those congressional districts where the Socialists were strong: the Twelfth, where the target of their wrath was incumbent Socialist Meyer London; the Thirteenth; the Fourteenth, Fiorello's own; and the Twentieth, where his bête noir, Morris Hillquit, was challenging Fiorello's close friend Isaac Siegel, the incumbent. Murphy ordered Tammany, "Sink all partisanship. [Send] only one hundred per cent Americans [like Fiorello H. La Guardia] to Congress. Elect them to help win the war and a victorious peace. America first!" Informed in Rome by a war correspondent that both major parties were backing him, La Guardia allowed as how he had "only one desire—to serve my country first and my district next." He went on to predict that an across-the-board fusionist victory would "prove wrong the Kaiser's dope [i.e., misinformation] on our country."[3]

Throughout the summer, prominent New Yorkers from every walk of life campaigned for La Guardia, including many who would ordinarily support opposing candidates on principle. While Sam Koenig marshaled the Republicans who had opposed Fiorello in 1916,

Charlie Murphy mobilized the Irish, who constituted just about the entire Tammany electorate. As for the Italo-Americans, including those of Socialist persuasion, the influential *Il Cittadino* demanded that all Italians get out the vote for "this official who honors two countries." The New York press warned that voting for Nearing ("a vassal of the Kaiser") "would justly lay the district open to taunts as a hotbed of disloyalty and sedition." The *New York Financial American* insisted he be turned over "for internment or the chain gang."[4]

2.

When the British ship carrying La Guardia docked in New York on October 27, 1918, less than two weeks before the election, his uniform was, for a change, immaculately pressed, his decorations, including three from the Italian government, glistened on his chest—and he was furious. There wasn't a soul to welcome him back. In fact, friends and reporters had turned out. But through some mixup, they thought he was coming in on a French liner that was docking that very moment at a different pier. Miffed, he grabbed a taxi and went to the Hotel Brevoort on Fifth Avenue and Eighth Street. (Why he did not go to his apartment on Charles Street is not known; most likely, he had sublet it.) Meanwhile, back at the French Line pier, his supporters were enraged, assuming he had been detained in Europe intentionally to keep him out of the campaign.

The mixup was soon resolved when Espresso, after several frantic phone calls, tracked him down at the Brevoort. Espresso headed there immediately, followed by a fleet of taxis commandeered by all the other friends and reporters. La Guardia was checking in when Espresso rushed up, hustled him to the men's room off the lobby, and quickly briefed him on how to handle the reporters. La Guardia assured Espresso he was already familiar with Nearing's antiwar record and had decided on how to destroy him as an opponent. He then went out to "say hello" to the reporters and asked, pretending not to know the identity of his opponent, "Who is Scott Nearing? If he is a young man, I shall ask him what regiment he comes from." The following day he convened a news conference at which he cautioned that "the question of patriotism must not be introduced into this campaign. Scott Nearing must have a fighting chance.... [R]emember this—under the laws of this country a man is innocent until he is proved guilty."[5] Then, trim in his uniform, the medals gleaming on his jacket—as he would shrewdly clothe himself for all public appearances until resigning his commission after reelection—Major Fiorello H. La Guardia announced, still straight-faced, that he had come home on military duty. Because his first priority was winning the war, he would not campaign actively.

Before any of the reporters could ask what *that* was all about, Espresso rushed him over to the Democratic clubhouse on West Twelfth Street. There, an overflow crowd of Tammany sachems and chiefs eagerly waited to give a rousing ovation and ear-shattering roar of support for the man they had dismissed as a "guinea" and "dago" and "wop" in previous campaigns. The rest of the day was devoted to being hailed by his own followers, meeting with campaign advisers and strategists, and squeezing in a few private moments with the forbearing Thea. She'd waited for him through one election and a war. She could handle waiting through yet another election.

Next day, apparently forgetting his avowal of the previous day not to campaign in earnest, Fiorello proceeded to do just that. He started by "crashing" a crowd of Republican supporters Governor Whitman was addressing. Whitman was in the midst of his speech when La Guardia strode into the ballroom and was given a fifteen-minute standing ovation. After Whitman finished his speech, La Guardia spoke briefly, saying he considered it his "patriotic duty" to oppose the candidacy of any Socialist. The crowd went wild. Moving on to a series of brief meetings through the day and into the evening, he intensified the attack on his opponent's war record (or lack of same), saying, for instance, "Scott Nearing is a man without a country unless he stands for what the American flag stands for." At an open-air meeting at Second Avenue and Tenth Street, he described Nearing as "a silk stocking university professor who condescends to come here and attempt to foist Bolshevism on America." Moving down the street, he told the Women's Republican Club, "I went into the war because I wanted to stop all wars. I think my remedy is better than that of the yellow dog Socialists." Though the hour was late, "the Major," as he preferred to be called, was willing to accommodate a crowd of two thousand people gathered at the corner of Stuyvesant Place and Second Avenue. "If Scott Nearing wants to try out his beautiful theories," he said with acrid sarcasm, "why doesn't he go to Russia?"[6]

La Guardia also campaigned with characteristic vigor in East Harlem's Twentieth Congressional District in support of his close friend Siegel, determined to squash Socialist challenger Morris Hillquit as if he were the most horrific of bugs. At a rally for Siegel he shouted proudly, "I have never taken a cent [in legal fees] from [any] labor organization," whereas Hillquit's "basement price" to represent a client was two thousand dollars. Then he dramatically said, "I charge Hillquit with being a tool and an ally of the Kaiser."[7] Over the following days Fiorello moved cyclonically from street corner to street corner, not so much campaigning for the office that had become his almost by default as attacking the Socialists mercilessly as servants of an enemy foreign power, dividing his bile between Nearing and Hillquit.

Fearful of being ignored and frantic to deliver his Socialist message, Nearing challenged La Guardia to a formal debate. Fiorello declined, feeling that to accept would be beneath his dignity: "I stand on my record." But Nearing persisted, and La Guardia felt he owed it to his loyalists—and to his own sense of satisfaction—not to pass up a confrontation with an opponent whose politics he so vehemently detested. With the Socialist Party as challenger agreeing to foot the bill, the two met on November 1 at Cooper Union, tickets having been distributed equally between the two opposing camps. The contrast between the two men was striking. Said the *New York American* next day, "Nearing in appearance is the typical man of letters. Blonde and slender, he looks almost boyish. La Guardia wins attention by the blunt, honest characteristics of the typical political haranguer. While Nearing's gestures are airy and graceful, La Guardia's convey simply the impression of strength and fighting energy."

In his memoirs, La Guardia claimed "the debate was courteous." It was anything but. Nearing started off by defending his antiwar stance and then presented the Socialist program. This earned him a hearty round of applause from his supporters in the audience. When it was La Guardia's turn to speak, he did not fall into the trap of deprecating pacifism, insisting that the war against the kaiser was designed to establish permanent peace. "The issue in the 14th Congressional District," he noted, "is the same as the issue on the Western and Austrian fronts. I am personally opposed to militarism, imperialism and all manner of oppression. I am against war, and because I am against war I went to war to fight against war."[8] In his rebuttal, Nearing attacked war profiteers (earning an emphatic nod from his opponent) and graciously pointed out that La Guardia had introduced a bill providing the death penalty for them in wartime.

Then all hell broke loose. Going for the jugular, La Guardia accused the German-American Socialists of supporting "the Vaterland's orgy of butchery." Someone shouted, "Liar!" As La Guardia's supporters, waving Italian and American flags, surged toward the platform, he went on to condemn the "miserable failure of socialism in Russia" and "the refusal of the German Socialists to protect against the butchery by German militarists [as] another outstanding instance of [socialism's] failure in a crisis," adding that it was nonsensical to hope, as the Nearingites seemed to be doing, that peace could be restored simply by "talking against war on the corners of [New York's] East Side." Then, concentrating more on Hillquit than on Nearing, he practically screamed that "the German who couldn't get back to fight for the Kaiser had tried to do his bit fighting under the banner of Hillquit." This almost precipitated a full-scale riot.

When moderator Jacob Panken managed to restore order, after a fashion, Nearing gave his rebuttal, basically a rehash of what he had been spouting since day one of his campaign. He hailed Soviet Russia for inaugurating the social millennium, contrasted the glories of socialism with Wall Street greed and exploitation, and demanded that the United States propose an immediate and nonimperialistic peace, conscript personal wealth to foot the bill for the war, and recognize the recently installed Lenin regime. His supporters applauded. La Guardia gave a simple surrebuttal, saying of Nearing in an admixture of condescension and contempt, "He's a poet, not a professor of economics." On that note, Panken adjourned the meeting with praise for "such a dignified manner and pleasing results." Fiorello left the podium feeling pleased as punch with himself. Nearing left the podium feeling not unlike a neophyte pugilist trashed by a champion who had never heard of the Marquis of Queensberry Rules—or had, but chose to ignore them.[9]

Was La Guardia behaving opportunistically by hitting below the belt, not only in the debate but throughout the campaign? Not really. As for going after the despised Hillquit, he was aiding Siegel, who was not only a close friend but a political and philosophical ally. As for going after Socialists, personified in Nearing, he passionately believed they seriously imperiled the war's successful prosecution. But on a deeper, more personal level, he saw his campaign as a struggle for the hearts and minds of underprivileged East Siders, who, he feared, might be deluded by the Marxists into actually believing the millennium was just around the corner. La Guardia's objection to millennialism was rooted in his concern for the suffering in the slums, not only in the Fourteenth but in all the polyglot districts with their preponderance of hyphenates who had not yet made it into the mainstream and, he feared, might never do so. The message he reiterated throughout the campaign was that he could do more good in Congress than could the Socialists, who would never be elected in large enough numbers to effect needed social change.

Karl Marx claimed that religion was the opiate of the people. La Guardia claimed that the true opiate of the people was Marxism itself. Given his contempt of professional politicians as mere theorists, and the distrust of the practical man for purely speculative intellectuals, he was obviously pleased with the following editorial comments in the November 2, 1918, issue of the *Brooklyn Eagle*: "Scott Nearing is a former college professor, an author, a professional sociologist. Fiorello La Guardia is just a fighting American, who got away from the halls of Congress to do his bit. . . . When La Guardia got his education in the public schools in Prescott, Arizona, they didn't teach much sociology. The ideal held up to the boys was, we imagine, straight shooting and telling the truth."

La Guardia's eight-thousand-plus plurality over Nearing (14,523 to 6,214) was hailed by the *Times* (November 7, 1918) as a triumph of patriotism over sedition. Adding the perfect fillip to La Guardia's victory, all the fusion candidates won, including the Tammany hack who was run against incumbent Meyer London.[10] The election was followed a few days later by the Armistice. The Major's resignation from the Army having been accepted on November 21, he returned to the House in December for the final session of the Sixty-fifth Congress. Its first order of business was to vote him his back pay.

On March 8, 1919, Fiorello and Thea were married in St. Patrick's Cathedral; he was thirty-five, she was twenty-four. The groom wore his uniform for the last time (cleaned and pressed for the occasion). Louis Espresso was best man.[11] After a brief honeymoon, the couple set up housekeeping at the groom's Charles Street apartment. According to unanimous reports of friends, the two were ecstatically happy.

Tragically, their happiness was fated to be short-lived.

3.

From Paris, where he was negotiating peace talks, President Wilson sent a call for the incoming Sixty-sixth Congress to convene prematurely in a special session to deal with a plethora of problems arising out of the war's conclusion. Among the measures to be resolved were new domestic appropriation bills (required before July 1, which was the start of the fiscal year), refinancing of the War Risk Insurance Bureau, taxes, the tariff, repeal of wartime prohibitions, labor legislation, and aid for returning soldiers in getting employment. The Democratic president was not going to have easy sailing. The Republicans had carried both chambers in the November 1918 election: 48 in the Senate, to 46 for the Democrats, and 239 House seats, to 190 for the Democrats, with the balance spread among a few miscellaneous fringe candidates and independents.

Fiorello's immediate reaction on returning to the House was to the locust-like swarm of "profiteers buzzing around the capital [who] were being better cared for than the men who fought the war." A great opportunity for profiteering was the liquidation of huge war supplies. Militating in favor of the profiteers, the public at large was sick of the war, wanted to forget Europe and its problems, and was in no mood to accept responsibility for postwar reconstruction of the devastated countries and their disrupted economies. La Guardia was both heartsick and disgusted that not enough Americans realized the great significance of these problems. He foresaw Europe becoming once more "a fertile breeding ground for world war." The American people's "indifference to Europe and the world situation in general was," he lamented, "astounding."

Even more than in his first term, La Guardia often shot from the hip in heated verbal exchanges, compromising his effectiveness by giving the impression that as an ex-major and ex–consular agent he was the best judge of how to deal with postwar Europe and that anyone who did not share his views was either a fool or a scoundrel. Significantly, not a single one of the many resolutions he introduced was voted out of committee. The first called for repeal of the Espionage Act—this at a time when prosecutions of radicals under the act were multiplying daily like the proverbial hangers in a clothes closet. Criticized by the conservative wing of his own party, he argued that the act's only benefit was to cover up the inefficiency of the Wilson administration. If, he insisted, it had been justified in wartime, it certainly was not necessary in the postwar period. "I suppose," he added laconically, "what I have said is indictable under the Espionage Act."[12]

Among the battles he waged was to show, by producing reams of statistics, how corporate profits had become bloated while the vast majority of the population did not share in the riches the war had harvested. Another was against the disposal of war surplus. As there had been no planning for the cancellation of war contracts, a bill granting authority to settle these contracts and claims had to be hurriedly cobbled together and passed. One scandal he exposed was the plan made by the Bureau of Supplies of the War Department to turn over Army surplus copper to the copper interests on terms that gave them fees they were not entitled to, thus enabling them to keep the price of copper higher than it should have been.

One government agency that wished La Guardia had never returned was the Bureau of Surplus Supplies. Cluttering the Army warehouses were millions of cans of beef and millions of pounds of bacon. He asked the packers, who had sold these supplies to the government at a handsome profit, how they were to be disposed of and was told that they could not be sold domestically because the beef came in six-pound cans and "no family in this country could use six pounds at a time." Retorted La Guardia, "Evidently the corps of experts are not familiar with vital statistics or appetites of families."

When the bureau director came to the House to testify personally in favor of a million-dollar salary appropriation—of which his share was twenty-five thousand dollars per annum—he was asked what he was going to do with all that surplus food. He replied vaguely that he thought he might find a market for it in Romania or Bosnia or Herzegovina. Even his supporters on the committee had to laugh at the poor man's expense when Congressman La Guardia jumped to his feet and with withering scorn remarked, "It surprises me you did not offer this bacon to some Jewish synagogue." He then suggested that if the gentleman would "put that stuff on the market in New

York City or Philadelphia or Boston" he would "find hungry people willing to buy it and eat it." He also gave his personal assurance that they would "be able to digest army bacon." Of course, he added with caustic irony, that might well "interfere with the profits of the [meat]packers," but he was "not interested in that." Nor did La Guardia look kindly on the Salvation Army being offered the surplus meat: "The Salvation Army specializes in doughnuts and not in bacon."

To La Guardia, an even more disgraceful deal in surplus supplies was the Army's disposal of airplanes it had purchased from the Curtiss Company for $22,631,200 to the same company at a 90 percent markdown. Adding insult to injury, the Curtiss Company threatened the government with a lawsuit if it tried to sell the planes to any other party, arguing that the cheap price was dictated by the fact that they were "junk." La Guardia insisted on the floor of the House that they could not be so considered, given that they had been safely flown by the Curtiss pilots after their purchase by the Army. Why a responsible company would want to invest millions in "junk" was never explained.

One minor victory La Guardia scored was over the authority sought by the Bureau of Post Exchanges of the Army to spend a million dollars to purchase buildings erected by the American Red Cross and the YMCA at Army posts. These buildings, he pointed out, had been gifts of the American people, who had raised the money for the Red Cross and YMCA, and thus already belonged to the government. He succeeded in cutting the overall Post Exchange appropriation from its requested $5.875 million to a mere $150,000.

Despite his differences with colleagues on many issues, there was, however, one in which he was in total agreement with the majority: dismantling America's war machine and returning the country to its pre-1917 isolationism. He led the fight to recall troops from Western Europe and Russia, where Wilson had sent an expeditionary force to assist in the failed attempt to put down the Soviet government. "Their duty is completed, it has been gloriously performed," La Guardia insisted. "The thing to do is to get the men back as quickly as we can and to demobilize the troops that we have here now." He added his conviction that the generals and admirals were slowing down the process because they didn't want to be cut back to their prewar rank. Some members tried to shout him down, but shouting

Fiorello down was about as effective as King Canute's demanding that the ocean recede. Besides, he was probably right.[13]

Among La Guardia's hallmark phrases was "When I make a mistake, it's a beaut!" One "beaut" he made took him an entire generation to own up to. In 1919 he was "proud of my role in reducing the [standing] Army of the United States . . . from 507,000 to an average of 300,000." In 1947, having gone through another war, he published an article in the April issue of Reader's Digest entitled "Why I Now Believe in Universal Military Training," in which he "confessed" that he had "helped my country to make one of the most serious mistakes in its history."

What could well qualify as yet another "serious mistake," though La Guardia did not see it that way and refused to rescind his position, was to join his colleagues in contributing to the postwar hysteria known as the Red Scare, when many aliens were rounded up for deportation to their native lands simply because xenophobia had ridden upon the American scene as if it were the Fifth Horseman of the Apocalypse. Emblematically dragging his cloak of superpatriotism through the mud, La Guardia was in the vanguard of a band of like-minded members in going after Commissioner of Immigration Frederic C. Howe. A veteran of the Progressive Era, Howe had delayed deportation of some five hundred detainees at Ellis Island. La Guardia tore into Howe for allowing the detainees to receive a "batch of anarchist literature" that included such titles as "Rebel Worker," "Red Dragon, The Truth About the I.W.W.," and "I.W.W. Songs." He then offered an amendment to an appropriations bill that would have cost Howe his $6,500-a-year job. More legal-minded members voted the amendment down, on the grounds that he should have the right to defend himself before a proper body. After an investigation by the House Committee on Immigration, Howe resigned. To La Guardia's satisfaction, Howe's "leniency" was "corrected" by his successor.[14]

La Guardia possessed an inflated jingoism and magnified arrogance that became manifest in his determination to deal with Mexico's President Venustiano Carranza. Carranza had incurred the United States' displeasure during the war by his pro–imperial Germany stance and his campaign against American oil companies. Strained relations climaxed in July 1918, when the Mexican government enacted a law heavily taxing American-owned petroleum companies. When the oil interests, backed by the secretary of the Navy, demanded military intervention, President Wilson vetoed the idea on the grounds that such an action would be as immoral as Germany's invasion of Belgium. This gave the Republican-dominated Congress of 1919 an issue: Charge the Wilson State Department with a weak and vacillating policy toward our neighbor to the south.[15]

La Guardia's role in the debate was a rather strange one, as it agreed in so many respects with the position of the American oil companies, which, like other exemplars of "special privilege," he had so often condemned. The Wilson administration was divided, with the president insisting on nonintervention while the Army prepared to take military action against Carranza. "Plans for throwing a new punitive expedition into Mexico, should the situation take a turn justifying such action, have been worked out by the General Staff," reported the *New York Times* on June 22, 1919. La Guardia charged that Wilson's policy toward Mexico had been "one series of inconsistencies," cited the "disorder, chaos, revolution and disease" prevalent under the Carranza regime, and insisted that Carranza "be told in plain terms that he cannot be tolerated a moment longer." He further insisted that the United States go into Mexico "with beans in one hand and, if necessary, hand grenades in the other, and put an end to the present situation."[16] Wiser heads prevailed in the House. Carranza died a year later after a bloody struggle for power with the legendary Pancho Villa, and the whole issue petered out, obviating the necessity for American troops to cross the Rio Grande with beans and grenades.

There were times when La Guardia deployed his patriotism in defense of admirable causes, such as the future of aviation. Claiming America must produce "a true American motor, a true American plane," he was instrumental in the cancellation of a government contract with one manufacturer whose product had proved inefficient during the war. His opinion was highly regarded by fellow congressmen, who knew that this man who had actually flown in combat might be over the top on many issues, but not when it came to aircraft. As chairman of the House Military Affairs Committee's Subcommittee on Aeronautics, he was the leading spokesman for, and a fervent enthusiast of, General Billy Mitchell, whose warning that American aviation lagged dangerously behind that of the major European nations was dismissed as heresy by the generals. Embracing Mitchell's advocacy of air power as the nation's first line of defense in future wars, La Guardia buttonholed in support of Mitchell's proposal that the various air services be brought together into a single department. Congress refused to organize a unified air force. It would take another war to validate Mitchell and La Guardia's foresightedness—and cast shame on the generals for court-martialing and suspending from the service for five years an authentic prophet in his area of expertise.[17]

At times La Guardia's patriotism revealed a less than full awareness of the facts, but still he roared forth. In a debate over an appropriations bill, he lambasted former American ambassador to Russia David Francis, claiming that under him the U.S. Embassy at Moscow had lost touch with the Russian people. Francis was attacked for advising the State Department to support the Kerensky government instead of General Kornilov, a White Russian officer who alone, La Guardia argued, might have prevented the collapse of the eastern front. In fact, nothing could have prevented the collapse. The Russian government had by then been fatally weakened by unrealistic autocracy, unbridled corruption, and the unstoppable forces of historical inevitability. When the chairman of the Committee on Foreign Affairs defended Ambassador Francis, La Guardia lost his temper and defied him to "stand up and give us the names of the Provinces of Russia and their capitals and their races, or explain recent changes there." The chairman dismissed the challenge as not germane to the issue and just plain silly. It was.[18]

Thea remained in New York when Congress was in session. As a "bachelor" congressman, Fiorello was on a number of Washington A-lists. He said no to most of the many invitations that came his way. His constituents, he insisted, had sent him to Congress to represent their interests, not to ride the social circuit. Occasionally, though, he accepted an invitation, such as one to a dinner he was urged to attend by New York's Senator William M. Calder, who had served in the House for years and had befriended him. Much as he liked Fiorello, by the end of the evening Calder rather wished he'd left him home.

While cocktails were being served, La Guardia got into conversation about Croatia and Dalmatia with a gentleman who rubbed him the wrong way. He asked belligerently, "What do you know about Croatia and Dalmatia? I've lived in that part of the world for three years, and I know what I'm talking about." Replied the stranger with great indignation, "I am the Serbian Ambassador here." La Guardia was convinced he was still more of an authority on the area but decided the point wasn't worth pursuing. Moments later, as the guests were entering the dining room, he got into conversation with the lady on his left about aviation—specifically, about Liberty motors for airplanes. He "sounded off and told her how rotten I thought they were, and tore into General Motors in particular." (It will be recalled Fiorello had been instrumental in having GM's contracts with the U.S. Army cancelled.) He soon learned the lady was "related to one of the big shots" at General Motors. Was he embarrassed? Not in the least. If the lady was upset, that was her problem, not his. After dinner, when Fiorello went to the men's room, a man came in and engaged him in conversation. "How do you like the party?" he asked. Replied Fiorello, "Why, I never saw such a bunch of nuts before. I'm going. Want to come along?" Said the man, "I can't. I'm your host."[19]

La Guardia "thought my social career was ruined forever." Surprisingly, he soon learned that the same host and hostess wanted to give a dinner party for him as guest of honor—because he had been "so amusing." But not even Senator Calder could get him "to submit to that one." Socializing ranked very low on Fiorello's list of priorities. High on that list were the pressing issues to be addressed by this session of Congress, of which pride of place went to the debate on the National Prohibition Act. Its purpose was to put into effect the Eighteenth Amendment, which proscribed "the manufacture, sale, or transportation of intoxicating liquors."

When the enabling act was introduced in 1919 by Congressman Andrew J. Volstead, La Guardia was in the vanguard of opposition. While he foresaw, prophetically, the resultant lawlessness, he was preternaturally inflamed by what he perceived to be the overt hostility of Prohibition's supporters toward "foreigners" living in major cities, like his own beloved New York, whom backers of the bill, and the various national "dry" organizations that had lobbied it through Congress, held responsible for "drinking habits that tore at the very heart of Anglo-Saxon Protestant standards of morality." La Guardia rose to say that "this so-called foreign element was not the consumer of hard liquor." How could he be so sure? "They can't afford it!"

In the House, the issue of Prohibition was factionalized along urban/rural lines. Playing to representatives of the big cities like a vaudevillian playing to the balcony, Fiorello resorted to a string of one-liners that convulsed his sympathizers with laughter. When the debate turned at one point to how much alcohol it took to get a man drunk, he claimed to have no personal knowledge on the question because drunkenness was unknown among his family or friends. He added, "None of my ancestors had that failing. I traced it way back and the only one of my ancestors I could find who drank to excess was a certain [Emperor] Nero, and he got the habit from his mother [Agrippina the Younger] who was born on the Rhine." He then took on one of the act's leading advocates, Congressman William D. Upshaw of Georgia—whom he described as "a stereotypical hayseed"—and soon, as the saying goes, had 'em rolling in the aisles.

"The gentleman," La Guardia began the mini-debate, "knows that the moonshiners of the South are very anxious to get this bill through, because their business will increase." He asserted that "if the people traveling from other states would keep out of New York City, we would have no drunks in the streets." Asked Upshaw, "Does the gentleman intend to suggest that he does not want the financial patronage of the glorious 'Dry South' in the cities?" La Guardia shot back, "Absolutely not! It keeps our courts congested!"

But La Guardia exposed himself to charges of ignorance and bigotry when he opined in all seriousness that most of the nation's drunkards were "native Nordics" and not working-class European immigrants, who, might consume beer and light wines but had "nothing left [from their pay envelopes] with which to buy booze and strong drink." It was his conviction that the Prohibitionists could best accomplish their purpose through an educational program designed "to teach Anglo-Saxons how to drink and remain sober."[20]

Paradoxically, while La Guardia was a superpatriot, he was a staunch internationalist, most notably when it came to issues involving simple humanity. A steadfast idealist in the Wilsonian mode, he was eloquent in his defense of an appropriation bill to feed Europe that was under attack by a powerful coalition of isolationists, racists, and state-of-the-art xenophobes. "We did not intend to liberate [the Europeans] from Hapsburg or Hohenzollern oppression and stand idly by and permit them to starve," he shouted on the floor of the House. Then, in an obvious allusion to the specter of bolshevism looming on the horizon, he piercingly warned his colleagues in his best finger-waving manner: "You can not preach self-government and liberty to people in a starving land." Thanks to La Guardia's support, the bill was enacted.[21]

Another passion was to curb the anti-Semitism rampant in the new nations created out of the former European empires. In this, he was motivated strictly by a keen sense of morality, not ethnic heritage. Indeed, La Guardia never practiced Judaism or went out of his way to identify himself as a Jew the way he did as an Italian—though it must be stressed that he never so much as hinted at being ashamed of, or attempting to hide, his maternal ancestry. When anti-Semitic riots broke out in Poland soon after the end of the war, he introduced a resolution in the House instructing the U.S. delegation to the Paris Peace Conference "to communicate in clear and non-equivocal language to the representatives of the newly formed governments in whose countries these unfortunate acts have taken place that . . . the people of the United States can have no friendship for the people of any country who will permit or tolerate such conduct in their country."[22]

The resolution was considered by the House Committee on Foreign Affairs and reported out favorably. Within two weeks the State Department issued a statement declaring that "satisfactory assurances had been obtained from the Polish government that there would be no repetition of the Jewish pogroms." The fact that reconstituted Poland went on to become an anti-Semite's paradise, followed closely by Hungary and Austria, would more than suggest that those "satisfactory assurances" were so much twaddle.

While in Europe in April 1919, with the House Military Affairs Committee investigating Army camps, La Guardia stopped off in Paris to see President Wilson's aide, Colonel Edward M. House. (He couldn't see Wilson, who was in the process of reorganizing the map of Europe.) La Guardia expressed to House the hope that a compromise might be worked out whereby Fiume would be reconstituted as an independent city, but with the king of Italy as its sovereign and its defense and foreign affairs to be handled by the Italian government. Whether Wilson was made aware of the proposal is not known; the point is moot. Because the Treaty of London of 1915, to which

Italy was a signatory, promised Fiume to Yugoslavia, that's where Wilson decided it would go. When the Italian delegation at Paris walked out in protest, Wilson appealed over their heads to the Italian people. The appeal went ignored. La Guardia would later denounce Wilson for treating Italy shabbily.[23]

In fact, he would come to detest Wilson. And therein lies an irony.

Prior to the Fiume settlement, Fiorello was a staunch Wilson supporter. On March 3, 1919, he rose to plead for bipartisan support of the League of Nations: "In the war the great cry was to stand back of the President and win the war. We want to stand back of him and put through an arrangement that will prevent another war."[24] Not that La Guardia feared the United States becoming caught once again in Europe's perennial conflicts. Rather, he hoped that if nations could unite to wage war, they could unite to avert war. On June 29, the day after the Germans signed the Versailles Treaty, which included the Covenant of the League, La Guardia told a New York audience that in the League, which Wilson saw as the capstone of his career and of his life's work, he saw the only hope for peace. He dismissed as rubbish the charge by critics of both the League and its author that Article 10, which guaranteed the territorial sovereignty of the member nations, was in fact a device to interfere in the internal affairs of a sovereign state. "It is simply designed to prevent a repetition of the Belgian outrages and such outrageous terms as [those] submitted by Austria-Hungary to Serbia" that were the directly precipitating factor in the war's outbreak, La Guardia insisted passionately. That speech marked the last time La Guardia would have a good word for Wilson and his blueprint for peace.[25]

Before sailing off to the Paris Peace Conference, Wilson told a press conference aboard the *George Washington* that he would do "what's right" for the various minorities and irredentists poised to rise phoenix-like from the ashes of the autocracies. But, owing to the ambitions of the major allies and, of greater consequence, to his own arrogance-tinged blunders, the promise fell miserably short of achievement. When Wilson returned to the United States in the summer of 1919, he was greeted and attacked by liberals, intellectuals, progressives, and hyphenate Americans of every European derivation, Eastern and Western alike, for having betrayed his own Fourteen Points. Whether he alone deserved all the opprobrium, or whether the major allies deserved much of the blame, is debatable.

La Guardia shared the outrage and sense of betrayal felt by all the American hyphenates. But his priority was, naturally, New York's Italo-American colony. Testifying on September 5, 1919, before the Senate Committee on Foreign Relations, whose chairman, Henry Cabot Lodge, had sworn to the heavens that the United States would never join the League of Nations (it never did), Congressman La Guardia reminded the committee that, both during the war and after the announcement of his Fourteen Points, Wilson had promised that, if Italy stayed in the war after threatening to pull out after the disaster at Caporetto, the United States would help her regain Fiume from the moribund Austria-Hungary. Fiume, La Guardia insisted, was "Italian in spirit, blood, language, and in every way," no matter what that damn 1915 Treaty of London had to say on the subject. Three weeks later, he told a partisan audience at New York's Hotel Commodore, "We must have a Republican [victory at the polls] this year, to show the whole world that President Woodrow Wilson is discredited at home."[26]

La Guardia was not only arguing a point, he was, in a sense campaigning, in particular for the benefit of the people of New York City, as distinct from only the Fourteenth Congressional District. For by then he was running not for Congress but for the presidency of the New York City Board of Aldermen.

CHAPTER TEN

"I can outdemagogue the best of demagogues"

1.

In 1919, a special election was called to fill the office of president of New York City's Board of Aldermen, which fell vacant when Alfred Emanuel "Al" Smith defeated Charles S. Whitman for the New York governorship. Republican national leader Will Hays and New York County leader Sam Koenig saw an opportunity to break Tammany's hold on this, the city's second-highest office. While there were many local issues involved, the issue that would dominate the election was Woodrow Wilson's Peace Plan. New York's immigrants and first-generation Americans blamed Wilson for what they considered his craven betrayal of their native lands: the Italians, for his failure to secure Fiume for Italy; the Irish, for his failure to press for Eire's independence from Great Britain; and the Germans, for the harsh Versailles Treaty. These were three huge voting blocs. (Lest today's readers wonder why the Jews did not figure in this equation, the fight for a national homeland was at this point in time only a promise made by the British government, which held the mandate over Palestine.)

No Republican had ever won a city election. Still, the local leadership felt that with the right candidate they had at least the semblance of a fighting chance. And if such a candidate could unite the hyphenates, thus keeping the "melting pot" boiling, their hatred of Wilson could well play a decisive role in the upcoming presidential election. Koenig saw only one man capable of pulling it off: Fiorello H. La Guardia, Italo- and Jewish-American war hero, champion of the Democratic as well as Republican hyphenates (recall how the Tammany Irish helped send him to Congress in the previous year), and highly vocal and palpably virulent anti-Wilsonian. Few among the GOP national leadership, including Hays, were overly optimistic about La Guardia's chances. They did, though, see the ethnic vote he would presumably lock up as potentially decisive in carrying New York for the Republicans in the 1920 presidential election.

When told by Koenig that he had been anointed with Will Hays's blessing, Fiorello had two words: not interested. His seat in Congress gave him what amounted to a national forum. As the second-highest New York City official, his opinions would hardly be heard west of the Hudson River. But Koenig argued that he was not only the best man for the job, he owed it to his fellow hyphenates. There were other factors to consider. Thea was taken with the possibility of having Fiorello at home year-round, instead of his being away when Congress was in session; if he lost, he would still retain his seat in the House; and Koenig had gotten the four other county leaders to enter Fiorello in the midsummer primary. Fiorello was "quite unhappy" at the assignment but would accept it "as a Party proposition."[1] The deciding factor was the understanding that if he won, the GOP nomination for mayor in 1921 would be his. The deal was struck.

Brooklyn's wily Republican boss, Jake Livingston, selected Paul Windels to manage Fiorello's campaign. Understating the candidate's drawing power, Windels felt that "the nomination was intended merely as a political gesture to please the very large Italian vote which up to that time had had no political recognition. It was also thought that it might be helpful in building interest among the Italians in the approaching Presidential election."[2] That pessimism notwithstanding, Windels's selection was an inspired one. He and La Guardia were as antipodal in appearance and style as any two humans could be. A politically ambitious conservative lawyer, son of an American mother and a German father who had fought in the Franco-Prussian War, the trim thirty-four-year-old Windels was blond, blue-eyed, six feet tall, and always impeccably turned out. A Progressive in the mold of Robert La Follette and George Norris, La Guardia was dark, short, and pudgy, dressed like an unmade bed, and was as well known for his choppy gait and aggressive manner as for his high-pitched voice. But—and this was the overriding factor—the Teutonic aristocrat and the Latin man-of-the-streets, united in their antagonism toward Wilson, were clear symbols of opposition to the Paris peace treaties. The two meshed perfectly: Windels tended to matters of detail and finance, La Guardia tended to campaigning.[3]

One possible problem, which Koenig easily disposed of, was William M. Bennett, with whom, it will be recalled, Fiorello had shared law offices. When he entered the 1919 primary in defiance of the machine, Koenig saw to it that Bennett failed to receive so much as a single vote in lower Manhattan's ethnic districts. Authorities investigated but found no evidence of voting irregularity. Unwilling to pay for a recount, Bennett withdrew. The Democratic candidate, Robert L. Moran, was a bland florist from the Bronx whose health was so precarious as to preclude campaigning. There are those who believe Tammany was willing to go with so pathetic a candidate out of confidence that it would score its usual victory. It's more likely that Boss Murphy was resigned to the party losing this one. Given the antagonism to Wilson among the hyphenates, including even the Irish and German sachems and braves, one didn't have to be proficient in reading the entrails of chickens to know that even the strongest Democratic candidate didn't stand much of a chance, no matter how many votes were cast by "repeaters."

With a pledge of thirty-five thousand dollars from the state's Republican leaders, La Guardia opened headquarters early in September at the Imperial Hotel at Thirty-first Street and Broadway. Besides Windels, the old La Guardia crowd was on hand: Harry Andrews, Louis Espresso, and the ever reliable Marie Fisher. Fiorello kicked off his campaign on September 8. Racing from street corner to street corner—and remember, he was covering an entire city, not just a district—he flew in and out of churches, synagogues, political clubs, social halls, weddings, wakes, bar mitzvahs, wherever he could gather an audience, making his pitch about how he was going to clean up the city Tammany had so despoiled.

Fiorello followed a fixed routine: He would go out after lunch to make any number of speeches all around town, then return to headquarters. There Thea would force-feed him a sandwich and Marie would brief him on the evening schedule while Frank "Ciccio" Giordano, his Army orderly, had to practically tie him to a chair so that he could get "the Major" shaved and "in presentable shape" for the dozen or more meetings slated for that evening. One night he spoke at sixteen. "He was a man of inexhaustible mental and nervous energy and physical strength."[4]

When he popped up in the ethnic districts—the so-called Little Europes—La Guardia, speaking in the appropriate languages, confined his attacks to Woodrow Wilson and his Peace Plan, and by extension the Democratic Party, thus playing into the fierce resentments of the hyphenates. He took an almost fiendish delight in stampeding his Italo-American audiences into a frenzy merely by mentioning Fiume; likewise, where appropriate, his mention of Wilson's inability (or perhaps unwillingness) to speak out forcefully against anti-Semitism in Eastern Europe, lack of support for Irish independence, and the unrealistic vengeance visited upon the Germans by the Versailles Treaty. To suffragettes he vowed to support their cause (which in fact he was on record as doing in Congress) and, if elected, to appoint women to his staff. When addressing audiences whose priority was good government, he branded Tammany the fountainhead of municipal corruption, waste, inefficiency, and stupidity, as when he fairly screeched in graphic metaphor to one reform-minded gathering, "The 1920 budget of the Hylan administration, conceived in the bowels of darkness, is more than enough to stagger the public."

La Guardia offered no alternate philosophy of government other than a heartfelt commitment to be honest. He was for more and better schools, raising the salaries of public employees, eliminating corruption in the police force, balancing the city's budget, lowering municipal taxes, and much more. But when it came to the city's complex, in some cases unique, problems his comprehension was minimal. Example: Senator Calder urged that he stress maintenance of the five-cent transit fare. Fiorello had to concede that he knew practically nothing about this issue, which was of no little importance to most New Yorkers.[5]

Not unexpectedly, he received the support of the city's major Italian-language newspapers and the pro-Democratic German-language *Staats-Zeitung*. What *was* unexpected was his endorsement by the normally Democratic Hearst papers. Vehemently opposed to everything Wilsonian, Hearst urged his readers to express their disapproval of the president by voting for Congressman La Guardia, party affiliation notwithstanding. But then, Hearst would have urged voting for Kermit the Frog, if he were the GOP candidate. Anyone who opposed Wilson was okay with him.[6]

Resorting to a scheme that can be described as either an act of desperation or an act of stupidity, Tammany circularized the city with a broadsheet asking Italo-Americans to elect Moran so that La Guardia could continue to represent them in Congress. La Guardia wrote the author that if he'd send along "a few hundred thousand of this circular," he would "be glad to see that they are properly placed."[7] Recalled Windels, "Whenever we had a discouraging evening or colorless Republican meeting, we always wound up as [sic] a nightcap at an Italian meeting where the enthusiasm was overwhelming." There La Guardia would "provoke the audience to Dionysian delirium" in such words (in Italian) as "Any Italo-American who votes the Democratic ticket this year is an Austrian bastard!" At the conclusion of one such session, he asked Louis Espresso, "How did I do?" Espresso, who found his friend's "excessive Italianness" embarrassing, replied, "Gee, F.H., you were lousy." La Guardia turned to Windels and said proudly, "I can outdemagogue the best of demagogues."[8]

Notwithstanding his confidence, always his strongest suit, there were times when Fiorello would slip into a blue funk. Despite Windels's reassurances, he knew that "the club house boys" seriously doubted he could win. While there's no doubt that the national leadership had all but written him off, La Guardia had to have been heartened by a shrewd ploy by Major Michael A. Kelly, an honored veteran of New York's venerable Old Fighting Sixty-ninth. Kelly created the Liberty Party for the express purpose of entering the race. He knew he had no chance of winning—even of placing. His purpose was to defeat Moran, and by extension Wilson, by siphoning off the traditional Irish vote that couldn't in all conscience go Republican. His platform—oppose the Versailles Treaty and the League of Nations and support independence for Ireland—was like a godsend to the many extremist Irish nationalists who ordinarily would have supported Moran. Also militating in La Guardia's favor was the inefficient administration of mayor John F. Hylan, which won him the endorsement of the Citizens Union, a blue-ribbon aggregation of those politically significant old-line New York families known popularly as silk-stocking Republicans. Hylan was also a concern to the *New York Times*, which endorsed Fiorello on the eve of the election.[9]

On Election Day, November 4, 1919, Fiorello and Thea voted early at their polling place in the Village and then posed for pictures: he looking confident, his fingers gripping his talismanic ten-gallon Stetson, she looking especially radiant, having learned only days before that she was pregnant. While Thea rested, Fiorello spent the day racing between campaign headquarters and polling places throughout the city where he suspected, or had been given to suspect, there might be some Tammany-inspired "monkey business." When the polls closed, he and Thea and his closest advisers checked into a suite at the Hotel Brevoort to await returns telephoned in by Sam Koenig, who had established himself at police headquarters, where the official count was being tallied. The night was long and hell on the nerves, as neither candidate was able to pull ahead in a convincing lead. It was not until four A.M. that Koenig phoned in with the succinct message, "F.H., you're in."

Just as La Guardia had become the first Republican elected to Congress from New York's Fourteenth Congressional District, albeit on a fusionist ticket, he was now the first man running on a straight Republican ticket to win citywide office since the five counties united in 1898 to become Greater New York City.

It was not an overwhelming victory. He lost Queens, the Bronx, and Staten Island. What put him over was his sweep of the Italian districts in Brooklyn and Manhattan. The final tally: Fiorello, 145,108; Moran, 142,501; and Socialist candidate James O'Neal, 45,112. As for Kelly and his Liberty Party, though thrown off the ballot by Charlie Murphy through a technicality, he achieved his purpose of siphoning off Democratic votes by telling his supporters to write in his own name or vote for any candidate other than Moran. After La Guardia's victory was announced, Kelly had the pleasure of wiring Murphy, "You put me off the ballot, but look what I did to you." La Guardia nodded in vigorous agreement when Kelly boasted to the press, "The Liberty Party not only furnished the lid for Tammany's coffin, but we nailed it down."[10]

There is no denying Fiorello's talents as a vote-getter, but there is also no doubt that party affiliation and loyal district captains played a prominent role in his victory. The year 1919 saw an unanticipated Republican success. His two most important running mates in what had become known as the Campaign of the Three Majors—Major La Guardia, Major Henry H. Curran, candidate for Manhattan borough president, and Major Philip J. McCook, candidate for the State Supreme Court—also won. In fact, they ran ahead of him. Even Fiorello's Socialist adversary for aldermanic president showed surprising strength. Tammany was done in simply because it was identified with Wilson and the so-called Peace That Failed.

La Guardia's win was perceived by the professional pols as a sign of the coming radical shift in New York politics. Richard Croker, the Tammany Terror of the 1880s and 1890s, now living in retirement, told Fiorello, "Some day an Italian and a Jew will be mayors of New York, and the Italian will come first." (In fact, given La Guardia's dual heritage, they both came first.) Tom Foley, Democratic leader of the East Side, eschewed prophecy for pragmatism when he admitted that Tammany would be in heavy trouble unless the Irish made room in the tent for the Italians and promised, "Show me another La Guardia, and I'll run him."[11]

2.

It was no less an authority on municipal sleaze than Boss Tweed who said famously, "There never was a time when you couldn't buy the Board of Aldermen." By the time La Guardia assumed the presidency, having resigned his congressional seat the day before, its original power, which included making up the city budget, fixing the tax rate, granting franchises, and awarding contracts, had been given to the Board of Estimate, for which the aldermanic board was now a rubber stamp. It was also a joke, a disgrace, a parody of free government, a three-ring circus, and, above all, a dumping ground for political hacks for services rendered to their respective parties. When La Guardia took over, the board's political makeup was thirty-seven Democrats, twenty-six Republicans (himself included), and four Socialists, whose influence was negligible since the others invariably voted along party lines. In his presidential address at the opening day of the session, La Guardia promised that, as Republican minority leader, he would cooperate with the Democrats on all matters of a constructive nature and, moreover, would "try to prevent waste and unwise appropriations." The Tammany majority responded to this piece of news by taking away his power to appoint committees. La

Guardia didn't even object. To do so would be futile, given the numbers.

Indeed, he could do little but sit back and suppress yawns as a whole slew of ordinances and resolutions, which it was the board's major business to pass, came flying in from all directions, the vast majority of them decidedly partisan. For example, the Hibernian members resolved to honor St. Patrick's Day, while their Italo-American coevals introduced a resolution to condemn a U.S. senator from Tennessee for having called Italians "dagoes." There were ordinances dealing with place-name changes (for example, Blackwell's Island to Welfare Island). And then there were the animal rights activists, one of whose number urged that La Guardia use his "utmost influence to have an ordinance passed making it compulsory for drivers to have their horses either rough-shod or provided with one of the many contrivances to prevent horses slipping during frosty weather." (The activist did not request that horses be prevented from having to labor "during frosty weather.")

On one occasion some of the members almost came to blows. In April of 1921, the Board debated whether it should resolve to give Albert Einstein and Chaim Weizmann, then visiting the country, the "Freedom of the City." Wall Street lawyer Bruce M. Falconer protested honoring these two eminent scientists, simply because he had never heard of them. Learning who the two visitors were, he said, "If anyone in my hearing had said that it was Professor Einstein, the scientist, who was to be honored, I would not have objected." After all, he pointed out, by way of explaining away his ignorance, Weizmann and Einstein were "common names in the New York telephone directory, like Smith and Jones."[12]

The question now obtrudes: Why did La Guardia put up with—let alone expend so much energy on—such nonsense? His workday averaged between eight and twelve hours. His desk, where he usually lunched on a sandwich and a bottle of milk while talking to the reporters, was all but buried under a pile of correspondence, memoranda, newspapers, ordinances, and, it would seem, anything else the wind had blown in. Evenings were invariably given over to off-the-cuff speeches all around town, wherever he was asked. And he didn't have to be asked twice. When a reporter wondered, "What do you do when you have no work to do?" the answer was a crisp "Work."

Explained the reporter, "I mean, recreation." Explained La Guardia, "That's it, work. There's nothing I enjoy better than good hard work, and believe me, there is plenty of it around here."[13]

That there was. And it can be summed up as a crash course in preparing himself for his ultimate goal: becoming mayor. Paul Windels gave La Guardia a copy of the city charter that he "went around with under his arm, day and night. He just made a study of it."[14] And he studied well. Within a year of taking office, he had become an expert on any number of issues of which he was practically ignorant when he ran in 1919—the transit problem, to cite but one. When he ran again in 1921, he was able to offer viable plans to modernize municipal government. These included abolishing the board over which he now presided, something he would do as mayor a dozen years down the road. His ambition was to preside over City Hall. For now he must preside over an anachronistic, largely ceremonial municipal entity whose antics amused half the citizenry and nauseated the other.

Which brings us back to our initial question: Why did Fiorello expend so much energy coping with such antics? Especially since he could vote only to break a tie, and the rules precluded his right to speak on any matter (a rule he pointedly ignored—constantly). The answer is quite simple: As president of the Board of Aldermen—in itself a stepping-stone to higher office, viz. his immediate predecessor, Al Smith—he served in the mayor's absence, which made him the city's second-highest official. Also, as aldermanic president he was automatically a member of the Board of Estimate, the city's true governing body. This positioned him to acquire firsthand the knowledge of how the city was run. And with his sights on the mayoralty, such knowledge was a categorical imperative. He helped to prepare the budget, observed the operation of the various city departments and agencies, familiarized himself with the myriad problems that devolved upon keeping the city clean and in good running order, and learned all there was to learn about such problems involving a large population as education, transportation, taxation, feeding and housing, et al.

The Board of Estimate, which was to the Board of Aldermen like a powerful legislative upper house to an emasculated lower house, was comprised of the mayor, city comptroller, president of the Board of Aldermen, and the five borough presidents and was both a legislative and executive entity. As a result of the special 1919 election, La Guardia and Manhattan Borough President Henry Curran were the sole Republicans. The Democrats were Mayor Hylan, Comptroller Charles L. Craig, and the other four borough presidents. La Guardia and Curran saw their duties on the board as being twofold: to keep an eye on the Democrats and, if humanly possible, nail Tammany to the wall with a scandal or two.

Most of the Board of Estimate could have been said to qualify as experts in municipal government. Though politicians, not students of political science, they were superior to the average alderman in education, experience, and responsibility. For that reason, logic would dictate that, unlike the aldermanic board, where stupidity and outrageousness were the norm, the upper chamber would behave like gentlemen and confine their mutual detestations to ironical retorts and clever put-downs, as is the practice in the British House of Commons. But not this crew, thanks in large measure to a triangular mutual hate society consisting of the city's three top officials: the mayor, the comptroller, and the president of the Board of Aldermen.

Mayor Hylan, known as "Honest John" for reasons that had nothing to do with his probity, was a well-intentioned but rather dim-witted stooge of William Randolph Hearst, self-anointed leader of the Democratic Party's left wing in New York. Best remembered today for baiting Reds, hating FDR's New Deal, and propagandizing the pre–World War II isolationists, from the 1880s to the 1930s this creator of the world's greatest news empire was a confrontational social muckraker. Hearst used that empire to support every demand of the Progressive Era, from the direct primary to regulating big business. Though Tammany loathed Hearst as a Jeffersonian Democrat, the sachems agreed, in the immortal epigram of Lyndon Johnson, that they'd "rather have him inside the tent pissing out, than outside the tent pissing in." In 1906, Hearst was given the party's nomination for the New York governorship. (He lost.) In 1917, Tammany agreed to run Hearst's pawn "Honest John" Hylan for mayor. It was his relationship to Hearst that enabled Hylan to be chosen— and elected. As mayor, he accomplished nothing constructive.

Comptroller Craig, who owed his election to his connection with Tammany boss Charlie Murphy, was a sharp-tongued bully. To Honest John, whom he considered the village idiot, Craig was not so much an unmitigated horror as an absolute nightmare. Their horrendous intra-Tammany feud had been going on for two years when La Guardia arrived on the scene. With his arrival, the feud became even worse.

Though a Tammany puppet, Hylan took a liking to the vehemently anti-Tammany La Guardia. Why? Perhaps he found it a novelty encountering something he had never met before: an honest politician. More than likely, it was because La Guardia took a liking to him, after an initial disagreement that was quickly patched up, and because—this is only conjecture—he perceived in the hapless mayor an integrity, albeit a muddled one. But when all's said and done, what doubtless was the greatest factor in bringing these two into harmony, after a fashion, was their shared loathing of Craig. Fiorello, who always lined up with Hylan against the comptroller, "hated Craig with such a perfect hatred, which Craig returned, that it would require a Dr. Freud to untangle the snarl."[15]

Since the minutes of the Board of Estimate show that they agreed on most issues though they fought over policy, it's quite probable that the La Guardia–Craig feud was a personal one. Again, questions that cannot be answered definitively: Did each see in the other qualities he subconsciously disliked in himself? Each, for instance, tossed brickbats like Michael Jackson tossing kisses, and insulted opponents as if commanded to do so by a Higher Power, yet was easily offended when insulted in return. Given that they were the two most able officials on the board, did both realize there wasn't room enough for two men who each wanted to run the show as a solo act? Is it possible that race played a part—may well have been the root cause? Consider: On one occasion, Craig blurted out to Hylan of La Guardia, "Will you please hit that little wop over the head with the gavel!" This last, incidentally, was the interpretation placed on the feud by the Italo-American press, though the claim that La Guardia endured the ordeal of bigotry "with Roman stoicism" was far-fetched.[16]

That "Roman stoicism" was disproved a day later when Craig tried to defer discussion of a pet project that La Guardia had made up his mind to kill. Fiorello screamed, "Don't try to pull that stuff! You said I hadn't been here for three meetings and you would take up this business today. Now take it up!" To which Craig warned, "You say that again, and you will get what you deserve." Whereupon La Guardia made a lunge for the comptroller but was held back by Borough President Curran. Meanwhile, Craig's secretary, Charles L.

Kerrigan, slipped behind La Guardia's chair. La Guardia turned on Kerrigan and threatened, "If you try to start anything with me, you'll go out of that window, you bootlicking valet!" Kerrigan shot back, "I'm no wop." Screamed La Guardia, "What's that you say? What's that you say? What's that you say?" Curran had to restrain him from crawling all over the man. Hylan, who was presiding, sat back enjoying the floor show.[17]

It was more than a floor show. It was a display of partisanship out of control. In American politics, professionals who trash each other for public consumption may well share a convivial drink or two out of the public eye. Not so La Guardia and Craig, who were bent on destroying each other. Their feud was played out in the press. New Yorkers read one day that Craig camouflaged an appointment for purposes of getting himself a new car; the next day, that La Guardia billed the city for personal telephone calls and telegrams. La Guardia accused Craig of endorsing a loan to the Brooklyn Rapid Transit Company without consulting the Board of Estimate. When Craig claimed to have dug up some dirt on La Guardia, the latter threatened to vote against giving Craig's favorite company the contract to heat City Hall. Craig informed the reporters, "If I had my way they would shut off the heat in City Hall," to which La Guardia replied, via the press, "Nothing you could do would make me mad. You're a complete and official failure."[18]

Though rhetorically their public feud was a tie, La Guardia was the clear winner when the battles involved policy as distinct from personality. With Hylan's support, he defeated Craig on a few major issues, such as the comptroller's attempts to raise the salaries of already overpaid officials and exempt a number of positions from civil service. A triumph for the Little Flower came when he linked Craig with a scandal involving construction of a new county courthouse. La Guardia and Curran stood alone in opposition to the Tammany-inspired project, which had been authorized before their election to the Board of Estimate and for which contracts had already been signed. La Guardia persuaded Hylan to authorize an investigation, which disclosed major corruption. Hylan canceled the contracts, a grand jury handed down sixty-nine indictments, and the chief offenders, many of them Craig cronies, were dispatched to the penitentiary. La Guardia, exulting with the words "I said some time ago that this courthouse would out-Tweed-Tweed," blamed Craig (who was not one of the grafters) for having dismissed the warning that something was amiss.

Ironically, La Guardia came in for some carping at the highest echelons of the state Republican Party for having acted prematurely. Had he held back until election time, the wasted city funds, not to mention the scandal itself, would have given them a sensational campaign issue. La Guardia termed this "the doctrine of the old school of politics" and shouted, "I consider that it is my duty to serve the city first and look for campaign issues afterward!" The state bosses wisely let the matter drop. Besides, they already had their issue for the 1920 contest: Woodrow Wilson.[19]

Prior to exposing the courthouse scandal La Guardia was perceived, even by his own party, as a convulsive street brawler who screamed, lunged, and otherwise played the roughneck if that's what it took to aggrandize himself in the political arena. But now the perception changed. Save to his most obdurate antagonists across the entire political spectrum, he was seen as that rarity of rarities, an honest politician. True, he never lost that predilection to dramatize himself as well as an issue. But improving his image (not that *he* ever felt it needed improvement) was bottommost on his political agenda. Uppermost was a program for municipal reform.

Its nucleus was the simultaneous streamlining and expansion of government functions. To force speculators to build desperately needed housing, he proposed a tax on unused property. To eliminate corruption, inefficiency, and periodic brutality in the police department, he proposed its reorganization along military lines. He called for enlargement of the port facilities, creation of a municipal garbage and rubbish disposal facility, and bringing together all forms of rapid transit (subways, surface buses, and elevated trains, or "els") in a single operating company under the city's supervision. And finally, warning of the necessity to prevent the city from sliding into bankruptcy, a warning prompted by the huge deficit revealed after the 1921 budget, he proposed a revision of the city charter to purge the municipal payroll of its superfluous positions and the "leeches" who occupied them, by consolidating departments that overlapped in responsibility and were shockingly overstaffed.[20] But these reforms, he was realistic enough to know, must wait until he was mayor to be pushed through.

La Guardia had grown in office, as demonstrated by the fact that the bulk of his reform proposals derived from more than a year's close scrutiny of mismanagement of the city's affairs. He could never be considered an intellectual in politics. He learned not from what was gleaned from the literature of reform but from experience, especially by noting the errors of others. Fiorello La Guardia was like a man who learns to build a house not by studying architecture and scanning blueprints but by watching the professionals carry out the actual construction and even offering to lend a hand. Maverick that he was, he still played within the system, supremely confident that he could be a loyal Republican without compromising his ideals and integrity. Sam Koenig and all the other GOP bosses were eminently pleased. Granted, he effected departures from the norm, like fulfilling his campaign promise to the suffragists by allowing an aide, a leader of the League of Women Voters, to serve four o'clock tea at City Hall—an astonishment to the pols that was exceeded only by his order to toss out all the cuspidors. But these were gnomic aberrations, more than offset by his making the expected party appointments to his staff. In addition, he dispensed patronage to Paul Windels, thereby boosting his campaign manager's stock with the party's Brooklyn leaders.

In September, Fiorello was elected national chairman of the Italo-American Republican League, established with one objective: to exploit the Fiume issue. Among those welcoming the group into the fold were Republican presidential nominee Warren G. Harding, his running mate, Calvin Coolidge, and, of all people, Henry Cabot Lodge. The senator from Massachusetts, leader and most vociferous of the nation's anti-Wilsonites, was only too happy to make common cause with an ethnic group he had spent a career vilifying. (Though to be accurate, he had spent a career vilifying immigrants of all ethnicities.) Here indeed was validation of the old political dictum "The enemy of my enemy is my friend." And under the aegis of La Guardia, the Italo-Americans became Lodge's ideal of an enemy to befriend. Stumping for Harding not only in New York but nationwide, wherever there was a sizeable colony of Italo-Americans, La Guardia fulminated against Wilson, more often than not in Italian, for "screwing" their homeland. The hope of the American people, he insisted, lay entirely in the Republican Party. Only by electing Harding would the requisite wooden stake be driven through the heart of the vampire Wilson.

La Guardia's sincerity in backing Harding is open to question, given his preference for the Progressive Senator Irvine Lenroot at the 1920 nominating convention. But the idea of letting the party down was unthinkable, even though the party had on occasion let *him* down. He considered himself a true loyalist. Besides, to do so would be tantamount to supporting, albeit tacitly, the treachery of Wilson. Not open to question, however, is that La Guardia would have liked to have it both ways, being at one and the same time a loyal Republican and a Progressive, as he now openly identified himself. He thought that while he could force himself to vote for the party's choice, he could still buck the party on his home grounds; that is to say, pursue a Progressive agenda that ran counter to the will of the party yet still remain a member in good standing. Such a feat was not impossible, if undertaken by a charismatic leader who knew when and how to compromise and conciliate and, in the bargain, had the magnetism to draw the party along in his wake, should the necessity arise. Like a Theodore Roosevelt.

But La Guardia was no Theodore Roosevelt. La Guardia was La Guardia. And that he would overreach, and bring disaster not to the party but to himself, became an inevitability with the changing of the guard at Albany. Nathan L. Miller, a McKinley Republican, succeeded Democrat Al Smith as governor in the 1921 election. Though La Guardia had campaigned as vigorously for Miller as he had for Harding, the two would become mortal enemies. As Miller prepared to move into the executive mansion, La Guardia prepared to buck the party machine he had served faithfully for a decade.

Led by Miller, the party machine crushed the Little Flower.

3.

The New York State Republican leadership had been growing suspicious of this I'm-my-own-man dynamo. For openers, he had gone after powerful Republican-oriented businesses like the telephone company, lashing out at the profits they were piling up. Learning that a family was burned to death while the mother tried without success to reach the Fire Department, he insinuated that the telephone company was guilty of murder. He questioned the fifty-thousand-dollar annual salary multimillionaire GOP bigwig August Belmont received as president of the Interborough Rapid Transit. Testifying before a state legislative hearing on rent control—an idea the predominantly Republican property owners detested—he said, "I come not to praise the landlord, but to bury him!"[21] And this was before he began to clash with Miller.

Shortly after the new year of 1921 opened, Fiorello set himself on a disastrous course when he protested the Republican-controlled legislature's unseating of five legally elected Socialist assemblymen for being members of "a subversive and unpatriotic organization." Argued La Guardia, "The ballot is the legitimate weapon of the Socialists just as it is of the general public"—a view shared, it might be noted, by such prominent New York City Republicans as Charles Evans Hughes and Henry L. Stimson, along with President-elect Harding and a host of conservative GOP newspapers and magazines. Even A. Mitchell Palmer, the man most responsible for the postwar Red Scare ("Palmer Raids") joined in what quickly became a national outcry against the Albany legislature's brainless exercise in illegal paranoia.

What made La Guardia, who had eagerly joined the posse dispatched by the Sixty-ninth Congress to run to ground all "reds," do this volte-face? The answer is that the onetime conservative was in the final stages of his metamorphosis into a passionate Progressive—a Progressive, what is more, who had awakened to the awareness that anyone who hated radicals would think no less charitably of immigrants. As he protested at one meeting, "All you hear up-State is: 'We were born here, they were not.' " He did not consider Socialists and anarchists fellow-travelers. The former, he noted, believed in the ballot, whereas the latter believed in the bomb.[22] The onetime outspoken anti-Socialist now insisted that unless the Republican Party gave every law-abiding citizen "a chance to play, a chance to educate himself and a chance to be happy," it would suffer the fate of the Whigs, whose death gave the GOP its birth. Operating on the theory that the best way to dramatize a stance is to lead by example, Fiorello arbitrated a strike in the shoe industry, submitted a plan for municipal housing (turned down in short order by the state legislature), and led the fight to raise the minimum salary of municipal employees to $1,500.[23]

Then came his clash with Governor Nathan L. Miller, champion of Old Guard conservatism. A corporation lawyer who admired Calvin Coolidge and suspected Teddy Roosevelt and men who shared his thinking of being "overly complicated" (a stupefying euphemism for "too progressive"), Miller endorsed Prohibition, defended censorship, loathed socialism, detested welfare legislation, contemplated direct primaries as one would contemplate bubonic plague, and viewed New York City, epicenter of the immigrant masses, with total revulsion. Rounding out his catalogue of troglodytic postures, he condemned the League of Women Voters for "promoting radicalism."

Beginning in midwinter 1921, he and La Guardia clashed over two issues: repeal of the Direct Primary Law of 1914, which gave registered voters the right to choose their party's candidates for elective office, and the Knight-Adler Act. This piece of traction (anti-home-rule) legislation vested in the state legislature control over New York City's transit system. It offered no guarantee of a continued five-cent fare. Even before Miller took office, La Guardia had been sounding the alarm that only "reactionary groups" would insist upon a repeal of the primary law. In 1921, while the question was under consideration in the legislature, he warned, "The direct primary is the salvation of American politics. It vests responsibility where it belongs—in the people." He might as well have been shouting to the wind. Miller had been put into office by upstate voters and the large business interests to dismantle the social welfare programs established by Al Smith, and he was only too happy to oblige. Imposing loyalty pledges for teachers and scaling back social programs reflected his fear for the spirit of American self-reliance; he saw in such areas as city-financed health centers and milk stations for the poor threats to freedom and the American way of life. In bringing the primary system of nomination back to the clubhouse, where he felt it properly belonged, Miller ameliorated his apprehension about the power growing numbers of the proletariat had to foster larger government and social welfare programs. The classes, Miller and the GOP hierarchy insisted, knew what was best for the masses—which meant for themselves.[24]

As for the transit issue, facilities—especially on the subways—had not kept pace with population growth, equipment had depreciated in quality, public control was spread among three agencies, and some transit companies were either in bankruptcy or headed there. This last factor was an especial cause for concern. Should the Brooklyn Rapid Transit and Interborough Rapid Transit companies fail, both of which leased the subways the city had constructed at a cost of three hundred million dollars, the city would have to default on the interest it paid on the subway bonds funded in the permanent debt.

In his Second Annual Message to the Board of Aldermen, on January 3, 1921, La Guardia called for a single operating company to purchase the existing companies, subject to the following conditions: Cost was to be determined by physical evaluation of all equipment and ancillary factors (i.e., conditions of the rails and tunnels) and not on the basis of capitalization, which had become inflated due to obsolescence of equipment, deterioration of rails, and waste. Also called for was retention of the five-cent fare on all forms of transit. In view of its initial investment, La Guardia insisted, the city must have the right of representation on the proposed new corporation's board of directors. "Let us hope," he concluded, "that there will be no interference by the State Legislature in this very important city matter."[25]

He hoped in vain. The Knight-Adler traction bill, which was passed a few months later, not only remained silent about the nickel fare, it vested authority in a three-man commission to be appointed by the governor. Here, indeed, was a slap in the face of New Yorkers. Miller's determination to control a city that was so irremediably controlled by the political opposition was not only unacceptable, it was downright inexplicable. "The man who introduced this bill, Senator Knight of [upstate] Wyoming County, comes from a little town in that county that cannot even boast of one street car, and yet he proposes to tell us what we should do," noted La Guardia. Rather than "submit to rule of the yokels upstate," he suggested in all seriousness that the five counties that comprised New York City secede and reconstitute themselves as a sovereign state.[26]

Convinced that in the next mayoral election the Knight-Adler Act would hand the office to the incumbent Hylan on a gold platter, La Guardia tried the soft approach first. He proposed a sit-down with Miller to point out that the traction bill would so alienate the majority of the electorate as to in effect cede total control of the city to Tammany and thus destroy GOP influence in the component boroughs. Miller not only rebuffed La Guardia, he brought pressure on the county leaders to fall into line. First to fall was Brooklyn's Jake Livingston, "after an intensive three-minute survey of the plan from the engineering, sociological, banking and actuarial standpoints." Sam Koenig, who like his protégé Fiorello feared that the governor was indeed unwittingly playing into the hands of the Democrats, underwent a sudden change of heart after Miller made it known that he was considering a judgeship for his brother Morris. Koenig begged Fiorello to go along "for the sake of party unity."[27]

Fiorello not only refused, he made the rounds of the Republican clubhouses urging that the men who got out the vote realize that Knight-Adler would sound the death knell for the city's GOP. In Brooklyn, he condemned Livingston as the party's Brutus. In the Bronx, he condemned "Saffron Yellow Republican Representatives [who] voted for the [transit] fare grab." At one Manhattan West Side clubhouse, his confrontational stance and language actually led to a brawl. It wasn't long before the clubhouses locked him out. Arriving at one in Brooklyn for a scheduled speech, Fiorello found the doors closed and the lights out. "This is the first time that anything like this has happened to me," he said with total chagrin. Then he murmured an unalloyed warning: "They will be sorry for it later on." As events would prove over time, they were.[28]

La Guardia now found himself in the same camp with not only Mayor Hylan (who had taken what amounted to a blood oath in promising the people "the preservation of democracy and decency and the retention of the five cent fare") but press baron Hearst, whose newspapers blasted Miller and the "Money Power." Fiorello repudiated any connection with Hearst. "No one expects that I will be nominated for mayor by the Democrats," he insisted sarcastically and went on to aver with passion, "I am a Republican." Republican newspapers denied the claim. Most vocal in this regard were Frank Munsey's *New York Herald* and *Evening Telegram,* which denounced him as noisy, stupid, ignorant, shallow, demagogic, and disloyal and—perhaps the unkindest cut of all—dismissed him as "La Guardia, the petty and the pitiful!"[29]

Now taking his fight directly to the people, La Guardia talked up the five-cent fare, home rule, the direct primary, and just about everything else Governor Miller stood for before church, fraternal, civic, women's, veterans', and ethnic groups from one end of the city to the other. Barely concealing his determination to succeed

Hylan in the coming mayoral election, he managed to get in quite a few examples of misadministration at City Hall and the need to revise the city charter. In fact, he had quite a lot to say on any subject that would appeal to a specific audience. Debating Jacob Panken and Seymour Stedman on their Socialist home ground, he promised that the progressivism he espoused would benefit the people more than the utopianism these two espoused. Denouncing the Russian Revolution, he argued that it had "not been proven that wholesale changes would benefit mankind," as it was "impossible to get imperfect human beings to live under any golden rule." Resorting at times to irony, he made fun of the Prohibitionists, disparaged upholders of out-of-date so-called blue laws, condemned Coney Island's "bathhouse barons," tore into those groups that wanted to abandon city colleges, and demanded pensions for "Gold Star mothers and the wounded and maimed boys." He took on the superintendent of schools when a minister was refused permission to speak at a school forum because of a complimentary remark he had made about Lenin. Tearing into film censorship, which Miller advocated, he facetiously expressed a total lack of concern before the American Motion Picture Association over "the number of seconds the censors decree a husband may kiss his wife." Condemning immigration restrictions, he vowed to oppose any attempt to alter the appearance of the old Castle Garden, cracking that he didn't "want the spot where my ancestors landed defaced; they didn't come over on the *Mayflower*."[30]

The anti-Republican press termed him "Champion of the People's Rights." Having gone to the political mat with Miller, and thus his own party, over flashpoint issues, Fiorello now took after the "stand-patters, reactionaries, and corporation bosses of the party," calling for a social revolution to carry on "the work of Theodore Roosevelt for a new school of politics." Still, politician that he was, Fiorello realized that despite his popularity it took power to fight power. In March, he called upon Senator Calder, the powerful Brooklynite who had been his mentor as a congressman. Calder, no Progressive but a virulent anti-Millerite, made public his considered opinion that "if the Republican Party does not make this little wop Mayor next fall, New York is going to hell."[31]

But so far as the party hierarchy was concerned, "the little wop" was dead meat. When word came down from Albany calling for his ostracism, many downstate Republicans, outraged by his conduct as president of the Board of Aldermen and member of the Board of Estimate, readily agreed. Even Senator Calder soon abandoned him, lest continued support jeopardize his own position with the party chieftains. On August 2, 1921, after weeks of negotiations with the most reputable anti-Tammany Democratic factions in the five boroughs, an agreement was reached whereby Republican Manhattan Borough President Henry Curran would be run for mayor on a fusion ticket.

4.

To accept the party's decision would make any struggle against the Albany autocracy by Fiorello come off as inane. Yet running as a Progressive would end not only in certain defeat but in political excommunication as well. He had no option but to run as an independent. Should he beat Curran in the September primary and then go on to oust Hylan in November, as mayor he would be the city's GOP leader as well as master of policy and patronage. The bosses in Albany would have no choice but to deal with him.

Sam Koenig begged him not to run. "The town isn't ready for an Italian mayor. You'll lose and you won't be able to make a living." Fiorello refused to be put off. "Sam, I'll run. So long as I have five dollars in my pocket I'm all right, and if I can't earn that, I've always got my service revolver."[32] He pledged to wage "a penniless primary," that is, one free from party backing. And that's exactly what it was. Even longtime partisans Louis Espresso, Paul Windels, and Harry G. Andrews dared not support him against the party bosses.

He established headquarters in the Hotel Netherland with the slogan "The Bosses Don't Want Him, but You, Mr. Knickerbocker, Do." For the first time, La Guardia was completely on his own. Also for the first time, he had an omnibus platform that was less a collection of planks than a veritable smorgasbord of promises: Better Transit for a Nickel; Direct Primaries for all Elective Offices; Home Rule without State Interference; Protection of All City Property Rights; Protection of City Water Supply; City Approval of All Local Legislation; Frequent Conferences of City Legislators; Universal Transfers on Surface Lines; Lower Gas, Electricity, and Telephone Bills; Efficient Municipal Management; Mayor's Advisory Counsel;

Bigger and Better Harbor Facilities; Economical Terminal Market System, Lowering Cost of Food; Improved Educational Opportunities and Seating Capacity; Profitable Municipal Disposal of Garbage and Rubbish; Municipal Operation for Snow Removal; Better Housing Facilities with Lower Rents; and Equalization of Taxation Burdens with Lower Taxes.

His organization, if such be the word, was hurriedly put together by the city's two politically conscious groups who most favored his candidacy, the Italo-Americans and the women, who were out to grasp a share of the political pie, thanks to the Nineteenth Amendment. Elizabeth Collier, a Republican leader in Brooklyn, organized a regiment of surrogate spokesmen and poll watchers. Dr. Vincent A. Caso, publisher of the *Bensonhurst Progress*, and Nicholas Selvaggi, an assistant district attorney in Brooklyn, founded the Kings County League of Italian-American Republican Clubs. Despite the enthusiasm, there was not enough time to form a truly strong organization in any of the five boroughs.[33]

Meanwhile, racing around the city, the candidate made apposite promises to all voting blocs: taxpayers, tenants, borough chauvinists, supporters of Irish freedom, Gold Star mothers, veterans—whatever the group, he had a pledge. Playing to one of the truly formidable components of his constituency, he promised to appoint women to his administration, especially in the departments of health, correction, welfare, education, and markets: "Who knows better about these subjects than women?" His appeal among the ladies was the promise of clean government and a major role for them. His appeal among his fellow hyphenates was simply being one of them. So far as the Italo-Americans were concerned, their *paisano* had been given the shaft by the bosses not only because of his opposition to Governor Miller—whom they had followed La Guardia in supporting in 1920—but also because of his ancestry. After an anti-Prohibition parade through the streets of South Brooklyn, Fiorello told some five thousand of them that the GOP bosses "seem to think an Italian, though he be an American, has no chance to be Mayor of New York, but they may have a Mayor of Italian descent after the next election!"[34]

It was a heartfelt boast, but an empty one. Curran not only had the machine support, he had women's divisions down to the precinct level and even a rival Italo-American league. Furthermore, he ignored La Guardia altogether, campaigning almost exclusively against Hylan and Tammany Hall. Worse, La Guardia, spouting threats and invective in Miller's direction, was barred from the clubhouses. Word was sent down from on high to "give the noisy, treacherous, little wop what he deserves," sneered Frank Munsey in his *New York Herald* (July 5, 1921). The *Brooklyn Daily Eagle* on that same day dismissed "the Little Flower" contemptuously as "the Little Garibaldi." La Guardia was trashed by the English-language press, save for a handful of papers including Hearst's. And Hearst was less interested in electing La Guardia than in antagonizing the Republicans.[35]

In early August, La Guardia made the first of two blunders, something hard to explain away in so seasoned a campaigner. Summoning two employees of his aldermanic office, he asked, "Have you decided what your district will do? If you haven't I'll give you ten minutes to make up your mind." The two replied they were for Curran and were fired summarily. When word got out, the Republican press took him to task. Wrote the *New York Evening Post* (August 4, 1921), "These boss tactics come with bad grace from one who spends most of his time denouncing the bosses." Three weeks later, having constantly declared himself to be a purer Republican than Miller, La Guardia endorsed for reelection two Democratic judges, because they were Italian.[36]

A week before the primary, in what can be interpreted as either playing one's trump card or acting out of desperation, La Guardia told a press conference that in 1919 the "bosses" had promised to give him the mayoral nomination if he won the presidency of the Board of Aldermen. Asked to confirm the story, Sam Koenig denied it. He did not, however, refute La Guardia's charge that after going up against Miller he "was marked for slaughter."[37] That he was is borne out by the primary results: Curran racked up three votes to his one. La Guardia failed to carry a single borough and won only twelve out of sixty-two assembly districts, all predominantly Italo-American.

La Guardia sought to mend fences, claiming, after a lunch with Curran, "Yes, we are all good Republicans." Also, he made a few speeches supporting Curran and gave interviews in which he voiced hope that Curran would win in the general election—and blasted his antagonist on the Board of Estimate, Charles Craig, who was seeking reelection. It didn't help.[38] Hylan buried Curran by more than four hundred thousand votes, and Craig did almost as well against Charles C. Lockwood, whose committee had investigated the courthouse contracts.

5.

While La Guardia's political collapse was self-inflicted, it was hardly suicidal. He was tough and seasoned, fully bent upon survival in the jungle of New York politics. Admittedly, he embraced lost causes when he felt they deserved his fiery advocacy. But playing the martyr was not his style. How, then, could a professional politician such as he have violated the elemental rule of never bucking your party's bosses, by taking on Governor Miller and the state organization? Four factors comprise the answer: principle, power, error in judgment, and personal tragedy.

When he first sought office, in 1914, Fiorello brought no political philosophy to the table. What he brought was resentment and distrust of powerful men and empathy with the underdog. It did not take a Cassandra to foretell an eventual clash between him and his polar opposite in the Republican hierarchy. Miller proved to be that polar opposite. When the clash came, La Guardia had not only conceived a program for municipal reform, he was convinced that unless the party adopted his program, and thereby became the party of the masses instead of the party of the classes, its days were numbered. Obviously, what he wanted his party to be and what the party was were irreversibly incompatible.

In terms of the power aspect of the equation, in 1921 La Guardia was confident he would succeed in seizing control of the downstate organization, a confidence fortified by his 1919 victory, his popularity with the hyphenates and women of all ethnicities, and the respect of the city bosses for services (and party loyalty) rendered during the 1920 presidential campaign. Did La Guardia desire power in part for the sheer joy that having it can bring a man? Was he, indeed, a perfect candidate for proving Lord Acton's hypothesis that power corrupts, and absolute power corrupts absolutely? The answer is unascertainable. What *is* ascertainable and thus relevant, though, is the joy he derived from throwing his weight around while ameliorating the plight of the downtrodden and disadvantaged, be they his "boys" at Camp Fiume or his constituents, first in the Fourteenth Congressional District, then in the five boroughs that comprised New York City.

As for La Guardia's mistake in judgment, the first major one of his career—attacking the Albany machine—it can be said to have been rooted in what was to be his greatest personal tragedy. He and Thea enjoyed a happy social life that revolved around a small circle of friends, most notably Green Geniuses Attilio Piccirilli and Onorio Ruotolo, Paul Windels, violinist Albert Spalding, Fiorello's wartime aide and companion, and, during his annual seasons at the Metropolitan Opera, legendary tenor Enrico Caruso. In June 1920, Thea gave birth to a daughter, Fioretta Thea. La Guardia simply adored her, more so because this middle-aged man so inordinately fond of children had doubted whether he would ever be a father.

The following winter, after campaigning for Harding, La Guardia learned that both his wife and infant daughter had contracted tuberculosis. Advised by doctors that the higher altitude of the Bronx might benefit them, he bought a six-room white stucco house in a semirural area at 1852 University Avenue, which cost him practically every cent he had. Although an invalid, Thea took care of the baby in the sun parlor Fiorello had built onto the house. The strain proved to be too much, and she suffered a breakdown. In desperation, La Guardia took her to Dr. Edward Trudeau's famed sanatorium at Saranac Lake. But Thea insisted on returning home so that she could care for the baby. On May 3, 1921, the disease having settled in little Fioretta's spine, she was rushed to Roosevelt Hospital, where she died five days later of tubercular meningitis.

Thea was so sick that the overwhelmed Fiorello had to attend their baby's funeral alone. Despite his frantic efforts to obtain the best medical care for her, Thea continued to fail. By the summer of 1921 Fiorello agonized over the realization that his beloved wife was doomed. He spent as much time as he could at her bedside, helpless to do anything but hold her hand and offer up silent prayers that he knew in his heart must go unanswered. On the morning of November 29, with her devastated husband at her side, the twenty-six-year-old Thea died of pulmonary tuberculosis.

It was during this year of personal tragedy that La Guardia recklessly took on the GOP machine. Small wonder that, as August Bellanca remembered, his behavior seemed more often than not that of a man who not only didn't care what happened to him but, in fact, seemed to expect the very worst. The quicker Thea declined, the more Fiorello baited his opponents, the more they punished him, and the more he flailed out in return; the baby's death exacerbated his wretchedness.[39]

Immediately following Thea's death, Ciccio Giordano moved in to offer La Guardia companionship. He recalled seeing him bend over Thea's coffin, which lay open in the dining room, kissing her corpse and breaking into heart-wrenching sobs. Thea's funeral on December 1, 1921, was, at Fiorello's insistence, a simple affair, requiring only three cars to transport their closest Italo-American friends and Thea's sister to Woodlawn Cemetery for interment. The ceremony was a double one. Little Fioretta's remains had been disinterred from another cemetery, and mother and child were buried together.[40]

On December 17, Attilio Piccirilli, Fiorello's closest friend dating back to his Greenwich Village days, took him to Cuba for a healing change of venue. But his grief was beyond assuaging. When he returned, his temper was out of control. Threats against Miller became vicious, his hatred for Craig became even more pronounced, and innocent city employees were victims of his unhappiness for no other reason than that they seemed to be in his way. To onlookers, friends and foes alike, Fiorello gave every indication of unraveling before their eyes.

Despite his political rage and personal pain, La Guardia had acquired a realistic understanding of the city's needs. The bosses had forced him into City Hall (where the Board of Aldermen met) in 1919. Two years later, he left City Hall convinced that was where he belonged. Many of the reforms he would push through as mayor he proposed for the first time in the 1921 primary. He may have lost that race, but he gained something that would have salubrious consequences for the city a dozen years down the line: an important ideological awakening. "The Republican Party," he told the Board of Aldermen in his farewell address, "will go back into history for the ideals of Roosevelt and Abraham Lincoln."[41] Given his sentimental nature, he would associate the cause of humane government with the memory of his wife and daughter, who, along with his father, had been, as he saw it, victims of social murder. Asked by Zoe Beckley of the *Evening Mail* if he thought he could make New York City into something physically beautiful and societally rewarding, La Guardia exclaimed:

> Could I? Could I? Say—first I would tear out about five square miles of filthy tenements, so that fewer would be infected with tuberculosis like that beautiful girl of mine, my wife, who died—and my baby. . . . Then I would establish "lungs" in crowded neighborhoods—a breathing park here, another there, based on the density of population. . . . Milk stations next. One wherever needed, where pure, cheap milk can be bought for babies and mothers learn how to take care of them. After that the schools! I would keep every child in school, to the eighth grade at least, well-fed and in health. Then we could provide widows' pensions and support enough schools for every child in New York. . . . I would remove censorship from movie films. . . . I would provide more music and beauty for the people, more parks and more light and more air and all the things the framers of the constitution meant . . . when they put in that phrase "life, liberty, and the pursuit of happiness."[42]

Noble as those sentiments were, as well as eerily prescient, they were the sentiments of a man who all his life dreamed of achieving success in doing good but now appeared to be on a downward escalator to oblivion. Wife, child, career, standing in the party—all were gone. He was no longer young, nor a young man of promise. Crowed his nemesis, City Comptroller Craig, "The trouble is that he wanted to be Mayor and the people gave him the answer. Now he is sore. He's the 'late lamented La Guardia!' "[43]

Hateful as they were, the words could have served as La Guardia's political epitaph—which all the newspapers were now writing. Reflecting their general tenor, the *Westchester Globe* editorialized, "The prestige of a La Guardia in office has gone and will not return. A political party, in the march onward, has little use for the man who denounces the party which gave him office, when he goes out of that office. . . . The Republican Party will live on, while individuals drop out of sight."[44]

Everyone shared these sentiments. Everyone, that is, but the man himself. Fiorello H. La Guardia, broken in spirit, was now considered by one and all to be politically dead.

PART III

1922-1933

Return to Congress,
Champion of the People

CHAPTER ELEVEN

"I would rather be right than regular"

1.

La Guardia worked out his grief through frenetic activity. He resumed his private practice with the new law firm La Guardia, Sepinsky & Armour, was made consul for the Free State of Fiume, taught English at the Columbia Grammar School, lectured to Italian immigrant groups, joined enthusiastically in street games with neighborhood children in his spare time—and confronted his one obsessive desire: to get back into politics. Friends urged that he seek the governorship, or perhaps a return to Congress. But though he had plenty of volunteers to mount a campaign for any office, he lacked the most important component—a party. The GOP hierarchy wanted no part of him. To stage a comeback, La Guardia had to seek organizational support outside the party. He found it in the Italian immigrant community. Though their number now topped one million, of whom one hundred thousand were registered voters, they lacked a single district leadership in either the Democratic or Republican party. If they wanted political power, they would have to fight for it. The Little Flower didn't have to be asked twice to lead that fight.

Four days after Thea's death, he was elected honorary president by acclamation of the Kings County League of Italo-Americans Brooklyn Club. In his acceptance speech he hammered home that Italians would never count in New York politics until they organized themselves statewide. Two months later, the league was organized in all twenty-three of the borough's assembly districts "and they were ready to go." La Guardia established a Bronx branch of the league and then undertook a tour of the state, establishing small but effective organizations of Republican Italians. No more, he insisted, must they accept their lowly positions within the GOP machine, let alone the Old Guard's blatant racism.[1]

By early spring, he was garnering headlines as he rushed about the city and state speaking his mind on just about everything. He insisted that the people must be exposed to more classical music: Jazz's "discordant, strict, ear-racking noises are typical only of barbarous tendencies, and indeed a poor imitation of some of the most primitive tribes." He defended pacifism: "Wars are directed by bankers." He testified before Congress on behalf of legislation calling for the pensioned retirement of disabled men who had been commissioned for war service but did not remain in the military: "I am appearing in behalf of men who served under my command." He headed the Salvation Army Drive, led the male membership of the League of Women Voters, and stumped for a soldiers' bonus. He called for higher wages for government-paid laborers, the use of U.S. Army aircraft to transport the mails, municipal control over utilities, an updated snow removal system, milk stations, infant care centers, rent controls.[2]

The press speculated that all this headline grabbing was preparation for a run as an independent against his nemesis, Governor Nathan Miller, who was up for reelection. La Guardia encouraged such speculation. He hoped to use the threat of a vendetta against Miller and the Old Guard to force the party to buy him off, as it were, by nominating him for what he really wanted: a return to Congress. But not from his old Fourteenth Congressional District. He had his eyes on his old friend Isaac Siegel's Twentieth (East Harlem), the city's largest Italo-American congressional district. Siegel was not seeking reelection, in order to accept a judgeship.

La Guardia still considered himself a proud Republican. He was not after revenge but, rather, wanted to bring the party into line. *His* line. His pendulum had begun moving toward the left of the political spectrum, and he was determined that the party climb aboard. This high-profile controversial Republican now made common cause with inarguably the highest-profile controversial Democrat in modern American journalism: William Randolph Hearst. For all the Hall's accommodation to curry his favor and keep him happy, Hearst had no qualms about bolting the party when he thought it was turning conservative, as when he ran for the New York mayoralty as an independent on a municipal socialist platform. (He lost.)

In May 1922, Hearst invited La Guardia to write for his *New York Evening Standard* on any topic of his choosing. The invitation was readily accepted. Next, he called upon the Republicans to run La Guardia for the governorship, hinting that were his "suggestion" turned down he might personally finance him as an independent candidate. Party leaders went into a collective sweat over the realization that the rambunctious little Italo-American they thought they had rid themselves of could seriously vitiate their man Miller's strength with the backing of the powerful Hearst. Returning from a European vacation, Hearst boosted La Guardia when he told a press conference, "This is emphatically a progressive year. The people have been plundered by profiteers. . . . [What I say] is not demagogy; it is democracy—the democracy of Jefferson. It is not radicalism; it is republicanism—the republicanism of Lincoln."[3]

It was something else, and Tammany knew it. Hearst wanted to be the Democrats' choice for governor or, should that fail, for senator. To that end he was prepared to dip into his enormous fortune to use La Guardia to splinter the Republican vote. Clearly Hearst was using La Guardia for his own Machiavellian purpose.

Not so clearly, either to Hearst or the GOP hierarchy, Fiorello was allowing himself to be so used for *his* own Machiavellian purpose. He couldn't have cared less that he had no chance of being his party's choice for the executive mansion at Albany. He had his eyes on that East Harlem congressional seat.

Now supported by a personal organization and the state's most powerful newspaper chain, La Guardia made his move to spook the party bosses into giving him the gubernatorial nomination. In late June, with the election just four months off, he issued a pamphlet, "Proposed Plans for Republican State Platform," along with an announcement—a threat, actually—that he would challenge Miller if the governor were renominated by the party on a "reactionary" platform. The Forty-Two Planks, as they were known, began by condemning "the illogical, unscientific, wholesale prohibition of immigration on the quota system, based upon narrow-mindedness and bigotry," and went on to demand, among other items, the direct primary, the short ballot, municipal home rule, an eight-hour day, equal rights for women, freedom of speech and action for Socialists, repeal of the state's motion picture censorship law, old age pensions, workmen's compensation, a tax on unimproved land, a city water and ice works, municipal multiunit housing, state ownership of electric companies, limitations on injunctions in labor disputes and jury trials in contempt cases arising out of such disputes, a generous tax credit to farmers (a powerful voting bloc upstate), rent controls, exemption from state income taxes on incomes under five thousand dollars, a minimum wage, and the abolition of child labor.[4]

The newspapers—Hearst's excepted—treated the proposals as a joke. Leading the pack was the *Times* (July 14, 1922), which feigned surprise that the platform had excluded "municipal ice cream sherbet at cost, or, preferably, free." Not so the GOP hierarchy, which began to squirm when Fiorello's articles, under the overall title "The New School of Politics," began to appear in the *Evening Standard*, written in the style that endeared Hearst's papers to the masses— simple sentences, short paragraphs, figures of speech reflecting the flavor of the city, an evangelical spirit, and aphorisms aimed at the politicians: "Do after election as before election you said you would"; "Make New York the City Beautiful—the Home of Happiness"; "Put into practice ideals that others have preached for ages." Their content offered bold innovations reflecting old values, an approach that La Guardia shared with his generation of liberals; indeed, with reformers in general. The *Times* (August 31, 1922) dismissed the articles as "full of noble and Hearstian thoughts." (If so, then, as Teddy Roosevelt might have said, "Bully for Hearstian thoughts!")

In the articles, which appeared regularly until he began to campaign actively at summer's end, La Guardia allowed as how he would clear the slums, provide school children with free lunches, establish stations for the purchase of cheap milk, put all rapid transit underground, and place all public utilities under city ownership and management. He also called for more parks and playgrounds, schools, open-air concerts, and a music and art center so that "New Yorkers could live beautifully and creatively." Anticipating the federal Work

Projects Administration by more than a decade, he insisted that "parks, driveways, municipal farms, stadiums, boulevards, memorials, bridges, tunnels and all works of embellishment and construction should be provided for so as to absorb unemployment." Here we can see how the *Evening Journal* articles, which were in fact an explication and elaboration of his "Proposed Planks," not only prefigured the societal insurgency of the city's masses against the domination of its classes, an insurgency of which La Guardia was in the vanguard throughout the 1920s and on into FDR's New Deal, but also can be said to have prefigured the New Deal itself.

In one article that raised indignation among the classes and cries of hallelujah from readers of the Hearst papers, he reminded Anglo-Saxon Protestants, "Whether you came over on the [luxury liner] *Aquitania* or your ancestors came over on the *Santa Maria* or the *Mayflower* or the *Half Moon*, you are an immigrant or the descendant of immigrants. Bear that in mind." Overall, however, the articles stressed economics over politics; for example, "Only a well-fed, well-housed, well-schooled people can enjoy the blessings of liberty." Elaborating on this theme (August 19, 1922), he wrote, "The American people are having a hard time making both ends meet . . . Every daily paper contains advice on how to get along with less food owing to the high cost of necessities. . . . It is the proper function of government to prevent monopolies and profiteering on food." On September 14, he urged that the price of coal be kept down. La Guardia's ultimate goal was the welfare state. A necessary first step toward effecting such a state was the elimination of "reactionaryism, standpatism and the supremacy of the powerful privileged few."[5]

It is an axiom of American presidential politics that a viable enough third party can split the votes of one of the two traditional parties and throw the election to the other, as when Republican Teddy Roosevelt's Bull Moose Party siphoned off votes from the incumbent Taft and put Woodrow Wilson into office. In La Guardia's announced candidacy for the gubernatorial nomination, backed by Hearst and the powerful immigrant blocs plus defecting reform Republicans, the state hierarchy was faced with having a wrench flung into their hopes to reelect Nathan Miller. They knew he could not possibly be elected—La Guardia would have been the first to concede that—but they also knew that his independent candidacy would defeat Miller, and with him the Republican ticket. The man whose political obituary they now realized they had written prematurely had to be given what he was really after. Sam Koenig was delegated to give it to him.

La Guardia insisted that if he ran it must be on his own program, reserving the right to repudiate the party's platform in toto. Koenig agreed, with an understandably spectacular lack of enthusiasm, and on August 30 announced that the Republican County Committee was "proud to nominate the distinguished former President of the Board of Aldermen for Congress from East Harlem." The party's earlier designated candidate, a political nonentity, immediately withdrew, and La Guardia entered the primary uncontested. He would make no more attacks on Governor Miller, a condition for being taken back into the party fold he had agreed to. It didn't matter; he was confident the Democratic candidate would trash Miller quite effectively.

It had played out exactly as the shrewd Little Flower planned from the outset, with the bosses forced to buy him out with the congressional nomination for the sake of Governor Miller. As for Hearst, *his* scheme for the governorship failed miserably. Former governor Al Smith, who hated Hearst for accusing him of allowing the distribution of poisoned milk to New York City children—a charge as ill founded as it was libelous—made known his availability for the Democratic gubernatorial nomination. Tammany Grand Sachem Charlie Murphy spread the word at the Syracuse nominating convention that he favored Hearst, as a sort of consolation prize, but Smith persuaded the delegates otherwise, and Hearst withdrew. Meanwhile, La Guardia was in the third week of his own campaign. Lest there be any doubt that he was running not as a hard-core Republican but as a Progressive, he told the *New York World* (October 1, 1922), "I stand for the Republicanism of Abraham Lincoln, and let me tell you that the average Republican leader east of the Mississippi doesn't know anything more about Abraham Lincoln than Henry Ford knows about the Talmud."

2.

Opposing La Guardia were Henry Frank, a politically unknown lawyer fielded by Tammany Hall, and William Karlin, a respected but colorless labor lawyer nominated by the Socialist and Farmer-Labor parties. The three candidates—an Italian, a Jew, and a Socialist—reflected the character of East Harlem. With more than 250,000 people packed into an area of less than a square mile on New York's Upper East Side, the Twentieth Congressional District—running from 99th Street north to 120th and from the East River to Fifth Avenue—was, after the Lower East Side, the nation's most congested slum. Of the twenty-seven nationalities, each in its own ghetto-like enclave, two predominated: the Italians, surrounding Jefferson Park along the river, and the Jews, concentrated off Fifth Avenue. The Italians were the more numerous, constituting a majority in thirty of the forty-two election districts. However, they were more apathetic than the Jews when it came to political involvement.[6]

To La Guardia headquarters in a vacant store on Madison Avenue near 109th Street flocked on Day One a horde of Italo-Americans who immediately rushed throughout the district ringing doorbells, distributing campaign literature, and for the remainder of the campaign following their *paisano* as he moved by flatbed truck from street corner to street corner speaking—at times ranting—to audiences his troops had prearranged or crowds he quickly drew on the strength of his powerful, albeit high-pitched, voice. At the outset, he promised there would be no mudslinging. He had met his opponents and found them to be "fine gentlemen," he told the *World* on October 1. In a friendly debate before three thousand at the New Star Casino on the subject "Which Party Can Best Defend the Interests of Labor—Republican or Socialist?" he said, "Mr. Karlin is a conservative running on a radical ticket. I am a radical running on a conservative ticket." Admitting that Karlin would "represent to the best of his ability some of the very ideas which I represent," he warned, though, that if Karlan were elected to Congress "he would be alone," whereas La Guardia "shall go there to work with the progressive group represented now by such men as Senators Borah, Johnson, Brookhart and La Follette, all Republicans. As a man, Mr. Karlin is very capable. As a Congressman he would be powerless."[7]

Frank, like Karlin, also promised publicly to avoid personal abuse and to campaign strictly on the issues. Karlin kept to his word. Frank didn't. Fiorello regarded Frank as the more formidable of his two opponents. He had gone into the campaign with the Socialist Party's welfare state platform, which had great appeal to the large number of the Twentieth's Jewish voters who were either Socialist or pro-

Socialist. Also, he was endorsed by the International Ladies' Garment Workers Union, the Amalgamated Clothing Workers of America, and the Central Trades Labor Council of Harlem, a special Italo-American labor committee representing locals in the building trades.

For the most part, La Guardia's platform was the same as Karlin's and the Socialists'. Among the planks were repeal of Prohibition and anti-immigration laws, minimum wage laws, old age pensions, distribution of electricity at cost, legislation to protect indigent new mothers, and stricter laws on child labor and labor injunctions. In hopes of persuading the voters to put aside party labels and compare his brand of progressivism with Karlin's, La Guardia reiterated at meeting after meeting that he was not running on his party's platform, he was running on his own platform. While he managed to bring over some of the Socialists through such argumentation, his appeal for the Italo-Americans was primarily emotional. On October 9, 1922, *Il Pubilo* editorialized, "What better opportunity to create more favorable relations between the sons of the New World and the adopted children of Italian origin in the United States than to have La Guardia in Congress as an exponent of Italian psychology and tradition?" Through the efforts of Marie Fisher, his name and accomplishments were brought to the attention of the Daughters of Italy, an organization of former Sicilian and Calabrian peasants who customarily voted Democratic. The community's professional men—lawyers, teachers, doctors, social workers—were drawn to his liberalism.

In order to induce Italo-Americans to shake off their characteristic apathy when it came to turning out at the polls, well-known outsiders were brought into the district, ranging from the famed Italian movie lover Rudolph Valentino to Mayor Hylan. The Democrat mayor, who had run strong in the Twentieth, told a meeting of the Sons of Columbus at the New Star Casino, "There is no office within the gift of the people that's too good for him. Now that he is running for Congress, I hope that all my friends in Harlem, *regardless of party* [italics added], will vote for him."[8] Hylan's endorsement infuriated his fellow Democrat Frank. Neither did it go down well with Tammany. But there was little they could do about it: Hylan, after all, was Hearst's man. Compounding Frank's problems, he had been losing ground among the Jewish voters, particularly those not committed to the Socialist Party. And his charge that La Guardia was an anti-Semite proved to be as ineffective as it was unfounded.

Prior to the Hylan speech, Fiorello had made the rounds of the district's synagogues dismissing Frank's qualifications in Yiddish— which, he reminded his audiences, his Jewish opponent could not even speak. On October 28, the campaign became downright vicious when Frank openly accused La Guardia of having said at an open meeting, "I would rather cut off my right arm than ask an Italian to vote for anybody but an Italian candidate." La Guardia issued an immediate denial, insisting that Frank, and Frank alone, was now making a "racial-religious appeal for sympathy votes." Next day, Frank made sure that every fellow Jew in the Twentieth received the following postcard:

> The most important office in this country for Judaism is the Congressman. Our flesh and blood are united with our own on the other side of the ocean. Only through our Congressman can we go to their rescue.
>
> There are three candidates who are seeking your vote: One is Karlin, the atheist. The second is the Italian La Guardia, who is a pronounced anti-Semite and Jew-hater.
>
> Be careful how you vote.
>
> Our candidate is Henry Frank, who is a Jew with a Jewish heart, and who does good for us. Therefore it is up to you and your friends to vote for our friend and beloved one, Henry Frank, for Congressman.
>
> (Signed) THE JEWISH COMMITTEE

A few days later Tammany announced that Frank and other Democrats had received a letter from the Black Hand, the secret Italian society, warning them to "get out of La Guardia's way." Though it was just another spurious Tammany kick below the belt, La Guardia realized that such a letter coming days before the election could well signal his defeat. The Jews of the Twentieth did not know he was half-Jewish. Given his name, his appearance, his friends and supporters, and his overall identification, some of the Jews might well believe Frank's charge that he was an anti-Semite.

Seething with rage, Fiorello rushed into the Jewish quarter to denounce Frank's "cowardly attempt to create racial prejudice" against him; the story of the Black Hand letter was "an aspersion upon every voter in the district of foreign extraction . . . a clumsy dying attempt of a beaten candidate to get votes." What's more, he asked, where was Frank when Congressman La Guardia was denouncing the Polish pogroms in 1919? La Guardia then wrote "An Open Letter to Henry Frank"—in Yiddish—in which he challenged Frank "to publicly and openly debate the issues of the campaign, THE DEBATE TO BE CONDUCTED BY YOU AND ME ENTIRELY IN THE YIDDISH LANGUAGE—the subject of the debate to be, 'Who is Best Qualified to Represent All the People of the Twentieth Congressional District.' "

Frank, who knew not a word of the language, responded that he would not demean himself by occupying the same platform with a Bronx carpetbagger and traitor to the Republican Party whose stock in trade was to burlesque the Jews. "A challenge from you, with your well-known anti-Semitic tendencies, to debate in Yiddish is an insult and an affront to the Jewish electorate in our community. You are certainly not qualified to represent the people and you will know it on Election Day when the people send you back, bag and baggage, to your little cottage and sun parlor on University Avenue in the Bronx."

Fiorello rushed into the Jewish quarter shouting, "For Frank to refer to a 'sun parlor' in my house is as low and unmanly an act as a man could resort to. I was compelled to move out of my district and purchase a house with a sun parlor in an effort to save the life of my poor wife." Sensing that Frank had gone too far this time— the family-oriented Jews were sympathetic—La Guardia then ridiculed his opponent for believing that only a Jew could represent Jews in Washington, getting off a Yiddish-flavored crack that would elicit chuckles in the Twentieth for years to come. "After all," he asked of his opponent, "is he looking for a job as a *shamas* [a synagogue custodian] or does he want to be elected Congressman?" Just before election, a Yiddish-language newspaper hailed Fiorello as an old and trusted friend of the Jews, going on to describe him as a Zionist, a student of Jewish history, a foe of anti-Semitism, and one who "speaks Yiddish like a true Jew." As demonstrated by his record in Congress and on the Board of Aldermen, the paper stressed, he was indeed the champion of all humble and persecuted people, no matter their religion or ethnicity.[9]

La Guardia was tense on Election Day, fearful that with Tammany on the scene, and because some of the East Harlem Republican leaders had been out to destroy him politically, many of his ballots might wind up in the sewer or the river. All day, the usually cheerful but now grim-faced candidate toured the district with a patrolman and a plainclothesman (thoughtfully provided by Mayor Hylan), encountering at many of the polling stations acrimonious accusations and counteraccusations, open threats, and near-violence. The count was so close, and thus took so long, it was not until the second day after the polls closed that the final results were announced.

The Jewish assembly districts, which were the smallest and reported earliest, gave Frank what looked like a commanding lead. La Guardia's margin of victory must come from the mixed but predominantly Italo-American Eighteenth and Twentieth districts, which cast 72 percent of the total vote. Both came through, giving him a plurality of 1,220 over Frank. The total count: La Guardia, 8,492; Frank, 8,324; Karlin, 5,260. Fiorello won by a narrow margin of 168 votes. Frank sued for a recount on the grounds of gross fraud, bribery, and intimidation of election officials and party watchers, which Fiorello dismissed as "the perfect zenith of idiocy." The Tammany-controlled Board of Elections cut down his lead, but the House of Representatives, to whom Frank appealed, seated the winner after investigating the charges.

3.

A Democratic resurgence cut the Republican majority in Congress to a fraction of what it had been since 1920. La Guardia attributed this, as well as his victory, to being part of a nationwide repudiation of the Republican Old Guard. Perhaps. More likely, it was the fact that midterm elections invariably favor the party out of power. Compounding the concern of the party was the Harding administration's fear that the agrarian radicals, in concert with the already existing nonpartisan farmer-labor bloc, would hold the balance of power in the Sixty-eighth Congress. It was to this bloc that La Guardia offered himself in the service of its leader, Wisconsin's Senator Robert La Follette. A product of the Populist uprising that had begun in the West during the last part of the previous century, this radical anti-monopolist, now in his fourth consecutive term, was hailed as a latter-day Thomas Jefferson for his determination to destroy privilege and expand economic opportunities for the masses. Like his new friend from East Harlem, La Follette did not question the capitalist system, only the right of the classes to expand their power at the expense of the masses. Though a confirmed pacifist and militant reformer, La Follette was no pie-in-the-sky fantasist. A lifelong professional politician who had built up his own powerful machine in Wisconsin, he took a back seat to no man when it came to legislative tactics.

By 1922, with Teddy Roosevelt dead, Woodrow Wilson in near-vegetative isolation, and William Jennings Bryan (one of the founders of the Populist movement) devoting himself full-time to defending fundamentalism and touting Florida real estate, "Fighting Bob" sought to imbue younger men with the passion of his generation of reformers to keep alive the ideals of the Progressive Era after the demise of the Bull Moose Party. Among those younger men, Fiorello H. La Guardia was the most vocal of some sixty-five congressional colleagues from both major parties dedicated to driving special privilege out of government control and returning it to the people. Being an unknown quantity to most of the veterans of the Era, Fiorello was not assigned to any of the congressional committees whose function it was to draw up programs pertinent to their cause: agriculture, taxation, railroads, the judiciary, and the like.

But he was not to remain long in obscurity. What's more, he knew it. Convinced that these were his kind of people, he returned to New York to tell the Harlem Board of Commerce they were not "wild-eyed radicals" but "serious-minded men who believe that Congress must do something constructive and who have definite ideas of what shall be done."[10] In a December 10 speech in his home district, "The Awakening of the Progressive Spirit in This Country," he reiterated Jefferson's thesis that malignant plutocrats were determined to have the New World emulate the class-ridden Old World, adding that "history is conspiratorial," and the conspirators can be destroyed only through a popular (but *never* anarchical) uprising. As La Guardia saw it, a conspiratorial "go-back movement, deliberately calculating and cruel," was begun with the conclusion of our participation in the First World War. "The war barons—yes, we had and have war barons in this country—the profiteers and the interests controlling monopolies on the necessities of life, were busy getting control of State and National governments." Their purpose? To turn the hands of the economic and political clock back to McKinley Republicanism.

But, La Guardia reassured his audience, thanks to the bloc with which he was now allied, "the awakening of the progressive spirit throughout the country" was in fact "the arousing of a united protest against conditions which [had] become intolerable." Exploitation, the result of favored legislation; poverty, the result of the greed of monopolies; dissatisfaction, the result of privileged government—all had "resulted in the alliance between farmers, industrial producers, the believers in democracy, and the true lovers of America." In the land of plenty, he went on—"richest in the world in national resources, with less density of population than any other country, producing enough food not only to feed itself, but a quarter of the world"—a large part of the population, though working and producing, still lacked "proper and sufficient nourishment [and] proper and cheerful living accommodations."

Obviously there was "something wrong with its government, which must be righted and corrected without delay." The Progressive group in the next Congress, he vowed, had "not only the desire to do good, but the absolute power to do it." The solution, as he saw it, was not socialization of the means of production and exchange but implementation of the Populist program to give the government back to the people and then have the state help only those who couldn't help themselves. He promised to work with the Progressives to secure direct primaries for all offices up to the presidency, abolish the electoral college so that the majority would rule, and create a better understanding and close cooperation between farmers and urbanites by maintaining a decent price for food without raising the cost of living—which he insisted could be accomplished by restricting such "parasitical intermediaries" as "banks, loans, railroads, profiteering, and speculating." Finally, La Guardia promised, he and his colleagues would fight for tax relief for low-income groups, a child labor law, and government control of all fuel.[11]

The man who had supported the League of Nations and European cooperation in the maintenance of, hopefully, perpetual peace was now a pacifist/isolationist in the La Follette mode: Europe's affairs were not America's affairs. Though empathizing with the westerners on such demands as government warehouses for agricultural produce and farm subsidies, he was essentially an urban reformer. Instead of speaking out on problems that remained far west of the Hudson River while waiting for the new Congress to convene, he used the time to help the Amalgamated Clothing Workers of America win recognition in Buffalo for their union, fight for maintenance of rent controls in New York City and repeal of the Knight-Adler transit law, and propose that the islands in the East River be converted into public parks.[12] He also played a prominent role in the strike against meat packers that resulted in the reduction of price by five to ten cents a pound. "Call me a radical, if you will, call me anything," he told reporters, "but when there are people right in my own district who are working day and night and can't earn enough for their families to eat, something is wrong. Such conditions should not exist and they are conditions I am determined to change."[13]

Thus did Fiorello add a new dimension to the La Follette movement: viewing the nation through the lenses of its big cities, in particular its slums, with himself a link between the East and the West. In the process, his own recognition in the Progressive movement was rapidly escalating. When, on February 24, 1923, some three hundred Republican women, many of them Italo-Americans, tendered a banquet in his honor at the Hotel Pennsylvania, the main speaker, Senator Smith Brookhart, a close ally of La Follette, promised that with eastern allies like La Guardia in Congress there would be a "people's bloc" to thwart the schemes of "the tobacco bloc, the steel bloc . . . the Wall Street bloc." All the speakers predicted La Guardia's term in Congress would see the enactment of much Progressive legislation. Fiorello wrote enthusiastically to La Follette, "I am firmly convinced that there will be quite a rush to get on the Progressive band-wagon at the next session of Congress."[14]

La Guardia was quickly emerging as a national populist figure. On March 2, 1923, he warned President Harding that unless the administration and its Congress approved the La Follette program, "a Progressive [third-party] ticket might be put in the field, as in 1912," the allusion being to the Roosevelt-led Bull Moose Party, which split the Republican vote and put a Democrat in the White House. Meanwhile, until Congress convened, he continued to make headlines by addressing himself to issues beyond the bounds of the Twentieth. Numerous press interviews, along with a veritable blizzard of messages to government figures, revealed that even before taking his seat in the Sixty-eighth Congress, Fiorello was taking on his party's Old Guard.

Unwilling to be elliptical, he came right out and named names, as when he told one reporter, "Secretary of War Weeks is forever making war. Pacifism is patriotism." He wrote to Colonel C. R. Forbes, director of the U.S. Veterans Bureau, "Perhaps if we had less filing, less officials, less examinations disabled veterans might fare better. . . . It's a damned shame." House majority floor leader Frank W. Mondell received a scathing letter attacking a proposed immigration bill as "DISCRIMINATORY AGAINST JEWS AND ITALIANS." The Army Air Service was excoriated for the expense—and stupidity—of a recent test conducted off Cape Hatteras: "We all knew that a bomb dropped from the air would sink a battleship." Dozens of letters went flying off to the White House concerning deportation cases. He even threatened the Supreme Court that on the day Congress convened he would introduce a bill curbing its power to declare social welfare legislation unconstitutional. Though all were released to the press, the letters rarely elicited a reply (as was the case with the Harding "warning"), and those few that came in were never to his satisfaction. He didn't care. His intent was to lay down a fusillade to discredit the politics of President Harding's "normalcy."[15] Though up to his eyelashes with that epistolary bombardment of the Harding administration, heralding the coming of a necessary third party, playing an active role in municipal affairs, and corresponding with his western colleagues, La Guardia never for a moment ignored his constituents in the Twentieth. A well-oiled personal machine would come later; for now, he ran the district with the politically correct help of one Italo-American and one Jewish-American.

When the Sixty-eighth Congress convened in December 1923, four months into the Coolidge presidency, Fiorello, along with John M. Nelson of Wisconsin and Roy O. Woodruff of Michigan, was an acknowledged spokesman of the House's twenty-three midwestern insurgent Republicans (most of them from Michigan and Wisconsin).* They immediately announced their program for populist reform. But first on their agenda was to alter the House rules under which the Old Guard, through the Speaker, majority leader, and

---

*Coolidge succeeded to the presidency that year when Harding, while on a fishing trip to Alaska, died under circumstances that have never been definitively resolved.

chairmen of the Rules and Steering committees, could kill legislation they didn't like merely by bottling it up in committee. The Progressives demanded a change that would empower the floor to discharge a bill from committee if a hundred representatives voted it. Their strategy was to hold up election of a Republican Speaker of the House until the demand was met.

After two days of futile balloting, majority leader Nicholas Longworth conceded the impossibility of organizing the House without the support of the insurgents. After conferring with La Guardia and his two colleagues, a compromise was worked out: The old rules would be in effect for thirty days, after which there would be an open debate on proposed changes. Frederick H. Gillett was elected Speaker. After the thirty days, following a long debate, La Guardia and his colleagues had to admit failure. La Guardia, who was viewed as the insurgents' leader (he was certainly their most vocal and abrasive torchbearer), was denied a seat he wanted on the Judiciary Committee. By way of punishment, he was put on the insignificant Committee on the Post Office and Poor Roads. The reactionaries had succeeding in arrogating to themselves total control of the major committees.[16]

When the House finally got down to business, they defeated the Progressive bloc's program: judicial reform, welfare legislation, direct presidential primaries, et al. Even modifying Prohibition, however slightly, was turned down (though the members did not turn down the celebratory libations). For Fiorello the most horrendous bill of the Sixty-eighth Congress was the Johnson-Reed Act, which drastically curtailed immigration and assigned higher quotas to immigrants from Anglo-Saxon countries. Equally outrageous was Treasury Secretary Andrew Mellon's tax plan, that which favored higher incomes, and President Coolidge's veto of the Bonus Bill. (These issues will be dealt with in the next chapter.)

On March 2, 1924, the *New York Times* headlined its coverage of a speech Fiorello gave at the International Synagogue in his district "La Guardia Reveals New National Plot." The plot: Four pillars of the Republican Party—Henry Ford, Frank Munsey, Andrew Mellon, and Interior Secretary Edward Doheny—were conspiring to divide the universe four ways. Ford would take industry, Munsey the newspapers, Mellon the finances, and Doheny the natural resources. La Guardia insisted "it was all plotted," just as the Ku Klux Klan was plotting the passage of the proposed Johnson-Reed Bill to keep out Jewish and Italian immigrants. Then, praising those congressmen who opposed the bill, he promised, "Whether St. Peter is a *goy* or a Roman Catholic, he'll let them into heaven for that!" To his constituents, their Little Flower was a hero. To party regulars, he was a traitor.

In order to build up independent organizational strength, La Guardia okayed formation of the Twentieth's Eighteenth Assembly District Men's Progressive Club to work for him and La Follette. Such were his differences with his party, he refused to attend the Cleveland convention in June, where Coolidge was nominated as a matter of course. On June 15, Fiorello tossed an SRO audience at the New Star Casino one of his typical zingers: "Photographs were transmitted from the Cleveland Convention by telephone, but it would seem that the platform was written in long hand with a quill pen."[17]

The following week, he watched the Democratic convention at New York's Madison Square Garden all but self-destruct over Prohibition, fundamentalism, xenophobia, and the cult of big business, unable to come up with a nominee through an incredible 102 ballots. Out of sheer exasperation, if not terminal exhaustion, they settled on John W. Davis, a New York corporate lawyer who represented such financial titans as J. P. Morgan. On the Fourth of July weekend La Guardia went to Cleveland for the Conference for Progressive Political Action, at which La Follette won that third party's nomination by acclamation. As his running mate he chose Democratic insurgent Senator Burton K. Wheeler, who had bolted his party after Davis's nomination because he could not "represent any candidate representing the House of Morgan."

When La Guardia's turn came to speak, he predicted victory for their candidate and concluded with what became his signature epigram: "I would rather be right than regular." In fact, Fiorello hoped to be both regular *and* right. He did not follow La Follette in bolting the Republican Party at this time, as there was no independent organization he could join. La Follette, over opposition from the Socialists, opposed the CPPA's fielding a full slate of candidates. What historians refer to as the Progressive Party was actually a coalition of Socialists, insurgents from the two major parties, trade unionists, and old-time reformers committed only to the La Follette–Wheeler ticket.[18]

As late as the end of July, though cochairman of the La Follette campaign in the East, La Guardia had not yet said whether he would seek reelection as a Republican or as an independent. The Socialist Party, which was planning to place La Follette at the head of its line on the ballot, promised Fiorello the 1924 nomination for the House—on condition that he refuse to enter the Republican primary. Sam Koenig, on the other hand, assured him of the party's support for a second term—if he came out for Coolidge. On August 10 he made his decision, which the *New York Times* announced in a front-page headline: "La Guardia Bolts Republican Party." "Desirable and comfortable as a [Republican] party nomination may be," Fiorello wrote Koenig, he could not "sacrifice principle for the sake of a party nomination or anything else." Believing that the Republican Party platform made "no appeal to the hope of the people whom I represent," he could not "conscientiously pledge myself to support that platform and to limit my legislative activities within the narrow confines of that document." Admitting the obvious—that he "did not support the reactionary attitude of the Republican majority" while in Congress—he added, "If honest independence of action in the fulfillment of a legislator's duty in his representative capacity disqualifies a candidate and prevents his renomination, on that too I am ready to go before the people of the Twentieth Congressional District." As to whom he would support for president of the United States, "I beg to state that the platform adopted by the Conference for Progressive Political Action contains an economic and political program which comes nearer fitting our present time and conditions than any platform presented to the voters of this country since 1912, when the late Theodore Roosevelt set the example of righteousness rather than regularity. I shall therefore support the CPPA platform and the candidacy of Robert M. La Follette for President."[19]

The Republican nomination for the Twentieth went to Fiorello's friend Isaac Siegel, who had carried the district in 1918 and 1920. Drafted by the Republicans to step down from the bench and seek his old seat, Siegel told his wife, "Damnation! You know I don't want to run against the Major but someone has to put up a fight against this confounded third party."[20] Henry Frank was again Tammany's choice. The next day (August 12, 1924), as reported in the *Times*, the American Labor Party—a New York City umbrella group of Socialists, single-taxers, trade unionists, and Farmer-Laborites—convened and endorsed by acclamation the New York Socialist ticket and nominated La Follette, Wheeler, and La Guardia. But since it had no place on the ballot, Fiorello's name was entered on the Socialist line, even though the party's decision to support a non-Socialist was unprecedented. Admittedly, La Guardia courted Marxist support, but only because he needed it. The Socialist banner was not the one he cared to march under. For the moment, he had entered into an alliance of conscience and expediency. He opted for the Liberty Bell, the emblem of Western reform, whose line on the ballot also carried his name.

4.

La Guardia spent nearly four thousand dollars—a goodly sum for a candidate in a poverty-ridden district with no organized party support—donated by trade unions, fraternal groups, and individuals, mostly a dollar here, a dollar there. It covered the expenses of campaign paraphernalia (posters, displays, etc.) and the rental for headquarters in a vacant store on the corner of Madison Avenue and 106th Street. Speakers, poll watchers, doorbell ringers, secretaries, and solicitors donated their service gratis. Included were such old out-of-the-district friends as sculptor Attilio Piccirilli and August Bellanca, the latter a rapidly rising eminence in the Amalgamated Clothing Workers of America. Running the headquarters was the faithful and efficient Marie Fisher. Fiorello was attacked by mainstream Republicans, but it meant little to him and even less to his East Harlem constituency. (Of course, La Guardia could not have foreseen his return to the GOP fold two years down the road, after the Progressive movement collapsed.)

While Fiorello did not yet have a well-oiled political machine, he had the nucleus of one in the Eighteenth Assembly District Men's Progressive Club. Predominantly Italo-American—its literature was in Italian—the club included some politically active Jews. What soon evolved into the F. H. La Guardia Political Club was almost single-handedly created by a twenty-two-year-old Harlem-born Italo-American who under La Guardia's mentorship would emerge as leader of East Harlem and one of the city's most colorful, most controversial politicians: Vito "Marco" Marcantonio.

The two had met three years previously when Fiorello, then president of the Board of Aldermen, addressed a student assembly at De

Witt Clinton High School, where Marcantonio, a fervent radical Socialist, was a student activist. As head of the Tenants' League in Harlem, he joined the La Guardia reelection campaign when it won the Socialist Party's endorsement. One of his first undertakings was to organize a corps of young fellow militants, the *Gibboni*. (After winning a baseball game, the club earned the reputation of being *campioni* ["champions"], but on a subsequent occasion some kibitzer said they looked more like *gibboni* [gibbons, or "apes"], and the highly amused crew adopted the name.)[21]

Like Fiorello, who came to look upon him as a surrogate son, Marcantonio was a short, tough polemicist who resented privilege and was preternaturally ambitious. Also like the man who would in time take him into his law firm as clerk, foster his advancement over the opposition of the other partners, and launch him on a political career that included succeeding La Guardia in representing the Twentieth in Congress, young Vito spoke up for the underprivileged people like himself, knew Yiddish and Italian (he would learn Spanish when the Puerto Ricans flooded into his district), and was a natural-born speaker with a gift for articulation and rhetoric "and a natural-born leader to whom the common people were attracted because they knew he was one of them but only smarter."[22]

While Congress was not in session, La Guardia would be back in his district speaking throughout the day and into the night translating the CPPA Cleveland platform into the brand of progressivism those who believed in him could understand in the context of their own immediate concerns. A master of the dramatic effect, often he would thrust the microphone aside and shout aloud in his high-pitched voice, "My speech to you tonight is . . . a crusade to save the Republic, a war, if you please, against privilege, against legalized exploitation." Often he would launch into the trust-busting mode, a sort of Teddy Roosevelt *redivivus*, but in straightforward terms the voters of his district could appreciate: "If you don't like the sodas on the corner, you can go to the other corner and pay less, but if you don't like the gas, you've got to buy it anyway."

The master of the metaphor was also a pioneer in the use of visual aids. One day there appeared in the window of his dingy headquarters the "La Guardia Exhibit": a cut of meat symbolizing his opposition to the meat packers, a lump of coal to remind his constituents of how he'd fought the fuel monopolies, and a beer stein to remind them of his demand for real beer, instead of the Prohibition-mandated, barely potable "near beer." Simultaneously a huge billboard was erected on the street corner with the legend "Who wants to keep La Guardia out of Congress?" On successive days the names of J. P. Morgan & Co., the Coal Barons, Andrew W. Mellon, and others of similar bent were chalked in. When the legend "Who wants to keep La Guardia *in* [author's italics added] Congress?" was added, such names as the American Federation of Labor, the Immigrants Protective Association, the Consumer's League, and the Labor Committee of the Conference for Progressive Political Action were chalked in. There was also a campaign song, sung up and down the streets of the district, more often than not by choruses of up to 150 people accompanied by ukuleles, guitars, and mandolins, which while not of Tin Pan Alley caliber was nevertheless effective: "Fiorello H. La Guardia, / Harlem needs a man like you in Congress; / You voted for the Soldier's Bonus, / Helped the Immigrant, / And fought in Congress for us! . . . With a record like yours, / Harlem needs you!"[23]

Though the Socialist vote in the Twentieth was primarily Jewish, an even larger number of Jews were either Democrats or Republicans or simply voted for a Jewish candidate. Fiorello's opponents were both Jewish and both proven vote-getters. As he had in 1916, Fiorello presented himself to the district's west side as a champion of the Jews. Had anyone, he asked rhetorically, fought with greater fervor against immigration restrictions that favored Europe's Anglo-Saxons? Was anyone more critical of that arch anti-Semite Henry Ford, the American who did more than any man to popularize that vicious forgery *The Protocols of the Elders of Zion*, Czarist Russia's "documented proof" that the Jews were out to dominate the world? These were the themes of La Guardia's many appearances throughout the Jewish quarter, complemented by a display in his headquarters of copies of his congressional speeches favoring Jewish immigration, along with laudatory editorials in the Jewish press.

Accused by his opponents of being a carpetbagger (he still lived in the Bronx), La Guardia described how he had served the cause of the hyphenates while in Congress. Charged with being absent from a meeting memorializing war veterans at a ceremony in the Italian quarter, he had the local American Legion post produce newspaper photographs proving he had indeed attended. When "the dangerous radical" La Follette's "disloyalty" for having opposed

America's entering the war was thrown in his face, La Guardia's brilliant war record was recalled. In any event, East Harlem was pacifistic, and, what's more, the Twentieth was a slum for which the bonanza of the postwar boom and Jazz Age 1920s was mythic. What had *they* to fear from radicalism?

Just over half of the eligible voters nationwide went to the polls. Coolidge won overwhelmingly with 15,275,003 votes to 8,385,586 for Davis and 4,826,471 for La Follette, who carried only his home state of Wisconsin. Not only was his national campaign poorly planned and underfunded, it was a disorganized mess. A mishmash of Marxists, single-taxers, vegetarians, theophists, and radicals of all persuasions gathered under La Follette emblems to preach their diverse philosophies.[24] By contrast, the Twentieth gave La Guardia the greatest margin of victory it ever would.

With a goodly share of just about every political, philosophical, and ethnic group in his corner except the most parochial Democrats and his own hidebound fellow Republicans, his win was almost predictable. The final vote was 10,756 for Fiorello, 7,141 for Frank, and 7,099 for Siegel. Not only did La Guardia do better in the Italo-American wards than he had in 1912, but, of greater consequence, the Jewish wards, which he had failed to carry that first time out, now gave him decided pluralities in five of the six assembly districts; the sixth went for Siegel, but by a plurality of less than a hundred votes.[25]

The Republican sweep of Congress gave them a majority of four in the Senate and forty-seven in the House, leaving the Progressives holding the balance of power in the upper chamber but not in the lower. The lineup in the House was now 241 Republicans, 188 Democrats, 3 Farmer-Laborites, and 2 Socialists—one of them La Guardia. When he insisted on being listed as a Progressive, the House clerk—a Republican—put him down as a Socialist. His successful campaign ended on a La Guardian note, when he sued the arch-Republican *New York Tribune* for *six cents* for libeling him with the charges of "electioneering in a battered, rusty, old automobile" and going around "without a collar." The *Tribune* agreed to settle out of court, but Fiorello insisted on having a verdict officially recorded: "I know this does not mean a damn thing, but it is my only chance to get a crack at them."[26]

CHAPTER TWELVE

"I am doomed to live in a hopeless minority for most of my legislative days"

1.

That the nation's greatest mayor was also one of the nation's greatest congressmen seems to be little known except by historians of the Jazz Age, which extended over his entire postwar career in the House. The headlines he made and the mirth he raised in registering opposition to odious legislation served a shrewdly calculated objective: to publicly identify censoriously, and thereby hopefully humiliate, the bigots, racists, moral cretins, and egregious hypocrites in Congress to whom this legislation was deemed to be Received Wisdom. Because so many of his battles extended over two or more terms, we shall treat his five-term "second" congressional career by topic instead of chronologically.

Both on and off the House floor Fiorello was at times exasperating, at times irritating, at times seemingly bent not so much on defending an attitude as grabbing a headline, at times downright hilarious, at times eloquently moving. Often his well-publicized antics outdid those of such Jazz Age icons as, say, professional gold-digger Peggy Hopkins Joyce and her libido-driven hijinks, silent screen star Mabel Normand and her drug-driven hijinks, "Public Enemy Number One" Al Capone and his crime-driven hijinks, author and chronicler of the age F. Scott Fitzgerald and his wife Zelda's alcohol-driven hijinks—indeed, the entire class of tabloid headliners on whom the nation's press depended for elevated circulation, and on whose hijinks the average readers fed like vultures dining on the choicest carrion. But with Fiorello, there was a difference. His hijinks were motivated by an obsessive determination to protect the little people against the Interests. At times he played the gadfly, the clown, or the stand-up comic, often with a nasty edge. Fellow legislators laughed either with him or at him, unless they failed to get his point—or chose to miss it.

For example, the obsession with Anglo-Saxon superiority was a major component of the *Zeitgeist* of the times. When the *New York World* asked each member of New York's congressional legislation to trace his descent, La Guardia airily showed his contempt for such matters by responding, "I have no family tree. The only member of my family who has is my dog Yank [a German shepherd]. He is the son of Doughboy, who was the son of Siegfried, who was the son of Tannhauser, who was the son of Wotan. It's a distinguished family tree, to be sure—but after all he's only a son of a bitch."[1]

Fiorello was a favorite of the journalists who covered Capitol Hill, what with his dash, color, and temperament complemented by a round, full face atop a round, full, but very short body, a habit of dashing instead of walking, and a falsetto voice that could be heard above the wildest din. While colleagues, even Democrats, had a portrait of President Coolidge on the walls of their offices, a picture of Rudolph Valentino graced the wall of Room 150 of the House Office Building, the domain of Congressman Fiorello La Guardia, where he could often be found—more often than not simultaneously—dictating correspondence, posing for photographers, flapping his hands as if semaphoring some arcane message while explaining something in Italian or Yiddish to a visiting constituent, hastily dashing off an article for publication or a radio talk, mimicking mercilessly such targets of his scorn as Coolidge, Treasury Secretary Andrew W. Mellon, Henry Ford, or those of his colleagues he particularly detested, and disposing hastily of his mail with terse observations like "Bunk!" or, if they were appeals from religious groups, "Nice boy, Jesus!" [2]

When it came to a social life, he showed a calculated disrespect for such prerogatives of his official position as White House invitations (he gave them to page boys as souvenirs) and sedulously avoided the Washington cocktail and official dinner party circuits, which he accused of "ruining more Congressmen than anything else." He preferred to take in a movie or enjoy an informal dinner, accompanied by serious but lively conversation, with friends, who included a few newspapermen and fellow Progressive lawmakers. Notable among the latter was his roommate, Minnesota's Ole J. Kvale, an ordained Lutheran minister who defeated Andrew J. Volstead (author of the Eighteenth "Prohibition" Amendment) in 1922. But even these activities were kept to a minimum. Fiorello was a workaholic, preparing for congressional sessions even on Sunday like a student cramming for finals. Unlike the student, though, he could hardly wait to get to the business at hand. The moment the convening gong was sounded, he could be seen scurrying down the House corridors on his short legs; more often than not, he was the first into the chamber and the last to leave.[3]

Thanks to an innate genius for trigger-fast, often mordant repartee, he invariably left an opponent reeling like a boxer who's been given the decisive punch and cannot for one brief moment decide whether to try fleeing for his life or simply falling in a heap on the canvas. Like the time he had a go at handsome, narcissistic Otis T. Wingo, hailed (especially by himself) as the Adonis of Arkansas, over an appropriation for a federal office building in New York City:

LA GUARDIA: Apparently, you know nothing about the bill.

WINGO: Yes, I know about that bill. . . . They came in here and wanted $385,000 for the adornment of the façade. Does the gentleman from New York know what a façade is?

LA GUARDIA: Of course he does. Does the gentleman from Arkansas?

WINGO: Yes. That is the same thing to a building that a snout is to a hog. It is the front part of it. And a pork eater ought to know what the façade is.

LA GUARDIA: If the gentleman from Arkansas were less interested in his own façade and more in the inside of his head, he would be a better legislator.

As the House broke into laughter, the ensuing exchange between the enraged, wild-swinging Arkansan and the enraging, counter-punching New Yorker became so "ungentlemanly" it was expunged from the *Congressional Record*.[4]

Dramas such as this—and there were many—went down well with the two groups La Guardia always played to, since they comprised the majority of his admirers on the Hill: the Visitors' Gallery and the Press Gallery. But a price had to be paid. For Fiorello, it was not until 1926, when he returned to the Republican Party, that he was given a seat on a reasonably important committee, that on alcoholic traffic. Running true to form, he used it to censure the Coolidge administration, thus further alienating him from his party's leaders. With the Progressive bloc, which had lost two years previously what little power it once enjoyed, La Guardia was in agreement only on legislation of an economic nature. When it came to two of his primary targets, immigration restrictions and Prohibition, these rural members from the South and West voted against him. "I am doomed to live in a hopeless minority for most of my legislative days," he once said, his tone one of pride tempered by more than a dash of sorrow.

La Guardia mastered a number of areas. As one of the most garrulous of all representatives, he introduced an exhaustive—one might say, exhausting—cornucopia of amendments, resolutions, and objections on pending bills plus a few bills of his own on a broad variety of topics. In addition, he elected himself an investigative committee of one, a kind of roving member-at-large, which saw him probing such disparate issues as New York speakeasies, Pennsylvania coal strikes, Chicago's Beef Trust, even the accidental sinking of a submarine off Cape Cod.

Of all the issues La Guardia felt most committed to, the primary one involved a sociopolitical policy dating to the nineteenth century that favored the interests of native inhabitants over those of immigrants. (In treating with this subject it is necessary to abandon as an exercise in futility the possibility of convincing nativists that the only *true* native Americans are the Native Americans.) Complementing the activities of the Ku Klux Klan were learned men—scientists and educators—who preached that only the Nordic race, or Anglo-Saxons, had made viable contributions to Western civilization. The so-called Nordic craze peaked around the time La Guardia returned to Congress in 1923. The nation had seen an unrestricted immigration of thirty-five million predominantly non-Nordics from Southern and Eastern Europe. Congress decided it was time for the Statue of Liberty to, in a sense, turn her back. Jumping into the debate, Fiorello accused all "Anglo-Saxon-on-the-brain" colleagues of suffering mental retardation and went on to remind them the Nordics were barbarians when the Romans were in England "civilizing that country."[5]

An earlier law of 1921, based on the 1910 census, had allowed for larger quotas. A bill introduced by Congressman Albert Johnson of Washington, chairman of the House Immigration Committee, called for lowering the quotas drastically by basing them on the 1890 census, which was before the great mass immigration, when newcomers constituted a much smaller minority of the overall population. This slashed Italian, Jewish, Slavic, and Greek immigration by as much as 90 percent, with 85 percent of the quotas going to the Nordics from Western and Northern Europe. For more than two decades an aggregation of Yankee blue bloods, disillusioned Populists and Progressives, labor leaders, and sociologists, their attitudes intensified by the Klan, the so-called Red Scare, and Henry Ford's anti-Semitic crusade, suffered an irrational fear. This was that a land that had been (or so they believed) free of the vice and crime and slums and inebriates that to them defined the non-Nordic mind-set was about to fall victim to the shock troops of the pope and that insidious bugaboo the Great International Jewish Conspiracy. Their only salvation, as they saw it, lay in keeping the new immigrants out.

La Guardia knew from the outset that fighting the Johnson Bill was futile, but fight it he must. He introduced amendments and resolutions in hopes of at least vitiating its overall effect. All of them, like his proposal to change the quota year used as a yardstick from 1890 to 1910, which would reflect the greater number of naturalized immigrants, were voted down. Still, he succeeded in drumming up support from, in addition to Jewish and Italo-American organizations, such truly Nordic groups as the United Swedish Party, the Sons of Norway, the Steuben Society, the American Irish Republican League, and various Lutheran religious groups. But to no avail.[6]

What particularly rankled La Guardia was that not one of the leading Progressives voted against the bill, which, after being joined with the similar Reed Bill in the Senate, was signed by President

Coolidge, himself a proud Nordic, on May 26, 1924. In a speech before the Brooklyn Jewish Center two months previously, La Guardia admitted that "this piece of Ku Klux Klanism" would surely pass, but dignity demanded that he condemn it.[7] He spoke out because he wanted the bill's proponents to articulate their prejudices openly so that they could be placed in the *Congressional Record* for everyone to see and for posterity to judge. While he might not beat back his adversaries in the congressional arena, he hoped at least to humiliate them in the public arena.

Ever the optimist, La Guardia never abandoned hope that in time the nation would revert to its "melting pot" tradition. He persistently introduced and reintroduced legislation and amendments to the proposals of other legislation dealing with the "Nordic business," in the process heckling the Nordic-oriented Coolidge administration. Not that he anticipated success. "They serve for educational purposes," he explained to one interviewer. "The function of a progressive is to keep on protesting until things get so bad that a reactionary demands reform."[8] What he didn't tell the interviewer—perhaps it was a given among all who knew him either personally or by reputation—was that the Little Flower had a talent for dramatizing the issues that were among his highest priorities.

Like doing away with Prohibition.

2.

In the summer of 1919, during the bitter floor fight over the Eighteenth Amendment, La Guardia prophesied that it would "create contempt and disregard for law all over the country."[9] It created much more: a growth industry in bootlegging, gangsterism, the illicit manufacture of real beer (as distinct from the legal "near beer" with its much lower alcohol content), and resultant street wars. On the floor of the House and in the appropriate committee chambers, at public meetings, and in the newspapers, he hammered away incessantly at the imbecility, as well as the unenforceability, of a law that only a few wished to see perpetuated. La Guardia not only attacked the law verbally, he sought to do so legislatively. For example, he demanded huge sums for the Prohibition Bureau, once going so far as to propose an increase in annual appropriation from less than twelve million dollars to three hundred million—to prove the utter futility of enforcement. He expected to be voted down, as indeed he was. He merely wanted to show the nation what the law's proponents either could not or would not see: In a misguided attempt to legislate morality, there was no amount of money and no staff large enough to police a nation that, the "drys" and the gangsters always excepted, stood squarely behind the "wets."[10]

Trying to reform personal habits by legal proscription was not the only aspect to Prohibition that lay at the root of La Guardia's contempt for its proponents, the drys, whom he looked upon as fools and bigots as well as hypocrites "who voted dry and lived wet." There was the issue of governmental corruption by moneyed interests. "Gentlemen," he asked the House in February 1925, "what is the use of closing our eyes to the existing conditions? The importation of liquor into this country is of such magnitude, it comes in such enormous quantities, involving the use of a fleet of steamships, involving enormous banking operations, involving hundreds of millions of dollars, that it could not carry on without the knowledge if not the connivance of the authorities entrusted with the enforcement of the law." He was quick to seize upon the fact that Prohibition involved class and economic issues. Atlantic luxury liners, he told the House, were involved in rum-running, delivering the finest European liquors to New York patrons who had money enough to pay the going prices.

Fiorello's attacks were getting on the nerves of Grant M. Hudson of Michigan, chairman of the House Committee on Alcoholic Liquor Traffic, of which the gentleman from East Harlem was the single "wet." On June 17, 1926, outraged by his claim that the gangsters were the only ones to share the Prohibitionists' enthusiasm for the Volstead Act, Hudson ordered him to "behave." Said La Guardia in the parliamentary third person, "The gentleman is sore because I have shown how his sacred Prohibition law is being violated." Insisted Hudson impatiently, "I am not irritated. Good God, if you want to get drunk every day, go and do it. I do not know personally that the dry laws are being violated." Shouted Fiorello, "Then go learn something! You are probably the only man in the United States who would make such a statement."

He then staged an attention-grabbing dog-and-pony show to demonstrate how easy it was to brew "legal" beer and, by extension, how stupid the law prohibiting its manufacture was. In his House office, before some forty photographers and reporters and an ex-brewer,

La Guardia would combine two legal drinks to create one illegal drink. Announcing grandiloquently, "Gentlemen, we are about to begin. You needn't feel anxious. There will be at least a little for all of us," the ad hoc East Harlem brewmeister took from a pail a well-iced bottle of near beer (Budweiser), which contained one half of 1 percent alcohol, and one bottle of malt tonic, which contained 3.75 percent alcohol. Next, he poured a water glass two-thirds full with the malt, topped it off with the legal Budweiser, and stirred with a pencil. A rich, dark foam rose to the rim and overflowed to the carpet. The result "was beer," exulted the Associated Press reporter. The ex-brewer testified, "It tastes delightful." But there was more. Fiorello announced, "Now I'll make Pilsner," and added a pinch of salt. Other refinements produced a Würzburger and something "reminiscent of stout." The photographers alternated between sipping the brew and snapping away with their cameras. A good time was had by all, especially La Guardia, less because he had grabbed yet another slew of headlines—for him, that was no novelty—than because he had proved a point.

Because the farce was staged practically within sight of the national headquarters of the Anti-Saloon League, its director, Wayne B. Wheeler, demanded legal action against the congressman. But General Lincoln C. Andrews, the nation's chief Prohibition law enforcement officer, refused to initiate proceedings, ostensibly on the grounds that Fiorello's brew was so awful it would make people sick before it could make them inebriated. In fact, Andrews was determined to avoid giving La Guardia a chance to appear in court not only as defendant but as defendant's legal counsel as well.

In Albany, the New York Prohibition unit threatened arrest for anyone who used the "La Guardia formula" in the state. Wanting the publicity of being jailed, Forello showed up at a drugstore in his home district and gave a repeat performance. Surrounded by a mob of neighbors, newsmen, and photographers, even a motion-picture photographer, he challenged the cop on the beat to arrest him. The officer declined on the grounds that he guessed "that's a job for a Prohibition agent." The agent in charge of the New York office followed General Andrews's line, insisting that if La Guardia's illegal brew violated anything, it was the Pure Food and Drug statutes. That department decided to pretend the whole exhibition had never taken place.[11]

Much as he enjoyed the mirth he had created, La Guardia's tomfoolery posed a logical thesis: if illegal beer (2.75 percent alcohol)—whose domestic manufacture was the core of Prohibition's greatest evil, the gang wars—could be blended from two legally acquired beverages, then why not amend the Volstead Act to allow people to get from one bottle what they got less conveniently from two and, in the process, put the mobsters out of business and thus reduce the crime rate? He introduced an amendment to that effect, warning that the only alternative was a brewery in every American home and place of business. *New York Daily Graphic*'s editor Emile Gauvreau wired him, "Whole staff trying experiment. Remarkable results." Drugstores reported a run on malt tonic. The amendment was defeated.[12]

That didn't slow down Fiorello. He now exchanged the hat of brew master for that of professor of geography and public administration. On June 26, 1926, during a debate over an appropriation bill for the Prohibition Bureau, he put on another show-and-tell. Using a large colored map of the United States, he illustrated the complete ineffectiveness, let alone impossibility, of policing close to eighteen thousand miles of seacoast and land borders to interdict illegal importation of alcoholic products from abroad. Then he lectured the House on how many agents were available: twenty-four for the nearly thousand-mile Mexican border, ten for the four hundred miles of the Gulf Coast, twenty-five for Florida's 950-mile peninsula, seven for the 890 miles that separated southern Georgia from Philadelphia—and so on around the map until he had completed the point he was trying to make: "If we are to have Prohibition, enforce the law." The lecture left his colleagues unimpressed; when he proposed to increase the bureau's staff from around 2,000 to 250,000, that, too, was voted down.[13]

La Guardia, meanwhile, had donned yet another symbolic hat—that of sleuth. Based on information forwarded by well-placed people throughout the country, and after poring over official but seldom referred-to documents, he charged that along with totally ignoring geographical considerations, congressional obtuseness, and the American public's drinking habits, the Volstead Act had spawned a band of corrupt federal officers. There is little doubt that he went over the top in insinuating that the Treasury Department, which was in charge of enforcing Prohibition, was slipshod in performance be-

cause Secretary Mellon—another favorite La Guardia target—was
"formerly a whisky distiller himself" and his chief lieutenant, General
Andrews, was a "typical cringing officeholder seeking to please his
boss."[14]

However, he came closer to the truth when he assumed the role
of prosecutor, drawing up legal arguments in three cases, the first of
which he was given a half-hour to present on the floor of the House on
March 24, 1926. It involved a well-known bootlegger, his previously
married wife, and one of the Justice Department's top investigators,
and it all sounded like some present-day TV movie-of-the-week on the
Roaring Twenties. It seems that a few years earlier a midwestern whiskey baron named George Demus had been apprehended by the Justice Department's top Prohibition enforcement officer, Franklin L.
Dodge. While Demus was sitting in jail, according to La Guardia's
brief, Dodge confiscated some two hundred thousand dollars' worth
of the confiscated whiskey for himself, then left the Justice Department and set up housekeeping in another state with Mrs. Demus,
whom he had seduced (willingly) in the warden's office. La Guardia
asked his colleagues what they intended to do about Dodge now that
he was "violating both the Mann and Volstead Acts."

By way of response, the "drys" accused La Guardia of gloating
over the breakdown of the law instead of working to uphold it.
Speaking for the majority, Representative Blandon of Texas demanded, "Ought we not to hold the infamous liquor traffic responsible for seducing the Government agent and leading him astray?"

Retorted La Guardia, "Do you want to give him a congressional
medal for his behavior? I would put him in jail!"

The question was treated as rhetorical, and there the matter
ended, so far as the House was concerned. Dodge denied the allegation and was never brought to trial. On October 6, 1927, in Cincinnati, a black touring car forced a taxicab to the curb. Mrs. Demus
ran screaming from the cab as George Demus, having been released
from jail, jumped out of the car, gave chase, and shot her dead.
Demus got off with an insanity plea and was confined to a state
asylum, from which he was shortly released after regaining his "san-
ity."[15]

Having gone after others like Dodge, and with better results, La
Guardia suddenly switched tactics and went after enforcement offi-

cials he felt were being criminally overzealous. In 1925, hoping to dry up the sources of illegal beer and liquor, the government resorted to a novel form of entrapment: opening and running speakeasies as a means of snaring the big wholesalers. La Guardia charged government agents with illegally operating a whiskey-selling speakeasy in New York, a whiskey-selling poolroom in Norfolk, Virginia, and a distillery at Elizabeth City, North Carolina. This business, he charged, amounting to half a million dollars a week, was conducted by a syndicate traffic manager at 32 Broadway. The New York "speak" was the Bridge Whist Club on East Forty-fourth Street, one of the city's more upscale watering holes.

La Guardia arose on the House floor to seek prosecution of A. Bruce Bielaski, head of the New York undercover office, who had been the club's "proprietor." Insisted Fiorello, perhaps a bit hyperbolically, "This thing has become bigger than a question of booze; it involves the stability of government." His investigation also revealed that in addition to contravening the law by operating a "speak"—financed by the taxpayers!—Bielaski's sting operation included a dictograph in a booth to eavesdrop on the more eminent bootleggers, and he was therefore guilty of yet another federal crime: wiretapping without a court-ordered warrant.

Amid the tumult that followed this disclosure of government agents functioning as agents provocateurs, La Guardia took off after yet another form of entrapment. The culprit was Frank Cooper, a judge of the United States District Court of Northern New York. On January 28, 1927, La Guardia introduced articles of impeachment against Cooper for instructing Prohibition agents to infiltrate rum-running groups in order to goad them to bring in liquor over the New York–Canada border so that they would be arraigned and tried in his court. At La Guardia's insistence and despite some grousing in the House, the matter was referred to the Judiciary Committee.

Cooper and Bielaski both had an impressive number of convictions and were fiercely defended by the "drys," who argued that if the two descended into the sewer in their pursuit of criminals, it was the fault of the criminals because they operated from that venue. Leading the nationwide chorus of those from all walks of life who defended the two men's sterling characters, one prominent Episcopalian cleric castigated La Guardia. After screaming to the heavens, "Crucify him, crucify him," the cleric wrote to La Guardia the caveat that "you are crucifying Jesus Christ afresh!" But for La Guardia, the issue here was not another Crucifixion but an indictment of the Anglo-American principle of jurisprudence. Cooper had compromised himself as a judge by playing the multiple role of detective, prosecutor, material witness, and principal to a federal crime that he had abetted. In addition, like Bielaski he was an illegal wiretapper.

La Guardia triumphed after weeks of at times acrimonious name-calling in the Judiciary Committee hearings (every one of which he attended, occupying the front seat and with body language almost daring the members not to let Cooper and Bielaski off the hook). Bielaski resigned, and his office, along with that Bridge Whist Club, was put out of business. As for Judge Cooper, while the committee refused to impeach him, it did express official disapproval of his methods. La Guardia was satisfied. "I consider that the committee's decision places Judge Cooper, and all other Judges inclined to act as investigators instead of Judges, upon probation. This resolution is a warning," he went on, spelling it out: "But unless Judge Cooper mends his ways in this regard I shall have some more charges to make next December."[16]

La Guardia's anti-Prohibition stance made many a headline but barely a splash. The Eighteenth Amendment remained firmly fixed in the nation's legal canon. As he put it to his colleagues in 1928, "Politicians are ducking, candidates are hedging, the Anti-Saloon League prospering, people are being poisoned, bootleggers are being enriched, and Government officials are being corrupted."[17] Nevertheless, he had realized his paramount intention, which was to dramatize the hypocrisy, stupidity, waste of money, and utter futility of trying to dry up the sources of liquor and illegally produced beer, all in the hope that the American public, realizing that the law was unenforceable, would demand its repeal. Thus it can be hypothesized that La Guardia more than any other member of Congress was responsible for discrediting this so-called Noble Experiment to the extent that it was eventually rescinded by the Twenty-first (Repeal) Amendment on December 5, 1933.

3.

Another major battle La Guardia fought was for a more equitable tax structure that did not favor the rich over the poor. In so doing, he was fighting against his own party, which was the party of oligarchy. But his first loyalty was to his East Harlem constituents.

After years of being investigated, punished, taxed, regulated, and generally berated during the Progressive Era, the nation's industrial movers and shakers had staged a comeback with the election of Warren Harding, whose slogan was "This is essentially a business country." Coolidge took care not to drop the ball when, upon his accession to the White House, he enthused with an almost religious fervor, "The man who builds a factory builds a temple, the man who works there worships there, and to each is due not scorn and blame, but reverence and praise." The so-called New Gospel was expounded by the National Association of Manufacturers in tandem with the U.S. Chamber of Commerce in a deluge of books, pamphlets, magazines, and stump speakers. Their credo: The soldier, the clergyman, and the statesman must relinquish leadership to the businessman, who, extolling the blessings of unregulated capitalism, alone knew what was best for the nation.

The nation's economy had been expanding rapidly since the post–Civil War era. Employment, wages, profits, and dividends had been on a steady upward climb. After World War I the United States became a creditor nation for the first time in its history, and the succeeding years saw a soaring economic growth. The conservative reaction of the 1920s was a kind of social reform, led by radical utopian capitalists whose belief in the power of unregulated free enterprise was as passionate as the most committed evangelical fundamentalist's belief that the world began, as Bishop Ussher "proved" through Old Testament genealogy, on an October day in the year 4004 B.C. (he couldn't quite decide whether in the morning or the afternoon) and not, as science has proved, a few billion years earlier. Thus was Herbert Hoover moved to prophesy in 1928 that "with the policies of the last eight years we shall soon with the help of God be in sight of the day when poverty will be banished from this nation."[18]

La Guardia knew that these policies of the Republican Party, which he considered the paid whore of big business, did absolutely nothing to relieve the economic plight of Americans who shared a low rung on the socioeconomic ladder. The White House, insisting that what was good for business was good for America, raised tariffs, lowered taxes, fostered monopolies, colluded in price fixing, opposed farm relief, and ignored the needs of labor. Throughout most of the decade, the fight between the Coolidge-era policy of budget-balancing and tax reduction (especially in the higher brackets) and the La Guardian insistence that the burden of taxation be lifted from the nation's lower-income groups was, for all intents and purposes, an ongoing duel between the blunt-talking representative from New York's tenement district and one of America's two or three richest magnates. Of these, La Guardia believed, the man most responsible for these ills was Treasury Secretary Andrew W. Mellon, whose remarkable eleven-year career began under Harding and ended under Hoover.

The vast Mellon empire included coal, coke, gas, oil, and aluminum. War contracts had increased his already considerable fortune. Simply stated, Mellon was convinced that if the government kept taxes down and left the economy alone, "any man of energy and initiative in this country [could] get what he wants out of life."[19] First proposed to the Sixty-seventh Congress but not enacted in its essential aspects until the Sixty-ninth and Seventieth Congresses, the "Mellon Plan," as it came to be known, was ostensibly intended to reward and encourage initiative, thus stimulating investment. In his first report, in 1921, to the House Ways and Means Committee and the Senate Finance Committee, Mellon recommended the repeal of wartime excess-profit taxes and a cut to a 40 percent ceiling on income surtaxes. However, there would be no tax cuts for anyone earning less than sixty-six thousand dollars per year. To compensate for the loss in revenue, he also proposed a two-cent postal card, a license tax on motor vehicles, and several other taxes.

Though members accepted most of Mellon's ideas, the excess profits tax was eventually removed and the top surtax cut to 50 percent.

On November 25, 1923, a few months after La Guardia's return to Congress, the Mellon Plan was reported out of committee. As revised, thanks to the efforts of the La Follette–led Progressives and the Democrats, the plan now called for a reduction of the top income surtax from 50 percent to 25 percent; incomes under eight thousand dollars were to have their tax rates lowered from 8 percent to 6 percent and incomes under four thousand dollars from 4 percent to 3 percent. The Democratic caucus decided to battle for a 44 percent surtax ceiling, while the White House insisted on Mellon's 40 percent. The House began a long debate.[20]

LaGuardia told the House he was more interested in the tax on low incomes, which he believed should be lowered even more. Insisting that the Mellon Plan was deliberately conceived as a weapon for redistribution of wealth, he charged that its author's idea of reducing taxes to stimulate the economy by encouraging business was "based on a historical untruth, because men of wealth never took genuine risks; they let others, including the government, initiate hazardous ventures before moving in; and even then stockholders incurred the risk while the men behind the enterprise held bonds, backed by the physical properties of the enterprise." Retorted Mellon, "I have never viewed taxation as a means of rewarding one class of taxpayers or punishing another." Though admitting that higher taxation on the rich was ultimately borne by the consumer, he insisted it would nevertheless prove beneficial over time as it would lead to a stronger economy.[21]

With a Republican majority, and over the vociferous objections of La Guardia and his fellow Progressives, the House passed the Mellon tax. In the Senate, a Progressive-Democratic coalition forced the adoption of a substitute bill, and the final bill as passed by both chambers after conference called for a reduction of the top surtax to 40 percent, with an increase in the inheritance tax from 25 percent to 40 percent. Said the highly displeased Treasury secretary, "Estate taxes, carried to an excess, in no way differ from the methods of the revolutionists in Russia."[22] Despite its having been watered down, the plan as it now stood was a victory for those favoring the easing of taxes on higher incomes.

But Mellon was still not satisfied. In October 1925, he sent to Congress a new tax plan that would lower the maximum surtax on high incomes to 20 percent, establish a basic 5 percent rate on low incomes, reduce and eventually repeal the inheritance tax, and repeal the gift tax. When the plan won unanimous support of the House Ways and Means Committee, La Guardia again went forth to do battle: "I do not want to destroy wealth, but I do want to abolish poverty." He then noted sardonically Coolidge's recent plea for charity to dependent widows and orphans at the same time his Treasury secretary was taking steps to reduce by close to eight million dollars the taxes of the six men who had made more than four million dollars each in 1924. Mellon's latest program also eliminated the publicity clause by which the government was required to reveal the amount of taxes paid by each taxpayer. This led to a heated debate on December 15, 1925, with the Ways and Means Committee chairman that accomplished little more than allowing La Guardia to let off steam.[23]

Some colleagues from working-class districts rose to support his tirades against Mellon's ideas. It didn't help. On December 17, anxious for quick action, the House moved to limit debate on the tax bill. This prompted the furious Fiorello to decry the limitation, albeit with an uncharacteristic outer calm as a restraint on his anger: "And I say now in the best of humor and in all kindliness that if this condition continues, well then the fight is on. We will keep a quorum here and make objection to every unanimous consent request made." Again he spoke in vain. The new tax bill, containing not only the essential features of the original Mellon proposal intact but an additional reduction in the surtax, more drastic than the administration had sought, was brought before the House for final passage and approved overwhelmingly by a vote of 355 to 28. In early 1926 the revised Mellon Plan became the law of the land. Two years later, Mellon, *still* not satisfied with what he had wrought in behalf of the rich at the expense of the poor, proposed added tax reductions for high incomes. La Guardia quickly offered in counter proposal an amendment establishing a 30 percent surtax on incomes over $1.5 million, which the House just as quickly rejected with a vote of 366 to 24. Yet again La Guardia and his fellow Progressives could do little but engage in an orgy of frustration and hand-wringing.[24]

As Coolidge prepared to turn the White House over to his successor, Commerce Secretary Herbert Hoover, the nation's business interests could reflect with great satisfaction on the benefits derived from six years of operation of the Mellon program. While persons earning five thousand dollars per annum had benefited from tax reduction to the extent of a 1 percent gain in income after taxes, the gains for those with higher incomes were progressively larger until those whose earnings exceeded a million dollars a year paid 31 percent in taxes. As the decade drew to a close, 25 percent of the nation's annual income was earned by but 5 percent of the population. La Guardia's heroic stand against the unequal distribution of wealth had been blown away by the heavy artillery of Mellon and prosperity.[25]

But La Guardia was not one to give up easily. So far as he was concerned, while there was nothing he could do about the Mellon tax program, there was at least something he believed he could do about this "man whom he viewed as the spinal column holding together the heartless skeleton of presidential leadership since the war."[26] Having amassed a veritable library of data on Mellon, he ordered his young secretary, Ernest Cuneo, to prepare a case for the impeachment of the Treasury secretary.

Cuneo had to report back that he could find no specific statue that Mellon had violated by his stock-holding ventures (he had given up his many directorships on taking office, in compliance with the law). This did not daunt La Guardia, who now began a series of scathing attacks on Mellon on the House floor calling for his impeachment. Were his facts well checked out? (La Guardia had a penchant for sometimes going off half-cocked.) We'll never know. On February 3, 1932, just as he was getting warmed up, President Hoover suddenly announced Mellon's appointment as ambassador to Great Britain.

CHAPTER THIRTEEN

"Asbestos will not hold the statements I shall make on the floor of the House!"

1.

To La Guardia, the most effective government was one that administers with both a big heart and a big stick, with a moral obligation to put the protection of the interests of the people before the interests of the Interests. While battling throughout the 1920s against Prohibition, inequitable taxation, and privatization of public resources and utilities, he was active on a number of other fronts simultaneously.

There was, for example, his fight against the McNary-Haugen plan, which was intended to address the desperate need of the nation's farmers for relief in light of the fact that agricultural prices had plummeted by almost 50 percent following World War I. The first of five such bills introduced yearly from 1924 to 1928, McNary-Haugen proposed to aid the farmers by having the government dump surpluses abroad in order to keep domestic farm prices high. Any losses sustained on the free world market would have to be absorbed by the farmers involved. Every time the bill came up for debate, La Guardia argued that the plan would raise the price of

food for domestic city workers without giving true relief to the farmers.

In May of 1924, he delivered on the floor of the House a major
attack on the bill that was at the same time a response to the attacks
he had come under from the press, in his mail, and on the floor of
Congress itself for being branded a radical. Defining himself as "a
progressive in every sense of the word," he was "not at all shocked
by being called a radical" if that meant he was "asking radical
changes in the very conditions which brought about the disparity
between the exorbitant retail prices of food and the starvation prices
paid to the farmer." He charged that "something is radically wrong
when a condition exists that permits the manipulation of prices, the
creation of monopolies on food to the extent of driving the farmer
off his farm by foreclosure and having thousands of underfed and
ill-nourished children in the public schools of our cities."

He then went on to lambaste "a vicious, unfair, unbalanced economic system," which favored neither the farmer nor the consumer,
catering instead to such parasitical groups as the bankers, meat packers, warehouse owners, and shippers. The McNary-Haugen Bill, he
insisted, would simply raise farm prices, thus hurting the consumer,
without protecting both groups from the evil trusts. "Take control of
all transportation of the country," he urged, "take all the [grain]
elevators and storages, and eliminate entirely the middleman and
banking industry." The laws had not kept pace with the development
of the modern industrial system, he contended. "You have protected
the dollar and disregarded the producers," he accused the bill's supporters. "You have protected prosperity and forgotten the human
being, with the result that we have legalized a cruel system of exploitation. Now we are approaching the time when a real change is
necessary."[1]

Here is one time when Fiorello had failed to do his homework
thoroughly, relying instead on the passionate rhetoric of radicalism.
There were already regulatory laws in place; if by "control" he meant
government ownership, he was not prepared to amend the McNary-
Haugen Bill to that effect. The best he could come up with, in the
spring of 1926 and again in early 1927, was an amendment to the
bill that would mandate a five-year prison term and five-thousand-
dollar fine for any one of a series of acts intended to raise the price,

restrict the supply, hoard or monopolize, or set any unreasonable charge for farm products. "The only purpose of the amendment," he said, "is to protect the consumer against gougers, profiteers, monopolies, food manipulators, speculators and gamblers." Congressman Gilbert Haugen of Iowa, author of the House version of the bill, opposed it, and the House voted it down quickly. Not only was the proposal unrealistic (as well as incapable of being passed), it ignored the true root of the farm problem, one that obtains to this day: overproduction. Having voted against McNary-Haugen in 1924 and 1926, La Guardia finally joined in passing it in 1927 "for the simple reason there was nothing else before us that promised any relief at all."[2]

In August of 1925, as the Jazz Age with its attendant prosperity was rapidly approaching the alpine peak from which it would descend by degrees into the abyss of the Great Depression, Fiorello was inundated by complaints that hundreds of thousands of New Yorkers had been hit by a nine- to ten-cent jump in the retail price of meat. After ascertaining from a number of Texas colleagues in the House that the price of cattle had not gone up, and launching an investigation of New York's retail butchers that cleared them of profiteering, he identified the true culprits: the meat packers. He organized a citywide protest meeting in his New York district office and called for the city's major newspapers to consider advocating a strike against what he called the Beef Trust.

Then, after a series of frank but fruitless talks in Chicago with Armour, the nation's largest meat packer, he asked William M. Jardine, secretary of agriculture, to investigate not only Armour but all the meat packers. Jardine responded that such an investigation "would entail a great deal of time and expense, and I regret that we are not in a position to undertake a study of this kind." He enclosed copies of the department's publications "Use of Meat in the Home" and "Lamb and Mutton and Their Uses in the Diet."

"I asked for help and you send me a bulletin," La Guardia shot back in a blistering letter. "The [tenement dwellers] of New York City cannot feed their children on [your] bulletins." They had long been "trained by hard experience on the economical use of meat" without the need for agricultural bulletins. What was wanted was "to bring the pressure of the United States government on the meat profiteers who are keeping the hard-working people of this city from obtaining proper nourishment."³

The threatened strike failed to come off. But this did not deter Fiorello. He was only waiting for the right moment to bring the matter before the House. The moment came the following January in a debate over an appropriation bill for the Department of Agriculture. "Mr. Chairman and gentlemen," he began with biting sarcasm on taking the floor, "now that the House is engaged in its favorite indoor sport of fooling the farmer, I want to take the opportunity to say just a few words for the consumer." Once again denouncing the jobbers, commission merchants, bankers, railroads, canning companies, and food monopolies for the plight of the farmers, and by extension the plight of the consumers, he asked for a change in the distribution of food. "*This* is the help I got," he fairly screeched, waving the pamphlet on the economical use of meat. As his colleagues roared with laughter, La Guardia waved the other pamphlet, "Lamb and Mutton and Their Uses in the Diet," over his head while informing the House that 90 percent of the people in New York could not afford lamb chops. Whereupon he performed a show-and-tell that convulsed the chamber:

"Why, I have right here with me now—where is it? Oh, yes, here it is in my vest pocket." He dramatically extracted a miniscule chop that cost thirty cents. Scarcely had the laughter died down when he reached into another pocket and extracted a diminutive cut, with the words, "Here is $1.75 worth of steak," and from yet another pocket, a scrawny slice of beef: "Now here is a roast—three dollars worth of roast." What workingman's family, he demanded to know, "can afford to pay three dollars for a roast of this size?" The cattle grazer was getting two and a half to five and a half cents a pound, while the consumer was paying seventy-five to eighty cents a pound. Therefore, he concluded, quoting from bills of sale and documentation of the packers' profits from hoofs, horns, and intestines as well as from the edible meat itself, it was obvious that the packing-house monopolies—the Beef Trust—were raking in outrageously unjustified profits and could afford to cut prices substantially while continuing to realize adequate returns. Concluding on a personal note, he recalled how, "when I was a kid out in Arizona," he "enjoyed an American breakfast—ham and eggs, bread and butter [that] are luxuries in New York City today. The American breakfast has almost disappeared. If we continue along these lines, we will . . . soon go on the rice diet of the Chinese coolie." He called for "a readjustment of the present system, and . . . to restore the American breakfast to the children of this age."[4]

La Guardia's figures were questioned by two letters from the Institute of American Meat Packers, which elicited a scornful letter to Norman Draper, its Washington representative: "Both of your letters display the arrogant attitude of the packers." Maintaining he had told the Armour people in Chicago "that the packers have it in their power to reduce the retail cost of meat in New York City from 25% to 33½%," La Guardia warned, "some of these days we will simply stop eating meat in New York City and perhaps then we may arrive at a fair level of prices."[5] Predictably, there was no congressional investigation of the meat packers.

Fiorello next aimed his heaviest artillery at yet another target: the Bread Trust. "Bread King" William B. Ward, together with his associates, controlled the nation's three leading baking corporations—Ward Baking, General Baking, and Continental Baking—with combined assets totaling nearly a billion dollars. La Guardia expressed "shock" that the Federal Trade Commission had voted to end its investigation of the combine, which had been ordered in 1924 by a Senate resolution. On February 1, 1926, he introduced two resolutions. One called on the Federal Trade Commission to determine whether the Ward combine was acting in restraint of trade. The other asked the Department of Justice if it had taken any action against Ward. Both bills were buried in committee. When La Guardia moved to bring them to the floor, a point of order against such a motion was sustained by Speaker Nicholas Longworth. However, a few days later, at La Guardia's insistence, the Department of Justice filed a petition charging Ward and his associates with conspiracy in restraint of trade. On April 3, 1926, the government succeeded in having a consent decree entered in federal court dissolving the Ward monopoly.

Here, as when he successfully took on so many other targets with similar results, La Guardia had prepared himself well, carefully amassing documentary evidence and soliciting indisputable facts and figures from reliable groups and other sources. This gives the lie to the charge by his enemies that, particularly when most aroused by an issue, he shot from the hip. Ignoring the charge, and the fact that on occasion he did indeed shoot from the hip, Fiorello would augment his research by organizing support, particularly among responsible social workers, as evidence that he was not alone but was leading a crusade. "When Fiorello was in his best form, it was often because he had studied hard and knew his lines by heart."[6] He was in particularly good form when he joined the fight over the extension of rent controls in the District of Columbia, excoriating "landlords [who are] determined to exact a pound of flesh from their tenants."

Yelling ouch before they had been pinched, the Real Estate Board of New York City sent a letter protesting against rent control as "radical." La Guardia replied that he considered their protest "the same old whining, cringing plea presented by the New York landlords who have thrived on the housing situation." So far as he was concerned, "nothing better in support of the Bill" could have reached Congress "than a protest from the landlords of New York City." He concluded his letter with the ironic exhortation, "Please keep up your good work."[7]

There was not a group with a legitimate battle to wage that could not count on Congressman La Guardia to arrogate to himself the role of first among equals in the trenches. During New York City's 1926 garment strike he not only walked the picket line, he protested at a Madison Square Garden meeting the use of antipicketing injunctions, doing the same a few months later in support of striking makers of paper boxes. He condemned the use of "kidnapped" Chinese strikebreakers to replace striking American merchant mariners. He went after the Pullman Company when it prevented twelve thousand Pullman porters from unionizing. He fought to raise the pay of government workers.[8]

La Guardia garnered more headlines than any other congressman throughout the 1920s, whether in commendation of his various positions or condemnation of his various tactics, on the House floor and off. Perhaps ironically, it was his efforts in behalf of one group, far removed not only geographically but in just about every other aspect from his East Harlem constituents, that solidified his status as every American working man's (and woman's) paramount advocate on Capitol Hill: the coal miners of Pennsylvania, West Virginia, and Kentucky.

Due to high unemployment and competition from other power

sources, after World War I the coal industry was one of the country's sickest industries—a sickness exacerbated by the mine owners, who often sought to alleviate the problem by periodic cutting of labor costs.[9] In August 1925, anthracite workers in eastern Pennsylvania went on strike. On December 2, in a column he wrote for Hearst's *Evening Graphic*, La Guardia castigated the "arbitrary, brazen and willful refusal of the operators" to accept Governor Gifford Pinchot's terms for a settlement. There appeared to be "one solution only": The government "should step in at this time, compel a settlement of existing differences and immediately commence a survey of available coal fields now in operation and take such action as eventually will put the government in possession of the gift of God that surely was intended to be used for the benefit of all American people." In other words, nationalization of the coal industry.[10]

Though the strike ended the following February, La Guardia felt, and rightfully so, that the settlement finally arrived at was not in the best interests of the miners. He again urged nationalization of the industry on the grounds that the resources were God's gift to the American people, and not a beneficence bestowed by the greedy mine operators. Two years later, in February 1928, when the Pennsylvania fields were tied up by another strike, this time against yet another round of wage cuts, La Guardia rushed out to the strike area. Trailed by a host of reporters and photographers, he toured the most affected coal towns interviewing the strikers and their families. Many of them—including women and children—he watched being arrested by state police merely for picketing in contravention of a federal court injunction. He saw children literally hiding in terror under their beds in the barely habitable miners' shacks. On the previous day strikebreakers had fired a barrage of bullets through the windows of the school at Broughton just before the 350 pupils were to be dismissed. "I have never seen such thought-out, deliberate cruelty in my life as that displayed against the unfortunate strikers by the coal operators and their army of coal and iron police," La Guardia seethed to the newspapermen. "Asbestos will not hold the statements I shall make on the floor of the House!"[11]

He immediately telegraphed the House requesting passage of a resolution to investigate the strike. He also submitted an affidavit signed by a strikebreaker swearing that he and another strikebreaker had each been paid twenty-five-dollars by the mine operators' "police" for firing into the miners' barracks. Nothing came of the request. Rushing back to Washington, La Guardia took the floor four days later (February 8). By then his colleagues already knew the horrible details of his exposé through the headlines his dramatic visit to western Pennsylvania had engendered. Also by this time, he had been inundated with pleas from West Virginia and Kentucky miners to investigate their equally wretched lives and the subhuman level of existence to which they and their families had been reduced.

Tearing into the mine owners and operators on the floor while waving a fistful of photographs and affidavits to buttress his charges, La Guardia denounced the use of the injunction in labor disputes, noting that it barred the union from retaining attorneys and paying strike benefits and prohibited even the singing of hymns. He called down the wrath of heaven upon the appalling poverty and exploitation of the company towns, in which the miners and their families were forced to live, at outrageous rentals, in substandard company-owned shacks and purchase, at outrageously inflated prices, the necessities of life from company-owned stores; reviled the private police ("crazed with hootch") for shooting into schools; and damned the mine owners for importing Negro strikebreakers from the South whom they then kept in "peonage" by enticing them into exhausting their wages on "carloads" of prostitutes, both white and black, who were brought in by the companies to transform every payday into a mass orgy. "An industry," he shouted in peroration, "that can not pay its workers a decent living wage has no right to exist!"[12]

While the House dragged its feet, the Senate, goaded by Burton Wheeler and his fellow Progressives and liberal Democrats, authorized an investigation. Collecting over three thousand pages of contradictory testimony from miners and operators, the Senate Committee on Interstate Commerce found enough evidence to introduce a bill that would license coal operators in interstate commerce, enable the formation of mergers, and recognize the right of labor to organize and bargain collectively. The bill went nowhere. In the meantime, at the invitation of publisher Oswald Garrison Villard, La Guardia wrote an article for *The Nation* on the investigation, in which he urged the government to "step in and take possession of all natural resources, coal, oil, water, and gas."[13] La Guardia, of course, realized that he had a better chance of seeing pigs fly than such an idea coming to pass. Here, again, he was using the newspapers and his legislative status to ventilate dreadful dirty dealings in high places, in hopes that Congress would be forced by enlightened public opinion to do what humaneness, let alone common decency, demanded it should.

But for now, despite all the turbulence and inequities in the coal industry, it was America's newest economic leviathan that was to provoke the big debate over public ownership in the 1920s: electricity. Fiorello jumped into the dispute with the alacrity of an evangelical environmentalist fleeing the home he suddenly discovers sits astride a toxic waste dumpsite. He would not only be fighting an issue in which he believed passionately, it would give him the chance to go after the man he considered the Industrialist from Hell: Henry Ford.

3.

By the end of the 1920s, despite agitation by reformers during the Progressive Era for nationalization of utilities. more than 80 percent of the nation's electricity was generated by a mere dozen holding companies. A pro-public-power bloc in Congress was determined to see government construction and management of river valley projects through the country for generating electricity. Out of this would evolve the great Tennessee Valley Authority and the power project on the Colorado River we know as Boulder Dam. The TVA, an independent agency of the executive branch, operates fifty hydroelectric dams in a region encompassing Tennessee and parts of Alabama, Virginia, Georgia, Kentucky, North Carolina, and Mississippi, with an aggregate population of more than seven million.

The dams provide electricity, control flooding, increase the region's water supply, and operate nuclear-powered electric generating plants; its power system annually produces more than 125 billion kilowatt-hours of electricity, almost ninety times as much as was generated in the same region in 1933, thereby boosting the area's annual home usage of electricity from six hundred kilowatt-hours in that year to some fifteen thousand kilowatt-hours today. Also, through cooperation with state and other agencies, TVA conducts research and development programs in forestry, fish and wildlife preservation, watershed protection, and air and water quality control. Ancillary activities include reforestation, industrial and community development, the development of fertilizers, and the establishment of recreational facilities. This "social resurrection," as economist Broadus Mitchell termed it,[14] was owing to two factors: the formulation of plans, marshaling of public opinion, and introduction of legislation for government operation of this and the Boulder Dam projects; and the frustration of efforts by the private sector to lease Muscle Shoals on the Tennessee River. These factors, in turn, were owing in large measure to the perseverance, at times seemingly pathological, of the leaders of that pro-public-power bloc in Congress— George Norris in the Senate and his chief lieutenant in the House, Fiorello La Guardia, who was determined to keep Muscle Shoals out of the hands of Henry Ford.

When it appeared that the United States must eventually become caught up in the European war, Congress authorized government construction of a hydroelectric plant and two nitrate plants to increase the production of explosives at Muscle Shoals, Alabama, an undeveloped area of the Tennessee Valley that yearly was alternately arid and flooded. At war's end, and after an expenditure of $150 million, Congress terminated further funding of the unfinished dam. Soon a number of private companies, foreseeing a tremendous potential in the valley, descended on the now idle Muscle Shoals project. By 1924, the leading contender was Henry Ford. The Coolidge administration, unwilling to go into the hydroelectric business, agreed to Ford's proposal to sign a hundred-year lease at an annual rental of $1.5 million to manufacture nitrates for cheap fertilizer and construct a large city in the Tennessee Valley. Since Coolidge could not act on this without legislative approval, he had an administration-supported bill introduced in the Senate directing the War Department to accept the Ford offer.

While Norris, who in 1922 had introduced his first bill for government development of Muscle Shoals on a multipurpose basis, led the opposition in the Senate, La Guardia did likewise in the House. The five-day debate opened on March 5, 1924, with a typical La Guardia salvo of unalloyed derision, characterizing the Ford offer as "a bill to make Henry Ford the industrial king of the United States. . . . *Be it further resolved* [emphasis in the original] that it is necessary to bunco the farmers of America." Pointing out that the bill's language, as reported out of committee, was precisely the language of Ford's published request to the White House, he warned that the bill's promise to guarantee cheap fertilizer for the farmer was an empty promise and urged instead that the Department of Agriculture be empowered to manufacture the fertilizer.

He then noted that, with built-in production cost guarantees, Ford's actual profit would amount to more than 50 percent on his initial investment. Already an automobile czar, Ford would now become overlord of the electricity, labor force, navigation, and fertilizer industries of the Tennessee Valley. "If you pass this bill," Fiorello warned his colleagues, "you should replace that flag on the wall of this house with a great big dollar sign." Seizing upon Ford's well-known virulent anti-Semitism to support his argument, La Guardia called him a man with "hatred in his heart [whose] ignorance of history, literature, and religion" was equaled only by his "consummate arrogance." Far from being a great American, he was a miserable bigot waging "nefarious warfare against the Jews" and doing more "to create strife and hatred in this country among the races than any man in the United States." La Guardia opposed not only Ford's offer but any offer by private companies to produce fertilizer and power in the Tennessee Valley. He was "not for the operation of this great plan by anyone or any corporation except the United States Government."

But the House was hostile to the idea. It was also hostile to La Guardia's throwing up roadblocks in the path of the Ford steamroller by popping up and down like a jumping-jack proposing one amendment after another—a favorite tactic he employed to forestall any legislative act he despised but knew must pass nevertheless. On May 10, patience having run out, the House voted to close debate on all amendments. As La Guardia jumped up with yet another amendment, cries of "Vote! Vote! Vote!" ricocheted round the chamber.

"Oh, you can holler 'Vote' as much as you like," he yelled back, "but you will all live to rue the day that you railroaded and jammed this bill through."[15]

The House went ahead and passed it that same day. But a determined opposition led by George Norris prevented its Senate passage through adroit maneuvering. In April, the Senate Agricultural Committee, now dominated by Norris and other Progressives, began hearings on Muscle Shoals. Expert after expert testified on the unsuitability of the area for fertilizer production. However, this became a side issue when it quickly became apparent that the controversy's overriding—indeed, crucial—factor was not fertilizer but electric power, which the Norris Committee saw as Ford's true interest in the project. That opinion was shared by southern manufacturers who feared competition from any Ford-electricity-powered enterprises in their front yard. Norris succeeded in burying the original Ford offer in committee and then offered his own substitute proposal: government ownership and operation of Muscle Shoals.

While the Senate debated Norris's bill, La Guardia led the fight in the House: "The sooner we decide to take God's gift to the people of America and operate it for the enjoyment of all the people instead of for the profit of private corporations, the better it will be for the people of this country." A month later he insisted that the claim by proponents that private operation of the area would greatly benefit the farmers was nothing more than an attempt to delude the nation's agricultural producers. Their primary goal, he further insisted, was to control the manufacture of power: "Muscle Shoals is a water-power project first, and incidentally a nitrogen plant. There is no fooling ourselves, and there is no use continuing to fool the farmer."[16]

By now, with a veritable "electrical revolution" having taken place in the United States, the emphasis had shifted to the development's power possibilities. With the Ford deal dead and Norris's bill getting nowhere, President Coolidge established a board of inquiry. Out of this came yet another bill that would set up a joint committee of Congress authorized to lease the site. La Guardia was no less relentless than Norris and their allies in both chambers in opposing the idea. On March 11, 1926, he took the floor to tell his colleagues, "You cannot find any corporation in business for love, for philanthropy, or for patriotism. The lessee will want to make money and they will make it on the farmers and the consumers. The lessee corporation will make money and the farmers will pay."[17]

The Norris plan received a welcome boost toward the end of that year when the Coolidge White House's effort to dispose of the dam and nitrate plants to private interests collapsed and Ford withdrew his offer. Moreover, the 1926 congressional elections had strengthened the antiprivatization farm bloc in Congress. This paved the way for Norris and La Guardia to introduce a joint resolution for government development of Muscle Shoals for the production of both power and fertilizer.

Testifying for the resolution before the House Committee on Military Affairs, La Guardia warned that whoever gained control of Muscle Shoals, "the greatest power plant in the country [, would] have the absolute control of the industry of that whole section of the country, within the radius of the transmission of power." Congress, he reiterated, "cannot afford to give that power to any one group of men."[18] When it was proposed to amend his resolution to replace the word "fertilizer" with "nitrogen products," La Guardia was outraged by what he saw as a ruse by fertilizer companies to prevent government production of their product: "I want to say, gentlemen, that the conduct of the lobby of the Power Trust and the conduct of the lobby of the Fertilizer Trust is living proof that the world's oldest profession is not limited to any one sex."

Defending the Boulder Dam Bill, for which he labored concurrently, La Guardia tried to dismiss the opposition through ridicule: "Oh, of course, great and many are the arguments against Government operation. Oh, it is unconstitutional, oh, it is wasteful; oh, it is inefficient, oh, it is uneconomic, says the Power Trust and the power lobby"—which groups, he concluded, "are really nothing else but social cooties [bedbugs]."[19] La Guardia was a loose constructionist who argued that each age must eschew older dogmas and determine for itself the meaning of constitutional limitations, rather than feel bound by precedents from ages gone by. "Constitutional limitations must necessarily be construed in the light of changed conditions," he declared on May 24, 1928. "It is left for each age to say what the laws of that age shall be." There then followed one of the most powerful speeches of his entire congressional career. Foreseeing a future in which government scientists would harness nature to serve the best interests of the people, he called upon his colleagues to visualize the results of the government-owned and government-managed Boulder Dam project:

> Imagine this huge canyon to be damned by a wall over six hundred feet high, creating a gigantic natural reservoir site impounding twenty-six million acre-feet of water. Millions and millions of horsepower now going to waste year after year will be harnessed and utilized to generate electricity which will be sent hundreds of miles and bring cheer, comfort, and move the wheels of industry. Just think of . . . a magnificent stream, with a daily uniform flow of water throughout the year to be

utilized as a great artery of commerce for the region of the country. The Imperial Valley, now threatened by flood, to be secured in its safety. . . . The project is thrilling.[20]

Congress passed both the Muscle Shoals and Boulder Dam bills. Coolidge pocket-vetoed the first, on the grounds that while the business of the federal government was business, it was not "the retail business." He did, though, sign the second bill, which authorized the government to erect a huge dam in Boulder Canyon on the Colorado River for water, irrigation, and power purposes. Influencing his decision was pressure from businessmen and politicians from the Southwest clamoring for electricity and water, which were not being supplied by private companies. The bill left to the secretary of the interior the decision of whether the power stations should be operated by government or private companies. It was not until Coolidge's successor turned the White House over to Roosevelt that the Boulder Dam project went into operation. The era of the TVA was several years down the road. Still, La Guardia had the satisfaction of being around when both projects were serving the purpose for which he had waged the good fight.

4.

There was much of the old-fashioned philosophy of such western radicals as La Follette, Norris, and Wheeler that La Guardia could not share—for instance, issues involving race and nationality in American life.

These were new issues for the twentieth-century liberals but nonissues for the westerners in Congress, who were locked into their own agendas. The majority of these populists largely ignored the demands of Negroes for the first-class citizenship they had been constitutionally guaranteed by the so-called Civil War Amendments (Thirteenth, Fourteenth, and Fifteenth). This attitude, like their lack of La Guardia's passion on the question of immigration, was a matter of profound sensitivity for the hyphenate Progressive and his hyphenate constituents in East Harlem, who to the Nordics, many of whom could trace their lineage back to the republic's beginnings, were practically an alien species. In 1929, when several of his colleagues refused to have Chicago's newly elected Negro representative

Oscar De Priest occupy office space next to theirs, La Guardia informed Speaker Longworth, "I shall be glad to have him next to my office."[21] La Guardia was neither grandstanding nor condescending. He was making manifest yet again his repugnance with the power of Anglo-Saxon America.

Another difference between La Guardia and most of his fellow Progressives was that whereas their priorities were to a great extent regionally oriented, Fiorello was all over the map. In addition to his battles on the major issues we have already discussed, he fought simultaneously for a multiplicity of causes not yet mentioned. These included legalizing sex education, establishing federal summer camps for slum girls, making Columbus Day a national holiday, providing free transportation for Gold Star mothers visiting the graves of their sons in European cemeteries, changing bankruptcy proceedings, and standing up for the rights of downtrodden Native Americans. He even took on the "baseball trust." After introducing a bill that would place a 90 percent tax on the sale of baseball players, he wondered if he was "up against the same kind of proposition as I am when I am fighting the steel trust, the railroad, or other corporate interests." He was.[22]

Still another way La Guardia differed from the pacifist Progressives was in his ambivalence toward the military. Though opposing a big Army and Navy, he favored an expanded and unified Air Corps and was, as has been noted, General Billy Mitchell's most avid spokesman in Congress to that end. Also an enthusiastic exponent of submarines, "the Major" loved to talk about military preparation, strategy, and tactics. Though repelled by the cost in lives and resources and the attendant horror and destruction that were the natural consequences of war, as a topic it never failed to fascinate him. The man who had entered the postwar Congress as a confirmed isolationist was now an internationalist—provided it served America's best interests.

Preoccupied as he was with issues of national concern, La Guardia never for a moment forgot the people who had sent him to Congress. Particularly relevant were municipal problems, especially those that impinged upon the "bread and butter" needs of low-income groups, such as a court decision that allowed the IRT subway line to raise its fare to seven cents. La Guardia promptly attacked the decision while introducing a bill to prevent federal courts from aiding "greedy public service corporations."[23] His constituents looked upon him as their *padrone*—the benevolent village headman back in the old country to whom they could bring their problems secure in the knowledge that he would try to resolve them. Mail from his district flowed into his office daily. Rare was the letter that concerned public ownership of utilities or any other of the national issues. Rather, they were requests for passports, visas for visiting kinsmen, naturalization papers, veterans' benefits, information about Civil Service examinations, complaints about high rents, evictions, the price of meat, milk, ice, and coal, the fear of a mother about her daughter staying out of trouble, the fear of a father about losing control over his children—and, of course, jobs. La Guardia selected lieutenants to tend to specific requests and problems, with orders to satisfy the petitioner where humanly possible. When in the city, he made himself personally available to constituents at one of the district clubs or at his downtown law office.

Addressing the cares of the people does not explain completely the control he held over East Harlem. Tammany Hall had been the first to address those cares. But Tammany, thirsting only for patronage and power, made promises it had no intention of keeping. La Guardia thirsted only for reform and sought to fulfill every pledge. Every spring at the New Star Casino he gave an accounting of his activities in that year's congressional session and familiarized his voters with the names and achievements of men whose philosophy and labors gave them promise of a rewarding life in the country of their adoption. He captured their imaginations with the hope that better times lay ahead, along with their share in the American dream.

Helping and educating the voters were but two devices by which La Guardia controlled East Harlem. There was a third, and perhaps most consequential: a personal organization.

It was one of La Guardia's many inconsistencies that a man so contemptuous of political machines would construct one of the best in the business. What separated his from just about all others was that La Guardia's ultimately served the people and not the pols. His organization, which enabled him to be elected to the House for five straight terms from a three-party district (Democrats, Republicans, Socialists), was, it need hardly be noted, the result of pragmatism, as distinct from opportunism. He had vowed never to repeat the mistake he made in 1921 of being an organizationless man. Even after he returned to the Republican Party he continued to mistrust the Twentieth's GOP district leaders. To him they were no more than a pack of self-aggrandizing ward heelers. Besides, he knew they did not care for his brand of politics. All they cared about was that he was a winner. And in overwhelmingly Democratic New York City, any Republican winner, no matter how distasteful to the hierarchy, was to be, if not treasured, then certainly tolerated.

Though his organization was well in place and functioning smoothly, until 1929 La Guardia had but one aide in Washington. This was, of course, Marie Fisher, his secretary since 1916. Having, in her words, "grown up with the work," Marie was not only Fiorello's entire "Washington staff," she performed the multiple duties of receptionist, stenographer, typist, and research assistant. She also continued as his personal secretary at his New York law office. Fiorello was the first to admit she was as knowledgeable as he himself about legislation as well as what was going on back in East Harlem. On February 28, 1929, Marie, who at thirty-three was thirteen years his junior, retired as Fiorello's factotum and became his wife. Although she devoted much of her leisure time to reading and taking courses at Columbia University, she continued to help her husband campaign.

The couple kept a suite in the Potomac Park Apartments for when Congress was in session. In New York, Fiorello sold the Bronx house and took a four-room apartment in an East Harlem tenement at 109th Street just east of Fifth Avenue. He and Marie were ideally matched, and not only politically. (And, it must be added, not in a culinary sense either. La Guardia often claimed only half-jokingly, "When I married, I lost a good secretary and got a lousy cook.") Both were uncaring of creature comforts and accumulating possessions. They were, by mutual consent, quasi-bohemian and quasi-spartan. Their clothes were "off the rack." Their sparse furniture suggested a few quick trips to discount stores and garage sales. Close friends—with whom they enjoyed socializing often—included Fiorello's fellow Green Geniuses and a number of liberal journalists, two of whom, Lowell Limpus and Maurice G. Postley, functioned unofficially as his PR men. Postley publicized La Guardia's activities in the *Bronx Home News*, billed as the largest "home-town" paper in

America, and later in the *Evening Journal* when he moved to that paper. Limpus, as editor of the *New York Daily News,* was equally generous to this "humane spokesman for inarticulate workingmen" and "barrel of fun" in what was the nation's most popular tabloid.[24]

Marie's place in La Guardia's Washington office was taken by two men just out of college, Dominick ("Mimi") Felitti and Eugene R. Canudo, son of one of Fiorello's first law partners, Raimondo Canudo. In New York, the team included Nicholas Saldiveri, who handled all veterans' affairs for La Guardia, and Ernest Cuneo, a former cub reporter on the *New York Daily News* who had been an All-American (Columbia University) and professional football player. According to Cuneo, who began his legal career clerking for La Guardia in the early years of the Depression, Fiorello ran his organization like a benevolent despot, alternating abuse and temper with lavish praise: "Our love for him was something like that of the Old Guards' for Napoleon."[25]

Of the inner circle, the earliest to come aboard, the most dynamic, and the one who would go furthest politically was the aforementioned Vito Marcantonio. In 1924, while "Marco" was attending NYU Law School, Fiorello installed him in Foster, La Guardia & Cutler though he was two years away from being admitted to the bar. "I am going to take this boy on eventually," La Guardia explained to Cutler, "as I want to make him my professional heir."[26] When La Guardia became mayor, Marcantonio won his seat in Congress. He held it for five terms, becoming in the process a controversial figure in New York politics. Under Marcantonio, the F. H. La Guardia Political Club, which he organized in 1924 with his *Gibboni* and which launched his own political career, became the city's most effective machine after Tammany Hall.

The club's rank-and-file were a cross-section of the Italo-American community, both native-born and naturalized—laborers, students, mailmen, schoolteachers, doctors, and lawyers. Most were young and politically ambitious. Also included were a fair number of professional pugilists and street brawlers. La Guardia recognized this as a necessity to offset the tactics of his Tammany enemies, who were not above dropping milk bottles and baby carriages from tenement roofs on his street-corner meetings and then setting off false alarms, which resulted in firemen dispersing the crowd. They also served the necessary function of watching the polls on Election Day, lest Tammany goons fail to give an honest vote count or, on occasion, seek to keep La Guardia's supporters from casting their ballots.

As we have seen, La Guardia's easiest election win was in 1924. Thereafter, though he appealed to all ethnic groups in his district, it was only the Italians he could count on. And even there he ran into heavy opposition. Many of them resented his being a Protestant and a Mason. Many took their cue from *Il Progresso*, the city's most popular Italian-language newspaper, whose owner, Generoso Pope, not only supported Mussolini (whom Fiorello openly condemned) but supported Tammany in return for lucrative advertising contracts. Though La Guardia did so well with the Jewish vote in the 1924 La Follette campaign, the Jewish districts returned to the Democratic fold in subsequent elections. This was offset, to a degree, by La Guardia's bringing many Socialists over to his cause.

By the mid-1920s a new group, the Puerto Ricans, was moving into the district. La Guardia lost no time entering into a dialogue with their leaders, expressing his concern for their welfare and equitable treatment. On March 17, 1928, at the suggestion of the island's leadership, he introduced a bill in Congress requiring that the governor of Puerto Rico, appointed by Washington because Puerto Rico was a territory, be a native-born citizen of the island. (The bill failed to pass.) To the Puerto Rican Brotherhood of America Incorporated, located in his district, he promised to do all within his power to curb the power of the avaricious sugar companies he held responsible for the island's poverty. When, in September 1928, the island was battered by a hurricane, La Guardia took the lead in Congress to appropriate relief funds and volunteered his services in the field to the Red Cross. (They were politely declined.) Despite their growing numbers, Fiorello failed to organize the Puerto Ricans in his district as he organized the other ethnics. It was a failure he would come to regret.

La Guardia was returned to Congress every two years by pluralities, not majorities. (In 1926 he won reelection by a mere fifty-five votes.) Did he ever consider the possible consequences of his limited appeal? Probably not. What he considered was the bottom line: He always won. He was the most successful vote-getter in Manhattan's Republican Party—and this despite the fact that the party supported its maverick congressman out of practicality, certainly not ideology. Convinced that his district's melting pot looked to him for leadership, La Guardia now became convinced that the whole melting pot that was New York City saw him in that same light.

He set his sights on City Hall.

La Guardia and Hearst were no longer on speaking terms, dating back to 1925, when the press lord, failing to win the renomination of his mayoral marionette, Honest John Hylan, wanted to run Fiorello against Jimmy Walker, the Tammany choice. Fiorello declined, and wisely so. His organization was in no way strong enough to go up against Tammany. Besides, he distrusted Hearst's motives. Hearst retaliated by ordering his editors that La Guardia's name was never to be mentioned favorably in any of his publications. Fiorello tried to buy the *Bollettino della Sera,* so that he would have a forum to get across his views. When that failed, he founded the La Guardia Publishing Company and published an Italian-language weekly, *L'Americolo.* He had, he explained, only one purpose: "the protection, the well-being, the happiness of the great mass of Italians in the United States." *L'Americolo* succumbed after a year, despite heroic efforts and an expenditure of money Fiorello could ill afford.

Fortunately, two nationwide publications that represented the highest standards of liberal journalism, *The Nation* and *The New Republic,* not only publicized and celebrated La Guardia's many activities, as well as his record in Congress, but also invited him to contribute articles and opinion pieces. La Guardia had plenty of opinions. This went a long way toward getting across the message that here was a politician who could be all things to all people, yet never compromise his ideals and always remain his own man.

Since winning his first election in 1916, Fiorello had proved he could work at one and the same time with politicians who were themselves antipathetic philosophically and ideologically. Party labels were of no consideration. If he thought he could win, he would run on any ticket, not excluding one from the local Chinese laundry. Though neither a Socialist nor a Progressive by party affiliation, he courted and won their support and gave his imprimatur to their causes. He may have been a Republican, but this did not inhibit his dismissing GOP Presidents Harding, Coolidge, and Hoover and their cabinet members in terms that reeked of ridicule. Fiorello H. La Guardia, in summation, was crafty and unbreakable, a political guru, a certifiable reformer, and a confrontational liberal. He was also resolute in his belief that he was the only man capable of taking on Jimmy Walker and breaking Tammany's stranglehold on New York City in the 1929 mayoral race. (Because the New York contests are held in noncongressional election years, La Guardia did not have to give up his seat to run.)

His desire to be mayor was more than a political ambition. It was a political obsession, complemented by a need to achieve the personal power and opportunity to do good for the people of the city he so loved that he had been denied in 1921 by the bosses. Besides, constantly fighting for the Progressive cause in Congress had after six years become by degrees frustrating and lonely.

CHAPTER FOURTEEN

"I would hang a banker who stole from the people"

1.

A drive to get La Guardia the Republican mayoral nomination was launched in April by Ed Corsi and his Columbian Republican League, with Fiorello's active encouragement. Support came from such influential organizations as the New York Republican Club, the Kings County League of Italian-American Republican Clubs, a group of powerful Brooklyn county committeemen, and even silk-stocking Republicans who preferred La Guardia with all his rough edges to surrendering control of the city yet again to the Tammany machine. There was a spasm of opposition from Fiorello's former law partner William M. Bennett, the perennial antimachine conservative, but his campaign never got off the ground.

A far greater threat came from the party's Old Guard. Despite Sam Koenig's reminder that La Guardia was not only a proven winner, with that large following among the city's ethnic groups, the hierarchs could not accept the nomination of a man so opposed to the present occupant of the White House. They beat the bushes for a Hoover Republican to back and came up with a few prospective candidates. Pausing only long enough to undergo a tonsillectomy, Fiorello scared them off by barnstorming the city from one clubhouse to another with the threat of a rough-and-tumble, no-holds-barred fight in the primary. However, like all smart politicians, he was not above striking a deal. To appease the Hooverites he proposed that one of their own, National City Bank president Charles E. Mitchell, run on his ticket for city comptroller. The proposal was declined.

On the evening of August 1, 1,519 influential clubhouse leaders convened unofficially and heard Koenig declare that Fiorello "represents the desires of the rank and file of the party and of the plain people." State Senator Cortlandt Nicoll of the silk-stocking district nominated him. Only five delegates registered opposition. A riotous ovation followed. In his acceptance speech, he thanked the delegates, joked that he had "survived an orthodox Republican convention" (a joke the orthodox Republicans, having been presented with a fait accompli, did not find particularly amusing), praised the hastily constructed party platform as Progressive (a bit of dissembling here, since it contained only vague generalities), and served notice to Walker: "Jimmy, this fight is on the level."[1]

Early next morning, operating out of headquarters in the Hotel Cadillac in Times Square, Fiorello launched what even he realized was an uphill battle. First, there were the cold statistics: 1,265,423 registered Democrats (some of whom could doubtless be counted on by Tammany to vote more than once) versus 601,719 Republicans. Also, any hope of attracting Socialist support was vitiated when that party fielded the capable Norman Thomas. Even the normally pro-Fiorello *Nation*, while lauding his "independence, courage, [and] true liberalism," backed Thomas because "the Republican machine is not one whit better and is far less able than Tammany. Hall."[2] Furthermore, William Randolph Hearst made his peace with Tammany after six years of bitter feuding and got behind Walker.

Within his own party, Fiorello was anathema to what the press called "the better element." They found repellent the loudmouthed, rambunctious little Latin hyphenate who had bolted the party in 1924, backed a Socialist for mayor a year later, and took potshots at President Hoover. To them he was "a radical," "a foreigner." To the city's three Republican newspapers—the *Herald Tribune, Evening Post,* and *Evening Sun*—he was an opportunistic agitator. Conservatives in his party could not back Fiorello because of his Progressive views; liberals, because the Republican machine had nominated him.

To add to his woes, the wealthy, upscale Fifteenth Assembly District, from which came the party's biggest financial support, was in open rebellion against his candidacy. La Guardia sought to resolve party opposition by staffing the highest echelons of his campaign and selecting as running mates for comptroller, president of the Board of Aldermen, and district attorney a respected trio whose conservative credentials were impeccable. It didn't work. But then, neither would having made his selections from among the Twelve Apostles. For with all the obstacles facing him, by far the most formidable was the man Fiorello hoped to unseat.

Born in Greenwich Village of Irish immigrant parents, James John "Jimmy" Walker, a year Fiorello's senior, was the darling of the people. Though his family had ties to Tammany (his father had been a ward leader, alderman, and state assemblyman), Walker decided, upon graduation from NYU Law School in 1904, that his future lay not in the political theater but in the Broadway theater. After a few years of self-indulgence along the Rialto that included much boozing and womanizing, cultivating important friendships, and songwriting (his chef d'oeuvre: "Will You Love Me in December as You Do in May?"), Walker realized he could enter the (Tammany) family business, toward which he had been gravitating, without having to abandon show business. His father was pleased. So, too, was Grand Sachem Charlie Murphy. Jimmy was personable, popular, politically oriented, and—to Murphy, a plus factor of no mean significance— inherently convinced that corruption and venality were simply excusable minor forays into piddling naughtiness.

Starting out as a district captain, Walker was elected to the New York Assembly and four years later, under the tutelage of Al Smith, to the State Senate. In 1925, backed by the Tammany organization and now Governor Smith, Walker won his first of two terms as mayor. While he made a horrific mess of the second term, the first was fairly creditable. Among his accomplishments were creation of the Department of Sanitation, unification of the city's public hospitals, and improvements in the playgrounds and park systems. Strictly a night person, spending more evenings in the Central Park Casino than days in City Hall, here was a mayor who refused to let hedonism get in the way of municipal responsibility. And oh! how the people loved their "Gentleman Jimmy." Said famed saloon restaurateur Toots Shor, voicing the consensus of opinion, "Jimmy! Jimmy! When you walked into the room you brightened up the joint!"[3]

There were portents. Despite a wife and his Catholicism, Walker openly took as his mistress Broadway semistar Betty Compton. Al Smith believed that his public behavior not only harmed the Democratic Party but also jeopardized Smith's own presidential ambitions. When Jimmy pledged to be "a Tammany Hall Mayor" who would follow faithfully the sachems' "leadership and advice," Smith warned him bluntly, "The wind is getting stronger and you're going to be blown sky-high."[4] Walker couldn't quite share that vision. Neither could the people. He was their Jazz Age avatar, their symbol of the times.

Determined to win despite formidable odds, Fiorello made more than four hundred campaign speeches, taking to the stump as often as fifteen times a day. Rushing from one end of the city to the other, he appealed to every social and ethnic group in every language at his command. His primary target audience was the city's slum dwellers, for whom he concentrated on the issues that most affected them: food, housing, schools, parks—and dirty politics. Of the lot, by far the one of most concern was the high cost of food. The methods of distribution, Fiorello disclosed after a characteristically intensive study, were a scandal, with the produce going from farmer to commission merchant to wholesaler to jobber to retailer to consumer, amassing added charges along the way. After a three-hundred-page report in 1912 followed a barrel of spinach and found that it was loaded and reloaded nine times between farmer and consumer, the Bronx Terminal Market was built, during Mayor Hylan's administration, where freight cars and cargo ships could unload their produce directly for purchase by retailers. But, charged La Guardia, Mayor Walker had taken no step to open the market or to have additional ones built. As a result, working New Yorkers, with no savings or investments to fall back on, were paying 43 percent of their income just to feed themselves.[5]

In the city's worst slum-ridden areas he would point dramatically to the "thousands of sunless, fire-exposed houses with yard toilets and dark and ill-kept public halls," which he branded "an everlasting disgrace to the richest city in the world." Mayor Walker, he noted contemptuously, had fought against the Multiple Dwelling Bill, which established standards for improving tenements. After the bill became law, his administration joined realty interests in attacking it in the courts. When it came to housing, "the Walker administration has

made a record of callous indifference and malevolent sabotage un-
equaled by any administration in the history of the city."[6]

Another major target group was the middle-class Republicans, for
whom Fiorello stressed a different set of issues. In his official acceptance speech before the party regulars at Town Hall on September
20, he charged the Walker administration with hindering business
enterprise and then announced a catalogue of promises. He would,
if elected, reorganize overlapping municipal departments, establish
a regional planning commission, unify the transit system, clean up
the Police Department, eliminate graft, and solve the housing problem through private enterprise. Merciless in his attacks on Tammany
Hall and its long history of graft and corruption, he cited meticu-
lously harvested facts and figures on the mismanagement of various
municipal departments under the Walker administration. He even
charged the administration with strong ties to the underworld.[7]

In his speeches to orthodox Republicans, La Guardia was re-
strained in diction and verbiage. Not so when addressing "the plain
people," as in the middle of a speech to an East Side Italo-American
Republican Club, when, making a point about corruption in the police department, he shouted, "Why, I can take you to a crap game
less than two hundred feet from here. And the bosses of Tammany
Hall know it!"[8] Before labor groups he tore into Walker's failure to
put up low-cost housing and promised to end once and for all time
the union-busting activities of the police force and the shaking down
of workers on city contracts. He reminded veterans' groups of the
fights he had waged in their behalf in Congress. He addressed for
the first time the African Americans, who were steadily abandoning
the Republican Party, vowing to one Harlem audience, "If I have
anything to do with this city's administration, you will get a different
deal." Protesting discrimination in a Brooklyn Episcopal church, he
shouted, "Christ would have hung his head in shame." To Jewish
audiences, he denounced anti-Semitism. To Italians, he reminded
them he would be the first of their descent to preside over City Hall.[9]

La Guardia's strong appeal to the underprivileged was somewhat
compromised by the strong support he had among the elite. His
campaign manager, for one, Keyes Winter, was leader of the Fifteenth ("Silk-Stocking") Assembly District. Allying himself with the
party's conservatives alienated the left, while his radical record in
Congress alienated many of the Hoover Republicans. They endorsed

him only out of party loyalty but would not campaign for him. Adding to his troubles, although La Guardia came up with evidence of the connection between Tammany and the underworld, he was unable to convince Governor Franklin D. Roosevelt to investigate the Walker administration. Roosevelt claimed he lacked enough facts to warrant such a probe. It's possible that a contributory reason was that he had his eyes on the White House and was not yet in a strong enough position to antagonize further the powerful downstate Democratic machine, which disliked him intensely.

In its early stages, the campaign was kept well within acceptable bounds. In fact, the rhetoric was one-sided. Walker, who didn't even open his campaign until less than a month before Election Day, was rather amused by the slogan his opponent had placed in front of his Hotel Cadillac headquarters: "Elect a full-time mayor who will sleep at night and work in the daytime." The temperature was raised considerably when La Guardia, furious over his refusal to respond to the charges of corruption, began to attack Walker instead of sticking to the issues. A week before election, the campaign got rather silly. It was taken to that level by Fiorello, who was showing signs of desperation.

In a speech to the Irish-Republican League of New York in Bryant Hall, he accused Walker of being a renegade to his "race," charging that he had a "British peeress," one Lady Armstrong, on his campaign committee. As if *that* weren't enough to demonstrate the man's infidelity to the Irish Republic, La Guardia fairly screeched, "If you go to the Mayor's apartment, you will find an autographed photograph of the Prince of Wales!" Then he attacked Walker's reputation as a dandy: "He is not a well-dressed man, according to the standards of American gentlemen. He is a loudly dressed man—displaying all the bad taste and vanity of the political parvenu who got rich quick. . . . He is the loudly dressed man according to the styles of the English fop or the Paris gigolo."[10] To which Walker responded, "If I thought that I might serve the taxpayers better by appearing at City Hall clad in overalls, or even a snood, I should do so. But until we have an ordinance to the contrary, I shall bathe frequently, as is my custom, and change my linen often, as is perhaps my eccentric desire, and patronize the tailor of my own choice."[11] Perhaps because he liked La Guardia personally, Walker was decent enough not to note that his opponent was the last man to pass judgment on matters of dress. Perhaps he felt the personal attacks made no difference. They didn't. The final vote: 865,549 for Walker to 368,384 for La Guardia. (Thomas got 174,931, most of them from his fellow Socialists but a not inconsiderable number from voters disgusted with both the other candidates.)

For La Guardia it was more than a loss. It was a humiliation. He failed to carry a single assembly district, and he accounted for only 26 percent of the total vote, the lowest figure for any mayoral candidate since the creation of Greater New York in 1898. Though having accepted from the outset that he was at best a long shot, the degree by which he lost was both unanticipated and personally devastating, so much so that when he emerged from his headquarters to thank his followers after wiring his concession to Walker, there were tears on his cheeks.[12]

How is it that this proven vote-getter lost, and so humiliatingly?

The fact that New York was not yet ready for an Italian mayor is only part of the answer. He had the Republican nomination but not the party's rank-and-file, who either sat out the election or voted for one of the other two candidates. He did well in the Italo-American districts, but there weren't enough of them to send him to City Hall. Two major faults can be attributed to La Guardia himself. Though nominally a Republican, he went into the race as a bogus reform fusionist, trying to please nearly everyone. He pleased practically no one but those Italian hyphenates, who would have voted for him regardless of what he said and who as a group were repugnant to too many of New York's Anglos and other hyphenates.

In the final analysis, though, three factors overrode all other considerations: Walker's immense popularity, the normally huge Democratic majority, and Governor Roosevelt's refusal to authorize an investigation of the downstate Tammany machine. As the *New York Times* noted on November 6, 1929, as soon as the results were announced, "No one could have been surprised—not even Major La Guardia really—at the reelection of Mayor Walker. If ever there was a foregone conclusion it was this one. The stars in their courses fought for Mr. Walker."

But perhaps the last word should go to Sam Koenig. A week before the election, the stock market had collapsed, and the Great Depression of which it was a harbinger, in tandem with the split in the Tammany machine and the incontestable proof of massive municipal corruption, would create a radically different political climate in New York City four years down the line. It was something that could not have been foreseen on that November Tuesday that was for La Guardia the saddest of his political life to date. Only in retrospect could Koenig say, "We were too soon with the right man."[13]

2.

Following his return to Washington, La Guardia emerged as one of the most influential of congressmen. It was not his methodology that changed. It was the times. Until the Great Depression he had enjoyed little success as a leader on his own terms. Despite his blend of paternalism and progressivism, even in his home district he was considered rather underwhelming by many except the Italo-Americans. In Congress, his parliamentary tactics and in-your-face oratory, along with his occasional dog-and-pony shows, were often considered more irritating than persuasive. They led many colleagues to see him as a gadfly who played to the balcony, a nuisance, and worse: a gnomic alien with logorrhea who dared patronize them as being beneath him intellectually and morally. But this did not deter him. By the time he left Capitol Hill for good, his importance in Congress would be conceded by even those newspapers most hostile to him throughout the 1920s.

The stock market crash of October 1929 was seen by President Hoover, his cabinet, and the nation's leading financiers as a storm that would soon blow over. All that was required of the nation was courage and confidence. Optimism for a return of prosperity in the coming year was shared by the leading bankers and merchants. To the financial world, the Wall Street convulsion following a time of great prosperity was as mysterious as it was unexpected.[14]

But not to La Guardia. While the financiers and their champion in the White House had been reading reports and articles that bolstered their confidence in the nation's continuing good economic health, La Guardia had been reading better indicators: letters that came in daily from his constituents, jobless and in dire economic straits even before the Crash. Typical was this one: "My husband is out of work for the last four weeks and I have seven children none able to work and we are constantly down and up against the rent and everything." Less than a week later came a letter signed by four sons seeking his assistance in getting a job for their father, who had been out of work for three years. Complaints poured in daily, such as this one, scrawled in Italian on cheap note paper, from a tenement dweller who "used to get pension from the government and they stopped. It is now seven months I am out of work. . . . I have four children who are in dire need of clothes and food. . . . My daughter who is eight is very ill and not recovering. My rent is due two months and I am afraid of being put out."[15]

After the Crash the letters came in more frequently and with a greater sense of urgency. Not only East Harlem but the entire country was in a crisis. The nation's first unemployment census, taken in April of 1930, showed three million unemployed, with 180,000 people without jobs in Manhattan alone. But the rate at which unemployment rose made these statistics outdated as soon as they were tabularized. Nine months later, a special census showed six million unemployed—and the figures were rising steadily.[16] As conditions worsened, soup lines became more numerous and the sidewalks were littered with the furniture of evicted families.

Radical groups encountered little argument when they charged that all this economic misery was proof positive of the breakdown of the capitalist system. The ensuing three years would see the already fragile economy tottering like a drunk down a dark street before collapsing in a gutter. Agriculture, long in one of its periodic slumps, would hit bottom. Eighty-five thousand businesses would fail. Nine million savings accounts would be wiped out. Nearly thirteen million Americans would be unemployed. When in 1932 FDR entered the White House and La Guardia exited Congress, the national income would be down by 50 percent, suffering in every part of the country would be horrific—and one of the hit tunes of the year would be the appropriately ironic "Brother, Can You Spare a Dime?"

To condemn Herbert Hoover for the smashup of the American economy and resultant Great Depression is not only unfair, it is ludicrous. Where Hoover is to be condemned is for the way he faced the problem as president. It was, in a word, appalling. His contention that the First World War and the collapse of the European banking community were important contributory causes is irrefutable. But, in all fairness to Hoover, ultimate responsibility in the United States must be imputed to the New Era politics and economics to which he fell heir as Coolidge's successor. The failure of farm income and wages to keep pace proportionately with dividends and profits deprived the market of consumer power to sustain good times. High tariffs prevented Europeans from selling enough goods to acquire money to buy in turn American products. Huge profits amassed by the Mellon tax plan went into Wall Street instead of "trickling down" into the general economy. Unwillingness to regulate industry "trusts" contributed to the unhealthy pyramiding of corporations. The Coolidge administration's fiscal policies encouraged blatant gambling in the bull market. When the market crashed it brought down the gamblers and exposed the weakness of the economy, thereby shattering the nation's confidence.

Inheriting a mess is one thing. Dealing with that inheritance is something else. And the way Hoover dealt with his did him in. Despite his overly confident public assurances, he quickly began to perceive the seriousness of the situation. On November 21, 1929, a month after Black Tuesday, he convened a White House meeting of business leaders and urged that employment and wage levels be maintained, on humanitarian as well as economic grounds. That same afternoon he asked the leaders of the American Federation of Labor and the Railroad Brotherhoods to cooperate in restraining demands for wage increases. Twelve days later, in his first annual message to Congress, he conceded that "uncontrolled speculation" had precipitated plunging farm prices and rising unemployment, called attention to his efforts to stimulate state and local governments as well as leaders in the private sector to encourage production of vital goods, and recommended an increase in public works programs, banking reform, and administrative reorganization to further strengthen the economy.[17]

The one thing he did not call for was the one thing most urgently needed to effect a quantum jump toward reviving the economy: a massive infusion of federal funds. President Hoover felt that the best way to go was a program of voluntary action. It wasn't. Industry, despite assurances to the contrary, found it impossible to expand employment. In fact, employment levels went in the opposite direction. The promise not to cut wages was broken across the board, although dividends continued to be paid at elevated levels for two years. Telegrams to governors and mayors requesting expansion of public works programs elicited universally a "cordial but vague" response.[18] Now, as the president insisted that the voluntary approach was the only logical approach, and the Depression crossed the Hudson River and headed west like an express train with a dead engineer at the controls, Congressman Fiorello H. La Guardia underwent a drastic reevaluation in the eyes of those who had denounced him throughout the years of Coolidge prosperity as a Socialist, a Communist, a demagogue, an obnoxious hyphenate, and a man to be avoided, like the policies he propounded and the prudence he promulgated.

Suddenly it was recalled that he had gone after the taxing, tariff, farm, labor, and monopoly policies of his own party—the party that held the White House between Wilson and Roosevelt and had, in fact, held it prior to Wilson since the Civil War except for the two nonconsecutive presidencies of Grover Cleveland (1885–89, 1893–97); that he had reviled the lopsided Jazz Age prosperity, exposing the frightful poverty of the urban slums and the exurban farms and coal mines; and that he had argued vehemently against the assumption that business interests and the national interest, more than being conjoined, were one and the same. Overnight, he was being bombarded from around the country with letters and wires of support and encouragement, and admiration for the battles he was waging, from people representing all walks of life—from tenement dwellers evicted from their hovels and farmers evicted from their land through foreclosure to such men of influence and foresight as philosopher John Dewey and theologian Reinhold Niebuhr.

Like an impatient racehorse in top form kept waiting at the starting gate, La Guardia sprang into action when he resumed his seat in Congress. In going after Hoover's mishandling of the crisis—a mishandling rooted in the tacit conviction of the GOP leadership that the egg Wall Street laid, to paraphrase *Variety*'s immortal headline, was simply one of those terribly unpleasant realities of life that must be gotten through, like childhood illness and adult divorce— La Guardia had a champion in a fellow New Yorker, Senator Robert F. Wagner. A Democrat, yes, but an ideological comrade-in-arms. In the early months of 1930 Fiorello worked nonstop to get House action on several measures introduced by Wagner and approved by the Senate that embodied principles La Guardia had already made his own.

One that raised dust in the House called for establishing a free national employment service, locally managed, to serve as a clearinghouse for jobs and job seekers. After a stubborn fight in the Judiciary Committee, of which he was a member, to force the bill before the full House, La Guardia led the fight for its adoption. On June 10, 1930, when the National Association of Manufacturers insisted that the bill was in violation of states' rights, La Guardia noted caustically that other federal activities were carried on within state perimeters, such as flood control, farm relief, and the public health service. The economy, he pointed out, having been nationalized by the growth of giant industry, demanded that activities heretofore considered local be subject to federal regulation: "Unemployment in one state is a matter which concerns every other state. I believe it is one of the most important functions of government to deal with the question of employment and unemployment."

Reiterating what he had been saying for years—that the nation's entire economic system had to be revamped to meet new conditions—he added, "There is no more justification for unemployment in this day and age than there is for epidemics of preventable diseases. . . . If it is necessary for the War Department to prepare careful plans for wars which will probably never occur, it is surely much more necessary to provide in advance for the relief of industrial depressions which are sure to come." At the same time, he introduced a resolution calling on President Hoover to convene a nationwide conference of governors to prepare and submit uniform labor laws to be enacted by the state legislatures. What La Guardia wanted was agreement on factory regulations, a short-hour day and five-day week (to open up jobs to alleviate the huge unemployment), abolition of child labor, minimum wages, old age pensions, and unemployment insurance for factory and farm workers to be financed by contributions from employees, employers, and the federal government.[19]

Though he was the minority member of the committee before which the bills were being considered, La Guardia wielded great influence because of his ability to attract the kind of headlines that held great appeal for those Americans most in need of such legislation. He was not above publicly branding the bankers and their allies in Congress "stock peddlers," "bond-mongers," and "public utilities whores," corporation lawyers as "pimps for Wall Street," and federal judges as "thieving sons of bitches in robes." To one of his closest aides he barked, "The bastards broke the People's back with their usury. . . . Let them die; the People will survive." But despite his every effort, and over his scathing minority report, the Wagner bills were passed in severely emasculated form. It probably did not matter. Hoover vetoed them anyway, arguing that they were too expensive and gave the federal government too much power. La Guardia's acerbic reaction: "The smallest thing ever performed by a big man in history."[20]

Fiorello not only publicly identified "the bastards," he went after them like an avenging angel. As already noted, the articles of impeachment he had drawn up against Treasury Secretary Mellon became moot when Hoover moved Mellon out of harm's way by naming him ambassador to Great Britain. Utilities tycoon Samuel Insull, attacked by La Guardia in a nationwide broadcast a year before the Chicago industrialist's enormous empire collapsed in ruins through his manipulative corruption, fled to Greece. La Guardia caused three of those "thieving sons of bitches in robes" to be reprimanded by the Judiciary Committee for shady handling of bankruptcy cases. (One narrowly escaped conviction in the Senate after his impeachment by the House.) Another La Guardia target was Richard Whitney, president of the New York Stock Exchange, whom he cross-examined before a congressional committee as if he were a common thief. When New York University conferred an honorary degree on Whitney, La Guardia inquired by letter, "Through what oversight did you overlook [honoring with a degree] gangster Alphonse Capone of Chicago?" In 1939, convicted of stock fraud and manipulation, Whitney and his degree wound up where they belonged—in Sing Sing.[21]

To support his unemployment insurance bill, La Guardia amassed much useful information through correspondence with the British Ministry of Labor on how the problem was handled in England. (In the summer of 1930, he attended the Inter-Parliamentary Union in London, taking Marie along on a sort of second honeymoon.) In addition, he studied reams of documentation on our own depressions of 1893 and 1907 in hopes of learning lessons from the past. But the bill was allowed to die in committee. Moreover, his resolution for a White House–hosted conference on labor legislation was completely ignored by Hoover. Hoover would doubtless have vetoed any insurance compensation bill that might have come across his desk. He considered such insurance a dole, the gravest threat to the American spirit of self-reliance.

This elicited from La Guardia a shrieked "Dole! dole! dole! That is all one hears at every discussion of an unemployment insurance plan." Demanding to know, "What is there so novel and radical about it?" he argued that if Americans can insure themselves against fire, theft, assault, and, death, as well as natural phenomena like hurricanes, then why shouldn't they be allowed to insure themselves against the hazards of industry? It was fine for the president to assure stockholders that prosperity was imminent, but the poor were "not interested in words. They want food, clothing, and shelter."[22]

In a speech on the House floor (March 3, 1931), La Guardia trashed the Power Trust as an "active, well-organized continuation of power, gas, electric and trolley corporations united in a common purpose of keeping private control of public utilities—maintaining high rates, influencing legislation, and fighting public ownership." Claiming that this monopoly resulted in exorbitant costs for public utilities, he added, "There is not a mother keeping house in the country but dreads the moment when the gas and electric bills come."[23] But the president was "firmly opposed to the government entering into any business, the major purpose of which is competition with our citizens." He added, "I hesitate to contemplate the future of our institutions, of our government, and of our country if the preoccupation of its officials is to be no longer the promotion of justice and equal opportunity, but is to be devoted to barter in the markets." That, to Hoover, was "not liberalism, that is degeneration."[24]

For the 1930 congressional campaign, John F. Curry, the new Tammany Grand Sachem, picked an attractive young Italian, Vincent Auletta, to replace the Hall's Number One Irritant. But popular sentiment was running in the Irritant's favor, not only among the voters but in the press. The *World-Telegram* (November 1, 1930) warned, "A little man would leave a big hole in Congress if La Guardia was defeated." Also militating in Fiorello's favor were the daily airings of the scandals being unearthed by Judge Samuel Seabury, appointed by the Appellate Division of the Supreme Court earlier that year to investigate New York City's Tammany-tainted Magistrate's Courts and the Walker administration. This prompted the *New York Times* to declare (August 30, 1930) that Congressman La Guardia was the only one who had the right "to stand up in New York City today and say, 'I told you so.' Recent disclosures of corruption in the municipal government...seem to furnish full justification for the charges which Mr. La Guardia freely made in the last Mayoralty campaign."

The campaign was waged in an atmosphere of the laboring class's growing resentment against the rising toll of joblessness and evictions and what seemed like a total inability on the government's part to stop the downhill slide. When the International Apple Shippers Association offered fruit on credit to the jobless to sell at five cents each, the rush to accept was overwhelming; by election time, some six thousand persons were selling apples on New York City's streets.[25] The *Evening Journal* claimed that during the eight-month Congressional session that ended in July, La Guardia made 970 speeches—an awesome average of more than three a day—against high prices and profiteering and in favor of protecting living standards. While Washington VIPs and their wives attended important social functions, Congressman La Guardia attended the Library of Congress to immerse himself in documents to root out facts and figures to buttress whatever he had to say on the House floor and the streets of East Harlem. Some of his suggestions elicited amused skepticism from the press, like the suggestion that every employed man buy a suit for an unemployed one, who would buy a suit for another man when he secured a job. To dramatize this idea, Fiorello had his picture taken at Harlem House, showing him buying a suit for an unemployed neighbor.[26]

His reelection campaign was run from a vacant store at 106th Street and Madison Avenue with La Guardia directing every move, paying his characteristically meticulous attention to every detail, while wife Marie and Edward Corsi flooded the district with placards and posters and arranged street-corner speeches at every intersection. Meanwhile, Vito Marcantonio had his *Gibboni* fan out through the Twentieth in quest of possible Tammany hanky-panky, besides marching up and down the streets morning, noon, and night singing their anthem, "Fiorello H. La Guardia, Harlem needs a man like you in Congress."

On October 24, 1930, the *Daily Mirror*, a powerful influence among laborers and the jobless, came out for La Guardia, saying it would be "a tragic thing for the people of New York if Mr. La Guardia is defeated." Categorizing him as "the only real liberal in the delegation from this state—one of the few in the whole House," the editorial went on to say he had "maintained vigilance against the plots of predatory wealth, food profiteers, and grafters of all kinds. . . . He is incorruptible. Citizens, do not let this worthy public servant be destroyed!"

The citizens obeyed. La Guardia was reelected with his largest plurality since 1924: 9,934, to 8,217 for Auletta (the Socialist candidate, Frank Porce, received 849 votes).[27] Meanwhile Hoover, who had won office with a majority of one hundred in the House and seventeen in the Senate, was handed what amounted to a vote of no confidence in this off-year election. The Democrats captured the House. The majority of one that the Republicans had in the Senate was irrelevant. Facing Hoover in both chambers was a bloc of western and midwestern insurgents who found his policies abhorrent. They were given the derisive label "Sons of the Wild Jackass" by one Hooverite, an appellation they bore with pride. Included in their number were the likes of such legendary Populist/Progressive senators as George Norris, William E. Borah, Burton K. Wheeler, Hiram Johnson, and Robert "Young Bob" La Follette Jr., successor to his father, "Fighting Bob," who had died in 1925. Among the congressmen was Paul J. Kvale, son of the now deceased congressman who had once roomed with La Guardia and officiated at his marriage to Marie.

In the House, where they were called the Allied Progressives, La Guardia assumed command of the insurgents. It was a natural and well-received assumption. He was older than most, had more seniority and experience in parliamentary tactics, and had researched and studied to a greater degree the problems of the Depression. In addition, he had many friends among the Washington press corps, and even those who wrote adversely about him wound up eliciting sympathy for his views from their readers. La Guardia's office became the war room where the insurgents mapped their anti–White House strategy. Pledging his group to fight Hooverism on every level, he declared unequivocally, "Congress must stop playing the cities against the farmers and the farmers against the cities."[28]

When the lame-duck session of the Seventy-first Congress ended in March 1931, the Sons of the Wild Jackass called for a convention in Washington. Attending, in addition to members of the House, were prominent reformers from every walk of life across the nation's entire political spectrum. With unemployment spiking to eight million, conditions for a political realignment seemed as "indicated" as a biopsy for a suspected cancer patient. Not in attendance was Fiorello, hospitalized because of a flare-up of his war-related hip injury. On March 31, 1931, in a three-page letter to Norris from his hospital bed summarizing his economic philosophy and outlining a program of action for his Progressive colleagues in both chambers of Congress, Fiorello wrote of "a tendency on the part of leaders in both of the major parties to continue to legislate on fundamentals laid down in the age of the stage coach, the spinning wheel, and tallow candles." This had "resulted in the concentration of great wealth under the control of a few families in this country with large masses of workers entirely at their mercy for their very existence." Legislation had not kept pace with progress in mechanics, electricity, chemistry, transportation, and the sciences. "The result is that we find ourselves with an unprecedented wealth, with warehouses full and millions of willing workers out of employment and large numbers dependent upon private charities." With millions of workers through no fault of their own being "thrown out of employment," it was the government's obligation "to give them relief and not force them to apply for private charity."

He then went on to propose as a minimum program closer cooperation between the Progressives in both houses of Congress, a national conference on labor legislation, unemployment insurance, lower interest rates, electric power, the outlawing of private employment agencies, a national system of employment agencies, and even liberalization of rules in the House. When the new Congress convened at the end of the year, he vowed, he would fight for an anti-injunction law, the five-day week, a multibillion-dollar public works program to be financed by higher taxes on the rich, the policing of the stock exchange, and government-backed insurance for savings accounts. "The salvation of this country," he concluded, "depends on Congress."[29]

Despite the even more precipitous downturn in the summer of 1931, Progressives of both main political parties—including both La Guardia and Governor Roosevelt—were reluctant to push government spending even for purposes of amelioration beyond the limits of a balanced budget. In response to a proposal by the Hearst newspapers that the government spend five billion dollars immediately to restore prosperity, La Guardia said that public works should be financed out of current appropriations, bond issues, and taxes in the higher brackets (the latter suggestion did not go down too well with Hearst). Increasing the national debt, he argued, would be "bad financing" and "bad statesmanship."[30]

A few months later, with unemployment in New York State having reached the million mark and local relief efforts no longer capable of meeting the need, Roosevelt called a special session of the state legislature. Here for the first time he expounded his (and La Guardia's) theory that it was the government's moral obligation to prevent starvation. He proposed, and battled the legislature through to final passage, the Wicks Bill, which established a Temporary Emergency Relief Administration for direct aid and work relief. La Guardia, who had urged Republicans to support it, lauded Roosevelt's insistence that the twenty-million-dollar relief program be financed out of an income tax increase, with the burden borne by those who "have benefited by our industrial and economic system." The act marked the first time any of the states accepted a significant share of responsibility for welfare and established the concept of work relief as a major method of public aid.

3.

When the Seventy-second Congress opened in December 1931, the two major parties were so closely matched in strength that La Guardia and his fellow Progressives enjoyed a political clout far in excess of their numbers. In the Senate, the balance between 36 Republicans and 47 Democrats (plus one Farmer-Labor man) was held by 12 Progressives, led by Norris. In the House, the count was 219 Democrats, 192 Republicans, and 15 Progressives under La Guardia's aegis, who tipped the balance by a three-vote margin in favor of electing John Nance Garner of Texas as Speaker of the House. (He would be elected FDR's vice president in the following year.)

In his message to the new Congress on December 8, President Hoover offered assurances that Congress could "now stimulate employment and agriculture more effectually and speedily through the voluntary measures in progress, through the thawing out of credit, through the building up of stability abroad, through the Home Loan Discount Banks, through an emergency finance corporation, and the rehabilitation of the railways and other such directions." A committee he appointed to consider public works expansion harshly condemned, not surprisingly, Senator Robert Wagner's two-billion-dollar public works program, on the grounds that "in the long run the real problem of unemployment must be met by private business interests if it is to be permanent." It was their—and Hoover's—considered opinion that the problem of massive unemployment could not be solved "by any magic of appropriation from the public treasury."[31]

On the same day the committee's report was made public, La Guardia delivered a major speech on the economic crisis in which he demanded bold action by Congress on a number of fronts. Blasting Assistant Secretary of Commerce Julius Klein, whom he described as "the bed-time story teller of the Administration" and a "Baron Munchausen" for feeding the nation optimistic reports about the state of its economic health, La Guardia declared the urgent need for fundamental and sweeping measures: "Near palliatives will not do; a major operation is necessary. . . . The entire financial structure of the world has collapsed; the present economic system is not adequate to meet the industrial age in which we are living and it may be necessary to go into the very fundamentals of our system and bring about an economic readjustment." He likened Hoover's thesis that the crisis could be ameliorated by depending upon voluntary action in the private sector to trying to plug a hole in a dike with one's thumb.

The only solution to the unemployment crisis, the crux of the dilemma, was a great government-funded public works program that "may run into billions but would be worth it." Admitting that such a comprehensive program would require increased taxation, he insisted the burden be placed on the wealthy. It was "unwholesome in any republic" that 5 percent of the nation's citizens owned 80 percent of the nation's wealth. In the speech's peroration La Guardia proposed yet again a national system of unemployment insurance. Employers kept their idle machinery well oiled, housed, and insured against fire and theft, while the human beings who operated that machinery were not only ignored but left to wallow in a misery not of their creation.

He was attacked by the opposition on the grounds that his suggestions were unconstitutional. "If the Constitution stands in the way," he shouted with asperity, "well, the Constitution will simply have to get out of the way." President Hoover's response to this as well as all other remedial measures called for in both chambers of Congress was his formulaic "We cannot squander ourselves into prosperity."[32]

With the nation in the third winter of the Depression, Hoover conceded the need for more government spending. But he remained resolutely opposed to direct federal relief for the unemployed, convinced that the economy could be restored from above, through business enterprise. The resultant clash with La Guardia came over a bill authorizing creation of the Reconstruction Finance Corporation with a capital of two billion dollars to extend credit to banks, insurance and mortgage companies, and railroads. Hoover's reasoning: If industry recovered—and it needed such credit to do so—then employment would rise, as would purchasing power, and the country would emerge from the economic chaos to a restored prosperity. To the press, by and large, the proposal was hailed as the boldest to issue forth from Washington since the economy plummeted following the Crash of '29.

To La Guardia, it was a "ruthless, cruel coercion on the part of bankers," a "millionaire's dole" for the bankers and their allies: double-dealing criminals who had caused the Depression in the first place, miserable vermin who had sold worthless securities, gambling with—and losing—the people's money. And here the White House was rewarding them with loans while their victims—farmers, workers, small businessmen, and destitute depositors—were begging an overburdened Red Cross for whatever assistance they might provide! Out west where he was raised, he screamed, they had a word for such a breed: horse thieves. When asked by one member, "Would the gentleman hang the bankers?" the gentleman shot back: "What would you do? Give them a medal? Yes, I would hang a banker who stole from the people!"[33]

During the debate over the bill, La Guardia offered a series of crippling amendments, all of which were voted down. The bill passed both chambers and was signed into law by the president on January 22, 1931. This did not stop La Guardia. He continued to heap abuse on the "financial incurables" as mail poured into his office daily from across the country hailing him as the people's last hope, describing foreclosures on homes and farms despite the founding of the RFC, which he referred to contemptuously as "the hospital for the rehabilitation of commerce and industry."[34]

Not even La Guardia at his most confident could have foreseen he was on the verge of his most spectacular victory since joining the House in 1917.

This time his clash with Hoover was over the Revenue Bill of 1932.

So great had the national income declined, the government was now in danger of ending the year in the red. And Hoover, committed as he was to lending money to big business, regarded a balanced budget as the sine qua non for recovery. To raise some six hundred million dollars, more than half the total tax bill, the White House approved, after initial reluctance, a sales tax on manufactured goods. Even Speaker Garner, who opposed raising revenue by this means, as it would impose an added burden on even the lowest economic class, thought it a lesser evil than an unbalanced budget and agreed to lead the president's fight in the House. The measure had been reported out favorably by the Ways and Means Committee with only one dissenting vote, and when debate began on March 10 an easy victory was foreseen. Not only was the organization and leadership of both parties behind the president on this one, even those newspapers that supported the common man, like the *New York Daily News* and *Chicago Tribune*, along with the Hearst empire, insisted the measure was the only way of preventing the nation from going into bankruptcy.

Not so the Allied Progressives, whose leader, La Guardia, waged a two-week battle that outdid David's celebrated joust with the Philistine Goliath. Never leaving the floor (he munched on peanuts for sustenance), he rallied his heavily outnumbered troops, at times with wisecracks at the opposition's expense, at times rising to heights of eloquence as he condemned the inequality of making the poor carry the rich on their backs. Naming names, he claimed it was all a plot on the part of the powerful few to scuttle the income tax through the sales tax. Indicative of the effect he was having, by the second week the opposition leaders could not hold their men in line. Bedlam became the order of the House as members cheered, jeered, shouted, and questioned not only the political loyalties but the very patriotism of colleagues. As the opposition fell like a picket fence in a tornado, Garner was forced to admit defeat. On March 24, westerners and southerners, giving vent to old Populist resentments, supplied the votes to defeat the bill.[35] Said the *St. Louis Post-Dispatch* (March 26, 1932): "Among the strange aspects of a confusing situation it appeared that virtually the sole member who still excited an effective influence on both sides of the chamber was Representative La Guardia, an uncompromising Republican Progressive ... [t]he only leader who appears to have a plan for carrying it out."

There was one more attempt a month later to reintroduce the sales tax. Fiorello jumped up, held his hands high like a football player about to punt, kicked vigorously with his right foot at an imaginary football, and shouted to his colleagues, "That is the way the sales tax will be booted out of this house."[36] Day after day he sat in the chamber in the front row, subsisting on peanuts, until he was satisfied that the sales tax was dead and buried.

Beating back the sales tax imbued La Guardia with a prestige that enabled him to trash the president's Omnibus Economy Bill. Intended to balance the budget, it asked Congress to save some three hundred million dollars by cutting the salaries of federal employees, consolidating overlapping departments, and cutting funds for veterans and vocational schools plus a variety of administrative agencies. Under the personal direction of La Guardia, who had armed himself with facts and figures from trade unionists, educators, veterans, government workers, and reformers, the bill was rewritten on the floor of the House. Though he did not get everything he wanted—salaries for government employees were cut—he got enough. When Hoover signed the bill in June, the original figure he had wanted cut from the budget had been reduced by 90 percent.[37]

In summing up his battles with Hoover to stand up for the little man against the oligarchs—and only the constraints of space inhibit an examination, however cursory, of all the battles he waged—it must be admitted, without detracting from La Guardia's parliamentary talents, that the victories in which he had assumed leadership could well have wound up as defeats if the direction he was moving in had been opposite that of the current tide. Or put another way, in La Guardia biographer Arthur Mann's felicitous words, "Fiorello could lead only when he moved in the direction already taken by the mob."[38] As we have seen, it was not La Guardia who had changed when he returned to Congress in 1922. It was the times that had changed, especially during the Hoover years.

Was Fiorello a verifiable demagogue, as Hoover categorized him? No more than he can be accused of having been a verifiable Socialist, as so many observers alleged. He was for regulation of institutions that he insisted were responsible for the collapse of the economy, not government ownership. The stock exchange, banking, and taxing reforms he fought for were designed to prevent what he considered "the Irresponsible Rich" from causing another depression. He also attributed the hard times to the depressed condition of low-income groups, which informed his fight to boost their purchasing power. Thus, La Guardia's overall program had a dual purpose: to police and tax the top of the economic order while at the same time protecting and bolstering the bottom. These two aims he had pursued throughout the 1920s, even during the best of economic times. Now, as the nation was going through the worst of economic times, it can be said that the country had caught up with him.

In concluding this section dealing with Fiorello La Guardia the congressman, let us look at what may stand as his valedictory to a seven-term career: the Norris–La Guardia Anti-Injunction Act of 1932.

As a former labor lawyer, La Guardia had long insisted that trade unions were the best way for working men and women to raise their standard of living. Congress shared this view during the Wilson years when, by the Clayton Act of 1914, it exempted organized labor from the antitrust laws. This attempt at reform was no more than a brief respite from the long-standing governmental indifference to, and collusion in, attacks dating back to the first attempts at trade unionism in the previous century. Congress may have spoken, but the courts spoke with a louder, more authoritative voice. And what they spoke can be encapsulated in the phrase "court-imposed injunction."

This was the chief instrument of the antiunionists, which La Guardia bore witness to as far back as the pre–World War I garment workers' strike. As a congressman, he denounced its use against railroad workers during the Harding administration and, in the Coolidge years, against Pennsylvania coal miners. Starting in 1923, and in every succeeding House session, he introduced anti-injunction legislation. It was always quickly interred in the files of the House Judiciary Committee.

In 1928, the Senate subcommittee chaired by George Norris submitted a comprehensive reform bill. But first Norris held extensive hearings in which leading attorneys and scholars on the subject gave the assurance he wanted that the bill would withstand judicial review. La Guardia introduced a companion measure in the House. The bill failed to pass both chambers. On January 5, 1932, as the Seventy-second Congress was getting under way, Norris felt the time was right for another try. Conferring often and coordinating their efforts, he and La Guardia presented the bill in their respective chambers. To rectify the ineffectual wording that had doomed the Clayton Act, the new measure specifically barred the use of injunctions to prevent union organizing or strikes, limited the application of any injunction to the charges specified in the complaint (thus barring the catchall injunction), provided jury trials for those charged with violating injunctions, stipulated that any judicial invalidation of any section of the measure would still leave other sections intact, and barred yellow-dog contracts (agreements in which an employee promised his employer not to join a union while in his employ). Of particular note was Section Two of the bill, which declared as a matter of "public policy" that because individual unorganized workers were "commonly helpless" they had the right to organize into unions, to enter into collective bargaining with an employer, and were to be free from coercion in these activities. Here was a direct precursor to the more sweeping Wagner Act of 1935.

When debate opened in the Senate on February 23, 1932, Norris, anticipating attacks on the bill's constitutionality, forcefully insisted that Congress had the right to declare public policy on any subject where it had the right to legislate. Averring that the bill was to "have the same rule of law apply to the poor as to the rich," he said it "prevents great aggregations of capital from combining against the weak and the poor in any way which would deprive them of the ordinary rights of free citizens."[39] One week after its introduction, despite a number of proposed amendments intended to weaken it, the Norris bill was adopted by the Senate by a vote of seventy-five to five, with sixteen abstentions. But there still remained the crucial battle in the House.

Here La Guardia took the lead. The rather brief debate climaxed on March 8, three days after its passage in the Senate, when the bill's chief opponent, James M. Beck of Pennsylvania, defended the use of injunctions in labor disputes with the argument that labor should not be given privileges denied to others. "What," he asked rhetorically, "could be more humane and beneficent than this [present] method of dealing with a labor controversy? The court . . . only commands [the laborer] to refrain from interfering with his employer's property and with the liberty of other workmen to work for his employer."

Rising to offer the chief rebuttal, La Guardia began by emphasizing that "this bill does not—and I cannot repeat it too many times—this bill does not prevent the court from being used as an agency for strike-breaking purposes and as an employment agent for scabs to break a lawful strike." What made the bill necessary, he charged, was that a few federal judges had sought to win the favor of financially powerful interests by adjudicating strikes in their favor through use of the injunction. Important declarations of policy, he went on, should be made by the elected representatives of the American people and not by a politically appointed federal judge.[40] The House passed the bill that same day (March 9, 1932) by an overwhelming vote of 362 yeas to 14 nays. Reported the *New York Times*, "Today's victory was the climax of an eight-year effort by Mr. La Guardia." President Hoover signed the bill exactly two weeks later. Administration supporters claimed that he was sympathetic to the bill's aims. Norris, on the other hand, claimed that Hoover signed reluctantly in the face of certainty that a veto would be easily overridden. The decisive pressure on him to sign, Norris maintained, came from the American people, who were acquiring a new awareness of "the inequalities which then existed in the economic structure."[41]

Between then and July, when Congress went into summer recess and members prepared for the upcoming elections, La Guardia continued to add to his luster by speaking out forcefully on a number of additional bills intended to benefit those suffering most from the Depression. Indeed, with his dramatic victories on the sales tax and labor injunction, he had by now emerged as one of the nation's most forceful and prominent leaders of a new, dynamic progressivism. He was also the most highly publicized congressman in the country: the man whose mission in life was to help the masses, not the classes;

the man whose rallying cry was "No doles for millionaires!"

The Republican president whom the Republican congressman from East Harlem had routed on so many fronts was by now totally discredited for one reason and one reason alone: He had failed to stem, let alone roll back, the Depression. In all fairness, it must be admitted that the charge that he lacked compassion and did nothing to that end is—and there is simply no other way to put it—rubbish. He did in fact sign some legislation that helped ameliorate the situation, such as the Glass-Steagal Act, which liberalized the credit regulations of the Federal Reserve Board, and agricultural and limited public works programs. He certainly did not deserve the opprobrium that history has heaped upon him. He was an intelligent man, a decent man, and a humane man, as his prepresidential career, both in the private sector and as director of Belgian war relief during the First World War, amply proves.

But Herbert Hoover was also a tragic man. His tragedy? That he held himself hostage to his own principles and failed to understand that what the ordinary people—the masses who decide who shall preside over their nation as its chief magistrate—wanted was what their thirty-first chief magistrate was inherently incapable of giving them: immediate, extensive, and direct government aid to get them through the most devastating economic downturn in the nation's history. Since the people who were most turned off by Hoover—and most turned on by their Little Flower's anti-Hooverism—comprised the population of East Harlem, La Guardia's reelection to Congress should have been a cakewalk. Indeed, when he returned home in July to campaign he was like a victorious Roman general returning home for a well-earned *ovatio.*

He was in for the shock of his life.

CHAPTER FIFTEEN

"The capitalist, if he does not invest his money, cannot eat it"

1.

The question fairly leaps off the page: How could *this* have ever happened?

Though confident of victory, Fiorello knew it would not be easily won. All signs pointed to Franklin Delano Roosevelt taking the White House, and the popular Democratic ex–New York governor had exceptionally long political coattails. The Republicans' party hierarchy, though not enchanted with Fiorello, were impressed with his record in the Seventy-second Congress; moreover, they realized that they must elect every Republican possible, in light of that dreaded coming Democratic avalanche. In October, Vito Marcantonio, La Guardia's campaign manager, collected enough signatures to place his name on the ballot under the Liberty Bell icon of the Liberal Party. With that and the GOP nomination secure, La Guardia began to maneuver toward capturing the Democratic nomination as well!

It was not an act of foolhardiness, nor arrogance, nor chutzpah. He had the backing of Senator Robert F. Wagner, the darling of the New York Democrats. He even had the support of one of his primary antagonists, Tammany's Brooklyn boss John McCooey. Not that McCooey liked La Guardia. In fact, he loathed him. His support was consonant with the longtime "gentlemen's agreement" whereby Tammany conceded the national offices to the GOP, which in turn gave the sachems the city's spoils in return. "Mr. La Guardia," McCooey told him, "I'd like to see you made Ambassador to Australia, but failing that, I'll try to send you back to Washington. Anywhere, just so long as you're kept out of New York City!"[1] But the final decision had to come from Tammany Hall. Boss Jimmy Hines gave the request an emphatic thumbs-down. Tammany chose political neophyte James Lanzetta.

La Guardia may not have gotten the Democratic slot on the ballot, but he certainly got Democratic backing of an impressive magnitude, not only in the state but nationwide, from such powerful labor leaders as John L. Lewis and William Green, whom twenty-one railroad unions followed in announcing for the congressman. Endorsements came in from influential Progressive senators, both Republican and Democrat, such as the letter from George Norris that was run in the *New York Telegram* on October 27: "The good you have done for the common, ordinary citizen, often under difficult and trying circumstances, certainly marks you as one of the advance leaders in honest government and progressive legislation." In addition, he had the support of the Roosevelt New Dealers, the influential pro-Roosevelt, anti-Tammany *New York Evening Journal*, and men like *Labor* editor Edward Keating, who were actively campaigning for FDR but openly urged Democrats to help return La Guardia to Congress.

While Vito Marcantonio tended to the mechanics of the campaign, the candidate rushed up and down long flights of East Harlem tenement stairs to interview Depression-ridden families. And there was, of course, his customary street-corner stumping as he stressed repeatedly the war cry that his constituents could never tire of hearing: The economic system had "to get in line. The people will refuse to be poor!" Fiorello was "a dynamo throughout the campaign—absolutely tireless. People waited to see him in long lines, and he saw every one of them. He kept tabs on the smallest detail, but could switch from a trivial question to a fiery speech concerning basic issues on no notice at all. He was everywhere at once, encouraging, strengthening, and inspiring us all."[2]

As Election Day drew closer, the campaign approached an emotional boiling point that burst into violence in the last week, courtesy of Tammany. While La Guardia was addressing a large crowd at 113th

Street and Madison Avenue, heart of the district's Puerto Rican section, a cascade of bricks, bottles, and assorted junk came flying down from a nearby roof, sending a few in the audience to the hospital. The *Gibboni* rushed to the rooftop in pursuit of the culprits, and the meeting ended in a real melee. At another street-corner rally, a baby carriage was flung down from a rooftop. La Guardia's boys contributed to the violence, going so far as to smash plate glass windows displaying pictures of his opponent. On one occasion, while tearing a Lanzetta poster attached to a fire escape, they pulled down the fire escape as well. We shall never know how many voters stayed home on Election Day out of fear of being physically intimidated, even mauled. Nor, for that matter, will we ever know how this fear affected the outcome.[3]

On November 7, led by the *Gibboni* holding torches on high, a crowd numbering in the thousands marched to La Guardia's tenement and shouted for "the Major." When he joined them, his ear-to-ear smile compounded in equal doses of gratitude for their support and confidence in the outcome, they all marched to 116th and Lexington—the candidate's lucky corner, where he gave his customary election-eve speech. Surveying the sea of faces, Marcantonio cried out ecstatically, "Man, how can we lose!"

Next day, when the returns came in, Fiorello asked, "How did we lose? Who were all those people in the parade?" One of his loyalists voiced the suspicion, "Maybe they weren't citizens."[4]

The final count was 15,277 for La Guardia, 16,477 for Lanzetta.

As an impromptu Lanzetta victory parade snaked its way through the district, Fiorello's supporters remained indoors, their window shades drawn in protest and mourning. When the parade, now numbering in the thousands, swung past his house, Fiorello drew a window shade aside and peered down, then turned away and said bitterly, according to comedian and raconteur Joey Adams, at the time a La Guardia acolyte, "What good's doing anything for the people? They don't appreciate it. I'm going to quit and work for myself and my family for a change."[5]

The *New York Times*, which over the years alternately lauded and condemned him, ran an editorial headlined "Exit One Gadfly" (November 15, 1932) that admitted La Guardia had been "in many ways, the most effective leader in the House. His influence was sought; the House hung upon his words." Still, his defeat "will be a source of relief to many of [those] who often found themselves unable or fearful to answer him when he was in full flight of oratory." No longer would his opponents have to face "his colossal energy and industry." La Guardia's unanticipated defeat made news throughout the country, whence came some consolation in the form of letters from people reflecting every walk of life and every socioeconomic stratum, Democrats as well as Republicans.

Ironically, La Guardia never ran a better campaign. Having shrewdly selected an executive committee that covered all ethnic bases in the district except, inexplicably, the Puerto Ricans, he made sure his many achievements in Congress were repeatedly celebrated. He was the same unorthodox Republican who beat Tammany five times in a row by making the normally Democratic Twentieth vote a split ticket. And he was more of a political force now than earlier in his congressional career. Not only was Congress heeding him for the first time, liberals and Progressives regardless of party affiliation were looking to him for the kind of resolution to the times that should have come from the White House.

This brings us back to the question: What caused La Guardia to lose?

His apologists attributed the defeat to two factors: Roosevelt's landslide election and a move to the left under the impact of the Depression. This latter excuse can be disposed of summarily, in view of the fact that Earl Browder, the Communist candidate, got all of 309 votes, and Socialist Frank Porce got even less. Besides, Lanzetta was not a leftist. Roosevelt's taking East Harlem by a margin of twenty thousand votes did not redound appreciably to Lanzetta's advantage. Not only did the New Dealers vote for Fiorello, many top echelon Roosevelt lieutenants actively and openly supported him with FDR's tacit blessing. The answer to La Guardia's defeat is threefold: his opponent, his precampaign mistakes, and his district's change demographically. To this can be added voter fraud, but since it cannot be quantified, it has no place in the equation.

The thirty-eight-year-old Lanzetta, virtually unknown until his Tammany-engineered election to the Board of Aldermen in the previous year, was a dream come true for a Tammany machine aching to dispose of the despised La Guardia. East Harlem born and raised, Columbia University trained (engineering and law), this handsome and personable second-generation Catholic Italo-American, lacking any

articulate public philosophy, had on entering politics endeared himself to his congressional district by cultivating it family by family. While
Congressman La Guardia was popping up and down in the House going after everyone on his hit list from crooked federal judges to the
president of the United States, and running around the country
speaking out on a catalogue of national issues, Lanzetta followed the
same route taken by La Guardia himself when the Little Flower started
his own political career: covering the district like crabgrass to win support among the voters and cultivating the right people. Lanzetta was
able to charge that La Guardia was so busy being a "statesman" that he
had ignored a cardinal rule among pragmatic congressmen: "Pork-
barrel" your district. Equally advantageous to Lanzetta was his popularity with the younger Italo-Americans. The mostly immigrant older
generation gave to the war hero major the brand of reverence and awe
ordinarily reserved for a Mafia don, whereas their children, having
come of voting age in the years of prosperity, and in the process having
become Americanized, did not hold him in the same veneration. La
Guardia, like their parents, represented the past. Lanzetta represented the future. He was one of their own.

La Guardia's failure to bring home the pork was in itself a serious
precampaign mistake, but inarguably his worst was to lose personal
touch with the voters. This brings us to the third reason for his defeat. The district had undergone a radical change in complexion,
one so rapid as to have seemingly happened while no one was looking. Two years previously, 21,304 East Harlemites had voted. This
time around, there was a dramatic increase of 12,866. Of these, between six and eight thousand were Puerto Ricans, who had displaced
the Jews in the district's western and northern precincts. Tammany
was quick to organize these newcomers and welcome them into the
fold. The new playing field was to become, in a sense, the ambitious,
aggressive Lanzetta's by default.

Once Fiorello perceived what had happened, he went on the offensive. He added a prominent Puerto Rican to his executive committee; he reminded the Puerto Ricans of all he had done for them
in Congress, including seeking dominion status; and—a bit cynical,
perhaps, but politically correct—he invited the world's featherweight
boxing champion, Cuba's Kid Chocolate, to stump the Hispanics on
the Little Flower's behalf, with an emphasis on those of black extraction. But it was too late. The damage was done. Lanzetta carried
the predominantly Puerto Rican Seventeenth Assembly District by

nearly three thousand votes. Not only was La Guardia's loss in the Seventeenth greater than when it was predominantly Jewish, the predominantly Italo-American Eighteenth, his power base for a decade, split between the two candidates. In previous elections Fiorello usually won by a margin of between 1,500 and 2,200 of the 15,000 votes cast in the Eighteenth. This year, 21,994 votes were cast, and his margin sank to 1,430. In this, his *annus horribilis*, Fiorello ran behind himself in not only the Puerto Rican district but—and more humiliating—in the Italo-American district.[6]

"I was beaten by the importation of floaters and repeaters," he told a friend. "Together with the Puerto Rican vote." La Guardia contested the election, and evidence of fraud at the polls was uncovered by the U.S. attorney for New York. The main offenders were men claiming to be election inspectors who gave fake addresses and were nowhere to be found; in some cases, more votes were cast for the Tammany candidate than there were voters in that particular district. Also, it was charged—never proved, but probable—that before the election Tammany city relief officials threatened to terminate welfare benefits to Puerto Ricans who did not vote for Lanzetta.[7] An official canvass failed to result in any substantial change in the final tally, and Lanzetta was certified as the duly elected representative from East Harlem. Thus the irony that Fiorello La Guardia left Congress as he had entered it ten years previously—as the result of a contested election!

Some weeks after his defeat, La Guardia served notice on Tammany Hall that he would lead a movement to reform the election laws so that New York City could "enjoy the exhilarating experience of a clean campaign."[8] So much for his "threat" to quit politics. Since the cleansing of New York City election laws did not come under the purview of the United States Congress, it would be permissible to suspect, as he departed for Washington as a lame duck, that the Little Flower had decided to take on once again the man who so roundly defeated him for mayor three years previously but was now on the verge of having to pay for his corrupt brand of politics: "Gentleman Jimmy" Walker.

2.

This would be the last lame-duck congressional session. The Twentieth Amendment to the Constitution, moving the presidential inauguration date from March 4 to January 20, would be ratified by the requisite three-quarters of the states toward the end of 1933 and become effective in 1936. Beginning in 1935, the new Congress would convene on the January 3 following election.

The session's opening was one of the most chaotic on record, coinciding as it did with a much publicized "hunger march" on the capital by three thousand jobless who paraded for six miles through the city under what the *New York Times* (December 7, 1932) described as "the most rigid police supervision on record in Washington." Given the behavior of the police, "supervision" was a euphemism for "corralling." The marchers were maneuvered into a dead-end street and forced to halt. They had no choice. On one side was a railroad embankment; on the other, cordons of police wielding—and threatening to use, if need be—tear gas and nightsticks. Representatives of the marchers presented to Vice President Charles Curtis (as president of the Senate) and House Speaker Garner petitions for unemployment insurance legislation and a direct disbursement of fifty dollars for every jobless family to help purchase food and fuel to get through the winter.

La Guardia demanded to be heard, Garner gladly obliged, and Fiorello launched into a denunciation of how the Washington police had handled the marchers, charging that they had resorted to "exaggerated" precautions because some officials got "panicky." He conceded what was general knowledge—that the Communist Party had played a major role in organizing and leading the march. But, as he wanted made crystal clear, while he disagreed emphatically with Communist philosophy, the constitutional right of petition should apply to all men, regardless of political creed. More than thirteen million Americans, he reminded the House, were jobless. Factoring in families, this meant that thirty-six to forty million people were affected. And that number did not include the indigent farm population, many of whom had lost their farms to foreclosure. "The unemployment situation," he said in summation, "is not going to be solved by a policeman's night stick."[9]

Three days later, in a radio address from Washington to a New York luncheon of the League for Industrial Democracy, La Guardia went after the "privileged classes and the small minority who have caused the financial decline," citing as proof "the collapse of their economic system." Those same groups, he went on, were bringing into play constitutional arguments to block the very legislation that would rectify the damage. His high-pitched voice now approaching a decibel level audible only to bats, La Guardia insisted that economic progress should not be inhibited either by states' rights arguments or other constitutional obstructions. Back on the House floor, he added to his demands that action be taken for alleviating the economic distress not only by the federal government but on the local level. To show he was doing more than merely suggesting, he got New York's Emergency Employment Relief Committee to purchase cotton for unemployed garment workers to make into clothes. Thus were seven thousand workers given eight to ten weeks' employment, in the shank of the winter. Here, he said, was an example of how action on the local level could help turn the tide—if enough local organizations were willing to pitch in.[10]

Fiorello's tirade was followed by chaos. The House gallery emptied in moments, and the members on the floor literally fled for their lives, breaking the hinges of the chamber's central door in the process. One terrified member from New England, apparently not wanting to be caught up in the stampede, stuck a cuspidor on his head and crawled under a desk for cover.

What caused the sudden interruption in the proceedings was a young man in the gallery who had jumped up, waved a revolver, and demanded the right to make a speech. Only two members did not panic: La Guardia and a colleague from Massachusetts. While La Guardia rushed up the stairs to disarm the man, his colleague shouted up for him to drop the weapon. After twirling it a moment—and perhaps realizing that even if he did make his speech his audience would be minimal in the extreme—he dropped it as La Guardia entered the gallery. The weapon was fully cocked and ready to be fired. A medical examination revealed that the armed intruder was certifiably unstable. Few doubted his condition was a consequence of the times.

By now the Depression had reached its nadir: Unemployment was almost 25 percent, local relief agencies were rapidly running out of funds, and banks were foreclosing at a historically unprecedented rate. Particularly affected were the farmers, so desperate that many sheriffs and marshals sent to execute foreclosure proceedings feared—and in some cases were actually warned—that it was they who would be executed, by lynching.

In his broadcast to the League for Industrial Democracy, La Guardia had claimed he was not simply a champion of narrow urban interests: "The farmers and the industrial workers have been kept apart by the stock ticker [which is to say, the moguls of Wall Street] long enough." A month later, he jumped into the battle being waged in the House by the farm bloc that capped their decade-long battle to convince three Republican administrations of the absolute necessity of farm relief legislation. At issue was the so-called farm domestic allotment plan, by which cotton, wheat, tobacco, and hog producers would limit their cultivable acreage by 20 percent in exchange for a subsidy, to be financed by a special processing tax. The bill's broadest opposition came, not unexpectedly, from urban congressmen.

Rising to offer a vigorous defense of the plan, La Guardia insisted that "a fundamental conflict of philosophies" was involved and assailed the doctrine of "rugged individualism." Asked what he thought the urban workers would do if prices rose, he replied, "We will demand increased wages," and added that since banks, industries, and railroads had come to the government for aid, "Why not the farmer?" When Congressman Robert Luce of Massachusetts argued that the bill favored a "minority," La Guardia retorted that the blame must be attributed to another minority: the nation's corporate interests. "That is the minority, Mr. Luce, that is threatening the country; that is the group that had long obtained class legislation. The minority that owns the wealth of the country has ruined our country, and not the minority that produces food."

La Guardia then predicted with confidence that the nation had arrived at a time "when those who owned and controlled the finances and wealth of the land are to be stripped of their arrogance. They are to be controlled instead of controlling." He admitted that the domestic allotment plan was more or less a stopgap measure and would not be really effective unless accompanied by more drastic measures. Personally, he further admitted, he would have preferred, instead of this limited plan, "straight price-fixing for all surplus agricultural commodities," adding, "The habit of thinking along constitutional lines makes many timid." In lieu of that, he said in summation, Congress was obligated to approve the plan. The House agreed, by a vote of 204 to 151, but the farm bill failed to pass the Senate.[11]

Early in February, La Guardia rose to link the plight of the farmer with the concentration of landed wealth in the nation, insisting that the Depression had "created a new class of profiteers—a small group of people who are able to exploit the misery of the American people and who are slowly but gradually increasing their holdings of the property of this country. Every foreclosure means that property is being concentrated into fewer hands in this country." He then tore into the Home Loan Bank Act enacted in the last session of Congress: "To date it has relieved only the money lenders—the high interest sharks." Then, noting that he had long been investigating the Prudence Corporation of New York, which held many mortgages, he announced that it had received eighteen million dollars in loans from the Reconstruction Finance Corporation—"and there is not a more despicable, lower gang of loan sharks and usurers in the whole country." With $9.5 billion held in mortgages throughout the nation, he urged, there should be a gigantic refinancing at interest rates of 2 to 3 percent. When doubt was expressed that businessmen would invest in 2 percent mortgages, he delivered a classic La Guardian retort: "The capitalist, if he does not invest his money, cannot eat it!"[12]

Given his record, it is not as ironic as it might seem that La Guardia was chosen to launch President-elect Roosevelt's New Deal in Congress even before he took office. Granted, he had got out the vital New York Italo-American vote to oppose the 1920 presidential ticket on which Roosevelt had run for vice president. And nine years later, Governor Roosevelt's refusal to investigate Tammany Hall destroyed La Guardia's only chance of taking the mayoralty from Jimmy Walker. Still, the two were not enemies, merely impersonal opposition party antagonists.

The fact that prior to 1932–33 they shared ideologies is not what brought these two forceful New York reform politicians together. What did so was the repercussions of the Great Depression. In 1931, Roosevelt had earned La Guardia's gratitude for calling a national governors' conference to address the problems of massive unemployment and devise a uniform program for labor legislation. The following September La Guardia urged New York State Republican legislators to support the Democratic governor's proposed tripartite program for direct government relief that included a five-day week, a public works program that private industry should emulate, and self-liquidation through taxation (with emphasis on the high-income earners) so that the current generation would not burden future ones. Here was the boldest proposal taken to date to put relief where it belonged, with the federal government, instead of its remaining, as Hoover insisted, with such publicly supported agencies as the Salvation Army and the Red Cross.[13]

Throughout his congressional career, long before Roosevelt had formulated an elaborate plan to end the Depression, La Guardia had introduced, in one form or another, a number of resolutions similar to what would emerge as such New Deal components as the TVA (Tennessee Valley Authority), the NLRA (National Labor Relations Act), and the FHA (Federal Housing Authority), among others. Informing his thinking were the three paramount early New Deal principles: plan, spend, and prime the pump from the bottom instead of from the top. Also like Roosevelt, La Guardia deplored the Keynesian philosophy of deficit spending and believed the incoming administration could do a better job than Hoover at balancing the budget.

La Guardia also shared New Deal opposition to Prohibition. Not only was it a failure that had given birth to a crime wave of cosmic proportions, it was draining away Treasury funds to fight the losing war for enforcement, funds that were needed to help balance the budget. He insisted that this highly divisive issue be subjected to a quick and merciful demise and interment so that the legislative branch could concentrate on what truly ailed the nation. On February 20, 1933, when the first thing the lame-duck House easily approved was the Twenty-first Amendment, repealing Prohibition by more than the obligatory two-thirds vote, La Guardia commented, "Congress will now be able to give its undivided attention to economical matters, less controversial and far more important."[14]

3.

La Guardia and Roosevelt first met during the First World War when the latter, while assistant secretary of the Navy, passed through Turin when the Major happened to be there on official business. According to Marie La Guardia, the two came to know each other a few years later when Roosevelt was convalescing from his polio attack. "Roosevelt would come down to Washington and stay at the Continental Hotel. Fiorello was living there at the time," she recalled. However, though each followed the other's career, they did not travel in the same political and social circles.[15] Enter Adolf A. Berle Jr., a young

Columbia University professor of corporation law, and charter member of the "Brain Trust," that cadre of brilliant academicians and intellectuals Roosevelt recruited as his inner circle of advisors. Prior to the 1932 election Berle invited La Guardia to his East Nineteenth Street town house for dinner, and the two hit it off at once.

Descended from German liberals on his father's side and New Englanders on his mother's, the thirty-seven-year-old Berle, equally at home in the back room of politics and the groves of academe, endeared himself to Fiorello, whose attitude toward intellectuals ranged from indifference to wariness. He particularly admired Berle's recently published *The Modern Corporation and Private Property*, whose thesis mirrored his own. Berle, for his part, warmed immediately to "the tempestuous, passionate honesty of the Little Flower"; if he was a demagogue, as his enemies charged, he "was certainly demagogic in the right direction." The friendship begun that evening would lead to Berle playing a major role in La Guardia's mayoralty and last until the latter's death.[16]

When the Seventy-second Congress convened for its lame-duck session, Berle was dispatched by FDR to Washington as his point man in getting legislation passed that would jump-start the New Deal before he was sworn in. Berle told House Speaker and Vice President–elect Garner that he thought La Guardia was the best man but would defer to Garner's opinion. The crusty old Texan replied that if anyone, party affiliation notwithstanding, could make the "hog wild" Congress do anything for the New Dealers, it was La Guardia—"a good little wop" who of all the representatives was the only one held in high regard by westerners, southerners, and easterners alike. If proof was wanted, added Garner, one need look back no further than the "good little wop's" success in transcending both sectional and political lines to make hash of Hoover's sales tax.[17]

La Guardia and Berle went to work at once, determined to prevent a wild liquidation of capital while at the same time holding the line until Roosevelt took office. One proposal, designed to halt the flood of foreclosures, was the Farm and Home Credit Bank, to be capitalized by the government at two hundred million dollars, to refinance farm and home mortgages at an interest rate of 3 percent. The proposal was sent to the House Finance Committee for consideration, and there it remained bottled up until the Seventy-second Congress expired. (A similar measure would be enacted by the Roosevelt Congress in April.) More successful—indeed, their major achievement—was an amendment to the National Bankruptcy Act of 1898. An improvement over all previous legislation, by 1933 the act was sadly flawed in two aspects: It did not cover corporations, and its liquidation procedures did not take into account the Depression-inspired need to keep operational as many businesses as possible. Updating the bankruptcy laws was considered crucial not only by the New Dealers but by the Hoover administration as well.

La Guardia's resolution empowered the courts to relieve debtors by granting credit extensions and thus defer liquidation procedures even when the creditors filed petitions of disapproval. (The act in its final form applied only to farmers and individuals; the Senate version eliminated the coverage of corporations.) An accompanying amendment transferred the reorganization of defunct railroads from the control of private bankers to the control of the Interstate Commerce Commission. "Within the next few days several railroads—it is now no secret—will be in the hands of receivers," La Guardia told the House in urging passage of the measure, Section Seventy-seven. It was now five days before Hoover was to surrender the White House to Roosevelt, and banks were closing hourly all across the country. "This is your choice," he warned colleagues. "Are you going to leave the management of the reorganization and receivership of these railroads in the hands of the gang that has ruined the railroads, or are you going to take it out of the hands of that gang . . . and put such control and supervision in the hands of a government agency [the ICC]?"[18] Three days later, in the closing hours of his presidency, Hoover signed the proposed amendment, and the revised bankruptcy statutes became the law of the land.

Adding to his success with Section Seventy-seven was the surprise registered by Fiorello's colleagues that he, of all people, should suddenly come to the aid of the railroads, part of the Interests which had long been his primary bête noire. His explanation: Investment bankers had in the past realized handsome profits for themselves in fees, commissions, and loans when reorganizing railroads. Section Seventy-seven would break up this "receivership racket" by requiring proof be submitted to the ICC that any liquidation petitions would serve the best interests of the four entities most concerned: the stockholders, the bondholders, the bankrupt business itself—and the general public. Also, La Guardia feared that if the railroads collapsed—

and many were on the verge of doing just that—it would create a domino effect, pulling down the banks, insurance companies, and other institutions that held railroad securities. While staunchly sponsoring a relief measure in behalf of big business, Fiorello, characteristically, was fighting to prevent the financial marauders from doing what they did so well when confronting a defenseless opponent: sail in for a freewheeling pillage. La Guardia was not against capitalism, as he was so often accused. He was against opportunistic grifters who filled their coffers at the expense of their stricken brethren.

With Berle's assistance, and the tacit approval of Roosevelt, La Guardia worked ceaselessly as the clock ran out on the so-called Hoover Congress. On February 25, a week before it was to become history, he proposed that Congress, in light of the severity of the economic crisis, invite the president-elect and his cabinet to Washington to begin working at once with the expiring administration. Time was of the absolute essence: With millions of Americans going hungry and financial panic imminent, Congress, he insisted, should prepare for morning, afternoon, and evening sessions.[19] His colleagues, however, let the suggestion go in one ear and out the other. Also in the closing days, La Guardia arrogated to himself the role of watchdog for the American Civil Liberties Union, scrutinizing any and every bill in which he perceived a suspected threat to the Bill of Rights.[20]

The Seventy-second Congress—and Fiorello H. La Guardia's congressional career—came to an end at twelve noon on March 4, 1933, with Franklin Delano Roosevelt's inauguration as the nation's thirty-second president. As the Little Flower and Marie left for New York, their pain of defeat was mitigated by the thousands of letters and telegrams that had come in since November from people representing all walks of life across the nation—legislators, judges, miners, garment workers, farmers, the jobless—all expressing profound regret that he was leaving Congress and wishing him good fortune in whatever endeavor he would be undertaking.

Little did he realize—or any of his well-wishers, for that matter—that ten months later he would be commencing a collaboration between New York's City Hall and the White House that it would in no way be hyperbolic to characterize as unique.

PART IV

1934-1943

The Great Mayor

CHAPTER SIXTEEN

"They didn't elect me for my looks"

1.

Shortly after midnight of the first day of the year 1934, in the study of an East Sixty-third Street town house, Fiorello Henry La Guardia was sworn in as the ninety-ninth mayor of New York City. It was, at his insistence, the simplest, quietest mayoral inauguration in the city's history. Except for Marie and a few close friends, the attendees were fewer than a dozen men of great influence. As was their custom when attending evening functions, all wore tuxedos. (Fiorello wore an ordinary business suit. In concession to sartorial propriety—many suspect it was at Marie's insistence—his suit was pressed, his tie was properly knotted, his shirt ironed, his shoes shined.) Progressive reformers of both major parties, the tuxedo-clad men, known derisively as the "Goo-Goos"—a scornful abbreviation coined by their ideological foes for "Good Government"—were pragmatic enough to accept that only by playing the game like the Tammany Democrats, albeit in a rather less sullied manner, could they constitute themselves a political force. The elite of the group that had elected Fiorello, they included Adolf Berle; *World-Telegram* publisher Roy Howard, foremost of the liberal newspaper barons; the venerable Nestor of political reformers, Charles Culp ("C. C.") Burlingham; and the owner of the house and the evening's host, Judge Samuel Seabury.

After taking the oath of office, Fiorello kissed his wife and announced, "The Fusionist administration is now in charge of our city. We are embarked on an experiment to try to show that a nonpartisan, nonpolitical local government is possible, and, if we succeed, I am sure that success in other cities is possible." With that, he and Marie made their good-byes and went home to their modest East Harlem apartment so that he could get a few hours' sleep before commencing what he had promised the electorate: a cleanup of the city that the Tammany-dominated Democratic Party had befouled.[1]

But how, you ask, did the contentious, confrontational fifty-one-year-old Little Flower become mayor? In two words, Judge Seabury. In style and substance, the two could not have been more disparate had they come from different planets. The tall Seabury, patrician in every sense of the word, could have graced the cover of *Gentleman's Quarterly*. La Guardia, conversely, could have graced the cover of— of what? Short (five feet two), disproportionately corpulent, a sartorial underachiever in what looked suspiciously to the casual observer like a state of perpetual motion who discharged words the way a machine gun discharges bullets, in a falsetto voice that in moments of anger caused him literally to shriek, La Guardia was a man to whom being disagreed with was an alien concept; a man who could devastate verbally (and at times threaten physically) a foe. The two were not even of the same party, Seabury being a Democrat. Yet they were in total accord. Appalled by Tammany's hold on the Democratic Party, and thus the city, both men were determined to end poverty and political monopoly and to eliminate the sordid machine politics that concentrated not on issues but on interparty rivalries over patronage.

Born on Washington's birthday, 1873, in the gentrified section of the Fourteenth Congressional District a dozen or so blocks to the north of where Fiorello was born nine years later, Seabury was a direct descendant of John and Priscilla Alden of *Mayflower* fame. His ancestors on both sides had given seventeenth-century New England and thereafter New York a plethora of physicians, lawyers, college professors—and clerics. His father and five lineal paternal antecedents served with distinction as Episcopalian ministers; his great-great

grandfather and namesake was the first bishop of the Protestant Episcopalian Church in America.

Young Samuel, who once said, "I will not be exceeded in courtesy," was raised in genteel poverty. Being rector of a Lower East Side
church with a less than affluent congregation necessitated the elder
Seabury having to educate his son at home. Like Fiorello, he worked
his way through law school and plunged at once into politics. Just as
La Guardia would be an independent Republican, Seabury would be
an independent Democrat. But unlike La Guardia, he was willing to
accept reform piecemeal instead of demanding an all-out, immediate, fight-to-the-death populist upheaval. He supported virtually
every movement whose intention was to promote the elimination of
social injustice, rein in big business, and/or reconstitute the oligar-
chic class to whom, it can be said, the masses were in thrall.

Seabury was elected to the City Court at the age of twenty-eight.
Five years later he won a seat on the State Supreme Court. Eight
years later—the same year in which La Guardia made his first failed
run for Congress—he was elected to the state's highest tribunal, the
Court of Appeals. Theodore Roosevelt, having bolted the Republican
Party, joined his Progressive Party with the Democrats to make the
nomination. In 1916, Roosevelt persuaded Seabury to step down
from the court and run for governor against the incumbent Old
Guard Republican, Charles S. Whitman, promising Progressive backing with these words: "You may assuredly count upon it, I will never
give my support to Whitman."[2] Seabury took Roosevelt at his word,
secured the Democratic nomination, and campaigned strongly—and
in vain. Because Seabury supported the reelection of Woodrow Wilson, New York City's Democratic machine sat out the election, and
the duplicitous Roosevelt abruptly rejoined the GOP, commanding
his followers to support Whitman. Losing the election so embittered
Seabury that he retired into private life, taking with him an inerad-
icable antipathy for Whitman, Tammany, and, above all, Roosevelt.

This was the year that La Guardia made his long-sought political
breakthrough by winning election to the House of Representatives
from the Fourteenth Congressional District. As he went on to pursue
the career already covered, Seabury went on to amass a fortune as
an attorney. He bought a mansion off Central Park and an elaborate
Long Island estate. Clothed by the best London tailors, on his nose

a pince-nez, in his hands a cane, the tall, portly, white-haired Seabury was pronounced by *Literary Digest* to be "perhaps the most thoroughly patrician figure in our public life today—at a period when any hint of aristocracy is supposed to be fatal."[3]

The reader will recall that when La Guardia was seeking to take City Hall from Jimmy Walker in 1929, his appeal that then Governor Franklin Delano Roosevelt investigate his charges of corruption in the city's judiciary was turned down. When evidence of Fiorello's charges in some of the city's fifty or so Magistrate's Courts began to make headlines in the following year, Roosevelt had no choice but to act. The Tammany-hating Seabury was asked to head the investigation and accepted. When it became apparent that crime and corruption had thoroughly metastasized municipal government, Seabury expanded his inquiry into Tammany itself. He did so thorough an investigation of Mayor Walker that "Jimmy" was told he must resign for the good of the party or face removal from office by Governor Roosevelt. Walker resigned and fled to Europe.

Stepping in as acting mayor was Joseph Vincent McKee. He was Roman Catholic, attractive, and personable, had a law degree from Fordham and an impressive record as an educator with a number of published articles and a history book to his credit, and enjoyed the backing of the Bronx's Edward J. Flynn, most powerful of the Democratic bosses. What is more, he was everything Walker was not: dedicated to his wife and children and possessed of a strong sense of municipal responsibility. As president of the Board of Aldermen Mckee had developed a program to modernize the city's mass transportation, hospitals, and bridges. "Holy Joe," as he became known because of his intense religiosity, went about his acting mayoralty with dedication and diligence, slashing the salaries of a number of political parasites, eliminating the use of taxpayer-financed sedans by Tammany officials (McKee personally commuted to City Hall by subway), and, all in all, throwing out a signal warmly received by the general public: New York at long last had an honest chief executive.

That's why he lasted but four months.

Through the judges who resided in its pocket, Tammany orchestrated a special election to fill Walker's vacancy until the 1933 general election. The sachems nominated John Patrick O'Brien, a Surrogate Court judge with a thirty-year record of reliability as a Tammany stooge. Like McKee, he was a good Catholic and a good family man, but there the similarity ended. O'Brien was not only physically unattractive, he was of questionable intelligence. Asked by a news reporter whom he would name as his police commissioner, O'Brien replied, "I don't know. I haven't gotten the word yet." In pushing aside McKee for O'Brien, the sachems proved what was long an open secret: They did not believe in permitting pragmatism to get in the way of politics Tammany style.

O'Brien beat the Republican candidate, an elderly nonentity, by a margin exceeding half a million votes. For Tammany, in the context of the coming regular election a year later, that was the good news. The bad news: McKee—though not on the ballot, *and not even an undeclared candidate*—received an incredible 234,000-plus write-in votes.[4] The write-in demonstrated it was arithmetically irrefutable that a fusion ticket combining reform Republicans, Socialists, and pro-McKee write-in Democrats could rescue the city from Tammany's soiled clutches.

Fiorello H. La Guardia believed he was the man to head such a ticket.

There was, though, one problem. The City Fusion Party wanted no part of him. Said one of their number, expressing the consensus of opinion, "I want to defeat Tammany [but] I feel as I did in the beginning that a crude, brawling, loud-mouthed person like La Guardia is the surest way to defeat that end."[5]

2.

The City Fusion Party, founded immediately after O'Brien's victory in 1932, grew out of a number of reform groups, mainly anti-Tammany Democrats but embracing the entire political spectrum, dedicated to charter revision, Civil Service reform, proportional representation, and consolidation of overlapping municipal offices. Originally the City Party, it was renamed in 1933 when it agreed to run a joint ticket with the Republicans in that year's mayoral election. It was not the city's first such reform group. Fusionists had elected two mayors in the past, Seth Low and John Purroy Mitchell; post–La Guardia they would elect yet another, John Lindsay.

The Fusion Conference Committee, the party's dominant Republican voice, found La Guardia personally objectionable, as did the Old Guard Republican gentry for whom they spoke. They had never been comfortable with either his style or his insurgency. They hadn't forgotten how he bolted to the Progressive Party while in Congress and, though he returned to the GOP fold, continued to espouse the cause of progressivism until his defeat in 1932. Especially grievous in their eyes was the lead he played in killing the Hoover sales tax. Too, there was an element of prejudice. The conservatives among them, according to Ed Corsi, La Guardia's close political aide and former commissioner of immigration and naturalization, despised him as "Half Wop, Half American, Half Republican."[6] Militating in his favor, though—and the Fusionists knew it, though they pretended otherwise—La Guardia's record in Congress had won him the support of a number of major newspapers and, perhaps even more consequential, of the marginally poor and the bottom-of-the-economic-barrel slum dwellers who were the majority of the city's inhabitants.

With the Democrats enjoying numerical superiority, even orthodox Republicans among the Fusionists realized that Tammany's hold on City Hall could be broken only if the Fusion could settle on a man who could bring to the party enough independents and disaffected Democrats as well as Republicans of all political gradations. The choice of such a man would lie with Judge Samuel Seabury. It was he who had exposed the Tiger, to give Tammany its popular appellative. Why not, the reader may ask, the judge himself? Seabury, as has been noted, had withdrawn from the lists seventeen years previously (though it was fairly well known that he would have accepted a presidential nomination). That left but one logical choice: Joseph V. McKee.

The four-month mayor had not protested when the Democrats forced that special election and nominated O'Brien over him. He did have a lot to say, though, after racking up those astonishing voter write-ins. And what he had to say, in a speech before the state chamber of commerce, was so fervently anti-Tammany that the Fusionists believed he was ready to bolt the Democratic Party. Overnight he became their torchbearer. Even La Guardia said he would support McKee's candidacy if he ran on "an anti-Tammany ticket with a platform pledging the removal of all incompetent, unfit office holders, with a constructive platform rehabilitating the finances and morale of our city."[7] All he asked was that McKee make known his intentions by May 1.

Before his willingness to forego the Democratic Party for the Fusion could be ascertained, McKee dropped a bombshell. He withdrew from politics to take a fifty-thousand-dollar-a-year job with one of the city's leading banks.

"This is no time for experienced, competent and honest men to leave the public service," La Guardia announced. "Mr. McKee's action is a loss to the city and must be a disappointment to his friends." On the eighth of May, he made yet another public statement: "The hopes of six million people surely cannot be deflated because one individual has voluntarily removed himself from the fight. . . . We should not be preparing for a front parlor reception when there is a dirty backyard to be cleaned."

Three days later Fiorello proposed a ticket that was the stuff of which fantasies are made: Al Smith for Mayor, Socialist Norman Thomas for president of the Board of Aldermen, Republican Robert Moses for comptroller, former Democratic mayor John F. Hylan for Queens borough president. When Smith immediately made it known that he was not interested (nor were the others), La Guardia proposed Judge Seabury—who on that same day released a statement to the press that he was not interested either, nor would he accept a draft. Then, abandoning what was little more than an exercise in cynicism—he already knew, for instance, that Seabury would never consider the idea, and had not bothered to ask the others if they would, doubtless convinced they wouldn't—La Guardia said that if Smith would not change his mind, he would run.[8]

Here indeed was a case of letting the cat out of a cellophane bag. He had already told A. A. Berle, "Adolf, I'm going in," even if it meant running as an independent Republican. Lauding his decision to run, yet knowing that to buck his own party would be futile, Berle determined to do what he could to get his friend what both men realized was the only thing that could possibly give him a chance: the Fusion nomination. And that, they realized, was unobtainable without Judge Seabury's blessing.

Asked by Berle "for your consideration" of La Guardia, "a man I have come to admire," Seabury said he was as yet favoring no candidate. He then asked if there were any truth to the charge made by many that La Guardia, whom he had never met, was a raucous, sleazy, self-aggrandizing politician in the most pejorative sense of the word. He was, of course, familiar with Fiorello's praiseworthy congressional record. But praiseworthy records are often achieved by the type of pols that Seabury would never invite to his home, let alone support politically.

Berle assured him La Guardia's methodology was a façade, behind which flourished an honest, honorable, dedicated political reformer who deserved to be judged not on his style but on his substance. To this Seabury responded, "I haven't foreclosed my decision on anyone yet. I'm still open and will give [him] very careful consideration," adding: "As you know, there are several other people looking for it."[9]

Seabury agreed to interview La Guardia, and the meeting was cordial. Despite their dissimilarity in lineage, personality, and overall tone, their shared lifelong, implacable abhorrence of Tammany put to rest any and all other considerations. But, as Seabury told Berle, he was not ready to commit himself. La Guardia understood and took great comfort in not having been dismissed peremptorily. His hopes rose, however, when shortly after their meeting Seabury invited Berle to join a small circle of influential Fusionists of which he was the epicenter—the circle that would ultimately arrogate to themselves the decision as to who would be the party's candidate.

Meanwhile, Fiorello had begun his own campaign for the nomination, speaking all over the city in quest of popular support and keeping his name alive in the newspapers. In running for mayor, he had to concern himself with issues that transcended the ethnic concerns that had marked his congressional candidacies. He acquitted himself admirably, delivering a series of lectures before audiences concerned with more than the standard bread-and-butter issues. He condemned the poor reportage of financial news in the family press (Columbia University's School of Journalism), pushed the need for massive government action to replace the Depression with prosperity (Yale), called for the reorganization of child welfare (the Broadway Temple Methodist Group), and appealed for funds at the request of the Salvation Army (broadcast over commercial radio). There was even an article solicited by *Scribner's* on the role of the Army and Navy in politics. In a rally of one hundred thousand at Battery Park to protest Germany's treatment of its Jews, he warned that the Nazis were threatening world peace—"America must not permit this to happen"—and pronounced Hitler a "perverted maniac."[10]

Concurrently, he sought to build a bridge to the Republican Old

Guard leadership. The groundwork was laid again by his Democratic mainstay, Adolf Berle, who arranged for him to meet one of the GOP's most influential comers, thirty-one-year-old Newbold Morris. Himself one of the Old Guard by virtue of both maternal and paternal lineage, Morris was another politician who could not have been more La Guardia's antithesis in appearance and ancestry. He was six feet five, blue-eyed, and blond, an alumnus of the best schools (Groton, Yale, Columbia University Law School), a member of one of the city's most venerable law firms, and the scion of an even more venerable New York family that included a signer of the Declaration of Independence and a former New York City mayor. The reform-minded Morris, seeking a career in politics, took at once to La Guardia. Hoping to soften the image that conservative Republicans had of La Guardia as not only a political embarrassment but also a dangerous man, Morris invited Fiorello to address his club, a bastion of GOP gentry in the "Silk-Stocking" Assembly District, the Fifteenth, where dwelled so many who had opposed him in his failed 1929 mayoral race.[11]

La Guardia was ten minutes late for the May 19 confrontation, and Morris feared he might deliver one of his well-known antioligarchic rants and send the formally dressed audience stampeding for the nearest exit. Morris had obviously underestimated the man or perhaps was unaware that he was a protean politician who could adapt his style to the setting. In a well-modulated baritone voice, La Guardia began by apologizing for being late, but it seemed that "Marie, my wife, sent my suit to be pressed, and it didn't come back until a few minutes ago. I couldn't leave the house until it was returned."

The apology elicited good-natured laughter. Fiorello said that he was "very proud to be here tonight," then went on, "but I don't know whether you ladies and gentlemen have decided to admit me to the Social Register, or whether you just wanted to go slumming with me." The ladies and gentlemen responded with greater laughter. Then came a sober, provocative analysis of the crisis the city now faced, starting with the basic premise that what was required was government by nonpartisan experts, not the substitution of one set of clubhouse slackers and freeloaders by another; an administration based not on cronyism and palm-greasing but on sound business and executive values. Taking care not to attack the Fusion leadership, he called for the party's expansion to include women and other unrepresentative groups. Then he concluded with his choice as candidate for mayor. Not himself—but Judge Seabury![12]

So effective was the speech, the audience (knowing full well that Seabury had gone so far as to transfer his legal address to his Long Island estate so that he would not even be eligible for a draft) awarded La Guardia with a rousing standing ovation. So overwhelmed by La Guardia's remarks were they, it seemed to have gone unnoticed that he had tactlessly ignored the conservatives present by speaking of the numbers of the unemployed and the fact that federal aid was absolutely vital to the alleviation of wide-scale economic misery in what was now the depths of the Great Depression.

Newbold Morris had asked him to prove to an unsympathetic group that he was, despite his celebrated sound and fury, a judicious political reformer whose character and judgment they could trust. Fiorello had presented that side of himself with a brilliance that surpassed Morris's fondest hopes. Said Stanley Isaacs, a Teddy Roosevelt Progressive who would be one of the key players in the La Guardia mayoralty, "He had this facility . . . of speaking the way the audience which he was addressing would like him to talk."[13] Isaacs was so impressed with what he had just heard that he shortly joined Morris and other reform Republicans in following La Guardia's suggestion to enlarge the Fusion Conference Committee, in the process outfoxing its prime mover, ex-Governor Whitman, and transferring to Seabury absolute leadership of the kingmakers.

While waiting to see whether he could expect more from the Social Register Republicans than a standing ovation, and hoping for a Seabury endorsement, Fiorello knew he could at least count on fellow Republicans in his home district of East Harlem: the F. H. La Guardia Political Club. Led by Vito Marcantonio, the club began a citywide movement among Latinate voters to draft the Little Flower for mayor. According to W. Kingsland Macy, New York State Republican Party chairman, the signed petitions were sent "by the wheelbarrow" to Seabury, apparently to great effect. One day in June Seabury remarked to Macy, "There seems to be a recurrent demand for La Guardia."[14]

Others sought to prevail upon Seabury in La Guardia's behalf, such as the esteemed Professor Wallace S. Sayre of New York University, who wrote him that the ex-congressman was the most capable campaigner the Fusion could find. Moreover, he had "a splendid record" and was a sincere, well-informed Progressive who had both an appeal to the left and, no mean consideration, the assured votes of four hundred thousand Italo-Americans: "This group, I am convinced, from studies of electoral behavior in New York City, is the most important to the Fusion—for it is both highly cohesive and in a mood for revolt against the dominant [Tammany] machine."[15]

Of course, the City Fusion Party was also in revolt against the dominant machine, but it was determined that La Guardia not lead it. While reports came in almost daily that he was becoming rather appealing to reformers, the party, devastated that it had lost McKee, was seeking out a possible nominee from among a group of respectable—and respected—independent Democrats. All declined, for a number of reasons ranging from health concerns to unavailability. According to Maurice P. Davidson, the Fusion Party's grand panjandrum, "We went all the way down the line, and we couldn't get anybody. All the time this was happening, Fiorello H. La Guardia was standing in the wings—not standing, but moving around very, very rapidly." He would ask Davidson every once in a while, "Well, who's your latest mayor[al choice]?" Davidson would tell him, and Fiorello would jump around and shake his fist and say, "Well, there's only one man going to be the candidate, and I'm the man. I'm going to run. I want to be mayor." Davidson went on to recall how La Guardia "wanted the nomination! He wanted it! God! Nobody else wanted it! They were afraid of it—afraid of being licked, afraid they couldn't carry it through. There were lots of reasons they always gave, sometimes personal. But here we had a man all the time who knew he wanted it. He wanted it!"[16]

To say that he wanted it was understatement. He browbeat the committee, he lined up Italo-American support, he courted the silk-stocking Republicans, he appealed to the public in every way and in every venue imaginable. Yet he knew he could not get to City Hall without the Fusion nomination. And he could not get that nomination without the nod from Judge Seabury.

Adolf Berle told an interviewer in 1960 that Seabury thought long and hard before coming out for La Guardia. He vetted the Fusion Conference Committee's offering the nomination to a dozen or so men. As late as July 22, 1933, when it was offered to Nathan Straus

Jr., Seabury told him to accept. Straus, scion of New York's leading merchant family, declined out of concern that with the recent election of Herbert H. Lehman as governor, another Jew seeking high public office would rile the state's anti-Semites.[17] C. C. Burlingham told fellow Fusionist Richard Welling that Seabury, who by now had been interviewing Fiorello on a fairly regular basis, "wonder[ed] whether businessmen would accept La Guardia." A week later (July 22) Welling wrote to Ben Howe, director of organization for the City Fusion Party, that Burlingham "tells me that S.S. does not want La Guardia." Everybody seemed to know who they should not name, replied Howe, but no one could agree on one who could win; he added that while he knew "all the answers" against La Guardia's nomination, "it seems to be going to [him] by default." Howe then asked what Welling thought would happen "if we turned La Guardia down on the ground that we do not want an Italian for Mayor at this particular time when the Italians have such a big [war] chest. You can imagine what Generoso Pope would do with his three Italian newspapers screaming about La Guardia being turned down because he was an italian [sic]. We are in a tough spot I can assure you."[18]

"Going to La Guardia by default" is exactly what happened. By the first week of August the field of willing potential contenders had narrowed down to three: La Guardia, Robert Moses, and John F. O'Ryan. Moses was an independent Republican who had been Democrat Al Smith's right-hand man when he was governor. The more conservative Republican O'Ryan, a retired general and attorney, was now vice chairman of the City Fusion Party and puppet of ex-governor Whitman.

Events began moving toward a climax on July 16 when the Fusion Conference Committee agreed to give Moses the nomination without consulting Seabury. On being told, Seabury was enraged. His distaste for Moses was threefold: Moses opposed a pet Seabury reform goal of proportional representation; he was contemptuous of Goo-Goos in general; and—to Seabury, arguably the most heinous of his faults—there was Moses's relationship with Al Smith. Seabury would never forgive the Democrats for abandoning him in 1916, causing him to lose the governorship to Whitman, toward whom he felt a revulsion that was pathological.

The day after Moses's selection, Seabury lunched with Davidson and demanded the nomination go to La Guardia. Davidson said

Whitman would never agree, and Whitman had the clout to lead the Republicans out of the Fusion. Seabury pounded the table with such force that not only Davidson but the dishes, glasses, and flatware jumped, along with a few diners in close proximity. "You sold out to Tammany Hall!" he shouted. "I'll denounce you and everybody else! You sold out the movement to Tammany Hall!" With that, he got to his feet and exited the restaurant, with a protesting Davidson in hot pursuit. Seabury had nothing further to say except to repeat, as the elevator door closed, "You sold out! Goodbye!"[19]

La Guardia publicly expressed amazement that the committee had dared to pick Moses, knowing Seabury's opposition to him, and announced he would "stand shoulder to shoulder" with the judge, adding that he would back any "genuine anti-Tammany candidate."[20] Meanwhile, Moses had rushed to remind *his* patron, Al Smith, that he owed it to Moses to back his candidacy. Smith's response was that his being a Democratic regular obliged him to support the party's choice. (There was, as it turned out, a limit to Smith's sense of obligation. Since he couldn't stomach the party's choice, O'Brien, he endorsed no one that year.) Moses had no option but to withdraw his name from consideration. The Fusion Conference Committee now turned to the only alternative it would consider, O'Ryan, whose quick acceptance pleased Whitman and sent Seabury into another rage. So far as he was concerned, O'Ryan was inexperienced, insipid, overly conservative, and colorless, and he advocated a higher subway fare. Since he was a Whitman man, one suspects Seabury would have rejected O'Ryan even if he were St. John the Divine.

La Guardia, still up to his old game of pretending his only concern was that Fusion field *any* candidate who could beat Tammany's, told the press that "the momentary issue is between the judgment, sincerity, vision, unselfishness of Mr. Charles Whitman and Judge Samuel Seabury."[21] In fact, that was not "the momentary issue," and Fiorello knew it. At issue was which of the two power brokers, the ex-judge or the ex-governor, would decide the Fusion nomination.

On August 2, Seabury and Burlingham formed a "harmony committee" to include, but also to supersede, the Fusion Conference Committee. The idea was that if the Fusion could not come up with a unanimous choice, they might just as well hand over to Tammany Hall the keys to City Hall and not go through the pretense of an election. O'Ryan promised to withdraw, provided he could not be guaranteed a "convincing unanimity."[22] La Guardia immediately issued a press release to the effect that if he were refused the nomination he would fight it out with O'Ryan in the Republican primary and, if unsuccessful, in the general election as an independent.

But this was, to put it simply, just so much bravado and blather. As he told Adolf Berle over dinner that night, La Guardia believed that a dark horse would emerge as a compromise Fusion choice. Berle sought to reassure him that Seabury and Burlingham would make sure he got the nod. But Fiorello was convinced that this was impossible, that his political career was dead. Later, as the two enjoyed a postprandial stroll in the warm summer night, La Guardia's despair turned acidic: "Why is it that every time you get to a point where you can do some good the *nice people* [La Guardia's emphasis] move in and block you? That's what drives a man like me to be a demagogue, smacking into things."[23]

Within forty-eight hours, on the afternoon of August 3, the Republican Mayoralty Committee met at the National Republican Club. It was chaired by Whitman, who introduced a resolution endorsing O'Ryan. Vito Marcantonio and Ed Corsi led a filibuster, joined by Stanley Isaacs and Charles H. Tuttle. Argued Tuttle, one of the most respected party elders, "The one man Tammany is afraid of is Seabury. Why take action here which Tammany would give its eye-teeth to have us take?" After a heated debate that lasted hours without anyone receiving the Republican endorsement, an uncommitted delegation led by Tuttle and Kingsland Macy (both members of the Seabury circle) was authorized to join the Burlingham-led Democratic "harmony committee," which met at six P.M. in the Bar Association Building.[24]

At this meeting, also a heated one, Seabury was urged to accept the nomination but refused. What's more, he vetoed the majority choice of O'Ryan, as well as that of a few other compromise candidates. After hours of squabbling that at times threatened to get out of control, Adolf Berle nominated La Guardia with an eloquent discourse on his magnificent record in Congress. Seabury seconded the motion. Around midnight, with a few of the hard-liners, led by Davidson, holding out, the majority agreed on La Guardia. After telephoning O'Ryan, who agreed to release his supporters in the cause of promoting harmony, Davidson changed his vote. The other fiercely anti–La Guardia Republicans came around.

La Guardia was at home, with Marcantonio, Ed Corsi, and a few other friends, silently watching the clock tick and all but convinced that his political future was on a treadmill to oblivion, when the telephone rang shortly after midnight. It was Seabury, offering him the Fusion nomination. "I promise you faithfully you will never regret this," La Guardia told Seabury in all sincerity. "I hope I shall be able to make you proud of me."[25] Next day the Republican and City Fusion Parties made it official, giving La Guardia two lines on the ballot.

La Guardia knew he had been forced upon the gentry. Now he had to win them over. He also had to appeal to disparate elements including New Deal Democrats, Old Guard Republicans, and people of all political stripes who opposed him either because of his aggressive style (which they deemed more appropriate for a Tammany ward heeler than a respectable candidate for what is generally conceded to be the most important political office in the United States after the presidency) or simply because of his ethnic background.

But he knew he would succeed. The times called for a rough-and-tumble brawler who could beat the Tammany Tiger at its own game and was at one and the same time the progressive leader the city so desperately needed. He vowed that the campaign would not be "merely a political contest but a citizens' movement for the salvation of the city."[26]

That it would.

It would also be one big mess.

3.

La Guardia set out at once to build a citywide organization and mount a voter registration drive that would push enrollment to a record high. It is estimated that of the 3.5 million eligible voters, only 1.5 million ordinarily registered for municipal elections. Tammany was confident that the tradition of a light turnout would hold and that the majority of those who bothered to vote would, as in the past, go Democratic. Moreover, they were confident they had a sure winner in the incumbent, John Patrick O'Brien, despite the warning of Bronx boss Ed Flynn that he was a sure loser.[27] During his year in office O'Brien had mortgaged the city to the bankers. He was not only a failure, he was, albeit unintentionally, something of a clown. Every time he put his foot in his mouth the newspapers gleefully recorded it for posterity. Even those papers that supported Tammany found him fair game for comic relief. Like the time he hailed the greatest genius since Newton "that scientist of scientists, Albert Weinstein." Or boasted to a Greek-American audience of having won a medal in college for translating "that great Greek poet Horace" (who was, of course, Roman). Or tried to curry favor with an Afro-American audience by describing Harlem glowingly as "the garden spot of New York." Or told a group of reporters covering the City Hall beat, "Oh, I would love to be a newspaperman, because I love the classics and I love good literature."[28]

La Guardia wisely decided to ignore his opponent and focus his attacks on Tammany's fraudulence. Another decision was to drench the voters in a brief but intensive precampaign canvass. On September 1, a month before he officially opened his campaign, a *Daily News* straw poll revealed that he already enjoyed a commanding lead over the inept O'Brien. His advisers, associates, and admirers all urged that he not limit his campaign to Tammany misrule but concentrate on other issues. He refused, reasoning that the *only* issue was to "throw the rascals out of office." Stressing the point, he told a luncheon of fellow Fusion candidates, "There is only one issue, and that issue is . . . Tammany Hall."[29]

Barring minor concessions to the large Jewish community, which always voted in numbers proportionately larger than any other minority, Tammany's Celtic-oriented nominations and appointments had long been informed by its conviction that "the Irish are natural leaders" and, what's more, all other groups "want to be ruled by them." This despite the fact that the Irish were outnumbered by the Italians, who were, in turn, outnumbered by the Jews, and that, furthermore, there was a considerable minority of old-line American Protestants who resented not having had representation in the city's Tammany governance. La Guardia selected running mates from each of the city's numerically significant ethnic communities.

For the first time in New York's history an Italian, an Irishman, a Jew, and a white Anglo-Saxon Protestant were running on the same ticket for the four top posts: La Guardia, the Italian independent Republican; Queens banker W. Arthur Cunningham, an independent Irish Democrat, for comptroller; lawyer Bernard S. Deutsch, chairman of the Bronx's City Fusion Party and president of the American Jewish Congress, for president of the Board of Aldermen;

Farley and Flynn, however, admitted in their memoirs that Roosevelt hoped for a McKee victory in order to finesse a Republican victory and, in the process, remove New York City from a Democratic machine that was not only corrupt and embarrassingly inept but, save for Flynn, had opposed Roosevelt's and Lehman's nominations the year before. To Roosevelt it was intolerable that this miserable crowd was running for mayor a shoe-in loser like O'Brien and, come November, the nation's largest Democratic city would be handed over to a nominal Republican who had the GOP's official endorsement.[32] With the state's Democratic organization already subject to him through Farley and Lehman, he was determined to control the city's party organization through Flynn and McKee.

Fiorello despaired. The man he had to beat was no longer the ridiculous O'Brien but a man who had amassed some quarter of a million write-in votes without even being a candidate; a man with enormous appeal to conservative Republicans who had grudgingly accepted La Guardia only because he'd been foisted off on them by Judge Seabury (a Democrat yet!); a man—and herein lay the crux of Fiorello's despair—who could well divide both the independent and anti-Tammany Democratic vote. In sum: the man—the *only* man—who could quite conceivably beat the Fusion.

Despair quickly gave way to determination. When it came to acceptable running mates, advisers, organization, voter registration, and poll watchers, Fiorello had it all over "Holy Joe." Also, unlike La Guardia's ticket, McKee's had no Republicans, no one from the City Fusion Party, no one from the Seabury camp, and not a single Anglo-Saxon Protestant. Not only was his ticket all Democratic, it was skeletal. Having jumped into the contest late, McKee was unable to collect a full team of aldermanic nominees. He could not even fill all the candidacies for the borough presidencies. Were he to be elected, he could not enter office, as could La Guardia, with a majority on the Board of Aldermen or a complete Board of Estimate. The latter, comprised of the mayor, the comptroller, the president of the Board of Aldermen, and the five borough presidents, functioned as the city's chief legislative and executive body.

La Guardia campaigned as he had against Walker, covering the city like crabgrass, delivering four speeches to McKee's one. Disregarding the pleas of his advisers that he abandon his characteristic slashing and, for district attorney of New York County, Manhattan WASP Republican Jacob Gould Schumann Jr., of Dutch colonial stock. For the five borough presidents, La Guardia also chose men on the basis of ethnic, religious, and political considerations (of the five, four were independent Democrats).

Other men entered the primary, notably Chase Mellen Jr., a thirty-five-year-old Republican insurgent who led an uprising in the party that overthrew the Lower East Side's archaic and rotting machine run by Sam Koenig, one of Fiorello's earliest champions. Even the Democrats had their problems. When the primary was over, three of eight incumbent district leaders were defeated; so was the Tammany designee for comptroller, by a Brooklyn independent. O'Brien managed to beat back unexpected opposition, as did La Guardia. The Fusion ticket went forward toward the general election intact and unified.[30] By the last week in September his lead over O'Brien had soared to four to one, and Tammany chief John F. Curry was beginning to accept that O'Brien was going to fail, along with the rest of the ticket.

Then the picture changed radically, sending La Guardia into a tailspin and Seabury into a monumental rage, thanks to the man referred to by his enemies as "that cripple in the White House."

As soon as the primary results were known, Roosevelt gave an order to his two top New York lieutenants, Postmaster General James A. Farley, who doubled as chairman of the state Democratic Party, and Ed Flynn, the only one of the city's five county bosses loyal to the president. The order: Persuade Joe McKee to abandon his banking career and jump into the mayoral race. McKee stood as candidate of the newly created Recovery Party. La Guardia had appealed to Roosevelt and his "persuaders" not to field another anti-Tammany ticket. Farley denied any part in the McKee "boom." Roosevelt refused to see Fiorello's emissaries, sending word through his press secretary, Steve Early, that he was maintaining a strict neutrality in the New York mayoral campaign. This was, of course, a flat-out lie.

The question now arises: Why did the president—who certainly "owed one" to Fiorello for his support of the New Deal—abandon that alleged "strict neutrality"? Such apologists as biographer James MacGregor Burns assert that it was all a Machiavellian scheme to assure a La Guardia victory by splitting the Democratic vote.[31] Both

La Guardia in a characteristic confrontational pose as he opened his mayoral campaign in Brooklyn in September 1933. Racing from street corner to street corner, he flew in and out of churches, synagogues, political clubs, social halls, weddings, wakes, and bar mitzvahs (wherever he could gather an audience). There he would make his pitch about how he was going to clean up the city that Tammany Hall (referring to New York City's Democratic Party) had so despoiled for nearly a century.

La Guardia being sworn in as mayor of New York City by Justice Philip J. McCook, shortly after midnight, New Year's Eve, 1934. Standing between the two directly to La Guardia's left is Judge Samuel Seabury, the man most responsible for his choice as the Fusion candidate. The oath-taking took place in Seabury's mansion. Note that La Guardia is the only one not wearing formal attire, which he detested.

One of the new mayor's first acts was to swear in Paul Windels as the city's new corporation counsel. Windels stampeded the powerful Brooklyn machine to back La Guardia in a mass meeting that nearly degenerated into a donnybrook when its power brokers threatened to torpedo his Fusion candidacy. Thus, Windels deserves a great deal of credit for La Guardia becoming the third Fusion mayor in the city's history (as well as the first one to succeed himself twice).

Adolf A. Berle, one of the leading members of President Franklin Delano Roosevelt's "Brain Trust" and the Republican La Guardia's chief Democratic booster, at the time he was named by the mayor-elect to clean up the city's financial mess as city chamberlain. It was Berle who worked with La Guardia, at the time a lame-duck congressman, in laying the groundwork in Congress for FDR's New Deal even before Roosevelt was sworn in as the nation's thirty-second president.

————————

La Guardia had his official city car fitted out as an office, so that, as shown here, he could get down to the task of running the city from the moment he stepped off the curb in front of his unpretentious East Side building. There, he and his family lived in a small, spartan fourth-floor walk-up apartment surrounded by working-class families.

————————

La Guardia and Robert Moses, the man who built New York City's infrastructure, parks, and housing, pose when Moses announced his candidacy for governor. He went on to suffer the most humiliating defeat in the state's gubernatorial history. The smiles here are forced. Both men needed each other to create one city from five semiautonomous boroughs, but they did not need to like each other—and didn't.

La Guardia, his second wife, Marie, and their adopted children, Jean and Eric, pose for the press after Fiorello voted in the 1937 primary that resulted in his second term as mayor. Marie started out as La Guardia's secretary when he first went into law practice, efficiently ran both his law office and his congressional office, and retired to become a homemaker when her husband first became mayor.

La Guardia making a last plea for reelection in 1937 at his "lucky corner"—the intersection of East 116 Street and Lexington Avenue. He had established the tradition of doing so on the eve of every one of his mayoral elections. Here, as on the other occasions, he ends his last-minute plea with a "benediction." Though a Republican, La Guardia depended upon the support of the American Labor Party to put him over the top.

La Guardia began his first mayoral term going after the mobsters—the "tinhorns" he so hated. Here he shows he means business by personally smashing a pile of slot machines, after which he ordered them ceremoniously dumped into the waters off Long Island Sound.

The hyperkinetic La Guardia—the city's beloved "Little Flower"—is shown here, midway through his second term of office, in an uncharacteristic pose. Though he may look calm on the outside, inwardly his mind was churning as he sought to cram forty-eight hours into every twenty-four-hour day in his determination to "clean up" the city and make it a model for all municipalities.

Sketches by the illustrator James Montgomery Flagg, dating from La Guardia's second term, to which Flagg appended the caption: "This is my impression of our quadruple-motored Flying Fortress, the Mayor. With a mixture of fun and admiration, we call him 'the Little Flower'—no one says what flower! Can it be the 'Red Hot Poker?' At least it is surely a Hardy Perennial."

La Guardia discusses the great Harlem riot of the summer of 1943 at the makeshift command post he established in the district in order to personally supervise its containment. Facing the camera, to the mayor's immediate right, is his—and New York City's greatest—police commissioner, Lewis J. Valentine.

La Guardia is with President Franklin Delano Roosevelt and the
Democratic governor Herbert Lehman. Lehman's smile is guarded; he
had his problems with La Guardia on a number of city-versus-state
issues. FDR's is genuine; he admired La Guardia, who in turn adored
the President—from whom he managed to get more federal aid for
New York City than went to any state during the Depression.

La Guardia in an atypical pose while visiting Guthrie, Oklahoma, early in
his second term. He always remembered with great fondness and nostalgia
his days as a child on what was then the Western Frontier, which he
memorialized by always wearing a ten-gallon Stetson hat, even as a
congressman and later as New York's mayor.

Shown here with La Guardia at a first-year anniversary memorial of Pearl Harbor is Senator George W. Norris of Nebraska. He was one of the nation's leading Progressives and La Guardia's mentor during his congressional years. The two coauthored the Norris-La Guardia Act, one of the greatest pieces of prolabor legislation.

———————

La Guardia gleefully smokes an uncharacteristic pipe (he preferred cigars) to celebrate his defeat of Tammany Hall, symbolized by the frayed tiger skin sprawled on the floor. It appeared in his office with a note attached: "Wounded in 1933—killed in 1937" (i.e., La Guardia's first term). The tiger was a traditional emblem of Tammany Hall, the most corrupt political machine in American municipal history.

———————

La Guardia was great music lover who would conduct a band or orchestra whenever the opportunity arose. He is shown here, at the start of his unprecedented third mayoral term and shortly after being named director of civilian defense, rehearsing for his debut with the National Symphony Orchestra. Asked if he would like any special attention or effects, La Guardia replied, "No. Just treat me like you treat Toscanini."

La Guardia looks on exultantly as FDR's interior secretary, Harold Ickes, signs yet another federal funding package for New York City, this time for a low-rent housing project in the Williamsburg section of Brooklyn. Known as "the Old Curmudgeon," Ickes sometimes acted as if the federal funds he was responsible for disbursing came from his own pocket, but he greatly admired La Guardia, and the two shared a cordial relationship.

In another uncharacteristic moment, La Guardia poses to mark the completion of his three terms as New York's ninety-ninth mayor (he declined to seek a fourth). His face is a study in pride and personal satisfaction at what he accomplished as the city's first Italian, first Jewish, and most successful reform chief magistrate in the city's history.

This eight-foot-high marble sculpture by the noted Spanish sculptor Luis A. Sanguino, commissioned by the Port of New York Authority, now stands in the passenger terminal building of La Guardia Airport. Its eponym, a great believer in the future of aviation when it was in its infancy, conceived and built this modern air complex.

In one of many instances where he would clap his hands together for attention and beam at having succeeded, La Guardia prepares to argue before a state Constitutional Convention in favor of broader home rule for his city. This was an issue that brought him into conflict with the Democrat-controlled state legislature, but failed to deter the Republican La Guardia.

Almost with a sense of relief, La Guardia prepares to close out an extraordinary political career that included an unprecedented twelve years as New York's mayor, fourteen years as a United States congressman, three years in the U.S. Diplomatic Service, three years in the U.S. Immigration Service, two years as president of the Board of Aldermen (later the City Council, under charter reform), and two years as New York deputy attorney general.

After leaving office, La Guardia became a radio commentator. He would mix national and local political news with advice to housewives on the latest grocery bargains, harangue inefficient political leaders, and speak out on just about anything and everything that came to his mind. Made from his Riverdale home, the broadcasts continued almost until the day he died.

In this photo, taken during La Guardia's postmayoral tour of duty as director general of the United Nations Relief and Rehabilitation Association (UNRRA), can be seen an exhausted man who managed to squeeze a hectic hundred years into a mere sixty-five. Also apparent are the incipient signs of the pancreatic cancer that would carry him off in 1947, a year later.

This is one of the last known candid snapshots of Fiorello H. La Guardia. In it we see a plethora of feelings and attitudes that in the aggregate seem to sum up a man who knows he has done his very best, despite overwhelming odds, and wishes he had more time to continue his fight for the rights of the People against the Interests. Perhaps, he also wishes to slay a few more dragons, in particular the politicians, including leaders of his own party, who over the years were his greatest *bêtes noir*.

Testimony to the love he evoked in the people as New York's—and the nation's—greatest mayor, long lines extended for blocks around the Cathedral of St. John the Divine to pay tribute at the bier of their "Little Flower" on September 21, 1947. Son of a Jewish mother and lapsed Catholic Italian father, La Guardia, whose first wife was Roman Catholic and second wife was Lutheran, was himself an unconfirmed Episcopalian, thus his burial from this great cathedral.

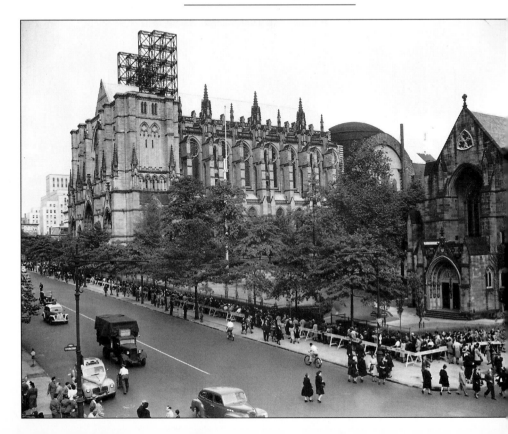

style and try to behave with a sense of decorum, he traded insults with hecklers and pointed a finger, waved an arm, stomped a foot—sometimes simultaneously—as he warned New Yorkers that their city was dying from "Tammanyitis." "Ours is not a political contest," he told the audience at the official opening of his campaign at Cooper Union. "It is a crusade. We are not fighting against particular candidates. We are fighting against a cruel, vicious political system. We want to wrest control from the political bosses and make our city what we want it to be, a great, big, beautiful, kind New York."[33]

Unlike in the 1929 campaign, La Guardia did not confine his stumping to street corners. He took his message to merchants, bankers, businessmen, and men and women in the professions, preaching the absolute need for efficiency, honesty, economy, and a balanced budget. He vowed to reform real estate assessment rates, restore the city's credit rating, unify the transit system, and shrink the bureaucracy by eliminating unproductive jobs held by Tammany hacks, political tinhorns, and crooked oligarchs he called "an army of parasites fattening at the trough of the city treasury." Only workers of proved ability would be tolerated by a Fusion administration.[34]

The campaign had come down to the question of which candidate could best give the city the responsible, independent, politically untainted administration it so desperately needed. As for La Guardia challenging McKee on a personal basis, that was left to such backers as Adolf Berle, who questioned his qualifications to lead an anti-Tammany crusade, and Seabury, who dismissed the Recovery candidate as the "pliant, subservient and vacillating tool" of the "adroit and sinister Flynn"—who, Seabury went on to charge, was conspiring to take over City Hall so that he could plunder the city in ways that Boss Curry and Boss Tweed had never imagined possible.[35]

In the battle for editorial support, La Guardia had the support of the city's most prestigious editorial pages. But those papers' combined circulation totaled a shade fewer than 1,371,000. Those for McKee boasted an aggregate readership of almost 4,137,800. (O'Brien had the support of one paper, the Tammany *Democrat*.) This factor, in tandem with his endorsement by a host of the leading Goo-Goos of the day from the worlds of academia, the arts, social activism, and business, meant that while La Guardia had the "haves" in his corner, the "have-nots" were another matter. Another *urgent* matter.

There were now, in this Depression winter of 1933, as many New Yorkers on relief as the total population of Buffalo. Moreover, an estimated one-third of the city's population lived in slums "unfit for human habitation."[36] Many of the poor could be depended upon to vote Democrat. Tammany had made it a practice of befriending them by purchasing their votes with anything from Thanksgiving and Christmas turkeys to political favors. La Guardia had to correlate their aspirations with those of the Fusionist reformers. Making the rounds of the slums—and all five boroughs had their share of them—he reminded the inhabitants of all he had done in their be-half as "America's Most Liberal Congressman," promised to take politics out of relief, restore the city's credit so that it would be eligible for federal public works programs that would reduce unemployment, reform and enlarge the city's health services, increase the number of playgrounds, create green parks where now stood miserable mud flats, provide free legal aid in the courts where needed, and clear the slums through tax-supported housing. Again, he was offering more than just an appealing laundry list of promises. He was proposing what was tantamount to a welfare state. What the masses needed, he insisted, was not charity but a reformed society in which they could better their lives.

As for McKee, the slum dwellers heard and saw much less of him. Though he claimed to be a New Dealer, he was not the social and economic reformer La Guardia had been for most of his political life. He was as successful at courting the slum dwellers (most of them in their mother tongue) as he had been with the intellectuals, the Republicans, and the Goo-Goos. But in courting the pro-Tammany ethnic vote, he unleashed an issue that had no acceptable place in this or any other political campaign. In the process, he demonstrated he had not lost his ability to go for the jugular.

The issue was anti-Semitism.

4.

All three candidates played tribal politics: calling forth immigrant parents and delivering dithyrambs in celebration of all that the hyphenates had given to, and received in turn from, the land of their adoption. But when it came to playing the game, neither opponent was in La Guardia's league. There was hardly an ethnic community

that did not have a committee in his corner, along with their particular foreign-language newspaper.

Of the city's major ethnic groups, attention must now be focused
on the two that were most affected by Hitler's rise to power during
this period: the German-Americans, most of whose roots went back
to the late eighteenth and early nineteenth centuries, and the Jewish-
Americans, most of whom were first or second generation. The
German-Americans were still attached emotionally to their
homeland. The Jews felt no loyalty to the Eastern and Southern European nations of the now deceased Austro-Hungarian and Russian
empires whose abhorrent treatment had precipitated their mass emigration in the closing years of the nineteenth century and opening
years of the twentieth. For every Jewish voter he won over with his
attacks on Hitler, La Guardia alienated one pro-Nazi German. He
considered this too insignificant to influence the election's outcome.

What he did consider significant, however, was an article that was
brought to his attention a few weeks before Election Day. Written
eighteen years earlier by McKee when he was a high school teacher,
it questioned the moral and political reliability of the city's Jewish
youth. Throughout the current campaign—by which time the Jews
constituted more than a fourth of the electorate—Holy Joe had
sought to identify himself not only with President Roosevelt but with
Governor Lehman, who was the idol of New York's Jewish voters.
Concurrently, Seabury was speaking out against Lehman for not
prosecuting the Tammany leaders whose nefarious deeds his investigations had brought to light. Some of McKee's supporters insinuated that the attacks were symptomatic of Seabury's anti-Semitism.
Though he knew this to be fallacious, La Guardia pleaded with him
to stop the anti-Lehman attacks, lest the Fusion antagonize the Jewish voters. Seabury refused. La Guardia was on the verge of publicly
disavowing them when Paul Windels, one of the major Fusion strategists, argued that a rupture between him and Seabury could only
benefit the Recovery Party.

In an attempt to provoke just such a rupture, McKee sent a tele-
gram demanding that La Guardia repudiate Seabury's "base and
reckless slander" of so honorable and committed a public servant as
Lehman: THE CHARGE IS UTTERLY AND CONTEMPTUOUSLY FALSE AND
I DENOUNCE, HERE AND NOW, SAMUEL SEABURY FOR MAKING IT. WHAT
DO YOU SAY?[37]

"I told you something like this would happen," shrieked Fiorello to Windels. "I should have disavowed Seabury's speeches a couple of days ago."

Windels now revealed that ever since McKee entered the race, Fusion had been keeping a copy of his 1915 article on tap, should its use become necessary. "Here," he told La Guardia, "is the opportunity to put McKee's own record right up to him."[38]

La Guardia called for a stenographer at once and dictated a response to McKee's telegram:

YOUR SILLY EFFORT TO CREATE A FALSE ISSUE NOW THAT THE FLYNN-FARLEY CAMPAIGN HAS BLOWN UP, WILL NOT BE TAKEN SERIOUSLY BY ANY ONE IN NEW YORK. ARE YOU TRYING TO DRAW A RED HERRING ACROSS THE COWARDLY, CONTEMPTIBLE AND UNJUST ATTACK THAT YOU HAVE MADE AND PUBLISHED AGAINST A GREAT RACE GLORIOUSLY REPRESENTED BY OUR GOVERNOR? ANSWER THAT, MR. MCKEE, AND THINK TWICE BEFORE YOU SEND ME ANOTHER TELEGRAM.[39]

The newspapers ran not only La Guardia's wire but the article itself. In the piece, written for *Catholic World* and titled "A Serious Question," McKee urged Catholic families to support the city's high school system in larger numbers, claiming that for every Christian high school student there were three Jews, who "in overwhelming numbers" were abandoning Judaism, embracing Godless socialism, and defending the practice of lying and cheating in the materialist pursuit of money. "Surely we cannot look for ideal results from such material," the author warned, adding that "it is such as these that our [Catholic] children, who are without the benefits of education, must bow in later years."[40]

Stunned by the charge of being an anti-Semite, McKee was advised by some to ignore the whole thing and by others to start a whispering campaign against his Fusion opponent. He decided to meet the charge head-on in a major radio address in which he protested that his words had been taken out of context. Reading a paragraph from the article in which he commended Jews for their pursuit of education and as "excellent students and often profound scholars," he insisted that he "did not criticize Jews or Judaism" but "criticized only those Jews who abandoned Judaism," adding, "Do Jews do less?"[41]

Noted Democratic lawyer (and later judge) Samuel Untermyer, a McKee supporter, who had denounced the article as "a reverberation of Hitlerism" when it was republished in the *Times*, told the press that while he'd been willing to forgive and forget "a youthful indiscretion," he was astonished that McKee should defend his sentiments eighteen years later: "Mr. McKee's explanation explains nothing." Asked to comment, La Guardia agreed and went on to remark that "McKee ought to be twice ashamed of himself." But prominent men of the faith such as noted Rabbi Jonah B. Wise, banker Henry Morgenthau Sr. (father of FDR's Treasury secretary), and Nathan Straus Jr., testified publicly to McKee's friendship with Jews and sympathy for their institutions and causes. In a letter to the *Times*, one orthodox believer rapped his critics as enemies of God and Judaism. It took the *American Hebrew and Jewish Tribune*, however, to remind the electorate that the article had been brought to light when McKee ran successfully for president of the Board of Aldermen, and the Jewish community had given him a clean bill of health: "To dig it up now is a contemptible attempt to drag the anti-Semitic herring across the trail of paramount local, civic issues that should dominate the campaign."[42]

Whether La Guardia did a contemptible thing in resurrecting the article or whether McKee got what he deserved is secondary to the question: Was McKee an anti-Semite? The answer would depend on one's definition of the term, the context in which McKee aired his sentiments, and if there was any difference between the twenty-six-year-old teacher and the forty-four-year-old politician. There is no gainsaying that his attitude toward Jewish students was informed by this very conservative Catholic's enmity toward secularism, socialism, and materialism in general. These attitudes can be inferred from other articles he wrote for the *Catholic World* on topics that ranged from "the license of Luther" to the "pernicious" Jean-Jacques Rousseau to "the mad desire" for women's suffrage and birth control, which he saw as "destroyers" of the family. Most telling was an article on the role he claimed was played by his coreligionists in the nation's origins: "By Catholic daring and enterprise, America was discovered; by Catholic explorers its realms were traversed and its wealth and beauty pictured to the world; by Jesuit missionaries the light of Christ was first brought to its shores, and by Catholic subjects its first colony was founded. Now by Catholic help [in the Revolution] a glorious nation was established on its shores."[43]

That McKee's thesis was ridiculous is inarguable. Still, nowhere in his early writings is to be found any evidence of his being an anti-Semite. Furthermore, if he disliked Jews in 1915, which is also arguable, it is inarguable that by 1933 no reliable testimony exists that he deserved to be so charged. Thus it would not be unreasonable to dismiss La Guardia's insinuation as the worst excesses of tossing mud at the opposition.

Not to defend La Guardia, but McKee tossed quite a few buckets as well. Calling Fiorello "a Communist at heart" who if elected would be "a Moscow Mayor," McKee promised that he would "be an American Mayor." Moreover, he accused La Guardia of being part of a GOP plot to capture City Hall in order to swing New York behind a Republican to run against Roosevelt in 1936.[44] Also to McKee's discredit, it was he who led in the injection of bigotry into the campaign by attempting to force La Guardia to sacrifice either Seabury or the Jewish vote. The bottom line is that both men took the low road with charges that ranged from the defamatory to the absurd and were in any event extraneous. Neither came off looking good.

Whether it was ironic or a matter of what goes around comes around, the end result was that the Little Flower destroyed any chances Holy Joe may have had to capture City Hall with White House backing. When Roosevelt gave Farley and Flynn their marching orders back in September to get McKee into the race, he promised to invite him to Washington as a tacit sign of his approval. Following on the heels of La Guardia's accusation of McKee as an anti-Semite, the invitation was withdrawn, despite Ed Flynn's importuning that the president's intervention was all the more crucial to reestablish McKee's connection with the Jewish electorate.[45] In seeking to isolate his opponent from Seabury, McKee wound up being isolated from the White House by his opponent.

5.

Realizing they could not win the election, Tammanyites set out to steal it. Along with its standard practice of bribing Bowery bums to vote a few times, the Hall had the services of no less an eminence than racketeer and beer baron extraordinaire Arthur Flegenheimer (alias Dutch Schultz) who had purchased from the sachems for a reported fifteen thousand dollars the election of his candidate for district attorney. But Tammany had no exclusive when it came to gangster support. The notorious Joe Adonis was all for his *compadre* Fiorello, though purely for chauvinistic reasons: "There is no reason for the Italians to support anybody but La Guardia."[46]

Election Day, November 7, was a day of shooting matches, fist-fights, black eyes, cracked skulls, police arrests, even one reported stabbing, as a record number of New Yorkers for a municipal election turned out. In the slums, where Tammany's strength lay, Dutch Schultz's mob, joined by other mobs that enjoyed Tammany protection, turned what was supposed to be a peaceful, orderly exercise in the democratic process into an exercise in turbulence, intimidation, fraud, and violence. In one slum district south of Washington Square, Boss Al Marinelli materialized at the polling places with some two hundred of his underworld playmates sporting identical pearl-gray fedoras and hobnailed shoes and proceeded to dissuade Fusion and Recovery voters with a show of brass knuckles, lead pipes, and blackjacks.[47] Whether Joe Adonis and *his* mob went forth into battle that day is not known. Judge Eugene R. Canudo, the Fusion cochairman in Brooklyn (Adonis's home turf), recalled being "in the field that day, all over Brooklyn and I don't remember seeing any of these gangsters on our side."[48] Of course, that was only Brooklyn, and there *were* four other boroughs.

Tammany's mischief was no match for the Fusion, whose poll watchers outnumbered the opposition and, in addition, had at their disposal blue bloods in the upscale districts and, in the downscale districts, Vito Marcantonio's *Gibboni* and the likes of prizefighter Tony Canzoneri. La Guardia, accompanied by his wife and an aide, spent the day making the rounds of the toughest precincts, where the most trouble could be anticipated. At one polling place in an East Harlem school, he pushed his way through a crowd and faced down a man almost twice his size sporting the badge of a Tammany poll watcher. Reaching up and tearing the badge from the man's coat, the fearless Fiorello screamed in his high-pitched voice, "You're a thug! Now get out of here and keep away!" Then, turning on a dozen or so others in the crowd, he fairly shrieked, "I know you! You get out of here and keep moving!"[49] By ten o'clock, with his lead now well above the two hundred thousand mark and soaring, the apparent mayor-elect was back at his Paramount Building headquarters. Only a flying wedge formed by police officers kept him from being crushed by his hysterically joyous admirers.

McKee didn't even put in an appearance at Recovery headquarters. O'Brien appeared at Tammany headquarters around nine o'clock and joined Curry and the other chiefs for what was rapidly evolving into a deathwatch. Two hours later came the word: The La Guardia juggernaut was unstoppable. O'Brien wrote a congratulatory message of concession to La Guardia and then told reporters, "The man who takes over the City Hall now will have an easier job. . . . I ironed out the worst problems."[50] Curry and the others stared at him as if he were some hitherto unidentified species. Back at the Paramount Building, La Guardia received a phone call from the Hotel Astor, where the Fusion victory celebration was already in full swing: Get over here on the double!

At the Astor, La Guardia learned from W. Arthur Cunningham, his ticket mate for comptroller, that Tammany was trying to steal the office in Queens, where Cunningham, a Catholic, had expected that county's large Catholic vote. His enormous lead of fifty thousand had dropped to four thousand—and the returns from four hundred precincts were being held up. Fiorello said crisply, "Come on, Arthur. I'll get those four hundred precincts for you!" Off they sped to police headquarters in downtown Manhattan and up to the fifth floor, where the Tammany-controlled Board of Elections was doing its dirty work. The moment they entered the room, there was a shocked silence, and then the police began to fawn all over La Guardia. Though he had no right to give orders until he had been sworn in, he shouted, "I want four hundred patrolmen mobilized behind headquarters just as fast as they can get here!"

Said a captain, reaching for a phone, "Yes—Mr. Mayor." Meanwhile, Mr. Mayor ordered an inspector, "Get me four hundred patrol wagons! Roll 'em into the alley behind headquarters as fast as God will let you!"

"Yes, Mr. Mayor."

"As fast as each patrolman gets here, send 'em to one of the four hundred precincts in which the count for Comptroller is being held up! Tell 'em to mount guard over that voting machine with drawn guns!"

"Yes, Mr. Mayor."

"As fast as the patrol wagons get here, send one of them to each precinct! In every case the cops are to load the voting machine into the patrol wagon and bring it here at once!"

"Yes, Mr. Mayor."

"By God, I'm going to count those votes for Comptroller myself!"

And he would have, too. But that didn't prove necessary. Word of what he was up to spread rapidly. The returns that had been held up came flying in. Cunningham was the new comptroller.

"There you are, Arthur," La Guardia said as they prepared to return to the Astor Hotel, "you're elected. Let's all get a drink."

Back at the Astor, La Guardia pushed his way through the jam-packed ballroom, climbed atop a table, and, after managing to silence the wild cheering, said that he wanted them all to "remember that a cause, not a man, has succeeded. It will not be easy for our administration to say to you, after this successful campaign, 'Sorry, there is nothing in this for you who made the success possible.' But that is the way it must be. I will have the best men for every job, even if they happened to vote against me." This was not the only statement he made. Another was "They didn't elect me for my looks. They wanted things done [to make a bankrupt city solvent] and they knew damn well I'd do them." With both opponents having by now conceded, he reminded his campaign workers that although "we licked both wings of Tammany," he had "only the votes of a plurality." He was "determined to give this city the kind of administration that will provide me with a thumping majority four years from now." The final vote: La Guardia 868,522, McKee 609,053, and O'Brien 586,622.[51]

After fighting their way out of the crush of well-wishers, La Guardia and Marie, accompanied by her sister Elsie, who served as Fiorello's office manager, and one reporter friend, returned to their East Harlem apartment for a private celebration. Immediately on arriving, Fiorello shed his coat and vest, donned one of Marie's aprons, and hurried into the kitchen. As happy when preparing a meal as he was when haranguing a crowd, Fiorello H. La Guardia remains to this day New York's only mayor-elect known to have cooked his own election night victory dinner.

Later, as they sat around the table, congratulating him on his triumph and cooking impartially, Marie said, "Do you folks know what I think is the best thing of all about today's events?" "Why," said the reporter, "Fiorello has won the second most important post in America." "Oh, that's nice," replied Marie. "But the really important thing is that now we can afford to get a new rug for the living room. You all know how long I have wanted it." This was no posturing. The La Guardias were so impoverished when he took office, they couldn't afford a car. Winning an office that had paid Jimmy Walker forty thousand dollars was quite a step up the financial ladder. Still, his first official action was to cut his own salary by half. Marie got her new rug anyway.

Next day, while Marie packed for a two-week cruise of the Caribbean the exhausted couple was taking with a few friends, the new mayor was asked who his appointees would be. Replying that it was too premature to say, he grinned slyly and tossed off a characteristic one-liner: "We may have a literacy test for some."[52]

CHAPTER SEVENTEEN

"I'm the majority of this administration!"

1.

The New York La Guardia inherited was in essence an aggregation of five quasi-autonomous boroughs, four of which were among the eight most populous U.S. cities, extending over 229 square miles with a total population greater than the fourteen smallest states combined. The city was on the verge of expiring from terminal corruption and incompetence after decades of Tammany's public-be-damned rule. The sachems had elevated bribery, wire pulling, and influence peddling to an art form, be it fixing traffic tickets or buying judgeships, all with the collusion of compliant politicians. With the Great Depression now at its lowest point, New York City was particularly hard hit as unemployment nationwide stood at eighteen million. A sixth of the population—more than four hundred thousand families—was on some form of relief. This was a number equivalent to the population of Detroit and larger than that of Los Angeles.[1] The most to be expected from the private sector—what might be termed "the Hoover approach"—would amount, at best, to Band-Aid surgery. La Guardia's solution was direct government aid. Even before being sworn in, he had readied himself to do battle with Washington to get people back to work and jump-start the near-moribund economy. Before we follow him into battle, let us see what kind of administration he put together.

Most of the commissioners La Guardia chose were regarded as expert in their areas of responsibility, in itself a major change from the norm in New York politics. Some were not even New Yorkers. La Guardia could be intensely demanding. His mercurial temper and not infrequent unreasonableness were as much aspects of his persona as his rapid gait, falsetto voice, and omnipresent ten-gallon Stetson. Rexford Tugwell recalled that, "he often treated his commissioners like dogs" and held them "accountable to himself" in the belief that he was "incorruptible and infallible. It would be almost but not quite fair to say that he was an instinctive dictator."[2]

A number of them couldn't take Fiorello's style and quit. A few took it and accepted it as part of the job. Most not only took it, they gave as well as they got. When subjected to one of his temper tantrums, they'd react in kind. Invariably, after matching him shout for shout, those who succeeded in convincing His Honor that he was being mulish or unreasonable got a compromise. Never an apology, though; but then, they never expected one.

Two top appointments were in payment of political debts. John O'Ryan, who had stepped aside as Republican nominee to make way for La Guardia's GOP support as the Fusion candidate, was named police commissioner. Fellow reform Republican Robert Moses, who had wisely chosen not to contest La Guardia for the Fusion nomination, was named to the newly created post of city parks commissioner. Another Fusionist mayoral candidate, Langdon Post, was named housing commissioner, but his was not a political payoff. Post was an expert in his field—as Moses was in his. O'Ryan was disposed of early in the administration; La Guardia didn't want a commissioner who was more concerned with his men's uniforms than with ridding the city, as far as humanly possible, of crime and crookedness on every level. To his credit, he did not humiliate O'Ryan by firing him. He just drove him into resigning.

In selecting his fire commissioner, La Guardia broke precedent by elevating from the ranks John J. McElligot, with the command to run his department hands-on: "You can't fight fire from a swivel chair in a political club." Department officers carped at the job going to "an enlisted man," but the appointment proved to be exceptional; McElligot cleaned up the corrupted Fire Department.

For corporation counsel, La Guardia turned to Paul Windels. Windels was reluctant to enter the new administration, pleading business and family reasons, but was persuaded by Seabury to do so, conditional on running his office without interference from anyone—including the mayor. Fiorello told him, "I don't care whether the Law Department is the biggest law office in the world; I want it to be the best." He then asked wistfully if he might be allowed to make an occasional suggestion. Windels agreed provided it was only occasional and only a suggestion. La Guardia agreed and kept to his promise. Windels proved to be one of the best corporation counsels in the city's history, as well as a brilliant campaign strategist and one of Fiorello's closest personal friends.

Adolf Berle was prevailed upon to accept the newly created office of city chamberlain, a post that would be abolished once he had restored New York's ailing fiscal condition to good health. "There's something wrong in the tax department," he was told, "but I don't know what it is. See if you can find out." Berle was also La Guardia's intermediary with the White House.

For markets commissioner, La Guardia chose William Fellowes Morgan Jr., scion of one of the city's oldest aristocratic families, whom he referred to fondly as "my Social Register commissioner." Morgan became one of La Guardia's most faithful lieutenants, serving as his link with the consumer against the graft and artificially elevated prices that had plagued the poor throughout the years of Tammany control. Another aristocrat invited to join the administration was William F. Carey, a millionaire builder who sometimes riled La Guardia by treating the poor with condescension and a degree of detachment. As commissioner of sanitation, he managed to keep the streets at least as clean as they had been in recent memory.

To head the top four remaining departments, La Guardia conducted a nationwide search, which caused a furor among the city's politicians. He ignored the furor and persuaded to come to New York Austin H. McCormick as corrections commissioner, John L. Rice as commissioner of health, Sigismund S. Goldwater as commissioner of hospitals, and William Hodson as commissioner of welfare. In time, even his critics had to admit that "importing" the four was one of La Guardia's wisest moves. All succeeded in undoing the calamitous consequences of Tammany's long rule in their respective areas of responsibility.[3]

"Perhaps never before did a mayor of New York begin his term with such an air of getting down to business and enforcing industry and honesty on the part of every municipal employee." So wrote the *Times* on January 2, 1934, the day after La Guardia began his mayoral career. In the words of the *Daily News* written on that same day, La Guardia began with a "lion-like charge into the arena." Bounding out of his East Harlem building at 8:30 A.M., he jumped into his official car—in which he'd ordered installed a folding table so that he could work en route, and a police radio that kept him in touch so that he could, if he felt it necessary, rush off to supervise an emergency involving cops or firefighters. (Later in his term, he freed his personal guard of police officers for other duties. When fears were expressed for his safety, he brandished the pistol he packed and assured one and all he could take care of himself.)[4]

First stop was police headquarters, where, after swearing in Commissioner O'Ryan, he told two hundred ranking officers, "Drive out the racketeers or get out yourselves!" As recompense for proper payoffs, organized crime had been treated by the politicians with benign neglect. He added, "We are removing that protection. Now see that that kind of crime is ably handled!" Any cop who accepted "even a dime" could expect instant dismissal. To make certain his orders were followed scrupulously La Guardia selected a low-ranking officer known as an "honest cop" to be chief inspector. This was Lewis J. Valentine, who would replace O'Ryan and go on to become New York's greatest police commissioner since Theodore Roosevelt. Valentine was given a five-word command: "Be good or be gone!" Then the new mayor was off on a whirlwind round of his other commissioners' offices to swear them in and offer each a terse but trenchant comment. His health commissioner was told, "I know you'll not try to advertise quack medicine or practice medicine by correspondence. That would be contrary to the policy of my administration." His commissioner of corrections was told to "remove every one from top to bottom, if necessary, to straighten out this department."[5]

Fiorello interrupted the swearing-in of his top men to broadcast his inaugural address from an NBC studio. After calling attention to "these times of stress and troubles," and promising to cooperate with President Roosevelt and Governor Lehman, he concluded on a rather dramatic note by taking the Oath of the Young Men of Athens: "We will never bring disgrace to this, our city, by any act of dishonesty or cowardice nor ever desert our suffering comrades in the ranks. . . ." Then he dashed from the studio to City Hall, where he broke precedent by personally addressing the Board of Aldermen. When he demanded they support his program to preclude the city's going into bankruptcy by slashing salaries and ridding the public payroll of "leeches," the Democrats declared that, as the board's majority, their function was to lead, not to follow. To this La Guardia snapped crisply, "I'm the majority of this administration!" After a pit stop at his office for a hastily gobbled sandwich and glass of milk, he was off to finish swearing in his commissioners, all of whom were ordered, in variations on a La Guardian theme, to throw out the "deadbeats" in their respective departments or throw themselves out.

Later that afternoon a visitor found La Guardia at his desk tossing letters at a secretary while shouting such commands as "Say yes! Say no! Throw it away! Tell him to go to hell!" Meanwhile, three stenographers were taking dictation as he tore through a pile of correspondence barking out such "responses" as "Nuts," "Regrets," Thanks"—and the query: "Where's the waste basket? That's going to be the most important file around City Hall!" Irritated by the number of telephones and jumble of wires on his desk, he screeched, "One's enough, I can't work with all this junk around." Said the visitor, in retrospect, "The Fusion engine was warming up."[6] Said the *Daily News* in the next morning's edition, "You've got to hand it, we'd say, to Mayor Fiorello H. La Guardia for the way he went about taking charge of New York City."

Soon after the election, Burlingham wrote to Felix Frankfurter, "I don't expect to have too much to do with La Guardia."[7] In fact, he had very much to do with La Guardia, offering support and constructive criticism. Burlingham was the only man who could get away with this, partly because what he had to say was never gratuitous and always on target, mainly because he was the only man La Guardia would take it from. Even President Roosevelt heeded C. C. Burlingham's counsel. On Day Three of the new administration the

Times noted incredulously that the city's commissioners were actually "spending a full day at their desks." This was something city workers had not done during the Tammany years.

La Guardia took Burlingham's advice to create a Civil Service Commission. Chosen to head it was James Finegan, a respected Brooklyn attorney with a background in fusion politics, who quickly transformed what had been for decades a sleazily run, practically all-Irish sandbox into a highly effective municipal bureaucracy open, for the first time, to Jews, Italians, and Negroes. By the time Fiorello left office twelve years later, "county [i.e., borough] offices and county government had been wiped out or placed on a civil service basis [and] there was not . . . a single person outside of the state and county courts who owed his job" to Tammany Hall.[8]

Fiorello established a routine that would last throughout his three mayoralties. At precisely eight A.M., after a working breakfast that involved either studying reports or meeting with a department head or trusted adviser, he would grab his black hat, rush down to his waiting official car, and while en route to City Hall either tend to paperwork or confer with a municipal official summoned for that purpose. More often than not, he had his driver alter course, be it down to the East Side to check progress at a housing construction site, through a main artery to supervise, say, snow removal or traffic flow, or to the site of an ongoing federally funded work project to ascertain no one was goldbricking. At other times he would have his chauffeur pull over and then eject himself from the car to, say, query a patrolman about his "beat," solicit a sanitation worker's opinion on his equipment, or simply to call out to some "kiddies" to ask them about school—and remind them to be good students and good children "and listen to your mommies and daddies."

On one occasion he was berating the driver of a speeding taxi he had flagged down when a policeman, happening upon the scene, quickly pulled out his book to write the driver a citation. "Get the hell outta here," La Guardia shouted, "this is my case!" Summing up his mayoral philosophy, he liked to remind people that "running a city resembles running a house [, and] if the servants are honest . . . then the house can be managed well and economically run." Here was a hands-on mayor determined to see that the servants were well supervised, the house well run.[9] Confident his commissioners would perform to the best of their ability, La Guardia bolstered that confidence by stealthily (and sometimes not so stealthily) looking over their shoulders. As for the civil servants, he ensured that they kept up to speed—*his* speed—by staging unannounced inspections.

Lowell Limpus recalls accompanying the mayor to a Lower East Side relief station, where, after he ordered his car be parked a block away, they joined a line of jobless awaiting assistance. The line was moving at the pace of a paralytic sloth because one or two clerks were lackadaisically interviewing the applicants while other clerks were just hanging out, like back in the good old Tammany days. An enraged La Guardia barreled his way to the front of the line, knocking one attendant back into the crowd, and another who came to the first man's aid. Responding to the commotion, a supervisor sporting a derby hat and with a cigar in is mouth came to investigate. La Guardia knocked the cigar and hat to the ground and shouted, "Take your hat off, when you speak to a citizen!" It was only then that the supervisor recognized the citizen. Scurrying to the director's office and learning he was not in, La Guardia ordered a secretary to summon the welfare commissioner on the double. Meanwhile, he went back to the front of the line, perched on a stool, took out his watch, and commanded the clerks, "Now let me see how fast you can clear up the applicants!" In under a half-hour, many had been processed and were on their way, while others were being rushed through. When the commissioner arrived he was ordered by the irate La Guardia to wait until the director got there and then fire him unless he produced a doctor's note justifying his absence. Then he gave a tongue-lashing to those clerks who had been sitting idle when he arrived and strode out to his car, pointing en route to the man with the derby and calling back to the commissioner, "Oh yes. . . . There's another S.O.B. that [as of now] has no job!"[10]

Then it was on to City Hall, where La Guardia would bound up the steps and into his office, barely acknowledging the chorus of "Good morning, Mayor," call for two stenographers (sometimes four, if needed), put on his horn-rim glasses, sink into a chair (his short legs did not quite reach the floor), and in less than an hour dispose of his inordinately heavy load of mail—mostly grievances that after a year with the Little Flower at the helm dropped off by 90 percent. Then he would launch a nonstop round of discussions with his com-

missioners, civic group meetings, Board of Estimate sessions, whatever—in short, get down to the business of conducting the city's
business.

Insisting on a new spirit of civic responsibility, municipal workers
were told, "For doing your duty, you deserve no special thanks; that's
what we pay you for. Your excellences are taken for granted; they
will not offset your negative characteristics." Supervisors were told,
"You men cannot relax, you cannot get chummy with your subordinates and you cannot expect them to buy you a drink when the day's
work is done. You cannot accept any favors, even a cigar from those
who work under you." Executives were told to "get your coats off and
pitch in."

The idea of vacations annoyed him. To his budget director, Kenneth Dayton, La Guardia said, "I don't see how you can conscientiously go on vacation at this time. You may stay away permanently
if you do." Even medical leaves he found intolerable. Fire Commissioner McElligot, confined to a hospital bed, was ordered to resume
his duties "to the extent of your physical capabilities. This can be
done from the hospital." Another was told, "I hope they will do a
good repair job because [when you get out of the hospital there'll
be] no more loafing and you will have to work for a living. I mean
business and you will have to get down to business when you come
back." All men in a supervisory capacity were expected to be at the
mayor's beck and call—night as well as day. And forget about attending any occasion short of the funeral of a loved one. After failing
to locate Police Commissioner Valentine when he wanted him—and
when he wanted anyone, that person was well advised to materialize
on the spot—La Guardia sent him a crisp, hand-scrawled note: "I
fear you have not quite fully understood my policy that a city official
is on duty all the time."[11]

Fiorello's intrusive presence was notorious. No city worker, be it
a city commissioner or a garbage collector, was spared the experience, not even a vendor with whom the city did business. He once
refused to okay payment on delivery of three new ferry boats until
he rode in the engine room of each one for a few hours, taking
notes; he then called in the shipbuilder's representatives, handed
them a detailed list of shortcomings and imperfections—and negotiated a large reduction in the price. He did not confine inspections
to the big-ticket items. He was known to criticize the door designs

on the Women's House of Detention, check personally the material used for policemen's blouses, and even call his own emergency fire drills to make sure everything was up to snuff in that area.

La Guardia came down mercilessly on his commissioners, if he felt such action was warranted, since he insisted they set the proper example by which all other workers were to comport themselves. One day—actually, it was three o'clock in the morning—he telephoned the commissioner of sanitation to inquire if he had a snow alarm plan. "Sure," replied the commissioner groggily, "I'm called as soon as the first flake falls." Said the mayor, bristling with sarcasm, "Wonderful. Stick your head out the window," and hung up. Then there was the time the assistant commissioner of markets, having arrived late for a ceremony, received a newspaper clipping in the mail that told how a Japanese official, tardy for a public function, committed hara-kiri by way of atonement. Across the margin, La Guardia had scrawled, "That is what I call class!" On occasion his temper became positively volcanic, as when he shouted "Murderer!" at his hospitals commissioner on learning from an indigent father that his son had died unattended in a city hospital. The commissioner checked the records, found that every possible medical assistance had been provided, and asked, "And for this you call me a murderer?" Replied La Guardia, with not the slightest hint of an apology, "What do you expect from a grieving father?"

At times, his methodology approached the absurd, as when he ordered his secretary to locate a certain commissioner and have him report to City Hall on the double. The commissioner was at his out-of-state weekend home. He arrived at City Hall a few hours later after driving way in excess of the speed limit, only to be asked a few trivial questions and then dismissed. When the door closed, La Guardia said with a sheepish "oops!" grin to a visitor who was present, "Wrong commissioner."[12]

Though the ambience of hell fire and brimstone he created was more often than not the order of the day, there were times when even Fiorello realized he might—but *only* might—be putting too much pressure on his people, so he occasionally relieved the tension, as he did with the Order of the Shank Bone. In a beautifully wrapped and beribboned box he kept the shiny shank bone of a sheep, which he would present to a commissioner who slipped up or simply goofed inconsequentially. The Shank Bone would be returned the next day, to be passed on to another victim. (There was always another victim.) Fire Commissioner McElligott, as an example, received it for getting burned with a Roman candle after sending out word that the Fourth of July was to be "safe and sane."[13]

Like most bullies—and say what you will about the man, he could be, and often was, a bully—La Guardia tended to humiliate and otherwise harass those who were in no position to fight back. One day he called in a stenographer and shouted at her before a mortified department head, "If you were any dumber, I would make you a commissioner." But those who stood up to him, like Paul Windels and Robert Moses—especially Robert Moses—managed to convince him he had gone too far. Recalled Justice Frances Bloustein, his first female court appointee, "He liked to see people . . . cringe."[14]

Granted, this was hardly the most admirable approach. But it's what it took for La Guardia to create one large city out of five component counties and, in the progress, strip Tammany of its powers to skim and graft. Lamented Jimmy Walker, "I never thought I'd live to see the Tiger skinned." To preclude its bones from disappearing altogether, the Tiger leapt into the embrace of the underworld. The price it paid was, ironically, its Irish identity. In its heyday Tammany sold protection to organized crime. By the 1940s, the gangster Frank Costello, Italian despite his assumed Irish name, was playing the pipes to which the sachems danced. Henceforth, until its remains were interred for all time, the once uniquely Hibernian gang would speak like an adjunct to the uniquely Italian Mafia.

2.

In La Guardia's war to transform New York, his first battle was over seeking federal grants. Prior to his inauguration, while in Washington he was told by Interior Secretary Harold Ickes, who was in charge of the Public Works Administration, "Go home and balance your [city's] budget, [its] credit is no good."[15] La Guardia and Berle worked out the Emergency Economy Bill, which would empower the mayor to reorganize the city bureaucracy by instituting an enforced month each year without pay for city workers, fix the pay rate of any city or county employee, and eliminate up to ten thousand city jobs by executive order. The draconian bill was drafted only as an emergency measure, to expire after two years when, it was presumed, the city's fiscal crisis would be resolved. Its passage was imperative. The difference between municipal receipts and expenditures was around thirty million dollars, and its bonds could not be sold. The city was unable to meet its current bills because of an arrangement worked out with the bankers by La Guardia's predecessor giving them right of approval on withdrawals from a reserve fund—provided the budget was balanced.

On his second day in office, La Guardia appeared before the Board of Estimate to personally seek approval of the Economy Bill. It had already been sent to the state legislature for consideration, and Governor Lehman, having been previously consulted, had indicated his readiness to send the "home rule" message necessary for its passage. La Guardia's confidence that the voters would not tolerate obstruction of the Economy Bill was sadly misplaced. Next day the Board of Estimate, by a margin of twelve to four, passed an amendment limiting the mayor's emergency powers to nine months instead of two years. Five days later came a letter from Governor Lehman that sent La Guardia into a monumental rage.

Having silently expressed his doubts about the bill, Lehman now wrote, "No man in this country had ever asked for or received the dictatorial powers which would be yours through the enactment of this bill." While expressing sympathy for the city's economic predicament, Lehman believed that its mayor was exaggerating the fiscal crisis in order to seize dictatorial powers. Despite the urging of his advisers that he tread cautiously with La Guardia, Lehman further warned that "this bill will obviously afford you the means of completely scrapping the present city charter and give you the authority, single handed and with full dictatorial powers, to set up another charter [which the governor regarded] as not only entirely unnecessary but essentially un-American."[16]

La Guardia's immediate reaction was to consider a radio appeal to the people. Berle wisely dissuaded him. He was, after all, a Republican and could ill afford to ignore not only a Democratic governor but also a Democratic-controlled state legislature. Determined to fight for the bill as it stood, La Guardia wrote Lehman rather sharply, "Your charge of dictatorship comes as a hollow mockery to overburdened homeowners, taxpayers, rent payers, and wage earners, who for more than a decade have suffered under as cruel and vicious a secret [for which read Tammany Democratic] political dic-

tatorship as has ever existed in an American community." Suggesting
that the governor had been motivated by politics—a suggestion that
offended the straight-laced Lehman—the letter continued, "There
is no point making political capital out of the situation, and I
therefore overlook many of your statements." The letter ended with
the mollifying assurance that he was still the governor's "humble
servant."

The city had been in default since mid-December when it was
unable to pay revenue bills totaling $4.5 million that had come due;
security holders were demanding payment, the bankers were now
free to renege on their four-year agreement, and Washington would
surely withhold essential loans. Furthermore, the majority of the voters of the state's largest city were out of jobs, on enforced minimum
maintenance diets, and without fuel in this, one of the worst winters
in recent memory.

La Guardia proposed a meeting between himself and Lehman to
resolve the impasse. With Lehman insisting he would never sanction
the Economy Bill as drawn, La Guardia suggested that the powers it
invested in the mayor might be invested in the Board of Estimate.
He could afford to make such a concession; Fusion held a safe majority of the board's votes. Both camps eagerly seized on the idea,
and a sit-down was arranged for January 10 in Albany. Setting out
for the capital, La Guardia could not resist telling reporters, "The
humble mayor of New York, a city of seven million, is crawling up to
Albany, hat in hand to beg the right to go to our own legislature . . .
for a bill in keeping with the Governor's own view of Constitutional
democracy."[17]

After the all-day meeting, the two concluded an agreement granting all powers originally sought by La Guardia to the Board of Estimate, conditional on their being exercised by at least ten of its
sixteen votes. La Guardia, who could easily live with this—he controlled twelve—announced that the city budget would be balanced
on February 1 and said he was confident the federal government
would thus come through with a loan of twenty-three million dollars
to complete the city's subway system, plus other needed grants—for
openers.

Now that La Guardia and Lehman had come through their first
showdown commendably, the White House, having remained aloof
from the entanglement, let it be known it would support the former

should further difficulties with the latter arise. Difficulties did indeed arise, though the malefactor was not the governor but the state legislature. There the Economy Bill was perceived as essentially a political act, with the battle not over dollars but over votes—and, ultimately, over power. Assemblymen and state senators were less concerned with saving New York City's credit than with their own political futures. The Democrats saw in La Guardia's determination to eliminate useless jobs a basic threat to their position, a view that had the support of municipal employees, the overwhelmingly preponderance of them Tammanyites, for whom the bill meant salary cuts and job furloughs. Tammany's primary concern was to keep forty-five county jobs from the mayor's control. Their abolition would save over five hundred thousand dollars annually. Most were sinecures, some were purely honorary or "no-show," all were patronage plums. Throughout that winter, while fighting a nasty cold, La Guardia would periodically rush off to Albany bearing reams of facts and figures to support his insistence that the bill simply must be passed. "Wear your rubbers, Mr. Mayor," counseled the *Daily News* (January 26, 1934). "You're turning out to be too good a mayor to lose."

In the Assembly the bill won only eighty of the required one hundred votes for passage. Sending Berle to Albany to negotiate behind the scenes, La Guardia launched a campaign to win public opinion with a radio broadcast on the evening of February 10 in which he denounced as "beyond decency" a system that put incompetents and "no show-ers" in highly paid county jobs. And, he demanded rhetorically, what else, in tandem with deeply ingrained dishonest political traditions, had reduced the city to its present financial pickle? Why, such sanctuaries of patronage as the Boards of Water Supply and Education, whose members were accorded limousines, chauffeurs, and secretarial services. These tinhorns, he noted with disgust, had few official places to be driven to (in which event they could damn well take a subway) and not much of an official nature to enter into any correspondence about that could not be handled capably in the aggregate by one or two competent stenographers.

Telling his listeners that there wasn't "a well-conducted business or a well-regulated family in the country that has not reduced expenses," La Guardia carefully laid out, step by step, how his Economy Bill would reduce city expenses by consolidating city departments, thereby eliminating unnecessary jobs. Wisely playing to one of his major strengths—employing conciliation and modified obsequiousness where he might feel inclined to jeopardize his position on a major issue by letting loose with both barrels—he had kind words for Governor Lehman, whose help, he admitted, obviated the city having to declare insolvency. He expressed the hope that with such an ally in Albany, eliminating the city's deficit and bringing the budget into balance would lead to the granting of federal funding for a desperately needed increase in jobs. Maintaining a nonpolitical stance, La Guardia managed to condemn both major parties for practicing machine politics in times of crisis. And it worked. Civic leaders, good government groups, and men of the cloth implored the public to demand passage of the bill. The public came through. All that was needed now was the support of the major political leaders.[18]

Of these, two Democrats stand out in bold relief, James J. Farley and Ed Flynn. Neither was a La Guardia admirer. Farley, one of FDR's closest advisers, played a double game: publicly urging New Yorkers to unite behind their mayor while privately indicating that his urging not be taken too literally. Flynn, also an FDR favorite, hinted to Lehman that he wasn't eager to see the bill passed, despite Lehman's amendments that would preserve Civil Service pension rights and, of greater concern to any political boss, limit controversial payless furloughs. Two upstate leaders and Farley loyalists, the O'Connell brothers (Daniel P. and Edward J.), publicly denounced any measure that did not guarantee complete protection against jobless furloughs to teachers, firemen, and policemen and condemned any other measure that gave the mayor powers over borough officers. Berle and Corporation Counsel Paul Windels remained in Albany in constant negotiations with minority leaders Irwin Steingut and Lewis Dunnigan. La Guardia and Lehman kept in close telephone contact.

In February, the revised bill was again defeated, though this time by a narrower margin than the first go-around, with all but seven Democrats failing to follow Lehman's floor leader. On March 6, the day after a third defeat, obviously orchestrated by Farley, La Guardia vented his spleen at a public dinner in the Bronx. He blasted both Farley (who was in attendance) and Flynn (who wisely took the precaution not to attend) with the charge that if the two had lined up seven Bronx Democratic votes, the city would be on the way to balancing its budget and qualifying for federal aid. The audience cheered. Farley replied with the lame excuse that he lacked the "power" ascribed to him by the mayor.[19]

Lehman now decided to appeal to Roosevelt, inviting Steingut and Dunnigan to accompany him on the pretext of discussing federal relief funds for the state. Though he had remained distant from the Albany debates, the president told the two minority leaders in no uncertain terms that unless New York City was put on a sound basis it would lose federal loans, and the blame for the suffering jobless would be attributed solely to them. The two met with La Guardia at City Hall. Also attending was Windels, aldermanic board president Deutsch, Flynn (a sign that the Bronx leader was prepared to relent, quite probably given Roosevelt's position), and representatives of teachers and other Civil Service groups. Together they hammered out a bill that all sides could live with.

Despite FDR's warning and La Guardia's willingness to make some concessions, the Democrats at Albany scrapped the compromise version, and the bill was defeated. La Guardia, backed by Lehman, refused to let it die. Rushing to Albany, he confronted the legislators in a bitter six-hour face-off. Though the Democrats handled him roughly, he managed to maintain his composure, knowing that for the sake of the city he must, if needs be, appease. To drive home the point that he meant business, before leaving for Albany he had four hundred pink slips sent out to city transit workers, whose jobs depended on federal grants. The public pressure this precipitated brought the Democrats back to the bargaining table.[20]

On April 5, the Assembly passed the bill by a vote of 120 to 23; four days later, after an all-night session, the Senate grudgingly followed suit. It was not the bill La Guardia originally wanted. For one, it placed stringent curbs on the mayor. Also, a dozen amendments tacked on to win the bill's passage left the county bosses with their offices intact. La Guardia accepted his defeat philosophically, equating the result with a "small, puny, anemic, undernourished, undersized baby." Hinting that he had expected too much to begin with, he continued with the metaphor: "I love the little brat. I will try to nourish it into something useful."[21]

The day after the bill's passage, he obtained from the Board of Estimate a provision for unpaid leaves ranging from seven days to a month for all city employees earning more than twelve hundred dollars a year. In addition, over a thousand jobs were cut from the pay-roll, and salaries above three thousand dollars, including the mayor's, were reduced.[22] Throughout April, further pay cuts were announced, usually at top levels, and superfluous or redundant jobs were abolished in almost every city department. In all, the bill made up some thirty million dollars, roughly half the city deficit. Higher taxes would make up the rest.[23] Tammany scored a minor victory in that the county offices remained beyond the range of La Guardia's ax. La Guardia scored a greater victory in that he managed to regain control of the city's finances from the bankers and put it back into the hands of the elected officials where it belonged.

3.

La Guardia's six months of aggravation over the Economic Bill were compensated for by increased support at home and the personal satisfaction derived from the city's dramatic turnabout. Bankers were now amenable to reducing the interest rate on city borrowing, which led in turn to improved sales of city bonds. Thanks to Parks Com-missioner Moses, who refused to be inhibited by the lack of adequate funds—with La Guardia's concurrence he merely acquisitioned every strip of vacant public land—1,700 recreational renovation pro-jects were completed, including Central Park, which had been al-lowed to deteriorate. In addition, 69 new small parks and play areas had been developed. Within the year, the number of playgrounds alone had risen by 60 to 179.

Throughout the long, hot summer there were free street shows by hired musicians and actors, dancing on the Central Park Mall, sunbathing on the Great Lawn (an enormous plot from which ho-boes encamped there since the Hoover days had been evicted), and free concerts. At one, the music-loving (and headline-grabbing) mayor seized the conductor's baton and led the Goldman Band in a souring Sousa march that won him an ovation from the audience. In an August radio speech summing up those first six months, he was able to inform the people that, besides parks and playground development, major reform had been undertaken in city hospitals, citywide purchasing, and health plans. There was, of course, much more to be accomplished, he admitted, promising it would be. Asked by a reporter after the broadcast which aspect of his job annoyed him most, he snapped, "Limitation of power."[24]

With the onset of his first autumn as mayor, La Guardia became caught up in a twofold political dilemma that made him feel as Odysseus must have felt while navigating the passage between Scylla and Charybdis. It began on a May afternoon when fellow Fusionist City Comptroller Cunningham died suddenly at the age of thirty-nine. La Guardia named Deputy Comptroller Joseph P. McGoldrick, a dedicated Fusionist, as Cunningham's temporary successor, with the hope that he would move into the position permanently in the court-ordered November election. Tammany, then in the throes of reorganization after being trounced in the previous year's mayoral election, saw an opportunity to regain its influence at La Guardia's expense by denying him the three votes on the Board of Estimate that went with the office. In July, leadership fell to forty-one-year-old James J. Dooling, a pragmatist whose first step was to pledge the Hall's full support to President Roosevelt (a pledge FDR accepted for what it was worth, which he doubted was very much). Of greater concern for La Guardia, three popular Democrats often at odds with the old Tammany leadership—Senator Robert F. Wagner, Alfred E. Smith, and Surrogate James A. Foley—had rejoined the fold. The Democratic nomination for comptroller went to Frank J. Taylor.

Fighting to keep those three seats on the Board of Estimate was problem enough for Fiorello and the Fusion. Magnifying the problem was the upcoming gubernatorial election. The Democratic standard bearer would be the incumbent Herbert Lehman. Judge Seabury, deciding after all to get back into the political wars, sought the Republican nomination. But the GOP's Old Guard, not wanting the Democrat on a Republican-Fusion ticket, turned to Robert Moses, who though a Fusionist was at least a Republican Fusionist. This put La Guardia in a bind. He owed much to Seabury—in fact, his very office—but he felt he owed loyalty to his parks commissioner. Maintaining an unaccustomed silence, he sent Paul Windels to the Republican nominating convention in Rochester, to work with W. Kingsland Macy, who was leading the party's liberal wing in behalf of Seabury. Windels, as the saying goes, could've stayed home. Moses won the nomination with 824 votes to Seabury's mortifying 57. La

Guardia, who must have suspected he was wasting Windels's time, had paid his debt to Seabury. But he was not off the hook. On the one hand, Moses was doing a superb job as parks commissioner. "I can't get along with him," La Guardia told Windels, "and I can't get along without him."[25] But then there was Lehman, whom he needed almost as much as he needed Moses, given Lehman's close ties to the White House. In the end, La Guardia voted for Moses with a spectacular lack of enthusiasm, then directed all his energies to getting McGoldrick elected.

Moses proved to be the worst possible GOP choice, as evidenced by the fact that he got the smallest percentage of votes polled by a gubernatorial candidate in the state's history. It's questionable whether his biggest problem was his superciliousness, his vituperative attacks on Lehman, or his general lack of knowledge of or even interest in political issues that did not devolve upon him personally, if not a combination thereof. For La Guardia, the loss was good news. The bad news was McGoldrick's defeat by Frank Taylor, which gave Tammany those three votes on the Board of Estimate, greatly diminishing the mayor's influence with that all-important municipal body.

In an August 22 radio broadcast, La Guardia pleaded for new general taxes on business to finance the city's relief costs, which were climbing daily. The storm of protest his speech raised, led by Tammany, was particularly intensive as the media and business community weighed in against the idea. La Guardia was willing to make compromises. Proposals ranging from sales taxes to taxes on subway fares were sent up as trial balloons. None would fly. On September 14, the Board of Estimate turned down any compromise. La Guardia retaliated with one of those dramatic moves that characterized his leadership. He ordered the termination of all relief payments—a sum of nearly a million dollars covering four hundred thousand families—as of nine o'clock the following morning. The federal government let it be known that its 50 percent share of relief for New York City would also cease, and there would be no more grant funds forthcoming unless the city continued to meet its agreed upon 25 percent share.

So great was the uproar, it went hardly noticed that the relief payments were resumed four days later. The whole stunt had been La Guardia's characteristic way of dramatizing an important issue in order to raise questions that must be debated, on the national as well as local levels. It was now accepted by even the staunchest oppositionists that some type of tax would have to be levied. Just exactly what kind was a subject of debate for weeks. The immediate crisis was relieved on November 10, when a loan by the bankers of two million dollars was approved. But this was only a stopgap measure. Vehemently opposed to "going to the bankers with my hat in my hand to borrow money for relief," La Guardia went instead to Washington. Though a fifty-four-million-dollar loan for public works had already been approved for New York, and an additional fifty million was on its way, he argued before the Committee on Economic Security that additional *loans* to municipalities would not resolve the crisis: "You can't have relief on a four percent interest basis." The answer was direct relief allotments. New York, he pointed out, was not the only city suffering. His arguments went unheeded.

A week later he was in Chicago, to lay the problem before the U.S. Conference of Mayors. Proving himself a militant well versed in the problems facing all cities, he criticized the terms on which the Ickes-controlled Public Works Administration was making funds available. Led by La Guardia, the conference forced a reevaluation on Washington's part and, for the first time, was given representation on the advisory committee on allotments, the policy body for the vast public works program. La Guardia was named the mayors' representative. That he was held to be the man most responsible for this fortuitous turn of events added to his popularity. In time, New York's mayor would be looked upon, in a sense, as the nation's mayor.

Back home, when it became evident that a projected 2 percent sales tax seemed most likely to win the necessary legislative and public support, La Guardia went along. It was not lost on anyone—particularly his antagonists—that as a lame-duck congressman he had almost single-handedly doomed Hoover's proposed sales tax. In taking responsibility for the New York City tax, La Guardia did what he did whenever faced with a Hobson's choice: He neither apologized nor explained but just accepted the unavoidable.

Early in December he secured a loan from the bankers of fifteen million dollars at 1.75 percent interest, and the sales tax went into effect without serious public opposition and with no appreciable falloff in business. With Christmas coming on, the city was permeated with something it hadn't known since the close of the Jazz Age: an air of goodwill. For thousands there were even pay raises and bonuses. When, joined by Marie, Fiorello presided at the annual lighting of the Christmas tree in front of City Hall, he revealed to the public for the first time the two children they had recently adopted: three-year-old Eric, a "Nordic" type who came from an orphanage, and Jean, a few years his senior, the daughter of La Guardia's first wife's sister, who was unable to raise her.[26]

4.

In his 1925 State of the Union Address, Calvin Coolidge voiced opposition to federal intervention in local matters: "It does not follow that because abuses exist it is the concern of the Federal Government to attempt their reform." Legally, he was correct. Because the Founding Fathers looked upon America's cities as wards of the states, no provision was made for them in the Constitution. An 1868 Iowa court decision established as case law that "municipal corporations owe their origins to, and derive their powers and rights wholly from, the [state] legislature [and thus] are the mere tenants at the will of the legislature." The law was upheld at the beginning of the twentieth century when the U.S. Supreme Court ruled that the state "at its pleasure" could "modify or withdraw all [city] powers [as well as] expand or contract the territorial area, unite the whole or a part with another municipality, repeal the character and destroy the corporation," this "without the consent of the [city's] citizens, or even against their protest."[27]

Two months after President Roosevelt took office, big-city mayors persuaded him that with their resources exhausted, it was the federal government's *moral obligation* to contravene this tradition that the cities were the responsibility of the states and assume direct responsibility for cities in such crises. Roosevelt agreed. He ordered the Reconstruction Finance Corporation to make available millions in the form of loans, and created the vast Public Works Administration under Ickes. In his famously pompous fashion, the well-intentioned interior secretary moved the millions entrusted to him with the alacrity of drying cement.

Not that he opposed the program; in fact, he was one of its strongest supporters. It's just that he wanted to do it his way—and his way meant binding disbursements in red tape. Meanwhile, unemployment was going through the roof, cities were going broke, and people were going to bed at night hungry. Prompted by the demand of municipal reformers nationwide, led by La Guardia, for a massive program of direct federal relief, Roosevelt created the five-hundred-million-dollar Federal Emergency Relief Administration to distribute assistance grants through the states. Brought in to administer the program was Harry Hopkins, at the time New York State's temporary relief administrator, who was to emerge as FDR's most trusted aide and confidant.[28]

While Ickes dithered, Hopkins disbursed. Within two hours of starting the job, he handed out five million dollars. That was only the beginning. He ran roughshod over bureaucrats who got in his way, and he bent to his purpose rules that he considered a hindrance: "People have to eat, so I'll do as I please."[29] As the 1933 Depression winter worsened, Hopkins argued for even more relief for the unemployed. The president approved, and a Civil Works Administration was established for the singular purpose of creating jobs for four million unemployed by funding federal improvements (post offices, courthouses, highways, and the like). Previous such programs had been administered through the states. The new CWA offered outright grants directly to the cities. Hopkins was familiar with La Guardia's compassion for the unemployed. Shortly after his election—the first New York mayor to have been previously a Washington figure—La Guardia was asked by Hopkins to help plan the new CWA. He wrote proposals for the employment of workers to clean and refurbish the city's parks, restore its rotting docks, construct covered municipal markets, establish temporary shelters for the homeless, and repair public buildings.

Though Ickes was making large-scale allocations for public works, New York was not a priority city. Its applications, so horribly cobbled together by hack politicians, were hardly guaranteed to win confidence in Washington; moreover, the city's credit had practically been exhausted. Still a month from taking office, La Guardia submitted a long list for Ickes—subways, bridges, slum clearance, street repair, airfields—that was carefully thought out, detailing costs, projection of labor needs, and the like. (It was then that Ickes told the mayor-elect, "Go home and balance your budget, your credit is no good.")

On February 5, 1934, Fiorello made his first visit to Washington as mayor of the nation's largest city, to claim its share of the available allotments. Unable to see the president, who was ill with a cold, he did see Hopkins and Ickes, as well as Hugh Johnson, then head of the National Recovery Administration. It was not only a busy day, it was a highly remunerative one. He brought home assurances of sixty-eight million dollars in loans for New York, including twenty million for the proposed New York City Housing Authority and a million and a half for the Triborough Bridge, which had been stalled due to wholesale corruption and resultant lack of funds. On the same day, Congress authorized an additional $950 million for the CWA. Thanks to his quickly gelled friendship with Hopkins, Fiorello would see that New York got its fair share and then some.

But the PWA funds promised by Ickes, who was eminently satisfied that the grant proposals could not have been better presented, were not forthcoming. Known as "the Old Curmudgeon," he always seemed to behave as if the money he was authorized to disburse was coming not out of the U.S. Treasury but out of his own pocket. In May, with the Economy Bill having finally passed, La Guardia returned to Washington to convince Ickes to release the promised funds, which would put three thousand men to work on subway construction, with prospects of an additional four thousand on other PWA projects.

The visit was capped by a genial interview with the president. Roosevelt would have preferred a Democrat in New York's City Hall. Still, as Hopkins, Ickes, and Berle convinced him, they could not have a better man at the city's helm in fostering his New Deal—of which New York would be both testing ground and showcase—than this progressive Republican. Roosevelt came to genuinely like La Guardia, though he did find him at times irksome. Over time, their close personal relationship would redound to New York's advantage to the extent that the city would get more federal funding throughout the Depression than any other city, and what it got was out of proportion to that of all the other states.

But first, the funding was imperiled by La Guardia's becoming innocently caught up in a vicious feud between the president he not only needed but admired and the parks commissioner he also needed but detested yet had to tolerate.

Robert Moses was imaginative, intellectually gifted, supercilious, power hungry, cruelly insulting and dismissive, an arrogant egomaniac: in sum, a brilliant one-man horror show, whose relationship with La Guardia was a reluctant yet incredibly productive symbiosis. Moses, to his credit, would speak admiringly of La Guardia, albeit in retrospect, as if speaking of a friend. But as the old cliché goes, with friends like that, who needs enemies?

"There were times," recalled one who knew both of them well, "when you could swear they were going to come to blows." After one confrontation Moses raged to an associate, "Someday I'm going to hit that son-of-a-bitch and knock him through the door." La Guardia treated him with sarcasm, referring to him as "His Grace." Determined always to have his way, Moses would threaten to resign unless some project was approved, money made available, or rule bent. After a while, La Guardia made up a batch of preprinted resignation forms: "I, Robert Moses do hereby resign as _____ effective _____." The next time Moses issued a threat, La Guardia pulled out the pad. Moses glanced at the proffered form and flung it across the room. No man who ever worked for La Guardia was given as free a reign. But then, no man ever accomplished so much for the city in a physical sense. Their collaboration would be monumental, painful, turbulent—but, in the final analysis, successful beyond the dreams of both, or of anyone else.[30]

He transformed the city, creating parks where slums and mud pits existed, housing projects in place of ramshackle tenements, and an incredible network of highways and bridges that gave New York a cohesion that many had considered impossible. A reform Republican, he had been chief aide and confidant to the reform-minded Tammany governor Al Smith. Having established a remarkable statewide parks system, Moses managed, with incoming Mayor La Guardia's blessing, to have the state legislature combine the offices of New York City's five borough parks commissioners into one, under his authority.

Forty-five when sworn in as parks commissioner, he made himself, in the words of his greatest biographer, Robert Caro, "the ward boss of the inner circle, the bankroller of the Four Hundred of politics." He bestowed retainers, fees, and commissions upon city and state political leaders "on the basis of a very exact appraisal of their place in the political pecking order." Not unremarkably, it was they who saw to it that his power was maintained. Moses was also a genius at "using the wealth of his public authorities to unite behind his aims banks, labor unions, contractors, bond underwriters, insurance firms, the great retail stores, real estate manipulators—all the forces with sufficient weight to . . . insure that, in deciding on such projects, the decisive voice would be that of the people."

Often overlooked is the irony that in rebuilding New York City, Moses made inevitable its decline into decrepitude in our time. To build his highways, 250,000 immigrants and low-income people were forced to leave their homes, destroying many a neighborhood community, some the size of small cities themselves, which had been lively, congenial residential areas. Those highways flooded the city with cars, caused traffic to grow to city-destroying dimensions by raising the air pollution level, and also systematically starved the subways and suburban commuter railroads. Writes Caro, "By making sure that the vast suburbs, rural and empty when he came to power, were filled on a sprawling, low-density development pattern relying primarily on roads instead of mass transportation, he insured that that flood would continue for generations if not centuries, that the New York metropolitan area would be—perhaps forever—an area in which transportation—getting from one place to another—would be an irritating, life-consuming concern for its 14,000,000 residents."

For other major projects—Lincoln Center, the United Nations, the Fordham, Pratt, and Long Island University campuses, and a dozen mammoth urban renewal housing projects—he dispossessed tens of thousands more. While no accurate figures are available on the total number of people evicted from their homes for all of Robert Moses's public works, the total is almost certainly close to half a million. A disproportionate number of blacks, Puerto Ricans, and the poor of all ethnicities were forced to make way for housing for the rich. Barred from many areas of the city by their color and their poverty, they had nowhere to relocate but already overcrowded slums—or "soft" borderline areas that then became slums. Consequently, Moses's heralded "slum clearance programs" created new slums as fast as they were clearing the old. What's more, the housing he built for the poor was drab, sterile, and shoddy, in areas that contributed to the ghettoizing of the city by color and income. Parks and playgrounds were intended for the economically advantaged.

For the economically disadvantaged he created recreational facilities that left much to be desired and little to be appreciated. After four decades of Robert Moses's power, a city so bright with promise when he began to rebuild it was in physical decline. The highways and tunnels he created were collectively the history's most awesome urban improvement, but even more awesome was the congestion on them. While he had built more housing than any public official in history, the city was starved for housing for the underprivileged, whom Moses always looked upon with undisguised condescension; more starved, it can be said, than when he started building.[31]

Thus the man of whom Fiorello La Guardia literally screamed to Paul Windels on February 22, 1934, "Jesus Christ, of all the people in the City of New York I had to pick the one man who Roosevelt won't stand for and he won't give me any more money unless I get rid of him. . . . Seven million people in the city and I had to pick the one Roosevelt can't stand!"[32]

The Moses-Roosevelt feud had started when Roosevelt was recovering from the polio that seemed to end his promising political career, and then-Governor Al Smith, wanting to help get him back into politics, persuaded him to assume chairmanship of the Taconic State Park Commission. Roosevelt accepted, on two conditions: approval of a Taconic Parkway through the scenic Hudson region he loved so passionately, and a place on the commission for his political adviser Louis Howe, the man most responsible for his rise to political eminence after what threatened to be a retreat into invalidism. As president of the State Parks Commission, Moses vetoed the Howe appointment with the snide observation that if Roosevelt wanted "a secretary and personal valet," he would have to stand the cost himself. Roosevelt did not press the matter. When Moses became New York's secretary of state, he blocked approval of the Taconic Parkway. Roosevelt submitted his resignation but withdrew it at Smith's personal request. He did not, however, rescind his ill feelings toward Moses.

Those feelings turned into mutual hatred when Smith decided to run for the presidency in 1928 and passed over Moses to anoint Roosevelt as his gubernatorial successor. Moses's private comments—which he took no pains to keep private—were brutal: FDR was "a crippled patrician," "a poor excuse for a man"; what's more, his wife, Eleanor, was "a gawky caricature of a woman." Roosevelt had had to accept as best he could such nasty ridicule. But now he was president of the United States and in a position to settle old scores with Moses.

La Guardia obviously knew nothing of this when he made Moses his parks commissioner. He learned of it on February 21, when summoned to Washington by Ickes at the president's command and informed of "the Boss's" feelings about Moses—and ordered to dismiss Moses as head of the PWA-financed Triborough Bridge Authority. Roosevelt could not, of course, make any federal funding contingent upon a city commissioner being fired. But using the TBA as leverage was effectively the same thing. The Triborough was intended to link Manhattan with Queens and the Bronx. (Brooklyn was already linked by the Brooklyn Bridge, and Staten Island would remain linked by ferry until construction of the Verrazano Narrows Bridge decades in the future.) First conceived in 1916, work was not begun until a decade later during the Walker mayoralty, then had to be put on hold due to corruption and consequent lack of funding. La Guardia revived the vital project and, on February 4, 1934, appointed Moses to head the TBA. Moses came up with an elaborate—and quite brilliant—plan involving four interconnecting spans. But this could be achieved only with federal funding of some fifty million dollars that would, in the bargain, generate employment for thousands.

When Ickes told La Guardia that either Moses must go or the project would not be funded, he also made it clear that millions more in loans from the Ickes-controlled PWA would not be forthcoming either. La Guardia asked for "a few days to see what he might work out." But nothing could be worked out. The president was unyielding. Adolf Berle tried to reason with him that threatening to cut off federal aid unless Moses was fired would have grave consequences both for the La Guardia administration and the president himself, given that New York was the showplace of his New Deal. Even Ickes, uncomfortable at having to play the heavy in FDR's Machiavellian scheme, wanted him to back off. He wouldn't.[33]

La Guardia could not force the resignation of Moses, who had constituted the TBA so that commissioners could be removed only following specific charges and a formal hearing. He could, though, fire a city commissioner. He threatened to remove Moses as parks commissioner unless he voluntarily stepped down from the TBA. Falling back on his standard threat, Moses said that if the mayor insisted, he would resign from the TBA—but would also resign as parks commissioner. What's more, he would make it known that the city's chief executive had surrendered to federal pressure to remove an official who had not done a thing to justify such treatment.

La Guardia was urged by all his most trusted advisers not to give in to the White House. "There is only one course to pursue, and that is to stand like a rock against Ickes and all the rest," said C. C. Cunningham, reflecting the consensus.[34] Realizing that giving in to Roosevelt would compromise his standing with the fusion that had put him into office, and knowing that Moses was indispensable as parks commissioner, La Guardia heeded his advisers. Meanwhile, as the drama dragged on through the summer, with neither side budging, Ickes had undercover investigators seek out any evidence of wrongdoing on Moses's part that could cause his removal from the TBA.

They came up with nothing. The Master Builder may have been a Master Monster, but he was a scrupulously honest one. Furthermore, he had the people on his side. Desperate for that funding, as it would help ease unemployment, they agreed that the White House had no right to maltreat a man who might have made a lousy governor but was a superb city planner. If the White House wanted Moses fired, it would have to come out and say so publicly—and face the consequences. This put FDR in a bind. He could not antagonize his home state, where the majority of the people loved him—but loved more the idea of federal funding and jobs.

The drama approached a climax on November 21, when the PWA board met to approve a long list of projects, and Ickes personally slashed from it every single proposed project for New York City. La Guardia was now huddling daily with his closest advisers. Windels argued that, on political grounds, he could not knuckle under to the president. Burlingham posited the same argument on grounds of principle. Then, the day after Christmas 1934, he received from Ickes an official Administrative Order Number 129. Obviously the work of FDR, it stated unequivocally, "Hereafter no funds shall be advanced to any authority, board or commission constituting an independent corporation or entity created for a specific purpose wholly within the confines of a municipality, any of the members of the governing body of which authority, board or commission holds any public office under said municipality." Translation: Moses could not hold simultaneously the job of parks commissioner and chairman of the TBA.

Roosevelt, who had let Ickes take all the fire, now directly involved himself. Shrewd enough a politician to realize that some compromise had best be arrived at, he told La Guardia that if he felt he could not force the Moses resignation, he would be satisfied with a promise to Ickes—in writing—not to reappoint Moses when his chairmanship came up for renewal on June 30, 1935, which would be well in advance of the bridge's completion. Though Order Number 129 had not been made public, La Guardia showed it to Moses, in hopes of making him realize he had no choice but to give in and resign from the TBA, and then rushed down to Washington and secretly swore to Ickes that he would promise in writing not to reappoint Moses.

But Moses could be every bit as conniving as the president he so loathed. While La Guardia was returning from Washington, Moses secretly leaked the order to the press, gambling on a violent public reaction in his favor. The gamble paid off. New York newspapers joined the public in condemning the order, insisting that under no conditions must their mayor give in to the White House. Representatives from every conceivable civic group, political affiliation notwithstanding, agreed. Compounding the situation, newspapers around the country saw in the whole imbroglio the threat of FDR withholding funds capriciously out of dislike for an individual in any city. A way out of the maelstrom was imperative.

As it happens, Order Number 129 also applied to Housing Commissioner Langdon W. Post, who was also a member of the Municipal Housing Authority, which received federal funds. Ickes assured La Guardia that 129 would not apply to Post. This only reinforced the obvious: that the order was simply a device on Roosevelt's part to get back at Moses. With the chorus of criticism reaching a crescendo, Roosevelt summoned La Guardia to a secret meeting (February 24, 1935) aboard a train carrying him to Harvard for a speech, in hopes they could jointly resolve the issue so that both—but in particular the president—might save face.

La Guardia brought along a letter that he thought might do the trick. Addressed to Ickes, he agreed to conform with Order Number 129 in the future and never again appoint a city official to a federally funded authority. However, he went on, applying it retroactively created a problem in the case of Post, who was quite familiar with the city's entire housing program; "what is more, he is enthusiastic, zealous and energetic in his work. It would be a pity to displace him at this time." Might he, wondered La Guardia, possibly ask for a "modification" of 129 that would permit "officials of existing commissions or authorities to continue their work until completion?" He added shrewdly as a P.S. that there was one other official who would be affected by the modification: Robert Moses. "I assume the ruling on one will be applicable to the other."[35]

Such an attempt to cover a retreat on Moses by pretending the battle was really over Post was an obvious smoke screen that FDR was reluctant to use. He did nothing about it over the ensuing three days other than to vet La Guardia's shrewd letter to Ickes. Meanwhile, requisition slips that Moses had sent to Ickes for his signature four months previously lay unsigned on his desk. Contracts for the next stages of the Triborough Bridge could not be let, and the threat of layoffs loomed large. Then, on February 26, two days after the secret meeting aboard the presidential train, Al Smith told a press conference it was "ridiculous" not to let Moses finish the Triborough. What's more, Ickes's order was "narrow, political and vindictive."

When Smith's statement made national headlines the next day, FDR, in Ickes's words, "came to a conclusion that a retreat was in order." Summoning Ickes to the White House, he called in a stenographer and dictated a reply to La Guardia's letter, to go out over Ickes's signature, in which he agreed to solve "the problem created as the result of the expiration of the term of Commissioner Langdon Post" by ruling that since Post had been appointed to both his city and authority posts prior to the order's issue, he should be allowed to keep them. "Since a like situation exists with reference to Mr. Moses of the Triborough Bridge Authority, that interpretation shall also apply to him," the letter added. Ickes predated the letter to February 26—"so as to antedate by one day the blast let out . . . by Al Smith," adding lamely that "the whole thing was a mistake from the start."[36] For Moses, it was an obvious victory, sweetened by the fact that in seeking to cut him off at the knees, his mortal enemy had restored him in the eyes of the public. It was also a victory for La Guardia: "THE MAYOR WINS," exclaimed the *Times* (March 12, 1935), averring, "By persistence and persuasion he at last won his point." By then, a check for the necessary TBA funding was in the mail, and checks to fund millions for other projects were being prepared.

The whole affair had a coda that bordered on comic opera. Moses's term on the TBA ran out in June, and La Guardia, out of consideration for FDR's and Ickes's feelings, decided that a second swearing-in was unnecessary. A letter of reappointment would suffice. But not for Moses. He demanded not only another swearing-in but also a formal ceremony to boot, falling back on his standard threat to resign both as TBA chairman and as parks commissioner unless he got it. La Guardia denounced the latest Moses tempest as "childishness" but went along with the formal swearing-in. When photographers grouped the two, Moses was asked to put his arm around the mayor's shoulder. La Guardia, who was a foot shorter, squeaked, "Nothing doing!" Whereupon Moses draped a long arm around the Little Flower and said with a huge smile, "If the Mayor can stand it, I guess I can." The mayor put on a game smile.[37]

One year later, on July 11, 1936, the ceremony celebrating the opening of the Triborough Bridge was held on the central span. Roosevelt at first refused to attend but, facing political realities, agreed at the last minute, on the condition that La Guardia and not Moses, who was the presiding master of ceremonies, introduce him. Also in attendance was Ickes, who had first declined because the master of ceremonies, out of spite, had invited him only as a "general spectator," relenting only when La Guardia arranged that he be sent a special guest ticket and be permitted to make a five-minute speech. Said Ickes, "The Triborough Bridge is a wonderful affair. From the engineering point of view, it is one of the greatest in the world as it is the biggest."[38]

5.

A week after the Moses controversy was resolved, La Guardia was faced with his first explosive crisis, the Harlem Riot.

Once a thriving white middle-class community, Harlem was by now a congested community of roughly three hundred thousand, almost entirely black, 90 percent having migrated there primarily from the South after the First World War. This reflected a sixfold population increase over three decades. Formerly attractive single-family brownstone houses had become run-down multiple-family dwellings. Almost entirely a bedroom community, with 95 percent of its working population commuting to jobs in other parts of the city, Harlem was of all New York City communities the hardest hit by the Depression.

La Guardia's attitude toward the blacks had always been exemplary. Back in 1931, he was hailed by the influential and highly respected black New York daily, the *Amsterdam News*, as "one of the most fearless friends the Negro has ever had in our Congress." On becoming mayor, he named blacks to important posts in his administration. The highest ranking, Tax Commissioner Hubert T. Delaney, was considered unofficial ombudsman for the black community. A year before the riot, in response to complaints of discrimination in the Board of Transportation, La Guardia ordered its chairman to end all bias in job assignments. His relations with leaders of such organizations as the NAACP, the Urban League, and black churches were warm, and he took liberal positions on racial issues, challenging established biases and urging Americans to greater tolerance. Still, while he empathized sincerely with the plight of urban blacks, insisting they be accorded the same rights and an equality accorded all minorities, his focus was primarily on the other ethnic groups. But the blacks were not like all other ethnics. They had their own problems—problems La Guardia offered no special program to alleviate.

Due to the heavy migration from the South, there was greater competition within low-skilled occupations open to blacks, as well as for housing. The level of unemployment among blacks was by 1935 three times the rate for whites. Eight Harlem blocks were jammed with more than three thousand residents each; one block held close to four thousand. These were figures faced by no other section of the city, even the Lower East Side and East Harlem slums.[39] Men unable to find jobs left their families, and mothers were forced to go out and work, leaving their children to fend for themselves. Forty-three percent of Harlem's black families depended upon relief for their very survival. Programs established to help the poor openly discriminated against them. The Civil Works Administration program initially required New York blacks to come to Harlem to register regardless of where they lived and consistently placed them in positions below their skill level. Women applying for relief were asked by receptionists, "Have you tried the streets?"[40]

Entire industries were closed to them, even for menial jobs. The Metropolitan Insurance Company hired no blacks—despite its more than one hundred thousand policyholders in Harlem alone. The Fifth Avenue Coach Company refused even to discuss its hiring practices with investigators from a commission set up by La Guardia to look into the entire problem; the commission reported that this and other corporations "may be divided into two classes . . . those that employ Negroes in menial positions, and those that employ no Negroes at all." Macy's gladly accepted blacks' patronage but hired them only for cleaning floors and routine maintenance. Gimbels, like its traditional competitor, likewise welcomed blacks as customers but hired none at all. Of ten thousand workers with New York's Consolidated Edison, only sixty-five were black (porters or janitors). New York Telephone had not a single black operator (described by one executive as "customary practice"). New York's subway and surface transit carriers counted but a handful on their payrolls—all on their janitorial staffs, all closed out of any advancement to mid-level positions, and all assigned to Harlem stations. Many employers were quite open in justifying their antiblack prejudice, claiming that Negroes were "inferior" or that the public would not tolerate integration or that integrating would harm employee relations. Blacks were explicitly barred from membership in twenty-four unions.[41]

Six months into his administration, having received an alarming report on the disproportionate crime rate among black children, La Guardia commissioned a study, "The Negro Problem as Reflected in the Functioning of the Domestic Relations Court of the City of New York." The study revealed that childhood crime among blacks over the previous thirteen years had risen by more than 240 percent. In Manhattan alone, one of every four juveniles arraigned in children's court was black. One of every four nonsupport cases in the city involved black families. La Guardia passed the report on to his assistant Louis Dunham, who recommended, "further study."[42]

The blacks had by now turned increasingly to racial solidarity, led by the clergy advocating "Don't Buy Where You Can't Work" actions. The Rev. Adam Clayton Powell Jr., assistant pastor (to his father) of the Abyssinian Baptist Church, who was beginning his meteoric rise to political eminence and eventual decline into ignominy, said that his parishioners were "as much at home on the picket line as they are in church." The growing militancy led to at times inflammatory contact with the one city agency the blacks least trusted, the New York Police Department. One demonstration, in March 1934, degenerated into an hour-long physical confrontation when a police officer tossed tear gas into a peaceful Harlem rally of more than five thousand honoring the mother of one of the Scottsboro Boys (nine Alabama black youths convicted of raping two white women and sentenced to seventy-year terms on manufactured evidence).

When the officer was called on the carpet by Chief Inspector Valentine and asked if he regretted so impulsive an act of force, he replied, "I can't say I do. It was the only way of dispersing them without injuring them." Why he felt the obviously nonviolent crowd had to be dispersed was never questioned. Valentine found the use of tear gas unjustified but took no disciplinary action. As relations between the people of Harlem and the police deteriorated, complaints came in of police breaking into apartments without warrants, conducting illegal searches of persons and property, and referring to the community collectively, often within earshot, as "black bastards." Traditionally the department did not discipline police on these charges or complaints. Exacerbating the problem, Valentine made it a practice to banish cops from other commands with poor records or bad judgment to Harlem beats.[43]

On March 19, 1935, at 3:30 in the afternoon, an undersized sixteen-year-old Puerto Rican youth named Lino Rivera stole a ten-cent penknife from Kress's on 125th Street: "I wanted it and so I took it." Grabbed by workers who saw him do it, he bit both before they managed to subdue him and summon a policeman, who took the boy back into the store for questioning. As a crowd of curious gathered, a woman yelled that his captors "were taking the boy to the basement to beat him up." Someone shouted that the cops had killed the boy. Another cried out, "It's just like down South where they lynch us." The police ordered the crowd to mind their own business and disperse.[44]

The Kress manager decided not to press charges, and Rivera was escorted by the police from the store through a back entrance to avoid the milling crowd out front and told to go home. When an ambulance arrived to treat the two employees he had scratched and bitten, blacks in the crowd were convinced that a nonwhite child had been arrested for a petty charge and billy-clubbed to death in the back room of the store by the police. Believing the rumor, crowds stormed the store, overturning counters and spilling merchandise on the floor, and began looting. It took police more than an hour to clear the store and lock the doors.

Contributing to the chaos, an activist group known as the Young Liberators set up a picket line before the store and waved hastily painted placards protesting the brutal beating of a Negro child, passing out handbills that said, "The boy is near death. . . . A Negro woman had her arm broken." The situation was further inflamed by the Young Communist League, which issued a hastily prepared diatribe to the effect that "the brutal beating" of the boy by the Kress guards "again proves the increasing terror against the Negro people of Harlem. [White] Bosses, who deny the most immediate necessities . . . who throw workers out of employment, who pay not enough to live on, are protecting their so-called property rights with brutal beatings. . . . They lynch Negro people in the South on framed up charges."[45]

By sundown, as a small group of terrified white police tried to keep order, people returning home from work joined the mob. One man egged the crowd on with tales of brutality and discrimination. Suddenly bottles started flying through the air, Kress's plate glass windows were shattered, and the looters moved in en masse. As word spread quickly, residents poured out of their apartment buildings while others heaved bottles, bricks, and other items from their windows onto the police below. When a black station wagon appeared, a woman screamed, "There's the hearse come to take the boy's body." This sent looters rampaging through the neighborhood, smashing plate glass shop windows, carting off loot, setting fires, and otherwise feeding the riot with their wrath.

At some point it occurred to the police to prove the Rivera boy was alive and well. After a search, he was found at two in the morning and brought to the front of Kress's. But due to years of blatant discrimination and bad feelings between black residents and neighborhood white storekeepers, the riot had by then taken on a dynamic of its own. Black merchants put up signs: "Run by COLORED People." Several white-owned establishments put up signs: "This store employs Negro workers." Whites who chanced to be in the area were attacked simply because they were the wrong color in the wrong place on the wrong night. Snipers from rooftops fired down into the street. Police reinforcements rushed into the area and charged the mobs in phalanxes, clubbing rioters on the head with their gun butts. When order was finally restored next morning and the streets cleared, the casualty count stood at more than 100 stabbed, beaten, or shot; 125 men, mostly young and black, had been arrested for disorderly conduct, inciting to riot, and looting; 250 shop windows were smashed—and three blacks had been killed by the police.[46]

District Attorney William C. Dodge was convinced that the Communists were behind the riot. Whether they were is highly questionable. Not questionable is that they exploited the situation. Blared the Communist *Daily Worker* (March 22, 1935), "Negro Harlem Terrorized." Other, more responsible papers, sought deeper cause for the rage, among them the *Herald Tribune* (March 22, 1935): "The factors lying behind this situation are rooted in the economic problems of a poverty stricken area within which a vast population is squeezed." Powell took a different tack: "Continued exploitation of the Negro is at the bottom of all the trouble, exploitation as regards wages, jobs, working conditions." Local businesses, he was convinced, utilized even government-assisted programs to discriminate against Harlem's population while taking its money and its votes. The people were "finally fed up."[47]

The long-festering situation in Harlem had not occupied La Guardia's thinking, due to failure by police and other officials to keep him informed and his preoccupation with other municipal interests and concerns, not the least of which was the playing out of the Moses TBA drama. The events of March 19 changed that. His gut reaction was to blame "a few irresponsible individuals" who spread false rumors of race discrimination. On consideration, he concluded that what occurred at Kress's could not be dismissed as just a Communist plot. Conceding that the grim conditions in the Harlem community had contributed to the riot, La Guardia established a Commission on Conditions in Harlem, chaired by a prominent black dentist, Dr. Charles Roberts, to study the precipitating causes for the riot. Noted Negro sociologist E. Franklin Frazier was named to conduct the actual research.[48]

After twenty-five hearings at which testimony was taken from some 160 witnesses, "The Negro in Harlem: A Report on Social and Economic Conditions Responsible for the Outbreak of March 19, 1935" was presented. Describing the riot as the black community's inarticulate response to unemployment and blatant racism, it made a poignant plea for municipal action to combat job discrimination, build decent affordable housing, and resolve the entwined problems of crime and insensitive police. The report also called for improved health care, more schools and parks, and a concerted effort to eliminate the prejudice that was prevalent in all municipal services from relief to medical assistance and so poisoned relations between the races. Criticizing some of the city's best-qualified commissioners as being insensitive to the problem, the report went on to note that even after the already projected Harlem River Houses project was completed, and even if rents were reduced throughout the community and the housing code was strictly enforced, "the fundamental problems will not have changed." Only a subsidized housing program for its fifty-six thousand depressed families at the very least would address the appalling effects of poverty, racism, and slum conditions prevalent in Harlem.

La Guardia concurred. But there were limits to what he could do. Comprehensive solutions to all the major problems facing the city at this point in time were impossible. To one conference of Negro church leaders he said that he carried "no illusions about the difficulties facing your people in New York," while to a delegation of prominent black leaders he admitted to being "as helpless in handling large scale economic problems as the League of Nations was in preventing the war between Italy and Libya."[49] The report also condemned the police for their "shocking barbarity," averring, "It is a grave state of affairs when the inhabitants of a large section of the city have come to look at the . . . police . . . as lawless oppressors who stop at no brutality or at the taking of human life." It recommended setting up a biracial citizens' committee to investigate regularly complaints against the NYPD. But La Guardia feared this would weaken his efforts to go after the rackets, including those based in Harlem, and would create problems with Valentine (soon to succeed O'Ryan as police commissioner), whom he thought was doing, by and large, a superb job, even though O'Ryan had criticized him, and justifiably so, for being "too busy, unsympathetic or uninterested" to cooperate with the blacks. [50]

When a number of his commissioners disputed the report's findings, La Guardia asked Howard University professor Alain Locke, famous for his study of the "New Negro," to evaluate the report in the context of its critics' comments. After a full review, Locke agreed with most of its conclusions and offered a number of remedial prescriptions. While La Guardia could not adopt the list in its entirety, he did commit the city to allocating more resources to Harlem than ever before. Despite strong resistance, over the next four years he built, in addition to Harlem River Houses, the Central Harlem Health Center, a new Women's Pavilion for Harlem Hospital, and two new schools for the area. He also integrated the all-white staffs of city hospitals, expanded Civil Service opportunities for blacks, attacked discrimination in relief programs, and appointed blacks to the Emergency Relief Board, to supervisory posts in the fire and sanitation departments, and to jobs in the offices of the city marshal, district attorney, and corporation counsel. In 1936 he named the city's first black magistrate, and a few years later he appointed the first black woman judge.[51]

Admittedly, these appointments were tokenism. There is no gainsaying that La Guardia "played the ethnic card" when it came to appointments, even though he said, "I have never appointed and never will appoint a man to office because of his color."[52] Still, it took courage to make such symbolic breakthroughs in the 1930s, when segregation was practiced in New York City as it was in, say, Montgomery, Alabama. On June 25, 1936, the *Amsterdam News* commended La Guardia "for naming more Negroes to big, responsible jobs in city government . . . than all other mayors of the city combined." On December 5, 1940, Walter White, executive secretary of the NAACP, wrote the mayor that his forward-looking policies on civil rights were influencing officials across the country.[53] But New York's—and La Guardia's—"black problem" was not resolved definitively. An even greater upheaval lay in the future.

CHAPTER EIGHTEEN

"The only ultimate cure for them is dynamite"

1.

When La Guardia came into office, he enjoyed a majority of thirteen to three on the Board of Estimate, the upper house of the city's legislature. The lower chamber, the Board of Aldermen, was already dominated by Tammany, but this was of lesser consequence since it functioned as little more than a rubber stamp. As already noted, on the Board of Estimate the mayor, city comptroller, and aldermanic president had three votes each, the borough presidents of Manhattan and Brooklyn each had two, and the Bronx, Queens, and Richmond presidents had a single vote each. The failure of Joseph P. McGoldrick to win election as Comptroller W. Arthur Cunningham's successor reduced La Guardia's majority to ten. In November, Aldermanic President Bernard S. Deutsch died suddenly, and the office automatically devolved upon Timothy J. Sullivan, the board's Democratic majority leader. La Guardia's original thirteen-to-three majority was now a seven-to-nine minority. Then two of his allies, George U. Harvey and Joseph A. Palma, borough presidents of Queens and Staten Island respectively, began voting with the Democratic majority. With only the loyalty of Brooklyn Borough President Raymond Ingersoll, the most votes that La Guardia could now count on was five.

Before his term was half over, with the Democrats dominating both houses of the legislature, Tammany had effectively wrested from La Guardia control of the city government and was more obsessed with seeing him fail for the Hall's own sake than seeing him succeed for the city's.

This made him more than ever determined to fulfill the promise of Fusion reform—what he liked to call "scientific government"—he had made to the voters. Signs of such reform were clearly discernible. Drastic improvements in health services were moving ahead for those New Yorkers most in need of them. Work was progressing on a new Hospital for Chronic Diseases and new, sorely needed general hospitals in Jamaica (in Queens) and Harlem. Other facilities, including regional clinics in all the boroughs, were either being planned, on the drawing board, or in various stages of construction. La Guardia set as a goal achieving in municipal hospitals the norm for patients in private hospitals. It was a rash goal, and from today's point of view illusory. But this did not stop his pressing on with an agenda that also included major laboratory additions, expanding the nursing force, and developing an extensive scientific research development program.

The success he was to realize in the area of public health was never replicated in another high-priority area: sanitation and waste disposal. Dissatisfied with the garbage-littered streets, the cleaning of which was still largely carried out by some six thousand sweepers, and the fact that snow removal was always a problem despite the availability of a large volunteer force, La Guardia went through two commissioners before settling on William F. Carey, a former chief of excavations for the Panama Canal. Try as he might, Carey managed to introduce only minimal efficiency into the army of sweepers and fared little better in the purchase of heavy equipment due to financial constraints. In time, a construction program for large incinerators was begun following a ruling by the U.S. Supreme Court that terminated the dumping of garbage at sea and discharge of polluted waters into the city's rivers. It was to achieve no more than a dent in the problem.

Of the three fields of reform that were La Guardia's main priorities—housing, transit, and public power—the last two provided unsatisfactory results despite the energy and optimism with which he approached them. Of his catalogue of goals to unify the boroughs, he considered unification of public transit facilities the most urgent—and the easiest to accomplish. The problem of inter- as well as intraborough auto traffic was being resolved now that the Triborough Bridge was becoming a reality. Most New Yorkers, though, depended upon public transport, primarily the subway system, especially workers commuting to Manhattan from the outer boroughs. And that mode left a lot to be desired, mainly because it had never been systematically planned but had, like Mrs. Stowe's Topsy, just growed and growed.

The three principal lines—the IRT, BMT and Independent—were built at the beginning of the twentieth century by the city, entering into a complex partnership with private interests for both construction and operation of routes. La Guardia hoped to unify and expand the three lines under public ownership and management, in combination with surface routes (buses and elevated trains—the "els"). This envisioned single authority would open new lines to accommodate the city's growth, set a single fare, and establish a level of highest efficiency in all operational aspects.

As a first step, La Guardia authorized his two most capable advisers, Adolf Berle and Judge Seabury, to negotiate a purchase price for one of the lines. Told that an acceptable figure had been agreed upon, he exulted, "A good day's work. Now we must see there is no delay."[1] Legislation was immediately prepared and submitted to the city and state legislatures. The Board of Estimate shared the mayor's enthusiasm. Not so the state-appointed Transit Commission. La Guardia's appeal to Governor Lehman to push the transit bill, along with his willingness to compromise in the face of opposition from the legislature, was practically a replay of the Economy Bill fight. Berle and Seabury were ordered to plow ahead. Two years later, they completed the proposals for takeover of the private lines. The Transit Commission again rejected their report.

La Guardia demanded that either the commission come up with an acceptable proposal of its own within ninety days or he would move heaven and earth to get the commission abolished. The threat got him nowhere. In May 1938, he dealt directly with the commission. It was a pleasant meeting—but that was about the extent of it. La Guardia would eventually get the unification he wanted, but only after protracted delays and few of the benefits he hoped for. There was a moral in this that could apply to any and all other battles waged by the Little Flower in behalf of the masses: People do not set policy; they live in accordance with policy set by the politicians. Would it be overly cynical to murmur a silent "Amen!" to Swift's observation in *Voyage to Brobdingnag*: "And he gave it for his opinion, that whoever could make two ears of corn or two blades of grass to grow upon a spot of ground where only one grew before, would deserve better of mankind, and do more essential service to his country than the whole race of politicians put together"?

Equally frustrating as the transit issue to La Guardia was his attempt to establish a city-owned power plant. In December 1934, he ordered rejection of all bids by the privately owned utilities companies to supply electric power for the city's use because he deemed the proposed rates exorbitant. The White House tentatively promised to fund a public power plant.[2] A euphoric La Guardia selected a site for the new plant, the construction of which he anticipated the moment plans were finalized. The project had the support of the public and the press. Not so the politicians, who were lobbied vigorously by the utility companies.

Faced with the will of the people, criticism by the press, and the fiscal support of the White House pending application for a loan, the utilities offered to cut their rates for electricity supplied to the city. What's more, within three months they were offering a general reduction for the consumer. But La Guardia could not be swayed from his intention that the city construct its own power plant, even when the newspapers urged that he accept the "peace offer" and doubted the wisdom of burdening the city with the costs and risks of such a venture. When the state legislature and then the Board of Estimate denied him the necessary authority, he continued the fight by letting the voters decide.

At the end of March he went to Albany to seek the required referendum and was confronted by a stonewalling power lobby. "That's what these gentlemen appearing in the opposition are bent upon," he all but screamed for the benefit of the press, "nipping in the bud any project for the municipalities to protect themselves against the extortion of the power companies." The courts rejected the referendum on a technicality. The mayor persevered. "This is not final. I see the day when we will own all Consolidated Edison. It may not come in my time. . . ." Two years later a drastically reduced proposal to acquire a utility plant on Staten Island was blocked by the Democratic-controlled municipal legislature. La Guardia's words proved to be prophetic: It did not come in his time.[3]

Transit unification at least had results, albeit limited, and his fight for a municipal power plant, though it failed, at least reestablished La Guardia in good standing with the political left. It was in creating decent housing for the poor that he scored his greatest success.

It is estimated that a million children were being raised in horrific slums that comprised in aggregate seventeen square miles within the five boroughs and would cost some fifteen million dollars to eliminate. Ten acres of these slums were pronounced "unfit for human habitation," as well as unprofitable for their owners. Of the worst, 4.4 square miles were in Manhattan, 5.3 miles in Brooklyn. The 516,000 families that lived amidst this squalor earned an estimated average yearly income of seven hundred dollars. According to prevailing formulas, they could afford only seven dollars a room per month for rent.[4] La Guardia wanted that rental to be in decent housing. The $150 million required for the first stage seemed obtainable from Washington, given its anxiety to ameliorate the city's unemployment.

In the second month of his administration, La Guardia had the city pass a law to carry out "the clearance, replanning, and reconsideration of the areas in which unsanitary or substandard housing conditions exist." A New York City Housing Authority was established, and Housing Commissioner Langdon Post was named chairman of this semiautonomous authority. Where feasible, La Guardia personally ordered landlords to make improvements. He had "no sympathy for them," said Post; they had allowed their property to run down, and thus had only themselves to blame. When the landlords whose properties were not too old and could be made properly habitable refused, La Guardia told Post, "The only ultimate cure for them is dynamite."[5]

In selecting Langdon Post to head the New York City Housing Authority, Fiorello had an ideal commissioner. In Secretary of Commerce Ickes, he had, as we have seen, a major headache. Unsure of when or even whether Ickes would release the funds already authorized, and in any event impatient to get started, La Guardia turned to private funding. With loans from Vincent Astor, the city's largest landholder, and financier Bernard Baruch, he was able to begin the pioneering project, First Houses, in Manhattan's East Village (at Avenue A and East Third Street). Dedicated in December 1935, it contained 120 sunlit apartments, with modern sanitary facilities, which rented for $6.05 per room to families whose weekly income averaged twenty-three dollars. It was, comparatively speaking, a milestone of minuscule proportions, but a milestone nevertheless, and convinced the public as well as the White House that La Guardia meant business. What's more, it got the ball rolling. Williamsburg (Brooklyn) and Harlem River Houses (Manhattan) followed, built directly by the PWA instead of grants to the city, and thus owned by the federal government.

Thanks to La Guardia's perseverance, and the fact that he was admired by Roosevelt, Ickes, and in particular Harry Hopkins, the U.S. Housing Authority, along with a state authority, was soon funding housing directly, and on a scale that could not be faulted. Red Hook contained more than nine thousand units; Queensbridge Houses, more than eleven thousand (and, an innovation in public housing, elevators). The floodgate was open. While it must be conceded that none of this could have been accomplished without the New Deal, the credit for initiating the reform and goading Washington into taking action belongs to La Guardia. Other American cities, facing the same problem, got the same *kind* of assistance from Washington, but proportionately New York received much more than its share.

In November 1935, La Guardia became president of the U.S. Conference of Mayors, an office he would hold for ten years. Here, reasoned the mayors, was a man with a big mouth out of all proportion to his diminutive stature who successfully led the cities' fight to bypass their states for access to federal assistance. One of the new president's first acts was to petition Harry Hopkins to create independent WPA units for the twenty-five largest cities on an equal level with the forty-eight states. On June 26, 1936, Hopkins announced that the WPA would award the privilege of administering its own federal relief operations to but one of the cities: New York. The city would, in effect, be treated as "the forty-ninth state." Hopkins's made his decision not because of his personal fondness for La Guardia but because the mayor had developed a wide range of WPA projects and administered them honestly and efficiently. Here was testimony to La Guardia's tireless efforts to put New York in the vanguard of the emerging partnership between the White House and the cities.[6]

2.

Let us pause to take a closer look at this man who seemed capable
of functioning only in a state of perpetual motion. It was said that
on any day scores of New Yorkers were prepared to swear they had
spotted their pudgy little mayor in his high black Stetson and rum-
pled suit dashing in or out of any number of locations throughout
the five boroughs—simultaneously. La Guardia was a study in ubiq-
uity who truly cared about his constituents. And *all* New Yorkers were
his constituents, whether or not they had voted for him or, for that
matter, whether or not they even *liked* him. He not only gave new
meaning to the term hands-on executive, he gave new meaning to
the term executive intervention.

He personally intervened, for example, on learning that a neighbor's daughter had been denied a surgical residency at Bellevue by
its all-male department; as a result, the city hospital hired its first
woman surgeon. La Guardia appointed more women to responsible
city posts than any previous mayor. "City government is just housekeeping," he believed, "and women knew best about that sort of
thing."[7] He personally stepped in to settle strikes among elevator
operators, hotel employees, taxi drivers, furriers, and various garment trades workers. During a laundry strike he threatened to have
the business's hot water turned off unless management settled. When
hotel owners refused to honor a compromise labor commitment,
they were paid surprise visits by city health and labor inspectors. Taxi
owners were warned that unless they came to terms with the justified
demands of the drivers, receivers would be sent in to seize uncol-
lected taxes. He pressured distributors to sell cut-rate milk at city-
operated baby health stations by threatening to establish municipal
milk depots unless prices were kept reasonable.[8]

He even took on the New York City Bar Association, suggesting
that juridical appointments were drawn from the old-boy establishment lawyers, and subsequently resigned from the American Bar Association with the public charge that it was devoting "its efforts to
special interests rather than to the uplift and welfare of the profession." He went after doctors for being preoccupied with profits and
displaying "stubborn resistance to new ideas" such as group health
care and expanded public health services. He stood up to the New
York Firsters by opposing a bill that would have required municipal

employees to live within the city limits, arguing that this was "inappropriate" for a metropolis like New York, in which only the very rich could afford the few private homes.⁹ When the Fire Department received thirteen identical bids for rubber-lined water hoses, he organized a national campaign against what he termed the "Fire Hose Trust," going so far as to draft a bill that would have put the city into the business of manufacturing its own hoses. The Federal Trade Commission investigated. This resulted in antitrust actions against the companies. Six months later the monopolists signed a consent agreement to cease price-fixing.¹⁰

Other targets included "raw magazines" like the *Police Gazette*, drunk drivers, water pollution, high city insurance rates, and inefficient sanitation disposal. The police commissioner was commanded not to let "technicalities, nor lack of evidence" stand in the way of prosecuting offenders and to be particularly hard on the "tinhorns and horse thieves" responsible for street gambling. On occasion, La Guardia would don judicial robes and take to the bench in Magistrate's Court, a prerogative to which his office as the city's chief magistrate entitled him. A bus driver went through a red light when La Guardia happened to be on the scene. He noted the license number, had the offender hauled before him, and imposed—and collected on the spot—a two-dollar fine. Inspecting the Bronx Terminal Market and finding private guards carrying billy clubs, he personally confiscated the weapons, lest the city markets look like a patrolled danger zone. There was, surprisingly, a limit to how far and into what areas La Guardia would inject himself. When Ernest Cuneo wrote suggesting it might be a good idea to extend daylight saving time, he wrote back testily that he declined to "fiddle with the calendar."¹¹

Recalling the placid rural ambience in which he had grown up in Arizona, La Guardia hoped to temper New York's hectic urban life. The city, he decided, was a difficult enough place to live in without its citizens being subjected constantly to car horns honking, jackhammering in the streets, construction clamor, and the various aspects of pedestrian noisemaking that can raise decibels to near-intolerable levels. In addition to calling for the formation of committees, to include schoolchildren, to agitate for noise reduction, he inundated the newspapers with official pronouncements urging calm and serenity. More effective was his order that, for openers, the police issue summonses for unnecessary tooting of horns by motorists, loud radio playing, the unlicensed use of loudspeakers, and even, around the Yuletide season, "disturbing caroling."[12]

The Little Flower had a special place in his heart for his younger, more vulnerable citizens—the "kiddies." There are many today, the writer included, who recall fondly how during a protracted newspaper strike he read the Sunday comics over the radio, replete with appropriate dramatic intonation and grave suspense, so that "all the little boys and girls" were kept up to date on the trials and tribulations of their favorite characters—and derived from them a sense of morality. "Ahh! What do we have here? The gardener! Stabbed! . . . But Dick Tracy is on the trail! And say, children, what does it all mean? It means that dirty money never brings any luck."[13] To teach youngsters the workings of government and imbue them with a positive attitude about serving the people, high school students were hired as City Hall interns and personally lectured to by His Honor from time to time on the proper management of municipal government. He always took particular pleasure in opening a new park, playground, or community health center, convinced that exposing children to wholesome recreation, fresh air, and affordable health went further toward combating juvenile delinquency than sentencing them to serve time in juvenile homes or jails.

La Guardia had a special tolerance for children who committed crimes of a nonviolent nature. He saw no reason for making it a court case should a child "break a window or hook an apple." He told one audience of jurists, "Nothing has such a tendency to make a boy a criminal as to arrest him and lock him up." Arguing that juvenile delinquency was too complex an issue to be resolved with narrow-mindedness, he urged, "Remember we are dealing with human beings. Give these kids a chance to be born right. See that they get proper nourishment in their infancy. . . . See that their families have decent homes in which to live." He told one graduating class from the Central Needle Trades High School, "A first-class tailor is worth more than a third-class lawyer." To accommodate high school graduates whose parents could not afford a proper education, La Guardia refused to permit budget-minded reformers to establish tuition at the city colleges.[14]

Just as he wanted the children not to miss the "funnies" during the newspaper strike, he did not want them to miss one of the great pleasures: a circus under the big tent. When License Commissioner Paul Moss, acceding to complaints of residents in the Flatbush section of Brooklyn that the annual visit of the Ringling Brothers Circus would disturb their quiet neighborhood, refused permission for the setting up of the three-ring tent, La Guardia became furious. Ruling that "the circus under canvas is an American institution," he canceled Moss's injunction. The Big Show went on.

His concern for children's enjoyment was complemented by a concern for their morals. A city prohibition forbade movie houses admitting unaccompanied children, since many of the films were considered too adult and the mid-afternoon adult crowds were often of the "objectionable variety." To contravene the ban, kids often prevailed upon strangers to bring them into the theaters as their own, thus exposing them not only to films they shouldn't be seeing but also to possible molestation. La Guardia had new laws passed that allowed children to enter movie houses on their own—but only after school hours and only so long as the films being shown "were proper for young minds." The law also called for stationing a uniformed matron or guard at a specially marked children's section. He personally led a police inspection of the movie houses to ensure that these safeguards had been initiated.[15]

The ubiquitous mayor was also a plebeian mayor. When his official car was undergoing maintenance, he rode around in a police sidecar. His comment, "I ain't no sissy," elicited from the *Times* the next day (July 15, 1936) commendation that he stuck to his job even while hospitalized on occasion due to his wartime injury, whereas his predecessors in office had been given to seeking pleasures, including world cruises, at the people's expense. When an aide happened to mention he would be playing several rounds of golf the following Sunday, La Guardia responded with genuine incredulity, "I thought you did that *last* week." Legendary showman Billy Rose invited Fiorello and Marie to be his guests at a Broadway opening night; La Guardia turned him down with thanks: "We never attend first nights. They are for the social registerites. We will go along with the common people some time later on." It didn't bother Marie, who preferred to remain out of the spotlight. The couple was in total agreement that his job was to run the city, hers to take care of the children and run the house—although, Fiorello being Fiorello, there was often spousal interference on his part in her area. But this did not faze Marie in the least. She knew the kind of man she had married. Besides, he was a better cook and, more important, a good father.[16]

The ubiquitous mayor and plebeian mayor was also very much the peripatetic mayor. Though centralizing the city government on Manhattan, he would relocate it in toto if he felt the occasion demanded. When, for example, Brooklyn celebrated its centenary, he relocated the entire government to the Kings County borough hall for five days, moving himself, with Marie and the children, into a Brooklyn hotel. He later did the same in the Bronx and Queens. During the summers, he would relocate City Hall, as if it were a traveling circus, to exurban or resort areas. His rented summer home would be surrounded by rented houses and hotels into which those officials who did not want to make the daily trek from the city installed themselves and their staffs. And all officials of his administration knew they were on call, not the normal five days a week but seven. Just like their mayor.

La Guardia considered anything and everything going on in the city worthy of, if not in fact demanding, his official attention, even if it did not fall within his mayoral responsibilities. New Yorkers were accustomed to the sight of their mayor materializing genie-like at some disaster, be it the collapse of a tenement roof, a railroad wreck, or a conflagration that threatened surrounding buildings. He would not supervise from the sidelines. He would leap in, screaming advice or lending a helping hand, as he did one day at Radio City Music Hall. He had just settled in to enjoy the show when a note was slipped to him that a building in the vicinity was on fire. Fiorello leaped from his seat, barreled his way up the aisle to the nearest exit, and rushed to where smoke was pouring from a restaurant, into which he disappeared. As the firemen came out a few hours later after extinguishing the blaze, one of them yelled, "Will someone get the mayor out of there!" When the last fireman emerged, with still no sign of the mayor, there was great consternation. He finally appeared, soot-covered, and explained, "I gave the refrigeration system a personal going over. I wanted to find out whether the building code had been violated." On another occasion, a Bronx building collapsed, and La Guardia climbed an unsteady ladder and comforted a man pinned by the beams as rescuers worked around him for two hours.[17] His presence at every major emergency (and even a few comparatively minor ones) was something New Yorkers came to expect; his fearlessness and concern for others, something they came to respect.

He also had a dramatic side—some might call it melodramatic. "I am like the boys in the trenches at zero hour," he would say. "It is not time to hesitate or reflect. It is not time to consider one's self. I am going [into battle] because it is my duty. If I succumb it will be in a worthy cause." To numerous interviewers and in response to countless messages of congratulations for a particular deed or overall performance, he would respond, "It is a most discouraging feeling to be at the head of the largest and richest city in the world and find yourself helpless just because you want to clean the city, and it would be so easy if you could only eliminate the selfish greed of politicians." Another oft-reiterated claim in the same vein: "There are few compensations in public life to offset the sacrifice, the unjust criticisms and the daily anxieties, but occasionally there are compensations and one of them is to receive such a fine letter as yours."[18]

3.

On January 20, 1935, under the headline "Can One Spunky Little Mayor Show the World?" the *Brooklyn Eagle* editorialized in jocular admiration on La Guardia's determination to put New York City on a par with the world's great metropolises in the arts, particularly the performing arts: "He wants to spend some of the people's money in ways calculated to increase the public's taste, enrich its mentality and encourage its esthetic impulses. What a cockeyed idea for a Mayor." Then, in a thinly veiled swipe at Jimmy Walker, it went on:

> The little man with the dark double chin is a curious anomaly. He cares more about art than the crease in his pants. He had rather give the city a municipal art center than to get somehow, by ways politicians know, the money it would cost in[to] his own pocket. He'd rather give the people of New York [the opportunity] to listen cheaply to a symphony by Beethoven than to hear them sing in his honor, "The Sidewalks of New York." He actually considers Wagner better music than "Will

You Love Me in December As You Do in May?" I guess the man is crazy.

La Guardia initiated his program to elevate the city's cultural level early in his administration. Because he was wrestling with his Economy Bill and the myriad problems arising out of the Great Depression, he started out on a modest scale, ordering the cleaning and regilding of city sculptures and the creation of new murals and statues in the zoos Robert Moses was creating. But Fiorello's dreams soared above the zoos. In the autumn of 1934, he named the city's first Municipal Arts Committee. Among its more than a hundred members were such cultural icons of the day as writer John Erskine, scenic designers Donald Oenslager and Robert Edmond Jones, composer Douglas Moore, actor Otis Skinner, and Brooke (Mrs. Vincent) Astor, the civic benefactress whose support of the New York City library system has extended down to our own time. He stipulated that the committee should "endeavor through art to increase the grace, happiness, and beauty of our municipal life."[19]

At the committee's first meeting, he set forth three major objectives: establishing a city art center, a special high school for music and art, and an educational and cultural program aired by the city-owned radio station, WNYC. It was also directed to develop low-priced symphony concerts and establish a municipal orchestra. Faced with the jealousy of the already established (but far from ambitious) Art Commission, a lack of funds, and a membership so large (118) and disparate that any attempt at a given project was an adventure in contention, the committee found the going rough. It did, though, sponsor several excellent events, among them an exhibition of American art at Rockefeller Center and a July music festival, at which the soloist in the opening concert was the virtuoso violinist Albert Spalding, La Guardia's wartime aide. Also, it opened the first municipal art gallery in the United States.[20]

La Guardia could hardly be considered an all-around lover of the arts. His greatest love was classical music. Besides attending performances, when he could find a free moment he liked to sneak off to rehearsals of the New York Philharmonic. He also liked to conduct a number of orchestras and bands, jokingly telling the musicians, "Just treat me like Toscanini." As for the other performing arts, he liked theater but detested ballet; he did not like "to see American young men leaping around the stage in those white tights exhibiting their crotches."[21] When it came to the plastic arts he was the arch-conservative: "I think that a work of art should be beautiful, should inspire instead of distress and please instead of annoy." While attending an outdoor art show, he stood stone-like as sculptor William Zorach explained the appeal of one piece—an avant-garde avian representation—in esoteric terms. Asked to comment, La Guardia replied, "If that's a bird, I'm Hitler."[22]

La Guardia's cultural program was motivated not only by his insistence that New York City achieve world-class status in the arts but by more practical factors as well. Though the New Deal's Federal Arts Project gave employment to creative and performing artists (a program that would eventually be abandoned), the financial rewards were minimal. Too, there were plenty of others that he wanted to get off relief. Patrons of cultural institutions, always a source for funding promising creativity through private grants and scholarships, were also suffering from the Depression. La Guardia wanted to pick up the slack and thus ensure talented young people the opportunity to initiate and pursue their careers. He also wanted all the city's schoolchildren to be taught skills in the artistic field of their choice, as well as a high school of their own for the more gifted.

After a four-year study, the Municipal Arts Committee made its mandated report, which included the recommendation, unrealistic for the times, that 1 percent of the city's annual budget be appropriated for the arts. It called for an all-inclusive municipal art center, a special Harlem art center, a municipal orchestra, and the expansion of community drama and contemporary dance programs beyond current levels. Among its recommendations, in addition to one that theaters be included in high-rise office buildings, were a few that would be effected over time to the appreciation of modern-day audiences, such as that curtain times for the theater and opera be earlier and that serving alcoholic beverages in theater lobbies and foyers during intermissions be allowed.

But by the time he was given the report, the ever-impatient La Guardia had already begun implementing his initial three major objectives. On February 14, 1936, he dedicated the High School of Music and Art at St. Nicholas Terrace and 135th Street, the first high school where students could major in music and the performing arts. "I believe this to be one of the best contributions that I will be able to make as long as I am mayor of New York City," he declared in dedicating the school.[23] The school, bearing his name, flourishes today across the street from the Lincoln Center for the Performing Arts on Manhattan's Upper West Side, and is considered a model of its kind nationwide. Also already begun was the broadcasting of cultural programs over the city-owned WNYC.

Not so easily realized was La Guardia's dream of an all-inclusive art center for opera, symphonic concerts, and theater, where the people could enjoy the best in the performing arts at the most affordable price. Here was yet another instance of his insisting that the have-nots were as entitled to exposure to culture as the haves. Funding was to come from private donors. By 1936, pledges of fourteen million dollars had been amassed, but they were never honored after it became known that the site of the proposed center would be in Central Park. It was hoped by some people that it would be part of a wide group of cultural locations located on Fifty-third Street just west of Fifth Avenue, where the Museum of Modern Art acquired its present location that same year. Though a branch of the public library (today the Donnell Branch) was built across the street from the museum, his dream for a performing arts center there failed to materialize.

La Guardia continued to push the idea for five years before being forced to give up in 1940, lamenting the failed plan as the "one great setback in my administration." Still, the dream was not entirely doomed in his lifetime. In the early 1940s, the city took over the Mecca Temple on West Fifty-fifth Street, headquarters of the Masonic Shriners, for nonpayment of taxes. When a purchaser could not be found to make a satisfactory bid for what was a white elephant the city was anxious to unload, Newbold Morris came up with a novel suggestion: Convert the temple into a theater of music and drama, with admission prices to be kept at a bare-bones minimum. Though at first skeptical, La Guardia soon got behind the idea. A nonprofit corporation to manage the venture was set up, and the Board of Estimate agreed to lease the building, accepting as rent from the corporation a sum equivalent to its assessed yearly taxes. It was further stipulated that the corporation be self-supporting, whether by ticket sales or passing the hat among the city's culturally sympathetic elite. The stipulation was met by a combination of the two. At La Guardia's insistence, the city helped launch the venture with a sixty-five-thousand-dollar grant to help the corporation remodel the faux-Moorish structure.[24]

On December 11, 1943, his sixty-first birthday, La Guardia presided over the opening of the New York City Center of Music and Drama. Addressing the audience with emotion, he asked rhetorically, "Is it not time for us of the older generation to keep burning the flame of art ... to hold on until the younger generation lay down their arms and come back [from war] to the peaceful, spiritual, and happy things of life?" As he was about to leave the stage, amidst the thunderous applause of an audience moved by words so transparently heartfelt, the orchestra rendered him a deafening "Happy Birthday to You."[25]

La Guardia promised that "some day the great Art Center will be housed in a magnificent structure and will combine all the activities originally planned." The City Center, as it became popularly known, proved to be immensely successful. Its offshoot, the New York City Ballet, went on to become a world-class dance company. (The entire operation was transferred to the Lincoln Center for the Performing Arts when it was built in the 1960s—"the great Art Center" that La Guardia envisioned but sadly did not live to see realized.)

4.

Of all the battles La Guardia waged, none was pursued with greater determination than the one against the "chiselers" and "punks" who had infested the city over decades of Tammany rule. Collusion between politicians and the underworld was manifest in everything from bankrupt finances to dilapidated housing to exploiting merchants through intimidation to allowing workers in the construction industry to keep their jobs only at the price of kickbacks to contractors. Merchants, wage earners, and businessmen were forced to go along with their exploiters because they feared testifying against them and knew they could expect less than reassuring protection from the police and the courts.

Prior to the 1920s, crime was a growth industry among independent bands of hoodlums conjoined by neighborhood and nationality, principally the sons of immigrants. The Lower East Side gangs were predominantly Italian and Jewish; the most powerful and dreaded of them was the United States chapter of the Mafia, of Sicilian origin, whose exclusively Italian members terrorized through bombing, blackmail, and murder. The West Side gangs, like the infamous Gophers and the Hudson Dusters, were predominantly Irish. Out of all these lower Manhattan gangs came such notorious figures as Irving Wexler (alias Waxey Gordon), Louis "Lepke" Buchalter, Jacob "Gurrah" Shapiro, Owen "Owney the Killer" Madden, and Jack "Legs" Diamond—to cite but a few among many. The East Siders were primarily racketeers. The West Siders, given their proximity to the Hudson River wharves and New York Central freight yards, began in their teens as package and freight-yard thieves and graduated into big-time burglary and armed robbery. Prostitution transcended geographical demarcations. Narcotics would come later.[26]

With Prohibition, New York's crime became big business. Supplying alcoholic products—whether the illegal import of hard liquor from Europe or the domestic manufacture of beer and "rotgut" whiskey—was not only safe but also, thanks in large measure to a small cadre of collusive law enforcement officials, enormously profitable. Almost all underworld characters got into bootlegging to some extent, and virtually everyone cleaned up. They corrupted Coast Guardsmen into looking the other way when the product brought in from Europe on luxury liners was off-loaded onto cutters just outside the three-mile continental limit; and policemen into ignoring, if not helping pave the way, for the product that was landed in Canada and trucked across the border. Through a combination of business smarts and utter mercilessness that bordered on the sociopathic, many became millionaires through control of beer distribution, a share of the prostitution trade, and a near-monopoly in the numbers racket that was predominant in Harlem and the Bronx.

In "the numbers," also known as "the policy game," a player bet he could guess a number, which originally consisted of three digits computed from the betting odds on pari-mutuel machines at various racetracks around the country but subsequently was based on other computations. Though the odds against hitting the three digits were a thousand to one, the game was popular among many people, especially the poor, because bets could be as small as a penny and the payoff was six hundred to one. It differed from today's lottery, legal in many states, only in that lottery numbers are drawn in full view and thus cannot be "fixed," and the odds of winning are astronomical in comparison to "The Policy Game."

With the end of Prohibition, the bootleggers turned from the now profitless bootlegging to the enormously profitable operation of slot machines. Repeal also accelerated a movement that had been steadily growing since the mid-twenties: racketeering. By the time La Guardia came into office, one of the most lucrative forms was "shylocking." The crime lords ("loan sharks") loaned money to small businessmen and others at high rates of interest, with payment secured by terror and beatings—sometimes, as a last resort, murder. This posed no financial hardship, as the interest ("vigorish") already collected would be greater by far than the sum of the original loan. Gross income from the loan shark racket in New York City alone in 1935 was ten million dollars a year. Dutch Schultz, hardly the epitome of modesty, was able to brag that his yearly take from the numbers racket was ten times that amount, a figure accepted as indisputable.[27]

Other rackets, even more profitable than the highly lucrative selling of protection to small shop owners, was the restaurant racket organized by Schultz. Here the mobsters not only controlled the waiters' and cafeteria workers' unions, they forced the owners to join an "association" to which they had to pay "dues" and "tolls" or run the risk of strikes and having their establishments emptied by stink bombs during rush hours. Another hugely rewarding source of income was the garment industry, where millions were made from such activities as gaining control of the truckers' union (call a strike and force manufacturers into settling), stealing payrolls, selling protection, even exacting tribute from the manufacturers and jobbers as an alternative to either taking control of their firms or forcing them out of business. From the garment industry it was an inevitable move into motion picture theaters and just about every other form of industrial endeavor including the cleaning and dyeing industry. In fact, it was easier to identify what forms of commercial endeavor were *not* in thrall to what was referred to collectively as "the mob."

Still other rackets included control of downtown Manhattan fish markets, especially the Fulton Fish Market, by Joseph "Socks" Lanza. Lanza's thousand foot soldiers forced fishing boat owners to pay ten dollars a load into his union's "benevolent fund," operated a "watchman's service" for the automobiles of retailers who came to the markets, and "allowed" vendors to operate in the large open-air pushcart market. Some of the vendors were friends acting as "fences" for fish stolen by Socks's men. Another foodstuff that fell into the hands of organized crime was the artichoke, whose overlord, Ciro Terranova, forced shippers and merchants to deal only with his Union Pacific Produce Company by intimidating buyers into boycotting other sources. Terranova, the "boss of bosses" in Harlem and the Bronx during the La Guardia years, enjoyed the added distinction of being related by marriage to Ignazio "Lupo the Wolf" Saietta, founder of the American branch of the Mafia and the man most responsible for the rise of the infamous Charles "Lucky" Luciano, king of the prostitution and narcotics trades. Still another victimized comestible was kosher poultry, controlled by Arthur "Tootsie" Herbert. Employing standard industrial racketeering methods, Tootsie's hoods maintained monopolies in feeding and trucking the chickens. Labor gangsters like Joe Adonis and Albert Anastasia controlled the Brooklyn waterfront. They dominated the International Longshoremen's Association, extorting huge profits both from their own longshoremen, dependent upon them for jobs, and the stevedoring and shipping companies.[28]

Repeal also brought about the organization of crime into "families," thus eliminating the dog-eat-dog mentality of the individual gangs for territorial control. But these could not have functioned without official "protection," which machine politicians saw was provided for a price. Of these, the most powerful by far was Tammany boss James J. "Jimmy" Hines. Hines, who, it will be remembered, paved the way for La Guardia's first defeat for reelection to Congress, was Dutch Schultz's "protector." He had been, at one time or another, protector of many of the most notorious crime figures. The underworld received "dispensation" through corrupt police, "bought" judges, and especially William C. Dodge. Dodge, Manhattan district attorney during the first La Guardia administration, had been anointed by Hines and elected with the aid of Dutch Schultz's money and men. In Brooklyn, the district attorney, William F. X. Geoghan (who served from 1931 to 1939) was no less tainted.[29]

As mayor, La Guardia had no jurisdiction over the district attorney, and only limited control over some of the courts, specifically the Magistrate's Courts, which handled nothing more significant in the area of crime than misdemeanors. La Guardia's principal ally was the Police Department. His chief agents at the outset were Police Commissioner O'Ryan (whom he drove into resigning nine months into the administration) and his commissioner of investigations, Paul Blanshard. In his choice of Lewis Valentine as O'Ryan's successor, La Guardia found a perfect collaborator. Blanshard, a former clergyman and close friend of Socialist leader Norman Thomas, was, in Thomas's own words, "a terrible man to work with."[30] Nevertheless, La Guardia did the best he could under the circumstances. But the circumstances involved a mayor who, more often than not, believed that the cause was best served by being his own chief crime buster. Blanshard, like O'Ryan, threw in the towel before the end of the first term. Valentine, obviously a man of stronger fiber, stuck it out to the end, doubtless because City Hall backed him to the fullest. Like La Guardia, he loathed criminals and could not be "bought." He was Fiorello's kind of man.

It was Fiorello who decided which issues that fell within his purview were to be attacked, and in what manner. His greatest crusade was against gambling. And there was no more pernicious form of the sport than slot machines. These "mechanical bandits" (also known as "one-armed bandits") were found in even the smallest retail establishment, under the threat of property damage if the merchants objected. So many people, especially the poor, were pouring money into them with no chance of a payoff that their eradication became a major La Guardia concern. "The slots" constituted arguably the most lucrative underworld gambling enterprise in New York City, where there were between twenty thousand and thirty thousand machines. A single machine in a reasonably good location could take in twenty dollars a day. And Frank Costello had his goons make sure they were placed in thousands of small shops, restaurants, candy stores, and poolrooms. Not only a source of great criminal profit, the slot machines ensnared young people into stealing in order to play them. To La Guardia's way of thinking, slots launched young people on a career in crime.

Shortly after entering City Hall, La Guardia ordered Valentine, in his capacity as chief of detectives, to raid the True Mint Company, where 450 slot machines were found, along with a set of books revealing the racket's operations. In a two-week period, his men arrested 714 slot machine operators together with hundreds of crapshooters, policy and numbers runners, and bookmakers. To circumvent the police, Costello converted fifteen thousand of his slot machines into "candy machines" and won a court injunction against further police action on the grounds that they could not be seized unless it was proved they were used for gambling. La Guardia ordered Corporation Counsel Windels to take an appeal as far as the Supreme Court, if need be. In the meantime he directed Valentine to confiscate the machines and notify him personally as soon as the first arrest was made. He meant business, and he wanted the criminals, the patrons, the lawbreakers, and the courts to know it. Another bit of street theater was called for.

This time, before a crowd of news reporters summoned for the occasion, he had a number of the confiscated machines loaded onto a barge and towed out to sea, where he attacked them with a sledgehammer and consigned them to a watery grave. "These machines," he declared, "were controlled by the most vicious of criminal elements."[31] La Guardia's persistence and Windels's adeptness as a litigator paid off. The Supreme Court ordered that the lower court's injunction be vacated. Next, with the cooperation of the state's attorney general and various social agencies, La Guardia succeeded in getting an amendment to the state penal code, effective May 7, 1934, which made possible an even more effective drive against the machines. By the end of his first full year in office, slot machines were eliminated as an issue. Costello and his friends moved their operation to Louisiana.

La Guardia next launched his campaign against pinball machines. Apparently innocuous, they were owned by gangsters and, as La Guardia saw it, exerted a deleterious influence on young people. Placed on a commission basis in cigar stores, bars, grills, and similar places, each brought in between forty dollars or more a week, with some reaching as much as a hundred. In the aggregate the total yearly take was more than twenty-three million dollars.[32] His campaign extended over his three terms. In 1939, the Police Department made 2,229 arrests, 84 percent of which resulted in convictions; in 1940, 22,295 arrests with 82 percent convictions. Thereafter the fight became bogged down in the courts by a sympathetic judge until a justice in the Court of Special Sessions ruled that mere possession of a pinball machine was illegal and the government was not obliged to show that it was used for gambling. The arrests continued and, along with the War Production Board's ban on further manufacture of the machines, resulted in ridding the city of this large source of illicit revenue.

So relentless was his war on gamblers that La Guardia sometimes ran roughshod over the rights of individuals, as when police raided a private poker party. This caused Magistrate Anna Kross, a La Guardia appointee and the first woman to become a New York City judge, to rebuke him for "lawless law enforcement."[33] He ignored the rebuke and persevered, forcing some of the city's big gamblers to relocate to New Jersey by keeping them under steady pressure and making it harder for them to operate. (La Guardia's biggest frustration when leaving office after three terms was that he had not achieved the success in combating crime that he set out to. What success he had was commendable enough, certainly more than any other mayor's. He could never purge the people of their deep-rooted craving to gamble nor eliminate the ability of the criminals to influence some police, and especially some judges. But not for lack of trying—especially in the area of political corruption.)

When the Democrats gained control of the city legislature, La Guardia vowed to Tammany, "You're going to see one hell of a fight." It was no idle threat. With his full backing, Commissioner of Investigations Blanshard launched an investigation, with orders to run to ground racketeers who had infiltrated the city's markets, while La Guardia ordered Valentine personally to "get" the gangsters whose connection to Tammany was an open secret. In November 1934, Valentine issued his famous "muss 'em up" order. Indicating an impeccably attired gunman in that day's lineup, he said, "When you meet men like that, don't be afraid to muss 'em up. Blood should be smeared all over that man's velvet collar. . . . With killers, racketeers, and gangsters the sky's the limit." He added, for the benefit of cops who walked beats, that here was a breed of people without rights: "You can club them with impunity."[34]

Reaction in the press of Valentine's comments ranged from strong criticism to shock. La Guardia openly supported Valentine, telling the *Times* on January 27, 1935, that "numerous recent killings" of policemen by criminals were proof that the city and the underworld were now in a state of war. "This is no time for coddling crooks. When the war is on you cannot stand by and expect that a police officer is going to be shot by a cowardly crook." A few weeks later Valentine added a disquieting variation on the mayor's theme: "Barbarians and savages," he averred, were walking the city's streets.

Given their sheer numbers, Tammany-bought judges, and clever criminal lawyers, Valentine went on, the scales of justice were balanced in their favor instead of the people's: "It's about time we gave honest people a break."[35]

Valentine's pronouncement was followed by the rounding up of three hundred "undesirables," under a section of the penal code that made it unlawful for people with criminal records to assemble in public places. Their jail time lasted until the following day. La Guardia remained silent, as he did when half a million dollars' worth of books considered obscene by "the courts and the police" (among them works by Mark Twain!) were committed to the Police Department furnaces. Subsequently, a mass raid of city parks netted some seven hundred panhandlers, beggars, and drunks, who were stuffed sardine-like into cells. It was after this incident that La Guardia "conferred" with Valentine on his tactics. But neither then nor following any of the subsequent incidents cited did he issue a public disclaimer.[36]

In June 1935, the war against crime became a major political issue. District Attorney Dodge, who as already indicated was "in the pocket" of Tammany's crime boss Jimmy Hines, had been at odds with the New York County grand jury appointed to investigate racketeering. When Dodge ignored its call that he appoint a special prosecutor to continue its investigations, the jury, out of sheer disgust, was dismissed at its own request, and Governor Lehman stepped in. He summoned La Guardia and Valentine to his New York apartment and demanded a report on what the administration had been doing to fight vice and crime. La Guardia, uncharacteristically, maintained a stance of discretion and cooperation in public. It is not difficult to imagine his private thoughts, however, when shortly after the meeting Lehman sent a letter to Valentine on the overall crime issue. La Guardia wrote Lehman, with acerbity, that the letter had been forwarded to him unanswered by Valentine "in accordance with the customs and usual channels of communication."[37] The implication was obvious: He resented being bypassed or even being treated on a par with any of his commissioners.

The next move was Lehman's. He ordered Dodge, on threat of dismissal from office, to appoint a special prosecutor. He even proposed four names for consideration. All refused on the grounds that they were too busy to accept the assignment. Moreover, all regretted that Lehman had not included in his list the only man recommended by the Bar Association to head the rackets inquiry. Lehman replied he had withheld the name—thirty-three-year-old Thomas E. Dewey—"because he was not sufficiently known to inspire public confidence." Dewey, it should be noted, was a Republican.

He was named nevertheless and thus launched on the career that was to make his reputation as a crime buster and lead to two failed attempts to be elected president. La Guardia promised, and gave, full cooperation, though he did consider Dewey's demands for funds, furniture, and office space excessive. It must have been painful to have Dewey conferring directly with Valentine, as if he were part of his staff. Even so, La Guardia made no apparent objection. Much as he hated to accept it, New York's mayor could have only a limited role in rooting out major crime, but he had strongly focused public attention on the issue. Perhaps this was his most solid contribution to the cause.

In the last month of 1935, La Guardia once more seized the headlines with the kind of street theater at which he was so proficient, a device that could be more effective than some people were prepared to admit. The theme of this latest production was the miniature artichoke, and the villain of the piece was the aforementioned Bronx and Harlem crime boss Ciro Terranova, who through his Union Pacific Produce Company exacted a tribute from every retailer who purchased, under force, this delicacy especially valued by the Italian community. La Guardia kept his plans secret even from Commissioner of Markets Fellowes Morgan until he was told to be at the mayor's home at six A.M. on December 20. "I remember it well," Morgan wrote many years later; "it was the shortest and coldest day of the year." When both arrived at the Bronx Terminal Market, it was evident to Fellowes that the mayor had arranged for some sort of ceremony. Under his arm were large proclamations. Policemen with bugles stood by to herald the crowd to a place in front of the market restaurant. In the extreme cold the bugles (or bugle blowers) froze and had to be taken into the restaurant to be thawed out.

Undaunted, La Guardia climbed to the platform of a truck, dramatically unrolled one of the large proclamations, and read it to the astonished crowd: Under an archaic clause in the equally archaic city charter permitting the mayor in an emergency to ban the distribution of food, the sale of artichokes was now prohibited in the public markets. Scrolls were passed out to cops in squad cars, to be posted throughout the market area. Having declared war on the Union Pacific Produce Company, La Guardia told the market concessionaires and their workers, "I want it clearly understood that no bunch of racketeers, thugs and punks are going to intimidate you as long as I am the Mayor of the City of New York."[38]

The stunt received enormous publicity, though the press reaction was not entirely favorable. Next day, the *Herald Tribune* said, "It is impossible not to conclude that the world today is a bit mad," contemplating the spectacle of the mayor as "protector of the virtue of artichokes." Thundered the *Post*, "Where does La Guardia get the idea that he had the right to keep merchants from selling artichokes? What induces him to believe that New York City can be ruled by proclamation?" Unnoticed was the fact that amid these theatricals La Guardia had dispatched Paul Kern to Washington to secure from the Department of Agriculture cancellation of Terranova's license to sell artichokes.

La Guardia was not a fool, and he well knew how to combine effective legal action with the politics of symbolism. In this case he not only ended the reign—at least over artichokes—of one racketeer who had been draining a million dollars a year from the pockets of consumers, he prepared the fall of others, including the notorious Socks Lanza, who had long ruled over the Fulton Fish Market. Such was La Guardia's hatred of the underworld, he once told his police, "I want you to put so much fear into the heart of every crook in New York that when he sees a cop he'll tip his hat." Though it never came to that, by the end of his first term as mayor crime in the city was down by 20 percent.[39] When La Guardia left office in 1945, New York City was no longer in thrall to the underworld. Thanks to him, the city had won its war against the slot and pinball machines, and although it had not been purged of other forms of gambling, their practitioners were constantly on the defensive. Against vice, he had done his best. That he failed to accomplish all that he desired is ascribable to the simple fact that that desire transcended the ability of any one person or any administration.

It must be conceded that most of the credit for putting away the master racketeers belongs to Dewey; still, as Charles Garrett put it, "one of the greatest legacies left to New York by the La Guardia period was the knowledge that the racketeers could be beaten."[40]

But, while he could take satisfaction in the knowledge that many of the top underworld figures were either in jail, in other states, or in their graves, he had to accept that the underworld was down but hardly out. With La Guardia inhibited by the scope of his mayoral authority, organized crime developed a greater influence in machine politics than it had enjoyed before. Frank Costello, who emerged in the forties as a power in Tammany, was not the only one to latch on to the Tiger. Indeed, it would stage a comeback some years later under Carmine DeSapio. But the comeback never achieved anything approaching the influence and power of its antecedents, and the city was put out of its Tammany-induced misery largely through the efforts of a later mayor, Ed Koch.

In all fairness, when summing up Fiorello La Guardia's role as crime fighter, it must be recorded that at times he came off as quite silly, as when he drove the famed Minsky brothers and their inimitable burlesque shows out of town. On April 30, 1937, when the six Minsky houses in New York were starring such entertainers as Abbott and Costello and the legendary ecdysiast Gypsy Rose Lee (who in fact never bared her all on stage) and no less a respected theater critic than the *New York Times*'s Brooks Atkinson was praising the genre for the good fun it offered, La Guardia refused to renew the Minsky theater licenses and banned the very use of the words "*Minsky*" and "*burlesque*" in theatrical advertising, thus putting them out of business. "No, he was not perfect," conceded one observer on reflection. "He could be cynical, churlish, hot-headed, petty and just plain wrong. At one time or another he antagonized everyone who ever worked for him. But he also gave us all a standard of excellence, a sense of adventure in government, pride in what we were doing. He was actually making New York a better place to live—and he made us part of the excitement."[41]

5.

Charter reform was long overdue. The two-thousand-page one in effect when La Guardia took office had gone into effect on January 1, 1898, when New York became a consolidated five-borough city. Aptly described by Al Smith as being "as big as a telephone book and making just about as much sense," it was a veritable salmagundi of overlapping, conflicting, and outdated laws, with hundreds of amendments having been grafted on willy-nilly without weeding out the irrelevant or the contradictory. Among the more than 1,700 sections and thousands of statutes were such exotic provisions as these: New Yorkers were prohibited from lodging their sheep and goats in boardinghouses; a dead horse left in the street had to have a light attached to it after dark; businesses with more than ten employees had to provide one cuspidor for every two persons; and anyone caught incinerating bones in Manhattan was automatically banished from the island.[42]

The movement for charter reform began with the election of the city's first Fusion mayor, Seth Low, in 1901, and met with little success other than the one-term mayoralty of John Purroy Mitchell (1913–15). When the Seabury-led Fusion won control of the city with La Guardia's election, it increased momentum in the state legislature to set up the requisite framework for revision. Governor Lehman recommended that the legislature establish a commission to draft one for submission to the city's voters in the upcoming (1934) off-year election. Legislators on both sides of the aisle concurred, but a hopeless deadlock loomed. The Republicans, cooperating with the La Guardia administration, still controlled the Assembly; the Democrats, the Senate. And a two-thirds vote in each chamber was required to enact such legislation. The Tammany Democrats, who willingly accepted Al Smith as chairman of the proposed twenty-eight-member commission, introduced the bill enthusiastically, in the belief that any reforms would be consonant with their self-serving conception of how the city should be run. Their enthusiasm dropped quite a few degrees when La Guardia succeeded in getting Judge Seabury named a member. The Tammany delegation balanced Seabury with Frank J. Prial, who had led the fight among the city's civil servants against the Economy Bill.

The reformers were determined to reshape the basic structure of municipal government by creating an efficient and largely nonpolitical system through reorganization of its powers. Some favored the so-called Cincinnati Experiment—a city manager responsible to a single legislative chamber elected by proportional representation. Other, wiser heads argued that abolishing what remained of borough autonomy, which would be one consequence, would not work (nor, for that matter, would it ever stand a chance of passage). The reformers, hoping to find ways to restrain borough partisanship and eliminate the political machines, pushed for a one-house legislative body for the city, under the chairmanship of the mayor. La Guardia remained uncharacteristically silent.

His championing of charter reform was tempered by his seeing in it a dramatic reduction of the mayor's power and prestige. He felt he could effect the most urgently needed changes, such as elimination of the county offices, albeit piecemeal, through the original Economy Bill and other ongoing measures. It is indicative of his basic attitude that when the proposed bill reached its crucial stage in the 1934 session of the state legislature, La Guardia, who was present, actually fell asleep.[43] A few days later Seabury announced that nowhere in any new charter would limitation of mayoral powers be acceptable; the present system of a strong mayor must be retained. Though he favored a one-chamber legislature, Seabury argued that there must be no city manager but the continuance of an elected mayor responsible for the city's administration through department heads over whom he had unlimited control. Despite opposition led by Seabury and Smith, the Tammany-dominated charter commission voted to maintain the Board of Estimate and the basic structure of the Board of Aldermen. This amounted to restoring the administrative and patronage powers of the borough presidents and the separate county bosses. Seabury, Smith, and four other members resigned from the commission.

With charter reform now on life support, Smith and Seabury urged that Lehman get from the legislature a law creating a newer, smaller commission, to be appointed by La Guardia or jointly by him and Lehman. Lehman yielded. His main concern at this point was to remove charter reform as an issue in the approaching gubernatorial campaign. With La Guardia's almost reluctant concurrence, he asked the legislature for a special amendment to the Home Rule Law enabling the mayor to name a new nine-member commission. The measure was passed unanimously, hopefully to put La Guardia on the spot. Consumed with the problems of relief and unemployment and noting that the earlier commission had suffered from trying to please everyone, he adopted the public attitude that, before naming the new commission, "we must first decide from what viewpoint charter reform is to be approached, and then get persons who are in accord with that viewpoint."[44]

La Guardia was quizzed almost daily by the newspapers on whom he would name as chairman and members of the new commission. His only response was to remind press and public alike that his immediate priority was addressing more pressing issues directly affecting the people. This was a smoke screen. There was no limit to the number of pressing issues he was eminently capable of addressing simultaneously. He wished simply to lower the temperature on the issue and then tackle charter reform with a fresh start. In January 1935, he announced his selections, under the chairmanship of former U.S. solicitor general Thomas D. Thacher. None of the original members were retained. In their stead he named a group of civic and political leaders acceptable to all factions and promised noninterference.

After a year's work, the reorganization plan was made public. Greatly reduced in pages and verbiage, it was essentially the same basic compromise that had led Smith, Seabury, and the others to resign from the first commission. Though it did call for more orderly government through the addition of a deputy mayor—La Guardia made no secret of what he thought of that idea—it failed to meet the mandate for a truly new charter. There was, however, one principle on which the proposed charter called for more than a simple retention of existing structures. That was its incorporation of a means to rein in and diminish the more traditionally hidebound borough interests.

Unlike the members of the first commission, all of whom had been condemned by Seabury as lackeys of the machine politicians, the new commissioners believed, perhaps with justification, that the five counties represented an important aspect of New York life and that what was essential was not the elimination of their influence but, rather, completion of the transformation that had begun in 1898—that is, to create one city while preserving borough diversity and local autonomy. The Board of Estimate, with the borough presidents securely fixed, remained the linchpin of city government. It was to continue in its old form, and with the same apportionment of votes, as the city's policy-making body, with general control over the city's finances. The Board of Aldermen was reduced from sixty-five members to twenty-one and renamed the City Council. It would have the sole power to initiate local laws, though its legislative power would be limited by a provision requiring that most local bills of any consequence be approved by the Board of Estimate before going to the mayor for his signature. Some departments were reorganized, and there were additional innovations. Proportional representation, which could modify considerably the aldermanic board, was recommended conditional to its being put before the voters as a separate issue.

It was also urged that the Board of Estimate be subject to control by confrontation "with the interests of the public at large." To secure such confrontation, a City Planning Commission was proposed. It was conceived as a strong body, with inherent powers to countervail political pressures. Included in those inherent powers were control of zoning, responsibility for the capital budget, and being in charge of the city map with authority to submit public and private changes to reviews and recommendations. Eight-year terms for members would remove them from political influences and thus assure long-range judgment. It was the most striking new creation of the charter's authors—and, as events played out over the long haul, the most naive, given the belief that a body of this nature would force the borough presidents to curtail their more drastic demands and thereby contribute to their own reduction in power and influence.

Immediate reaction from all sides was less than enthusiastic. Seabury, speaking for the Fusionists, expressed lukewarm approval. The borough presidents grumbled over the diminution of their power. Tammany had no choice but to "subside into sullen opposition." La Guardia wrote to Thacher: "To say I am disappointed is putting it mildly. I had looked forward to a healthy, robust, normal child. Not even a puny incubator infant has been produced. Just a Cesarean delivery out of the belly of the old Charter, with a bit of unscientific plastic surgery in-artistically applied. What a mess!" Signing the letter, "sincerely but unhappily," he did agree to be the first witness at the public hearings on the proposed new charter.[45]

While he denounced the borough presidents and party leaders and resented the inevitably of vetoes in the borough-dominated Board of Estimate, La Guardia realized that the system could work acceptably under a strong mayor. Being such a creature, he need not fear opposition from the borough machines. And while he resented the useless jobs the borough leaders needed in order to retain their power, he saw that power a priori as a fundamental element of political life. Besides, he was confident that when the time came to prepare for the 1937 mayoralty campaign, he would succeed in bringing the separate power centers over to his side and neutralize the local leaders one by one.

When the public hearings got under way in the following month, he admitted "it is not the Charter that I would have written" but realized that in a city like New York everybody could not agree on everything in a charter.[46] After getting off a few good one-liners about the protected "Borough Presidents' Union" he joined in support of what was, after all, the only new charter he was going to get. As the plebiscite neared, he campaigned for its passage: "The new Charter represents very substantial gains for the citizens." He particularly supported modifying Manhattan's dominance and enhancing the power of the city's minorities through proportional representation (the new plan replaced district races between paired opposition candidates with a boroughwide slate of candidates): "Proportional representation is in my judgment the greatest progressive step for labor and minority groups of all types that has ever been offered to the citizens of New York." Despite intense lobbying against it, led by four of the five borough presidents (only Ingersoll of Brooklyn backed it), and thanks to a massive effort led by La Guardia to educate the people as to the need for the new charter, imperfect though it was, a million voted for its approval and only six hundred thousand against.

More charter reform lay in the future. But we are now at a remove of a half-century and more from the La Guardia years, and our concern is with those years. While the reform charter adopted during his mayoralty was far from perfect, it was a quantum leap in the right direction. To deny him credit for instigating and all but personally orchestrating that leap would be unfair.

A mayoral election was coming up in November. Though Tammany had been beaten in 1933, the machine was still strong in the borough and county offices. In 1933, Fusion had won only 25 of a total of 94 elective offices, and in subsequent elections it had taken a mere 7 out of 109 positions. Manhattan, stronghold of Tammany, showed signs of losing its preeminent dominant position, with New Deal Tammany bosses and power brokers like Flynn and Farley having gained dominant influence in the other boroughs. By mid-1937, the various party chieftains and power brokers were organizing for a primary. There was little doubt La Guardia would seek reelection. In doubt, though, was which party's ticket he would run on.

CHAPTER NINETEEN

"I call a bluff every time I see one!"

1.

Meeting at the Hotel Astor on March 31, 1937, the Fusion Party, having already begun soliciting contributions and political support, praised La Guardia's administration as one of the finest in the city's history and called upon him to run again. He didn't have to be asked twice, but in terms of numbers he needed much more than Fusion backing. He hoped to win over Progressive and independent support, along with various unaffiliated pro–New Deal groups. Most needed, though, was the endorsement of his own Republican party, with its six hundred thousand votes. The GOP resented, however, his support of Roosevelt in 1932 and 1936 and his traveling around the country bringing the message of the New Deal to urban America. Moreover, the clubhouse leaders considered unforgivable his failure to repay their 1933 support by a suitable dispensation of patronage. They formed ABL clubs, "Anybody but La Guardia."[1]

The more pragmatic element, led by Corporation Counsel Windels, argued that the party could no more do without La Guardia than he could do without the party. But the powerful borough bosses were not buying that argument, with one exception: New York County's Kenneth Simpson. A successful lawyer with an impeccable pedigree as a member of the state's Republican aristocracy who favored Fusion and was particularly impressed with La Guardia's first-term performance, Simpson had recently taken command of Manhattan's organization—which, of the five county organizations, was so much the weakest that even fellow Republicans dismissed it as a joke.

Figuring prominently in the equation was the new and already quite powerful American Labor Party. The ALP had been formed in the previous summer by a coalition of organized labor Democrats and Roosevelt supporters covering the political spectrum from Socialists through independent liberal Democrats who were not happy with voting for FDR under the party banner because of their loathing of Tammany. Run by powerful leaders in the garment trade unions, the ALP had the backing of the CIO's most powerful chieftain, John L. Lewis of the United Mine Workers. In the 1936 election it gave FDR 239,000 votes and overnight became New York State's leading minority party. Assuming it had those votes in its pocket, Tammany launched its quadrennial scramble for the following year's mayoralty nomination. And while the sachems were trying to agree on a nominee, La Guardia pulled off one of the great feats of political grand larceny: He literally kidnapped the party from them.

Loyalists in the unions reminded labor of how much it had received from Fiorello during the various strikes that peppered his first administration—and even earlier in the century. Also stressed was how as mayor he had guaranteed "peaceful picketing" by prohibiting the use of billy clubs by policemen on strike duty. Then there was the Norris–La Guardia Act, all the trips he had made to Albany to plead for pro-labor legislation, and more: the sixty-million-dollar Triborough Bridge, slum clearance projects for three thousand families, eighteen miles of new subways, 235 new playgrounds, a 30 percent drop in street accidents and 40 percent decline in fire-related losses, and city bonds selling at par or better—much of this paid for with federal funds secured by La Guardia. For his part, La Guardia managed to place his brilliant young protégé Paul Kern on the ALP general staff even before the 1936 election, over the objection of James Farley, who had conceived the idea of the party in the first place solely as a means of guaranteeing Roosevelt those anti-Tammany labor votes. Kern established a dozen lines of communication between the party leadership and City Hall. What Farley feared came to pass when the ALP decided to support La Guardia's reelection.

When La Guardia ran in 1933, it was strictly as a Fusion candidate, and voters tended to see the race in terms of Tammany versus Reform. This time around, La Guardia ran as La Guardia with Fusion backing, and the voters tended to be for or against *him*. As the campaign progressed there was almost universal agreement that he was the best mayor in the city's history, as suggested by the fact that he was lauded by such disparate journals as the arch-Republican *Herald Tribune* and the Communist *Daily Worker*. Taking nothing for granted, La Guardia carried on with city business—and coped with unforeseen obstacles. Governor Lehman, a wily political animal despite his public holier-than-thou posture, went over La Guardia's head to the Board of Estimate with an appeal that it restore city salaries to their pre-1932 level. Caught by surprise and robbed of a popular, vote-getting issue, La Guardia was furious, having himself suggested restoration of the cuts in the previous October. He counteracted with a Lehmanesque mini-bombshell of his own: announcement of an eight-hour day for nurses and other employees in all city hospitals. The board passed the resolution unanimously. For La Guardia it was a small victory, but it was popular with labor, and in an intense political season like this one, any victory was valuable.

Next came an encounter that took on heavy political resonance. Robert Moses was up to his characteristic malicious troublemaking. This time it was over five thousand WPA workers removed from the parks by WPA Administrator Col. Brehon Sommervell in a series of economy moves. Instead of falling back on his old ploy of threatening to quit, Moses padlocked 142 parks and playgrounds. La Guardia, en route to a meeting of the U.S. Conference of Mayors in Los Angeles, had been kept informed of events by phone and was determined not to give in to what amounted to blackmail on Moses's part to increase the city budget in order to serve his purposes. When the train made a stop at Toledo, he phoned Police Commissioner Valentine to open the playgrounds and to see that they were kept open, with WPA workers assigned to assist the police. Moses received authorization for the requested funds. Adolf Berle was convinced, as were many, that Moses was plotting to unite Republican conservatives with the Al Smith Democratic irreconcilables to mount his own campaign for mayor at the least sign of La Guardia stumbling. Berle needn't have worried. La Guardia's vow that no playgrounds would be closed to "the kiddies" while *he* was mayor would be remembered by the voters come November.[2]

In June, gearing up for the coming campaign, La Guardia relocated his family to Asharoken Beach near Northport for the summer. He announced that the "Summer City Hall" would be set up at an old mansion belonging to the Parks Department located at nearby College Point in Queens. When he told the Board of Estimate at the last scheduled meeting of the relocation, William Brunner, Democratic president of the Board of Aldermen, said, in a bogus display of civic virtue, that he did not want a vacation. A few others agreed, and La Guardia all but screamed, "Very well! We'll have no adjournment at all this summer!" and announced that he would call regular weekly meetings at the Summer City Hall. "I call a bluff every time I see one!"[3]

For the primary, La Guardia set up no headquarters, appointed no campaign manager, solicited no contributions, and made few speeches. Here was the shrewd candidate demonstrating to the people that he was too busy running the city to partake in the standard preelection routine. But if the people were fooled, the politicians weren't. All knew that this hands-on mayor had his hands on his noncampaign. By mid-July he was assured endorsements by the Fusion and American Labor parties, but there remained the problem of the Republican nomination. His one hope lay in Simpson. Simpson announced he would consider it an act of treachery—and it would play directly into Tammany's hands—for the Republicans to field a candidate instead of supporting La Guardia in the primary. "Yes," he told them, making the rounds of the clubhouses, "he *is* an S.O.B. and all the things we have been saying about him are true, but he is *our* S.O.B. and we must stick with him for the good of the party!"[4]

The first crack in Republican opposition to their "turncoat mayor" came in the spring of 1937 when the Ninth Assembly District Republican Club voted to endorse him. The endorsement was not easily come by. The meeting was marked by violent language directed at the Little Flower, of the sort rarely heard outside a Lower West Side grog bar, verbal abuse of anyone who would consider the endorsement, flying fists, and the sight of women either ducking under chairs or making a dash for the nearest exit. La Guardia got the endorsement. Soon after, the Young Republicans also voted to endorse him, but only after two and a half hours of debate featuring repugnant charges that the mayor was a "double-crosser," "secret ally of Tammany," and "Communist." The endorsement was owing to an impassioned speech by Newbold Morris, who said that no matter what they thought of La Guardia, they had no alternative to endorsing him. Proceeding on the theory that the divided GOP rank-and-file would indeed reconcile themselves to that political reality, La Guardia organized a slate of running mates that would appeal to Republicans and Laborites alike.

At that point, Kenneth Simpson pulled off a political coup the equal of any that La Guardia had ever engineered. One evening, without warning, he summoned the press to meet the two reform Republican candidates *he* had selected to be La Guardia's running mates: Joseph McGoldrick, who had failed to be elected comptroller following the death of W. Arthur Cunningham, for that office; and Newbold Morris, as president of the new City Council. La Guardia was infuriated. Though both men were dedicated Fusionists, he had his own candidates for both offices, one of them Adolf Berle. Worse, to accept them would shut out the Laborites, who had demanded the right to name at least one of the candidates.

There now ensued a game of political two-man bluff poker, with each concealing an ace up his sleeve. Simpson's was public endorsement of Fiorello. Fiorello's was a threat not to run in the Republican primary unless he picked his own ticket, in which case the GOP would come in dead last. He might have antagonized the party's leadership, but he still had a following among the rank-and-file. After a week, both men realized that in trying to outbluff each other they ran the danger of jointly committing political suicide. Following a conciliatory meeting, La Guardia, with an okay from Seabury, agreed to accept the Simpson slate. The Labor Party leaders accepted the deal, albeit with ill grace. They had no choice if they were to stand any chance of success in November.

La Guardia could at least count on the Manhattan organization, but one in any of the three larger outer boroughs was an absolute sine qua non, not only in numbers but also in convincing the others to go along. The Bronx was out; GOP boss John Knewitz was uncompromising in his opposition. Queens was scratched; the organization had its own candidate and was prepared to drive too hard a bargain for abandoning him. That left Brooklyn, where John Crews, the county leader, was not all that opposed to La Guardia. But Crews chose to remain neutral in the face of a powerful, famously hostile faction headed by veteran Republican Jake Livingston. Livingston hated La Guardia, as did most of the Brooklyn clubhouse leaders, because of La Guardia's refusal to let them name Livingston's appointees to office and, in the bargain, publicly referring to their faction as "clubhouse loafers."

On the night of July 29, as three thousand members of the Kings County Republican Committee were filing into Brooklyn's Kismet Temple to pick a candidate, Windels, himself a Brooklynite, parleyed in an anteroom with the leaders of the Livingston forces. Livingston planned to push through a resolution publicly repudiating La Guardia. Windels knew that most of the leaders at the table were torn between an obsession with destroying La Guardia politically and an obsession with a Republican victory in a Democratic-controlled town. When Windels presented his case, Livingston's followers remained unyielding—until Windels announced that he had just spoken with Kenneth Simpson and that Manhattan would support La Guardia. He then threatened, "If you don't come along we'll go into the Primary and battle it out. You may whip us but you'll split the Republican Party and wreck your own organization in the battle."

Some found the argument compelling. But Livingston and a number of leaders so hated La Guardia, they were perfectly willing to destroy their party if in doing so they could destroy his career. Windels then came up with a compromise solution that was a marvel to behold because each side was convinced it was "putting something over" on the other. He suggested that the choice of a Republican nominee for mayor be referred back to the twenty-three Brooklyn district organizations. This satisfied the Livingston camp, which controlled two-thirds of the Republican committeemen and was sure they could destroy La Guardia either in the central committee or in the district organization. But Windels had carefully analyzed the makeup of each of the twenty-three organizations, and while La Guardia had no chance at all in eleven districts, he had managed to line up a slim majority in each of the remaining twelve. The Livingston men demanded permission to denounce La Guardia and say anything they pleased about him, with the promise that no attempt would be made to choke them off by parliamentary procedure. In return, they accepted Windels's insistence that Livingston himself open the meeting by introducing the resolution referring the nomination back to the districts. Then they went out to face the committeemen.[5]

With La Guardia's supporters outnumbered three to one by his foes, Windels's speech in response to the resolution was drowned out by a storm of hisses, while Livingston's attack upon the mayor provoked boisterous demonstrations. Windels began to panic when it became evident that if the opposition broke the agreement they could pass with ease a resolution denying La Guardia the party's nomination. His panic hit critical mass when some of the Livingston camp decided to stampede the meeting for that express purpose. At that point, what can only be described as "a La Guardia miracle" came to pass. One of his most zealous opponents, a district coleader named Grace Lesse, brought down the house with a splenetic condemnation of the mayor—and then blew it with a peroration in which she vowed that rather than support him, she was "willing to tie up with Tammany Hall." In the stunned silence that followed— if there was one thing the Republicans hated more than the Little Flower, it was the Tammany Tiger—a La Guardia supporter leapt upon his chair and howled, "Tammany sellout!"

La Guardia's thousand supporters picked up the chant. Windels's lieutenants scooted about the hall and quickly organized cheering sections. The opposition booed and hissed. Lesse's effort to explain was drowned out, as was the voice of every anti–La Guardia partisan who tried to follow her to the microphone. Faced with the threat of a full-scale riot, Chairman Crews announced that no one else would be permitted to address the meeting and ruled that the resolution introduced by Livingston had been carried—then adjourned the meeting. Much to the horror of the anti–La Guardia leaders, Windels had secured La Guardia the Republican nomination by the powerful Brooklyn machine.[6]

The ticket was completed with the selection of the patrician Stanley Isaacs as Manhattan borough president, to which La Guardia eagerly assented, and Thomas E. Dewey, who seemed the obvious choice, as district attorney. To this La Guardia assented also, though not all that eagerly. Because he was so popular due to his crime-busting activities, and knew it, and because he was a congenital prima donna, Dewey made some outrageous demands—including a guarantee of three hundred thousand dollars for campaign expenses and campaign quarters separate from the other Republican candidates. "Dewey's vanity, always disagreeable, was working overtime," Berle recalled. "My own thought was that it was better to drop him overboard." Though Fusion refused to accede to some of Dewey's terms, which were patently ridiculous, it was obvious he wanted to run. He allowed La Guardia to talk him into joining the ticket. According to Isaacs, Dewey "made a most uncongenial running mate."[7]

With his ticket now in place, La Guardia had one more hurdle to leap before the general campaign: entering the Republican primary race. To gather support, Simpson, accompanied by McGoldrick and Morris, made the rounds of every GOP clubhouse in all five boroughs to convince the La Guardia foes that their choice was limited to backing him or going down the electoral drain. In this, Simpson had the support of Dewey, and together they managed to win support among the professional pols.

La Guardia first had to win the Republican primary against an opponent who was running in the Democratic primary as well: U.S. Senator Royal Copeland, a physician who had achieved popularity through his newspaper column on health problems. An anti–New Deal Democrat who had been in the Senate since 1928, Copeland was the choice of the Democrats by default. The first to be offered the nomination was Grover Whalen, who had been Jimmy Walker's police commissioner. When he declined, the Democrats turned to the highly popular Senator Robert Wagner Sr. But Wagner did not want to run against La Guardia, as he saw no real issue between them. Besides, he preferred to remain in the Senate. Tammany boss James J. Dooling, literally rising from his deathbed, designated Copeland. The other Democratic leaders united on backing Whalen, who changed his mind about running, and were prepared to go up against the Tiger in the primary. Thereupon Dooling shrewdly offered La Guardia's Republican opposition a rallying point by entering Copeland in their primary as well.

Doubting that Copeland could carry his own suitcase, let alone a majority of the electorate, the Democrats found themselves caught up in a bitter contest of their own. Half a dozen of the party's most powerful district leaders threw their support to the Whalen backers, but reports they were getting from their precinct captains revealed that voters loyal to Tammany for years were moving toward La Guardia. The Italians wanted him for obvious reasons; the Jews favored him because of his frequent, forceful denunciations of Hitler and the Nazis. The Whalen backers withdrew and united behind moderate New Dealer Jeremiah T. Mahoney. A former law partner of Wagner's, State Supreme Court justice, and state counsel for the American Federation of Labor, Mahoney had a commendable anti-Nazi record. As president of the American Athletic Union, he had denounced Hitler and opposed American participation in the 1936 Berlin Olympics. This was no small consideration in a city where the Jewish vote was some 30 percent of the total. The Democrats hoped to strengthen their candidate by getting Al Smith's backing, but Smith wanted to humiliate Roosevelt, with whom he'd had a falling-out, by running an anti–New Deal Democrat in his home state.[8] He supported Copeland.

Not quite sure who his more formidable rival was, Copeland denounced both Mahoney and La Guardia with impartiality. While the other two went after each other for the Democratic nomination, La Guardia campaigned against Copeland for the Republican nomination by *not* campaigning. Simply ignoring the man, he concentrated on running the city and won the primary by more than thirty-five thousand votes (81,680 to 46,410).[9] Copeland didn't fare much better against Mahoney, who, backed by major New Deal figures, became the man La Guardia must beat in the November race.

It was almost a mathematical impossibility for La Guardia to lose the election. He was the choice of, in addition to the Fusion, American Labor, and Progressive parties, a good number of Republicans who would either vote for him over voting for a Democrat or would simply sit out the election. He even had the Socialist and Communist parties behind him. For the first time in their history the Socialists refrained from fielding a candidate and released their members from party loyalty so that they might support whomever they chose. They chose La Guardia. The Communist Party had denounced La Guardia mercilessly in the past. Now, on orders from Moscow, it adopted the new "popular front" policy of backing Progressives and endorsed him. La Guardia immediately repudiated the endorsement—though not to the extent of telling them to vote for Mahoney.[10] (As it turned out, their total vote was so negligible it was counted under the Progressive column. It's even questionable whether they cast any votes at all.)

The campaign was rather tepid. What genuine passion it involved occurred when the Democratic-controlled aldermen voted on October 5 for a reduction in the water rates. Though attractive to the voters, the cut was opposed by La Guardia, who counted on the full tax to balance his 1938 budget. When the matter came before the Board of Estimate in executive session two days later—two days during which La Guardia denounced the cuts as "a new low in legislative and political trickery"—the Democratic city comptroller urged that he make up for the twelve-million-dollar loss in water rates by a cut in government salaries. Realizing that the Democrats were attempting to blind-side him and curry favor for their candidate, and opposed at any rate to cuts of any kind at this of all times, La Guardia threw a monumental fit. Pounding on the table as if determined to atomize it, he shouted, "*You* cut the revenues, now you go ahead and cut the expenses!" According to one reporter present, "with a mighty tug the door of the chamber flew open," and La Guardia, his face a choleric red, his eyes brimming with tears of rage, charged out of the room, pushed past everyone in the corridor, and disappeared into his office.[11]

La Guardia convinced himself that even extremely unpopular acts could work to his advantage if executed with a flair. Averring with pride that "no matter what happens, my successor won't take over a bankrupt city," he vetoed a Tammany-inspired bill granting city workers a five-day week. Then, with puckish humor, he added, "Because I know I'm going to succeed myself."[12] Determined to win the mini Battle of the Budget, the Democrats waited until the last days of the campaign to announce restoration by the Board of Estimate of sixty-five county jobs and various pay raises. By then, La Guardia's lead was so commanding that it didn't matter.

Since Mahoney could not attack his opponent on substantive issues—both were in agreement on most points—he was reduced to personal attacks, all of them bordering on the ludicrous. He maintained that La Guardia continually broke promises and conducted the business of city government by caprice. When that failed to raise a stir, he sought to drive a wedge between La Guardia and the Jewish community by charging him with waffling on anti-Semitism and with not appointing more Jews to office. This was ridiculous, and the Jews knew it. La Guardia simply ignored the charges, having been advised by C. C. Burlingham, and correctly so, that "the Jews are yours, for the election."[13]

Next, Mahoney tried a new tack. He called the mayor a "coddler" of radicals under whom a happy, placid New York had been transmogrified into "a city of strife, [and] a haven for red agitators" and charged he was the candidate of an "active adjunct of the Communist party" (i.e., the American Labor Party). Former police commissioner O'Ryan, who had his own ax to grind, joined in these attacks, characterizing La Guardia as an "emotionally abnormal" individual who had destroyed a "magnificent Police Department" in order to satisfy "the red fringe." Also getting into the act was Mahoney's running mate for city comptroller, Frank J. Taylor, who called La Guardia "a crackpot."[14]

The Democrats were not without enormous political clout, namely, the president, the governor, and the extremely popular Senator Wagner. It was a given that Wagner would support his former law partner and that Lehman would support the straight party ticket. The unknown in this equation was what course Roosevelt would follow. Berle had written him, "I hope you keep out of this one. As in 1933, there is nothing in it for you; the alleged Democratic machine includes the very people who tried to cut you. . . . In return they are apparently asking you to give them the City."[15]

Though Roosevelt remained neutral, it is more than probable that he was for La Guardia. On the Saturday before election, he sent a special delivery letter that La Guardia interpreted as an endorsement and wished to have published. When he showed it to Windels, no Roosevelt admirer, Windels urged that he not do so. He saw it as an attempt by the president to cash in on the anticipated La Guardia victory the following Tuesday. Besides, he warned, it might offend many of Fiorello's Republican supporters. The letter was withheld. Roosevelt was not displeased.

On the evening of November 2, La Guardia closed the campaign at his "lucky corner" on 110th Street and Lexington Avenue in the heart of East Harlem. Joined by his protégé Vito Marcantonio, who now held his old congressional seat, the mayor thanked eight thousand friends and neighbors, bid them a fond good night, and went home to grab a few hours' sleep before rising early next morning to vote.

It was a complete rout. La Guardia's 1,344,630 votes to Mahoney's 890,756 gave him the largest electoral victory for mayor in the city's history. (His vote broke down as follows: Republican Party, 674, 611; American Labor Party, 482,790; City Fusion Party, 159,556; Progressive Party, 17,633.) At ten o'clock on election night Roosevelt telephoned his congratulations. Moments later, La Guardia went out to greet the cheering crowds who had gathered and to enjoy a mock-funeral procession that passed by with "pallbearers" carrying a long, black-draped coffin-like box that bore the legend "Tammany Rests in Peace."[16]

2.

The Little Flower had won more than a second term. He had won the inalterable love and respect of an electorate, in particular the most economically disadvantaged, who felt they could now look upon City Hall as a friend and ally, a source of aid and comfort instead of, as had been the case under Tammany domination, an employment agency for corrupt politicians. For the first time in the lives of the majority of them, people wrote to City Hall of their miseries and travails confident the letters would not wind up in the trash basket but would be read by—or their contents at least brought to the attention of—the head man himself. Where possible, frantic petitions for some help, *any* help, were disposed of humanely. The black wife of a WPA worker who had not been paid for two weeks wrote that the grocer was owed so much money he had cut off her credit. "Will you please help me, I have no food for my children. Tomorrow is Christmas, and we are starving." Back came a food package, paid for by La Guardia out of his own pocket. Learning that forty-nine-year-old former black boxing great Sam "Boston Tar Baby" Langford, now a blind pauper, had been struck down by an automobile on a Harlem street, La Guardia promised him a job as soon as he got out of the hospital. Told there would be a two-week wait before the job was to begin, he quietly paid Langford two weeks' salary out of his own pocket.[17]

One thing that gave La Guardia as much pleasure as helping the poor was sticking it to the privileged. Hearst publishing executive A. G. Newmeyer wrote to complain that every time his wife went shopping in midtown Manhattan the chauffeur had one hell of a time finding parking space for her limousine. Could Fiorello kindly provide a "parking courtesy card" like he received from mayors of other cities? La Guardia replied that in his administration the chauffeurs of everyone, "including Mrs. La Guardia," received no special privileges. He was, though, prepared to issue the kind of courtesy card that was available for pushing baby carriages through city playgrounds. "How many such cards can I send you?"[18]

While his humor, along with his mental state, was in top form, as much could not be said for Fiorello's physical state. Added to his old wartime injuries, which cropped up periodically, he had fallen victim to chronic rheumatism, arthritis, sciatica, kidney ailments, and mild diabetes, some of which sent him to the hospital (from where, despite great discomfort, he would conduct official business). Though ignoring his doctor's caveat about losing weight and neglecting his health, he did agree with one correspondent who warned that he must slow down—"but I do not think that there is anything I can do about it."[19]

Nor *would* do about it. When a disgruntled relief recipient shoved him down a flight of marble stairs while he was watching workmen tear down the old Federal Building at the south end of City Hall Park, the fifty-seven-year-old mayor rushed up the stairs ahead of the police officer accompanying him, grabbed his assailant by the throat, demanded, "Why did you hit me from behind?" and then held the door open while the cop dragged the attacker away. "All in a day's work," he remarked offhandedly to witnesses. "I've had worse blows than that below the belt."[20]

La Guardia's second swearing-in, just after midnight on January 1, 1938, was like his first, in the study of Judge Seabury's East Side town house. This time he was attended by a larger group of old friends, counselors and supporters, and new political allies like Kenneth Simpson and District Attorney Thomas Dewey (who was ignored by the mayor except for a perfunctory glad-you-could-make-it). The scene was one of jubilation. The Fusion government, the first in the city's history to succeed itself, had not only expanded its forces but flexed its muscles. The new city charter was now operative. La Guardia had built bridges to the Republican hierarchy and drawn up a circle of friends and advisers who would loyally serve not only him but the people of New York as well.

But before we examine the new administration La Guardia put together, it would be well to look at his actions immediately following reelection.

The logical move for any politician who has just won a campaign (or even, for that matter, lost one) is to take a brief vacation or, at the very least, a few days off to celebrate (or commiserate) with family and friends. La Guardia did neither. Instead, he spent the seven weeks until his second inauguration executing a series of actions that can only be described as impulsive and ill advised, prefiguring his later years, when petulance and enmity became a fixed aspect of his persona.

First he went after the Transit Commission for having turned down the Seabury-Berle plan for unification of the city's subways. He vowed to demand the commission's abolition and have no further dealings with it. It was all right with him if the state wanted to retain the commission—"but," he said, "let the state pay for it, as it pays for amusements in the state parks."[21] His next target was the Police Department, and here he did more than vent antipathy and issue threats it was not in his power to carry through on. He demanded the resignation of all detectives over sixty-three and all officers over sixty-five. To soften the blow, he sent a letter of assurance to each man that no stigma was attached to his forced retirement and that each was leaving city service "with a badge of honor." It was not lost on anyone that most of the men had acquitted themselves admirably throughout their careers, but their careers began under Tammany. While these actions, possibly justifiable from La Guardia's perspective, were nonetheless erratic, what he did next was bizarre: attacking the City Housing Authority.

Implementation of the National Housing Act, the first federal housing authority, was in its organizational phase under the chairmanship of Nathan Straus. When Straus invited heads of local housing authorities to meet with him in Washington, La Guardia, who liked him personally, threw one of his monumental fits. Insisting that Straus "quit star-gazing and get down to work," he announced that the only conference any New York official would attend would be a hearing on a concrete application of the law. "For ten years we have had nothing but conferences. The law is perfectly clear." The ban on the city's participation in the Washington conference led Charles Abrams, the highly respected expert on housing and counsel to the New York City Housing Authority, to resign in protest. This led La Guardia to threaten he'd get "damned rough" if federal officials did not stop "conferring" and get down at once to serving the purpose for which the National Housing Act had been passed: to speed up slum clearance and construction of low-cost public housing.

When Straus renewed the invitation, Langdon Post, La Guardia's handpicked chairman of the authority when it was first set up, protested La Guardia's intransigence, accusing him of trying to dominate the authority in a manner that contravened federal law. He urged the mayor to accept the invitation. The mayor's response was to call in the press and announce that he "accepted Mr. Post's resignation." Post protested that he had not resigned and would carry on until a successor was chosen. Said La Guardia, "Well, that's interesting." Whereupon he ordered his secretary, Lester Stone, "Raise your right hand," and swore him in as temporary chairman. Turning to the newsmen, La Guardia symbolically wiped his hands and said, "Well, that's that." Reminded that naming a chairman was exclusively the right of the authority's board, he shrieked, "Well, they'd better elect [Stone], or there will be a new board." The mayor was "being silly," murmured Post.[22]

When the first allocation of housing funds was made, to eight cities, New York was excluded from the list. Since its mayor had boycotted the conference, the city's applications had been withdrawn. La Guardia now took charge—which was doubtless his intention all along. He rushed down to Washington and personally presented to Straus two major projects, the costs of which just about equaled what the other eight cities had received in the aggregate. The meeting was quite amicable (though Straus couldn't resist remarking that New York was a few weeks late), the proposals were accepted, and from then on the two were on the best of terms and mutually cooperative. Furthermore, La Guardia, who had a history of redeeming his worst errors by pulling off surprises, sent Stone back to his secretarial duties and named Alfred Rheinstein, an able and experienced—as well as scrupulously honest and ethical—builder, who proved to be a first-class city housing administrator.

La Guardia may or may not have acted "silly," as Post charged, but he had certainly impinged upon the independence of the New York City Housing Authority. Mayors could arrogate to themselves a degree of autonomy in many areas, which La Guardia did with regularity, but not in the area of public housing, which involved attracting private capital. The selection of sites and choice of tenants was too conducive to political patronage and, even worse, corruption. But here, as in other instances, like his threat to "get" the Board of Education if its actions were not to his liking, the urge to exercise control outside the scope of his authority was frustrating almost beyond endurance. Deep within himself, La Guardia must have realized that in breaking with Post, to cite but one instance of stepping out of bounds, he was playing a dangerous game.

Not to excuse such behavior, but two factors must be borne in mind: He knew that the times were such that the people—the masses, *his* people—were thirsting for strong leadership, which would help explain Roosevelt's attraction. Second, while continuing to fight for everything he felt his city deserved, and then some, La Guardia had become a political figure of national importance. And a consequence of national importance was high national office. It was not a case of capitalizing on his position as leader of the nation's largest city and on the high esteem in which the White House held him. Rather, it was to him a natural—perhaps even an inevitable—career progression. This career progression was in fact an ambition La Guardia had been silently entertaining for quite a while, and it had been given impetus by his being one of Roosevelt's favorites—indeed, his chief New Deal surrogate not only at home but also throughout the country.

That Fiorello was thinking beyond City Hall was hardly a secret within his inner circle. Even before the votes were counted in 1937, he was discussing higher office—including the governorship and the vice presidency—with Berle. A week after his victorious reelection, Secretary of Interior Ickes intimated at a press conference that if Roosevelt did not seek a third term in 1940, La Guardia would make an ideal choice. And *Fortune* magazine ran a survey that showed many Americans were prepared to vote for the feisty Little Flower in 1940.[23] Whether Ickes meant what he said or was just blowing a little flattering smoke in the Little Flower's direction is as unascertainable as whether the Little Flower did or did not at this point in time entertain the ambition to follow Roosevelt into the White House come 1940.

La Guardia had carried every borough and could count on the support of—in addition to Comptroller McGoldrick and City Council President Newbold Morris—every borough president except James J. Lyons in the Bronx; his majority in the Board of Estimate was incontestable. He now put together an outstanding administration that pleased the Republicans, Fusionists, and New Deal Democrats—especially the Republicans, who had accounted for roughly half his total vote and thus can be said to have won him the election.

For the newly created post of deputy mayor, he chose Henry H. Curran, who had served as Manhattan borough president during La Guardia's term as president of the Board of Aldermen and defeated him in the bitter 1921 mayoral primary. The choice was both magnanimous and politically prudent. Still, the need for a deputy to free the mayor from burdensome detail was to this particular mayor the new charter's least laudable improvement. Burdensome the office of mayor may be, but La Guardia was not one to share power. Before long Curran was reduced to somewhat inane humor as an antidote to the frustration he felt at considering himself superfluous. La Guardia could have given him *some* authority, if only as an act of charity. What he gave him was a mild reprimand: "I understand the attempt to [employ] levity and humor . . . but remember there are several millions in New York who do not understand."[24]

Adolf Berle, whose office of city chamberlain in charge of finances had been abolished by the new charter, temporarily headed the innovative City Planning Commission. But Berle decided he'd had enough of New York politics and joined the Roosevelt administration as assistant secretary of state for Latin America. Rexford Guy Tugwell, shining light of FDR's New Deal "Brain Trust," then headed the commission. For the newly created post of city treasurer, Fiorello chose successful retired Republican coat manufacturer Almerindo Portfolio, a favorite of the city's Italian community. To replace Socialist reformer Paul Blanshard as commissioner of investigations, his former deputy, William B. Herlands, was brought aboard. The brilliant but often abrasive Paul Kern, La Guardia's young protégé, was made chairman of the Civil Service Commission. "The other Paul," Windels, wishing to return to his law practice, declined reappointment as corporation counsel. He did, though, continue as La Guardia's personal lawyer and ex officio adviser. Picked to replace Windels was his assistant, William C. Chanler. Chanler would have his share of battles with La Guardia but knew to back off when confronted by his overbearing will. Picked to succeed McGoldrick as budget director was Kenneth Dayton. Though one of the original Fusionists, he and La Guardia were known not to share a mutual admiration. But La Guardia admired his abilities, and Dayton, like Chanler, knew how to accommodate himself to the mayor's imperious ways without compromising his integrity: "The important thing is to keep alert . . . so that at the right time you can still say yes."[25]

La Guardia began his second term confident of the support of the City Council, especially now that it was under the chairmanship of Newbold Morris, described by Seabury as "one of the brightest stars in the Fusion administration."[26] With such reformers as Genevieve Earle, the only woman on the council, Robert K. Straus, and B. Charney Vladeck, La Guardia could not have hoped for a council more attuned to his philosophy of government. Earle, long active in nonpartisan politics, was celebrated for her fierce commitment to social causes. The thirty-two-year-old Straus, a graduate of Harvard and Cambridge, had served as secretary to the New Deal's original Berle-Moley-Tugwell Brain Trust. His initiative and social commitment particularly endeared him to La Guardia. Perhaps the most fascinating of the new breed was Vladeck, a brilliant scholar whose resumé included imprisonment for revolutionary activities in his native Russia, writer and lecturer, and business manager of the *Jewish Daily Forward*. In 1917, as the lone Socialist on the old Board of Aldermen, Vladeck managed to win the Tammany members' respect for his talents. Appointed by La Guardia to the newly created City Housing Authority in 1935, he served capably until his election to the City Council, on which he was minority leader.

At a dinner he gave for the council the night before its first meeting, Morris hoped they would "just debate quietly and objectively for the good of the city," instead of indulging in gutter politics.[27] His hope was not to be realized. The council was made up of two opposed groups, thirteen organization Democrats and a coalition of thirteen Republicans, American Labor Party members, and independents. The council president could vote only in the event of a tie. The Fusion was confident that with Morris it could invariably carry the day. But the Democrats, having lost control of the Board of Estimate along with City Hall, were not prepared to surrender the only forum left to them.

In the glory days of old, when the aldermanic council totaled sixty-five and Tammany called the shots, a few stray independents or Republicans never posed a problem. Now, thanks to proportional representation, monolithic rule by the Democrats was a matter of history. Or so Morris—and La Guardia—believed. But the picture changed dramatically over the presumably insignificant selection of vice chairman. The Democrats voted thirteen strong for their candidate, John Cashmore of Brooklyn. The opposition had only twelve votes for theirs, a Fusionist named James A. Burke. The thirteenth vote belonged to an ALP member, who was in Ireland getting married. This was future labor boss Michael Quill, who would become known to, and loathed by, a later generation of New Yorkers.

When the Democrats claimed victory, Chairman Morris reminded them that the new charter required a majority vote, and thirteen was not a majority of twenty-six. Countered the furious Democrats, it was in this instance a majority of those present and voting. For the next three months, the two sides fought it out in the media. Suits and countersuits were filed almost daily, and injunctions were issued and ignored with similar frequency. Finally the dispute went into litigation. The judges owed their positions to Tammany patronage, and on April 15 Cashmore's validity as elected vice chairman was upheld.

With its members in key positions, Tammany was now in complete control of the new and now quite powerful City Council. Any legislation that did not serve the Democratic leadership's purposes could not be voted out of committee and brought to a vote. They were able to defeat the county reform bill and, of greater significance, the 1938 budget, thus continuing the time-honored practice of protection for superfluous patronage. If the leadership allowed emergency relief measures and absolutely crucial new taxes to be favorably voted out and passed, they did so grudgingly and under great public pressure, much of it generated by minority leader Vladeck, the council's one-man conscience and center of moral gravity. Tragically, this voice of reason in an arena of ongoing contention was to die midway through the first term. La Guardia was reduced to either cajoling or raging if the council's actions displeased him—which was almost always the case—and as a last resort simply pretending it did not even exist and soliciting the support of the public.

La Guardia came into office this time with two preoccupations: solidifying control of the city's fate and solidifying his national reputation. When asked, at the end of his first year as mayor, what he most regretted about the job, he had replied unhesitatingly, "Lack of power." Now, at the start of his fifth year as mayor, he set out to expand the power he had gained and sought to increase it methodically and unremittingly as the ultimate tool with which to dispose of major political problems to his total satisfaction. But perhaps "political problems" should not be the operative phrase. Perhaps "enemies" would be more to the mark. And what a list of enemies! Agencies, boards, and institutions whose style he saw as an insupportable hindrance to clean government of and by the *people.* Topping his hit list were those who either purveyed or profited from patronage; a bloated bureaucracy; and, at the acme, state government, which to him was a secure bastion from which privileged politicians were able to treat the city like an unloved foster child.

Picking off his targets one by one, La Guardia took on the Transit Commission, which to him was an enclave of political parasites who thwarted the city's control of its own mass transportation system. Then came the Board of Education, which to him was a sanctuary for incompetent and inefficient bureaucrats and hacks who seemed to behave as if they had a divinely ordained mission to protect their turf at the expense of better and broader education of the city's youth. Next it was the turn of the county offices, that seemingly bottomless pit Tammany had sought heroically to fill in with unnecessary "payback" jobs, usually of the "no-show" genre. Then the courts, a veritable beehive of incompetents with a derisory knowledge of the law and dubious capacity to adjudicate, who were beyond the reach of the city government—which, as an added insult, had to finance the entire miserable system. And then there was the issue of home rule for a city that, with its immense wherewithal, he saw as being held hostage to an inherently insensitive and indifferent state government.

In some—but only some—battles, La Guardia came out the victor. On the plus side, the Transit Commission was eventually abolished (La Guardia saw to it that its more worthy members were given new government jobs). The Board of Education reorganized its building division, a sore point with the mayor, and launched a much-needed forty-million-dollar new-schools program. Street peddling was abolished, and large indoor markets were constructed where the peddlers could sell their wares without impeding traffic. Abolishing all those county offices proved problematic, given Tammany's control of the City Council. But at least La Guardia confronted that problem; and, when a referendum was held in 1941, they were finally eliminated.

But by far the most difficult problem was the courts, a complicated system of some 3,500 employees, with the lower courts (like the appointive Magistrate's Courts) financed by the city, while the State Supreme and Appellate courts were paid jointly by the city and the state. Since the entire system was exempt from budgetary auditing by the city, patronage and corruption could be—and flagrantly were—practiced free from reproof. Salaries were constantly being raised for court clerks, bailiffs, and stenographers. When La Guardia tried to halt them, obliging judges issued writs of mandamus, and the increases went through. On the state level, the Supreme Court justices earned much more than the Chief Justice of the United States. The salary of the surrogate clerks exceeded that of the city's parks or police commissioner.

In April, to dramatize the problem, La Guardia staged a two-hour show-and-tell before the New York Bar Association. Replete with charts and graphs, he challenged the illogicality of a bloated state juridical bureaucracy that cost more to maintain than the entire federal judiciary including the United States Supreme Court. The Bar Association listened politely; some even commended the mayor on his presentation. The following day, in what seemed suspiciously like an act of deliberate defiance, a local judge handed down a decision that allowed salary increases for twenty-one employees of the Brooklyn Supreme Court and directed the City Comptroller to provide salaries for three newly created positions. A furious La Guardia retaliated in the only way consonant with his official authority: He sent a letter to all the justices reminding them that official stationery was paid for by the city and was only for official use. "You will, therefore, keep a careful record," he advised, "accounting for such stationery and the nature of the official business for which it is used."[28]

There were more frustrations for Fiorello courtesy of the court system. Patronage had left Tammany Democrats well entrenched in most judicial posts. The courts had not only given the Democrats the balance of power in the City Council but also upheld the budget protecting the jobs of sixty-five useless county officials. All that La Guardia could do was fume, as he did when on occasion the judiciary exercised authority in matters he felt should come under the purview of the city executive, such as traffic control and what he considered to be the city's power to prevent dual job-holding, or, as we call it today, double-dipping.

The problem was not entirely political but reflected an ongoing effort to resolve categorically the relationship between the state and its cities. The original limitations between state and city powers were vague. The problem had become intensified due to the increasing complexity of government. To La Guardia's way of thinking, the only resolution lay in a reevaluation of the divided powers—and a strong crusade for home rule. He undertook leadership of that crusade shortly after commencing his second administration with an assault on Governor Lehman and the state legislature over taxes and the power to levy them.

La Guardia had come under attack for expenditures that raised the city property tax to the highest level in its history. Relief costs were rising, and the city's federal relief grants, already the nation's highest, were deemed inadequate to meet basic needs. Deprived of what it believed it had a right to receive in state aid, the city passed a 3 percent utility tax. Cottoning to the idea, the state imposed a 2 percent utility tax of its own. This left the city with the benefit of only 1 percent, which translated into an annual loss of twelve million dollars. La Guardia called the first press conference of his new term for the express purpose of warning that unless the state restored the utility taxes it had "carried off bodily" from the city, relief payments would have to be cut. "The mayor cannot print money, he cannot revise the multiplication tables." La Guardia took no questions. End of press conference.[29]

Over the next few weeks he and Lehman engaged in a public feud through the media, which sank to the level of name-calling and suggested the feud was but another round of political infighting. All but lost in the verbal melee was La Guardia's attempt to air the necessity for home rule. Finally, in a letter to Lehman he demanded that, having failed to restore the utility tax, the state should assume the full onus of the city's relief program. Finding the arguments "inaccurate and erroneous," Lehman took him to task for failing to properly supervise collection of the sales taxes. What's more, claimed Lehman, the city had adequate taxing power and should use it. Replied La Guardia, "I wrote a letter to a statesman and I received a reply from a politician!"[30]

By the end of March he was demanding a special session of the legislature to deal with the problem of relief. To drive home the point, he threatened to dim the streetlights and close some branches of the public library. In a more drastic gesture, he ordered a 10 percent cut in home relief benefits. When the legislature ignored his demand, the City Council had no choice but to come up with new taxes—which Fiorello made sure everyone knew were "Lehman taxes, not La Guardia taxes." The relief cuts were restored.[31] Though he had achieved a victory of sorts—public money had been raised, and he had dramatized the issue of home rule through the kind of infighting in which he had no peers—it was obvious that only a state constitutional convention could resolve the larger issues. The convention, called for the following month, the eighth since 1776, intended to adapt the 1894 revision to modern needs. Controlled by the upstate Republicans, it quickly became highly politicized. As a result, court reform was dead on arrival, and control by the cities over salaries and pensions and of the school systems was rejected.

Appearing unannounced before the convention, La Guardia demanded that at the very least the cities should be empowered to adopt laws amending or repealing state legislation as it affected them directly. Also, the state should be prohibited from enacting special legislation affecting the cities even despite requests from the governor. The Home Rule Amendment that would be adopted by the convention in August gave more satisfaction than had been hoped for, in that it accepted most of La Guardia's demands, notably empowering the cities to act in fields from which the state had been excluded. But the courts left subject to interpretation other areas in which he had hoped to close the gap between state and municipal control. This, complained the mayor, left "political hacks" frozen into city payrolls.[32]

Meanwhile, despite coping with a full plate both at home and in Albany, La Guardia was expanding his national political image. In a nationwide broadcast dealing with United States trade policy vis-à-vis Latin America, he urged that since Nazi Germany and Fascist Italy were subsidizing exports for the purpose of gaining new markets in that strategically important area, the United States should offer federal bounties to undercut the European dictators while at the same time expanding production as an amelioration to unemployment. Secretary of State Cordell Hull, a steadfast advocate of free trade, quashed the idea.

The question of the day became: What was the mayor of New York City up to now? There's no doubt that Assistant Secretary of State Adolf Berle, still very much a La Guardia partisan and off-the-record adviser, had a hand in the proposal. This led to another question: Was Berle, in collusion with his friend, out to undercut Hull and thereby finesse a 1940 presidential hopeful whose conservatism was a matter of public record? This in turn led to yet another question: Who did the two hope might benefit most from eradicating Hull's presidential aspirations? The incumbent, FDR, who had not yet even suggested—at least publicly—the possibility of seeking a third term? Or FLG, who had also not yet even suggested—at least publicly—a desire to abandon City Hall for the White House, but who, perhaps like Roosevelt, must surely have taken the 1940 race into some degree of consideration?

A few days after his radio broadcast, La Guardia headed west for a speech before the Wichita Falls, Texas, Chamber of Commerce in which he expounded his thesis that the nation's ills were owing to the lack of individual purchasing power, while the entire country shared a common interest: the needs of communities, be they urban or rural. As he moved about the West he not only dropped these ideas in the guise of what we today call "sound bites" for the benefit of local organizations and newspapers, he predicted that a major shake-up lay just beyond the horizon, with conservatives, a good number of them big businessmen and professional politicians, standing in opposition to an alliance of Progressives, laborers, and farmers. At Guthrie, Oklahoma, clad in boots, spurs, and sombrero, he pranced about on a pony before a huge crowd of cheering onlookers and was then christened Chief Rising Cloud by an ancient Cheyenne elder, Wolf Tooth—who, speaking in his native tongue, nominated La Guardia for president of the United States. Disclaiming any such political ambition after the proclamation had been translated, Chief Rising Cloud said, "I came out to get some western airs and some of the western virtues." Asked his opinion of Roosevelt, he replied, "I would consider him a very distinguished member of the faculty of my school of thought."[33]

Though he lingered in the region longer than planned, La Guardia turned down a request, on the grounds that he was needed back in New York, from the La Follette brothers, Phil the governor and Bob Jr. the senator, to attend the official launching at Madison, Wisconsin, of the National Progressives of America. He admired the La Follettes and the progressivism they practiced, but he believed they had acted prematurely within the context of the massive upheaval he foresaw in America's traditional basic two-party system. La Guardia the Republican preferred to remain within the Democratic New

Deal. Here he had a powerful base and powerful friends. This would certainly work more to his advantage in terms of his own political aspirations than involvement with any third party. Yet he told the La Follettes by telephone, when asked to comment on the Madison rally, "It's all right."

When La Guardia returned to New York with an enhanced, positive national reputation and a hankering for more such forays west of the Hudson, he was pleased to learn that his constituents had both enjoyed and admired the press coverage he had harvested, be it for political pronouncements, his no-holds-barred condemnation of Nazi Germany's treatment of the Jews, or merely prancing about on a pony. Also expressing admiration was a *Times* editorial on April 27, 1938, while he was still indulging himself beyond the Mississippi: "Mayor La Guardia works hard, often too hard. He recuperates by playing hard. His rest is largely motion. . . . His temper and constitution are equally suited for labor and for frolic. He deserves the good times he has had." The editorial noted that "his occasional discharge of political speeches was another relief to his system."

From our own perspective, we can wonder whether the *Times* missed the point in proclaiming that "occasional discharge" simply "another relief to his system" or whether, in fact, Mayor La Guardia intended it to have a more significant effect on a future that was as yet not discernible.

For the 1938 Summer City Hall La Guardia chose the New York City building at the as yet unfinished World's Fair. Grover Whalen, the fair's president, considered the whole idea an intrusion and showed his displeasure by not attending the brief welcoming ceremony. Fiorello couldn't have cared less, even though the air-conditioning had not been turned on. He enjoyed being in the middle of the bustle and construction. From there he not only conducted city business but, a more enjoyable "chore," rode forth periodically to officiate at cornerstone layings and dedicatory ceremonies of the many and varied projects—housing, hospitals, courthouses—funded by the federal government, through either loans or outright grants, for all of which he could claim credit. These occasions also gave him an opportunity to reiterate variations on a favorite theme: Many governmental problems that had been handled—often sloppily so—on a local basis prior to his coming into office were really federal responsibilities.

To stress the point, he went down to Washington a number of times to seek even more federal funding and touch base with the likes of Harry Hopkins, Harold Ickes, and, when he was available, Roosevelt. He also did quite a bit of traveling in the opposite direction: north to Albany, where the constitutional convention was dragging on, to appeal for amendments on child labor and the right of municipalities to raise money without having to come on a yearly begging expedition to the state legislature. "Why," he told the convention, "I have come up here not only on my hands and knees, but literally crawling on the floor." What disillusionment he had in the work of the convention was magnified when it became obvious that as it moved toward a conclusion of its labors, the only questions that seemed to preoccupy the politicians were redistricting and pari-mutuel betting. But apparently that disillusionment gave way to resignation tinged with cynicism, to judge by a remark La Guardia made to Lieutenant Governor Charles Poletti: "Don't worry too much about the convention, it will soon be forgotten."[34]

La Guardia allowed himself only one day of rest and relaxation that entire summer. This was at the insistence of Eric and Jean. Out at Northport, Long Island, with Marie, they complained they did not see enough of their father, but this happened to be a particularly hectic summer for him. Where possible, he would reserve summer weekends for them, organizing ball games with friends of theirs he brought along to their vacation homes, directing amateur theatrics, even cooking suppers. He was a concerned parent who took a special interest in their schooling and a giving parent who would take them on his lap when they were children and listen earnestly to their stories and adventures. Above all, he was determined that they not grow up as "special kids." Nor as privileged kids. After visiting the La Guardias one day in their modest apartment surrounded by those of blue-collar workers, pushcart peddlers, and one or two professionals, Harold Ickes noted, "He was lovely with his two adopted children."[35]

On September 2, La Guardia quit the Summer City Hall—ironically, the day the air-conditioning began to work—and went out to Northport to bring his family back to the city. Five days later he was on his way west for a return engagement.

3.

The purpose of the trip was to attend the national convention of the American Legion in Los Angeles. Accompanied by Marie, he quickly turned it into what could be termed a politician's version of a royal progress. Wherever he stopped en route to the West Coast, his reception was the stuff of which adoring headlines are made. Typically, in Shreveport, Louisiana, he was met at the airport by the state's governor, who introduced him as coming from "a little town in the northern corner of the country . . . a little town because it is so much smaller than the man who guides its destiny." The "guide" was then driven through town in an open car, along streets lined with onlookers whose enthusiasm was not dampened by heavy rains that caused cancellation of an aerial display planned in his honor. When his train made a brief stop at Chattanooga, reporters rushed aboard to inquire about his plans regarding the 1940 presidential election. Replied La Guardia, visibly amused, "I don't know anything about politics. Besides, I'm too busy running New York City."[36]

His false disclaimer about ignorance of politics aside, he was telling the truth about running New York, even from a distance. So that he might be constantly aware of what was happening back home, he wore two watches, one set on New York time, the other one local. He communicated frequently by phone with his commissioners. In Phoenix he greeted with what a *Times* reporter covering the trip termed a "rueful grin" the news that District Attorney Dewey's prosecution of Tammany boss James Hines on racketeering charges had resulted in a mistrial. The presiding judge had ruled that Dewey, whose reputation was riding on this high-profile case, had nullified the proceedings, "like a drop of poison in the human system." Enjoying the overly ambitious Dewey's public embarrassment, La Guardia added the zinger: "We spend a hundred dollars a day to air condition that courtroom, and now here's a mistrial."[37]

On the long-anticipated return to his boyhood town, Prescott, Arizona, Fiorello stepped from the train and onto a pony and, trailed by dignitaries and a school band, rode amidst cheering bystanders to the courthouse steps, where he was greeted as "a hometown boy who has achieved worldwide renown." In his reply, La Guardia fondly reminisced about his childhood in Prescott, where he formulated his political creed. It was a creed, he said, that derived from his resentment of the exploitation of the railroad workers he had observed as a child and of the graft he witnessed in the person of a federal agent cheating with food intended for the Indians. Later, when a rocky outcropping was dedicated to the memory of his father, La Guardia eulogized Achille as "the sort of man who loved to bring cheer and happiness to those around him" and then capped the occasion by grabbing a baton and leading the Prescott school band in a medley of marches.

Arriving at Los Angeles on September 10, La Guardia delivered a rousing speech at the opening of the convention, wildly cheered by the Legionnaires, in which he called for unqualified nonpartisan support of the government in its dealings with the European powers. That very week, Great Britain and France had caved in to Hitler's demands on Czechoslovakia—the so-called Munich Pact that British Prime Minister Neville Chamberlain promised would guarantee "peace in our time" but in fact guaranteed war in our time. One can only muse, doubtless unrealistically, on how history might have turned had Europe's appeasing leaders heeded La Guardia's pronouncement, made earlier in the trip at the time of the Dewey foulup of the Hines indictment, when he insisted that the same laws applying to criminals should apply to nations: "When an individual [in this instance Hitler] goes berserk, we take him in custody and put him in a place where he can do no harm."[38]

Throughout the trip La Guardia had kept on top of a New York trucking strike, ordering the deployment of police to protect the movement of essential goods. He even declared himself ready to rush back, should that be necessary. Yet, when the devastating hurricane of '38 struck the Northeast on September 21—described by the *Herald Tribune* as "sudden, unprecedented, and unbelievable"—causing 461 deaths (ten in New York City) and untold millions in property damage, La Guardia spent two days in a leisurely inspection of California's film industry instead of flying back to personally direct the massive cleanup. While his failure to do so is inexplicable, he was not faulted. The simple fact is that he had transformed himself from a purely local figure to a widely recognized national figure. His transformation from New York City's mayor to what was in effect America's mayor was complete.

Arriving back in New York on September 24, he jumped right into the trucking strike, which had resumed following a four-day truce. After a compromise settlement he presented was accepted by the drivers but rejected by the owners, he made one more appeal, in a stormy public meeting, which was loudly cheered. When that failed to move the trucking firms, he mobilized a thousand sanitation trucks plus equipment from other departments and manned them with strikers, who positioned themselves that very night in front of City Hall ready to respond to emergency needs. The trucking firms signed the compromise agreement.

4.

The 1938 midterm election was of particular concern to New York voters. Not only would they be electing an entire congressional delegation, they would be electing a senator and a governor. The senator up for reelection, considered a shoe-in, was the powerful and popular Robert Wagner Sr. Governor Lehman was expected to win reelection. Suddenly, the political picture changed when Senator Royal Copeland, not up for reelection until 1940, died unexpectedly. Chances spiked that a Democrat or at least an independent pro–New Deal liberal might capture that seat, especially if Lehman exercised his gubernatorial right to name an interim successor who would have the advantage of incumbency in November.

The whole business took on a new dynamic when Lehman said he would not name a successor but would seek the seat himself. Were he to lose, the Republicans could well capture both a Senate seat and the Albany executive mansion. Exacerbating the Democrats' concern, enthusiasm in the White House for Lehman was fading. The president had not forgiven Lehman's refusal to support a number of New Deal innovations, in particular his ill-advised attempt to "pack" the Supreme Court by increasing its constitutionally mandated membership in order to create a majority sympathetic to his political philosophy. The governor's enemies—and he had quite a few within the party—urged that Roosevelt back La Guardia for the senatorial seat. Much as he wanted a Senate seat to cap his long tenure in the House, La Guardia announced that he would not run at this time. But perhaps in 1940. . . . He reminded his constituents—and his enemies—that, having been reelected after promising to end the Tammany spoils system, polluted politics, and inefficient municipal government, he could not now renege on that promise. Knowing that there were many who would gladly help send him to the Senate in order to get him out of City Hall, he added in a parting shot, "I've been trained since boyhood that it's treason to give aid and comfort to the enemy."[39]

In the autumn, Lehman, having abandoned the Senate race, was renominated for the governorship. His Republican opponent was Thomas Dewey, who had won a second successful indictment and trial of James Hines and believed this increased his chances of defeating Lehman. Both men considered La Guardia's support vital, surely testimony to his political strength, but La Guardia felt it was in his best interests to remain neutral. In fact, he could not imagine himself endorsing either man. Though Dewey was a member of his own team, he had resisted a personal appeal to follow the mayor's example and stay on to finish the job for which he had been elected; he represented the party that had dominated the fruitless constitutional convention and supported amendments that to La Guardia were thoroughly odious; and he was one of those people only relatives and close friends can warm up to without difficulty. As for Lehman, La Guardia had not forgiven his persistent refusal to support the entire New Deal program. Roosevelt backed Lehman out of party loyalty and their long-standing friendship, and the American Labor Party gave its support, but La Guardia held back, promising to support Lehman if Lehman in turn promised to support the New Deal more forcefully.

Lehman finally came around to praising Roosevelt's "humanitarian policies," and Dewey ordered that his campaign was never to mention La Guardia by name. Yet, for reasons never explained, La Guardia's support of Lehman was not forthcoming. Lehman defeated Dewey by a narrow margin of sixty-seven thousand votes. In the congressional elections, the Republicans more than doubled their seats in the House (from 89 to 170) and gained eight seats in the Senate. Aggravating the loss to the Democrats was the defeat of a number of governorships. Having played a spectator's role during the campaign as opposed to a participant's, La Guardia now emerged as leader, under the Roosevelt banner, of the nation's progressive forces. Should the nation's thirty-second president follow the tradition established by the first and step down after two terms, he would be in the forefront of possible successors.

CHAPTER TWENTY

"I don't want any lawyer sitting around to decide what's in the city's best interest!"

1.

Ask anyone today what the name "La Guardia" summons to mind, and the answer is invariably, "The guy they named the airport for." He was not only its eponym, he was its creator. It started in November of 1934, when Fiorello boarded a flight at Chicago that terminated at Newark. Insisting that the terms of his ticket—"Chicago to New York"—be honored, he refused to get off. A hastily commandeered plane shuttled him to Floyd Bennett Field in Brooklyn, then used only for flight training. "And remember," he shouted while deplaning, "Newark is not New York!"[1]

Having once again staged a public incident to dramatize an issue—his insistence that New York assume preeminence in the rapidly expanding field of aviation—La Guardia bombarded postal authorities to switch their mail flights from Newark to Floyd Bennett. He also kept detailed records on all flights diverted from Newark because of fog and showered Postmaster General James Farley with telegrams to the effect that Floyd Bennett suffered less fog and offered superior flying conditions. Farley saw this all as yet another attempt by La Guardia to enhance his image and was having no part of it.

Failing to win federal officials over to converting Governor's Island in the East River to an airport, Fiorello trained his sights on the old Glenn Curtis Airport at North Beach in Queens. During the 1920s it had catered to wealthy sports flyers, but it was now on its last legs because of the effect of the Depression on its clientele. Lying along the east shore of Flushing Bay, and greater in area than Floyd Bennett, its low terrain and lack of high buildings precluded obstructions, and the surrounding marshlands could be filled in to make large runways. With completion of the Triborough Bridge, it would be a twenty-minute drive to midtown Manhattan. La Guardia envisioned North Shore as a colossal air- and seaplane complex that would serve the entire Northeast and assure his city's dominance over regional air commerce: "Nothing can stop it."[2]

Nothing could stop La Guardia either, though it was the height of the Depression, and municipal leaders were not about to expend the necessary forty-four million dollars for what became known as "Fiorello's Folly." He now had the support of President Roosevelt, himself an aviation enthusiast. The federal government contributed twenty-seven million dollars to underwrite filling in 357 acres of marshes and wastelands to create runways and apron space. This encouraged municipal authorities to come up with the balance of funding. Into the project went a thousand carloads of cement, twenty thousand tons of steel, two hundred miles of cable, twenty-five miles of underground piping, and enough electric power to provide lighting for fourteen thousand city streets. The massive project was completed in two years by five thousand men working three shifts six days a week—and an interfering mayor who spent almost every Sunday dashing out to the site for a personal inspection. He was determined to have it in operation for the second summer of the extended 1939 World's Fair.[3]

Named the North Beach Airport, its six-thousand-foot runway was the world's longest, with a load tolerance of twenty-five tons per square foot; its rotating tower beacon, the world's brightest, projected a shaft of light of more than thirteen million candlepower; its administration building was more than five times greater than most railroad terminals; and its hangars, in the aggregate, enclosed an area exceeding that of Madison Square Garden. At the formal dedication on October 15, 1939, before a crowd of 325,000, La Guardia was so pleased and proud, he magnanimously forgave those who had initially opposed the idea.

La Guardia then went after business, attracting the largest carriers away from Newark—and raising fees once vendors began competing for space. It wasn't long before North Beach could boast every conceivable type of store and boutique, even a brokerage office. When a terminal promenade designed to accommodate as many as five thousand people eager to see planes take off and land offered as a concession to any willing entrepreneur for twelve thousand dollars a year saw no takers, La Guardia had the city operate the promenade itself. It wasn't long before the "Sky Walk" was bringing in a hundred thousand dollars annually. By then it was the busiest airfield in the world, handling two hundred flights a day. Bronx Borough President James J. Lyons, one of the mayor's most obdurate antagonists, introduced a resolution in the Board of Estimate that the new airport be named "La Guardia Field," to honor "the Mayor of our city who conceived the idea . . . and who was solely responsible for its development."[4] Determined to create a ring of airports, La Guardia pushed through the Board of Estimate the purchase of a polluted bathing beach in Queens, which he envisioned as the site of an even larger international airport. The beach was known as Idlewild Point, and La Guardia's expanded vision came to fruition as Idlewild (today John F. Kennedy) Airport.

2.

With its theme of "Building the World of Tomorrow" against dwindling hopes for peace, the New York World's Fair of 1939 sought to promote the message of hope and prosperity with its exhibitions and demonstrations of the great technological advances to date and yet to come. Under Robert Moses's personal supervision, despite three years of problems including strikes and shortage of funds, an incredible aggregation of buildings, parks, and grounds—indeed, every aspect of a colossal undertaking of this nature—in addition to new highways and bridges, arose from a gigantic swamp and garbage dump of over a million acres, the so-called Valley of the Ashes.

La Guardia saw it as a great force for bringing enormous benefits to a great metropolis in the final stages of a reform-inspired renaissance. After making sure the city was cleaned up and new subway cars on new express lines were in place to bring visitors out to the fairgrounds, he traveled around the country publicizing the coming event—and garnering quite a bit of personal publicity that enhanced his national reputation. Along the way he announced that he would not permit Nazi Germany to have an exhibit at the fair, adding that if it somehow *were* to—and he had to have known he had absolutely no say in the matter—he would put a facsimile of Hitler, whom he referred to as "a brown-shirted" fanatic, in the Museum of Horrors. Hitler's top lieutenant, Hermann Goering, he described as "a perverted maniac." Goering vowed to bomb New York City to smithereens, if that's what it took to "stop somewhat the mouths of arrogant people over there."

When the German Consulate in New York asked for police protection against the possibility of attack by angered Jews, La Guardia generously provided an all-Jewish security detail under the command of Captain Max Finkelstein, president of the Police Department's Jewish fraternal organization, the Shomrin Society. Shortly thereafter, La Guardia received a .22-caliber cartridge, around which was wrapped a note: "You will get this if you continue to attack the German Nazi Party." Was he frightened? Not in the least. Was he happy about it? Was he ever! It earned him—and his city's forthcoming fair—the kind of headlines no amount of money could buy. The fair was declared officially open by President Roosevelt on April 30, 1939, before a massive crowd that included dignitaries representing every nation. His speech was a celebration of democracy and praise for the host country; a land of many tongues, a land that stood out in stark contrast to the European dictatorships. Speaking briefly after the president, La Guardia declared, "The city of today greets the world of tomorrow."[5]

La Guardia roamed the fairgrounds as often as official duties permitted, welcoming and hosting visiting dignitaries including foreign royalty and heads of state. He inspected exhibits to make sure those running them were in top form and visitors were being accorded all due respect. He rushed to attend to emergencies, be they plumbing problems or reuniting a temporarily misplaced child with its frantic parents. He even paraded about occasionally in western costume and had a few words for anything he personally considered "nasty," such as a beauty contest in which the contestants wore little more than a smile. And he made many a speech on topics pertinent to a World's Fair: international politics, economics, religious freedom, and the like. To promote the fair and celebrate its vision of the World of Tomorrow, he made a few quick trips across the nation and even to South America.

After only a brief period, the original premise evanesced as the fair, dedicated to technological progress and the vision of a future that would make the world even greater than could be imagined, quickly became dedicated to entertaining the masses. High-mindedness gave way to carnival as "bands of strolling players—singers, dancers, musicians, acrobats, clowns . . . roamed about . . . strumming banjoes, singing popular songs, giving out swing music . . . surrounded by crowds wherever they went."[6] There were vendors of every conceivable commodity from souvenirs to junk food, deluxe dining in elegant surroundings, and pay-for-view extravaganzas like Billy Rose's celebrated Aquacade. Though the sophisticated technology exhibitions drew long lines, they had to compete with the reality that, given a choice between being enlightened and being entertained, most people will favor entertainment over edification. Within two months of the opening, attendance dropped below expectations, and a financial shortfall necessitated laying off several hundred employees. La Guardia offered city employees Saturday off so they could attend with their families, but more was needed than Saturday visitors. In August, he undertook a hasty 1,700-mile selling trip. At Chicago, where he addressed a luncheon of seven hundred businessmen, he was introduced by Mayor Edward J. Kelly as not only the world's greatest mayor but also "the most dynamic personality in America."[7]

By now, war had broken out in Europe. Moving quickly to assure calm, La Guardia put police on emergency duty to maintain order and to guard bridges, tunnels, and piers. "Battles will be fought in Europe," he said, "not in the streets of New York."[8] Meantime, management of the fair's troubled finances was reorganized, and La Guardia received support from FDR for his idea that a second year might provide a morale booster. It may have boosted morale, but it did not boost net returns appreciably. The fair never achieved projected profits, having failed to attract the anticipated number of visitors. Wrote Bruce Bliven in the *New Republic*, summing up its achievements, or lack of same, "I imagine that the Fair will make a lovely park once the salesrooms are cleared away."[9]

3.

While coping with problems attendant upon the new airport, the fair, and the administration of a city that had yet to emerge from the Great Depression, La Guardia had to cope, yet again, with what one newspaper called "the city's No. 1 problem child"—Robert Moses.[10] Each man was determined that on any given issue, it must be, to inject a present-day locution, "my way or the highway." The confrontation that highlighted the second half of La Guardia's second term might be called "the great storm over the bridge versus the tunnel."

Constructing bridges and arterial routes was to Moses an obsession. All else was secondary. Fifty miles of arteries, including the Triborough Bridge, were by now completed, and the Whitestone Bridge linking the Bronx and Queens was well under way. Moses had plans for a hundred miles more. For these he not only needed more money, he demanded complete authority. Grants from Washington for development of arterial routes included funds for acquiring and developing adjacent land for recreational purposes; budget priority was for parkway maintenance and extensions. Moses juggled funds with the dexterity of a master tumbler working with a half-dozen Indian clubs. And he carried on feuds with the same arrogance—and total lack of charm.

When Paul Kern, chairman of the Civil Service Commission, issued a memorandum asking for the cooperation of all departments in reporting inefficiencies, Moses told him to send the communication to the OGPU in Russia, "whose representative you seem to be." When one young member of the corporation counsel's department suggested to La Guardia that under current law a certain course could not be pursued, he was fired on the spot: "I don't want any lawyer sitting around to decide what's in the city's best interest! Keep them out of my meetings!" Admiring the young official for standing up to the mayor, Moses hired him for his own department.[11] It was a department he had established as a quasi-autonomous entity within the city government. According to Moses's biographer, Robert Caro. he dealt with budgetary and personnel problems unique to all department heads by calling for more money and less red tape, going so far as to ignore judicial restraining orders, let alone orders from City Hall. For Wednesday meetings of department heads, he sent in his place a potted plant.[12]

Moses's thirst for power was by now running amok. He imposed himself as head of various independent authorities created to develop a single major public project that, when the project was completed and the bondholders paid off, was supposed to go out of existence. He managed to devise and push through the state legislature a series of laws that perpetuated these agencies under his authority, to go on from one project to another. This helped increase his power exponentially, as they were independent entities to begin with, exempt from most of the rules and restraints to which other city agencies were subjected.

But there was one authority he not only couldn't get his hands on, he couldn't get his hands *near:* the one responsible for building tunnels. La Guardia saw to that. When in 1936 he created the Tunnel Authority to build an underwater link connecting Queens and midtown Manhattan, he refused to put Moses on the board. "Leave the son-of-a-bitch off," he ordered the authority's chairman. Moses was not concerned with being left off the board. He was concerned only with either taking over the Tunnel Authority completely or merging it with his Triborough Bridge Authority. La Guardia was concerned with putting the brakes on Moses's shameless never-ending grab for power. He was also concerned with subverting Moses's attempt to undermine the Tunnel Authority's operations.

As work on the East River tunnel moved slowly toward completion, the two men moved rapidly toward confrontation over the issue that culminated in a heated exchange between the two involving La Guardia's protégé Paul Kern. At issue was Kern's ruling as Civil Service commissioner that toll collectors for the Triborough Bridge Authority must be selected from the Civil Service lists from which court attendants and prison guards were selected. Moses went over Kern's head and told La Guardia that unless he had his way on this matter, he would have no choice but to take it up with "the attorney for the bondholders." No one, least of all Kern, whom he despised, was going to tell Robert Moses whom *he* must hire on any of *his* projects.

Replied an enraged La Guardia, "I want it clearly understood that the city is not being run by attorneys for the authority bondholders.

... You are a city official, and will take up matters with the corporation counsel." Replied Moses, "I think you had better read the arrangements and contracts."[13] La Guardia didn't reply. He was in a problematical position. He knew that Kern, whom he had raised from office aide to one of the city's highest positions, and who was proving to be both independent and abrasive as the months passed, had brought on the current brouhaha by revising the mayor's lists from which the toll collectors were to be selected. Fiorello H. La Guardia did not take too kindly to independence on the part of his subordinates, even protégés. As for abrasiveness, that was something he tolerated only in himself.

Of greater consequence, La Guardia learned from his legal advisers that the recent amendments Moses had gotten through the state legislature greatly broadened the powers of various city authorities and specifically gave them the right to employ special counsel. Moses saw himself not as La Guardia's subordinate but at the very least his equal. The power to pursue his multitude of additional projects would be diminished during the war years due to constraints on personnel, materials, and funding, but at this point in time he was in a commanding enough position to be regarded as an adversary La Guardia must rein in, compromise with if necessary, and even, when presented with no alternative, join.

The next phase in the run-up to the great bridge-versus-tunnel confrontation came in the autumn. It involved extending a favorite Moses project, the "circumferential highway"—later the Belt Parkway—then running through the Gowanus section of Brooklyn and intended eventually to follow the shorelines of all four of the contiguous boroughs. Included in cuts in the capital budget La Guardia requested from the Board of Estimate were cuts in funding the Belt. He insisted that schools and health centers, as well as mass transportation extensions and other civic improvements, should have priority over building of additional automobile routes.

This was unacceptable to Moses. He rallied the support of the Municipal Arts Commission for 1938, which was enthusiastic over the idea of a waterfront Vienna-like "ringstrasse" that would circle the entire island of Manhattan. The commission was in fact reflecting the will of the people—and of La Guardia. Within two days he surrendered to Moses's vision and gave priority to the new road. But then, perhaps it was not so much sharing a vision as being unable to halt what was in effect a Moses steamroller.

When the proposal came before the Board of Estimate for consideration, Newbold Morris argued that the city had "a stupendous involvement in public bridges, buildings, and equipment which must be protected. Unless the plant is properly maintained we will undergo a repetition of the era when broken-down equipment and neglected buildings cost the taxpayers many needless millions." He further argued that under growing restrictions on capital expenditures, not a single school nor new hospital nor new police station or firehouse would be provided for in the next two years. In this he had the support of City Comptroller McGoldrick and Manhattan Borough President Isaacs—indeed, of the entire Fusion element on the board.[14]

Moses threatened that if his highway, whose cost was estimated at $105 million, were delayed he would make sure it was "dead for a long time." Here was one Moses threat that had to be taken in all seriousness. La Guardia had gotten Washington to pledge fifty-five million. Moses's various authorities were bringing in $4.5 million annually (the Triborough Bridge alone was earning $1.3, net). But these monies were used to pyramid his other projects, specifically by trading in old bonds and floating new ones. The balance needed to fund the Belt had to come from the city.

Anxious to avoid another damaging fight within his administration, and supportive of a heavy-duty construction project that would create more jobs, La Guardia, in one of his rare appearances before the Board of Estimate, imposed his will on the Fusion members, whose votes could determine the outcome. He asked them "to go along with me on this." They did. They also felt betrayed by the man the Fusion had made mayor in the first place. Recalled McGoldrick years later, they caved in "because—you know La Guardia was very intolerant of differences. . . . It would have thrown the entire administration into chaos."[15] Being forced to side with Moses infuriated La Guardia. Having to antagonize his fellow Fusionists made it worse. A month later he set out to redress this latest Moses *coup*.

At this point we must backtrack to the late spring, when Washington began to cut relief dollars, which had funded so many construction projects in La Guardia's first term. There still remained, though, funding for public housing. And Moses was determined to add *that* authority to his collection. On August 29, 1938, he wrote to La Guardia averring that "neither the City Housing Authority nor the State Housing Commission are properly constituted for any major construction," and suggesting the mayor "put all the city work under one man, which is really the only effective way of carrying out a program of this kind." Not surprisingly, Moses volunteered to serve on a committee to formulate "a program for the remaining years of this administration." If necessary, he would deign to accept a position as housing czar. La Guardia didn't bother to respond.

Meanwhile, Moses had a team of his own architects quietly design a comprehensive new public housing program—and developed a secret plan for reorganizing the New York City Housing Authority under his personal control. Then, consistent with his methodology when setting out to expand his power, he went after NYCHA chairman Alfred Rheinstein. Rheinstein sought to work harmoniously with Moses, but every time he tried to explore some avenue of cooperation, he received not teamwork but an abusive lecture—a Moses specialty—on how to run his department. Moses was determined to embarrass Rheinstein and undermine his confidence. Choice retorts included "The weather has gotten to you," "What you say makes no sense at all, and indicates again how inexperienced you are," and "Much as I like you personally, I don't know what the hell you are talking about." When Rheinstein learned Moses planned to make a speech on housing, he asked for an advance copy in his capacity as city housing boss. Moses ignored the request.[16]

Why he did so became clear after the November elections, when the voters approved a constitutional amendment that for the first time made state money available in ample sums for public housing. On November 22, before an invited audience of builders, real estate agents, and reformers, Moses delivered what his office had billed as "a talk on housing and recreation" but what was in fact a palpable move to usurp the city housing program. For the occasion, to which he had invited the press, he rented a wing of the Museum of Natural History and arranged for the municipal radio station, WNYC, to broadcast the speech live. Before the broadcast began, Moses's men distributed elaborate four-color brochures describing a $245 million program for ten specific housing projects—a subject that, so far as Moses was concerned, was closed to further discussion.

Striding to the microphone, he attacked public housing professionals as inept bureaucrats who had squandered millions with little to show for it. As an alternative, he offered a comprehensive system based on clearly defined principles of site selection, slum clearance, construction, and financing. He even went into details regarding exact dimensions, locations, and precise costs. More than making a case for his audience, he was making his case for the tens of thousands of radio listeners throughout the five boroughs whose support, he was convinced, would compel their mayor to add the position of housing czar to his already inflated list of titles.

But those tens of thousands never heard a thing. Their mayor was not about to let his power-hungry parks commissioner grab control of city housing. Having gotten wind of what he was up to, La Guardia ordered the WNYC station director to kill the Moses broadcast.

The Moses plan did, however, make headlines the next day. While most papers agreed it was the work of a master builder, they also agreed that this time the master builder had gone too far. The plan was attacked for imposing higher rentals than the poor people such housing was intended for could afford and for giving private investors an unfair advantage by relieving them of taxes as well as costs of the new parks that were obligatory concomitants of any new housing projects. Said the *New York Post*, reflecting the consensus, "We congratulate the mayor for socking the Moses plan and for socking it hard."

The mayor did more than sock it hard. He prevailed upon a powerful Housing Committee headed by Paul Windels to shoot down every single one of Moses's plans described in that elaborate brochure, which he facetiously dismissed as "a beautiful printing job" that was admirably long on imagination and public relations and pathetically short on familiarity with housing problems. Far from accepting the rebuff with his customary fusillade of insults, tantrums, and threats, Moses went on the offensive. Which brings us to the Great Bridge vs. Tunnel Controversy.[17]

Proposed as early as 1925, the Manhattan-Queens link was proceeding slowly and would require another two years to complete. But funding for the second tunnel—to connect Manhattan and Brooklyn—was unavailable. La Guardia's pleas for loans or grants from Washington to start that second link had been turned down by both

Jesse Jones of the Reconstruction Finance Corporation and Interior Secretary Ickes. Riding to the rescue, at least as *he* saw it, was Robert Moses. For a price—which included membership on the Tunnel Authority board—he would finance the new link by capitalizing the profits of the Triborough Bridge. La Guardia approved, the press approved, and the plans were approved by the War Department (without whose permission it could not be built). When it looked like another major La Guardia–Moses accomplishment was to come to fruition, Moses made a dramatic announcement on January 22, 1939: "After considerable study, we believe the soundness of the Brooklyn-Battery crossing lies in a bridge." (The Battery, for the benefit of those not familiar with New York, is the lower tip of Manhattan Island, where the bridge's approach would be situated.)

His "soundness" was not without logic. Cost of the bridge would be forty-one million dollars, as opposed to eighty-four million for the tunnel, maintenance costs would be halved, and it would have six lines instead of a tunnel's four. Opposition came from all directions. A coalition of civic-minded New Yorkers argued that such a structure, given the obligatory massive anchorage, extended approach ramps, and immense pier supports, would devastate the local ecology of the riverside area. In the Planning Commission opposition was led by Manhattan Borough President Stanley Isaacs, who questioned how the new traffic could be handled in the already congested streets that gave onto the area. Also, he and the other Fusionists were convinced that such a project was aesthetically unacceptable, and they asked for further study of the tunnel. Moses's arrogant response: "An absolutely silly argument. No one is interested in studying the tunnel because it simply doesn't make sense." He then lobbied for support in Albany, where he enjoyed no small measure of influence.

Two weeks later, on March 2, the Planning Commission finessed further study and prolonged hearings by supporting the bridge. On the previous day, in a letter to the chairman of the Tunnel Authority, La Guardia wrote, "It is unseemly to have two departments in conflict with each other. . . . If a generous grant were available a tunnel would be preferable. If no grant is available a tunnel is out of the question." He then turned to other municipal problems and responsibilities, as much out of calculation as a sense of mayoral responsibility, and let Moses take the full heat for a politically explosive project he also supported only because he was convinced it would be the bridge or nothing.

Moses's antagonists joined in applying the heat. The Regional Plan Commission, led by its much-respected reform chairman, George McAneny, opposed the bridge as a spoliation of the skyline and of historic Battery Park. The Citizens Union based its objection to the bridge on how it would affect adversely real estate values and property taxes and precipitate a diminution in the quality of life in the overall southern Manhattan area. Speaking for eighteen leading cultural groups, the Fine Arts Federation of New York warned that the bridge would "disfigure perhaps the most thrillingly beautiful and world renowned feature of this great city." Joining in the anti-bridge fray were the New York chapter of the American Institute of Architects, the Merchants Association, the Westside Chamber of Commerce, the Real Estate Board, the City Club, the New York Board of Trade—indeed, it would seem, every civic group that opposed Moses and the Planning Commission.

Referring to the controversy as "the same old tripe," Moses was confident he would carry the day when the City Council met on March 28 to consider legislation approving his Triborough Authority as the agency to construct his new bridge. Opposition was led by Isaacs and McAneny. When his turn came for rebuttal, Moses stressed categorically and unequivocally, "Either you want it or you don't want it, and either you want it now or you don't get it at all." Next came the verbal poison darts: George McAneny he categorized as "an exhumed mummy . . . an extinct volcano." As for the expertise of civil servants, he glared ferociously at the Manhattan borough president and likened the Civil Service to "nothing but a Communist state *pleasing to Mr. Isaacs.*"[18] Then, with a smirk of satisfaction on his face that was contrapuntal to the gapes of shock at the indecency of his behavior, Moses strode from the chamber. He knew—and he knew *they* knew—that the plans were ready, the pieces in place, and the federal funding available. Funding, he was confident, that would never be available for a tunnel.

And he was right. The bridge proposal carried in the council. Within two days, the state legislature passed the necessary enabling legislation and Moses was getting the approval of the War Department. Before the month was out, he was negotiating with the Reconstruction Finance Corporation and with private bankers for the $41.2 million funding. La Guardia rushed down to Washington to lobby for the bridge before the War Department review board. It was hardly a triumph, due in large measure to his denouncing its members as "swivel chair admirals."

Late in May, with the opening festivities of the World's Fair behind him, La Guardia appeared personally before the Board of Estimate to urge passage of a slightly revised bridge proposal, which hopefully would resolve the concerns of the opposition. Meanwhile, Moses was attacking his critics through letters in the press with a passion that caused the normally supportive *Herald Tribune* to conclude, "There is no point in arguing with a volcano. . . . We can't understand the present heat and the present hurry. All we ask is time for more study and more light. Why, therefore, the tantrums?"[19]

As the volcano's tantrums continued, along with La Guardia's support, both were unaware of developing events behind the scene. On April 5, two days after Governor Lehman approved the bridge bill, Eleanor Roosevelt mentioned casually in her newspaper column, "My Day," that "a man who is greatly interested in Manhattan Island" had called her attention to the controversy and urged that her fellow New Yorkers not disturb what remained of lower Manhattan's beauty and serenity and natural grace with the bridge's construction.

There's little doubt that the "man" who had called her attention to the bridge was C. C. Burlingham. A few days later, the *Herald Tribune* was only too happy to run a three-column letter to the editor from Burlingham seconding the first lady's viewpoint. Also, unbeknown to La Guardia, Burlingham wrote to his friend the president "in graveyard confidence" on April 10, arguing that "nobody fit to have an opinion wants the Battery Bridge." This was hardly the time to "spend millions for a scenic motorway" for Robert Moses. "It should have been stopped by the Planning Commission. . . . It can easily be stopped by the War Department. . . . The channel of the East River should be widened, not narrowed or obstructed." Burlingham concluded with the Latin phrase *Verb. Suf. Sup.* [Latin for a word to the wise is sufficient]—"especially when the sapient [man of great wisdom and discernment] is a lover of New York, as well as President of the United States and Commander in Chief of the Army."[20]

Hating Moses as he did, but wishing to do what was in the best interests of the city, Roosevelt, motivated by the Burlingham letter, solicited the opinions of others. La Guardia had his supporters in high places, especially Ickes. The interior secretary sought to rally the support of Labor Secretary Frances Perkins, whose opinions FDR particularly valued: "The President is going to kill this. I wish you would argue this out with him. . . . He's getting the military to . . . say that it interferes with navigable streams and it doesn't—not at all. . . . It's just that he so hates Moses." Perkins raised the issue with the president and was told he was "reliably informed" that such a bridge was a "very great hazard to navigation. In case of war we can't have any bridges around there. They'll drop bombs and so forth." Perkins reminded Ickes there were plenty of other major projects "not burdened with Moses's name" and suggested he focus on those.

By May, Secretary of War Harry H. Woodring had decided he would rule against the bridge despite recommendation of the Army engineers to the contrary. Whether he arrived at his decision independently or the president did in fact, as Ickes predicted, "kill this" is unascertainable—but the latter is probable. The president always took great care to cover his tracks. On July 17, Woodring made his ruling public, with the excuse that the bridge's construction would create a peril to navigation in wartime, being "seaward" of the Brooklyn Navy Yard, thereby creating "additional hazard and obstructions to the already congested water traffic at the locality." He added that under enemy attack the bridge could be tumbled to block the vital harbor. Moreover, it was fortunate that other "feasible alternatives" existed. He didn't feel obliged to mention the word "tunnel." When "reminded" that both the Brooklyn Bridge and the Manhattan Bridge already existed seaward of the Navy Yard, he brushed it off by saying the two bridges in question should eventually be demolished.[21]

Moses bitterly charged Woodring with "a comic opera theory of defense" worthy of being "immortalized by a new Gilbert and a new Sullivan" and ranted about "the kicking around, discourtesy, and insulting treatment" he had received from Washington. He turned to La Guardia for help. La Guardia told him, "This [i.e., New York City's] administration is never daunted by anything. We must go on to the next thing."[22] The "next thing" was that Manhattan-Brooklyn link.

With the help of friends in the White House, La Guardia got the tunnel option revived, now that the bridge was a dead issue. Adolf Berle obtained from Jesse Jones of the RFC a supplementary allocation; others took up the cause.[23] At the ceremony marking the completion of Moses's circumferential highway in the spring of 1940, La Guardia announced acceptance by the city of an RFC loan of fifty-seven million dollars at a favorable rate of interest for a tunnel linking Manhattan and Brooklyn. Moses, whose dream of a peripheral parkway system linking the boroughs—a dream he had had since 1927—was now a reality, had to accept that "the biggest, most beautiful bridge in the world" he had hoped to build would be a functional underground tunnel—in his words, "a tiled vehicular bathroom smelling faintly of carbon monoxide." Moses regarded it as his greatest defeat.

La Guardia, who had not enjoyed playing the role of the Judas goat on the bridge issue, took the opportunity to give his obnoxious parks commissioner a little comeuppance. He informed Moses there was only enough money to complete the tunnel and the Manhattan approaches, not for the Brooklyn approaches and Owl's Head Highway intended to connect the Battery crossing with the Belt Parkway. The Belt would have a five-mile gap. Moses offered to have the Triborough Authority build the connecting road—provided it could impose a toll to finance construction. No way, said La Guardia, unalterably opposed to the idea of tolls on city highways. Moses had no choice but to have the authority pick up the twelve-million-dollar tab for the highway.[24]

4.

Critics, including those closest to him, were becoming fed up with what they perceived as La Guardia's tendency to "check with the Chief"—FDR—before making decisions. More than merely checking with the Chief, he seemed, on occasion, to be doing the Chief's bidding, and it was the sort of bidding the reformers didn't like. Such as when he appointed his onetime Tammany antagonist Jimmy Walker to a twenty-thousand-dollar-a-year job mediating labor disputes as "impartial chairman" of the Women's Cloak Industry. La Guardia partisans insisted this was merely an act of magnanimity for the former playboy mayor, who had returned home from European exile practically penniless. But many argued it was a favor to Roosevelt, who had no great love for Walker but wished to appease New York City Democrats and the party's new national chairman, Bronx boss Ed Flynn. The appointment so disappointed Judge Seabury, he sadly equated La Guardia with the poet Tennyson, whom Robert Browning denounced in "The Lost Leader" for accepting the position of England's poet laureate: "Just for a handful of silver he left us, / Just for a riband to stick in his coat."[25]

In fact, Fiorello was undergoing a metamorphosis of sorts. Now at the peak of his power and popularity, he was approaching the apex of irascibility.

To win over the conservatives, he ordered officials to furnish Dun and Bradstreet with names of all patrons found in gambling places during police raids, even if they were only observers. At the urging of church groups, he ordered provocative magazines removed from newsstands: "There is no question of freedom of the press involved here. It isn't censorship I am seeking to invoke. The Mayor has no such power. But you know the Mayor has power of sewage disposal." Twenty-four garbage trucks were dispatched to seize the "offending literature."[26]

He interfered in the selection of a new president for CCNY, something not even Tammany had dared try. He ordered Commissioner of Investigation William Herlands to investigate individuals for no other reason than that they had made themselves unpopular with City Hall. "Unhappy about his own blocked ambitions," he "played cruel games with people, dangling promotions in front of them, forcing them to jump through hoops to show their personal loyalty. Even more than before, he humiliated his commissioners. In the presence of one of his deputies, [Herlands] was told that 'you let them shit all over you and pee all over you and you like it so much you lick it up.'" Newbold Morris was told, "You're so stupid it's an art."[27]

The former East Harlem congressman seemed to have abandoned his dislike of royalty and the highborn and his contempt for authoritarians, to judge by the gracious reception he accorded Rafael Trujillo when that Dominican dictator arrived on a visit. And the legendary champion of labor and energetic supporter of collective bargaining for federal employees was now downright hostile to municipal labor unions. In the struggle between the industrial unions that had coalesced as the CIO and the more conservative AFL, La Guardia sided with the latter.

And then there was his abrupt dismissal of a valued aide, which became one of the causes célèbres of his second term.

The aide in question was New York City Housing Authority Chairman Alfred Rheinstein. A builder with years of experience and a strong social conscience, Rheinstein was convinced construction costs could be lowered, and he set about to prove it by introducing innovative methods and techniques. At first, La Guardia backed Rheinstein, as his methods produced desired results. In the August 1939 issue of *Harper's*, Rheinstein published an article, "Why Slum Clearance May Fail," that severely criticized federal housing standards—which, he noted, were not applicable to Manhattan. Rigid limits on the cost of land meant that public housing could only be constructed in the outer boroughs, where they were least needed. Income levels prescribed for the entire nation were ill suited to New York's higher wage scale. Moreover, he argued, prospective tenants should be rated by a variety of human factors instead of merely by income alone. The article berated Federal Housing Administrator Nathan Straus, with whom he had had several confrontations over where to build new housing, for "sabotaging" the entire program. Straus retaliated by canceling approval for a major housing project in Brooklyn's Bedford-Stuyvesant area. La Guardia apologized to Straus for Rheinstein's behavior and expressed regret for the article "with reservation," terming it "mediocre" and "amateurish."[28] On October 8, Rheinstein resigned. La Guardia, who was in Cincinnati for a World Series game, sent him a two-word telegram: RESIGNATION ACCEPTED.

Rheinstein received support in the press. La Guardia received denunciation. Said the *Times* on October 12, when publishing the letter, "The evidence is overwhelming that Mr. Straus . . . treated Mr. Rheinstein as if he were a subordinate employee of the federal government [and] New York as if it were a federal pensioner." Calling the administration's subservience to Washington a special cause for concern, the *Times* went on, "If Mayor La Guardia had put himself on a doormat [and] prostrated himself on the White House steps, he could not have brought the point home more convincingly."

La Guardia was not overly perturbed by the criticism. Straus approved the Bedford-Stuyvesant project area and assured him federal funding would continue. Given that Rheinstein, who had fought against red tape and official constrictions, posed the threat of becoming another Moses—and having one commissioner with so many enemies in Washington was the last thing he needed—La Guardia was happy that events had made possible his removal and the resumption of funding. But the *Times* was convinced that in looking for a new NYCHA chairman, he would come up with one "who will not mind being dropped like a hot potato whenever his opinions fail to coincide with what the Mayor believes to be expedient." The new chairman was the recently retired president of General Electric, Gerard Swope, who admitted, "I have not the remotest idea of policy."[29] Swope nevertheless proved to be acceptable. He was highly thought of in Washington.

The Rheinstein affair left an acrid taste in the mouths of those wondering if Fiorello was indeed morphing into the "Lost Leader." Not content with having disposed of Rheinstein, La Guardia was determined to humiliate him. In an obvious move to create the impression of malfeasance, he ordered Rheinstein's office sealed off by the Department of Investigation. Rheinstein was convinced that "the Mayor is playing politics in Washington and doing somersaults to every one in the national administration." Many agreed, including Ickes: "I told him that I was now certain that he was a candidate for something, otherwise he would not have supported Straus at the expense of Rheinstein." Surely such thinking would jibe with the headline run by the Communist organ *Daily Worker* when La Guardia, who had built a political career on his condemnation of the "Interests," appointed twenty-four-year-old oil heir David Rockefeller to a municipal post: "His Honor, Eye on the Vice Presidency, Figures a Good 'In' with the Rockefeller Clan Won't Hurt Him One Little Bit."[30]

In the November elections of 1939, Fusion suffered a severe setback, with the Democrats electing all sixteen of their candidates for the municipal courts and all nine city Supreme Court justices. In the City Council, they won twelve of the contested twenty-one seats. The 1937 election had given the Democrats enough votes to tie up almost any legislative proposals not to their liking. During some of the darkest days in the city's history, the council racked up a record of stalemate and inconsequential undertakings. Forty of the seventy-four local laws adopted dealt with changing street names or designating new streets. Important issues they failed to act upon included revision of the city's pension system, reorganization of the courts, and elimination or consolidation of all those Tammany-held county jobs. Now they had the two-thirds majority necessary to override any mayoral veto. Within four years the Democrats had gone from being an albatross around the neck of municipal reform to being able to dictate their own programs and maneuvers.

Addressing the opening of the new council on January 1, 1940, La Guardia began in a mood of nostalgia, recalling that it was exactly twenty years since he had assumed presidency of the old Board of Aldermen and admitting, "I had all the defects then that I have to-day, and I haven't improved a bit." Then, in an uncharacteristic mode of accommodation, he promised he would "understand fully every blow" the City Council struck, "because it is necessary for an executive to work with a legislative body."[31] But the Democratic majority did not feel it necessary to work with this particular executive. As an indication of things to come, the council organized itself at its first regular meeting, on January 22, 1940, that lasted a bare twenty minutes.

To obviate repetition of the organizational squabbles of 1938, Newbold Morris was continued as president and Democratic majority leader John Cashmore was made vice-president. New resolutions were quickly referred to committees. Next, the WNYC microphones were removed from the chamber. During the preceding two years, the regularly broadcast council debates had provided New Yorkers with the same kind of laugh-evoking entertainment present-day TV viewers are provided by the likes of Leno and Letterman. Now in complete control, Tammany wanted an end to making public fools of themselves. Morris then suggested that the press be barred from meetings, leading the *Herald Tribune* to conclude (January 23, 1940) that members could only behave with decorum and sensibility when denied "the heady intoxication of having people listen to them."

Barely had it gotten itself organized when the council decided, on February 6, to take a month's vacation. When it reconvened, the newly elected Alfred E. Smith Jr. called for an investigation of the Civil Service Commission and in particular of its chairman, Paul Kern. The number of city jobs exempt from Civil Service when La Guardia first came to office was more than a thousand. By the end of his first term these had been cut to six hundred, and rapid progress was being made to meet the goal of 250. Smith's intention here was to strike a blow at the La Guardia reform movement while at the same time winning the support of patronage-starved Democrats. There is little doubt that the éminence grise behind Smith's action was Robert Moses, who had retained close ties to the Smith family. He was determined to embarrass La Guardia and go after Kern, his number one bête noire. In Smith, who was commencing a political career that would never equal his famous father's, he had a willing ally.

The thirty-year-old Kern was a rebel from his college days whose cavalier attitude and bored indifference at council meetings further antagonized many of the members already put off by his belief that Communist teachers should not be barred from the schools unless they sought to indoctrinate their students. A confirmed intellectual and dedicated reformer, on graduating from Columbia Law School he was hired by then-Congressman La Guardia's Washington office. After eight months, Kern returned to teach at Columbia, from where La Guardia recruited him as his secretary following his election as mayor. He became at once a protégé and member of Fiorello's inner circle. Two years later he was promoted to the Civil Service Commission, of which he soon became chairman.

Smith's investigation, which went on into 1940 with increasing bitterness, was highlighted by charges that included, along with irrelevant issues, a number of unproved matters of malfeasance and nonfeasance. Kern alternated between insolence in his replies and silence. When La Guardia reappointed Kern to a full six-year term as chairman, the City Council took this as a slap in the face and vindication for Kern. Nevertheless, erosion had begun in the relationship between mentor and protégé. The administration was beginning to look bad, what with Smith's constant haranguing and Kern's overall attitude. Kern began to change from a shining light to a liability. Though the Smith investigation produced little except much noise and many newspaper headlines, plus an appreciable amount of embarrassment for La Guardia, it did realize at least one desired intent, the eventual destruction of Kern's promising political career.

The council's powers, and its ability to go after La Guardia, were strengthened by favorable judicial decisions. As mayor he believed he had the authority, under the new city charter, to veto resolutions establishing investigative committees and that, moreover, he and his commissioners were empowered to withhold information they deemed to be confidential. In 1939 a court ruled that Commissioner of Investigations Herlands must heed the subpoena of a council committee and reveal the full results of an inquiry he was conducting. La Guardia was furious. A later court decision forced him to appear before a council committee and hand over documents he insisted were privileged.

These decisions served to broaden the council's powers and add fuel to its investigative zeal at a time when the Democratic majority was only too willing to abuse what powers it already possessed. Concomitant with hounding City Hall and the Civil Service Commission was a nonstop inquiry into the city's relief programs and cuts in a budget La Guardia insisted had already been cut to the bone. In 1940, he sent twenty-nine separate messages vetoing such cuts. Despite the Democrats' numeral superiority, a few broke away from the fold, and the council could not come up with sufficient votes to override the vetoes. In the end, they refused to vote at all, and the La Guardia budget was adopted by default. Victory though it might have been, it was hardly a sweet one. La Guardia was no longer the man of considerable power he'd been when he first assumed command of the city.

Even more problematic than the mayor's conflict with the City Council was his confrontation with former council member Michael Quill, head of the New York Transport Workers Union. Quill failed to be reelected in 1939 when the American Labor Party refused to endorse him. By then La Guardia's determination to unify the city's transit system had been realized. For $326 million the city purchased a system that carried almost two billion passengers a year, five times the total carried by all the nation's railroads. Requisite legal procedures would require several months more, running into the spring of 1940. But problems arose immediately involving the status of the TWU's thirty-thousand members. How were the existing contracts with the heretofore private owners to be handled? Were the workers to be integrated into the Civil Service? And if so, would their contractual rights be protected?

In June 1939, the state legislature passed the Wicks Bill providing Civil Service status for all transit workers. This presented La Guardia with a dilemma. The bill was opposed by the TWU, a powerful affiliate of the CIO, which had strongly supported him in the last election. The union felt it would lose traditional rights, such as the closed shop and the right to strike. Also feared was that with the system, and its fixed five-cent fare, now in city hands, the question of profits through higher fares was a moot point—except to the workers, who needed a higher fare to increase their bargaining power. La Guardia insisted that Civil Service status was the only means of preventing a massive increase of exempt positions, a potentially powerful instrument of patronage.[32]

Governor Lehman wanted his opinion. La Guardia considered the legislation premature, hoping that the city might be able to handle the problem by local legislation. As the deadline for signing or vetoing the bill neared, Lehman wired La Guardia for instructions. Waiting till the last day, he wired back that he favored the bill being signed "provided and if you can guarantee to keep the courts off my neck and that the courts will not interfere, disturb, or otherwise prevent carrying out exactly what you and I have done in this matter."[33] Lehman signed the bill, remarking that the mayor's telegram was "not clear." It was, in fact, an exercise in verbal gibberish. But it did serve a desired purpose: adding tens of thousands of transport workers to the Civil Service rolls.

Quill was furious. La Guardia promised him there would be no immediate changes in labor policy—with one exception: "No employee's [Civil Service] status will depend upon his affiliation with any labor union organization." Rejecting the right of transit workers to strike, he also stated categorically that the city would not tolerate the closed shop.[34] This from a staunchly prolabor congressman who had spoken out forcefully in favor of the closed shop. But La Guardia drew a distinction between private industry and the municipal workforce. A transit strike would cause undue hardship on the city, he could have argued, though whether that justified denying the basic right of the workers to strike was still a difficult stance for him of all people to defend.

Defiantly denouncing La Guardia as the "bankers' puppet," Quill got from his men blanket authorization for a strike, to be carried out at such time as their leaders might decide. For the present, he urged an immediate march on City Hall by the workers and their families to demonstrate just how large an army was ready to fight the administration. The demonstration, set for March 13 while the City

Council was away on its month-long vacation, went off peacefully as La Guardia, after crossing the picket line, announced that he would confer with Quill on the following Monday. The conference was attended by CIO head John L. Lewis, thus opening the way for a compromise settlement. It was agreed that the right to strike would be referred to lawyers on both sides. A second meeting was held March 26, at which La Guardia insisted that a closed shop and the right to strike were illegal and unconstitutional when applied to Civil Service.

After two hours of heated wrangling, La Guardia caved in to the extent of a willingness to submit to the Transit Commission the contracts of the transit workers as they existed under preunification private management. Nevertheless, Quill insisted his men would walk out. But not quite yet. An understanding was reached between La Guardia and Lewis that all unresolved issues would be referred to the courts as they arose. Next day, the *Times* termed this "postponement and evasion." Mayor La Guardia had undermined his brave stance in March that had brought on the crisis: "The right to strike against the government is not and cannot be recognized." Now he was saying it was the courts that would decide the existence of such a right.

A year later (March 1941) Quill called a strike of all bus lines, resulting in the severest transportation tie-up since the subway motormen's strike of 1926. The subways were dangerously jammed. After eleven days both sides agreed to binding arbitration, and again Quill came out the winner. He now threatened to follow up with a subway stoppage unless the city agreed to negotiate closed-shop agreements to replace those expiring on June 30. At a Madison Square Garden rally, La Guardia was charged with being a strikebreaker and his name was booed. Renegotiating of the contracts began, with union leaders arguing that nothing precluded negotiation of collective bargaining contracts with employees having Civil Service status, and again his "antilabor attitude" was condemned.

Infuriated by Quill's charge that he was "an erstwhile friend" of labor, La Guardia retorted that he was "not going to fail in my duty for the sake of mistaken popularity. I believe my contribution to American labor will long be remembered when present trends of force and violence have been eliminated from the American labor movement." Quill was not impressed. While the contract negotiations went on, La Guardia appealed to President Roosevelt that the subways be put in the business of carrying mail if the threatened strike were carried out. This would qualify them for federal protection. Roosevelt sent a memorandum to the postmaster general approving La Guardia's request, But after Ickes opposed it in a cabinet meeting the memorandum was ordered destroyed. John L. Lewis again entered the negotiations, the basic issues were left to the courts and to the future, and again a subway strike was averted. (There would not be one until more than a quarter of a century later, at the start of the Lindsay administration—with Quill still head of the TWU and making life miserable for all New Yorkers who depended upon the subways.)

The *Herald Tribune* (April 10, 1941) defined the course La Guardia had adopted as that of "a wise physician," adding, "Statesmanship is made up of that sort of thing." But in an article in the *New Republic* (May 5, 1941) he was accused of seeming to have forgotten everything he knew about collective bargaining, making eleventh-hour concessions to the transportation workers, attempting to cut the ground from under their leaders, and pushing through a bill mandating prison sentences for vandalism against subways, which was seen as a "clumsy club" to hold over the head of the unions. In short, "La Guardia was provocative in more than his usually picturesque way."

There is no denying that his behavior was influenced considerably by his feelings toward Quill. When John L. Lewis came to town to enter the negotiations, La Guardia said, "I want you to know, Lewis, that no one is going to pull a subway strike, especially not that goddamned friend of yours. . . . Tell him to take the next boat back to Ireland." When Lewis replied, "Come, come, we're reasonably good Americans," La Guardia screamed, "Reasonably good Americans!" and then let fly with a stream of obscenities.[35]

5.

La Guardia's next exercise in inducing justifiably adverse criticism was about, of all things, a teaching appointment at City College of New York.

On October 1, 1939, the Board of Higher Education of New York City named renowned British mathematician and philosopher Bertrand Russell as a professor in these disciplines at CCNY. Russell was a half-century ahead of his time when it came to sexual attitudes. In his *Education and the Good Life* and *Marriage and Morals*, published years before the CCNY appointment, he expressed confidence that "university life would be better, both intellectually and morally," if most students entered into temporary childless marriages "that would afford a solution to the sexual urge neither restless nor surreptitious, neither mercenary nor casual, and of such nature that it need not take up time that should be given to work." He advocated that all sexual practices that did not involve children should be regarded as a purely private matter. Adultery was not only permissible, it was even desirable. As for Christianity, "Through its whole history it has been a force tending toward mental disorders and unwholesome views of life."[36]

Though the books were attacked when published, by the time Russell accepted a position at the University of California at the start of World War II they were forgotten by all except the author's devotees—and William T. Manning, Episcopal Bishop of New York. Manning was one of those intolerant ecclesiastics to whom views contrary to their own are not only a personal affront but, more heinous, a mortal sin in the eyes of their Maker. When Russell's appointment was announced, Manning, joined by the Catholic clergy, set off an uproar that divided public opinion and put La Guardia in an embarrassing position—a position from which he would emerge less than honorably.

La Guardia's violent opposition to the suppression of free thought within the European dictatorships did not apply when controversial and unpopular opinions such as Russell's were being expressed closer to home. He complained to the Board of Higher Education, "Why is it that we always select someone with a boil on his neck or a blister on his fanny? I don't think we ought to get a collection of damaged goods."[37] In an address before news vendors La Guardia insisted, "I am not a prude." Fiorello may have believed that, but few concurred. When his secretary, Anna Clark, visited Washington, he demanded she stay at a hotel where residents had to be in by midnight. When he offered to drive his aide Mitzi Somach home at the end of the workday while going home himself in his city car, he made sure a third person in addition to the driver accompanied them. This sort of thing might have been viewed by his colleagues as one more of the mayor's amiable foibles that added to his charm. But with the Russell appointment, many others began to have second thoughts.[38]

On March 14, the City Council adopted a resolution ordering the Board of Higher Education to rescind the appointment. Three days later came a note from C. C. Burlingham: "I'm sure you won't let our anachronistic cinquecento [fifteenth century] Bishop or the Tammany Enquirer press you to press the Board of Higher Education to press the adulterous Peer out of his post."[39] But that is precisely what La Guardia did. He profusely apologized to Bishop Manning for the appointment and promised to act "within the limits of such powers as I have." These included pressure on the Board of Higher Education. The board voted eleven to seven against reconsidering the appointment. A taxpayer's suit brought the matter into the courts and led the state legislature to vote for an inquiry into the activities of Communists and other subversives in the New York City schools.

The court decision came rapidly. On March 31, Justice John E. McGeehan, a Catholic who once sought to have the portrait of Martin Luther deleted from a city mural illustrating the history of religions, ruled Lord Russell unfit for the position, as his attitudes toward sex were "immoral and salacious" and hiring him would be a "direct violation of the public health, safety and morals of the people." McGeehan also condemned CCNY for "in effect establishing a chair in indecency." Besides, he added, Russell wasn't an American citizen.[40] When La Guardia's budget for the coming fiscal year was presented on April 6, it was noted that he had ordered excision of the $8,800 funding for the Russell post, in keeping "with the policy to eliminate vacant positions." On the same day, two thousand CCNY students left their classrooms in protest and at a Carnegie Hall rally urged restoration of the funds and called for an appeal of the McGeehan decision.

Under pressure from La Guardia, Corporation Counsel Chanler announced that his office would not take the Russell case to a higher court, using as a face-saving excuse that it was a poor case on which to base an appeal, and there was "the gravest danger" that the lower court's decision might be sustained. When—again, on La Guardia's orders—Chanler refused permission for a special counsel to handle an appeal, the Board of Higher Education named a special counsel of its own. Meanwhile, at the University of California, Russell was barred from continuing in his post, which he had decided to do rather than "subvert" the people of New York.[41]

La Guardia was roundly taken to task, not only within his own official family but outside as well. What particularly hurt was a letter from John Dewey, one of the nation's foremost educators, who expressed shock at his refusal to allow an appeal and went on, "I have regarded you as a person who could be counted on to do the straightforward thing independent of political pressure." On April 18, Burlingham condemned Fiorello's denying the Board of Education the right to appeal "as high-handed." Burlingham admitted the Russell appointment was "foolish" and said he could appreciate "how abhorrent Russell's doctrines are to you." But why, he insisted, "should a man with your record in a free country do to the CCNY what the Nazis have done" to the universities of Heidelberg and Bonn? La Guardia's attempt, said Burlingham in summation, "to dispose of the case while it was in the courts was bad enough, but to prevent the Board appealing to higher courts is far worse. . . . It is not like *you*." La Guardia rebuffed his longtime mentor with the nonsensical charge that "the pressure groups are certainly bearing down on you. A lawyer [Chanler] has advised his client [the Mayor] not to appeal, and the client has accepted. . . . That is all there is to that."[42]

It was Russell himself who resolved the whole shameful episode by accepting a teaching position with the Barnes Foundation in Merion, Pennsylvania. The Board of Higher Education voted fifteen to two to drop the case. Overall, the entire Russell affair tarnished La Guardia's reputation as a man of integrity, but the damage was not fatal to his career. Indeed, he seemed to be as unaffected by the affair as he was by not being in top form physically, to the degree that his personal physician, Dr. George Baehr, was forbidding him to make any appointments at night. In May, Burlingham told him, "I am so worried that you are not taking proper care of yourself. Here you are, when you should be resting, in so many activities and giving so much of yourself to each of them."[43]

6.

Much of what La Guardia set out to do as mayor had been accomplished, and visions of high federal office were dancing in his head.

As president of the United States Conference of Mayors he spoke out on major issues of the day, especially the European war as it affected the United States. His style was less confrontational than that of his years in Congress. He delivered many a thoughtful speech, as when while in San Francisco he was asked to comment on the fascist regimes in Europe: "They are burning the books of the sages and the philosophers, but they must know that we are writing the history of their miserable deeds. . . . Oh, yes, the dictators are now in the limelight, but they are in the light of a setting sun; they are in a light that cannot endure."[44]

He supported President Roosevelt's call for a "quarantine" of aggressor nations and an end to the neutrality laws that prohibited the sale of much-needed planes to England and France. After Hitler's occupation of Czechoslovakia, La Guardia attacked American supporters of Germany as "international cooties." He advocated the idea that the country could neither stay out of a European war nor avoid taking sides. In doing so, he broke with his quondam congressional allies the midwestern Progressives, who were now among America's leading isolationists. Only a year before, he was being overwhelmed with adulation by many of the leading American universities. But in the spring of 1940, when C. C. Burlingham sounded out Harvard about awarding La Guardia an honorary law degree, they "looked him over, and decided he would not do."[45]

He was spending more time away from City Hall than had Jimmy Walker, and complaints were being raised, especially by the Democrats. Not that they missed him. They merely exploited a reason to condemn him. In fact, they would have supported him for higher office—as a way of getting him out of City Hall. Most New Yorkers didn't seem to mind their Little Flower's rushing around the country having his say. They understood his political ambitions. "Mayor's Views Have Received Attention as Those of a National Figure," ran a typical hometown newspaper headline.[46]

While his attitudes and opinions were not to be faulted—save by his targets, in particular the foreign dictators and the home-grown politicians whose bodies were in the twentieth century but whose thinking was in the tenth—there is no gainsaying that his eye was on the coming presidential election. Asked by a reporter in Louisiana about his plans for 1940, La Guardia replied he was too busy running New York City to give much thought to that: "The man in office who has his eye on another office is like the automobile driver with a pretty girl at his side—he can't keep his mind on his work."[47] But then, this was the man who stood up in public and said, "I am not a prude."

Whether Roosevelt had or had not by then decided to break with tradition and seek a third term is still a matter of conjecture for historians.[48] The popular assumption was that his second term was his last. Still, this was only an assumption. He seemed to be playing a suspiciously conniving game of suggesting and then discounting first one possibility, then another. Cordell Hull was most prominently mentioned, though few believed the secretary of state, known for being tight-lipped and void of passion, was presidential timber.

That Roosevelt might indeed seek a third term was an idea La Guardia apparently was not eager to entertain. Nor was he eager to embrace the idea of a La Guardia draft being entertained by many, an idea for which a convincing case was made by Rex Tugwell "on the ground of unfinished business," in a debate with fellow Brain Truster Raymond Moley before the *Herald Tribune* Forum in October 1938. There was a swift reaction from La Guardia. He called Tugwell in the next day "and denounced me furiously. It was the highest temper I had ever seen him display, and I had seen a number of such exhibitions. It took him about a week to calm down, during which he raged in diminuendo every day."

Tugwell told him "he was betraying a dangerous weakness, which he could not afford. He had set his heart on something so unlikely [occupying the White House] that he ought not to have entertained it even as a vague idea. I regretted his hurt." But a La Guardia candidacy "was just not possible." He would never get the Democratic nomination. "The politicians would be in control there. Roosevelt could force the selection of himself but he could not force anyone else's selection."[49]

When La Guardia calmed down after a week, he was realistic enough to accept that the country would never take seriously the candidacy of someone who was half-Italian and half-Jewish. But would ethnicity preclude his chances of getting the second spot on the ticket? Early in 1939 Adolf Berle came up from Washington to lunch with him and report that Roosevelt was not interested in a third term and would be satisfied with Hull—provided that the convention gave the second spot to a Progressive. Among those suggested by Roosevelt were Harry Hopkins and Fiorello H. La Guardia. La Guardia told Berle he could not envision getting through the convention: "The son of a wop who lives in a tenement doesn't become vice-president," he told one associate.[50]

Yet by the spring of 1940, involved as he was in the Quill and Russell messes, La Guardia appeared to be sending out mixed signals. Speaking in March before the City Affairs Committee, he described as the ideal candidate for the presidency a man who eschews "fads, fancies, and hobbies" and has "a brain, a heart, and a soul ready to deal with real problems." Lest the audience miss the point that the description was eminently applicable to him, he remarked somewhat ruefully that his current job was that of "a glorified janitor" with no power to affect directly political and economic issues on a national scale. "Yet, I must think about them." La Guardia was more than "thinking about them"—he was running around the country orating about them. When the names of Roosevelt and Garner were filed for the Illinois presidential primary, La Guardia's name also appeared, on a petition with four thousand signatures. "Are you kidding?" he commented when told, and immediately withdrew his name and reiterated his support for the Democratic ticket.

But the speculation about La Guardia went on—speculation he did little to stifle. At the end of April, he and Berle met again to talk over "various and strange things," of which the strangest was whether Fiorello could run as a vice presidential candidate on a ticket with Hull. "Of course," Berle confided to his diary, "it may not work out, for the President may decide to run."[51] With the political picture altered by the intensification of the European war, it soon became obvious Roosevelt would indeed run. Talk of a Hull-La Guardia ticket gave way to talk of a cabinet post for "my great friend Fiorello." Even before announcing for reelection, FDR decided to reorganize his cabinet and told Harold Ickes he had La Guardia in mind to replace Henry Woodring as secretary of war. It was a post La Guardia coveted, and one for which many close to FDR considered him quite suited.

When word got out, Roosevelt was bombarded by messages from La Guardia's closest friends high in Democratic circles that he was too important, too needed, as New York's mayor to be called to Washington. Even Berle had to admit that La Guardia leaving New

York posed the threat of a return to total Tammany control. Ickes, who knew how much La Guardia wanted a cabinet post, told FDR it was important he remain in New York where, with his liberal record, he could crack down on subversives: "Few men have the courage and intelligence to fight for ideals that La Guardia has." (Ickes also confided—not to the president but to his diary on March 15, 1940—that he opposed La Guardia as secretary of war, adding, "Besides, I'd like it myself.")

Even Governor Lehman told the president privately that La Guardia was the best man—perhaps the only man—qualified to handle the espionage and fifth column activity, as well as actions of the city's radical elements that were sure to become major problems as the nation moved toward war. (It is suspected that Lehman's support derived in large measure from being jealous of La Guardia's prospects.) Editorialized the *News* (January 11, 1941), "We don't . . . want Butch to get a Cabinet job. We want him to stay right on as Mayor of New York City. . . . La Guardia has been and is, in our estimation, the greatest mayor New York ever had. . . . He is the ideal Mayor for a time like this, when the war across the ocean is pulling the various racial groups' heartstrings every which way."

Also opposed to the idea, though for different reasons, was Burlingham, who told Seabury, "I hope he will not be such an ass as to go into Roosevelt's cabinet. He would only be a tool." He said as much to La Guardia: "You won't get anything by cuddling up to Franklin. He doesn't give a damn for you. I am perfectly sure he would chuck you out in a minute."[52] FDR's liking La Guardia notwithstanding, Burlingham's reading of the man was right on target. If La Guardia had been taken into the cabinet, he could well have learned the hard way—as Burlingham wisely perceived—what others had in the past and would in the future. Roosevelt was more than, in the words of Justice Oliver Wendell Holmes, "a second-rate intellect with a first-class temperament." He was also a crafty user of people with a charming faculty for ridding himself of those who no longer served his purpose, either suggesting, with a broad smile, that they submit their resignations or lauding them profusely while dumping them unceremoniously.

On June 20, 1940, Roosevelt named a nationally known and highly respected Republican, Henry Stimson, to replace Woodring. Whether he ever seriously considered Fiorello for the post is yet another matter best left to speculation. What most influenced his naming Stimson was the decision to form a coalition government as the nation moved toward war. (In addition to Stimson, fellow Republican Frank Knox was named secretary of the Navy.) Moreover, La Guardia was of greater value as the New Deal's leading booster in the nation's leading city. And not to be discounted is that, much as he liked and admired him, Roosevelt had to have been concerned about La Guardia's unpredictable temperament and willingness to work as a team member.

Whatever disappointment he felt—and it must have been considerable—La Guardia publicly supported the Stimson appointment. When the hope that he might succeed Secretary of Labor Frances Perkins, who was said to be resigning, petered out following her decision to stay on, he had to accept that there was no place for him in the president's official family—at this time. This did not deter him from campaigning vigorously for FDR and joining with Senator George Norris to form Independents for Roosevelt. He attacked the Republicans as the "kept party" of big business and their candidate, Wendell Willkie, as "the polished front of this shameful enterprise." Words of opprobrium like "pimp" and "whore" literally flew out of Fiorello's mouth. Recalls Paul Windels, "It was simply incredible how he spoke against Willkie—personally vituperative. . . . I suppose he wanted to make a big hit with Roosevelt." Windels noted that by now "FH," as La Guardia was known to intimates, was no longer the man "he used to be. The job was beginning to tell on him."[53]

FH's support for the Democratic ticket proved to be his undoing with the Fusion leadership, in particular Seabury, whom La Guardia accused of harboring an "obsessive hatred of Roosevelt." Obsessive hatred of some of the men around Roosevelt—in particular, the big-city "bosses"—would have been closer to the mark. Seabury and the other Fusion leaders resented what they saw as Fiorello's abandoning his reform principles to make a Faustian pact with the pro-Roosevelt likes of New York's Flynn, Jersey's Hague, Chicago's Kelly, Missouri's Pendergast, Tennessee's Crump, and "the remains of the Huey Long boodle organization in New Orleans." La Guardia's defense: "Hitler understands the language of Roosevelt."[54]

La Guardia could not be certain of reelection were he to go for his own third term. There was scant enthusiasm among the New Deal

Democrats. He had no support in his own Republican Party, save for the minority reformers. The Progressives had turned on him, and the Socialists and independents as political forces were insignificant. And now he had broken with the Fusion. Despite his prominence and popularity not only in New York City but throughout the country, Fiorello La Guardia had become, at this point in time, a man without a party.

But whether he even cared for a third term is questionable. "How could a man stand four more years in this office?" La Guardia demanded of columnist Marquis Childs. Adolf Berle, who was in constant contact with La Guardia and was privy to his thinking, noted in February 1941, "Marie does not want him to run for a third term in New York and neither does he." In fact, he had already promised Marie that he would not put them both through another campaign and another term of office. Whether he really meant it or was challenging Seabury and all those quondam boosters who had criticized his support of the New Deal to find a man better qualified to accomplish for the city all La Guardia had done in eight years is yet another of those unanswerable questions. But, giving him the benefit of the doubt, La Guardia was indeed speaking from the heart when he said, "It takes more than a human body to take eight years of that kind of punishment."[55]

Undecided about his future, consumed with helping reelect Roosevelt, continuing his fight against corruption, preparing the city for the coming war, coping not only with his Democratic enemies on the City Council but his disillusioned Fusion backers, further enhancing his national reputation through constant travel and speechifying—La Guardia may have lost his initial enthusiasm and was operating as mayor on half-speed. But he was still better at the job than any of his predecessors.

In August 1940 came another addition to an already full political plate when Roosevelt named him chairman of the American side of the U.S.-Canadian Joint Permanent Defense Board. He treated the challenge of planning the coordinated defense of the North American continent as a personal one. His take-charge leadership and penchant for bullying his way toward solutions endeared him to the board's members on both sides. They saw it as the only way of fulfilling their assigned task. Said the *Times* on August 27, just weeks after his appointment, "In exactly six and one-half minutes all the formalities were cleared and all the courtesies were accomplished. The board decided from the outset [at the American cochairman's far from subtle prodding] to use plain, everyday understandable English and to dispense with the complexities involved in diplomatic usage and in legalisms."

7.

After Roosevelt won his third term, the question of whether La Guardia would seek his own third term came again under scrutiny. Never the most forgiving of men, he took after those, including the Fusionists, who had accused him of siding with the Democratic bosses during the campaign, charges he described as "filth." In an open letter that Burlingham rightly described as the egregiously imprudent screed of an aggrieved, quarrelsome man whose rein on his emotions was appallingly frail, La Guardia condemned his critics for supporting Willkie, reminding them that he was a free man with the right to work for whomever he considered the best candidate, accused them of having done "irreparable damage" to the cause of reform, and took pride in having accomplished for New York what they had never achieved and would never have achieved without him. Finding comfort in the New Testament (2 Timothy 4:7), Fiorello more than implied that he would not run again: "I have fought the good fight. I have finished my course. I have kept the faith." Said Burlingham, "I wish you had a secretary or a friend who had the courage to tell you not to send a letter which you should destroy before you sign it."[56]

But he didn't. What's more, he meant it about not running again.

He was planning to relocate to Washington, more confident than ever that there would yet be a place for him in the new cabinet. But it was not to be. Roosevelt had decided that La Guardia properly belonged back in New York City. "Mr. La Guardia is understood to have been informed of the way the President feels about the situation through a third person," reported the *Times* on March 30, 1941. This was the day after Bronx boss Flynn, reflecting the view of others high in the Democratic political firmament that La Guardia should run for a third term, told an audience at Chapel Hill in North Carolina that the Little Flower was "one of the best mayors that New York ever had." Whether the fine hand of FDR was behind what seemed to be a movement to "draft" a reluctant La Guardia is anybody's guess. What is *not* anybody's guess was that within weeks La Guardia was backing away from his explicit avowals of the past. "In these days no one can say with any degree of certainty just what he will or will not do," he said, adding, "I prefer not to run again for Mayor of the City of New York."[57]

The key word here is "prefer." Simply stated, if those who were vocalizing about his indispensability really meant it, he would allow himself to be persuaded. The same day, as if having waited for the proper cue, a group of leading figures in the arts, business, and politics announced formation of the Citizens Non-Partisan Movement to Draft La Guardia for Mayor. La Guardia's response, issued that same day: Since a third term was all right in the case of the president, "it would be all right in my case [provided] we do not get into the habit of perpetuity in office."[58]

Meanwhile, he established plans for coping with the coming war. Unknown to the FBI and Army intelligence, he formed a "sabotage squad," made up of 180 specially trained police officers whose mission was to infiltrate and report on potentially subversive groups. In addition, he coordinated with the FBI surveillance activities in the city's German and Italian communities. His hint that he would seek a third term notwithstanding, La Guardia obviously still held out hope of a cabinet post. He wrote a memo to the president containing a detailed plan for a director of civil defense. "The new technique of war," he said, "has created the necessity for developing a new technique of civilian defense" that must be more than "just community singing, sweater knitting and basket weaving." What was needed was the creation of a home defense among the civilian population, "to be trained to meet any possibility of an air or naval attack in any of our cities." The plan was well thought out and patently logical in its approach to protecting the civilian population—and, believed La Guardia, who would "be very glad to cooperate and help" in its implementation, the post should be of cabinet level.[59]

A week later Anna Rosenberg, a trusted Roosevelt aide serving as confidential messenger between the White House and City Hall, assured the president, who was all for the plan, that Fiorello would accept appointment as director of the Office of Civilian Defense without cabinet status—provided he could sit in on cabinet meetings. Roosevelt approved. On May 18, after presiding over a mammoth preparedness rally of close to seven hundred New Yorkers, La Guardia flew to Washington and accepted the unpaid position of civil defense czar.[60]

His responsibilities embraced "everything from protecting civilians from bomb raids that may never come to seeing that babies get proper food, and includes the amorphous assignment of improving civilian morale." Structuring the administration alone would take four months—and La Guardia would be running for office at the same time.[61] Why he took on such a Herculean double task, especially in view of recurring health problems, can be explained away by the dream—admittedly fanciful but still one to be entertained—that he might become president in time. And if war came, which seemed logical, directorship of OCD could become one of the nation's most important posts—and keep him in the national spotlight. But whether he was up to handling both jobs, plus continuing as chairman of the U.S.-Canadian Joint Permanent Defense Board, remained to be seen.

Ickes, for one, thought it "absurd on the face of it." He conceded that no one was "better qualified to head Civilian Defense" than New York's mayor, but "he has to eat and sleep like other human beings."[62] The *Times*, in a piece by the esteemed columnist Arthur Krock (May 22, 1941), suggested La Guardia stick to running the city and leave the job of organizing civilian defense to others. La Guardia disagreed. What's more, his activities became even more frenzied, as indicated by a letter to Burlingham: "I am rushing for a meeting with the U.S.-Canadian Joint Defense Board. Am speaking in Philadelphia tonight and will return to Washington. Monday here [New York], Tuesday and Wednesday, Boston, Thursday here, Friday, Baltimore, and Saturday Columbus . . . most of next week in Washington."[63] He adhered to a schedule of flying to Washington early Tuesday morning for three days of work and returning to New York on Thursday nights, unless there was a cabinet meeting, when he would not return home until the next day. And then there were those numerous brief visits he made all around the country. To concerned friends telling him that he was doing too much, La Guardia insisted he was just putting in "a little overtime." The fervor with which he threw himself into his defense work suggests that here was a man whose total dedication to his mission was equaled by the feeling that he still had to prove himself.

He planned a force of United States Guards for around-the-clock protection of national defense plants, railroad beds, and reservoirs, coordinated emergency plans for the states, recruited fire and air raid wardens, studied defense and evacuation plans for the cities, and set into motion a program of lessons in defending against industrial and chemical espionage. He took it upon himself to mediate between the government and blacks who complained of being discriminated against in the defense industries. In his added position as "Protector of Morale," La Guardia precluded a threatened march on Washington by tens of thousands of blacks determined to publicize economic discrimination, by calling upon representatives from industry, labor, the black community, and government to "come in and thrash it out right then and there" at the White House. He also took it upon himself to advise the president on proposed changes in Social Security and what types of airplanes should be purchased. Tugwell found Fiorello "positively swollen with importance."[64]

According to Roosevelt confidant Bernard Baruch, Fiorello was getting in the president's hair. And in just about everyone else's as well. He was doing in OCD what he had done in New York: involving himself in even the minutest details instead of delegating authority. But whereas in New York he had only five boroughs to tear around in like a spastic hen, now he had forty-eight states. Baruch told Ickes in confidence, "He is too spectacular to keep his feet on the ground." La Guardia's OCD mandate called for coordinating regional defense groups through the governors. He irritated them by moving his own appointees into their states. He organized mock bombing raids and full-dress rescue drills that were laughable, since we were not yet at war, and being bombed by Germany, if we did get into the European war, was not even considered a remote possibility. He ran around the country, averaging two speeches a day, screaming about impending attacks, spending freely, and fairly screeching about awareness and readiness. It all smacked of scare tactics and manufactured crises. A people confident of the unlikelihood of an attack on the nation could not take him seriously. Yet here was this little dynamo rushing hither and yon, asking for fifty million gas masks for the entire Atlantic, Pacific, and Gulf coasts population and ordering hospitals to spend hours planning for emergencies and to set aside materials and equipment that could not be spared. His demand for a seventy-million-dollar home defense program struck many as excessive. One day he'd be planning recreation and health facilities in training camps, the next day he'd be involved in writing booklets outlining the duties of air raid wardens. That he was overstepping his bounds occurred to everyone except himself. Nor did it ever occur to him that when he did come up with an idea worthy of consideration, little heed was paid. According to Baruch, the president considered it a blessing he had not taken La Guardia into the cabinet![65]

The other half of his job as OCD head, that of establishing a propaganda bureau, had been allowed to languish as the FBI, the OSS (precursor of the CIA), and the OCD squabbled over how to divide up propaganda and internal surveillance. In what he intended as an astute move—in essence a way to raise OCD's visibility as well as heighten the president's interest in his work—La Guardia named the president's wife as codirector to handle the propaganda aspect of the job. The move was shrewd—but ill advised, given their differences in background and approach to public service.

Eleanor, who personally admired Fiorello, expected good manners from associates and believed that politics was an arena in which doing good work was the sine qua non. Fiorello saw politics as a profession and threw cold water on the rules of etiquette with his favorite expression, "lousy." It's possible—not necessarily probable, but possible—that the two might have arrived at some modus vivendi had they been able to sit down and iron out their different approaches to the job at hand. But La Guardia lacked the time and inclination to sit down and iron out. He could only make rapid-fire decisions and move on.

On top of everything, he was busy running for reelection.

CHAPTER TWENTY-ONE

"This is your friend La Guardia speaking"

1.

Few took seriously La Guardia's announcement that he would have preferred to retire but was unable to ignore "the call of the electorate." Especially when he publicly recited a list of his accomplishments over two terms and attacked "boss rule" as an epidemiologist would attack an outbreak of bubonic plague. Had he been given a federal post, he would not have run. But he wasn't, so he did. In the spring of 1941, Adolf Berle suggested to Ed Flynn the possibility of a Democratic endorsement. With Washington's tacit backing, La Guardia could be presented to the voters as the city's "defense mayor." Replied the Bronx boss and national party chairman, "The boys wouldn't stand for it."[1] The "boys" were, of course, the county bosses. As James A. Roe of Queens put it, they wanted a certified Democrat, not a Fusionist, a Socialist, or a Communist—which is to say, not a Little Flower. They chose Brooklyn district attorney William O'Dwyer, a future mayor.

Despite the feeling of their leaders toward Fiorello, the Republicans realized they could never hope to elect a candidate by themselves in a city where the Democrats outnumbered them five to one. Their only hope lay in allying themselves with the Fusion, which announced on July 21, 1941, that it would seek La Guardia's reelection. But the Fusion was a shadow of its former self: "Though it could still be counted upon, [it] had progressively declined as a political factor; it was now little more than a line on the ballot."[2] Militating in Fiorello's favor were his impressive record after almost eight years in office and his popularity, which had never waned. For the *Times*, his running again meant "a good day for New York." Full support was promised by the *Herald Tribune*, *P.M.*, and *World Telegram*. Of all the papers, the most laudable editorial came from the *Daily News* (May 24, 1941), which, ironically, would soon turn against him: "In New York City are to be found the country's widest extremes of wealth and poverty, plus the biggest assortment of racial stresses and strains. Yet it runs along on a good-natured, even keel, and La Guardia must be credited with much of that during his first two terms."

Organizing the ticket started with sharp controversy over renomination of Stanley Isaacs for Manhattan borough president. His record on the City Council was as faultless as the intelligence and capability he brought to his office, but he had rendered himself unacceptable by appointing Simon Gerson, an openly avowed Communist, to a confidential post. While admitting the appointment was a mistake, Isaacs refused to remove him. La Guardia had no choice but to drop Isaacs from the ticket. Not to do so could well have jeopardized his own reelection. Isaacs pleaded for the renomination, but in vain. The Fusionists were prepared to back him but decided it would be wise to defer to the Republicans, who insisted on Edgar Nathan, a prominent attorney. Isaacs ran for the City Council on an independent ticket, pledging his full support to La Guardia and his entire slate. It is testimony to the inflexible, imprudent, yet honorable Isaacs that he was not only elected to the council but served with distinction as minority leader until his death in 1962.

As for the rest of the slate, City Comptroller McGoldrick and City Council President Morris were renominated, and Republican Justice Matthew J. Troy was picked to run against Democrat John Cashmore for Brooklyn borough president. The choices for Queens, the Bronx, and Staten Island do not merit our attention. What does, though, is the other top spot on the ticket, that of Manhattan district attorney. Whether or not Dewey would run again with the Fusion was something he declined to divulge, and neither the Democrats nor Republicans had a prospective candidate on tap. Injecting a dollop of

surrealism, the Tammany Democrats announced that they were prepared to nominate Republican Dewey, conditional on his working
against La Guardia's candidacy. Appealing though the idea was,
Dewey feared this could prove disadvantageous to his own political
future. That, plus a canvass that revealed he had little to no support
from any other party, led Dewey to announce on July 3 that he would
not seek reelection and hoped one of his four assistants would succeed him. The picture became even more surreal the following day
when Tammany announced it would back one of the four—Frank S.
Hogan, who had distinguished himself by sending a number of sachems to jail!

Not only were the Republican and Fusion leaders bowled over, so
was Hogan. "In other words," observed the *Times* in summing up the
situation, "Tammany is ready to take a plea of guilty on all the political trials of the past six years if it can remove Mayor La Guardia
from City Hall."[3] The Republicans, now stuck with La Guardia, were
in a state of panic, but La Guardia's supporters saw a way out. If the
GOP also named Hogan, they assumed, what amounted to a vote of
confidence in Dewey's choice would get Dewey to campaign actively
for La Guardia. It turned out to be a wise assumption. Dewey told
Burlingham, "C. C., I shouldn't do this for the son-of-a-bitch, but
we're going to give him the endorsement again."[4]

The "son-of-a-bitch" had first to campaign in the primary, against the
ultra-conservative, isolationist Republican John R. Davies, who ran as
an independent. The party hierarchs hoped that somehow he might
win the GOP nomination and thus spare them from having to support La Guardia in the general election. La Guardia decided to be
an active nonparticipant in the primary, confident that he could take
the support of the voters for granted. He had no campaign headquarters, made no speeches, and continued with his routine of flying
regularly to Washington on OCD business and to attend cabinet
meetings, presiding over the U.S. Conference of Mayors, speaking at
Defense Day rallies in major cities, and, back home, fighting with
the City Council over county reform and with Michael Quill over
transit. Davies sang a set of variations on the theme: New Dealers
and left-wingers were an infinitely greater menace than "bosses" and
"ward heelers." La Guardia trounced Davies, but the voting was light,
with only 4 percent of the enrolled Republicans going to the polls.

Preelection estimates had been 23 to 30 percent. The GOP regulars were now left with the inevitable: Either back La Guardia or sit out the election and let the Democrats regain City Hall by default. They made the obvious choice. Three factors militated in their favor: a major voter registration drive led personally by La Guardia; his promise "to take up and lead the fight," warning his opponent, "Don't count on laryngitis"; and the Democratic candidate himself.

O'Dwyer, who as Brooklyn's district attorney had proved himself exceptionally good at crime busting, proved himself exceptionally bad at campaigning. His bringing nothing new to the table in the way of issues save criticism of the incumbent's management of the city went over with the electorate like a lead balloon. One new element the Democrats introduced into the campaign—Communism—proved disastrous. No one believed the charge that Fiorello was a party member any more than anyone believed James Farley's ludicrous claim that La Guardia was the "favorite son of Stalin." The more they knocked La Guardia, the broader his support grew among the Democratic voters. Labor backed him. Powerful civic groups backed him. Leading Republican figures backed him—including Robert Moses. Moses allowed he had "no brief for the Mayor's bad manners," criticized "his excursions into [Washington], where they give him nothing but the husks and the leavings," and even had a few choice words about the Little Flower's habit of rushing off to fires and thus taking up space that might be better allotted to a hook and ladder truck. But "in spite of his cussedness toward those whose support is indispensable in critical times . . . he has been the best mayor of New York in my lifetime."[5] On the day before the primary, Wendell Willkie announced he would fly to New York to cast his vote for La Guardia even though the mayor had openly denigrated the 1940 Republican presidential candidate. La Guardia pronounced Willkie's endorsement "the most generous and sporting attitude taken in politics for a long while."[6]

O'Dwyer, of course, had not only the Democratic Party but also the entire political hierarchy behind him including Farley, Flynn, and Governor Lehman. What he needed—what he fully expected—was the president's endorsement. What he didn't need was Roosevelt's telling a press conference on September 24 that he would not take sides in the New York election—and then expressing his "opinion" that the Little Flower had given the city the "most honest and,

I believe, the most efficient municipal government of any city within my recollection."[7] Next day, Fiorello sent him a one-word telegram, MERCI, while O'Dwyer nursed the bruises FDR had thus inflicted on him.

At this point, La Guardia was practically a shoe-in. All he need do was calm down, go about his business, and let O'Dwyer and Tammany self-destruct. But an inability to calm down was a congenital La Guardia affliction. So, too, was an inclination toward self-destruction. And this time around he almost succeeded, colliding head-on with Governor Lehman—and in the process nearly losing the election.

Being a loyal party man, Lehman endorsed O'Dwyer. It was a tepid endorsement at best. He knew in his heart that La Guardia was far and away the better man for the job. In announcing his stand on the campaign, the unkindest thing Lehman could find to say about La Guardia was that he was only human and could not be expected to handle both City Hall and the OCD. The subtext of Lehman's remarks could easily be read as an apology for not supporting him.[8]

But La Guardia didn't quite read it that way, as evidenced by his intemperate remark (without mentioning Lehman by name), "When you are once in a political organization . . . [y]ou have got to do what the political bosses tell you to. A politician always remains a politician." Adolf Berle, who should have known better, joined the one-man chorus with a stinging regret that Lehman was willing to "lend his name to reestablish the tin box politicians"—which is to say, the corrupt Tammany sachems of old.[9]*

Worse was yet to come. For that we must turn back to earlier in the year when New York State Comptroller Morris Tremaine of Buffalo died. Lehman picked Joseph O'Leary of the American Labor Party to replace him until the election, for which O'Leary was promised both Democratic and ALP backing. The Republicans nominated a respected upstate leader, Frank Moore. This put La Guardia in the position of having to choose between a member of the ALP that was backing him, thus jeopardizing Republican support, and backing a Republican, thus alienating the ALP. Fortunately for him, the state

---

*"Tin box" was an allusion to a popular refrain from the Seabury investigation of Tammany: Crooked defendants, asked to explain where they got all the money they had amassed through graft and fraud, replied blandly that they "found it in a little tin box."

Court of Appeals, with Justice Irving Lehman (the governor's brother) presiding, ruled that the election for comptroller must wait until the following year's general election.

Instead of letting well enough alone, La Guardia openly charged that Lehman had appointed O'Leary as a favor to Flynn and the other bosses to strengthen the O'Dwyer ticket. Now regretting the appointment, Lehman had the state's attorney general call for a special election to fill the office—and then changed his mind again and commanded that his brother's decision stand. Chortled La Guardia, "I think it's the funniest thing that has ever happened in American politics. . . . It's the first time a man has hit himself in the jaw and knocked himself out. . . . You've heard of *goniffs* [Yiddish for "thieves"] stealing from *goniffs*. Well now you are hearing of double-crossers double-crossing the double-crossers."[10]

Next day Lehman, characterizing La Guardia as "grossly abusive," issued a press statement in which, in an atypical paroxysm of anger, he charged that not only now but also for a long time he had treated everyone who opposed or criticized him with abuse and vilification. "Thief," "double-crosser," "crook," and "bum" were among the milder of the mayor's epithets. "Most people," added Lehman, "have no desire to compete with him in intemperate abuse and so they have permitted themselves to be intimidated into silence. But I cannot be intimidated. . . . New Yorkers are sick and tired of Mr. La Guardia's unbridled tongue."[11]

If anyone "hit himself in the jaw and knocked himself out," it was not the governor but the mayor. Lehman was a Democratic icon in a heavily Democratic city. To attack him so gratuitously as to call him a *goniff* was not only unjustified and intemperate, it was just plain stupid. Especially offended were the Jews, always a voting bloc to be contended with, who bitterly resented this attack on the first of their coreligionists to achieve the state's highest office. Polls showed a dramatic drop in support for La Guardia. In Jewish districts alone his popularity fell fifteen percentage points.

La Guardia was, of course, reelected—the first New York mayor to achieve a third term—in the closest election in more than three decades. With a plurality of but 132,000, he received about 53 percent of the vote—down seven percentage points from 1937. (The final count: La Guardia, 1,186,518 votes, of which the Republican Party accounted for 668,485, the ALP, 435,374, City Fusion Party,

63,367, and United City Party, 19,292. O'Dwyer won 1,054,235 votes.)[12] McGoldrick and Morris were reelected, and La Guardia carried in with him two of the five borough presidents, including Isaacs's successor Nathan as Manhattan borough president. While the Fusion retained control of the Board of Estimate, its strength there was reduced to twelve. In the City Council, the Democrats won a comfortable majority. There is no doubt that La Guardia's attack on Lehman was primarily the cause for his loss of strength from 1937. McGoldrick believed that Fiorello's remarks easily cost him a quarter of a million votes. Had they had been made earlier in the campaign, it is probable that La Guardia would never have been reelected.[13]

"The vote was a commendation of his record," wrote publisher Herbert Bayard Swope to Roosevelt, "and, at the same time, a rebuke for his intemperateness and his sometimes arrogant assumption of all that is virtuous. He deserved to win—but he deserved the slap." Tugwell put it more perceptively: "He was re-elected in 1941 not because of, but in spite of, his executive behavior; because of his performances in public, not because of his efficiency in office. He was still dedicated and still colorful, but he was against the bosses and had convinced the people that the bosses were their enemies as well as his. La Guardia, absurd and childish, was better than scoundrels and wasters."[14]

2.

La Guardia had been both criticized and ridiculed for trying to prepare the country for the likelihood of war, which seemed to most people unreal and remote. When the likelihood became reality with the attack on Pearl Harbor, he moved with characteristic speed. Immediately placing the city on a war footing, he convened his Emergency Control Board, which he kept in continuous session, and he ordered all Japanese nationals confined to their homes and put their clubs and other gathering places under police protection. (A little later the police, acting on FBI orders, rounded up 2,500 Japanese and moved them to Ellis Island.) By midnight air raid wardens were on duty and precautions against sabotage of bridges, tunnels, power plants, reservoirs, and railway stations were in force. The next day, in an address broadcast over the commercial NBC network as well as the city-owned WNYC, he said he "want[ed] to assure all persons who have been sneering and jeering at defense activities, and even those who have been objecting to them and placing obstacles in their path, that we will protect them now. But we expect their cooperation and there will be no fooling."[15]

Then, in his capacity as OCD director and president of the U.S. Conference of Mayors, he left Newbold Morris as acting mayor and took off for a five-day inspection of the West Coast. His first stop was Washington, where he dictated a memorandum for the president about seizing enemy merchant vessels docked in U.S. ports; he and Mrs. Roosevelt then flew off to Los Angeles, the nation's most vulnerable point. Mrs. Roosevelt recalls in her memoirs how Fiorello was asleep in his berth when the pilot received word that San Francisco was being bombed. She waited till the plane was about to land for refueling somewhere in Kansas before waking him. Sticking his head out of the berth—he looked "for all the world like a Kewpie doll"—he told her to leave the plane on landing and call Washington for verification. "If it is true, we will go direct to San Francisco." The report turned out not to be true, and the plane continued on to Los Angeles. Recalled Mrs. Roosevelt: "It was so characteristic of him, that I glowed inwardly. One could be exasperated with him at times, but one had to admire his real integrity and courage."[16]

Directly on landing, La Guardia bolted from the plane to check on the city's general state of defense preparedness, paying particular emphasis to firefighting equipment—a pet interest. Mrs. Roosevelt remembered, "His complete courage and lack of fear had an effect on everyone." He reorganized the fire department, organized doctors into emergency teams, ordered a shipment of medical supplies, and did much to lift the morale of a frightened and traumatized people, impressing one and all with his energy and decisiveness. But Mrs. Roosevelt wondered how much of his work was in vain since not enough had been done before. "I did not know and never have known how much all our plans, his and mine, really helped since so much of our equipment was lacking that they could not do the things that were considered essential." She suggested that more systematic planning in the months leading up to Pearl Harbor would have been infinitely more effective than all the comfort and courage they now offered.[17] She did not suggest it to Fiorello, though. She knew him well enough to expect a retort along the lines of "Spare me the hindsight, give me only the foresight."

Arriving back home on December 13, La Guardia took personal charge of New York's defense effort—planning blackouts, establishing air raid rules, ordering that illegal parking not obstruct emergency vehicles or picketing not detract from morale, reassuring parents that their children would be taken care of. Despite Washington's ban on all information regarding troop movements, he announced that the president had dispatched three thousand Army troops to New York to guard vital points. Some of his actions had about them the tone of opéra bouffe, like organizing a group of young volunteer women, known as "the Palace Guard," to serve as receptionists, messengers, clerical aides, and whatever else La Guardia might dream up. When they reported to City Hall each morning in their blue-gray uniforms, they saluted him smartly, then saluted each other!

Their first mission was to monitor the citywide air raid system scheduled for a trial run. When the sirens were meant to sound, not a one could be heard. Standing at one end of the Brooklyn Bridge with an ear cocked, Fiorello pronounced the test "an unqualified failure" and sighed, "I guess we'll have to try something else." Another action that earned him derision was to urge that gas masks be provided for every citizen, to be available in four sizes, from the "baby protector" to the "universal adult." (The idea was never pursued, as the city was deemed to be beyond the range of enemy planes.) And then there was the all-day session at City Hall of the U.S.-Canadian Joint Permanent Defense Board, presided over by La Guardia, following which he issued a "communiqué" assuring one and all that "military, air, and naval plans heretofore made are in satisfactory operation."[18] The World War II mayor was sounding more and more like the World War I major.

Meanwhile, the question of his ability to handle concurrently the demanding duties of directing the OCD and running New York City was being aired with increasing concern. That he had been, and was now more than ever, running helter-skelter in fulfilling both tasks prompted the *World-Telegram* to comment (December 23, 1941), "Temperamental civilian leaders, however politically gifted, are not always the best . . . in the stress of war peril. Nerves don't calm nerves." Three days later, the paper pressed the point: "The situation does not call for a dizzy show-off of one man juggling with multiple jobs." The *Times*, in a January 3, 1942, editorial, was more emphatic: "The Office of Civilian Defense and the office of Mayor of New York [have] ceased suddenly, definitely and irrevocably to be two offices that could be filled completely by a single man."

Intensifying the situation, La Guardia's behavior was becoming rather bizarre, to the degree that some feared he might be cracking up. The occasional displays of poor judgment and bullying that had begun to become manifest during his second term now burst into full flower. Having driven from office one of his original and most competent department heads, Fire Commissioner McElligot, he now went after another original and most distinguished appointee, City Markets Commissioner William Fellowes Morgan. This would create problems for La Guardia that many, including his own loyalists, believed he deserved.

Morgan had rid the markets of racketeers, gotten the pushcart peddlers off the streets and into roofed central markets, and pioneered in consumer education and information. The administration's most self-effacing commissioner, he had tolerated La Guardia's habit of making personnel appointments to his department without being consulted. After the 1941 election, La Guardia sent over three new appointees, at least one of whom (and possibly all three) was being rewarded for his efforts during the campaign. Morgan tried to make known his objections to the mayor but was told he was either out of town or too busy. He was not the first commissioner to be fobbed off with that lame and demonstrably spurious excuse, nor would he be the last. It's not that La Guardia shunned confrontations—to the contrary, as we have seen—but the choice of whom or what to confront, and when, had to be his and his alone.

Entering into the equation was Mrs. Preston Davie—a highly respected reformer and, it must be stressed, an unpaid volunteer—whom Morgan recruited into the city's conservation program. La Guardia's people wanted someone else, and he ordered Morgan to fire Mrs. Davie. Morgan refused, despite the mayor's reiterated hysterical screams of "Fire that dame, fire that dame!"[19] Morgan resigned, commenting sadly, "The unfortunate thing about it all is that the Mayor is so darned busy with other matters that he hasn't got the time to sit down and talk things over with his commissioners." La Guardia dismissed all questions about the Morgan affair with the melodramatic words "*E finita la commedia*" (the comedy is ended).

But it wasn't a comedy, and it wasn't ended. Morgan admitted to the press how La Guardia had pressured him into accepting spoils appointments. La Guardia angrily retaliated with the announcement that irregularities had been uncovered in Morgan's department and that the commissioner of investigations had been ordered to undertake a thorough probe. Only later would La Guardia admit that the "irregularities" were in fact one trivial charge that a tenant of the Bronx Terminal Market had illegally plugged into city electrical lines and Morgan might have known about it. (He probably didn't.)

Ending unpleasantness within his official family by dispatching his investigations commissioner to poke around was standard operating procedure for Fiorello. Morgan's inability to get the mayor's ear over those political payoffs added to the misgivings being bruited about over La Guardia's handling of two big jobs. The *Herald Tribune,* one of his most consistent supporters, editorialized (December 29, 1941), "We refuse to believe the Mayor has suddenly become a time-serving politician," and said the whole affair had brought "into sharp relief the deterioration of municipal rule." To assume he could continue to govern the city while running all around the country as an increasingly ineffective OCD director was, said the editorial, a "tragic absurdity."

La Guardia's gut reaction was to fall victim to self-pity. "I have suffered too much during the last six months, absorbing the criticism, the abuse, the sneers and jeers, including some from the press, when we were seeking to train people for just this emergency," he told the *Times* two days before year's end. He then went on to denounce "super patriots seeking to find flaws and to destroy the confidence of the people in this government. I'll have more to say about that."

That he did in a New Year's Day address over WNYC, in which he labeled his critics "some Jap or friend of a Jap," fell back on his suspiciously paranoid tactic of ascribing the least desirable motives to those who most disagreed with him, and took a swipe at the press, which he saw in the aggregate as "two-by-four editors," "swivel-chair scribes," and "liars" who refused to admit how "magnificently organized" were his great accomplishments with the OCD. He closed with the caveat that "the war will come to . . . our residential districts"—and *then* New Yorkers would appreciate their unique advantage in having their mayor as head of the nation's civil defense.[20]

That the two-by-four editors and swivel-chair scribes were unrelenting in their collective contention that La Guardia was too overwrought, overworked, and overtired to handle both jobs did not deter him. He had his press secretary, Lester Stone, inundate the media with favorable stories and pictures, while he himself finessed his more malleable critics by naming them to advisory positions and even moved his OCD headquarters to New York.

Meanwhile, unknown to him, the question of how La Guardia could handle both jobs was being resolved behind his back. Though Mrs. Roosevelt admired much about him, her admiration did not extend to his directorship of civil defense. Upon their return from the West Coast, she suggested to her husband and his advisers that what the OCD needed was not "reorganization" but "organization," stating in so many words that it had been chaos from the start.[21] Agreement was unanimous. On the first day of the new year, the president told La Guardia he had selected Dean James M. Landis of the Harvard Law School to take over OCD administrative duties with Mrs. Roosevelt remaining on as his assistant. La Guardia balked at being bumped up to nominal chairmanship, claiming he was the victim of unjust treatment by the press. The president remained firm. The Landis appointment was announced on January 10, 1942. Accepting the situation, La Guardia told a New York University alumni dinner a few weeks later, "Sin does not pay—I am about to give up the double life." On February 11, he resigned as OCD chief in Landis's favor, saying that his original assignment—preparing the nation for war—had been completed. (Mrs. Roosevelt herself quit ten days later, due to the demands of her numerous other activities and responsibilities.)[22]

Fellowes Morgan, despite their falling-out, was sincere in expressing an opinion shared by Fiorello's most zealous supporters. La Guardia had given his all for a cause that he believed in. He had tried to accomplish too much in the misguided, perhaps egotistical belief that only he could do it, in addition to governing the nation's most challenging—and in a sense most ungovernable—city. The overworked La Guardia's nerves, suggested Morgan, had been "shot to pieces." He was urged to go off for a much-needed rest: "When you come back, forgive and forget." But La Guardia could no more go off for a much-needed rest than he could forget that it was he who had set up the basics of home defense even before Pearl Harbor and that when war did come New York had in place fifty-six thousand volunteer air raid wardens—or forgive those he believed had shattered his political hopes and ambitions. What next occurred led many to fear that their Little Flower might be on the verge of imploding and, in the process, sacrificing his political integrity.

It involved his abrasive yet honorable protégé Paul Kern and his suave yet not quite so honorable political antagonist Ed Flynn. With Al Smith Jr. now in the Army, the investigation he had launched in the City Council against Kern and the whole question of Communists in the Civil Service Commission was renewed under another chairman. In a referendum on the County Reform Bill, which La Guardia had advocated since first coming to office in 1933, the voters had eliminated the offices of borough registrars and borough sheriffs and replaced them with two citywide offices. Since most of the eliminated officeholders were Democrats, Tammany prevailed upon the state Civil Service Commission, still a Democratic fiefdom, to have them transferred to the city Civil Service lists without competitive examinations.

Kern refused to accept the transfers. In the case of four, La Guardia overruled him. The four were close to Ed Flynn. As Kern saw it, since Flynn had managed Roosevelt's reelection, La Guardia had done it to keep himself in good stead with the president. When the names of the four transferees appeared on the payroll, Kern withheld approval. The four then secured a court order for release of their salaries. Kern resolved to appeal the decision. La Guardia ordered Corporation Counsel William Chanler not to undertake the appeal.[23] The Civil Service Commission then took legal action against Chanler. La Guardia suspended the entire Civil Service Commission for "insubordination" and ordered Chanler to seal the premises and "conduct an investigation." It was not lost on anyone that La Guardia had never suspended for "insubordination" commissioners more deserving of such reprimand. At a public hearing with his fellow commissioner Wallace Sayre, Kern warned La Guardia, "Your old friends are gone with the snows of yesteryear and you have surrounded yourself with sycophants who fawn on you." A few days later, though Kern, Sayre, and La Guardia all expressed regret over the whole incident, La Guardia formally removed them from office.

Kern openly denounced his onetime patron and protector as a leader who had abandoned his once commendable sense of fairness and dedication to fusion reform and become a practitioner of hot temper, political ambition of the basest genre, and sinister political deals. He then went on to accuse him of suspending officials who refused to be part of the "sinister hand" guiding his administration, denouncing respected judges "as low-grade thieves," sending "unspeakably vulgar notes to newspapers," and publicly referring to his own commissioners as "asses"—all on the "hollowest of pretexts." Kern further charged La Guardia with "keeping company" with men who were once his sworn enemies and were in politics for the money they could amass by means more foul than fair. At public hearings on his and Sayre's dismissal, Kern resumed the attack, warning La Guardia that "the same stiletto that you are now sticking in our backs will be stuck in yours by [your] sycophants," and then accused him of tampering with the merit system.

An even more spectacular charge concerned Ed Flynn. It seems Herlands had been quietly looking into charges that the Democratic boss and close Roosevelt adviser had misused city laborers and city material for work on his summer home at Lake Mahopac. Kern now claimed that he had himself looked into the charges and found that Herlands, who took his marching orders from the mayor, had deliberately delayed and blocked the inquiry. Why, wondered Kern with dripping sarcasm, had La Guardia been quick to dispose of such loyal fusionist commissioners as Rheinstein, Morgan, and McElligot, along with Kern himself—yet dithered on the Flynn investigation? Was it, he suggested, answering his own question, because Flynn had "gotten to" the mayor by offering to support him for the Democratic Senate nomination?[24]

The firing of Kern and Sayre was upheld by the appellate court, with the majority ruling that Kern's issuing "an obviously defamatory press statement attacking William C. Chanler" was cause for both his and Sayre's dismissal, which was further supported by La Guardia's testimony that "one agency of government cannot attack another and not impair its usefulness." But a strong dissenting opinion by Presiding Justice Francis Martin held that La Guardia's attack on

Chanler was patently used as a gambit to remove a commissioner "who would not perform the illegal acts directed by the Mayor." Civil Service commissioners, the opinion concluded, "are not under the personal supervision or control of the Mayor. They should be fearless and independent and not be mere pawns." More embarrassing for La Guardia, the Bronx grand jury found Kern's charges against Flynn to be valid—but also found that the prosecution failed to establish that Flynn had personally ordered the work to be done. In his memoirs, Flynn claimed that the use of the material in question—a few thousand Belgian granite blocks belonging to the city—"was all an innocent mistake."[25]

While Flynn was thus cleared, the impression was left that in coveting a national position La Guardia had somehow jumped into the political cesspool of power brokers and surrendered a piece of his soul in exchange for implied promises and transparent deals. Such an impression does not suggest that La Guardia had in fact lost his integrity or his probity. But it does suggest that he seemed to be in the process of losing his bearings.

3.

As La Guardia directed his attention and energy to getting New York through the war, he soon found his authority weakened, which added to the frustration that was starting to engulf him. The Board of Estimate had given him powers he asked for to move critical materials and supplies from one department to another—but only so long as he kept spending within the overall budget. These included $2.5 million for blackout and dimout precautions, installation of sirens, provisioning of buildings with firefighting equipment, and protection of the water system.

But political opposition soon intervened as the boroughs, taking their cue from what they perceived to be Washington's loss of confidence in La Guardia, petitioned that the War Department be given direction of the city's defenses. Then the press suggested that he delegate some of his responsibilities to a full-time civilian defense director for the city. La Guardia, however, would not even consider the idea. His police commissioner would remain in control of air raid wardens, and his Public Works Department would be in charge of salvage and clearing in case of an air raid. End of discussion. He did agree, however, to place the city under the jurisdiction of the state in such general matters as rationing and rent control—provided the city retain a degree of local autonomy. Then he lashed out at those who criticized his defense measures, charging that they had organized a campaign to discredit him.

To put the city on a wartime footing, the new budget he presented was several million dollars less than the current one, eliminating 5,600 jobs and mandating shorter paid vacations for all municipal employees. The cuts were across the board, affecting every department, and the various department heads stormed City Hall to protest. None stormed with greater force than Robert Moses. The idea of cuts in his Parks Commission budget was totally unacceptable, especially since his original budget demands had been reduced to a bare-bones minimum necessary to keep his department from, as he feared, collapsing.

More than fiscal considerations were in play. Moses's vision for the city had been curtailed by the war. Compounding his frustration, he had been denied a national post that he felt entitled to by virtue of his talents. Only Moses's arrogance could have led him to believe that his old nemesis, the president, might have mitigated his loathing for him. La Guardia refused to restore the budget cuts, but he did appreciate his parks commissioner's aching desire to do his part in the war effort. He put him in charge of the city's scrap metal drive. Moses being Moses, this was to be no standard drive for old pots and pans. Entire buildings, including historical ones, were stripped of all metal parts. Then, barely three weeks after taking over, he quit, blaming federal authorities for lack of cooperation and—as he told reporters—"because I have too much to do."[26]

Thanks to Moses's overzealousness, the city also had "much to do"—removing the veritable mountain of superfluous junk he had amassed in those three weeks. The junk dealers were unable or unwilling to handle it. La Guardia ordered five hundred Sanitation Department trucks to fan out over the city and collect the debris and successfully negotiated its sale to the dealers. In declaring the result of this somewhat aberrant scrap drive "magnificent," La Guardia had kind words for the press.

But "kind" was about the extent of it, and the words were few in number. His relations with the press had by then suffered an acute deterioration through the controversies surrounding his role in the nation's and city's defenses. The deterioration was aggravated by the way in which he dealt with reporters; he could be dismissive and downright insulting. A situation that had roots in his first administration now worsened; it was to leave scars that would never heal.

In the March 9, 1942, *New Republic*, George Britt wrote a provocative article, "What Has Happened to La Guardia?" Its gist was that the man who had won an unprecedented third term could not be returned to office if an election were held now. Britt's evaluation was not taken lightly. The strongest reform groups, including the City Club, the Women's City Club, the League of Women Voters, the City Affairs Committee, the Citizens Union, and the United Neighborhood Houses, were all complaining about Fiorello's behavior, in particular his crude language, abuse of commissioners, use of his Investigations Commission to "get back" at foes, and his bellicosity toward the press.

There had been scattered incidents over eight years pitting the man against the media, but these had been offset by his accomplishments in leading New York out of bankruptcy while creating from a congeries of autonomous counties a vital, unified, connected city. Now it seemed that his mayoral leadership threatened to give way to leadership by mayoral tantrum. Especially upsetting was his change of attitude toward the police. In his earlier years he had held them in check during labor confrontations. Now his attitude was that discretion in handling confrontations was best left to the arresting officers. He did not, of course, believe in brutalizing those arrested for minor offenses, but "the tough babies he thinks need a good working over."[27] In addition to condoning the beating of suspects, the one-time civil libertarian unilaterally ordered municipal employees to work a seven-day week, without discussions or negotiations. That this imposed hardships for many because of personal requirements or religious conviction concerned him not at all. Nor did the negative consensus of the press on his views.

In the fall of 1942, a year into his third term, the two major weekly newsmagazines, *Newsweek* (in a September 7 piece, "Hizzoner and the Press") and *Time* (October 5), stated what had long been an open secret: La Guardia had precipitated an irreparable break with the reporters who covered the City Hall beat. It was the inevitable consequence of a situation that had been going on since he first came to office in 1933. He and the press had rarely been on friendly terms.

The fault was primarily twofold and all his: In La Guardia's opinion, the press was an adjunct to his administration, especially when it came to supporting his programs; and in light of the results those programs engendered, he felt entitled to what amounted to an uncritical free ride.

Many of the newspapers liked him, as witness the spate of favorable editorials over the years, but the same cannot be said for the reporters, whom he kept at arm's length. During his first term, there were occasional verbal exchanges. Not long after coming into office La Guardia, irritated over one reporter's persistent questions on a political matter, restored a practice of his predecessors and demanded written questions. Would he respond in kind? "I don't have to write the answers. I *know* the answers."[28] In his second term, he did not hold his first press conference until several months after election—and ended it abruptly when but a single topic had been covered. Still, no matter what he said or did, he made good copy.

By the second year of his third administration, relations with the press had deteriorated almost to the point of no return. Stung by the pasting he had taken in connection with his OCD activities and the change in his once-egalitarian attitudes, he went after the newspapers with a vengeance. He refused to discuss an issue—*any* issue—until the reporters had "learned the ethics of their profession." He denounced stories critical of him as "smacking strongly of sabotage" and took to badgering publishers about "unfair reports" in their papers. At times, he behaved like someone throwing a monumental fit. On one occasion, infuriated by a question from *Times* City Hall reporter Paul Crowell, he snatched Crowell's notebook from his hands, threw it to the floor, and jumped up and down on it as if it were a cockroach that must be not only destroyed but also atomized. And then there was the incident—on the steps of City Hall before an audience of passersby—when the *World Telegram*'s Peter Kihss questioned La Guardia's Jimmy Walker appointment. La Guardia grabbed Kihss's arm and threatened "to throw [him] right down the steps" if he didn't stop pestering him. Robert Donovan of the *Herald Tribune* fared somewhat better. After a car door La Guardia slammed on him scratched his face, he received an apology.[29]

Reporters he considered offensive were barred from City Hall conferences and ceremonies. Others he complained about to their editors. Still others he called "pimps" and "punks" and "unethical liars"—at the top of his voice and before onlookers. On occasion, he even threatened libel suits that could never have held up in court. According to one veteran City Hall reporter, he did get "some news-papermen fired, had others transferred from City Hall, and intimi-dated a good many into reluctance to tell the whole truth about him." Wrote another, "Make no mistake about it, there is scarcely a man in the [City Hall press] corps who doesn't fear La Guardia's power of reprisal."[30]

The man who before becoming mayor had told a Columbia Uni-versity symposium that newspapers were too submissive to advertisers now took to complaining to advertisers about "false," "vicious," and "close to subversive" articles. To the president of Macy's he wrote, "I am appealing to you, because we had another case of sabotaging" in abetting "a deliberate plan to destroy confidence even at the expense of the morale of the business of New York City." The saboteurs? The city newspapers, "the *Times* in particular."[31] La Guardia was not being paranoid. He was being spiteful. Because reporters would not con-form to the demand that his statements be reported without com-ment or interpretation, he denied then access to himself and his commissioners and instead issued communiqués and press releases, thereby creating a tighter monopoly on the news than any Tammany boss had ever dared consider. Perhaps *Time* magazine summed it up best (October 5, 1942): The Little Flower was exhibiting "unmistak-able signs of being unable to distinguish between criticism of his public actions and of his oversensitive self."

This was a specific allusion to a fury that resulted from two minor incidents. The first came not long after Pearl Harbor when La Guar-dia announced that he would ration hot water. When the press car-ried strong protests, he changed his mind and said that Washington would decide the issue. He then denounced the reporters, charging that his initial statement had been inaccurately cited—it hadn't—and denying he had changed his view. When a reporter sought to discuss the matter, La Guardia shrieked, "You dare to want to talk to me?" The reporter declined to accept the dare.

The second incident was of far less consequence but enraged him even more. This was the so-called George Incident. In a September radio broadcast, La Guardia told of receiving a letter from a child complaining that his father gambled away the household money—and, what's more, didn't even have enough money left on payday for the lad's weekly allowance. Said La Guardia, "George, you must keep me informed." He also asked "other little boys [to] please also let me know" should their father gamble, and where. The press had a field day with this one, giving full coverage to James Marshall, former president of the Board of Education, who reproached the mayor for urging youngsters to inform on their parents, adding that it was abnormal behavior for youngsters to request a police investigation of their fathers if their allowance was not forthcoming. In his next broadcast, La Guardia accused the press of encouraging gambling.

People found it not only incredible but inconceivable that a one-time forthright Progressive and reformer who believed in the exercise of free speech and the right to express opinions, even those he opposed, now seemed determined to preside over a city where his orders were the only acceptable orders, and city councils did not make intrusive investigations (except at his instigation); where civil liberties must, if need be, cede precedence to his wishes and commands, and the press and his critics, whom he accused of "lying," were issued metaphorical muzzles.

4.

The decline of the area and the lack of security at the East Harlem apartment where the La Guardias had lived since their marriage convinced the city that its chief executive must occupy a more suitable home. He had balked at all previous suggestions about relocating to quarters more in keeping with his official position. He liked "the old neighborhood." But he realized the children would benefit from a better environment. After considering a few places, the Board of Estimate decided on Gracie Mansion, built by Alexander Gracie in 1799 on a promontory of land overlooking the East River, and allocated twenty thousand dollars to refurbish the house and grounds. The family moved in on May 14, 1942. La Guardia didn't much care for it, especially all the antiques. He was much more taken by his new official car, a small coupe with green body and white top, known as the Fiorellomobile. It had fire-engine-type emergency lights, with a red sign flashing MAYOR on its roof. That, plus five white stars painted on its hood, and its front and back bumpers covered with luminous black paint, made for easy identification in an emergency.[32]

La Guardia was obsessed with raising and keeping high the morale of New Yorkers. On January 18, 1942, he began a series of Sunday evening "Talks to the People" over the municipal radio station, WNYC. The fifteen-minute programs opened with the playing of the Marine Hymn followed by the mayor giving his favorite salutation, "Patience and fortitude." As many as two million New Yorkers tuned in weekly to hear advice and counsel on a variety of subjects, the latest war news, cracker-barrel philosophy, and anything else that occurred to the mayor. Knocking "the *really* bad people of our great city" was a favorite topic. Making it a point to address his audience as if addressing each listener directly, he would begin with a roundup of the latest war news, followed by a few health hints. "Ladies, I want to ask you a favor. I want you please to wear your rubbers when you go out in this weather. If you don't . . . you may slip and fall . . . and hurt yourselves. Then we'll have to take care of you and we don't like to ask our doctors and nurses to take care of any more patients. . . . So won't you please be sensible and wear your rubbers?"

Then he might segue into a condemnation of the "no good thieving, chiseling tinhorns" and scream at them into the microphone, "Cut it out right now. That sort of business don't [*sic*] go in New York. Not while I'm Mayor. Get me?" He gave names and addresses and ordered Police Commissioner Valentine, "Run these two out of town, will you, Lew?" Learning that gamblers used the phone booths at Yankee Stadium to call in their bets, he ordered the doors ripped off the booths so police could eavesdrop on the conversations. Informed that basketball fans at Madison Square Garden were calling New Jersey numbers to place bets, he disclosed the numbers on his program, advising his listeners to "Take your pencil. Here are some of the tinhorn telephone numbers. . . . Are you listening, New Jersey? Are you listening, Mr. Attorney General of New Jersey? . . . PAssaic 3-2590, PAssaic 3-1024, PAssaic 2-9333, LInden 2-3763. . . ." When a new ban was placed on sports events gambling, he warned: "I do not know what the firms of Chiselers, *Gonovim* [Yiddish] & *Imbroglioni* [Italian], unincorporated, are going to do, but we are going to watch. If you try any monkey business, we will grab you by the back of the neck and the seat of the pants and kick you out, do you hear?"

Told that Western Union was being used to transmit racetrack information, he used his Sunday evening bully pulpit to tell the company in no uncertain words, "Now Mr. Western Union let me tell you this. I think the law should compel refusal to take messages from gamblers and chiselers and tinhorns and touts, and also should prohibit transmitting . . . information of plugs trotting or creeping around a track in Havana or Tijuana." When Western Union ignored him, his listening audience was assured he had found a law that might sustain prosecution, "and I am going to try it out!" Were Western Union to continue transmitting such data over its wires, he threatened, he was "going to ask the police to . . . hold responsible the management of the company who gets the profit from these messages." Western Union agreed to cooperate. On one program he announced, "Oh, I've got to give a little notice now. Certain firms manufacturing stirrup pumps have raised their prices from eight to twenty dollars. . . . Cut it out. If you don't I'll tell [Office of Price Administration director] Leon Henderson. The two of us will get after you!"

Fiorello was the last thing one expected in a radio orator, what with his squeaky voice, sloppy syntax, and propensity for making a hash of the English language. But the audiences loved it. The ladies were especially fond of his tips on bargains ("Now about fish, you should take advantage of the low prices this week and buy fish.") and how to cope with three years of shortages and rationing. ("Hello, housewives. . . . Remember what I told you last Sunday about snap beans? Remember? They were asking fifty-four cents a pound and I told you to stop buying snap beans and the price'd come down— and you did, and it did. Look, we got them down to seventeen cents last Sunday.") He offered substitutes for more expensive or harder-to-come-by staples, and contributed gleanings from Marie's collection of recipes: new vegetables, little-known fish, new cuts of meat, and details on how to prepare the likes of "oxtail ragout," and "Jerusalem artichokes." Advocating the use of B-grade eggs with brown shells, he asked rhetorically, "Well, you don't eat the shells, do you?"

He urged his listeners to conserve electricity: "Turn off lights. Do not waste heat." He also urged housewives to save fat, advising categorically—no one knows where he came up with this one—that Germany lost World War I because of lack of fats. He did admonish, though, that the homemakers be sure not to use the same oils for preparing fish and meat. They were also advised not to waste bread: "There is such a thing as bread pudding."

Ere long La Guardia was attracting the highest ratings of any radio program in the city, and the adversarial Board of Estimate started attacking WNYC for functioning as "the Mayor's personal plaything [to] disseminate his own personal and political views." When they threatened to eliminate appropriation for the station from the budget, the mayor said he would find a way to communicate with the people, even if the station were boarded up. The Coty Perfume Corporation came forward with an offer of a thousand dollars a week to sponsor the program (La Guardia said he would give the money to the city), thousands of letters came in supporting the broadcasts, the embarrassed Board of Estimate revoked its threat, and "Talks to the People" continued.[33]

New Yorkers were not Fiorello's only radio audience. By the summer of 1942, his fifteen-minute "Mayor La Guardia Calling Rome," opened by a blare of trumpets and the words "This is your friend La Guardia speaking," was going out over shortwave. He hammered away at Mussolini and his German allies, reminding his listeners of their nation's glorious past, telling them that the Germans were stealing their food, instigating them to despise not only Mussolini but their ultimate "slave master," Hitler, and provoking them to "create . . . trouble and incite . . . to riot," lay down their weapons, and free themselves of "this fascist gang." In October 1943, the Office of War Information reported that La Guardia's weekly talks were the most popular of all American propaganda broadcasts to Italy. When one town was liberated by the U.S. Fifth Army, the townspeople told reporters of the broadcasts, "They were a great help to our morale . . . helping us understand that the Americans realized our plight."[34]

As the country's most visible Italian-American politician, La Guardia was asked if he would return the medals he had been awarded by the Italian government during World War I. He would not: "Italy was a nation then. It is only a colony of Germany now. Of course," he predicted confidently, "the people of Italy will get rid of Mussolini."[35] Even before the United States entered the war, he had cabled an urgent request to King Victor Emmanuel III "not to sacrifice [Italy's] sons for Hitler. . . . I appeal to you let us stand for peace and freedom as we did in nineteen eighteen." To the New York press he insisted that "no one can tell me that the Italian people were made to goose step in back of any dictator."[36]

He cooperated with the FBI and local law enforcement officials in seeking out fifth column activity and suspected sedition in New York, and he traveled around the country to dispel Fascist sentiments and "guide Italian American public opinion." His efforts in behalf of Italy's anti-Fascists were not confined to propaganda broadcasts. Receiving appeals for food and other necessities, he lobbied the State Department to alleviate the problem. When American bombers strafed Italian cities late in 1942, he implored Roosevelt to declare Rome an open city and thus save it from destruction. He also petitioned the White House in behalf of American Italians who wanted to send remittances to their relatives in the occupied territories, requested that the U.S. Navy distribute clothes, medicines, and other needed supplies to residents in those areas that had by then been liberated, and kept himself informed on Allied treatment of Italian civilians during the occupation.[37]

5.

Fiorello's actions in light of the horrors befalling the Jewish people— not only in Europe but also in America, though not to the horrific degree of the Holocaust—were less admirable. In fact, some verged on the deplorable.

La Guardia considered himself first and foremost an Italian, even though his mother was Jewish, albeit an Italian national. Though he never denied his Jewish ancestry, he never identified with Judaism. While he took justifiable pride as the first Italian elected mayor of New York City, that pride never extended to his being the first Jew elected to that office as well. To this day his Jewish background comes as a surprise to many. That is not to imply that he was an apostate. His record of speaking out early against the treatment of Jews in Hitler's Germany, and later those caught up in the occupied nations, was admirable. To the Jews, not only in Europe but in America as well, this was especially heartening.

In the years leading up to the war, the Nazis had strong support among Americans of German descent through the German-American Bund, headed by the infamous Fritz Kuhn. In 1939, before an audience of twenty thousand sympathizers jammed into Madison Square Garden, Kuhn praised Hitler and denounced Roosevelt.[38] La Guardia insisted, despite protests, on allowing the Bund to hold such public meetings. We were not yet in the war, and the Bund had a large following among the New York electorate. He did, though, have Investigations Commissioner Herlands study the group's records. As a result, Kuhn was jailed for embezzlement. But it did not stop there. During those years more than a hundred organizations were spreading hatred of the Jews across the country. Leading the pack was the malevolent Detroit-based Catholic priest Charles Coughlin, whose hatred of Jews and rabble-rousing to the effect that the nation must preserve the "Christian social order upon which it was founded" enjoyed the support of many church leaders. Significantly, the church hierarchy in this country, along with the Vatican, refused to speak out against the "golden-voiced radio priest." This encouraged Americans to coalesce in the so-called Christian Front, which fostered a program of anti-Jewish intimidation that resulted in stabbings, bashings, and random violence. Coughlin also had support on Capitol Hill, where Mississippi's John Rankin's hate-filled rants on the Senate floor included one of his favorite epithets, "kike," and Montana's Jacob Thorkelson ascribed to the Jews a massive invisible government that conjoined global banking operations with an international Communist conspiracy dedicated to world domination.

The Front, which was particularly active in New York, launched boycotts of Jewish merchants, encouraged an "employ Christians only" campaign, and harassed Jews, in particular the elderly and otherwise vulnerable, on the streets in ethnically mixed neighborhoods. In Washington Heights, site of a large middle-class Jewish population, Friday evening and Saturday morning religious services were disrupted by local youths barging in shouting, "Kill the Jews." Practically every synagogue in the community was desecrated; Jewish-owned businesses were vandalized. Reports of verbal and physical assaults on old and young alike and complaints to the local police were dismissed: "Ah, the boys are just playing."[39] Not only were the Jews appalled by what was happening to them, as well as the reaction—rather, lack of reaction—by the police, they were hurt that a mayor who stood so tall in favor of civic virtue and the happiness of all citizens remained surprisingly mute on the subject. While many insisted that those preaching and practicing hatred were merely exercising their First Amendment right, some concerned non-Jews demanded that the Front be shut down and its street orators either shut up or locked up.

Of all the influential publications, the *Nation* was in the vanguard in calling upon La Guardia to address the failure of the police to treat the whole issue as more than boys "just playing." One police officer hauling a prisoner into the station house was heard to say, "You people have gone too far, and we are going to stop you. . . . When the time comes I'll resign from the force and we'll settle the question our way." The prisoner's "crime": carrying a placard denouncing Father Coughlin! Detailing similar incidents of open police bigotry, the author demanded to know how the mayor was planning to deal with the problem. The mayor replied, "The police have rendered excellent service and have exerted the proper kind of restraint."[40] His words rang hollow not long afterward when twenty-six-year-old Joseph Schwartz was arrested for creating a disturbance while passing a street rally by "Christian Mobilizers." When one speaker declaimed that the only good Jews were to be found in cemeteries, Schwartz shouted back that he was a good Jew and still alive. In court under oath, the arresting policeman, one James Cavanaugh, who had been assigned to the rally "to guard the peace," admitted he had arrested Schwartz unjustly—but that he had only been acting on the orders of his fellow Hibernian Captain Michael McCarron.

The presiding magistrate was incredulous "that things of this kind can occur in the streets of this city." Urged to do more than quote the First Amendment grounds of free speech and lawful assembly, La Guardia promised to have advisers attend Christian Front meetings and report back to him. Equally disturbing to friends and loyalists was his reaction to a spate of written complaints. To one who urged his closer attention to the activities of the Christian Front and other anti-Semitic groups, he replied, "This report is typical of the exaggerated accounts circulated from some quarters."[41]

On January 11, 1940, the *Times* carried a letter to the editor in which the writer complained of having written fifteen letters to the mayor and other officials about the problem, all of which had gone ignored. Three days later the FBI arrested eighteen New Yorkers on charges of conspiring to bomb the *Jewish Daily Forward,* the *Daily Worker,* a Brooklyn movie house that showed Russian-made films, a number of Jewish-owned businesses, and even a few predominantly Jewish neighborhoods. It was further discovered that the conspirators planned to follow up their terrorist havoc with the assassination of Jewish congressmen, in hopes of igniting a nationwide uprising of anti-Semitic factions. Though the plot was considered too implausible to be taken seriously, it nevertheless indicated the extremes to which the Christian Front was prepared to go in furtherance of its depraved ideology.

At last convinced by the FBI roundup of the danger this lunatic fringe group posed, La Guardia told Commissioner Herlands to investigate police membership in the Christian Front. The investigation was limited and produced the sort of controversy La Guardia feared. The police were ordered to complete anonymously a simple questionnaire asking whether they belonged to the Front or any other "subversive, Communist, bund or fascist club or organization." This prompted the Brooklyn Tablet, house organ of that borough's Catholic diocese, to demand to know why the Front was thus being "maligned" and go on to suggest La Guardia was too concerned about Jewish opinion: "Let anyone be associated, directly or indirectly, with any movement or person which is reported to cherish dislike of some Jews then the Mayor and his whole spy system are turned loose on them." The journal then went on to denounce the questionnaire, in which four hundred police admitted to being Front members, as "infamous demoralizing, insulting, un-American, anti-Christian, and little less than a slander on all Christians."[42]

Remarkably, it took three years for Herlands to release an "Investigative Report on Anti-Semitism in New York City," detailing police negligence and incompetence in dealing with anti-Semitism, and for Commissioner Valentine to order steps taken against vandalism of Jewish businesses and desecration of Jewish houses of worship. Asked if he was responsible for the order, La Guardia ducked the question. Anti-Semitism was running rampant in the United States; according to surveys taken between 1938 and the war's end, it had the active support of 15 percent of Americans and the sympathy of another 20 to 25 percent. La Guardia was not only ignoring the issue, he was trying to distance himself from it.[43]

La Guardia's stance becomes even more embarrassing to record. Word was coming out of Europe about the German death camps. While proposing that the Nazis be warned that they would be held accountable, his position on aiding those Jews who could still be saved was a masterful act of ambivalence: "We cannot tell others to take in the doomed while we keep our own door closed. While we consider emigration and colonization, however, we must realize that taking the Jews and others out of terrorist controlled lands is not really the solution. The rights of Jews and other minorities must be made safe in every country in the world."

The threat was as irrelevant as his testimony some weeks later before Congress favoring creation of a commission to "save the Jewish people of Europe from extinction at the hands of Nazi Germany," then calling for the United States to permit immigration of the Jews *"in the same proportion that it asked other countries to do so"* [italics added]. It made for good headlines.[44] But—as La Guardia knew full well—the United States was not asking any country to open its doors. Although information about Nazi Germany's determination to eradicate European Jewry became public in November 1942, it took the United States fourteen months to do anything. And what was done was minimal and inadequate compared to what could have been done. Roosevelt was not an anti-Semite. Many of his closest advisers were Jews. His primary concern was oil for our war machine, and that meant not antagonizing the Arabs, most of whom supported Germany.[45]

If ever there was a time for the firebrand who had taken on the United States Army and, during his years in Congress, the entire government to unleash "his explosive resentment against the power and cruelty, the stupidity and arrogance of Anglo-Saxon America," the time was now.[46] But political daring had given way to political caution. Still fantasizing about a Washington appointment, the last thing La Guardia was prepared to do was challenge the president's discreditable policy on the rescue—actually the nonrescue—of Europe's condemned Jewry. La Guardia did not hesitate when it came to imposing upon the president a veritable deluge of ideas, suggestions, and opinions on the treatment of the Italians, European propaganda, military strategy, Latin America—indeed, a laundry list of issues that had nothing to do with New York City and were not matters that fell within his official parameters of responsibility. But when it came to the Holocaust, the most horrendously momentous historical event of the time, no memos issued forth from City Hall to the White House. There is no gainsaying that many leaders of American Jewry who had the president's ear did as little, or even less, to attempt to somehow force action on Roosevelt's part. But "the uncalculating passion that had ignited [La Guardia's] social conscience earlier had now been tamped by a shrewder politics and a wartime sensitivity to rocking the boat."[47]

PART V

1943-1947

The Last Years

CHAPTER TWENTY-TWO

"You can't stay in office indefinitely"

1.

Of all Fiorello La Guardia's stands on popular equality, the one with perhaps the greatest resonance for our times concerned black Americans. We have already seen how he coped with the Harlem Riot during his first term, named the first black magistrate in the city's history, appointed men and women of color to official positions, and was the first mayor to institute housing projects, hospitals, and recreational facilities in the black communities. He also signed petitions demanding that defense industries hire blacks, had choice words about employment agencies that openly discriminated against blacks, signed a public appeal to President Roosevelt that discrimination in the armed forces be eliminated, and pushed the President to meet with black leaders and establish a Fair Employment Practices Commission. When the FEPC was established, black labor leader A. Philip Randolph and NAACP head Walter White urged that La Guardia be named its chairman, maintaining he was the most resolute and effective public figure when it came to racial fairness. But, consistent with his policy of turning to southerners when it came to civil rights issues, Roosevelt named instead the *Louisville Courier Journal*'s liberal editor, Mark Etheridge.[1]

Meanwhile, the forces of history were moving the city toward its gravest crisis since the bloody Civil War riots, whose victims were primarily blacks, many of them innocent children. New York's black population had grown by 40 percent during the La Guardia years, with more than 145,000 relocating from the South, bringing the city's total to a half-million. Thanks to him, they were beneficiaries of, among other commendable achievements, the Harlem River Houses, the Central Harlem Center, a new wing at Harlem Hospital, and two new public schools. In addition, black doctors and nurses were brought into city hospitals, and more blacks were employed in police, transit, relief, and other services, not only in black neighborhoods but also throughout the city.[2]

The numbers were not satisfactory to the blacks, but there was a limit to how far any mayor could go beyond insisting upon a greater degree of integration. This was, let it be remembered, still a time when discrimination was endemic even in the North; when, for instance, blacks were restricted to the balcony in movie houses and not welcome at restaurants even in presumably more "tolerant" New York, and top-flight entertainers, denied lodging in hotels where they performed, had to make their entrances and exits via the back door and through the kitchen.

To La Guardia, as to other white egalitarians in positions of leadership, it was a tenet of faith that race should be not be significant: People were people when it came to needing a boost up the economic ladder and achieving equality. Admittedly, he could not comprehend, let alone exonerate, the illegitimacy, common-law marriage, gambling, drinking, lack of firm control of their children, and all other aspects of an unstable home life that were prevalent in the black community. But then, he could not excuse these factors in any community. What "problems" he had vis-à-vis the blacks had to do not so much with the lifestyle of so many of them, which conflicted with his own traditional values, as with the prejudice toward their community by so many Anglo-Saxon constituents whose aspirations he advocated.

Such prejudice was neither as blatant nor as horrendous as that of southern bigots whose out-and-out violence so often resulted in the sprouting from tree limbs of "strange fruit," the haunting metaphor for lynching victims. The prejudice of bigoted New Yorkers was no less impassioned but much more insidious. They denied blacks jobs, refused to tolerate them as neighbors, and rejected the moral and legal dicta that they were their equals and not their inferiors. Obviously, La Guardia neither shared these attitudes nor condoned them. But as Dominic J. Capeci Jr. has written authoritatively, in his capacity as mayor La Guardia not only worked with these people, he refused to believe they were fundamentally evil, and at times he compromised with them.[3] Was he being a hypocritical politician or a naive politician? Probably it was a combination of the two, albeit to a minimal degree. But the fact remains that he was sincere when it came to fostering parity, be it racial or ethnic.

By 1943, accepting, as did every other of the nation's municipal leaders, that the federal government was not going to fund enough public housing to ameliorate the chronic shortage, La Guardia turned to the Progressive Era practice of private interests developing low-rent tenements for the poor at modest profits—known as "philanthropy and five percent" projects. In June of that year he entered into an agreement with the Metropolitan Life Insurance Company to construct, at a cost of forty to fifty million dollars, a thirty-thousand tenant "quasi-public" low-rent complex on Manhattan's Lower East Side. The company, not the city, was to be responsible for clearing and rehabilitating the area and for management of the complex, to be known as Stuyvesant Town. The reader will recall that Metropolitan refused to hire blacks, even though it had in Harlem alone more than a hundred thousand policyholders. The company's chairman, Frederick Eckers, informed La Guardia that the company's policy of discrimination against blacks in the workplace extended to the dwelling place. Stuyvesant Town's resident population would be all white.[4]

La Guardia never expected the negative reaction from the black community, typified by letters from one housewife who asked, "Can it be, Mr. Mayor, that you of all people are approving . . . discrimination?" and from another who said Harlem boys would be coming home from the war to find "Hitler's policies right here in dear old New York." Unintentionally pouring salt on the wound, La Guardia had also foregone his practice of consulting the black community on interests of special concern to them, claiming he was too busy now to discuss Stuyvesant Town. In fact, he feared such discussions could sidetrack, possibly even compromise, so necessary a project. He did register his disapproval of tenant discrimination in a letter to Eckers, but this was as far as he could go. Tenant selection was contractually the prerogative of Metropolitan.[5]

Seizing upon the whole episode to further his political agenda, which was to become leader of the Harlem community, was the aforementioned Adam Clayton Powell Jr. As firebrands, he and La Guardia had much in common. Where they parted was on priorities. La Guardia saw the war as his paramount concern. Powell reflected the view of his constituency that while the United States was willing to fight globally for the rights of people against the forces of tyranny, discrimination flourished not only in the armed forces (which were not integrated until war's end, by President Truman) but on the home front as well. What could black GIs expect to return to but the same inequalities they left behind? As one resident put it, summing up the consensus, "I don't like goin' over there fightin' for the white man."[6]

The People's Committee, a grassroots organization that he put together and quickly transformed into a potent political force, helped the thirty-three-year-old Powell become the first black elected to the City Council. His superb oratory was devoted almost exclusively to lambasting the La Guardia administration for ignoring Harlem's needs. When he initiated his "Double V" campaign—victory overseas against the dictators and victory against what he saw as the racist administration at home—La Guardia became so embittered he refused to work in any way with Powell. For his part, Powell dismissed La Guardia as a Progressive who had either sold out or was burnt out, "one of the most pathetic figures on the current American scene."[7]

In the spring of 1943, race riots broke out in major cities around the country. By far the worst occurred in Detroit (June 21, 1943); it resulted in thirty-four deaths, most of them blacks killed by white police, another seven hundred injured, and property damage in the millions. Powell demanded that La Guardia meet with a biracial committee to thrash out the whole white-versus-black problem. The demand was ignored. La Guardia was determined to devise his own plans for confronting the issue, but with more moderate black leaders. What is more, he ignored Powell's warning that the Detroit riot had been caused by a weak mayor and out-of-control police force and that New York City with its "prima donna" mayor and racist police could expect the same. Powell insisted that La Guardia "get rid of your inferiority complex," then insisted his community prepare to defend itself.[8]

La Guardia broadcast a plea that New Yorkers maintain calm and ignore the "snakes" determined to foment trouble between the races. "Above all have an understanding of the other fellow's problems. . . . We have faults of our own, all of us, without being subjected to instigation or provocation of people who are not our friends and do not love our country." He assured the blacks that "if any white man provokes or instigates assaults against a Negro group, I will protect the Negro group and prosecute the white man," and implored patience: "We must not forget that in New York City we still have the aftermath of prejudice, racial hatred and exploitation that has existed in many parts of the country. I want to assure the people of this city that with just a bit of cooperation and understanding . . . we are able to cope with any situation."[9]

Six days after the broadcast, on the basis of reports he had ordered prepared on the Detroit riots, plus input from Walter White, La Guardia convened an interracial group to make plans for New York to avoid that other city's mistakes. At his request, White contacted leaders in the city's black districts to "see that our people so conduct themselves during the next few critical weeks and months [as to give] no cause for racial friction." La Guardia also announced new housing projects and had Police Commissioner Valentine appoint more black officers and establish rules to restrain police in the event of disorder. They were to protect property and were to use deadly force only in defense against bodily harm. Taverns were to be immediately closed down. Guns in sports and pawnshops were to be put under guard. Traffic was to be diverted around trouble spots. Passengers in public transport were to be protected. Tear gas was to be used only as a last resort.[10]

And then the roof fell in.

Sometime around 9:30 on the first Sunday evening of August 1943, a black woman named Marjorie Polite was arrested outside the Hotel Braddock on 126th Street and Eighth Avenue by white patrolman James Collins for creating a disturbance. After checking into the hotel, she was dissatisfied with her room, so demanded—and received—a refund. But when the return of a dollar tip she had given the elevator operator was not forthcoming, she left the hotel in a rage, screaming and cursing. Unable to calm her down, Officer Collins arrested her. Two bystanders, Mrs. Florine Roberts and her son, Private Robert Bandy, insisted that Polite be released.

There are two accounts of what happened next. According to the official police report, either the mother or son grabbed Collins's nightstick and beat him over the head, then both ran away, whereupon Collins drew his revolver and loosed a round at the fleeing pair. According to Bandy, he did not intercede until after Collins began to abuse Polite and angrily threw his nightstick at him, whereupon Bandy caught the stick and started running, prompting Collins to shoot him. Bandy's wounds were superficial.

Within minutes word spread through Harlem that a white cop had shot—some claimed killed—a black soldier who had simply been protecting his mother. Within an hour crowds numbering in the thousands massed menacingly at three points: the Braddock, Suydenham Hospital, and the Twenty-eighth Police Precinct on West 123rd Street. Meanwhile, people were running amok, smashing store windows, looting, setting stores afire, hurling stones and bottles from windows and rooftops. The hospitals were jammed, wholesale arrests were made, and armories were converted into temporary jails and warehouses where the overflow of arrested looters and their gleanings were held. Writer Ralph Ellison, author of the classic *The Invisible Man*, who happened to be on the scene, recalled, "In half an hour it seemed that all of Harlem was awake. Women stood on the stoops in their nightgowns and wrappers, and when the fire trucks went through with their flashing lights, you could see them framed in their tenement windows."[11]

La Guardia rushed with Valentine to the Twenty-eighth Precinct, which he immediately turned into an emergency command post. He ordered that all police who had finished their shifts be kept on duty and reinforcements brought in from other precincts. The police were ordered to move throughout Harlem to restore order and patrol the streets, assisted by an Army detachment hastily called in. A total of six thousand police and 1,500 deputized (mostly black) volunteers were deployed. Guards were placed on all subways that traveled through Harlem. Police from neighboring precincts were held in reserve. Along with White and other prominent black leaders, La Guardia toured the riot area on a flatbed truck ordering the crowds to return to their homes and assuring them that, rumors to the contrary, the soldier was only slightly wounded. He also went on the radio to dispel rumors and assure the people that life and property would be protected.

From Sunday night till Tuesday morning, when the situation was declared "under control," he remained in personal command. During that period he made five broadcasts, targeted mainly to the black community, blaming hoodlums for the riot, pleading for cooperation with authorities, and calmly describing the restrictions he had imposed. These included, in addition to contingency plans announced after the Detroit riot and orders he had given upon arriving at the Twenty-eighth Precinct, a community-wide curfew, sealing off the entire area, and special plans for the unimpeded flow of food and medical supplies. It took a week to return the community to normal. The cost of the "disturbance"—a word La Guardia preferred to "race riot"—was six dead, all blacks, 185 injured, and more than five million dollars in damage.[12]

Agreement was unanimous that La Guardia did a superb job confronting—and keeping from spreading to other black communities—the worst mayhem in Harlem's history, at the same time protecting area residents. Black leaders particularly appreciated that he did not condemn the community as a whole but reminded the rest of the city that the trouble was the work of a small group of hoodlums. Even Powell praised La Guardia's "wise and effective" leadership and the fact that the police avoided indiscriminate shooting. White promised, "The decent people of Harlem will stand by you and back you to the limit."[13]

Ten days after order was restored, La Guardia initiated his alternative to Powell's "Double V" campaign, which he felt had fed, if not directly precipitated, the riots. In a series of radio programs dedicated to "Unity at Home and Victory Abroad," he promised meaningful progress in better housing, more recreational facilities, better personnel in Harlem schools and hospitals, and more sensitivity on the part of the police. The Metropolitan Life Insurance Company was told he would oppose with all judicial powers at his disposal any discrimination in the selection of tenants for Stuyvesant Town. Also, he created, under the chairmanship of former Supreme Court justice Charles Evans Hughes, a Mayor's Committee on Unity to study the root causes of prejudice, discrimination, and exploitation: a kind of authoritative municipal institution to investigate the whole problem of American race relations and issue periodic reports based on exhaustive research. The idea that such a committee could actually influence public policy, let alone deracinate ingrained prejudices, was commendable. Whether La Guardia believed it actually could do so is open to doubt.

The fact remains that from the beginning of his first term in office he had been sensitive to the needs of the blacks and sought in many ways to bring them into the mainstream, but recommendations for meeting what were not so much demands for special treatment as demands for parity had gone largely ignored. For this, blame must be consigned to a combination of inaction by the City Council, arbitrary decisions by the likes of Robert Moses, and the prevailing sentiment of the times, both locally and on the national level, that effecting such parity was neither a priority nor, for that matter, of any undue concern. Above it all, in the eyes of New York's black community, stood one man, the city's chief magistrate, who by virtue of his position was the logical target. Charging La Guardia with the ultimate responsibility became almost a mantra among his critics following the Harlem "disturbance."

A Brooklyn grand jury convened after the riot blamed City Hall for the deteriorating problems in that borough's predominantly black Bedford-Stuyvesant neighborhood. Living conditions were deplorable, with three to eight families sharing a single bathroom in many of the once-grand mansions that had been converted into human rabbit warrens. Youths brandishing sharpened penknives roamed the streets in gangs terrorizing and assaulting passersby (on one occasion a sailor was stabbed to death for no discernible reason by a fourteen-year-old and some of his friends). The grand jury condemned the administration for failing to curb lawlessness in the borough and tolerating a lack of sensitivity toward blacks. The police, it was claimed, not only neglected the city but also on occasion verbally, and at times physically, abused black citizens.

Terming the problem one of crime, not of race, the grand jury made a number of recommendations: Increase the number of blacks in law enforcement agencies, require a permit to carry a knife, ban people from congregating in front of bars, toughen inspections of welfare recipients, promote special recreational and classroom activities, compel adolescent courts to hand down stiffer sentences, increase the staff of the Juvenile Delinquency Bureau, even interrupt radio programs at nine in the evening to ask parents if they knew where their children were. Other recommendations included calling in, when warranted, the National Guard (to include more black recruits) and canceling public events such as Mardi Gras, which often resulted in the coalescence of boisterous, at times near-uncontrollable mobs.[14]

The grand jury was dissolved before any of its recommendations could be acted on, presupposing they even could be without alienating the white community. But this was moot, since making findings and offering recommendations for prescriptive action was the extent of its authority. At a meeting in November attended by some five hundred people, most of them white, La Guardia defended his administration against the charge of failing to curb lawlessness. As for the grand jury's indictment of his administration, he made it clear that all he could do was enforce the laws regardless of race or ethnicity and treat those who broke them in the same way he treated, say, gamblers. Only with the passage of time could the problem of race relations achieve resolution.

La Guardia never denied the peril that would follow as a consequence of ignoring the needs and demands of New York's—indeed, the nation's—black population. He did what he could. It can be argued in hindsight that he might have done more, but two factors must be considered. To view through our own ethos what anyone of authority might have done for the betterment of race relations more than half a century ago is not only unfair, it is unrealistic. And it is to La Guardia's credit that he kept the city from exploding as a result of the Harlem riots.

2.

Midway through his third administration, which was coterminous with the midway point of America's participation in the war, Robert Moses, in an article titled "What's the Matter with New York," saw La Guardia as a conflicted man "uncertain as to whether to be a national, an international or a local character, whether to be a legislator whose every act is privileged or an executive who must be responsible for everything he does today, whether to be a conservative or a radical, an artist or a tough boss, a broad indeed cosmopolitan or an uncompromising reformer."[15] The article could just as well have been titled "What's the Matter with New York's Mayor." The matter was that things were not going precisely the way he wanted. And when they didn't, he would become frustrated. La Guardia transmuted that frustration into behavior that was at times outrageous, at times out of sync with his liberalism and tolerance of old, at times downright aberrant.

Instead of listening to the press, he treated it as an enemy. He stopped heeding the advice of friends, even such wise ones as Burlingham and Seabury. More than closing himself off from criticism, he became remote, isolated, and willful. An innate self-indulgence had given way to arrogance and incivility. Where once he rectified social injustice and trashed officials who deserved no better, now he struck out in all directions, seeming to take some inexplicable pleasure in pointing out the flaws and failures of others.

Ever the politician, he made every attempt to contain his vituperation if to do otherwise might be disadvantageous. When Dewey succeeded Lehman as governor, Fiorello wisely maintained an air of correctness in his dealings with a man, never one of his favorites, who was in a position to grant or withhold funding to the city. Though many in Washington officialdom were easy targets, he treaded cautiously when it came to the fact that while wartime spending had brought recovery from the Depression to many cities, New York did not initially share in the bonanza. Not only had financing the nation's defense led to a necessary cutting off of the relief and public works that had kept the city going during the 1930s—there were fifty thousand more persons unemployed in 1942 than in the Depression year of 1939—the city had no military contracts. Where housing had been in perilously short supply only a few years before, there were now more than seventy-five thousand vacant apartments and a glut of private homes.

La Guardia resolved the crisis through prudent yet insistent lobbying. Reminded of what he owed his old friend for his support of the New Deal, President Roosevelt ordered the appropriate agencies to confer with the mayor about the use of plant and manpower facilities in New York City. As a result, 12 percent of all Navy contracts were assigned to New York City firms and more than two hundred thousand New Yorkers were put to work. Roosevelt wanted it known that it was "Fiorello" who deserved much of the credit when full employment was realized in New York by the end of 1943. Fiorello was highly appreciative. But he felt that Roosevelt owed him more in the nature of personal favor. As we shall see shortly, when the president failed to come across, La Guardia sustained a humiliation and a letdown from which he would never quite recover.

His dealings with various city agencies and departments had become vexatious; none more so than with the Board of Education, prompting *Newsweek* (September 27, 1943) to comment that La Guardia spent much of his third term "barging like a small bee-stung [bull] around New York's educational china shop." For five years he had been attacking the board on grounds of inefficient methods of school construction. Now having found inefficiency and waste in the purchase of school supplies, he was determined to transfer this function to the city. When the education lobby defeated a bill to that effect introduced in the state legislature at his instigation, a furious La Guardia set out to wreak vengeance on all those who had opposed it, including board chairman Ellsworth Buck.

The public backed La Guardia to the hilt when he raged over the board's rejection of his insistence that Mark Starr, education director of the International Garment Workers Union, be named to the post of adult education director of the city school system, but it had little sympathy for La Guardia on the Buck issue. He overreacted, letting loose with both barrels on the board and its chairman. This led those who had supported him to now turn against him. They saw in his open contempt for the board a threat to the independence of the school system: "I had a friendly talk with Mr. Buck. He told me he would not resign and I told him the first time I got the chance I would fire him."[16]

There was no resignation and no firing. There was, though, more controversy. Instead of accepting defeat, La Guardia obdurately pushed ahead. After Starr was rejected a second time and Buck reelected chairman, La Guardia denied reappointment to labor representative Johanna Lindloff, because he did not like her "independence of speech and action." A rally in her honor degenerated into a strong condemnation of the mayor. His reaction was to have the city's budget director refuse authorization of funds for several of the board's appointments, among them Lindloff's confidential secretary, Trude Weil. When she sued the city for her $4,500 salary, funds were found available for her to become an adviser to City Hall on educational matters. La Guardia's reversal on Weil, whom he had specifically rejected, indicated a willingness to achieve some kind of understanding with the board. The board showed its willingness to cooperate by acceding to his insistence that its law secretary of more than twenty years' service be fired because of his role in the state's rejection of the purchasing department bill. Nevertheless, the situation was rapidly becoming intolerable.

When the influential National Education Association met in New York to investigate the whole squabble, most of those called upon to testify declined to do so, either out of hope that the rift between the board and City Hall could be healed or out of fear of retaliation by the man who ran City Hall. One who was only too happy to testify was Lindloff. She charged that La Guardia consistently sought to run the board and impede its legal authority. La Guardia was also asked to testify but chose instead to "testify" on one of his Sunday night broadcasts. The board members, he said homiletically, ought to be given "an old-fashioned course in good manners." He added that students should come to school with their hair combed and their shoes shined.[17]

In its report made public the following February, the NEA charged La Guardia with conduct "unprofessional and against public interest" in having forced the dismissal of the board's law secretary and initiating the bill transferring school purchases to the city. Shrugging off the report, La Guardia argued that since the NEA members came from smaller towns and cities, they did not fully understand New York, and therefore many of their judgments were easily refuted. Far from refuting them, however, he patronizingly played down their significance. In doing so, he threw away even more support with his glib remark that he had in fact been impressed by its chairman, a Miss Studebaker, "because she was wearing beautiful nylon stockings." The press took him to task for dismissing the report with "a quite graceless levity" and for being "gratuitously offensive" to Studebaker.[18]

Behind La Guardia's flippancy, his dismissal of criticism, his weariness with a job that was slowly but irrevocably becoming terminal, and others' suspicion that he may well have begun to come apart at the seams—in short, the answer to Moses's wondering what the matter was with New York, and by extension with its mayor—lay that profound frustration that began as wishful thinking and evolved into a pathological obsession: to go to war as a general.

3.

Urged by La Guardia, the president looked for a military position for him. With General Dwight D. Eisenhower having successfully landed forces in North Africa in the autumn of 1942, thus opening the Mediterranean, Roosevelt thought he had the perfect spot: sending his friend Fiorello to aid in the establishment of civilian government in Italy, once the North was occupied. The idea was passed on to Eisenhower, whose initial reaction was to hesitate "complicat[ing] my staff problems" with the battle of Tunisia at its height. He did agree, however, that La Guardia could eventually be quite useful in directing a separate staff operation over nonmilitary American activities in the war area. Telling La Guardia that he would be seeing action, but neglecting to tell him it would be as a civilian, the Army Department secretly advised him to begin "preparing to take over just as soon as the present phase of the Tunisia campaign is completed."[19] La Guardia gleefully ordered a uniform and polished the stars of a brigadier general to grace it. Little did he know the role his old foe Ed Flynn would play, albeit indirectly, in the fate of that uniform.

On January 3, 1943, Roosevelt nominated the Bronx boss to be ambassador to Australia and his personal representative in the Pacific area. Flynn thought he was eminently qualified for the post: "Australia is nearly fifty per cent Irish Catholic, and I am of that faith and people."[20] The Senate committee considering the confirmation thought otherwise. After three days of hearings on Flynn's political past and several charges of misconduct leveled against him, La Guardia was called on January 23 to testify as an expert on political bosses. This put him in a terrible bind. If he defended Flynn, whom he would gladly have recommended as ambassador to Hell, he would brand himself as a hypocrite, given his lifelong loathing of bosses. If he spoke against Flynn, he would upset Roosevelt, and thus compromise his chances of any Army commission.

To the inevitable question of whether he knew about those Belgian paving blocks for Flynn's summer home, La Guardia responded that he had *heard* of the charge but, lacking personal knowledge of the incident, passed on what information he had to the Bronx grand jury, over which he lacked control. Next question: Did he think that the United States should be represented abroad by "crooked and corrupt" individuals? His reply: "Your question answers itself." Realizing the witness was blatantly distancing himself from Flynn, and seeking to box him in, his interrogator reminded His Honor that it was in fact he who had openly characterized Flynn as "crooked and corrupt" in the past; did he consider Flynn suitable for the ambassadorship?

Replied His Honor, "I cannot qualify as a character witness, because of the bitterness that has existed for years between us and because of my prejudice against him." And that was that. Nine minutes after taking the witness chair, La Guardia was excused after having it both ways. He had avoided supporting Flynn and offending the president. He could now be assured of that military position he coveted. Or so he thought, as he continued to campaign for it shamelessly. On February 3, 1943, while Eisenhower's army pushed its way across North Africa toward Italy, La Guardia sent a hastily scrawled, messily punctuated "My dear Chief" note to Roosevelt:

> *I still believe General Eisenhower—can not get along without me and am awaiting your orders (but as a soldier)—*
>
> *Food, man-power, prices and wages are still our big trouble and headaches.*
>
> *Let me know how and when I can help.*
>
> *I hope to see you soon—in the meantime.*
>
>

Con amore

Fiorello[21]

In mid-March, La Guardia and Roosevelt had a long talk on Fiorello's presumably impending role of civil affairs director in liberated Italy—at his insistence, not as a civilian but as a brigadier general. He came away from the meeting convinced that his cherished goal was imminent, as witness the "Dear Harry" note he dashed off the next day to Harry Hopkins: "The Chief indicated I could be commissioned right after I finish the Executive Budget, in early April. I am to be assigned to General Eisenhower's staff and am confident that I will be able to do a good job and be really useful."[22] Talk of the proposed appointment soon found its way into the papers. "Clearly New York is about to lose a mayor and the army is about to gain an officer," wrote the *Herald Tribune* on March 28. But, as would soon become apparent, the newspaper was as premature in its comment as La Guardia was in his confidence.

Earlier in the month a law granting a mayor the right to a leave of absence was introduced into the state legislature and passed so quickly, and so obscurely, that barely any members were aware of what had been done. What had been done—without even mentioning New York City's mayor—was to enable the governor to name an acting mayor of the same party as the City Council president, should he, as La Guardia's mandated surrogate, also go off to war. Governor Dewey saw the opportunity to put a Republican of his choosing into City Hall and gladly signed the bill. The Democrats, realizing too late what they had allowed to sneak past them, shouted, "Treason!"

La Guardia would still be running the city from his post in Italy through a puppet mayor, the loyal Newbold Morris. This set off a firestorm in the press. To the *Times* it was a "flimsy law"; to the *Post,* "a sleazy deal" with "a strong odor of fascism about it." The *News* suggested it was time for Fiorello to leave office altogether. He not only seemed to have lost interest in the job, but "with his frequent air raid alarms and assorted mock-war goings on, his quarrels with the press . . . his [anti-Minsky] burlesque and [anti-]bingo crusades and his other interferences with our private lives," he had "got on the nerves of the city."

The legislation, along with La Guardia's determination to go off to war and still, in effect, remain mayor, troubled many. The office he had once looked upon as a sacred trust he now seemed to look upon as a private fiefdom, to pass around or retain at his own pleasure. Reformers, even among his inner circle, assailed this piece of legislative legerdemain as a flouting of democratic government. Those who still held to the idea of fusion and progressive government felt betrayed. Wrote one old acquaintance, reflecting the feelings of many, "You are the only man alive who can handle the affairs in New York City. . . . There's heroism in standing the abuse, the pestering, the boredom of your long term in New York City. . . . That's a bigger thing to consider than *how* you can *brigadier* anywhere on earth. Consider well before you just drop the world's greatest problem child at the most dangerous period of its life back into the lap of corrupt politics."[23] As other major supporters like Seabury and Windels added their objections, it was Burlingham who put it best: "What is this political streptococcus that is biting you? . . . You owe it to this City to stay right here and do your job."[24] Burlingham also told Secretary of War Stimson that taking La Guardia out of City Hall was a bad idea.

He needn't have bothered. Stimson had already decided he did not relish the prospect of contending with a loose cannon like Fiorello serving as what amounted to America's proconsul in Italy. He agreed with Navy Secretary James V. Forrestal that La Guardia could be sent to the Pacific, but as a civilian; the need for administration there would become a major issue, notably in the Philippines, following the end of the war. Other voices were chiming in urging that La Guardia be kept out of the military. But La Guardia was impervious to the crescendo of criticism as he busied himself with final fittings for his uniform and selecting his military aides (including World War I comrade Albert Spalding, who was prepared to put aside his flourishing career as a concert violinist to again serve "the Major"). His spirits soared when Roosevelt's press secretary, Steve Early, announced that "all indications point to service in the army for the mayor." Eisenhower and Army Chief of Staff George C. Marshall now added their objections. Then Senator Harry S. Truman, chairman of the powerful Committee to Investigate the National Defense Program, weighed in, expressing unequivocally his firm opposition to "political generals."[25]

Roosevelt had not expected such opposition; having just been embarrassed over rejection of the Flynn nomination, he was unwilling to get into another public ruckus over an appointment that showed every sign of being just as controversial—and unwinnable. During a press conference on April 6, 1943, three days after Truman made his views known, the president replied to a planted question that there were no plans to commission New York's mayor a brigadier general. Next day, Stimson announced that while La Guardia had patriotically offered his services to the War Department and to the nation, the Army was unable to find a position to match his efficacy as mayor of New York City.[26]

La Guardia happened to be in Washington—anticipating eagerly his travel orders. He gamely told reporters, "I'll carry on. I've got a uniform of my own up in New York, a street cleaner's uniform. That's my little army." But the hurt and embarrassment was almost too much to bear. Privately, he blamed Roosevelt for having abandoned him. "I burned all my bridges ahead of me for him," he told Burlingham. However, he would "continue to give him my utmost support during this war."[27]

The whole business was more than a public humiliation, it was a cruel letdown. His bitterness and self-pity would compromise his self-esteem and power to control events within his own city as he had managed to in the past. Being forced to don that metaphorical street cleaner's uniform instead of a brigadier general's was a defining moment in La Guardia's last years in public office. What the secretary of war did, he told Burlingham, was "just plain rotten," a "dirty deal." But "I have always been able to take care of myself. . . . I do hope you will understand. I am very unhappy."[28]

The starch had gone out of the Little Flower. He would never again be the man and mayor he'd been in his first two terms.

4.

Fiorello now began to fling irritability and arbitrariness in all directions like Jackson Pollock tossing paint in one of his more manic moments of creation. To the bitterness he felt over losing that commission and the directorship of the OCD was added the difficulty of running the city during wartime, plus his deteriorating health. All this cohered to make him even more antagonistic toward people around him and hypersensitive to the criticism such behavior provoked. His war with the press, and with city agencies that did not conform to his demands, heated up. Some aides felt that toward the end of his third term his actions bordered at times on the psychopathic, as when he fired an old and loyal friend simply because a third party had interceded in his behalf on learning that the man's position was threatened.[29]

What's more, the refreshing iconoclasm La Guardia was always prepared to unleash to the people's advantage had degenerated into callous arrogance and rudeness. He now summoned to mind an aging off-the-wall Dodge City marshal ready, nay, eager, to shoot whoever chanced to get caught in his gun sight. He could not take aim at Roosevelt. He still hoped the president would somehow get him into that uniform after all. In an almost pathetic "Dear Chief" note, he wrote that "Soldier La Guardia reports to the C[ommander] in C[hief] that he awaits orders. He believes General Eisenhower needs him now more than ever."[30] Roosevelt was sympathetic. But a canvass of his top people proved fruitless, and he simply would not impose any politician, let alone so problematical a politician as La Guardia, on any of his commanders. One can only imagine Fiorello's reaction upon learning that his last mayoral opponent, William O'Dwyer, who had been commissioned a major in the Army, had been rapidly bumped up to brigadier general.

The early skepticism that was a hallmark of Fiorello's political career had evolved into an unshakeable conviction that his way, and his way alone, was the only way. He was slipping into a me-against-them mode. Those he thought had hurt him (Truman, Stimson, the Board of Education, the press—the list reached almost as high as La Guardia himself) were, in his mind, demons to be exorcised. The exorcisms failed. Those demons simply dismissed La Guardia's every condemnation, be it a formal speech or an off-the-cuff remark, as the grousing of a man who refused to entertain the possibility, however remote, that he might be in error on a point. It was in attacking those he viewed as his paramount antagonists closer to home that he lost the goodwill of the public and, what was more consequential, of the reformers.

Locking horns with the Board of Education had only been a sign of things to come. La Guardia now became involved in an ugly dispute with New York firemen, over their refusal to work overtime. Even worse, he tore into some of the community's most influential movers and shakers, the department store heads, over their opposition to the sales tax and claimed that their stores were "groggy with profits" and that they sought to exert inordinate control over the press as major advertisers. The claim led the head of Tiffany's to say, "He's a liar [who] should be taken to Bellevue and have some of the competent [psychiatrists] there give him a couple of treatments."[31]

Many—including his own fellow reformers—were beginning to suspect a visit to Bellevue might not be a bad idea. Their suspicion accelerated following Fiorello's refusal to respond to a complaint by the Transport Workers Union about unfair labor practices that resulted in the War Labor Board censuring the city for failing to bargain in good faith. He threatened to go directly to the president. The threat, on which he wisely never followed through, was ignored by the WLB. But not by the people of New York, to whom their mayor's frequent outbursts were becoming daily fare. A concerned Burlingham urged that he "restore [his] badly shattered reputation." His reply was appalling: "Frankly, C. C., I am getting sick and tired of the whole thing. If people like you cannot understand and instead of giving aid and help, continue to listen to gossip and spread it and directly, or indirectly heap abuse, then let the [city] go back to Tammany."[32]

As La Guardia relied more and more on his own counsel, all but cutting off his commissioners and advisers, this most successful reform mayor in the city's history came under attack by the Progressives. Claiming that "we must not allow La Guardia to destroy the gains for which we fought," Roger Baldwin and the Rev. John Haynes Holmes of the American Civil Liberties Union petitioned the support of other reform leaders for a public rebuke, citing his "summary methods," "dictatorial shortcuts," and a "pattern of control widely condemned." In tandem with circularizing the reformers, Baldwin in a personal letter made a direct appeal to La Guardia. Acknowledging the mayor's unparalleled achievements, he suggested that they came at a high price, "for the precedents established by extralegal measures may be used for bad ends by your successors. As [William J.] Gaynor, your predecessor, remarked years ago, 'Good men in good times should not set precedents for bad men in bad times.' "

Among the accusations against La Guardia were cutting budgets to make independent agencies confirm to his wishes, paralyzing his own administration with fear and arbitrarily dismissing commissioners, interfering with the autonomy of the City Planning Commission, encouraging police violence, identifying as known gamblers on his Sunday broadcasts men who had not even been indicted, disregarding the civil liberties of others when it served his purpose, obstinately ignoring viable complaints by municipal unions, even ordering the seizure of what we today know as soft-porn magazines on the far from convincing grounds that "the Constitution and laws of the state do not apply to plain smut and filth" and, besides, "trials take too much time and advertise obscenity." After listing still other animadversions, the Baldwin letter begged that he "desist from arbitrary and lawless short-cuts which defy established rights. The temptation to do good, as you see it, by extralegal means—natural doubtless to a man of your temperament—will, we hope, be resisted in the interest of the larger democratic purposes which you have so long professed to serve."

La Guardia could not bring himself to accept either the censure or the counsel. To all recipients of the Baldwin-Holmes petition he sent a mimeographed note dismissing the charges as giving "comfort to the racketeers and gamblers . . . and producers of salacious and immoral stage productions."[33] The petition was circulated out of public view. For La Guardia to dismiss it as he did was unwise. There was much benefit to be gleaned from considering it, as many loyalists sought to make him appreciate. His old friend novelist Fannie Hurst suggested he meet with the Baldwin-Holmes faction. Surprisingly, he agreed. Despite an airing of grievances, nothing came of the meeting. La Guardia insisted that the disaffected reformers could not appreciate his position: "It is quite different to be in this seat."

In fact, they understood quite well. What *he* failed to understand was that being in "this seat" carried with it the obligation to employ more restraint in the exercise of power. When it became obvious that a meeting of minds was unachievable, the ACLU made the petition public in February 1944. This marked the final break between the reformers and the man they had put into City Hall and supported steadfastly for more than two terms.

With La Guardia now at his most vulnerable, the City Council, where his detractors easily outnumbered his admirers, went on the attack. Republican members, goaded by the Democrats, launched an investigation of the entire La Guardia administration. Previously, there had been probes of individual commissioners or particular policies, but this was something else. What it was, in fact, was a fishing expedition. Named to head the special committee was Walter Hart, Democrat from Brooklyn. Though it made a lot of unpleasant noise and precipitated some disagreeable headlines, it netted a small fish and a big fish. Both fish got away. The small fish was Commissioner of Finance Almerindo Portfolio, charged with going out to the racetrack in a city car. When this could not be proved conclusively, Hart decided Portfolio had committed a malfeasance anyway, even if he had *walked* to the track, since it was a violation of the city code for any city official to go watch the ponies during working hours in wartime.

The big fish was William Carey, commissioner of sanitation. Here the charges were more substantial: that he had conducted his private business affairs while in office and that he had mixed public and private monies to fund development of Sanita, a resort out on Long Island for the use of Sanitation Department personnel. The first charge Carey readily admitted to, having made this a precondition to accepting appointment as a commissioner. As for the second charge, Carey conceded that he may have violated the city charter, but the project was in the public interest, as it would lead to improvement in employer-employee relations. What's more, he planned to repay the public funds from proceeds of the department's annual baseball games. This led to a reminder from Hart that commissioners must be sure that their operations conform scrupulously to the provisions of the charter. To this Carey replied, "Well, let them fix up their City Charter to fit the public official."[34]

Here was the very logic that La Guardia had used since first coming into office. This argument, plus the revelation that Carey and his wife had loaned more than a hundred thousand dollars without security to allow work to continue on building Sanita, put an end to the issue—but not to the Hart Committee, which promised to unearth "more startling discoveries." Then Investigations Commissioner Herlands, who had looked into the charges against Carey and dismissed them as "honest mistakes," produced evidence that Hart had himself violated the city charter by appearing before a municipal agency as attorney for a bus line and should therefore be removed from office.

La Guardia, having remained aloof from the Hart investigations, called a special session of the City Council to consider Hart's removal. Backed—not unpredictably—by Robert Moses, Hart insisted it was Herlands who should be removed from office. At this point, the whole affair threatened to degenerate into travesty, with both Carey and La Guardia being charged with charter violations serious enough to constitute malfeasance and thus forfeiture of office: Carey for having engaged in private business while a commissioner, La Guardia for having allowed it. On December 28, voting along party lines, sixteen to six, the council adopted the Hart Committee's adverse report.

This was not unexpected by La Guardia. The remarks of old friend and fellow reformer Stanley Isaacs, though, were. Isaacs told a luncheon meeting of the National Lawyers Guild that henceforth the council's minority members could no longer follow the mayor "in blind loyalty . . . because he varies in loyalty to himself and to the things he used to stand for." Nor would they accept his word on budgets, on allocations, or even on the findings of his commissioner of investigations. "If they disagree with me I understand it," commented La Guardia. "If they agree with me I appreciate it. If they abuse me, I take it. And I still believe in democracy."[35]

That he still believed in democracy is beyond question. As for his pithy remarks preceding that statement, he was unprepared for Isaacs's telling a Citizens Union luncheon the following month, more in sadness than in anger, that La Guardia had given New York the finest administration in the city's history—"but now it has slumped, retrograded."[36] Fiorello wouldn't admit it, even to a confidant like Burlingham, but that last remark undoubtedly hurt.

5.

La Guardia's greatest accomplishments, like his best years, were behind him. His record as labor lawyer, congressman, and finally mayor of a city that was in a sense his creation, and whose greatness to this day is owing in large measure to his stewardship, speaks for itself. His last years should have been his happiest and most personally rewarding: the culmination of a brilliant career, one of the most brilliant in the nation's political history. But they were, in fact, his saddest. Whether he was able—or, for that matter, willing—to accept that the sadness was to a considerable degree self-inflicted is another matter. Chances are he wasn't.

At a City Hall reception on New Year's Day 1944, marking a full ten years in office, La Guardia, standing somewhat apart from the crowd, was caught in a reflective mood by a reporter for the *Times*. His account, published the following day, suggests that the mayor's pensive, rather solemn mien while making what amounted to "small talk" masked delight at an opportunity to unburden his mind. Describing his job as one of "heavy labor," "a heartbreaking work" with little of the glamour and satisfaction he had enjoyed as a congressman, La Guardia foresaw a time when mayors of great cities would be required to bring to the office specialized training in urban administration. It was not enough to be "a good orator or a likeable fellow," he insisted. "You just can't step into the job and learn over-night." Here he was echoing the Platonic thesis that we must train our leaders as we train our teachers, doctors, lawyers—all those we are dependent upon in the pursuit of learning and living.

La Guardia concluded the impromptu interview on a more posi-tive note: "But I'm really hopeful for the country," although he fore-saw, with prescience, difficulties that would come with the ending of the war. This would be especially true of the big cities, whose greatest priority would be to establish an entirely new relationship with the federal government. "Two years ago we were worried that no one was thinking about the future. Now everyone is, and out of it all I think we'll get something that is workable." After a moment's pause, he stressed, "It will be something entirely different from what we now have."

Over the ensuing months he warned that steps must be taken to confront a whole new set of problems that would be the inevitable outcome of the war's imminent conclusion and the resultant de-mobilization. "I can't impress upon you too strongly," he told a con-vention of the Hatters Union shortly before the collapse of Nazi Germany, "how serious that period is going to be." He called for, at the very minimum, uniform unemployment insurance, a well-thought-out program of public works, and national health insur-ance.[37] The easiest of the problems to solve was finding employment for New York's returning veterans. La Guardia already had a detailed seven-hundred-million-dollar program of construction of schools, hospitals, highways, and recreational facilities that had to be deferred by the war but might now at last be implemented. These would bring, perforce, needed improvements in water supply, sewage disposal, and the like. A secondary priority was halting the decline of estab-lished neighborhoods in the outlying areas. Expansion of the subway system would be limited until, as La Guardia put it, the city had "jelled."

What La Guardia failed to take into consideration was the need for a master plan, mainly because he did not think there was a need. One major consequence was that political pressures inevitably deter-mined construction priorities. Nor did he take into consideration how to preserve the new construction projects against the kind of decay prevalent when he first took office. Such costs were not fac-tored into his budgets. Within a generation, the entire city seemed to be falling into a state of disrepair that no funds available could prevent. Whether La Guardia assumed the federal government would support upkeep of rehabilitation is questionable. Unquestionably, though, he was no longer the budget-minded mayor he had been ten years earlier. Many sought to give him economic advice. They sought in vain. His last major reform to that end was fulfillment of a long-standing dream that resulted in the inception of group health insurance. Though elementary by today's standards, what is today referred to collectively as health insurance programs (HIPs) was not only revolutionary in and of itself, it set an example that would become nationwide.

With all that Fiorello had accomplished over twelve years, there was still more to be done. But he was tired. He was suffering intermittent bouts of illness. He had either driven off or lost by attrition many of his best men. He hadn't gotten over the disappointment of being denied a military role. The daily grind of political infighting that goes with the territory was wearing him down. He had lost the enthusiasm for municipal leadership that had swept him into office. And the people sensed it.

In the spring of 1945, with another election looming on the horizon, and raising the question of whether he would emulate Roosevelt and seek a fourth term, the *Daily News* ran a straw poll on mayoral candidates. William O'Dwyer, placing second in the three-man "race," came in with 30 percent, five points ahead of La Guardia. Leading the list, with 40 percent of the vote, was Jimmy Walker, even though it was known he was not even considering a run![38] The vote for Walker doubtless symbolized the general voter feeling that none of the candidates was particularly compelling, combined with a wistful look back to the golden days of the Roaring Twenties, before the Great Depression and a second world war made life so much more problematical and demanding. The low vote for La Guardia, far from being symbolic, was a reflection of the antagonism he had engendered in such episodes as the Lord Russell and Kern affairs, his suspension of the Civil Service Commission, his confrontation with the Board of Education, and his adversarial posture with his own commissioners and especially the press.

There were, of course, a number of people who wanted to see La Guardia make a fourth run. Others believed he wanted out because he foresaw the overwhelming economic burden that New York would in future years have to bear. Some who were close to him felt that the major factor was his health. One, an alderman, Murray Stand, told biographer Charles Garrett categorically that La Guardia would not have run even if he had sufficient encouragement because he felt his health would not permit it and that he would, like Roosevelt, die in office. Newbold Morris noted that in the spring of 1945 La Guardia was in great pain.[39] And not to be overlooked was the obvious: He claimed that if he chose to run he could be returned to office "without any trouble" and without the nomination of any regular political party. But like Lyndon Johnson, who in effect resigned from the presidency, La Guardia knew realistically that he simply could not be returned to office and could never accept the humiliation of rejection and defeat.

In his regularly scheduled Sunday night radio broadcast, on May 6, from his City Hall office in the Blue Room, surrounded by friends and city officials, with Marie and the children seated across the desk from him, La Guardia announced, after having kept the city guessing for months, "I am not going to run for Mayor this year." Among his stated reasons: his belief in rotation in office (he had supported FDR for a fourth term, he said, only because the country was still at war), a fear of growing stale in office, and the added fear of becoming bossy ("they tell me I am inclined that way at times"). He concluded, rather melodramatically, "Yes, my friends, you gave me a job and I did it."[40]

When journalist John Gunther asked him what he was most proud of in his three terms as mayor, Fiorello responded with what could well stand as his epitaph: "I raised the standard of municipal government everywhere in this country, by raising it in New York and so proving it could be raised."[41]

6.

The choice of O'Dwyer as Democratic mayoral nominee came as no surprise; party leaders in Washington as well as New York wanted him, as did the ALP. The Republican nominee, though, was rather bizarre: General Sessions Judge Jonah J. Goldstein, a lifelong Tammany Democrat, who also got the backing of the Liberal Party. The move had the support of Governor Dewey, who saw it as a boost to his own forthcoming campaign for reelection because it would bring over disaffected Democrats. In furtherance of that aim, the party chose for city comptroller Fusionists Joseph McGoldrick, who had held that post under La Guardia but broken with him in May, thereby ending La Guardia's control of the Board of Estimate. On hearing of Goldstein's nomination, Newbold Morris, who had planned to seek reelection to the presidency of the City Council, withdrew from the Republican-Liberal slate. Adding a dash more of bizarreness, Morris was asked by mutual friends of his and O'Dwyer's to run on the Democratic ticket, a blatant attempt to win over the remnants of the Fusion. Unwilling to do so, he discussed the matter with La Guardia and then jumped into the race for mayor as head of the new and hastily formed "No Deal Party."

Observers were convinced that Morris would not have made the move without La Guardia's urging. Some believed that the whole idea was La Guardia's, not Morris's, for a number of reasons: that he really wanted a fourth term but could not get Republican and Liberal support, so hoped to get back at them by launching a "spite ticket" and thus ensure O'Dwyer's election; that he wanted the Democrats to regain City Hall after twelve years because he was convinced that by the time they left office his own administration would stand out as glorious by comparison; that in splitting the Goldstein vote and ensuring an O'Dwyer victory, he hoped to gain Democratic backing for a race for the Senate in 1946, when one of New York's two seats would be up for contention. "These views are not far-fetched," one perceptive biographer has noted; "La Guardia was that egotistical."[42]

The result was that the Morris ticket split the supporters of Fusion and thus rendered the party moribund; the three-cornered race turned friends into enemies and proved again how politics makes strange bedfellows; a vituperative campaign was made even more so by wild charges and countercharges that flew about like a band of disoriented bats unable to find their home cave; and the entire flap generated about as much wattage among the voters as a flashlight bulb. Voter registration was the lowest since the days of Jimmy Walker. The results came as no surprise: O'Dwyer's total of 1,125,355 (867,426 by the Democratic Party, 257,929 by the ALP) was more than double the Goldstein and Morris totals combined. Goldstein got 301,144 from the Republicans, 122,316 from the Liberals, and 8,141 from the City Fusion Party.[43]

The big surprise was Morris's 408,404 votes—the surprise being that, on the assumption that not more than 100,000 came from independents and Democrats, it would appear that he received about as many Republican votes as Goldstein did. To Morris's credit (and La Guardia's delight), he had undercut Dewey. La Guardia, it should be noted, did little more than make a few speeches for Morris and try behind the scenes to solicit letters of endorsement. Many of those he failed to get were from old New Deal friends like Eleanor Roosevelt, who hewed to the party line. If the failure of Dewey and the Republicans to take New York's City Hall was the "good news," the "bad news" was the end of the Fusion cause. In the largest margin of victory in the city's history to that time, O'Dwyer also swept in a Democratic comptroller, City Council president, and four of the five borough presidents.

Had they been blessed with prescience, the Fusionists might have enjoyed great satisfaction knowing that, far from proving his boast that the Democrats could run the city honestly despite their long history of bossism and clubhouse cronyism, O'Dwyer, amid mounting rumors of public scandal, would resign the office at the start of his second term and be saved from probable criminal prosecution by President Truman's naming him U.S. ambassador to Mexico. While the Fusionists could not indulge in forethought, they *could* indulge in disappointment and disgust over the city's return to Democratic control, which they equated with return to the old Tammany way of political life. For this, La Guardia was held to be the chief culprit because of his failure to groom a successor and build a lasting party around his principles.

Was he in truth to be condemned? Fusion parties in the generic sense are by their very nature transitory political coalitions, inherently devoid of lasting power. Made up of disaffected reformers representing disparate political and civic groups who come together to confront problems of the moment, they lack cohesion, discipline, and solid organization. La Guardia himself was as ambivalent about a permanent City Fusion Party as he was about a permanent Progressive Party. He fought the good fight in behalf of both at those points in his political career when necessary. But he was a staunch believer in the two-party system, a system that may be the paramount reason the United States has a stability enjoyed by no other country where the multiparty system is the norm. While he believed in theory that a government could be drawn together from nonpolitical experts, he knew pragmatically that only cunning alignments keep a party in power.

The City Fusion Party had brought together good-government activists, reform-minded partisans, and disaffected Democrats to throw out the Tammany "tinhorns," and succeeded. It had served its purpose. La Guardia had lent cohesion to the Fusion by hitching it to his own Progressive reform agenda. But he left no party legacy, no structure, and no institutional urban reform movement. The Fusion can be likened to a great flashing star that tore across the firmament at a moment when the sky over New York was midnight dark, with its luminosity personified in an outspoken, gritty, politically fine-tuned mayor who perfectly reflected its demands for a municipal reformation. Simply stated, it effected great permanent changes in the city, but it effected little permanent change in the city's elective politics.

When reminded at the polling booth on Election Day that he was about to cast his final ballot as mayor, Fiorello replied, "You can't stay in office indefinitely." Asked what he would do next, he quipped, "I'm looking through the want ads."[44] On December 31, 1945, as they had done a dozen years before, La Guardia and Marie and a group of his closest friends gathered at Judge Seabury's home to toast out the old year and toast in the new. "The Mayor was tense, and as twelve o'clock approached, he sat immobile, doubled up, as if in great pain. One of those present asserts that an affliction of the mind and the soul troubled the Mayor, that he couldn't bear the thought of giving up all the power he had wielded for so long."[45]

7.

On January 2, 1946, La Guardia, who had turned in his special police car, drove down to City Hall with Marie in the family's Ford sedan and officially handed over the reins of power to O'Dwyer. In a show of magnanimity, immediately after the election he publicly urged citizenry and press alike, "Give the new mayor a chance to make good, be sure you have the facts before you start shooting off the ammunition." In a November 8, 1945, private "Dear Bill" letter, he offered full cooperation and assistance from himself and his commissioners during the transition period, adding homiletically, "At best, the job is tough. There can be but one mayor of the city and I certainly hope you will be it. The hardest part of the job is to say no, and to say it quickly, definitively, and emphatically."

Following the transfer-of-power ceremony, as the two posed for news photographers and reporters, the diminutive La Guardia remarked to his comparatively towering successor, "They're all waiting for me to sock you." Everyone laughed. With that, La Guardia reiterated his best wishes for the new mayor, flashed a wide smile, waved his black Stetson, and then, taking Marie by the arm, drove home to the forty-thousand-dollar house he had bought in the Riverdale section of the Bronx and out of political life.[46] He had but twenty months left to live.

The claim that he had been "looking through the want ads" was, of course, vintage La Guardia. On his plate even before leaving office was a book contract for his memoirs, carrying with it a ten-thousand-dollar advance and the assistance of two researchers and a writer/editor. The New York liberal afternoon paper *P.M.* took him on as a columnist, and he was invited by the Sachs Furniture Company to write a feature dealing with news issues, titled "Under the Hat," to be inserted in the company's regular print advertising. He signed a fifty-thousand-dollar-a-year contract to broadcast a local Sunday afternoon program on local affairs over commercial station WJZ, sponsored by June Dairy Products Company, and *Liberty* magazine signed him on for another series of fifteen-minute programs dealing with national affairs, to be aired over some two hundred stations of the nationwide ABC network, for $2,500 a week. All of his contracts carried the stipulation that he be uncensored and left free to speak on any topic. He hired a staff of six to assist with his "thinking, writing, and talking" and rented office space in Rockefeller Center.[47]

At the end of January, before undertaking this rather taxing schedule, La Guardia accepted an appointment, instigated by his old friend Adolf Berle, now U.S. ambassador to Brazil, to represent President Truman at the inauguration of that country's new president. During the mission La Guardia won over the people with his broad grin, broad hat, and broad gestures of friendship. There were some dicey moments when he fussed over attending official lunches, and he was reluctant when it came to donning formal clothes. Berle managed to get him where he was scheduled to appear, and properly attired.

Once launched upon his new writing profession, it did not take long for the Little Flower to offend. In his first column for *P.M.* on January 6, "How the *Daily News* Creates Dissension," he attacked that paper's ultraconservative publisher, Joseph Medill Patterson, as a malevolent bigot thriving on provoking prejudices who "would gladly [have] been singing *Deutschland Über Alles*" if America had not gone to war. It wasn't long before a number of papers refused to carry his Sachs pieces for fear of libel suits. La Guardia's characteristic reaction: "I am not writing news. I am giving my opinion, and I am going to nail every lie wherever I see it. Get me?"[48] *Liberty* "got" him by withdrawing its sponsorship after a few broadcasts, on the grounds that he was "too controversial" and made "reckless and irresponsible" statements about his old target, "the Interests," many of whom were important advertisers. La Guardia's reaction: "I have lost 'Liberty' but I retain my soul."[49]

Three years earlier, in an article for the January 1943 issue of *Free World* titled "A New Peace for a New Era," La Guardia had called for the American government to plan not only for its own postwar conversion to a peacetime economy but also for the millions of Europe's displaced survivors: "The moment that firing ceases we will have a great deal to do in getting food and medical supplies to millions and millions of people. We must all contribute. . . . We must see that millions of little children get as much of their childhood as is humanly possible. . . . We must provide for these children at once in all countries, even in the countries of our enemies." At the end of March, he was named by President Truman to replace Herbert Lehman as director general of the United Nations Relief and Rehabilitation Administration. Funded primarily by the United States and Great Britain, UNRRA was a commitment by forty-eight nations to aid in providing emergency food relief and facilitating the rehabilitation and reconstruction of the war-ravaged countries.

He toured the ravaged regions of Europe, then went on to Africa and the Far East, making snap decisions about food allocations, amassing reams of notes on how best to reconstruct the war-torn areas once the immediate problems had been resolved, and spouting advice in all directions. He knocked heads with Allied commanders on the scene and civilians in positions of authority with the U.S. State Department and the British Foreign Office—and invariably had his way. After getting the refugees fed, his first priority, La Guardia conferred with, among others, Stalin in Moscow, the Pope in Rome, and Marshal Tito in Yugoslavia. He was disgusted with all the "talk, talk, talk" he had been subjected to: "The people are crying for bread, not advice. I want plows, not typewriters. The people need relief, not sympathy. I want fast-moving ships, not slow-reading resolutions. People can't eat resolutions and even the people in our country have learned through a period of depression that ticker tape ain't spaghetti." He could pass himself off as an authority on immoral waste: "In my own city we waste enough food to feed a city of 350,000 people every day. That is a correct statement, I know. I picked up that garbage for twelve years." He refused "to be stopped by pettiness, the greed or selfishness of man."[50]

On a personal note, there was a reunion with his sister, Gemma Gluck. After being transferred from the Ravensbruck concentration camp, where her Jewish husband and son-in-law had perished, to a prison near Berlin, she was discovered wandering lost and helpless with a daughter and small grandchild when the Russians entered the capital. She managed to establish communications with her brother, who was still mayor at the time. He helped get her transferred to Stockholm to wait out formalities connected with her return to the United States. "Characteristically," Gemma wrote in her memoir, "he was unsentimental, brisk, and businesslike" when they met again after twenty years at the boardinghouse where she and the remnants of her family were living. She was told that he was doing all within his power to get them to the United States but that they would have to wait their turn in the visa quotas. They were to be treated no differently from thousands of other displaced persons.[51] In December, when it became evident that the United States and Great Britain, which had been supplying most of UNRRA's money and food, would no longer be doing so, La Guardia resigned in disgust and returned home.

8.

La Guardia had shown signs of aging in the year after he left City Hall. By the time he returned from his tour with UNRRA he looked like a man in the throes of physical decay. Still, he maintained his hectic schedule of broadcasting, writing, speaking out on issues of public concern, including testifying before Congress, and raising money for causes he favored. He continued to address problems facing the nation, which in recovering from the war was undergoing a social transformation, voicing demands for social justice and governmental intervention where necessary to correct whatever extreme hardships might arise. He campaigned nationwide for a program of federal health insurance, for a solution to the problem of unemployment brought on by advances in technology, and for an equitable uniform national welfare system that would protect areas like New York, which were being invaded locust-like by unemployed indigents because benefits were much higher than those in most other states.

By the spring, in a state of chronic abdominal pain, he was in Mount Sinai Hospital for tests. While awaiting results of one, then another, he would check himself out and fly off to raise money for a favorite cause, accept an honor, or give an address on what was wrong with the bureaucrats in Washington, then check back into the hospital for more tests and observation. Keeping his radio audience up to date, he reported that the doctors, with all their "puncturing and probing," had failed to reveal what was ailing him. He also lamented that there was "so much to be done in these days, and gosh I want to do it if I possibly can."[52]

But that possibility was rapidly dimming. On April 8, La Guardia was named winner of the One World Committee's annual Around the World Award for press and radio. Though but one of many awards he received over the years for various outstanding services, it gave him the greatest pleasure and satisfaction, though he admitted to suffering "hellish pain."[53] A few days later, back in Mount Sinai, his ailment was at last definitively diagnosed. His personal physician, Dr. George Baehr, told La Guardia he had a stone blocking the pancreas. He would, Baehr added, lose a lot of weight before the stone would pass; it would take time to do so, and he would have to endure severe pain. But the condition must be allowed to run its course since surgery was too dangerous.

In fact, the diagnosis was cancer of the pancreas, which to this day, despite great advances in medicine, remains an inoperable terminal illness. "I told his wife," recalls Baehr. "But I didn't tell Fiorello, because I thought that as long as he lasted he could earn some money for the first time in his life, and this was all the money, except for the pension amount, that would be left to his family. It was my duty to him. I knew he would want me to do it—not to tell him, to let him keep on working until he dropped." The press was told that La Guardia was suffering from inflammation of the pancreas, and subsequently that "further tests for a diabetic condition were being taken."

On May 1, Baehr reported that the ex-mayor "was doing very well." Though La Guardia persevered with his work, he knew otherwise. The pain was persisting, and his weight, which he had never managed to keep down to acceptable levels despite all kinds of diets (which he blithely ignored), was dropping dramatically. To keep up the pretense, Baehr "had to tell him a cock and bull story, that the duct from the pancreas had narrowed down and closed. But it was open again and the inflammation subsided. And since the digestive juice of the pancreas was not getting into his intestinal tract to digest food, he was losing weight for that reason." Whether Fiorello knew the truth but chose not to ask questions and instead assume a spurious faith and gullibility is questionable though probable. "George," he told Baehr, "I have great faith in you. If you tell me I have an inflammation of the pancreas and you're going to cure me, I believe you. But before you cure me, I'm going to die of malnutrition because I'm wasting away."[54]

Meanwhile, he pushed on with his autobiography, his column, and his radio broadcasts. On June 15, he told his listeners he was "back in the repair shop [i.e., Mount Sinai]. In all likelihood I will not be able to broadcast next week. I doubt very much I'll be able to even crawl to a microphone, but I'll keep you informed." When he couldn't do so directly, others were invited to take his place at the microphone, which was set up in the first-floor sunroom of his house. Newbold Morris recalls substituting on one occasion when, fifteen minutes into the program, he heard a thumping on the ceiling. It was Fiorello, monitoring the broadcast on a small bedside radio, who then shouted down: "Put more hell in it, Newbold, put more hell in it!"[55] Marie, who played magnificently the role of a wife unaware she was tending a dying husband, was not the only one Dr. Baehr confided in. He chose to tell Adolf Berle, as one of La Guardia's closest friends.

La Guardia had been scheduled for eight lectures on government and citizenship at Town Hall, beginning in October. It was also announced that he would advise Congress about reorganizing the District of Columbia government. In fact, his last public appearance was as commencement speaker at the Horace Mann School for Boys in the Bronx, on June 3, when he told the graduating class, "My generation has failed miserably. We've failed because of lack of courage and vision. It requires more courage to keep the peace than to go to war."

To others who came by to visit him, it was obvious that Baehr's "cock and bull story" was fooling no one. Robert Moses, for one, "was shocked to see the change in him. He was in bed, so shrunken ... and yet so spunky, and so obviously on the way out. To tell the truth, I felt like crying. It was a battle that not even the most courageous fighter could win."[56] On September 9, La Guardia wrote to Jack Kroll, director of the CIO's political action arm, "We must all get together. There is a deliberate and determined effort to revert back! The struggle is on. . . . I do so want to help in the big job ahead." One week later, he slipped into a coma. Four days later, surrounded by Marie, the children, and Marie's sister Elsie Fisher, who had long served as his office manager, the man eulogized by President Truman as "incorruptible as the sun" and by Secretary of State George C. Marshall as "a splendid product of our democracy" died in his sleep at 7:22 in the morning of September 20. While eulogies poured in—his old friend Harold Ickes said that "no one in his generation did more for the underprivileged or strove harder for justice and fair dealing"—the greatest tribute came from the common people of the city La Guardia so loved and in whose behalf he had so passionately labored.

Some forty-five thousand representing every ethnic and religious group, every profession and occupation, every way of life, every socioeconomic stratum, indeed, every age, stood patiently in line to say a simple but heartfelt good-bye to their Little Flower as he lay in state in the Cathedral of St. John the Divine. As they passed by the coffin, some offered a murmured prayer, some touched his lips gently, some said a private farewell, some wept openly. One woman gently tossed a rose into the coffin, saying, "Poor Mayor La Guardia. He's gone." One man recalled how as a congressman La Guardia had intervened to bring his mother out of Russia. Another said, "I feel he helped all of us." There was only one floral offering on the bier: a bank of roses bearing the legend "To Daddy" from eighteen-year-old Jean and fifteen-year-old Eric.[57] After the funeral services next day, the cortege passed through densely crowded streets to Woodlawn Cemetery, where the man Judge Samuel Seabury termed "the greatest mayor in the history of New York" was laid to rest.

Fiorello H. La Guardia was more than one small man who was larger than life. He was the sum total of many, often antipathetic, personalities. He was at times confrontational, at times cantankerous, at times downright crude. However, he was at all times brimming over with concern for, and prepared to do battle on behalf of, the economically underprivileged and socially disadvantaged, not only of his city but of all cities. Indeed, many considered New York's mayor the nation's mayor.

He cared not how he was perceived as a man but only how his battles to achieve reform on so many issues were perceived. And those battles were legion against the industrial oligarchs, the social oligarchs, and above all the political oligarchs. Be it as congressman, as mayor, or even in his prepolitical years as a young foreign service officer and then as a crusading lawyer, what obstacles he faced in fighting for the masses were, their number notwithstanding, dwarfed by what may be termed his Magnificent Obsession. That was to create out of a congeries of five quasi-independent, overly politicized counties one glorious city that would be a paradigm for all cities: the yardstick by which any metropolis not only *could* but *must* be measured. In giving New York the best government any city could have, he exemplified the best government all cities are entitled to have.

One of those rare creatures, a legend in his own time, La Guardia set the pace by which not only New York City but all other cities dealt with such overwhelming Depression-engendered crises in welfare and relief, health, housing, education, recreation, and the arts. Also, he led the nation's cities in what till then had been, thanks in great measure to the nation's Founding Fathers, an unknown concept: making the federal government responsible for providing the necessary funding to achieve those ends.

In creating—and there is simply no other way to put it—America's premier city, La Guardia persevered in the face of personal disappointment, powerful enemies, and a free-wheeling style that at times deservedly earned him criticism and condemnation. And in the end, despite, or perhaps because of, an unorthodox methodology that was subsumed by an inherent conviction that the Interests must be held accountable to the People, he triumphed.

That Fiorello La Guardia, the Little Flower, is known today primarily to a rapidly dwindling generation who flourished during his three mayoralties should not be interpreted in any way as a reflection of the man. Rather, it is a reflection of how fast truly great men— and let there be no doubt that La Guardia is to be counted among that effulgent band—often fade from our collective memory, along with an appreciation of their myriad accomplishments.

Editorializing on those accomplishments the day after his passing, the *New York Times* said in summation, "He did not find us brick and leave us marble [an allusion to the claim of the Emperor Augustus as to what he had made of Rome], but he rescued our public credit, put non-partisan experts in charge of city departments, expanded parks and playgrounds, developed clinics, public markets, housing projects, airports. He did much of this in an uproar of controversy but he did it."

No successor to date has come close to matching Mayor Fiorello H. La Guardia's record. It is doubtful, if not improbable, that any future successor will.

CHRONOLOGY

1882: December 11, La Guardia born in New York City.

1885: Family leaves New York for the American West.

1898: Family moves to Europe.

1901: La Guardia joins U.S. Foreign Service.

1906: La Guardia returns to New York City, joins U.S. Immigration Service.

1910: La Guardia admitted to bar, starts law practice, becomes politically active.

1914: La Guardia's first, failed run for Congress.

1916: La Guardia wins first of seven terms as congressman.

1917: La Guardia enlists in U.S. Army Air Service.

1919: La Guardia leaves Congress, is elected president of New York City Board of Aldermen, serves two terms.

1921–
1923: La Guardia political collapse and resurrection.

1923–
1933: La Guardia serves five terms as congressman.

1933–
1945: La Guardia serves an unprecedented three four-year terms as mayor of New York, plays major role in initiating Roosevelt's New Deal, becomes spokesman for the nation's mayors.

1941: La Guardia named cochairman of U.S.–Canadian Joint Permanent Defense Board, leads war preparations effort.

1942: La Guardia named to head Office of Civilian Defense.

1945–
1947: La Guardia leaves City Hall, does a stint with the United Nations Relief and Rehabilitation Administration, then retires to private life.

1947: September 20, La Guardia dies.

BIBLIOGRAPHY

BOOKS

Allen, Oliver E. *New York, New York: A History of the World's Most Exhilarating and Challenging City.* New York, 1990.

Bailey, Thomas A. *Woodrow Wilson and the Lost Peace.* New York, 1944.

Baylor, Ronald. *Neighbors in Conflict: The Irish, Germans, Jews, and Italians of New York City, 1929–1941.* Baltimore, 1978.

Bellush, Bernard. *Franklin D. Roosevelt as Governor of New York.* New York, 1955.

Berle, Beatrice Bishop, and Travis Beal Jacobs, eds. *Navigating the Rapids, 1918–1971, from the Papers of Adolf A. Berle.* New York, 1973.

Berman, Marshall. *All That Is Solid Melts Into Air: The Experience of Modernity.* New York, 1982.

Blanshard, Paul. *Personal and Controversial.* Boston, 1973.

Burns, James MacGregor. *Roosevelt: The Lion and the Fox.* New York, 1956.

Callow, Alexander B., Jr. *The Tweed Ring.* New York, 1966.

Caro, Robert A. *The Power Broker.* New York, 1974.

Capeci, Dominic J., Jr. *The Harlem Riot of 1943.* Philadelphia, 1977.

Chafee, Zechariah. *Free Speech in the United States.* Cambridge, MA, 1941.

Chambers, Walter. *Samuel Seabury: A Challenge.* New York, 1932.

Chudacoff, Howard. *Evolution of American Urban Society.* 2d ed. Englewood Cliffs, 1981.

Cline, Howard. *The United States and Mexico.* Cambridge, MA, 1953.

Coleman, McAlister. *Men and Coal.* New York, 1943.

Cuneo, Ernest. *Life with Fiorello.* New York, 1955.

Curran, Henry H. *Pillar to Post.* New York, 1941.

Dalrymple, Jean. *From the Last Row.* Clifton, 1975.

Dulles, Foster Rhea. *Labor in America.* New York, 1949.

Elliott, Lawrence. *Little Flower: The Life and Times of Fiorello La Guardia.* New York, 1983.

Ellis, Edward R. *Nation in Torment: The Great American Depresssion, 1929–1939*. New York, 1970.

Farley, James A. *Jim Farley's Story*. New York, 1948.

Fitch, Willis. *Wings in the Night*. Boston, 1938.

Flynn, Edward J. *You're the Boss*. New York, 1947.

Fowler, Gene. *Beau James: The Life and Times of Jimmy Walker*. New York, 1949.

Franklin, Jay [John Franklin Carter]. *La Guardia: A Biography*. New York, 1937.

Garrett, Charles. *The La Guardia Years: Machine and Reform Politics in New York City*. New Brunswick, 1961.

Gelfand, Mark I. *A Nation of Cities: The Federal Government and Urban America, 1933–1965*. New York, 1975.

Glazer, Nathan, and Daniel Patrick Moynihan. *Beyond the Melting Pot*. Boston, 1963.

Gluck, Gemma La Guardia. *My Story*. Ed. S. L. Schneiderman. New York, 1961.

Hamburger, Philip. *Mayor Watching and Other Pleasures*. New York, 1958.

Hays, Arthur Garfield. *City Lawyers*. New York, 1942.

Heckscher, August, with Phyllis Robinson. *When La Guardia Was Mayor: New York's Legendary Years*. New York, 1978.

Hofstadter, Richard. *The Age of Reform: From Bryan to FDR*. New York, 1955.

Howe, Irving. *World of Our Fathers*. New York, 1976.

Ickes, Harold. *The Secret Diary of Harold Ickes*: vol. 1, *The First Thousand Days, 1933–1936*; vol. 2: *The Inside Struggle, 1936–1939*; vol. 3, *The Lowering Clouds, 1939–1944*. New York, 1953–54.

Jackson, Anthony. *A Place Called Home: A History of Low-Cost Housing in Manhattan*. Cambridge, MA, 1976.

Josephson, Matthew. *Sidney Hillman, Statesman of American Labor*. New York, 1952.

Kessner, Thomas. *Fiorello H. La Guardia and the Making of Modern New York*. New York, 1989.

———. *The Golden Door: Italian and Jewish Immigrant Mobility in New York City, 1880–1915*. New York, 1977.

Kilroe, Edwin Patrick. *Saint Tammany and the Origin of the Society of Tammany, or Columbian Order in the City of New York*. New York, 1913.

Kroeger, Brooke. *Fannie: The Talent for Success of Writer Fannie Hurst*. New York, 1999.

La Guardia, Fiorello H. *The Making of an Insurgent: An Autobiography, 1882–1919*. Philadelphia, 1948.

Lash, Joseph. *Eleanor and Franklin.* New York, 1971.

Levine, Isaac Don. *Mitchell, Pioneer of Air Power.* New York, 1943.

Limpus, Lowell M. *Honest Cop, Lewis J. Valentine.* New York, 1939.

Limpus, Lowell M., and Burr Leyson. *This Man La Guardia.* New York, 1939.

Longstreet, Stephen. *City on Two Rivers: Profiles of New York—Yesterday and Today.* New York, 1975.

MacKay, Kenneth Campbell. *The Progressive Movement of 1924.* New York, 1947.

Mann, Arthur. *La Guardia: A Fighter Against His Times, 1882–1933.* Philadelphia, 1959.

———. *La Guardia Comes to Power: 1933.* Philadelphia, 1965.

Manners, William. *Patience and Fortitude.* New York, 1976.

Mellon, Andrew W. *Taxation: The People's Business.* New York, 1924.

Mitchell, Broadus. *Depression Decade.* New York, 1947.

Mitgang, Herbert. *The Man Who Rode the Tiger: The Life and Times of Judge Samuel Seabury.* Philadelphia, 1963.

———. *Once Upon a Time in New York: Jimmy Walker, Franklin Roosevelt, and the Last Great Battle of the Jazz Age.* New York, 2000.

Morris, Newbold, with Dana Lee Thomas. *Let the Chips Fall: My Battles Against Corruption.* New York, 1955.

Moscow, Warren. *Politics in the Empire State.* New York, 1948.

Moses, Robert. *La Guardia, a Salute and a Memoir.* New York, 1957.

Murray, Robert K. *Red Scare: A Study in National Hysteria, 1919–1920.* Minneapolis, 1955.

Myers, William Starr, and Walter H. Newton. *The Hoover Administration—A Documented Narrative.* New York, 1936.

Nearing, Scott. *The Making of a Radical.* New York, 1972.

Nevins, Allan. *Herbert H. Lehman and His Era.* New York, 1963.

Norris, George. *Fighting Liberal.* New York, 1945.

O'Connor, Harvey. *Mellon's Millions: The Biography of a Fortune.* New York, 1933.

Page, Thomas Nelson. *Italy and the World War.* New York, 1920.

Prothro, James Warren. *The Dollar Decade: Business Ideas in the 1920s.* Baton Rouge, 1954.

Radomski, Alexander. *Work Relief in New York State, 1931–1935.* New York, 1947.

Riis, Jacob. *How the Other Half Lives.* New York, 1890.

Riordon, William L. *Plunkitt of Tammany Hall.* New York, 1905.

Rodgers, Cleveland, and Rebecca Rankin. *New York: The World's Capital City.* New York, 1948.

Roosevelt, Eleanor. *This I Remember.* New York, 1949.

Rubenstein, Annette T., and associates, eds. *I Vote My Conscience: Debates, Speeches, and Writings of Vito Marcantonio, 1935–1950.* New York, 1956.

Salter, J. T., *The American Politician.* Chapel Hill, 1938.

Sayre, Wallace S., and Herbert Kaufman. *Governing New York City: Politics in the Metropolis.* New York, 1960.

Schlesinger, Arthur, Jr. *The Age of Roosevelt:* Vol. 1, *The Crisis of the Old Order, 1919–1933;* Vol. 2, *The Coming of the New Deal;* Vol. 3, *The Politics of Upheaval.* Boston, 1957–60.

Shaw, Frederick. *The History of the New York City Legislature.* New York, 1954.

Smith, Alfred Emanuel. *Up to Now.* New York, 1929.

Spalding, Albert. *Rise to Follow.* New York, 1943.

Speranza, Gino. *The Diary of Gino Speranza, Italy, 1915–1919.* Ed. Florence Colgate Speranza. New York, 1941.

Stoddard, Lothrop. *Master of Manhattan: The Life of Richard Croker.* New York, 1931.

Strong, George Templeton, *Diary.* Ed. Allan Nevins and Milton Halsey Thomas. New York, 1952.

Swanberg, W. A. *Citizen Hearst.* New York, 1961.

Thompson, Craig, and Allen Raymond. *Gang Rule in New York: The Story of a Lawless Era.* New York, 1940.

Tugwell, Rexford Guy. *The Art of Politics, as Practiced by Three Great Americans: Franklin Roosevelt, Luis Muñoz, and Fiorello H. La Guardia.* New York, 1958.

Valentine, Lewis Joseph. *Night Stick: The Autobiography of Lewis Joseph Valentine.* New York, 1947.

Ware, Caroline F. *Greenwich Village, 1920–1930.* Boston, 1935.

Wecter, Dixon. *The Age of the Great Depression.* New York, 1948.

Werner, Morris. *Tammany Hall.* New York, 1928.

Wharton, Edith. *A Backward Glance.* New York, 1934.

White, Walter F. *A Man Called White.* New York, 1948.

Wyman, David. *The Abandonment of the Jews: America and the Holocaust, 1941–1945.* New York, 1984.

Young, Alfred. *The Democratic Republicans of New York: The Origins, 1763–1797.* Chapel Hill, 1967.

Zinn, Howard. *La Guardia in Congress.* Ithaca, 1959.

PERIODICALS

Harper's Weekly	*Political Science Quarterly*
Mississippi Historical Review	*Antioch Review*
Literary Digest	*New York Historical Society Quarterly*
Outlook	*Survey Graphic*
The Nation	*Pegasus*
American Mercury	*New Republic*
Collier's	*Fortune*
Washington Literary Digest	*New Masses*
The Commonweal	*Saturday Evening Post*
Time	*Reader's Digest*
Newsweek	*Spotlight*
Catholic World	Newspapers quoted from are identified in the Notes.
American Hebrew and Jewish Tribune	

PUBLIC DOCUMENTS

Congressional Record

National Archives, Washington, D.C.

Various agencies of the government, e.g., U.S. State Department, Department of Defense

Papers of Fiorello H. La Guardia, Municipal Archives, New York

Franklin Delano Roosevelt Papers, FDR Library, Hyde Park, New York

Oral History Project, Columbia University, which contains *Reminiscences* of various people in La Guardia's life

Various private collections of papers of various prominent people in La Guardia's life, cited in the Reference Notes

NOTES

ABBREVIATIONS

Cong. Rec.: Congressional Record (Congress and Session are abbreviated; e.g., 65th Congress, Session 2, appears as 65:2)

FDR/HP: Franklin Delano Roosevelt Papers, FDR Library, Hyde Park, New York

FLG: Fiorello H. La Guardia

LGP: La Guardia Papers, in New York Municipal Archives

NY: New York

NYMA: New York Municipal Archives

OHP, CU: Oral History Project, Columbia University

PROLOGUE

1. All La Guardia quoted reminiscences, unless otherwise identified in the NOTES as being from other sources, are from his autobiographical *The Making of an Insurgent,* published in the year following his death (© 1948; see Bibliography). The memoirs carry his story only up to his military service during World War I. It is believed he would have continued on into his political years, had not death intervened.

CHAPTER ONE

1. Gemma La Guardia Gluck to Arthur Mann, in Mann, *A Fighter,* 30.
2. Copy of certificate in Military Pension File of Achille La Guardia, Spanish-American War, National Archives.
3. For a history of the Italian community in Greenwich Village, see Ware, 152. FLG's birth certificate is in the New York County Clerk Birth Records, NYMA.
4. Gluck, 4–5. For data on Achille's service, see Records of the Adjutant General's Office, U.S. Army, National Archives.
5. From stories dating from FLG's days at Sackets Harbor reprinted throughout the 1930s by the *Watertown Times.* See also news clippings, LGP.
6. *Bronx Home News,* Feb. 24, 1921.
7. Gluck, 3–4.
8. Ibid.
9. Mann, *A Fighter,* 30.

CHAPTER TWO

1. *St. Louis Post-Dispatch,* May 8, 1898.
2. Records of the Adjutant General's Office, U.S. Army, National Archives. See also Zinn, 3, n5.
3. Gluck, 8–9.

4. For correspondence relating to FLG's term at Fiume, see Consular Dispatches, vols. 3 and 4, Instructions to Consuls, vol. 175, U.S. Department of State, Record Group 59, National Archives.

5. Ibid.

6. Gluck, 10.

7. Consular Dispatches (see n. 4 above).

CHAPTER THREE

1. Allen, 250–51.

2. Wharton, 2, 11.

3. Riis, Chapter 1, "Genesis of the Tenement," 33.

4. Longstreet, 7.

5. Allen, 242.

6. Howe, 395.

7. Kilroe, 48.

8. Young, 202.

9. Callow, 74.

10. "Our City Government," *Harper's Weekly*, Jan. 1857, 34.

11. Quoted in Allen, 161.

12. Glazer & Moynihan, 217.

13. Riordon, 154. See also Morris R. Werner, "La Guardia," xvii, LGP. (Werner was editor of the FLG autobiography, *The Making of an Insurgent.* These notes did not make it into the book, which carries his story only until 1919, due to FLG's death before the story could be brought down to his years as mayor.)

14. Stoddard, 78.

CHAPTER FOUR

1. For FLG's application, qualifications, examination score, and official appointment at Ellis Island, see Fiorello H. La Guardia File, Records of the Immigration and Naturalization Service, National Archives.

2. Curran, 180.

3. Elliott, 55.

4. "I had no particular passion": James J. Ellmann, cited in Limpus and Leyson, 28. For FLG's final law school grades, see Mann, *A Fighter,* 341; FLG's letter of resignation, dated Nov. 20, 1910, is in NYMA.

5. Marie F. La Guardia, OHP, CU.

6. Kroeger, 25, 215; Hurst interview with Mann, Nov. 12, 1956, in Mann, *A Fighter,* 49; *NY World,* Oct. 13, 1929, Woman's Section, 1.

CHAPTER FIVE

1. Koenig, *Reminiscences,* OHP, CU.

2. Espresso interview with Mann, Nov. 24, 1955, *A Fighter,* 52–53.

3. For FLG's role in the campaign, see Limpus & Leyson, 30.

4. Quoted in Mann, *A Fighter,* 53–54.

5. Ibid., 55.

6. Quoted in La Guardia, *The Making of an Insurgent*, 94.

7. Interview with Bellanca, July 28, 1956, in Mann, *A Fighter*, 58–59.

8. Zinn, 12–13.

9. NY *Evening Journal*, Jan. 15, 1917; NY *American*, Jan. 1, 1917.

10. Letter to Tanner, dated July 16, 1914, in the Tanner Papers, Columbia University.

11. See *Annual Report of the Board of Elections of the City of New York, 1914*, NYMA.

CHAPTER SIX

1. Andrews interview in Mann, *A Fighter*, 66.

2. Hurst to Mann, ibid., 65; see also Limpus and Lowell, 44.

3. Ridder interview with Mann, *A Fighter*. 68–69.

4. Staats-Zeitung, Nov. 2, 1916.

5. *Annual Report of the Board of Elections . . . 1916*, NYMA.

6. Espresso interview with Mann, *A Fighter*, 72.

CHAPTER SEVEN

1. William E. Leuchtenburg, "Progressivism and Imperialism," *Mississippi Valley Historical Review*, Dec. 1952. For FLG's attraction to the Progressives, see Marie F. La Guardia, OHP, CU.

2. NY *Evening World*, March 11, 1917; NY *World*, undated clipping, LGP.

3. NY *Times*, April 3, 1917.

4. *Cong. Rec.*, 65:1, 106, passim, 168.

5. NY *Times*, April 17, 1917.

6. For a typical FLG locking-of-horns with the majority, see *Cong. Rec.*, 65:1, 2609.

7. NY *Evening World*, Dec. 21, 1917; *Il Telegrafo*, Jan. 3, 29, 1917; *Il Cittadino*, Feb. 15, March 15, 1917; *L'Araldo Italiano*, April 26, 1917; *I Giornale Italiano*, April 26, 1917.

8. *Cong. Rec.*, 65:1, 801, 804, 805, 818, Appendix, 108.

9. "I want to drive home": NY *Evening World*, May[?] 1917, "Scrapbook, 1916–1918," LGP. "But I started the policy": Mann, *A Fighter*, 78.

10. NY *Journal of Commerce*, June 22, 1917.

11. *Cong. Rec.*, 65:1, June 22, 323.

12. Ibid., 1700; for war loan, 676; for Espionage Act, 1602, 1604, 1696, 1701, 1711, 1712, 1841. For editorial comment, see following NY papers: *Journal of Commerce*, June 18, 1917; *Times*, April 17, May 27, 1917; *American*, July 10, 1917; *Record*, April 4, 1917. For FLG on other subjects, see: for food and fuel control, *Cong. Rec.*, 65:1, 3085, 4015–16, Index, 109, Appendix, 313–5; for bonds, 675–76; for taxes, 2298, 2487, 2488, 2609, 2691, 2694, 2714, 2748. See also LGP, 1917.

13. For a study of the Espionage Act of 1917 and its consequences, see Chafee.

14. Ibid.

CHAPTER EIGHT

1. *Bollettino della Sera*, Aug. 24, 1917. For other FLG activities during this period, see also the *Washington Herald*, Aug. 31, 1917, and the following NY papers:

Times, Tribune, Sep. 12, 1917; *Telegraph*, Sept. 14, 1917; *Evening Sun*, Aug. 15, 1917; *Evening Post*, Sept. 7, 1917.

2. Spalding, 213–15.

3. Ibid., 220–21.

4. Fitch, 39–40.

5. "Eighth A.I.C., Foggia, Italy—General History," Records of AEF, Air Service Historical Records, National Archives.

6. Ibid.

7. Ibid., Col. W. G. Kilner to Maj. Gen. William O. Ryan, May 30, 1918.

8. Spalding, 231–32.

9. For detailed account, see Page, 303–24.

10. Spalding, 252; *Literary Digest*, July 23, 1918.

11. For FLG as propagandist, see "Scrapbook, 1916–1918," LGP. See also NY *Times*, Feb. 4, 19, 1918; NY *American*, July 13, 1918; *Brooklyn Eagle*, May 15, 1918. For Trentino refugees, see *Cong. Rec.*, 65:2, 5620, 5590–91.

12. Speranza, II, 144.

13. *Brooklyn Eagle*, May 15, 1918.

14. Fitch, 114–17.

15. Espresso interview with Mann, Nov. 24, 1955, *A Fighter*, 52–53. The conversation is recalled by FLG in his memoirs.

16. Cablegram from War Department to AEF GHQ, Paris, Record Group No. 120, Records AEF, War Department Cables, National Archives.

CHAPTER NINE

1. For anti–La Guardia activities and the people involved, see *Philadelphia Record*, Jan. 17, 1918, and following NY papers: *Tribune*, Dec. 14, 1917; *Times*, Dec. 16, 1917; *Sun*, Jan. 9, 1918; *Call*, Jan. 16, 1918; *Evening Post*, March 27, 1918; *Evening Journal*, March 18, 1918. For FLG's response and that of his supporters, see *Globe*, Sept. 20, 1917; *Times*, Jan. 5, 1918; *American*, Jan. 9, 1918; *Evening Post*, Dec. 12, 1917; *Evening Journal*, Jan. 8, 1918; *Evening Telegram*, Jan. 17, 1918; *Sun*, March 17, 1918; *World*, Sept. 12, 1918. FLG's remark on the Socialist Party loyalty, *Times*, Sept. 17, 1918.

2. NY *Evening Journal*, July 16, 1918; NY *Times*, Sept. 17, 1918; NY *Evening Post*, Oct. 12, 1918.

3. "Sink all partisanship": NY *Evening Journal*, July 16, 1918; "Only one desire": NY *Times*, Sept. 5, 1918.

4. See *Il Cittadino*, Oct. 31, 1918, and following NY papers: *Times*, July 14, 15, 22, 31, 1918; *World*, July 21, 1918; *Globe*, July 15, 1918; *Herald*, Sept. 9, Oct. 14, 1918; *Tribune*, Oct. 23, 1918; *Financial American*, July 20, 1918.

5. NY *Times*, NY *American*, Oct. 29, 1918. See also NY *Tribune*, *Evening World*, both Oct. 29, 1918.

6. Quotes in order: NY *Tribune*, *Globe*, *Evening World*, *American*, Oct. 30, 1918.

7. NY *World*, Nov. 4, 1918.

8. NY *Evening Telegram*, Nov. 2, 1918.

9. NY *American, Tribune, World,* Nov. 2, 1918.
10. *Annual Report of the Board of Elections . . .* 1918, NYMA.
11. NY *Times,* March 9, 1919.
12. Ibid., Feb. 8, 1919.
13. *Cong. Rec.,* 65:3, 1152, 1231; 66:1, 876–81, 4796, 8609–10.
14. *Cong. Rec.,* 66:1, 1512–24; Murray, 205.
15. For a cogent analysis of U.S.-Mexican relations during this period, see Cline, 184–92.
16. For his entire speech against Mexico and related documents, see *Cong. Rec.,* 66:1, 2416–28.
17. *Cong. Rec.,* 65:3, 2835, 2836, 4168–69; 66:2, House Report #175, 3068, 3525, 8487, 8697. See also Levine, 175, 178–79, 182, 190, 284.
18. *Cong. Rec.,* 66:1, Jan 22, 1919.
19. Mann, *A Fighter,* 51–58.
20. Ibid., 2285, 2507.
21. *Cong. Rec.,* 66:3, 1366.
22. *Cong. Rec.,* 66:1, May 21, 1919.
23. M. R. Werner, "La Guardia," 98, LGP; see also Bailey, 257–70.
24. *Cong. Rec.,* 65:3, 4948–49.
25. NY *Times,* June 30, 1919.
26. Treaty of Peace with Germany, Hearings Before Senate Committee on Foreign Relations, *Cong. Rec.,* 66:1, 1109–12; NY *Times,* Sept. 30, 1919.

CHAPTER TEN

1. FLG to Nicholas Murray Butler, Aug. 11, 1919, cited in Zinn, 8.
2. Paul Windels, OHP, CU.
3. Windels to Arthur Mann, summer 1956, in Mann, *A Fighter,* 112.
4. Windels, OHP, CU.
5. For complete file of his campaign speeches in manuscript form, see "New York City Affairs (Correspondence and Statements of La Guardia), 1919–1920," LGP.
6. For an account of Hearst's role in the 1919 campaign, see Nancy Veeder, "William Randolph Hearst and the New York *Evening Journal:* A Progressive Voice, 1914–1920" (Smith College Honors Thesis, 1959), 41–53.
7. FLG to William Waller, Oct. 31, 1919, LGP.
8. Windels, OHP, CU.
9. Citizens Union endorsement, NY *Times,* Oct. 26, 1919; FLG endorsement, ibid., Nov. 3, 1919.
10. Final tallies, NY *Times,* Nov. 26, 1919; Kelly wire and boast, ibid., Nov. 5, 6, 1919.
11. M. R. Werner, "La Guardia," 118–19, LGP.
12. NY *Tribune,* April 6, 1921; NY *Call,* April 9, 1919. See also "Proceedings of the Board of Aldermen of the City of New York, January 5–March 30, 1921," I, 5–6, 155–56, passim, NYMA. For examples of the board's antics, see Shaw, 4, 12–13, 17, 26, 108–09, passim.
13. *Brooklyn Standard Union,* July 3, 1921.

14. Marie F. La Guardia, OHP, CU.

15. Mann, *A Fighter,* 121.

16. *Bollettino della Sera,* June 22, 1920. For more on the FLG-Craig feud, see Curran, 261–62, and Limpus and Leyson, 102–13.

17. NY *World Telegram,* June 22, 1920.

18. See NY *Times, American,* Feb. 6, 1921, *Herald,* Dec. 13, 1920. A whole file, "Craig, Charles—City Comptroller—1921," is to be found in NYMA.

19. Elliott, 113.

20. See "Proceedings of the Board of Aldermen of the City of New York, January 3–March 29, 1921": also "Jamaica Bay, Hudson Tunnel, and Staten Island Piers—1920–1921," NYMA. For news coverage, see *Brooklyn Citizen,* Jan. 19, 1921; *Brooklyn Daily Eagle,* April 20, 1921; NY *Telegram,* Jan. 3, 1921; NY *Sun,* Jan. 15, 1921.

21. NY *Times,* Feb. 7, 26, March 14, 1920.

22. Ibid., Feb. 13, 18, 29, 1920. See also M. R. Werner, "La Guardia," 132–33, LGP; Charles, 269–82; Murray, 241–45.

23. "a chance to play": NY *Times,* Feb. 20, 1921; see also March 24, 1921. For the shoe strike, see "Correspondence, 1919–1920," LGP.

24. NY *Herald, Times,* Nov. 11, 1921; *Brooklyn Eagle,* Feb. 15, March 2, 1921; *Brooklyn Standard Union,* April 2, 1921. See also Smith, 236–37, Mann, *A Fighter,* 128–29; Elliott, 107.

25. "Proceedings of the Board of Aldermen . . ." (see n12 above), I, 607.

26. *Brooklyn Eagle,* March 7, 1921.

27. "after an intensive": NY *World,* Feb. 19, 1921; "for the sake": NY *American,* Feb. 4, 1921

28. 'This is the first time": *Brooklyn Daily Times,* April 14, 1921; "Saffron Yellow" and "I could have been" from unidentified newspaper clippings in LGP, as are numerous clippings concerning the La Guardia–Miller feud, for which see the files "Traction News—January-March, 1921, and May-December, 1921" and "Home Rule and Traction News—November and December, 1921," NYMA.

29. Hylan quote: NY *Call,* Feb. 27, 1921; see also NY *American,* Feb. 2, 1921, *Evening Journal,* April 16, 1921, *Tribune,* April 17, 1921, *Herald,* Jan. 31, 1921.

30. See NY *Call,* Feb. 22, 25, 28, March 2, 3, 12, 1921; *Bronx Home News,* March 11, 12, 1921; NY *Herald,* April 21, Dec. 25, 1921; *Brooklyn Standard Union,* Jan. 30, Feb. 7, May 14, 1921; NY *World,* April 29, 1921; *Motion Picture News,* Aug. 10, 1921; NY *Times,* April 7, 1921; *Brooklyn Eagle,* Feb. 27, April 20, 1921; NY *Telegram,* Jan. 3, 1921; NY *Evening Mail,* March 11, 1921; *Brooklyn Daily Times,* April 22, 1921.

31. Quotes, in order: NY *Morning Telegraph,* April 8, *Sun,* March 23, *Evening Post,* Sept. 7, *American,* and *Call,* Sept. 8, 1921.

32. Edward Corsi to Mann, Dec. 27–28, 1956, in Mann, *A Fighter,* 132. Corsi got this story from Koenig.

33. For press coverage, see *Brooklyn Daily Eagle,* May 6, 1921; *Bensonhurst Standard Union,* April 10, 1921; *Bensonhurst Progress,* June 24, July 1, 1921; NY *Evening*

Journal, Aug. 12, 1921. See also "Italian Language Clippings, 1920–1921," NYMA.

34. *Brooklyn Standard Union,* July 1, *Brooklyn Daily Eagle,* Aug. 11, 1921.

35. For the rival Italian league, see *Brooklyn Citizen,* Oct. 3, 1921.

36. See also NY *Globe,* Aug, 3, 1921; NY *Times,* Aug. 27, 1921.

37. NY *American,* Sept. 8, 1921. See also NY *Evening Post,* Sept. 7, 1921.

38. NY *Times,* Sept. 11, 15, 1921; NY *Evening Mail,* Oct. 20, 1921. For FLG's helping Curran in the general election, see various letters in "Politics, 1921–1922," NYMA.

39. NY *Telegram,* Dec. 4, 1920.

40. A. Bellanca interview with Mann, *A Fighter,* 58–59.

41. Giordano interview with Mann, *A Fighter,* 58.

42. NY *Call,* Dec. 28, 1921.

43. Dec.[?] 1921, "Scrapbook, 1921–1922," LGP.

44. Quoted in Limpus & Leyson, 127.

45. Ibid., 128.

CHAPTER ELEVEN

1. FLG to Kings County League, "Scrapbook, December 1922–July 1923," LGP. Nicholas Selvaggi to FLG, Feb. 18, 1922, LGP. See also NY *American,* Dec. 4, 1921, March 3, 1922; *Bronx Home News,* March 16, April 9, Aug. 1, 1922; *New Rochelle Daily Star,* May 2, 1922. Press release "Republican Clubs of Bronx Form League," March 14, 1922, NYMA.

2. Limpus & Leyson, 132; see also following NY papers: *Evening Mail,* May 3, 1922; *Brooklyn Standard Union,* May 10, 1922; *Times,* May 8, 1922; *Daily News,* May 12, 1922; *American,* May 14, 31, 1922; *Tribune,* May 26, 1922. For FLG testimony in behalf of disabled emergency officers, see Retirement for Disabled Emergency Officers, Hearings Before the Committee on Military Affairs, House of Representatives, *Cong. Rec.,* 67:1, June 6, 19, 21, 1922.

3. *Brooklyn Daily Eagle,* July 13, 1922.

4. For copy of the "Proposed Planks," see LGP.

5. Copies of all the *Examiner* articles are in LGP. See also Mann, *A Fighter,* 148–49.

6. For an informative description of East Harlem during this era, see Edward Corsi's "My Neighborhood" in *Outlook,* Sept. 15, 1925, 90–92.

7. *Harlem Home News,* Oct. 25, 1922.

8. NY *Times,* Oct. 23, 1922.

9. For the Frank postcard, FLG challenge, and *shamas* crack, see Limpus & Leyson, 142, 144, 145; for "Open Letter to Henry Frank" and other quotes, see NY *Mail,* Oct. 21, 1922, *Harlem Home News,* Nov. 6, 1922, and unidentified Yiddish-language newspaper clipping, LGP.

10. *Harlem Home News,* Dec. 17, 1922. For discussions between FLG and La Follette, Nov. 24, 25, 1922, see LGP. See also Basil M. Manly, "Preliminary Report of the Proceedings, The Conferences of Progressivism," Dec. 1, 2, 1922, NYMA, and Hofstadter, 23 ff. It was Hofstadter who termed this belief the "Folklore of Populism."

11. Mimeograph copy of the speech and "Press Release for Dec. 11, 1922," LGP; see also NY *Times*, Dec. 11, 1922.

12. For Buffalo strike, see NY *Call*, June 14, 1913. For other activities in this vein, see LGP.

13. Quoted in Zinn, 72.

14. For the Hotel Pennsylvania affair and letter to La Follette (Feb. 21, 1923), see LGP; also Mann, *A Fighter*, 162–63.

15. Ibid., 163. Letter to Weeks, *Harlemite*, April 18, 1923. All others, LGP: to Forbes, Jan. 11, 1923; to Montell, Feb. 22, 1923; Army Air Service press release, Sept. 19, 1923. For headlines FLG generated, see "Scrapbook, December, 1922–July, 1923," LGP.

16. *Cong. Rec.*, 68:1, 14, 943–75, 994–1016, 1048–79, 1099–118, 1122–43.

17. NY *Times*, June 16, 1924.

18. See MacKay, 119–23; "A New Declaration of Independence," La Follette's Platform and Statement for the Cleveland Convention, NY *Herald Tribune*, July 6, 1924.

19. The letter was printed in its entirety in the Aug. 10 issue of the NY *Times*.

20. Quoted in Kessner, 105.

21. Canudo to Mann, Aug. 26,1957, *A Fighter*, 173.

22. Ibid., 175. For account of how FLG and Marcantonio met, see Rubenstein, 314–15.

23. Mann, *A Fighter*, 176–77.

24. Hays, 270.

25. For vote tally, see "The City Record: Official Canvass of the Votes Cast . . . ," 186–87, NYMA.

26. Mann, *A Fighter*, 10.

27. FLG letter to Cutler, Dec. 2, 1924, LGP.

CHAPTER TWELVE

1. Duff Gilfond, "Americans We Like, Congressman La Guardia," *Nation*, March 21, 1928, 320.

2. Duff Gordon, "La Guardia of Harlem," *American Mercury*, June 1927, 153.

3. Mann, *A Fighter*, 184–85.

4. Ibid., 185–86; *Cong. Rec.*, 69:1, 4351.

5. *Cong. Rec.*, 68:1, 5657, 5890.

6. For FLG correspondence with these so-called New Nordics, see "Immigration Correspondence Concerning Legislation on National Origins Plan," LGP.

7. NY *Herald*, March 3, 1928.

8. Quoted in "Americans We Like" *Nation*, March 21, 1928, 320.

9. *Cong. Rec.*, 66:1, Aug. 20, 1919.

10. *Cong. Rec.*, 68:2, Feb. 7, 1925; 69:1, March 24, 1926, 6175; 69:2, Sept. 1927, 2018–22.

11. NY *Times*, June 18, 20, 1926; *Washington Star*, June 19, 1926; NY *World*, June 10, 1926.

12. NY *Times*, July 18, 1926; New York *Evening Journal*, July 17, 1926; Gauvreau tele-

gram to FLG, quoted in M. R. Werner, "La Guardia," 255, LGP.

13. Mann, *A Fighter,* 202–203.

14. For speech on inadequacy of a force to police the Mexican border, *Cong. Rec.,* 69:1, 12057–62; for remarks on Mellon and Andrews, ibid., 12057–61.

15. FLG presentation, ibid., 6174–76; for Dodge's denial, 7480–82. For the Remus murder, which was so sensational it made the front page of the Oct. 7, 1927, NY *Times,* see also Oct. 16, 18, 25, 28, Dec. 21, 31, 1927, and for coverage of his release from the mental hospital, June 21, 1928.

16. *Cong. Rec.,* 69:2, 1001, 1121–34, 2018, 2019, 2011, 2487 ff., 3283 ff., 5463, 5799 ff., 5804 ff. See also John B. Kennedy, "Under Cover, an Interview with A. Bruce Bearskin," *Collier's,* Aug. 13, 1927, 14, 43–44; NY *Times,* Jan. 25, March 2, 26, 1927.

17. *Cong. Rec.,* 70:1, 2388.

18. See Prothro, 224, 225, 240.

19. O'Connor, 128.

20. Zinn, 150.

21. Ibid., 150–51. Mellon quote, and his theory on higher taxation, Mellon, 11, 21.

22. O'Connor, 135–36.

23. *Cong. Rec.,* 69:1, 889.

24. Ibid., Feb. 23, 1926, 4443; Dec. 12, 1927, 500; Dec. 15, 1927, 717–18.

25. Zinn, 153–54.

26. Ibid., 219.

CHAPTER THIRTEEN

1. *Cong. Rec.,* 69:1, 9773.

2. For FLG's voting record and remarks on this ongoing legislation, see also *Cong. Rec.,* 68:1, 10341; 69:1, 4098, 9863; 70:1, 8647. The remark to his constituent, B. F. Yokum, Aug. 26, 1927, LGP.

3. Jardine to FLG, Oct. 6, FLG to Jardine, Oct. 14, 1925, LGP.

4. *Cong. Rec.,* 69:1, 2772–73, 3052–53.

5. FLG to Draper, March 26, 1929, FLG.

6. Mann, *A Fighter,* 214.

7. Ibid.

8. On the garment strike: NY *Times,* Sept. 21, 1926; on the Chinese strikebreakers, July 16, 17, 1927, and the Pullman porters, July 16, 1927, on pay raise for government workers, NY *Evening Journal,* May 4, 1925; on unionizing baseball players, scope of resolution of Feb. 9, 1925, LGP; testimony before House Civil Service Commission, *Washington News,* March 29, 1928.

9. Dulles, 247.

10. *Cong. Rec.,* 69:1, June 17, 1926, 11472. Even before the strike, when trouble was looming in the coalfields between management and labor, he had urged the same resolution on Congress the year before (*Cong. Rec.,* 68:1, Jan. 3, 1924, 520) but to little avail.

11. Pittsburgh *Sun Telegraph,* Feb. 4, 1928. See also NY *Daily News,* Feb. 3, 1928. It

was at the urging of *News* editor and close friend Lowell Limpus that FLG visited the coalfields.

12. *Cong. Rec.*, 70:1, 2734–37.
13. *Nation* (April 4, 1928), 378–79. See also Coleman, 132–35.
14. Mitchell, 340.
15. *Cong. Rec.*, 68:1, 3704, 3706–09, 3838, 3903, 3904, 3919, 3925–3926.
16. *Cong. Rec.*, 68:2, 2542–43, 5181.
17. *Cong. Rec.*, 69:1, 5348–49.
18. Copy of the hearings, held Feb. 7, 1928, in LGP.
19. *Cong. Rec.*, 70:1, 8879.
20. Ibid., 9773–77.
21. Telegram dated April 10, 1929, quoted that day in the NY *Evening Journal.*
22. Quoted in manuscript, "Congressman La Guardia Getting Support from All Over the Country on His Baseball Bill," LGP. See also in the following folders: "Sex Education . . . ," "Columbus . . . ," "Equal Rights Amendment . . . ," "Gold Star Mothers . . . ," "Indians . . . ," NYMA.
23. NY *Times*, May 13, 21, 1928.
24. Ibid.; Maurice G. Postley to Arthur Mann, March 31, 1958.
25. Cuneo, x.
26. See FLG to Foster & Cutler, Jan. 19, 22, Feb. 24, 1926, and Cutler to FLG, Jan. 11, Feb. 24, 1925, LGP.

CHAPTER FOURTEEN

1. NY *Times*, Aug. 2, 1929.
2. *Nation*, Oct. 23, 1929.
3. Fowler, 379.
4. Mitgang, *Once Upon a Time . . .* , 45, 55.
5. Undated copy of this speech is in LGP.
6. Oct. 15, 16, 1929, LGP.
7. Copy of the "Acceptance Speech of Major F. H. La Guardia" is in LGP. See also manuscripts in "Mayoralty Campaign—1929, Speeches, Press Releases, etc.," LGP. His oratory was also fully covered in the New York City press.
8. NY *Times*, Aug. 28, 1929.
9. For his speeches before labor groups, see NY *Times*, Aug. 6, Sept. 3, 5, Oct. 19, 20, 24, 26, Nov. 3, 1929. Press releases for Oct. 19, Nov. 1, 1929, LGP. For his addresses to veterans, see NY *Times*, Oct. 19, Nov. 1, 1929; for ethnic groups, July 29, Sept. 23 (Negroes), Aug. 17, Sept. 3, 11 (Jews), Aug. 19 (Italians), 1929.
10. Speech of Oct. 26, 1929, LGP.
11. Fowler, 246.
12. NY *Times*, Nov. 6, 1929.
13. Koenig, OHP, CU.
14. See D. Werner, 12–13.
15. Feb. 14, Oct. 21, 27, 1929, LGP.
16. Zinn, 178.
17. Myers & Newton, 26–27.

18. Mitchell, 84–85.

19. *Cong. Rec.*, 71:2, 10407–11, 12444.

20. For his vituperation, see Cuneo, 39. FLG minority report, June 19, 1930, is in LGP; "The smallest thing" quote is in M. R. Werner, "La Guardia," 420, LGP.

21. Cuneo, 21, 54–56; *Cong. Rec.*, 71:3, 6691–92; 73:1, 4083–88.

22. "Statement of Representative F. H. La Guardia in Favor of Unemployment Insurance. At a Symposium over Radio Station WOR, Sunday, November 8, 1931," a manuscript of which is in NYMA.

23. *Cong. Rec.*, 71:3, 6691–92.

24. Hoover's comments, Myers & Newton, 197.

25. Zinn, 183.

26. NY *Daily News*, Sept. 20, 1930.

27. NY *Times*, Nov. 5, 1930.

28. March 24, 1931. For printed materials on the Allied Progressives see folder "Progressive Movement, Material and Correspondence . . . 1931–1932," LGP.

29. Letter to Norris, LGP.

30. Letter of June 19, 1931, LGP.

31. *Cong. Rec.*, 72:1, Dec. 21, 1931, 1933–36; Myers & Newton, 162.

32. For FLGs complete speech, see *Cong. Rec.*, 71:1, 1741–45.

33. Mann, *A Fighter*, 303.

34. For the actual debate, see *Cong. Rec.*, 72:1, 56 ff. For FLG role see also "The Soak-the-Rich Drive," *Washington Literary Digest*, April 2, 1932, 8–9; F. H. La Guardia, "Why I Fought the Sales Tax," *Spotlight*. Aug. 1932, reprinted in *Cong. Rec.*, 72:1, 15533–36; "Scrapbook 1930–1931," LGP; and three folders containing correspondence and press releases on "Sales Tax," NYMA.

35. *Washington Post*, April 18, 1932.

36. See Index of *Cong. Rec.* I, 72nd Congress, for FLG speeches, which are too numerous to cite individually; also Myers & Newton, 192–200, and five folders in LGP listed under "Economy Bill," NYMA.

37. Mann, *A Fighter*, 308.

38. NY *Times*, Feb. 24, 1932.

39. *Cong. Rec.*, 72:1, 5478–80.

40. Statement of March 24, 1932, Norris Papers.

CHAPTER FIFTEEN

1. Cuneo, 147–49.

2. NY *World Telegram*, Oct. 22, 1932; Cuneo, 166.

3. For press accounts of the campaign violence, see following NY papers: *Evening Post*, Oct. 26, *Sun, Herald*, and *Daily News*, Oct. 27, 1932.

4. Dominick Felitti to Arthur Mann, in Mann, *A Fighter*, 314.

5. Ibid., 315.

6. *Annual Report of the Board of Elections . . . 1930*; see also *Bronx Home News*, Nov. 4, 1932.

7. See M. R. Werner, "La Guardia," 512–15, LGP.

8. NY *Times*, Nov. 29, 1932.

9. *Cong. Rec.*, 72:2, 134–35.

10. Radio address, NY *Times*, Dec. 11, 1932; *Cong. Rec.*, 72:2, 712.

11. *Cong. Rec.*, 72:2, 1489–93, 1694.

12. Ibid., 3321–23.

13. Bellush, 185; see also NY *Times*, Sept. 15, 1921.

14. *Cong. Rec.*, 72:2, 4514.

15. FDR-FLG meeting: Schlesinger, *The Crisis of the Old Order*, 356; Marie F. La Guardia, OHP, CU.

16. Eugene Canudo interview, July 28, 1958, in Mann, *A Fighter*, 323.

17. Berle interview, Jan. 3., 1958, ibid., 324.

18. *Cong. Rec.*, 72:2, 5357–58.

19. Ibid., 5050.

20. FLG to Roger Baldwin, Feb. 27, 1933, LGP.

CHAPTER SIXTEEN

1. On the swearing-in: NY *Times*, Jan. 2, 1934. See also Mitgang, *The Man Who Rode the Tiger*, 296; on their return home, Marie F. La Guardia, OHP, CU.

2. Chambers, 180.

3. *Literary Digest*, Sept. 2, 1933, 7.

4. *Annual Report of the Board of Elections . . . 1932*, 46, 49, 82.

5. Mann, *La Guardia Comes to Power*, 67.

6. Ibid., Corsi interview, March 31, 1960, 69.

7. NY *Times*, April 3, 1933.

8. Ibid., May 4, 8, 11, 15, 20, 1933.

9. Manners, 144.

10. NY *Times*, March 25, 28, May 11, 18, 22, June 6, 1933.

11. Morris, 58–72; letter from Morris to FLG, May 15, 1933, LGP.

12. NY *Times*, May 20, 1933.

13. Stanley Isaacs, *Remembrances*, OHP, CU.

14. Macy to Arthur Mann, Sept. 14, 1959, Mann, *Power*, 78.

15. A carbon copy of the letter, dated July 18, 1933, with a covering note from Sayre to FLG, is in LGP.

16. Maurice P. Davidson, recorded interview with G. H. Silverburgh, 1953 manuscript, 24–25, 34, Davidson Papers, Columbia University.

17. Morris Ernst to C. C. Burlingham, April 13, 1933, LGP.

18. Mann, *Power*, 82–83.

19. Davidson (see n.16 above), 26.

20. NY *Times*, July 27, 1933.

21. Ibid., July 28, 29, 1933.

22. Burlingham deals in detail with all this maneuvering in his pamphlet, "Nomination of Fiorello H. La Guardia for Mayor of New York City in 1933" (1943), NYMA. See also NY *Times*, Aug. 3, 4, 1933.

23. Mann, *Power*, 86.

24. Ibid., based on interviews with Berle, Corsi, and Tuttle. See also NY *Times*, Aug. 4, 1933.

25. Quote in Paul J. Kern, "Fiorello H. La Guardia," in Salter, 18.

26. Manners, 149.

27. Flynn, 33.

28. Mann, *Power*, 90–91.

29. NY *Times*, Sept. 15, 1933.

30. *Ibid.*, Sept. 20, 23, 1933; see also *Time* Oct. 2, 1933, 13, and undated letter, 1933, from Case Mellen Jr. to FLG, in LGP.

31. Burns, 377.

32. Flynn, 132–33; Farley, 42–43.

33. NY *Times*, Oct. 3, 1933.

34. See Press Release, Oct. 19, 1933, LGP; also NY *Times*, Aug. 2, 1919, Oct. 21, 1933.

35. Berle's comments: "Address of Prof. A. A. Berle at Cooper Union, Monday, October 2, 1933," NYMA; for Seabury quotes, NY *Times*, Oct. 3, 1933.

36. See Rebecca B. Rankin, ed., *New York Advancing: A Scientific Approach to Municipal Government, 1934–1935* (New York, 1936), quoted in Mann, *Power*, 107.

37. Limpus & Leyson, 368.

38. Windels, OHP, CU. The Appendix to his *Reminiscences* (14–17) is the most comprehensive behind-the-scenes account of the anti-Semitism aspect of the 1933 campaign.

39. NY *Times*, Oct. 15, 1933. The two emphasized words are in the original.

40. Vol. CL (May 1915), 210–12. The full text was reprinted in the Oct. 17, 1933, NY *Times*.

41. From "A Straightforward Answer to Scurrilous Libel," radio address by Joseph Vincent McKee, Smith College Collection. See also Flynn, 137.

42. *American Hebrew and Jewish Tribune* Nov. 3, 1933, 405. For Untermeyer and FLG reaction, see NY *Times*, Oct. 17, 18, 20, 1933.

43. *Catholic World*, Oct. 1917, 89.

44. NY *Times*, Oct. 22, 23, 25, 26, 1933; see also "La Guardia Unmasked, Proof of his Affiliation with Communistic Organizations" (printed address by McKee) and "Let Us Look at the Record: A Few Cold Facts About a Republican-Progressive-Socialist-Fusionist" (Recovery Party campaign poster), Smith College Collection.

45. Flynn, 137–38.

46. On Dutch Schultz: Manners, 158; "There is no reason": quoted in Daniel Bell, "Crime as an American Way of Life," *Antioch Review*, Summer, 1953, 149.

47. NY *Times*, Nov. 8, 1933.

48. Canudo letter of April 21, 1965, in Mann, *Power*, 187n.

49. NY *Times*, Nov. 8, 1933.

50. NY *World Telegram* and *Times*, Nov. 7, 1933.

51. Limpus & Leyson, 371–74; *Annual Report of the Board of Elections . . . 1933*.

52. Limpus & Leyson, 376–77; the one-liner is quoted in NY *Evening Journal*, Nov. 8, 1933.

CHAPTER SEVENTEEN

1. Rodgers & Rankin, 119–20.
2. Tugwell, 48.
3. For these and other appointments, see Kessner, 274 ff.
4. NY *Times*, Feb. 28, 1935.
5. For press coverage of FLG's first day, see the following NY papers: *Times*, Jan. 2, 3, *Daily News*, Jan. 3, *American*, Jan. 3, *Herald Tribune*, Jan. 2, *World Telegram*, Jan. 2, and *Brooklyn Times Union*, Jan. 2, 1934; see also Henry Graff, "The Kind of Mayor La Guardia Was," *New York Times Magazine*, Oct. 22, 1964.
6. Moses, 19–20.
7. Burlingham Papers, Nov. 29, 1933, Columbia University.
8. Moscow, 126.
9. Quoted in Kessner, 272–73.
10. Limpus & Leyson, 380.
11. FLG to Dayton, July 11, 1938, FLG to McElligot, Feb. 27, 1940, FLG to Valentine, July 7, 1936, NYMA.
12. Kessner, 282–83.
13. Garrett, 130.
14. "If you were": Moses, 116; Blaustein to Thomas Kessner, May 3, 1983, in Kessner, 285.
15. Leonard Chalmers, "The Crucial Test of La Guardia's First Hundred Days: The Emergency Economy Bill," *New York Historical Society Quarterly* 57 (1973), 239–40.
16. For a detailed study of the events surrounding FLG's finance problems, see Garrett, 142 ff.
17. For Lehman-FLG exchange of letters, see Lehman Papers, Columbia University; also Lehman interview, OHP, CU. See also NY *World Telegram* and *Brooklyn Times Union*, Jan. 6, 1934.
18. Copy of the radio address is in NYMA.
19. NY *Herald Tribune*, March 8, 1934.
20. For press coverage, see NY *Times*, March 30, 31, April 1, 3, 6, *Herald Tribune* and *News*, March 31, 1934.
21. NY *Times*, April 6, 1934.
22. Ibid., April 17, 1934; *Brooklyn Eagle*, NY *World Telegram*, May 4, 1934.
23. Citizens Budget Committee, Annual Report, 1934, NYMA.
24. Quote in Heckscher, 72. Text of broadcast is in LGP.
25. Windels, OHP, CU.
26. Jean would die a young woman because of a congenital ailment. Eric went on to become an English literature professor at a western university. When contacted by the author, he declined to be interviewed for this book, or even to share any memories of his father, claiming he makes it a practice not to become involved in any such biographies. When Fiorello's brother, Richard, died at an early age, he took his nephew, also named Richard, into his home though he did not legally adopt him. Attempts by the author to contact Richard, if he is still alive, or his heirs, if he had any, proved fruitless, as did attempts to contact Fiorello's collateral descendants by his sister, Gemma, who is known to have been survived by a daughter and granddaughter.

27. Gelfand, 5–6, 22–23.
28. Chudacoff, 238; see also Schlesinger, *The Coming of the New Deal*, 264–65.
29. Ellis, 490.
30. Ibid., 215–16; Kessner, 304; Caro, 448.
31. Caro, 18–21.
32. Ibid., 42.
33. Berle letter to FDR, March 15, 1934, FDR/HP.
34. CCB to FLG, April 16, 1934, Burlingham Papers.
35. Caro, 438–39.
36. Ickes, I, 317; letter to FLG was published in the NY *Times*, March 12, 1935; see also Caro, 440–41.
37. NY *Times*, July 4, 6, 11, 1934; Marie F. La Guardia, OHP, CU.
38. Ickes, I, 637.
39. Capeci, 38.
40. Ibid., 35–36.
41. Charles Johnson, "Black Workers in the City," *Survey Graphic*, March 1925, 719. For a detailed discussion, see "The Complete Report of Mayor La Guardia's Commission on the Harlem Riot of March 19, 1935" (hereafter cited as "Report on the Harlem Riot"), 32–33, 50–52, 59–62, NYMA.
42. The report is in NYMA.
43. "Report on the Harlem Riot," 113–16, 118–21.
44. For press coverage of the riot, see NY *Herald Tribune* and NY *Times*, March 20, 21, 1935; quotes are from "Report on the Harlem Riot," 7–8. NYMA contains 193 police reports and commentaries from the community on the riot plus the report of the mayoral investigation and responses of city and state officials to the report.
45. "Report on the Harlem Riot," 10; NY *Times*, March 20, 1935. A copy of the Young Communist League handbill is in NYMA.
46. NY *Times*, March 21, 1935.
47. Ibid.
48. Ibid.; NY *Herald Tribune*, March 25, 26, 1935; see also Capeci, 4–5.
49. "Report on the Harlem Riot," 75–76; NY *Times*, May 7, 1936.
50. Ibid., 120; ibid, Aug. 20, 1935.
51. Ibid., June 25, July 1, Sept. 3, 1936.
52. Ibid., Sept. 6, 1935.
53. Letter now in NYMA.

CHAPTER EIGHTEEN

1. NY *Times*, Feb. 2, 1935.
2. Ibid., Dec. 20, 1934.
3. Quotes: NY *Times*, March 25, 1936, Feb. 26, 1940. For comprehensive background on the municipal power plant issue, see City Affairs Bulletin, "The Public Utilities Situation," Feb. 1935, NYMA.
4. New York City Housing Authority (NYCHA) Papers, NYMA.
5. NY *Times*, April 9, 1934.

6. For a complete history of the New York City housing program under FLG, see various NYCHA papers in NYMA. Also Jackson, and coverage in various issues of the NY *Times* covering this period.

7. NY *Sun*, March 2, 1935; NY *Times*, March 20, 1935.

8. For strikes, see following NY papers: truckers, *American*, Jan. 30, 1935; elevator operators, *Daily News* and *Mirror*, Feb. 19, 1935; waiters, *Times*, March 23, July 2, 1935; garment workers, *Post*, Jan. 24, *Herald Tribune*, Jan. 28, 1936; hotel employees, *Times*, April 19, 21, 26, May 3, 15, June 7, 8–10, 1934. See also Garrett, 122.

9. NY *Times*, Dec. 7–8, 1934, Jan. 22, 1935. See also correspondence CCB to FLG, Oct. 22, 1934, Oct. 5, 1935, FLG to CCB, Oct. 22, 1934, Oct. 5, 1935, and FLG to William L. Ransom, Oct. 4, 1935, LGP. The bulk of this correspondence deals with FLG's attack on the New York City Bar Association, which Burlingham found offensive, and his resignation from the ABA, which Burlingham praised.

10. NY *Times*, March 29, April 1, May 14, 18, Aug. 3, 15, 1935. "Fire Hose Bids," LGP.

11. "Other targets": NY *Times*, March 4, 1934, May 12, 17, 1935, May 10, July 26, 1936. Cuneo to FLG, April 4, 1934, FLG to Cuneo, April 5, 1935, NYMA.

12. NY *Times*, NY *Herald Tribune*, Sept. 15, 29, 30, Nov. 3, 1935.

13. Quoted in Elliott, 232.

14. NY *Times*, Jan. 3, June 26, 1935, March 12, 1936, Feb. 17, 1937. See Franklin, 125–127, for Central Needle Trades High School remarks.

15. NY *Times*, Dec. 24, 1935 (on delinquency), March 31 (on circus), and Oct. 10–11, 1936 (movies). See also Morris, 117.

16. Ibid., 118.

17. Ibid.; NY *Times*, June 20, 1936.

18. "I am like the boys": NY *Times*, March 21, 1934. For letters praising FLG that elicited the standard "few compensations" response, see "General" and "Miscellaneous" correspondence, LGP.

19. FLG to Erskine, Sept. 20, 1934, Erskine Collection, Columbia University.

20. See NY *Herald Tribune*, Jan. 16, 1935; NY *Times*, Jan. 16, June 27, 1935, Jan. 7, Feb. 15, May 19, 1936.

21. Dalrymple, 42.

22. NY *Times*, June 10, May 3, 1938.

23. Ibid., Feb. 15, 1936.

24. Garrett, 208; Morris, 161 ff.

25. NY *Times*, Dec. 12, 1943.

26. For a comprehensive study of the subject, see Thompson & Raymond.

27. Blanshard, "Investigating City Government in the La Guardia Administration. A Report of the Activities of the Department of Investigation and Accounts, 1934–1937," 51 ff., NYMA. For 1935 loan shark figures, see NY *Times*, Dec. 4, 1935.

28. Covered in various issues of NY *Times*, Dec. 1932–Jan. 1933.

29. Garrett, 159–60.

30. Thomas, OHP, CU.

31. Limpus & Leyson, 397.

32. See City of New York, Department of Investigation, "Report from Commissioner of Investigation William B. Herlands to Honorable Fiorello La Guardia, Mayor of the City of New York, on the Operation of Pinball Machines in the City of New York, Dec. 17, 1941," NYMA.

33. NY *Times*, Oct. 19, 1936.

34. "You're going to see": Limpus & Leyson, 397; "When you meet men like that": NY *Times*, Nov. 27, 1934. It was not the first time he used the "muss 'em up" phrase; see Valentine, 177 ff.

35. Ibid.

36. Heckscher, 110.

37. FLG to Lehman, July 3, 1935, LGP.

38. Morgan quote in Heckscher, 112; La Guardia quote, NY *Times*, Dec. 22, 1935.

39. Elliott, 221.

40. Garrett, 176.

41. Quoted in Elliott, 222.

42. Smith quote in Citizens Charter Campaign Committee Press Release, Sept. 4, 1936, NYMA.

43. NY *Times*, May 22, 1934.

44. Heckscher, 128.

45. FLG to Thatcher, April 27, 1936, LGP. See also Sayre & Kaufman, 17.

46. Garrett, 379–80, n15.

CHAPTER NINETEEN

1. NY *Sun*, June 19, 1937 (quote). See also Tugwell, 112–15.

2. NY *Times*, Feb. 13, April 7, 1937; Berle, 126–27; see also Caro, 450–52.

3. Heckscher, 167.

4. Garrett, 388, n18.

5. Windels, OHP, CU.

6. The scene is described in Limpus & Leyson, 407–10.

7. Berle, 130; Stanley Isaacs, OHP, CU.

8. Ickes, II, 162–63.

9. *Annual Report of the Board of Education . . . 1937.*

10. NY *Times*, Feb. 8, July 5, Aug. 27, Oct. 1, 1937.

11. Ibid., Oct., 1937.

12. Windels, OHP, CU.

13. In Yiddish article, "Sensational Facts: Why Has La Guardia Not Halted the Nazis in New York?" NYMA; CCB to FLG, May 14, 1937, Burlingham Papers, Columbia University.

14. NY *Times*, Sept. 29, Oct. 24–26, 1937; NY *Daily News*, Oct. 26, 1937.

15. Berle Diary, April 13, 1937, Berle Papers, FDR/HP.

16. Vote count: *Annual Report of the Board of Elections . . . 1937.* FDR phone call: Ickes, II, 71. "Funeral procession": NY *Times*, Nov. 3, 1937.

17. Kessner, 421.

18. A. G. Newmeyer to FLG, July 28, FLG to Newmeyer, July 29, 1937, LGP.

19. FLG to S. Tilden Levy, Aug. 11, 1939, LGP.

20. NY *Times*, Dec. 21, 1938.

21. Heckscher, 180.

21. For FLG on Abrams and Post, see NY *Times*, Nov. 19, 23, 24, Dec. 3 (quotes), 1937; see also *Nation*, Jan. 9, 1938, 143–46.

22. Berle, 136; Ickes, II, 404.

24. Letter to Curran, Dec. 7, 1939, in Burlingham Papers, Columbia University; see also "S.R.O. at City Hall," *New York Times Magazine*, Nov. 9, 1937, 8, 19.

25. NY *World Telegram*, Feb. 25, 1938.

26. NY *Times*, Jan. 1, 1938.

27. Morris, OHP, CU.

28. Copy of letter is in NYMA.

29. NY *Times*, Feb. 7, 1938.

30. For correspondence between the two, see NY *Times*, March 7, 11, 1938.

31. Ibid., Feb. 20, March 1, 1938.

32. Heckscher, 202.

33. Manners, 243; quote in Heckscher, 203.

34. FLG letter to Poletti, Aug. 26, 1938, in Herbert Lehman Papers, Columbia University.

35. Ickes, III, 47. For comments of the La Guardias; private family life, see Marie F. La Guardia, OHP, CU.

36. Manners, 245–46.

37. La Guardia's trip was widely covered in the press both locally and back in New York, whose major newspapers had sent along reporters to cover it.

CHAPTER TWENTY

1. NY *Times*, Nov. 25, 1934.

2. Ibid., Dec. 5, 1934, Jan. 6, April 30, 1935; NY *Herald Tribune*, May 1, 1935. For FLG's fight to bring an airport to New York City, see NY *Times*, Dec. 7, 1934; various correspondence, ibid., Oct. 21, 23, Nov. 2, 4, 24, 1936; NY *Herald Tribune*, Aug. 25, Dec. 13, 1935, March 2, July 9, 1936.; also pertinent letters in LGP.

3. Florence Teets, "The Little Flower's Folly," *Pegasus*, Oct. 1954, 2–7.

4. NY *Times*, Nov. 3, 1939.

5. Ibid., Nov. 11, 17, 1938; Manners, 245; on fair opening: NY *Times*, May 1, 1939.

6. Ibid., May 5, 1939.

7. Kelly quote in Heckscher, 247.

8. Ibid., 248.

9. Bliven, "Gone Tomorrow," *New Republic*, May 17, 1939, 42.

10. NY *Herald Tribune*, June 6, 1939.

11. Heckscher, 219. Heckscher recalls hearing directly of Moses's style and tactics from older employees still with the Parks Department when he became parks commissioner in 1967.

12. Caro, 268 ff.

13. Correspondence: April 7, 11, 12, 1939, LGP.

14. NY *Times*, Oct. 12, 1938.

15. Caro, 641–44, passim.

16. The Moses-Rheinstein correspondence is in NYCHA Papers, NYMA.

17. NY *Times*, Nov. 24, 25, 1938; Caro, 611–12, 666–68. See also Kessner, 456–59.

18. Caro, 641–44, passim; Berman, 303–04.

19. Berman, 303–4.

20. CCB to FLG, April 10, 1939, FDR/HP. See also Caro, 666–68, 672.

21. NY *Times*, July 18, 1939.

22. Moses, 116.

22. Berle, 267.

24. "Robert 'Or I'll Resign' Moses," *Fortune*, June 1938, 72; Caro, 641, 674–76.

25. NY *Times*, Nov. 1, 1940. See also Simon W. Gerson, "What Happened to La Guardia," *New Masses*, Oct. 2, 1940, 6; Ickes, II, 655.

26. NY *Times*, Sept. 26, Dec. 25, 1940; *Brooklyn Eagle*, Aug. 19, 1940.

27. Kessner, 476–77.

28. Letter to Straus, dated Sept. 27, published in NY *Times*, Oct. 12, 1939.

29. Ibid., Dec. 12, 1939.

30. Rheinstein quoted in NY *Times*, Oct. 12, 1939; Ickes, III, 47, 92; *Daily Worker*, May 3, 1940.

31. NY *Times*, Jan. 2, 1940.

32. For a thorough discussion of the transit issue, see Garrett, 210–18; Arthur W. McMahon, "The New York City Transit System: Public Ownership, Civil Service, and Collective Bargaining," *Political Science Quarterly*, June 1943, 161–90.

33. For the exchange of correspondence, see Lehman Papers, Columbia University.

34. McMahon (see n32 above).

35. Heckscher, 431n.

36. *Education and the Good Life*, 220–21; *Marriage and Morals*, 48, 63, 165, 166, 210.

37. FLG to Ordway Teal, March 5, 1940, NYMA.

38. Clark and Somach interviews in Heckscher, 271.

39. CCB to FLG, March 17, 1940, Burlingham Papers, Columbia University.

40. Copy of the court decision is in NYMA.

41. CCB letter to FLG in Burlingham Papers, Columbia University. Dewey letter to FLG, April 6, 1940, as well as letters from other leaders in all walks of life, LGP.

42. "The Russell Case," *Nation*, April 6, 1940.

43. Burlingham Papers, Columbia University.

44. NY *Times*, Oct. 4, 1938.

45. Berle, 308.

46. Schlesinger, *The Politics of Upheaval*, 56.

47. NY *Times*, Sept. 10, 1938.

48. Many historians, myself included, believe he had.

49. Tugwell, 141.

50. Berle, 194.

51. Ibid., 353.

52. Various letters recommending FLG dated May 21, June 3, July 5, Aug. 21, Sept. 18, Nov. 10, 11, 23, 25, 26, 27, 28, Dec. 28, 1940, are to be found in FDR/HP. For Lehman, OHP, CU. For Ickes, *Secret Diary*, III. Berle letter to FDR, May 20,

1940, FDR/HP; Burlingham letters to Seabury, May 24, 1940, and to FLG, Jan. 22, 1941, Burlingham Papers, Columbia University.

53. Windels, OHP, CU.

54. NY *Times*, Sept. 12 ("Hitler" quote), Oct. 14 ("boodle" quote), 1940.

55. FLG to Childs, NY *Sunday Star*, Jan. 4, 1940; Berle, 354, 358; FLG to Paul Windels, Dec. 23, 1939, in Windels, OHP, CU.

56. CCB to FLG, Dec. 5, 1940, Burlingham Papers, Columbia University.

57. NY *Times*, April 20, 1941.

58. Ibid.

59. FLG to FDR, April 25, 1941, NYMA.

60. Executive Order 8758, FDR/HP.

61. Ernest K. Lindley, "La Guardia and the Civilian Defense Program," *Washington Post*, May 25, 1941.

62. Ickes to FDR, May 22, 1941, FDR/HP; Ickes, III, 518.

63. FLG to CCB, May 28, 1941, Burlingham Papers, Columbia University.

64. NY *Times*, July 2, 1941; FLG memo to J. Edgar Hoover, July 16, 1941, FBI Files, National Archives; FLG to FDR, July 3, 1941, FDR/HP; *Time*, Oct. 27, 1941, 29; R. Tugwell Diary, July 3, 1941, Tugwell Papers, FDR Library, Hyde Park.

65. Baruch comment in Ickes, III, 572; NY *Times*, Sept. 3, 25, Oct. 10, 1941; memo, Director of the Budget to FDR, Sept. 5, 1941, FDR/HP. See also Heckscher, 299, Kessner, 493–95.

CHAPTER TWENTY-ONE

1. NY *Times*, Aug. 28, 1941; Berle, 373.

2. Garrett, 268.

3. NY *Times*, July 5, 1941.

4. Quoted in Kessner, 496.

5. NY *Times*, NY *Herald Tribune*, Sept. 16, 1941.

6. Elliott, 215.

7. Oct. 23, 1941; press clippings in FDR/HP.

8. NY *Times*, Oct. 22, 1941; see also Lehman, OHP, CU.

9. NY *World Telegram*, Oct. 28, 1941; Press Release, Nov. 1, 1941, Berle Papers, FDR/HP.

10. NY *Herald Tribune*, Oct. 28, 1941.

11. The press statement, dated Oct. 28, 1941, is in the Herbert Lehman Papers, Columbia University.

12. *Annual Report of the Board of Elections . . . 1941*.

13. McGoldrick to Charles Garrett, May 31, 1951, in Garrett, 273.

14. HBS to FDR, Nov. 5, 1941, FDR/HP; Tugwell, 102.

15. Transcript of radio broadcast in NYMA.

16. Roosevelt, 236–37, passim.

17. Ibid.

18. Heckscher, 315–16.

19. NY *Times*, Dec. 29, 1941, Jan. 3, 1942.

20. Ibid., Jan 2, 1942.

21. Roosevelt, 236–37, passim.

22. Lash, 646–48.

23. NY *Times*, Oct. 29, 1941, Feb. 10, Dec. 28, 1942.

24. For coverage of the entire affair, see following NY papers: *Times*, Feb. 10, 17, *Herald Tribune*, March 10, *Sun*, March 30, *World Telegram*, April 1, 1942.

25. Matter of Kern v. La Guardia, Appellate Division, 264 (1942), 630; Flynn, 170 ff.

26. NY *Times*, Sept. 23, 1942.

27. Memo for FBI Director J. Edgar Hoover, Aug. 2, 1939, FBI Files, National Archives.

28. NY *Times*, March 11, 1934.

29. See the *Time* and *Newsweek* articles; also Kessner, 510–11 and 662, n109 and n110.

30. William Conklin, "Fearless Fiorello," *Saturday Evening Post*, Sept. 16, 1941, 72; John Hennessey Walker, "The Men Who Cover the Mayor," NY *Sun*, Sept. 16, 1941.

31. FLG to Jack Straus, Aug. 10, 1942, NYMA.

32. NY *Times*, April 14, 1942.

33. Transcripts of the radio broadcasts are to be found in NYMA. See also S. J. Woolf, "The Mayor Talks About Our Town," *New York Times Magazine*, Sept. 30, 1945; John K. Hutchens, "His Honor the Radio Showman," ibid., July 16, 1944; Amy Porter, "Butch Says Cut It Out," *Collier's* April 28, 1945.

34. NY *Times*, Oct. 29, 1942.

35. Ibid., Oct. 21, 1942.

36. FLG to KVE, May 9, 1940, NYMA; NY *Sun*, June 18, 1940 (quote).

37. FLG to FDR, Dec. 27, FDR to FLG, Dec. 30, 1942, FDR/HP; FLG to FDR, Nov. 1, Dec. 31, 1943, FDR to FLG, Jan. 1, 1944, NYMA.

38. NY *Times*, March 2, 1939.

39. Baylor, 99–100, 124, 140, 155–56, 160–161, and Wyman, 10, 13–14. For a firsthand account of a Front meeting, see *Commonweal*, Sept. 1, 1939, 428–29.

40. James Wechsler, *Nation*, July 22, 1939, 87–97; NY *Times*, July 21, 1939.

41. NY *Sun*, Sept. 15, *Jewish Examiner*, Sept. 18, 1939; FLG to Isidore Fried, Nov. 13, 1939, NYMA.

42. *Brooklyn Tablet*, Feb. 17, 1940; see also NY *Times*, Feb. 10, 14, 24, 1940.

43. Wyman, 9–11, 15. For release of Herlands's report, Valentine's orders, and La Guardia's reaction, see NY *Times*, Jan. 3, 11, 12, 1944.

44. Ibid., July 26, 1943, Nov. 25, 1943.

45. See Wyman, vii, xiv, xvi, 5.

46. Mann, *Power*, 226.

47. Kessner, 526.

CHAPTER TWENTY-TWO

1. See NY *Times*, Aug. 8, 1938, Aug. 16, Dec. 28, 1939, May 7, 1941, Feb. 1, June 23, 1942 (on jobs for blacks), April 2, 1941, May 10, 1942 (on attitude of employment agencies), May 30, 1942 (on discrimination in the armed forces); FLG

to FDR, Aug. 10, 1942, FDR/HP. See also Kessner, 526–27. For Randolph to FDR, July 14, 1941, FDR/HP; Capeci, 1 (on White quote).

2. Capeci, 8–9, 12.

3. Capeci, "Fiorello H. La Guardia and the Harlem 'Crime Wave' of 1941," *New York Historical Quarterly,* Jan. 1980, 27–29; Capeci, 15.

4. Frederick Eckers to FLG, July 26, 1943, NYMA.

5. Ibid., For reaction, see Capeci, 14.

6. Ibid., 49–52.

7. Ibid., (quote, May 1942), 27.

8. Ibid., 70, 72–74.

9. Transcript of radio broadcast, June 22, 1943, in NYMA.

10. Capeci, 84, 86–87, 118.

11. Ibid., 127–28; NY *Post*, Aug. 2, 1943.

12. Capeci, 104; Kessner, 532; Heckscher, 357–61.

13. White, 102–4; Capeci, 117.

14. "Presentment of the August 1943 Grand Jury of Kings County in the Investigation of Crime and Disorderly Conditions of the Bedford-Stuyvesant Area of Brooklyn," 2–5, NYMA.

15. Robert Moses, "What's the Matter with New York," *New York Times Magazine,* Aug. 1, 1943, 29.

16. NY *Times*, April 19, 1943.

17. Heckscher, 347.

18. NY *Sun* ("graceless levity"), NY *Herald Tribune* ("gratuitously offensive"), Feb. 8, 1943.

19. Maj. Gen. George Strong to FLG, Dec. 7, 1942, LGP.

20. Flynn, 18.

21. "I cannot qualify": NY *Times*, Jan. 24, 1943; "My dear Chief": FLG to FDR, Feb. 3, 1943, FDR/HP.

22. FLG to HH, March 17, 1943, Hopkins Papers, FDR/HP.

23. W. N. Guthrie to FLG, April 2, 1943, NYMA.

24. CCB to FLG, Burlingham Papers, Columbia University.

25. NY *Times*, April 4, 1943.

26. Ibid., April 7, 1943. See also Burns, 491–92.

27. FLG to CCB, April 25, 1943, LGP. "I'll carry on": Heckscher, 351.

28. Letter dated July 17, 1943, in LGP.

29. Garrett, 284; see also "Little Caesar: La Guardia and the Press," *Time*, Oct. 5, 1942.

30. FLG to FDR, June 6, 1943, FDR/HP.

31. NY *Times*, April 15, 1943.

32. CCB to FLG, April 13, 1943, FLG to CCB, May 14, 1943, Burlingham Papers, Columbia University.

33. Baldwin letter to FLG of Sept. 18, 1943, and FLG's mimeographed note of the same date are in NYMA.

34. NY *Times*, Oct. 19, 1943.

35. Ibid., Dec. 15, 16, 1943.

36. Ibid., Jan. 9, 1944.
37. Ibid., May 2, 1944.
38. Garrett, 285.
39. Ibid., 291; Morris, 204.
40. NY *Times*, May 7, 1945.
41. Gunther, 622.
42. Garrett, 296; on the idea of FLG wanting a fourth term, see Moscow, 28; for Morris quote, see Morris, 206–7.
43. *Annual Report of the Board of Elections . . . 1945.*
44. Quoted in Heckscher, 400.
45. Garrett, 301. The speaker declined to be identified.
46. For the transfer of power, see Heckscher, 407.
47. NY *Times*, Dec. 3, 6, 16, 17, 30, 31, 1945.
48. Quoted in Kessner, 579.
49. Manners, 268.
50. Quotes in M. R. Werner, "La Guardia," 269–70, LGP. For an overview of FLG's work with UNRRA, see Kessner, 581–89.
51. Gluck, 86 ff.
52. Transcript of April 27, 1947, radio broadcast over WJZ.
53. NY *Times*, April 16, 1947.
54. Manners, 275.
55. Morris, "The Most Unforgettable Character I've Ever Met," *Reader's Digest,* June, 1960, 115.
56. "My generation has failed": NY *Times*, obituary, Sept. 21, 1947; "Robert Moses, for one": Moses, 118.
57. NY *Times*, Sept. 20–22, 1947.

INDEX